ASAD

OF SYRIA

THE STRUGGLE FOR THE MIDDLE EAST

ASAD

OF SYRIA

THE STRUGGLE FOR THE MIDDLE EAST

Patrick Seale

with the assistance of
MAUREEN McCONVILLE

University of California Press
Berkeley   Los Angeles

University of California Press
Berkeley and Los Angeles

First published 1988 by I.B. Tauris & Co. Ltd., London

First University of California Press edition published 1989

ISBN 0-520-06667-7

Printed in the United States of America

1   2   3   4   5   6   7   8   9

To Rana Kabbani

Contents

Preface

This book is an attempt to explain what the world looks like from the seat of power in Damascus. It is not an official biography of President Asad, but it could not have been written had he not agreed to talk to me, and for this direct access to him over several years I am grateful. I also valued the conversations I had with his two eldest children, Bushra and Basil.

My thanks are due to General Mustafa Tlas, the defence minister; Dr 'Abd al-Ra'uf al-Kasm, the former premier; Mr Faruq al-Shara', the foreign minister; the late Ahmad Iskandar Ahmad and his successor as minister of information, Mr Muhammad Salman; and Dr Najah al-'Attar, the minister of culture.

First-hand information generously given by men and women who participated in events or were able to observe them at close hand was an important source for this work. Some of my informants are mentioned in footnotes, others are not. To all I am deeply grateful.

A number of Syrian officials assisted me, whether by arranging interviews or helping to locate documents in the archives, or making arrangements for me to travel about the country. I would particularly like to thank the staff at the presidential palace, especially Mr Jubran Kuriyeh, Mr As'ad Kamil Elyas and Mr 'Adnan Barniyeh, and Dr Saber Falhut, head of the Syrian Arab News Agency, and his colleague Mr Zuhayr Jannan.

Among the many Syrians who made me personally welcome I must thank Dr Sabah Kabbani, Mr 'Adnan 'Umran, Dr Badi' al-Kasm, Dr Osman al 'A'idi, Dr George Huraniyeh, Dr Ghassan Maleh, Dr Nabil Sukkar, Dr Rateb Shallah, Mr Ghalib Kayyali, Mr George Antaki, Mr Naji Shawi, Dr Nagib Mura, Mr Wajih Mustafa, Mr Antoine Touma and Dr Nicolas Chahine.

Mr Albert Hourani, the most inspiring of teachers, guided my studies in modern Arab history over many years. The Hon. David

Astor, when he was editing *The Observer*, encouraged me to travel widely in the Middle East and write about it. To both I owe affectionate thanks.

Dr Rana Kabbani, Mr Albert Hourani and Mr Eli Ered read the manuscript before publication, making many corrections. Mrs Anne Enayat gave editorial advice, Mrs Margaret Cornell edited the text and Miss Elspeth Hyams at I.B.Tauris saw it through the press.

Finally, I owe a large debt of gratitude to my colleague, Miss Maureen McConville who, over more than twenty years, unstintingly lent me her research and writing skills.

Patrick Seale
London, June 1988

PART ONE

The Revolutionary

1

Coming Down the Mountain

Around the turn of the century, an itinerant Turkish wrestler came one day to a village in the mountains of north-west Syria and, in a voice which rang round the hamlet, offered to take on all comers. A powerfully built man already in his forties stepped forward, seized the wrestler by the middle and threw him to the ground. '*Wahhish!*', the villagers cried admiringly. 'He's a wild man!' Their champion's name was Sulayman. From then on he was known as Sulayman al-Wahhish, and Wahhish remained the family name until the 1920s.[1] This was Hafiz al-Asad's grandfather.

On unanimous testimony Sulayman was a man of exceptional strength and courage which in the village won him a place alongside greater families. As skilful with a gun as he was with his fists, he was considered an outstanding shot in a community in which shooting contests were a favourite pastime and every boy could handle a firearm. As a target, a long needle used for sewing up sacks of grain would be stuck into a mulberry tree, and the best marksmen would smash the needle. Once the Turkish governor sent a column to the village to collect taxes and round up army recruits, for this was before the First World War when Syria was still under Ottoman rule. It was fought off by Sulayman and his friends armed with sabres and ancient muskets.

The Turks sometimes found it wise to placate the firebrands. On one occasion the governor invited Sulayman to visit him at Jisr al-Shughur, a little town on the Orontes a hard day's ride from Sulayman's home village. When the swaggering Sulayman rode in with a posse of several dozen companions, he demanded what entertainment had been prepared for them. 'Lady dancers from Istanbul and Aleppo', he was told. Sulayman spat on the ground in contempt for such frivolities. To calm him down the governor said, 'Go to the market, take what you want and charge it to me'. So the company stormed through the souk, loading up saddlebags with chickpeas and lentils, bolts of cloth and other household provisions. The journey had been worthwhile after all.

In time Sulayman's authority, won by his physical strength, was exercised in peaceable ways. Neighbours in those parts quarrelled easily and frequently, over boundaries or water rights, over animals gone astray, over alleged insults, but for the most part reconciliations were also easy. But if it was not possible to come to terms, the opponents would appoint a third man as judge, or *qadi*, to arbitrate between them. Sulayman's standing and sense of fair play won him a reputation as a mediator which became so widely recognized that he was once summoned to make peace between two families of the village of Zayna, near Masyaf, a day's journey away, where the local notable, Muhammad Bey Junayd, had been unable to settle the quarrel.

The real rulers of the mountains were the heads of powerful families, each lording it over a *bayt*, literally a 'house' but in effect a group of lesser families related by blood through the male line, and constituting the basic unit of Arab society. Such mountain bosses (*zu'ama* in Arabic, singular *za'im*) gave protection, used their power to bestow or withhold favours, extorted tribute and demanded respect. Some were admired for their generosity, the noblest of Arab virtues, but more often these chieftains were petty tyrants, anxious to keep the people down and not at all pleased to see young men improve their lot. Upstarts could be slung out of the village neck and crop. With their guns and horses and hard-won positions, the bosses enslaved what peasantry they could and resisted change.

But leadership by inheritance could not be guaranteed, it had to be earned. From one generation to another families rose and fell on the social scale. The mountain way of life in which each field had to be won from the rock at the price of much labour and in which each man was master of his patch and of his gun bred individualism. A man's right arm could raise him above the common herd, a strong man could come to dominate the *bey*, or local lord. Such champions shone in troubled times, and times were often troubled. As the history of Asad's grandfather Sulayman showed, in the anarchic and isolated mountains which hug the Mediterranean coast between Turkey and Lebanon, a mere peasant could rise to be a petty chief.

For the most part the people of the mountains were left to themselves, which suited them well enough, but by the same token they were utterly neglected. Outside the cities of the plains, Ottoman government scarcely existed. In the upland settlements of the wild mountains the state provided no justice or education, no health care or roads or jobs or services of any sort. The only expression of authority was rapacious and oppressive: the tax collector or the mounted gendarme. It was not unknown for a single gendarme to ride into a village, assemble the villagers, take money if they had any, kill a chicken for his lunch, and make off back to civilization.

In Ottoman times the highlanders were so hard up that they could not even buy salt; they would walk down to the coast and carry back skins of sea water with which to flavour their dough. All were poor. Poorest of the poor were those who lived in the highest valleys and on the steep eastern slopes looking inland to the desert, people so deprived that over many generations they had been driven by hunger down to the central Syrian plain around Homs and Hama to work as virtual serfs for wealthy landowners. Well into this century there was no spare cash, no trade, no wealth other than what could be teased from the steep, stony fields. The only domestic craft was basket-making. Grain and goats were the twin foundations of this primitive economy, providing a year-round diet of bread, cracked wheat (*burghul*), yoghurt (*laban*), and clarified butter (*samneh*). The more prosperous might have a vine or two, a few fruit trees, a flock of sheep. Somewhat less wretched were the settlements on the western slopes of the mountains facing out to the Mediterranean. Sulayman's village of Qurdaha nestled in an almost Provençal landscape, although drier and whiter, little more than ten kilometres by donkey trail from the sea which could be glimpsed through a dip in the hills.

Asad's father, 'Ali Sulayman, inherited many of the characteristics of his own father: he was strong, brave, much respected and an excellent shot. Aged seventy he would pin a cigarette paper to a tree and put a pistol shot through it at a hundred paces to the admiration of the village boys. He continued the family tradition of mediating quarrels and giving protection to the weak, winning special praise in the early 1920s for helping the destitute refugees who flooded south when France surrendered parts of the former province of Aleppo to Turkey.

Born in 1875, 'Ali Sulayman knew Ottoman rule, briefly fought the French when they came, and lived on until 1963 (just long enough to witness the Ba'th party revolution of that year which brought his son to power). He married twice and over three decades fathered eleven children.[2] His first wife, Sa'da, from the district of Haffeh, bore him three sons and two daughters. Then there was a five-year gap separating this set of progeny from the children of his second wife, Na'isa, a strong, comely girl twenty years his junior, the daughter of 'Uthman 'Abbud from the village of Qutilba a dozen kilometres further up the mountain. She bore him a daughter and five sons. Hafiz, born on 6 October 1930, was the fourth child of this second union.

Shortly before Hafiz's birth, 'Ali Sulayman had managed to make the transition from simple peasant to minor notable, a reward for the esteem earned by the family over two generations. His promotion was signalled in 1927 by a change in the family's name from Wahhish, 'savage', to Asad, 'lion'. There are several versions of how this came about, all flattering to 'Ali Sulayman. The one most commonly repeated is that he had so distinguished himself as a pillar of village society that leaders of the four main families came to him and urged, 'You are not a Wahhish, you are an Asad!'[3]

Qurdaha at that time consisted of a hundred or so mud or rough stone houses at the end of a dirt track. There was no mosque or church, no shop, no café, no paved road, no village centre. The only places where people gathered were the spring, the cemetery and the *mazar*, the white-domed shrine of local saints which was the mountains' only form of religious architecture. The Asad family houses were grouped together in their clan quarter – uncles, aunts, cousins, half-brothers, nephews all living within hailing distance. By then the Asads owned a few fields which the now aging 'Ali Sulayman could just afford not to work himself. One or two seasonal workers were brought in at harvest time, although on a day-to-day basis the family planted, weeded and watered the vegetable patch and looked after the fruit trees. 'Ali Sulayman's wife, Na'isa, fed the chickens and fattened the lamb for feast days.

Hafiz al-Asad was born in a two-room flat-roofed house of undressed stone giving on to a front yard of beaten earth. On one side there was a mud extension for the animals. A rock-strewn path led away down the hill. The simplicity of this rough-hewn dwelling could be matched right across the uplands. Qurdaha owed its existence to a spring called 'Ayn Zarqa which rose just above the village in a cave adorned with stalactites and was prized for its digestive qualities. With a gentle climate and thirty days' rainfall a year, the village provided a healthy, simple life, even a degree of ease. A more varied agriculture was possible on these western and southern foothills than in the thin soil higher up the eroded mountains. Olives had long been the most important crop, the oil being used not only for cooking but also for lighting and soap-making. Vines and figs grew here and mulberry trees provided food for silk worms, but it was tobacco which was the cash crop, the real currency of the place.

As a small boy Asad lived in the warmth and bustle of an extended family.[4] Not only was he the ninth of 'Ali Sulayman's eleven children, but just down the road lived his Uncle 'Aziz Sulayman and his seven cousins of whom the eldest, Munira, was just a month younger than himself. His three aunts on his father's side had all married into families in nearby villages which provided the opportunity for visits to yet more cousins there. His Aunt Sa'da in particular was to be important in his life because she married Ahmad Makhluf of the village of Bustan al-Basha, a close relative of the girl who was to become his future wife. As for his father's first five children, all born before the First World War, they were less like brothers and sisters to Asad and more like uncles and aunts. Their swarming children, his nephews and nieces, added fresh faces every year to the extended family.

The centre of his young life was his father, the patriarch 'Ali Sulayman, who was already fifty-five when Asad was born and must always have seemed an old man to him. He was a dignified, rather austere, figure who on special occasions such as on visits to the French authorities in Latakia wore a fez and a tie. In traditional Arab fashion, 'Ali Sulayman was not only loved by his children but also, and perhaps more so, respected and obeyed. The boys would kiss his hand in the mornings, would not sit down in his presence and as they grew up would not dare to smoke in front of him. Asad's mother Na'isa, much younger than her husband, was a strong-minded woman in her own right who came increasingly to be the dominant parent – with particular influence over her two youngest sons, Jamil born in 1933 and Rif'at born in 1937. Rif'at, a mischievous, lively child and the benjamin of the clan, was her favourite.

Asad's early years were spent largely out of doors, perched on a donkey on the way to the fields, helping with the watering of the crops or the gathering of fruit, or just scampering about in the mountains with other children, in whose lives an education hardly featured. Illiteracy was almost universal in the mountain settlements at that time. Even in 1943–4 less than a quarter of all Syrian children between the ages of six and twelve attended school.[5] In Qurdaha as elsewhere, a man would have to go round the whole neighbourhood to find someone able to read a letter. The few people who could read were highly respected: looked to for news of the world outside, their advice was also sought on village affairs and in dealings with the government. They were even expected to provide entertainment. To pass the time in the evenings people would gather to hear tales of adventure read aloud from some old book. Asad's father was one of the literate few. There was no electricity at that time in Qurdaha and no radio, but this unusual villager subscribed to a newspaper which arrived several days late. He was the only man in the village to follow the ebb and flow of the Second World War, pin-pointing battles on a wall-map in the room where Asad slept as a boy.

'Ali Sulayman had a respect for book learning and was determined to give his younger sons an education. His first eight children had had no schooling to speak of because none had been available. The only education to be had in the mountains under the Turks and in the early years of French rule was that provided by the village prayer leader, who might gather half a dozen boys under a tree to teach them their letters and a few passages from the Qur'an. The Turkish authorities discouraged even such basic teaching and if they heard about it would send someone to give the shaykh a beating. However, when Asad was growing up under the more liberal French, open-air classes were common, and it was in one of these that he first learned to read. By the 1930s two new factors intervened to give him opportunities denied to older members of his family. The French brought education to remote villages for the first time, and his father was by then important enough to make sure Asad benefited. When a primary school was opened in Qurdaha, 'Ali Sulayman was able to secure Asad a place, thus making him the first of his children to start a formal education, one of a handful of boys in his village to be so fortunate.

The 'Alawis

The highlanders were in their great majority 'Alawis, members of an extreme Shi'i Muslim sect which, like the Druzes and the Isma'ilis, was a remnant of the Shi'i upsurge which had swept Islam a thousand years before: they were islands left by a tide which had receded. 'Alawis share with other Shi'a the belief that 'Ali, the Prophet Muhammad's cousin and son-in-law, was his rightful heir but was robbed of his inheritance by the first three Caliphs. They push reverence for the wronged 'Ali to extreme lengths by seeing him as infused with divine essence. Over the centuries this and other esoteric beliefs caused them to be denounced by Sunnis as infidels deserving death, and in self-defence they became secretive about their religion, adopting, like other extremist Shi'i sects, the doctrine of *taqiya*, that resort to a prudent duplicity which justified cloaking their true beliefs. When Sunni orthodoxy regained the upper hand from the thirteenth century onwards, pockets of sectarians took shelter where they could. No one is quite certain where exactly the 'Alawis came from or when they first occupied their mountains. They themselves say their ancestors came west to the Mediterranean several hundred years ago from the Jabal Sinjar, a mountainous redoubt in present-day Iraq between the Tigris and the Euphrates, and before that from Arabia itself where they claim parentage with the most ancient tribes. Such a lineage has been traced for Hasan bin Makzum, considered the father of one of the largest

'Alawi tribes, who died in 1240.[6] These ancestors, fleeing from stronger enemies or persecuted because of suspected heresies, found refuge in the inaccessible valleys high above the sea.

The names, values and tribal organization of the 'Alawis derive both from their distant nomadic background and from the experience of life in the mountains over the last few centuries. Today's 'Alawi tribal structures reflect what is left of this heritage. Most 'Alawis belong to one of four main tribal confederations, the Haddadin, the Matawira, the Khaiyatin, and the Kalbiya – and it is to the Kalbiya that Asad's grandfather Sulayman belonged. Originally each of the four big groupings was probably concentrated in a distinct part of the mountains, but over time the tribes intermingled so that even a hamlet of a hundred people might have Haddadin and Khaiyatin living side by side, if not in harmony. In addition, three smaller tribes, the Darawisa, the Mahaliba and the 'Amamira, settled at the northern end of the mountain range while several thousand 'Alawis lived, largely detribalized, on the plains outside the mountain areas. As a result tribal maps of the 'Alawi district are not neat affairs but show inextricable overlappings. Sulayman's village of Qurdaha, however, was less of a tribal mosaic than others. Overwhelmingly Kalbiya and the seat of the principal religious dignitary of the tribe, it was sometimes called Qurdaha al-Kalbiya.

'Alawis today are not always comfortable with the subject of tribal affiliations as the Ba'thist state has striven to replace such categories with the modern notion of citizenship, but if pressed every village boy could tell you to which tribe his family belongs. Asked to name the leading tribes and families of Qurdaha, the head of the municipality replied, 'We have no tribes or families here. We are all members of the Ba'th family under the leadership of Hafiz al-Asad.' Only then, after some coaxing, did he mention the Kalbiya clans which trace their lineage back hundreds of years.[7]

The name of the 'Alawi community is of recent coinage dating only from the French Mandate. Before the First World War the community was known either as the Nusayriya after its alleged founder Muhammad ibn Nusayr, a ninth-century religious propagandist, or, in a variant of the same word, as the Ansariya, the traditional name of the mountain range which they inhabited. Only in recent decades has a member of the community become known as an 'Alawi or Alawite, strictly speaking a follower of 'Ali, the fountainhead of Shi'ism, a name which places the 'Alawis within the family of Shi'i sects.

The history of 'Alawi or Nusayri beliefs is misty indeed. The earliest references come from Druze polemics against them in the eleventh century when, to the outrage of Druze theologians, Nusayri missionaries started proselytizing among the newly arrived Druzes in southern Lebanon. The Nusayris make a fleeting appearance in Crusader chronicles and later in a few travellers' tales and reports by European consuls, but it was not until the middle of the nineteenth century that a determined attempt to throw light on them was made by the Reverend Samuel Lyde in *The Asian Mystery*, published in London in 1860. He based his work on the first Nusayri text to come to the attention of Western scholars, a book called *The Manual of Shaykhs* which he bought from a Christian merchant of Latakia into whose hands it had fallen during the Egyptian conquest of Syria in the 1830s. The next breakthrough came with the publication in 1900 of René Dussaud's *Histoire et Religion des Nosairis*, itself based on a book published in Beirut in 1863 by Sulayman al-Adhana, a Nusayri turned Christian who was later killed for his apostasy. Adhana's book contained the Nusayris' principal prayers and instructions and an account of their fundamental beliefs. On these rather shaky foundations,[8] more recent scholars have built a fuller picture of the sect, although most readily admit that it remains, in Philip Hitti's words, a 'partially unsolved religious riddle'.[9]

There seems little doubt, however, that the Nusayris are a schismatic offshoot from mainstream 'Twelver' Shi'ism whose history for the last thousand years has been one of stubborn survival in the face of invasion and repression. The Franks of the First Crusade (1098) seized their strongpoints in the mountains and built castles on them. In the early twelfth century the then powerful Isma'ilis stormed up from their base in the plain at Salamiya and also built fortresses in Nusayri country, where pockets of them remain to this day still at odds with their neighbours. Saladin conquered the area in 1188 and demanded tribute. The Mamluk Sultans who followed him over the next century routed the Isma'ilis, drove out the last Crusaders, and tried forcibly to convert the Nusayri sectarians to orthodox Islam. When the fourteenth century traveller Ibn Battuta passed through the mountains he recorded that the Nusayris were compelled to build mosques. The Syrian theologian Ibn Taymiya (1263–1328), a champion of Sunni orthodoxy, condemned the Nusayris as more dangerous than the Christians and urged Muslims to make holy war on them – a text which still provides ammunition for their twentieth-century opponents.

Their next oppressors were the Ottoman Turks who conquered Syria at the beginning of the sixteenth century and made a new attempt to force orthodoxy on the Nusayris. Ottoman government, lasting until 1918, was interrupted briefly by a decade of Egyptian rule from 1832, which far from bringing relief meant better organized and still more severe repression. By this time the highlanders were widely despised as heretics and outcasts and it was only with the coming of the French Mandate after the First World War that the Nusayris felt free from persecution.

Education

In 1939–1940, when Asad was nine, his parents sent him away to school in Latakia on the coast. He was later to describe coming down the mountain to the city for the first time as 'the crucial turning point of my life'.[10] The boy spent the first three months with a married sister but when her husband had to move elsewhere, the young Asad was left without relations in the city and was put up in a humble lodging-house owned by a family acquaintance. He remembered that period as a sad one because of the distance from his family – 'In those days the thirty kilometres from Qurdaha to Latakia seemed almost as great as the distance today between Damascus and London' – but also as joyful because of the children of his own age with whom he ran about the town. It was a challenge for a child of the mountains to be thrown into urban life at the deep end. Asad now had his first lesson in what it was to be a member of an ill-regarded minority. 'Alawis were not well placed in Latakia, which was then three parts Sunni Muslim and one part made up of various Christian sects and denominations. Few in number, perhaps only some hundreds, the 'Alawis had little influence in the city and were generally sneered at. They did their best to keep out of trouble, living quietly in the poorer parts of town, and Asad was understandably homesick. He found himself there at a dramatic moment. Vichy France, then ruling Syria and living in fear of a British attack (which did not in fact come until the summer of 1941), built air-raid shelters, imposed a blackout and censorship and reinforced its troops. These warlike preparations unsettled the young Asad:[11]

> In the city I knew no one. With whom could I fight and against whom? I felt the village was a much safer place and wished I was back home. But I was not much concerned about the Second World War: I was far more worried about my homework.

These months in Latakia made him grow up faster than his village contemporaries. For the first time in his life he was away from his parents, and his eyes were opened to another way of life. He did well at school, winning several small certificates of merit which were the first things he presented to his father when he went home in the summer of 1940. After this instructive year he returned to his village school, and in that narrow setting he was already someone who had distinguished himself.

In 1942 Asad was one of only four boys from his village to sit the examination for the primary school certificate, a vital hurdle on the way to a secondary education. The candidates' documents had to be sent to Latakia well in advance and as a preliminary the four boys rode down the hill on donkeys to the coast to have their pictures taken by a pavement photographer. Then came the matter of the letters of application. Simply to be allowed to sit the examination required submitting a request, written in the pupil's own hand to 'His Excellency the Minister of Education' in the Latakia administration. The first paragraph had to begin so many millimetres in from the margin. This was the occasion of many false starts, many torn up sheets of paper. 'It took the four of us a whole day to write out our applications in a slow, meticulous hand. We believed that if we were one millimetre out or if we made a single mistake we would be rejected.'[12] The school principal took the letters, photographs and birth certificates in a large sealed envelope to Latakia.

All that remained now was the examination itself. In the 1940s there was only one secondary school along the whole length of the coast, from the northern frontier of Lebanon to Alexandretta, serving Latakia, Tartus, Jableh, and the entire mountain hinterland. Competition for admission was stiff, but Asad was good at arithmetic, Arabic and subjects which required learning by rote.

> I remember our headmaster took us aside and warned us not to get confused by the questions or be frightened by the sight of unfamiliar teachers in Western dress and speaking both French and Arabic. 'You are as good as the town boys' he told us, words we remembered when we went into the exam.

Indeed the country boys' results proved to be among the best.[13]

Asad inherited an important legacy from his grandfather and father – he was born into a family which was vigorously bettering itself at a time when the 'Alawi community as a whole was emerging from its long neglect. His grandfather Sulayman made the family's reputation for physical and moral strength. His muscular legacy offers an important clue to Asad's character. From his time on, the Asads became people who were not submissive, who did not defer or knuckle under, and who were not easily pushed around. They were a tough lot who were known to be moving up. Although their clan was smaller and poorer than many, they seized every opportunity for self-improvement.

The contribution of Asad's father, 'Ali Sulayman, was to make the family yet more prominent, to give his son an education which earned him self-respect and the respect of others. An official document of 1936 which lists leading figures of the region describes 'Ali Sulayman al-Asad as a *chef alaouite*, or head of a clan, although his position in the list indicates that he occupied a lesser place than the leading dignatories of the community.[14] A 1942 survey of 'Alawi tribes and clans, made by a wartime British Political Officer,[15] shows 'Ali Sulayman's family to be the head of the minor al-'A'ila clan of the Kalbiya tribe, a modest eminence but a real one. In their home village the Asads had carved out a place for themselves, even though they were still a good deal less influential than the leading Qurdaha families of Hassun, 'Uthman and al-Khayyir.

To his father's influence Asad owed a lifelong interest in books, poetry and the Arabic language. One day when he was in his teens, his father challenged him and one of his brothers to a memory competition: who would be first to learn a long poem by Hassan ibn Thabit (a friend of the Prophet Muhammad who followed him into battle and commemorated his deeds in verse). The poem was copied out and the boys went out of doors to study it. Asad was the first back but found that his father had already closed the book and was ready to recite. Developing a good memory became something of a family tradition and, in Asad's later years, his elephantine powers of recall were a source of uneasy admiration among his staff. It was also remarked that his accomplished use of classical Arabic, especially in off-the-cuff speeches, distinguished him in public life.

Because of his education and his vigorous personality, Asad was soon seen as the heir to Sulayman and 'Ali Sulayman. As his father was so old — eighty by the time Asad was twenty-five — the young man came to assume certain family responsibilities. In particular, he helped his mother with his two younger brothers, Jamil and Rif'at who, being less serious and single-minded, regarded him as a somewhat stern father-figure whose approval they sought but whose authority they liked to challenge. Asad was the first member of his family to leave the world of Qurdaha behind. His parents, aunts, uncles, cousins and half-brothers remained rooted in the village, but from an early age he was out on his own, learning to think for himself and acquiring interests and ambitions beyond their horizon.

2

The French Legacy

Asad grew up in one of the strangest political societies of modern times: an 'Alawi 'state' of some 300,000 people which France carved out of a backward corner of the Ottoman empire after the defeat of the Turks in the First World War. This unusual background was to have an enduring effect on him. The central paradox of his career was that as a man who was to claim to embody militant Arab nationalism he should have started life in an obscure backwater – separatist, Western-sponsored, and by definition sectarian, which held itself aloof from the Arab world in general and from the rest of Syria in particular. Separatism and unity, minority and majority, margin and mainstream, the part and the whole – these opposites still lie just below the surface of politics and society in the Arab world. Is that world a mosaic, a bewildering babble of ancient communities each at odds with the other? Or is it a unit, essentially one in way of life, language and aspirations? Most Arabs believe the second to be true and blame their fragmentation on the malevolent interference of foreigners. In Syria this feeling is particularly acute.

Every Syrian schoolchild is brought up to hate the Sykes-Picot Agreement of 1916 and the Balfour Declaration of 1917, the two instruments which in Arab eyes carved up and disposed of 'natural Syria'. Although natural Syria was almost never politically united, this vast area – bounded by the Taurus mountains to the north, the Mediterranean to the west, the Euphrates to the east, and the Arabian desert to the south – was in the minds of its inhabitants a whole, homogeneous in culture, threaded with economic ties and known for centuries as *bilad al-Sham*, 'the lands of Damascus'. Each of the main cities of the region had its own character and jealous particularity, and its constellation of leading families, but there was a sense in which Jerusalem and Jaffa, Tyre, Sidon, Beirut and Tripoli, Damascus, Homs and Hama, Latakia, Aleppo and Alexandretta were all kin, and of all these Damascus was acknowledged to be the most important.

For ten years in the 1830s natural Syria was ruled by Egypt from Damascus as a single unit for the first time since the reign of the Umayyad caliphs twelve hundred years earlier. When Egyptian occupation ended, *bilad al-Sham* reverted to Ottoman rule and was again subdivided into provinces, but these divisions were no more than local authority demarcations offering no obstacle to trade or settlement or family ties. (The real division at the time was between this 'natural Syria' and the Arab frontier provinces facing Persia – that is to say, present-day Iraq.) When the First World War finished off the 400-year-old Ottoman empire, its Arab provinces were left to the mercies of Britain and France, the victorious superpowers of the time, who had secretly arranged to share out natural Syria between them. France took the northern part which was to become the republics of Syria and Lebanon, while further south Britain seized what were to be Palestine and Transjordan.

The inhabitants of the whole region made it clear that they wanted natural Syria to be independent and undivided: in July 1919 an elected body calling itself the Syrian National Congress repudiated the Sykes-Picot Agreement and the Balfour Declaration and demanded sovereign status for a united Syria-Palestine. Overwhelming popular support for this demand was confirmed by the King-Crane commission, an American fact-finding team which visited scores of towns and villages and received nearly two thousand petitions. But in 1920, to the despair of the Syrians, the European powers were given Mandates over the new states carved out of the former Ottoman provinces. These Mandates were conceived as a form of guardianship of young nations, but France ousted the Arab administration which the Amir Faysal had established in Damascus and proceeded to set up a colonial regime, before reordering the region to suit itself and its local friends.[1]

First, in August 1920, it detached large areas from Syria – the ports of Tyre, Sidon, Beirut and Tripoli, the Biqa' valley, and the Shi'i region north of Palestine – and attached them to Mount Lebanon, the fief of its Maronite protégés, so as to create the State of Greater Lebanon. At a stroke Damascus lost its outlets to the sea and saw its horizons violently contract.

A second amputation occurred in October 1921 when France surrendered to Turkey large parts of the former province of Aleppo, bringing the Turks within fifty kilometres of the city. Aleppo's domain was further whittled away when France granted a special status to the Alexandretta-Antioch enclave of northern Syria because it contained a sizeable Turkish minority. (Less than twenty years later, the whole region was handed over to Turkey.) France then divided into four what remained of the country entrusted to it. In September 1920 Damascus and Aleppo were made the capitals of separate mini-states and in March 1922 the 'Alawi mountains and the Druze mountains were severed from Damascus and proclaimed 'independent'. In addition, the essentially tribal north-eastern part of Syria was brought under direct French rule and separatist sentiment encouraged by the settlement of Christians and Kurds.

These internal and wholly artificial frontiers were eventually swept away but Syria never regained its lost territories. When the French finally withdrew in 1946, the country had shrunk to 185,190 square kilometres from the 300,000 square kilometres which had been the extent of the Ottoman empire's Syrian provinces. The Syrians did not easily recover from the shock of this surgery, and the feeling that their country was made smaller than it was meant to be became a continued source of frustration.

The French influence

When France arrived as a mandatory power, it perceived itself as the protector of minorities and especially of the Maronites on whose behalf it had joined with other European powers in sponsoring a semi-autonomous Mount Lebanon after the 1860 massacres. It therefore proceeded to create a 'Greater Lebanon' in the 1920s. The benefits bestowed on the Maronites over the years could surely be extended to the backward 'Alawis just a step further up the Mediterranean coast. In French minds, the 'Alawis seemed to be crying out for the protector's touch. Thus a sort of political map took shape in French official thinking: the flatlands of Syria were largely Sunni and unfriendly, but skirting them were the mountain havens of the minorities, not only the 'Alawis but the Isma'ilis of the same area and the Druzes in their basalt hills in the south.

A French advance guard entered Latakia, the Mediterranean port which lies at the foot of the 'Alawi mountains, on 6 November 1918, a bare month after the defeated Turks had packed their bags. The interior of Syria was not occupied for another two years, a clear pointer to France's greater interest in the mountain minorities. In the 'Alawi area it set about trying to pacify the mountains, something the Turks had never managed, but faced immediate resistance which soon spread to the scattered villages of the uplands, finding a leader in an 'Alawi headman, the young Shaykh Salih al-'Ali. An old photograph shows this early nationalist wearing a curved sabre in his belt and a breastplate of beaten metal strapped over his *'abaya*. Terrain well suited to *maquisards* enabled him to defy France for over two years. Among his supporters was Asad's father, 'Ali Sulayman, who is remembered in local legend as riding off on horseback to raid a French position.

Eventually the French lost patience: in May 1921, three mobile columns were sent into the mountains to disarm one village after another, and by October it was all over. Shaykh Salih surrendered and was jailed in a Crusader castle on the small island of Arwad, just off the Syrian coast near Tartus, where a barracks still bears his name. Having imposed order on the 'Alawi district, the French could not make up their minds about its political destiny, an uncertainty reflected in frequent changes of name. In 1920 the area was called the 'Autonomous Territory of the 'Alawis', in 1922 it was renamed the 'State of the 'Alawis' and federated with the other Syrian statelets the French had created, only to be detached in 1924. In May 1930 it was named the 'Government of Latakia', in 1936 it was re-attached to the rest of Syria, but in 1939 had its autonomy largely restored. In 1942 it was brought yet again under the authority of Damascus in a last arrangement of the jigsaw before Syria won full independence from France in 1946. So the pendulum swung back and forth from separatism to unity, from part to whole.

The French put a stop to 'Alawi brigandage, introduced the rudiments of public administration, issued identity cards, and corralled the scattered and mistrustful mountain people into the statistics of a population census. They even gave them a postage stamp and a flag – a yellow sun on a white ground, a symbol which the local people must have found puzzling.

In Turkish times Sunni Muslims had been the privileged community, growing rich on 'Alawi labour. An 'Alawi highlander who ventured into the plains to look for work or to sell a basket of vegetables to buy the necessities of life could expect to be ground down by the Sunni or Christian merchant, money-lender or landowner with whom he had to deal. But once the territory was pacified in the early 1920s the French gave the 'Alawis privileges to the chagrin of both Sunnis and Christians, the latter in particular expecting better treatment at French hands. Perhaps with their missionary schools the French hoped to convert the 'Alawis to Christianity or at any rate turn them into clients. Be that as it may, the 'Alawis on the whole seized on the opportunity for self-improvement.

The port of Latakia acquired a traditional hold over the 'Alawi mountains through tobacco, the one export crop to find a market in Europe where it was especially favoured as pipe tobacco when the

American Civil War cut off supplies of Virginia leaf. In the last years of the Ottoman empire, France took over the Syrian tobacco trade and established a monopoly, the *Régie des Tabacs*, in a mansion built over a fourteenth century caravanserai in Latakia. When the empire collapsed and France inherited Syria, the French governor commandeered the handsome mansion as his residence.[2] For decades the *Régie* remained the growers' only customer and banker, and therefore the real master of the mountains whatever the political system at the time.

Another major instrument of French influence was the recruitment of young 'Alawis into the *Troupes spéciales du Levant*, a local force raised in 1921, in which they served under French officers together with Circassians, Armenians and other 'reliable' minorities. The auxiliaries totalled 7,000 in 1924 and double that number by the mid-1930s. Like the Circassians and Druzes, 'Alawis joined the *Troupes spéciales* because there was often no other employment and because the French deliberately sought them out, using the minorities as a fire brigade to suppress disorders elsewhere in the country. For the first time in their lives 'Alawi youths enjoyed some small but steady income, were disciplined, trained and exposed to new ideas. Service with the French established the beginnings of an 'Alawi military tradition central to the community's later ascent. Needless to say, the French made every effort to keep the *Troupes* immune from the Syrian nationalist ferment of the towns. When in 1925–7 the Druze revolt inflamed the whole south and beyond, even reaching the orchards of the Ghuta oasis around Damascus where the bloodiest battles were fought, most 'Alawi tribal leaders did not stir. And the community as a whole grew more separatist still in the 1930s when France faced a rising tide of opposition to its rule from a National Bloc of Syrian city notables campaigning for independence.

Between France and the nationalists

The great question facing the 'Alawis during the inter-war Mandate was where to position themselves between French power and the Syrian nationalists. Like the Ottomans before them, the French sought intermediaries through whom to rule the local population. While ultimate authority was in the hands of the French governor and his staff of native affairs officers, power at a local level lay with 'Alawis prepared to play France's game. Most 'Alawis were probably neither Syrian nationalists nor collaborators with France, wanting only to run their own affairs as they had for centuries. And among the political personalities of Asad's boyhood, some used the community's traditional assets, physical toughness, religious solidarity, the inaccessible mountains, to win what freedom they could. Others tilted one way or the other.

The most prominent men who chose to throw in their lot with the Mandate were the Kinj brothers,[3] shrewd peasants who backed the French from the moment of their arrival in 1918 and were rewarded with wealth and influence. Ibrahim al-Kinj, head of the family, was in 1931 appointed chairman of the Latakia Representative Council, a largely nominated body set up to advise the governor. He was awarded the Legion of Honour, acquired estates and rose to become the most influential chief of the Haddadin tribe. In his new role he had to be generous and hospitable, expensive virtues which he funded by smuggling tobacco and hashish from his own fields, and even arms and ammunition. His brother 'Ali was the ruthless director of the interior in the territory.

Another pillar of the French administration was the 'Abbas family, leaders of the largely religious Khaiyatin tribe, a very different breed from the jumped-up Kinj brothers. Learned and moderate, Shaykh Jabir al-'Abbas helped the French in their pacification campaign of the early 1920s and was made president of the Latakia Council. But in 1933 he broke with the French to advocate union with the Syrian Republic. While such families of the Haddadin and Khaiyatin tribes collaborated, the leading personality of the Matawira tribe did not. 'Aziz al-Hawwash, whose father and grandfather had been powerful chiefs in Turkish times, threw in his lot with the Syrian nationalists – the first important 'Alawi to do so.

In the Kalbiya confederation to which the Asad family belonged, both collaborators and nationalists were to be found. Two of the main figures of the tribe, Muhammad Bey Junayd and Saqr Khayr-Bek, spent the mandate years in veering from 'Alawi separatism to Syrian union and back again, but very probably prompted more by self-interest and jealousy of the Kinj and 'Abbas families than by conviction. The real luminary of the Kalbiya and one of its chief religious figures was the scholarly Shaykh Sulayman al-Ahmad, a member of the Arab Academy founded in Damascus in 1919 during Faysal's brief reign. The career of his son Ahmad, who won a reputation as a poet throughout the Arab world under the pen name of Badawi al-Jabal, illustrates the ebb and flow of 'Alawi allegiance under the Mandate. He was first a nationalist, then secretary to the collaborator Ibrahim al-Kinj until 1936, then again a violently anti-French nationalist and a member of the Damascus parliament before being appointed Professor of Arabic at Baghdad university in Iraq where he is said to have supported Rashid 'Ali's 1941 bid for greater freedom from Britain.

The Asad family was itself ambivalent in its attitude to the French authorities. Asad's grandfather, Sulayman, never came to terms with the Mandate or deferred to men who owed their prominence solely to the French connection. Asad's father, 'Ali Sulayman, fought the French at the start but was later drawn into French arrangements, being appointed in 1926 a member of a committee set up in Latakia to draft a constitution for the territory. He was one of eighty signatories of a letter which Ibrahim al-Kinj sent to the French Prime Minister in 1936 stating that the overwhelming majority of the 'Alawi people rejected attachment to Syria and wished to remain under French protection.

This was at a time when a Syrian delegation was in Paris trying to negotiate a treaty with France as a stepping stone to independence. A crucial issue between France and the nationalists was precisely the fate of the French-created 'Alawi and Druze mini-states: the nationalists wanted to reunite them with Syria while the French stressed their special status and wanted them to be garrisoned by French troops. When the National Bloc formed a government in Damascus, following the signature of the long-delayed treaty with Léon Blum's Popular Front government in 1936, it actively tried to reverse the separatist tide of the previous fifteen years. 'Aziz al-Hawwash, the most prominent 'Alawi to side with the Syrian nationalists, was rewarded by being appointed governor of Damascus. But in 1939 the French high commissioner brushed aside the never ratified treaty and named the French-educated Shawkat al-'Abbas as governor of a more or less autonomous 'Alawi statelet.

In Asad's youth when men talked politics Kinj, 'Abbas, Hawwash were the names to conjure with. But all these personalities, whether collaborators or nationalists, were overshadowed by the flamboyant figure of Sulayman Murshid,[4] the religio-political leader who himself walked a tightrope between French power and Damascus.

At the age of sixteen, when a shepherd boy in a wretched hamlet of the high mountains, Murshid fell ill and lost consciousness for a time. When he came round he claimed that he had descended from heaven and to the wonderment of the locals started to preach the end of the world and the coming of the Mahdi, a message which 'Alawi beliefs predisposed them to accept. His success was immediate. Within a few months religious enthusiasm turned political. Peasants took to arms, a couple of villages refused to pay their taxes, the white-domed shrines of holy men, such an architectural feature of the 'Alawi landscape, became venues for secret meetings. Fearing sedition, a French intelligence officer took the boy to Latakia where he was tried and sentenced to some months in jail. This was in 1923. Freed the following spring he returned to a triumphant welcome in the mountains where converts flocked to him. Murshid then began to perform miracles which greatly impressed the gullible common people, most of whom had hardly ventured beyond their villages. He would paint his legs with phosphorus to make them glow at night, or hide a pot of honey or butter in a mud wall, then, promising the villagers something good, give the wall a kick, and the food would tumble out to universal amazement.

His message sped rapidly down to the coast and to the 'Alawi share-croppers labouring in the Homs-Hama plain on the other side of the mountains. A leading shaykh gave him his daughter in marriage. In April 1924, in the small village of 'Alyat south of Homs, his disciples began slaughtering whoever would not convert to him. The French sent troops against them but Murshid's fanatics, believing that the sticks with which they were armed would turn into guns at the moment of combat, refused to surrender. Fifty were killed and as many wounded, and Murshid was sent into exile to the remote village of Raqqa on the Euphrates. But this only gave his cult a further impetus and on his return a few months later his following ran into thousands.

It was then that the French began to see that the young preacher was developing into a politician who could be put to use. His 'Alawi exclusiveness made him a potential ally against the Syrian nationalists. So the French built him up. The end of the world was deferred, miracles became rarer. Instead Murshid acquired a harem of thirteen wives in matrimonial alliances which extended his power. He set up his own courts, levied taxes on tobacco grown on his territory, gladly received gifts of money, livestock and land from his followers, became obese, built himself a Western-style villa in his village of Jawbat Burghal and opened a road to it. In 1937, although still illiterate, he was elected to parliament in Damascus. By 1939 he had 50,000 followers and an armoury of French-supplied weapons.

But after the last French troops withdrew in April 1946, Damascus set about subduing those parts of Syria where local sentiment and the French had encouraged separatism: the Jabal al-Duruz, the bedouin tribes of the desert, and of course the 'Alawi mountains. Troops were sent against Murshid's headquarters where one of his many wives, Umm Fatih, by all accounts a formidable personality, commanded his private army. She refused to surrender, and it is said that Murshid himself shot her. He was arrested, taken to Damascus and hanged in the main square in November 1946. (In 1952, during the regime of General Adib al-Shishakli, one of Murshid's sons, Mujib, was killed for allegedly trying to revive his father's separatist ambitions.)[5]

Such were the stars of the 'Alawi community when Asad was growing up. Even though Murshid came to a bad end, France's encouragement of separatism gave his people a new confidence in themselves. For generations they had been virtually beyond the pale of government, outlaws in their own country. The French brought them to Latakia and told them this 'capital' was theirs and this their 'state' — a revolutionary idea for people cooped up in their mountain hamlets who had hardly dared venture within the gates of the coastal cities. Now the movement down to the coast accelerated. 'Alawis acquired a sense of opportunities which in the anarchy and poverty of their lives they had never known before.

For almost the first time in their history a handful of them gained some small experience of public affairs, either with the French or with the nationalists, and their children used this springboard to get an education: two 'Abbas boys studied in France, two others at the American University of Beirut. Kinj al-Kinj, son of Ibrahim, was also a student at the AUB, as were no fewer than three sons of the ill-fated Sulayman Murshid. Power and influence were redistributed in the mountains. But, as in the past, what wealth the new chieftains could lay their hands on came mainly from tobacco: trading in it, levying private taxes on it, smuggling it, or extending protection to smugglers in return for a share of the loot.

The French did not bring much material improvement to the mountains. Dirt tracks were pushed into the foothills, the work often being done by gangs of men and women forcibly rounded up for the job on pain of a beating or a fine. The Latakia-Aleppo road was first built with such conscript labour. Villages further into the mountains, accessible only by donkey or mule, now saw the first motorcars, but here it would be the local notable who was the taskmaster, assembling young men from three or four villages to lay the track. The mountain fastness was breached, and the process of change could not be turned back.

In spite of this progress, most mountain 'Alawis were still abjectly poor at the end of the Second World War. A British officer who served in Syria wrote of an 'Alawi village:[6]

> The wretched inhabitants were in a deplorable state of misery, dejection and abandon . . . For a small country that had been under European mandate for twenty-two years the conditions everywhere were unbelievably bad.

Poverty led to a practice which was to bring the 'Alawis shame but also some indirect benefit. Destitute or landless families hired out their daughters as domestic servants from the age of six or seven, usually for ten years, sometimes for life. The trade probably began after 1921 when the French imposed collective fines upon rebellious villages: to pay peasants sold their sheep, their land, or their daughters. Hardly a well-to-do family in Latakia was without a little 'Alawi maidservant, while some unfortunate children were sent 'abroad', so to speak, to Aleppo, Tripoli, Damascus or Beirut. 'Alawis were not alone in providing child labour but it is they who are principally remembered for this practice. As late as 1950 there were some ten thousand 'Alawi girls working as domestic drudges in Damascus. What is rarely admitted is that domestic service was an education in its way, opening up wider horizons. It was discovered that mountain girls adapted rapidly to town life, learning to speak French in French-speaking households. Adaptability was to prove an 'Alawi characteristic.

The French connection may not have radically improved the 'Alawis' lot, but it made them *feel* different, and this in the long run may have been a more valuable bequest than prosperity. Yet when the French left there was a price to be paid. 'Alawis had always been disdained for their poverty and heretical beliefs; now they were condemned as disloyal to the political ideas of Syrian unity and Arab nationalism. Their service in the *Troupes spéciales*, the fact that they owed their first step up in the world to French colonial patronage, and their separatist sentiments all bred suspicion of them in other Syrians, widening even further the breach between 'Alawis and Sunnis. For a few years after the Second World War they found it necessary to lie low. It was not until the 1950s that a new 'Alawi generation, that of Hafiz al-Asad, began to elbow its way into the mainstream of Syrian life.

For their part the 'Alawis suffered from an acute sense of grievance, nourished over centuries, which explained the formidable energy, even the frenzy, with which this unfavoured community snatched at education, wealth and power once the wheel of fortune turned. With their history of oppression and exploitation, it was to be expected that 'Alawis should seek redress for the injustices of the past and should be utterly determined never to be subdued again.

No doubt the young Asad shared the feelings of his co-religionaries, resenting the past and suffering embarrassment on account of the ambiguous and unavowable French connection. But from his teens on he rebelled against this background, threw off his sectarian grudges and joined the most pan-Arab of parties, the Ba'th, eventually coming to rule Syria under its banner. Nevertheless despite his later nationalist credentials, the inescapable 'Alawi label was to be his burden. He had to work hard to convince his sceptical compatriots that he had left minority complexes behind him, had committed himself body and soul to the nationalist mainstream, and was indeed fit to lead them.

3

Party School and Army College

One morning in class a shabbily dressed teacher was failing to control the boys, and especially an insolent youth whose smart clothes marked him out as the son of a rich family. Swaggering in front of the others, he joked with his cronies and refused to sit down. At last the teacher had had enough. With trembling hands he bundled his papers into his briefcase and stalked out with the words, 'You can't buy my dignity for a few liras!' The boys knew he had thrown his job away: all were aware that his salary was paid by the fathers of rich boys such as the one who was tormenting him.

This little drama was played out in a long, rather battered yellow plastered building, set behind a row of palms a few streets in from the Latakia waterfront. The date was 1945 and among the boys in the classroom was Hafiz al-Asad, then in his first year at secondary school. Forty years on he still regarded that hard-pressed teacher as a hero.

Resentment at the unfairness of life, a nascent class-consciousness, was probably Asad's first political emotion. At home in Qurdaha he had not felt particularly underprivileged, but in town, where a handful of notables in league with the French lorded it over the poor, there were daily reminders of inequality. Every Syrian city had its elite of leading men – landowners, merchants, financiers, religious dignatories – many of whom could trace their prominence to the older Ottoman order which two decades of French rule had done little to disturb. Brought up to money and influence, their sons threw their weight about as playground bullies.

Asad recalled them:[1]

They took over the courtyard, beating up boys they didn't like and after school they would go to Abu 'Ali's foodshop to eat and feed their friends. Poor boys could only look on and go hungry. The sons of the rich changed their clothes once a week, or at the very least once a month, a sign of exceptional wealth at the time, but the less fortunate went to school in rags and couldn't even afford to buy books. Sometimes boys stayed away altogether because the fees could not be found. Rich boys didn't bother to work, but simply gave themselves what marks they wanted at the end of the year, and very few were the teachers who dared stand up to them.

'Alawi mountain boys like Asad studied hard because even getting into secondary school was a struggle and they had no thought of throwing away the chance to better themselves. In another country district, that of Zabadani, west of Damascus, only eight boys were admitted to secondary school in 1941 out of a population of some 40,000.[2] Asad's school reports for 1944–6 show that in those two years he consistently came top of the class. Poetry and literature were not forgotten. He spent hours after school gazing out at the Mediterranean and trying to put his emotions into verse (as he confided to a Syrian schoolgirl to whom he gave a poetry prize in 1974).

The injustice at school mirrored that of the world outside. The young Asad soon learned that what few jobs were available in Latakia were in the gift of notables, to be disposed of as their private property. If the Régie, for example, needed to take on more hands, the jobs would be shared out among the local bosses – ten for one, twenty for another – and they would then sell them to the highest bidder. A man might pay 200 liras for a job as a clerk or for the privilege of sweeping the tobacco warehouse floor, and then be sacked before he had had time to earn his money back. The same job would then be sold to another. And what was true of the Régie was true of the port, the gendarmerie, and what other few openings there were.

In those days Latakia was a sleepy Mediterranean town with little to boast of save a public garden and one or two government buildings in the French colonial style. But to a mountain boy it was the 'capital' of the 'Alawi state still in alien hands. Asad, then a tall brawny lad of fourteen, shared a room with a cousin of his own age in a poor quarter of the town. He was some two years older than most of his city classmates, no doubt the result of poor schooling in the village, but being with smaller boys had its advantages. He was strong enough to stand up to the playground bullies, and he began to be noticed for a spirit of defiance which got him into scrapes and scuffles, and which soon took on a political complexion.[3]

In the late 1940s Asad's school and others like it throughout Syria were noisy with political argument. To distinguish friend from foe, one boy might ask another, '*Shu dinak?*', literally 'What's your religion?' but meaning 'Where do you stand?' One of three answers could be expected: Communist, Ba'thist or Syrian Nationalist, rival ideological movements which competed with each other for young minds, while all opposed the ruling establishment of city notables and the religious zealots of the Muslim Brotherhood.[4] Young men from minority backgrounds, who were uncomfortable with the identification of Arab nationalism with Islam, found the secular doctrines of the ideological parties especially seductive.

The prophet of Syrian (in fact 'Greater Syrian') nationalism was Antun Sa'ada, a compelling Christian ideologue from Lebanon who taught that geography as much as history had bequeathed to the inhabitants of natural Syria a specific identity quite distinct from that of other Arabs. His bitterest opponent was the Communist leader, Khalid Bakdash, an eloquent Kurd who had steered the chequered fortunes of the Syrian party since 1930. The Ba'th's heroes were a clutch of schoolmasters: the ardent Zaki al-Arsuzi from Antioch and, from Damascus, Michel 'Aflaq and Salah al-Din Bitar whose pamphlets, passed from hand to hand, were eagerly discussed in Latakia. Another name to conjure with was that of Akram al-Hawrani, an agitator who was mobilizing landless peasants against their feudal lords in the plains of central Syria. All these thinkers and political activists were anti-French, all were disgusted with their political elders for the feebleness with which they had opposed the foreign carve-up of their country, all felt oppressed by the *ancien régime* and all were eager to put their imprint on independent Syria as it emerged from the Second World War.

It was a time of far-reaching change. The Ottoman empire had passed away a dozen years before Asad's birth, while the new states of the Levant won their independence a dozen years or so after it. In between were a couple of decades of French rule which undermined the old ways but failed to implant convincing new ones. The ideological movements of the 1940s which shaped Asad's adolescence were the midwives of an emerging society struggling to find answers to such fundamental questions as: What are the boundaries of our homeland? To what nation do we belong? How can the Arabs claim their rightful place in the world? But also, at home, how can the rule of the old oppressive class be overturned? From the clash of rival answers Asad acquired a political education, growing up in the school courtyard, fighting his first battles in the neighbouring streets, and making a lifelong commitment to a revolutionary party. He spent seven years at the Latakia secondary school, taking his baccalauréat in the summer of 1951 at the age of twenty. 'Those years formed my political thinking', he later declared. 'My political life started then and has not been interrupted since.'[5]

National renaissance

At the age of sixteen Asad took sides in the debate and joined the Ba'th. What was this movement and, more particularly, which Ba'th was it? For the party was not monolithic but was rent by internal schisms of which from the start the most enduring was the controversy about who could claim to be its founding father. In the lists were two rival schoolmasters, the 'Alawi from Antioch, Zaki al-Arsuzi, and the Damascene Christian, Michel 'Aflaq. For reasons which have to do with his own origins as well as with later party squabbles, Asad came down on the side of Arsuzi whom he never ceased to revere throughout his life, describing him as 'one of the greatest Syrians of his day and the first to conceive of the Ba'th as a political movement'.[6]

Zaki al-Arsuzi was a Syrian intellectual from a modest background who, in the late 1920s, won a place at the Sorbonne from which he emerged four years later with a philosophy degree and a boundless enthusiasm for French poetry, painting and civilization. In 1932 he was taken on as a teacher at his old school in Antioch where he had first shown promise. The awakening was brutal. French officials administering the Mandate were a different breed from the poets and professors he had worshipped in Paris. They were either low-grade *fonctionnaires*, ignorant of local custom, or else army officers with previous experience in North Africa whose most characteristic attitude was a contempt for the natives. 'How dare you teach here what you learned at the Sorbonne!' he was scolded when word leaked out of what went on in his classroom. 'What matters here is French interest, not French culture.' When a school inspector found him preaching to his pupils the ideas of the French Revolution, Arsuzi was stopped in mid-sentence and turned out of the classroom. Liberty, equality and fraternity were not for subject peoples.[7] In 1934 the young teacher founded a *Club des Beaux Arts* with the ambition of spreading art appreciation in his home town, but when this activity was also frowned on, he gave up French culture for Syrian politics and became a nationalist agitator.

The great issue of the time in Arsuzi's home province of Alexandretta was the battle between Arabs and Turks for political control. Turks formed the largest single community but the electoral rolls showed that non-Turks – Arabs and Armenians – were clearly the majority. However, as war with Germany was looming, France was anxious to conciliate Turkey and fell in with its demand that Alexandretta should not be absorbed into the Syrian Republic, as the Arab nationalists wanted, but should retain the 'special status' it had been granted under the Mandate. The nationalists were furious at what they saw as France's betrayal of their interests. Taking command of the protest movement, Arsuzi brought youngsters out on to the streets, provoked clashes between Arabs and Turks and landed himself in jail – to no avail; in July 1938, France and Turkey signed a treaty of friendship, whereupon Turkish troops marched into the province and, to the Arabs' astonishment and indignation, the electoral rolls suddenly revealed the Turks to be in the majority. The outcome was that in June 1939 Alexandretta began a new life as the Turkish province of Hatay: another greedy bite had been taken out of Syria's short coastline. By disregarding its pledge to protect the integrity of Syria, France had committed a flagrantly immoral political act.[8]

Unwilling to live under Turkish rule, thousands of Arabs left their homes in the province of Alexandretta and moved south to take refuge in Syria, Arsuzi among them. He arrived in Damascus at the outbreak of war with the aura of a nationalist saint, and set up his headquarters in the Havana, a political café in a main street of the capital. Soon he had gathered a circle of young followers to whom he explained that the 'renaissance' of the Arabs – that is what the word '*ba'th*' means – was in their grasp, and that once freedom from foreign rule had been secured, they would once more take part in the forward march of civilization, reviving their nation's ancient glories.[9] But Arsuzi's coterie never grew into a political movement, for the French would not leave him alone. Accusing him of poisoning young minds, they forbade him to teach in school or even to give private lessons, harried him from town to town, and reduced him to a life of penury and persecution. One of his disciples recalled that 'four or five of us youngsters shared rooms with him and saw his extreme poverty. He grew anxious and depressed, and more and more engrossed in his own imaginings.'[10] His sharpness in argument was not blunted but something, perhaps his hard life, unbalanced him. As he grew older he kept to himself and came to suffer from delusions. During the Second World War Arsuzi's interest in politics waned and, growing somewhat detached from daily life, he became absorbed in philological studies, examining the meanings of word-roots which are the most characteristic feature of the Arabic language and the base on which nuance, subtlety and variety are built. He expounded his ideas in a book, *Arab Genius in Language*.[11]

This eccentric thinker made a profound impression on a number of young people, among them a medical student, Wahib al-Ghanim, who had sat at his feet in Antioch in the late 1930s and then in Damascus in the early 1940s. Ghanim qualified as a doctor in 1943 and went to practise in Latakia, fired by Arsuzi's example of self-sacrifice and the dream of an Arab renaissance. As a student Ghanim had been a nationalist, his anti-French sentiments sharpened by the vexations of foreign rule. As he recounted, 'I once saw a French sergeant trying to pick up a girl. She ran off, he ran after her – and kicked her. He simply couldn't accept her daring to run away.'[12] But in Latakia, stripped bare by the war, people were starving. The nationalist became a militant socialist. From his clinic in the town the young doctor travelled on foot into the hills, bringing medicines to the stricken villagers and eventually winning their trust. They paid him return visits. Soon, like his master Arsuzi, Wahib al-Ghanim had his circle of followers. 'I couldn't resist giving free lessons to young men I hoped to win over', he explained. 'My father and brothers were all teachers and I tend to think like one.'[13] His most promising catch was a strong, lively village boy from Qurdaha, then at school in Latakia – Hafiz al-Asad.

In other parts of Syria the pattern was the same. Young nationalists were gathering still younger youths together to spread the gospel of Arab independence and social revolution. In Hama Akram al-Hawrani led a youth movement and across the desert, in the sleepy town of Dayr al-Zur on the Euphrates, a lawyer, Jalal al-Sayyid, started a boys' club with a strong nationalist flavour which was to be the first Ba'th party branch in eastern Syria.

But of all these youth groups, the most significant for the future was that of Michel 'Aflaq and Salah al-Din Bitar who, like Arsuzi graduates of the Sorbonne, on their return home to Damascus in 1934 became teachers at the Tajhiz al-'Ula, the most prestigious secondary school in Syria. 'Aflaq, a Greek Orthodox Christian born in 1910, taught history, while his friend Bitar, a Sunni Muslim two years younger, taught maths and physics. French oppression, Syrian backwardness, a political class unable to measure up to the challenge of the times were what persuaded them that a profound overhaul of society was required. Ridding Syria of the French was not enough to bring about an Arab rebirth: minds, attitudes, self-consciousness itself had to be radically reshaped.

By 1940 'Aflaq and Bitar had set up their own study circle which usually met on Fridays, the Muslim day of rest. They issued their first tracts in 1941 and, at the end of the school year in 1942, gave up teaching for full-time politics, to live henceforth the ill-fed but exhilarating life of professional agitators. 'Aflaq was a compelling speaker with a cunning use of the theatrical pause and a gift for handling abstract themes. At the start they called their group the Movement of Arab Revival (*harakat al-ihya' al-'arabi*), publishing their first tracts under that name. Then in May 1941 occurred Rashid 'Ali al-Kaylani's brief and stirring challenge to British ascendancy in Iraq. This act of defiance prompted 'Aflaq and Bitar to adopt the word *ba'th* as the name of their movement, to indicate that 'revival' had given way to something more fundamental, 'rebirth'. Zaki al-Arsuzi claimed they had stolen the name from him. Damascus was then a small city and people interested in the same cause could scarcely avoid getting acquainted. So there was an inevitable flow of disciples and ideas between 'Aflaq and Arsuzi. But the rival gurus were not on good terms. Rather small in stature, 'Aflaq was wont to wear an over-tall fez. 'How can anyone hope to lead a revolution in a fez?' Arsuzi was heard to sneer.

Ba'thist ideas

In spite of these squabbles, the ideas of the Ba'th excited the minds of a whole generation. What was it about them which earned the lifelong commitment of a man like Asad? The starting point of the argument was the abysmal depths to which the Arabs had sunk by the early twentieth century. After four centuries under the Turks, when many went hungry and few learned to read or write, they were forced to endure French rule and then watch powerlessly as the Turks seized one part of what they considered their homeland and the Zionists another. With such a degraded history, the Arabs lost faith in themselves. The reverse of the coin was an exaggerated respect for 'advanced' nations. 'Aflaq's and Arsuzi's achievement was to help lift this burden of guilt and inferiority. 'Aflaq formulated a theory and a programme to rouse the Arabs from what he considered a living death. That is what he meant by *ba'th* .[14]

The core of the theory was that the Arabs had every reason to feel proud since they belonged to an ancient race with many glorious achievements to its credit. The Arab nation, 'Aflaq taught, was millennial, eternal, and unique, stretching back into the mists of time and forward to a brighter future. To achieve deliverance from backwardness and foreign control the Arabs had to have faith in their nation and unstinting love for it.

To express his belief in the unity of Arab history, the Ba'th's founder coined the phrase: 'One Arab nation with an eternal message'. But 'Aflaq's nationalism was not based on any supposed purity of Arab race nor was it narrowly chauvinistic. He candidly defined the shackles of Arab society as tribalism, sectarianism, the oppression of women, and the supremacy of landowners, and in seeking to break them, turned for inspiration to the enlightened face of Europe which educated Arabs admired as much as they loathed its colonial face.

He also coined a three-word guide to action : 'Unity, Freedom, Socialism'. Unity was the necessary medicine for a sick and divided nation: Arabs from the Atlantic to the Gulf belonged together because of bonds of history, religion, language, tradition and common hopes. Freedom was first conceived as freedom from foreign domination, whether military, political or cultural; but it also came to mean the personal liberation of the individual from mental and social chains. As for socialism, it was the Ba'th's answer to the concentration of wealth and power in the hands of notables and much else that was exploitative in Syrian society. Although the Ba'th founders had read Marx, their socialism was put to work in the service not so much of internationalism as of nationalism.

Aflaq's advocacy of the primacy of national revival came up against the classic problem of how to reconcile the goals of Arab nationalism with the universal values of Islam so central to Arab life. What sense did it make to speak of the 'eternal message' of a distinct Arab nation when the Prophet's revelation was for all mankind? 'Aflaq's solution was to assert that Islam was the most sublime expression of Arabism: the one had grown out of the other and there could be no contradiction between them. Islam, he argued, was from its very beginning an Arab religion, revealed in an Arabic Qur'an, meeting Arab needs, embodying Arab values, and launching the Arabs on their conquest of the known world. Islam as a culture rather than as a faith had a special attraction for Arab Christians such as 'Aflaq himself. In any event, it demanded a rare measure of courage for a Christian to advance such views in a lecture at Damascus University on the anniversary of the Prophet's birth in 1943. It was hardly surprising that he offended devout Muslims in suggesting that Islam was a flowering of Arab genius rather than a revelation of God, while at the same time annoying his fellow Christians who accused him of selling out to the other side and nicknamed him 'Muhammad 'Aflaq'. But 'Aflaq knew what he was about. He reminded his Christian critics that Islam was the Arabs' history, their philosophy, their legal and social systems, a total heritage of which any nationalist, be he Christian or Muslim, should be immensely proud. Deference to Islam was also his way of countering the preaching of the Muslim Brothers who, with their Golden Age vision of a purged Islamic state, had gone to war against secular parties such as the Ba'th and were his most dangerous rivals.

'Aflaq and his inseparable associate Bitar were not simply classroom pundits: they took their cause into the streets. Their revivalism was essentially a movement of the young, even of the very young, building on a tradition of youth politics which, a decade earlier in Syria in the 1930s, had given every shade of opinion its regiment of schoolboy militants. Children as young as eight years old were organized into scout troops and political squads and were encouraged to join demonstrations, stop trams and throw stones. The schools were nurseries of national sentiment, ringing in the years of occupation and war with hymns to the homeland and exhortations to sacrifice, and offering teachers great opportunities to influence youngsters at an impressionable age. The years 1941-8 which witnessed the defeat of Vichy France in the Levant, the death of the interwar Mandates, Syrian and Lebanese independence and the emergence of Israel from the Palestine War, were a period of passionate excitement, almost daily agitation and remarkably free speech.

The Tajhiz in Damascus, the most important school in the country, found itself at the centre of the nationalist struggle. It provided shock troops to keep the capital on the boil while its graduates spread the nationalist message around the country. There were about 1,500 pupils, mainly sons of Damascus families but including some 200 boarders from different parts of the country, the lucky few who had managed to win a place. As many of these boarders came from deprived backgrounds and, separated from their families, were more open to the influence of agitators, they tended to be more militant than the day-boys. Most had stories to tell of ill treatment at the hands of the French or of local notables propped up by French power. One of these was Shakir Fahham, later Asad's Minister of Education for the best part of a decade. As a child of six in his native Homs, and living on little more than bread and water, he had suffered a painful experience which remained with him for years. A French officer had set his Alsatian dog on him. The shock had kept him in bed for two months.[15] Fahham arrived at the Tajhiz in 1940 spoiling for a fight, and sought out leading lights of the nationalist movement such as Arsuzi and 'Aflaq. He took part in violent demonstrations, was arrested and spent some time in jail.

Junior boys would haul baskets of stones up to the flat roof of the school where older boys would hurl them at the police below. Phalanxes of youngsters would then race across the river to the refuge of the university where demonstrators would gather before making their way downtown, while shopkeepers hurried to clang close their metal shutters. Usually the rioters headed for the parliament building where cordons of gendarmes and French Senegalese troops armed with batons and firearms awaited them.

One early Ba'thist recalled:[16]

> The first boy killed was a young teenager of twelve or thirteen called Fawzi al-Lahham, shot down in 1941 near the west gate of the Tajhiz. I saw Fawzi die. I had only just come to secondary school from my village of Surghaya.

'Aflaq and Bitar were often to be seen at the head of these demonstrations. Press cartoons of the time depicted them mercilessly but accurately as marching in crumpled clothes, with torn collars and dirty fezes. They were unemployed, unmarried, shabby, and living on a pittance. In cheap eating houses in those days one could buy a plate of *hummus* for fifteen piastres, and a loaf of bread for ten. But bread could be had at a nearby bakery for five piastres and one was allowed to bring it in, which is what 'Aflaq and Bitar used to do.[17]

The founding of the party

In 1941 British troops marched from Palestine into Syria to defeat Vichy forces suspected of pro-German sympathies. With their victory, Britain promised the country its longed-for independence from France. But French officials – Free French now, rather than Vichy – dragged their feet and continued to rule by decree with the hated apparatus of local stooges and intelligence officers. On being returned to power in July 1943 the Syrian nationalists rejected France's demand for a treaty and declared the Mandate at an end. But still France refused to relinquish its last bargaining card, control over the *Troupes spéciales*. Rioting broke out in Damascus in May 1945, whereupon the French commander shelled the capital, causing hundreds of casualties and destroying a large residential quarter. Britain imposed a ceasefire, bringing French authority to an end. The last French soldier left Syrian soil on 17 April 1946, a date since celebrated as Syria's National Day. In an orgy of nationalism schoolboys cheered the French off with a bonfire of textbooks – which goes some way to explain why boys of Asad's generation, and indeed Asad himself, never learned much French. 'We all threw away our French books that day', Asad recalled. The gap in foreign language teaching was not filled until English-speaking Palestinian refugees arrived in Syria after the 1948 war.

In late 1944 or early 1945 the Ba'th leaders began drawing up lists of their supporters and, in Ba'thist literature, the term '*haraka*' (movement) gave way to '*hizb*' (party). In July 1945 'Aflaq and Bitar applied for a licence to form a political party. Their application was rejected then, but was eventually granted once the French had left.

Disciples of both Arsuzi and 'Aflaq decided on a merger, and a drafting committee laboured for months to reconcile the views of the two camps. Some of Arsuzi's followers, notably Dr Wahib al-Ghanim, wanted a stronger dose of socialism than the Damascus leaders, essentially middle-class, reformist, bred in a milieu of traders and artisans, were ready for. But at last at a meeting in Latakia in early 1947 'Aflaq, Bitar and Ghanim agreed the text of a constitution and made arrangements for a founding conference. For three days of heady debate, from Friday 5 to Sunday 7 April, 247 young men from all over Syria, together with a handful from Transjordan, Lebanon and Iraq, crowded into the Rashid Coffee House in Damascus, which in those days opened on to a garden and outdoor cinema known as the Luna Park. (The Soviet cultural centre now stands on the spot.) By Easter Sunday the constitution had been adopted and a four-man executive committee elected, consisting of Michel 'Aflaq, as '*amid* or senior member, Salah al-Din Bitar as general secretary, and Wahib al-Ghanim and Jalal al-Sayyid as members. Zaki al-Arsuzi neither attended the conference nor was given a position in the new party.

After the founding conference, Dr Wahib al-Ghanim, then aged twenty-seven, set up a local Ba'th party headquarters in his clinic at Latakia and started recruiting in earnest. Asad was among the first boys to join, along with other young men from Qurdaha where Ghanim in his role of itinerant physician was already a familiar figure. This was a crucial moment. In this emerging revolutionary vanguard were fused the natural rebelliousness and independent spirit of mountain boys, the class grievances of rural have-nots, and the wider horizons opened up by French patronage and education. Ghanim remembered Asad as 'keen, devoted and strong, a useful aide in those difficult years'.

But there was little time for the task of party building. A national crisis immediately engulfed them. Syria had barely won the struggle for independence when it was confronted by the emerging Zionist state in Palestine. On 29 November 1947, the United Nations General Assembly adopted the Palestine Partition Resolution allocating more than half of Palestine to a Jewish state. A storm of protest swept across the Arab world and nowhere more violently than in Syria where Palestine was felt to be an organic part of *bilad al-Sham*. The instinct of many young men was to rush to defend the homeland against this most recent amputation. The Syrian army managed to put together an expeditionary force of some 1,800 men, including Wahib al-Ghanim and Akram al-Hawrani as volunteers. One of the first casualties was a young Ba'thist officer, Marcel Karameh.[18] Early in 1948 Asad and six other boys travelled down to Damascus to sign on for war service only to be sent tamely home, to their great disappointment.[19]

Defeat, the massive flood of terrified refugees from Palestine and the establishment of the State of Israel laid bare the reality of Arab helplessness in 1948. In Syria independence, so lately won from the French, was seen to be hollow. Facing up to militant Jewish nationalism became the most urgent and daunting of concerns. From then on the contest with Zionism became the major theme of Asad's life, but war had also to be waged at home against the old order. 'On both fronts', he lamented, 'we were confronted with the very opposite of what we aspired to.'[20]

The schoolboy politician

The founding of the Ba'th gave a great impetus to student politics in Latakia and set the young Asad on the first rung of the ladder. At sixteen he was already an unusual 'Alawi youth, confident, combative, class-conscious and unashamed of his background. He was physically robust, no doubt a gift from his grandfather's genes, and could hold his own in the rough and tumble of the schoolyard. He became a party stalwart, defending its cause on the street. 'He was one of our commandos', Wahib al-Ghanim recalled. 'We needed brave young men to fight for the party.'[21] Anti-government demonstrations, which could bring the whole city to a standstill, would end in running skirmishes with the police or brawls with rival gangs. If caught, student trouble-makers faced a beating or a night in jail, while Ba'thist workers risked being sacked from their jobs.

With a badge to wear and a structure through which to work, Asad and his friends daubed slogans on walls, collected signatures on petitions, smuggled Ba'thist tracts in from Damascus which they copied out and read at clandestine meetings often held in Asad's room. He wrote leaflets and distributed them, on one occasion planting them inside an army barracks, a feat which had never been attempted before and which won him much admiration. The young Ba'thists raised money for classmates whose parents had fallen behind with the school fees, and carried the party's message to poor neighbourhoods of the city and to outlying villages in the 'Alawi mountains. Ghanim was the directing mind, the link with Damascus, the fount of Ba'th doctrine. But as more enthusiasts were roped in, the centre of gravity shifted from Ghanim's clinic to the students themselves.

In 1949 the whole Asad family moved down from Qurdaha to Latakia for a year to look after the youngest child Rif'at, then starting secondary school. They took rooms in a lodging house from where they had a ringside view of their elder son's political activities, of which they did not wholly approve. Was it wise to get into so many fights and become known to the authorities? Was the boy wasting his time and throwing away the precious opportunity for betterment? His mother was somewhat more sympathetic to his politics than his father who, like most men of his generation, tended to see the ideological parties as dangerously subversive.

Within two years of the founding conference, the Ba'th in Latakia had outstripped its principal competitors, the Communists and the Syrian National Party, and was brought up hard against the fundamentalist Muslim Brothers, religious conservatives in alliance with the city elites, with whom it was thereafter to wage a war without quarter. The Ba'th, secular, minoritarian, aggressive, was a natural enemy of the Brothers, who picked out Asad, already something of a student leader, and repeatedly tried to beat him up. A friend who often fought shoulder to shoulder with him in these brawls was Mahmud 'Ujayl (later a member of the People's Assembly). But once in 1948 the Muslim Brothers caught Asad on his own and knifed him in the back. The wound took several weeks to heal.[22]

Although the Ba'th party in Latakia included a large number of 'Alawi boys, Ghanim was anxious that it should not be seen as a sectarian party. So when a fight was brewing with the Muslim Brothers, he urged 'Alawis to stay off the streets and let their Sunni comrades fight off the zealots. But Asad would have none of these timid tactics. His instincts rebelled against the built-in caution and defensiveness which had so long characterized his community. From those early beginnings he tried to break out of the constraints and inhibitions of his minority background, refusing to live, physically or mentally, in an 'Alawi ghetto but placing himself at the forefront of demonstrations and looking for street allies among Sunni toughs who were themselves equally opposed to the ruling establishment. Some of these Sunnis remained his friends into adult life. Even at an early age class alliances appear to have been more important for Asad than sectarian solidarity. Reaching out across the 'Alawi-Sunni divide in search of class or political allies was to be a characteristic of his adult politics.

In his last two years at school, 1949–51, Asad became an acknowledged schoolboy-politician and, in a free ballot, was elected head of his school's student affairs committee. In this role he was in touch with similar school committees across the country, co-ordinating tactics, deciding on slogans and agreeing secret codes so as to enable schools to communicate with each other and come out on strike at the same time. Hardly a political event took place in Syria in those years without drawing a response from the schoolboy militants. It was at this time that Asad struck up a friendship with another student Ba'thist, 'Abd al-Halim Khaddam, an energetic and aggressive young Sunni of humble background from the small coastal town of Banyas. He was later to serve as Asad's Foreign Minister for a dozen years and then as a Vice-President of the republic. Another Sunni acquaintance on the student circuit was 'Abd al-Ra'uf al-Kasm, a Ba'thist from a religious Damascus family, later to be Asad's longest-serving Prime Minister. Kasm remembered the committed, passionate, self-assertive Asad of those days: 'Everything about him then was black and white. He didn't like shades of grey.'[23]

Still a bit of an amateur poet, the head of the Latakia school committee wound up an angry meeting he was chairing by cursing the government — in verse:

> There is Damascus drinking the blood of its sons!
> Oh Guardians of Glory, where are the righteous rulers?
> The dogs have risen to the fount of life![24]

In 1951 Asad was elected president of the nation-wide Union of Syrian Students, a notable first for himself, his party and his community. Here was proof that he was politically the most important schoolboy of the day. It was to be a dozen years before he achieved such national prominence again. Experience as a student activist made a great and lasting impression, to the extent that he frequently referred to it in later life, insisting on its formative nature. He was bitten by politics and from that time on considered himself a politician first and foremost, even when he was wearing the uniform of the Syrian air force. The Ba'th's struggles of those years against pan-Syrians, Communists, and the whole of the Right with the Muslim Brothers in the van, gave him his political education and informed his attitudes to movements which forty years later were still present on the Syrian scene. Undoubtedly he tended to look back on his youth as a time of heroism and selfless duty in the nationalist and socialist cause, and this was the model he was to recommend to subsequent generations of young people. The early fights in the streets became part of the legitimacy he later claimed.

Enrolment in the air force

In the summer of 1951 Asad, aged twenty, left Latakia for his village of Qurdaha with a baccalauréat and the self-confidence of a student leader – but not much else. He was the first son of the poorer families of the village to climb to such academic heights and as such was someone of whom the *zuʻama* had to take notice. But what was there for this promising youth to do? Not for him the limited village horizons and the smalltime farming and trading pursuits of his uncles and elder brothers. His first ambitious thought was to become a doctor, a big leap into the professional middle class for an 'Alawi mountain lad to contemplate whatever his success at school. Asad may have thought to follow in the footsteps of his mentor Dr Wahib al-Ghanim or he may simply have been attracted to what was then, as it still is in Syria, a prestigious and high income profession. With his father's approval he telephoned to Beirut, to the Jesuit University of St Joseph to ask if he could enroll in its medical faculty. He was told that there were many papers to fill in and that it was best for him to come in person. But he was unable to get to Beirut. His father was already old and the family had little cash to spare. These circumstances pointed him in another direction.

The army was an attractive alternative because, since independence in 1946, fees had been abolished at the Military Academy at Homs which thus became the only institution to offer poor boys a start in life: the cadets were lodged, fed and even paid to be there. Young men from minority backgrounds made for the army in droves rather than for other professions because their families did not have the means to send them to university.[25] But the army, which had been thrust into the forefront of public life by the three military coups of 1949, had also become a leading national institution. Officers had improved their status and, in uneasy tandem with demoralized civilian politicians, were more or less running the country, a circumstance which prompted ideological parties to encourage their young members to go to military school and rise in the armed forces whose political importance could no longer be ignored. Thus the army barracks joined the secondary school as the nursery of a revolutionary vanguard.

When the French left Syria in 1946, there was no national army, simply a few hundred ex-members of the *Troupes* who were just about the only trained military manpower available to the new state, but who were also somewhat suspect because of the smell of separatism and collaboration which hung about them. The bloody clashes between France and Syria in the last days of the Mandate had shaken the loyalty of the force, with some soldiers deserting to the nationalists while others took up an offer of asylum in France. Yet, after 1946, country boys from the 'Alawi mountains, the Jabal al-Duruz and the largely bedouin north-east continued to provide the core of the regular army – the corporals, sergeants and junior officers. When the government called for volunteers in the early years of independence it was such young men who responded, not city boys with openings in trade, crafts or the professions. After military service was introduced in 1950, urban conscripts served their two-year term and then went back to softer, more profitable jobs in civilian life, but country boys stayed on. This was the historic mistake of the leading families and of the mercantile and landowning class to which they belonged: scorning the army as a profession, they allowed it to be captured by their class enemies who then went on to capture the state itself. At the Homs Military Academy where he enrolled in the autumn of 1951, one of an intake of ninety cadets, Asad met and befriended Mustafa Tlas, a young Sunni from the village of Rastan, near Homs, who was to be his staunch aide and ally for the next several decades. Like Asad, Tlas had been a Ba'thist schoolboy and had distinguished himself as a scout leader for the party. Their friendship was a cross-sectarian class alliance typical of the young revolutionaries of the time.

What finally tilted Asad towards the armed forces was his keenness to fly. But the air force he wanted to join was still in its infancy, as indeed was the army itself. When he enrolled at Homs there was still no air force academy, only a flying school at Aleppo to which a few cadets were transferred after passing a medical. Asad was one of fifteen to be chosen. One of his instructors, Fu'ad Kallas, remembered him as 'an absolutely straight young man with a touch of innocence who was very keen to learn and was ready to share everything he had with his fellow trainees'.[26] Pride as well as straightness prompted him to declare his party allegiance when filling out official forms. 'After my time as head of the students' union it would have been impossible to conceal it.'[27] With Syria then under the military dictatorship of Adib al-Shishakli, it was imprudent for a cadet to remind the authorities of his party membership.

The flying school Asad joined was that same year promoted to the status of an academy and a special curriculum devised for it. As there had been no applicants to the school the year before, the handful of cadets found themselves in a new institution with no seniors around to intimidate them and with instructors who were themselves not wholly clear about how to proceed. Should they be taught only to fly or should they also be given basic military training? Should infantry officers join the staff? Would hours of drill and running round the countryside with a heavy pack impair the cadets' ability to fly? How many flying hours needed to be clocked up before graduation? It was at length decided that Asad and his mates should be given military as well as flying instruction. There was no doubt which Asad preferred: 'Compared to the military side of things, the days spent learning to fly were like a holiday'.[28]

The smallness of the fifteen-strong outfit and the casualness of life made the years in Aleppo very agreeable. Competition was keen in the classroom and in the air. Asad passed out top of the class in each of the first two years and on graduation won a trophy for aerobatics. He found great freedom in flying, greater, he admitted, than air force cadets enjoyed later.

> We didn't stick very closely to the rules and the rules themselves were pretty lax. The technology was primitive. We would simply take off and, as there was no radar or ground control, nobody knew where we were.

The temptation to show off to family and friends was hard to resist. Why not put on a little display of trick-flying over one's native village? Several times Asad took up his propellor-driven trainer (Chipmunks in his first year, Harvards in the second) to cavort in the sky above Qurdaha and wave to friends – and then find himself out over the Mediterranean.

The young flyer narrowly escaped death on the eve of his graduation as a pilot officer in 1955. At the rehearsal two formations of four aircraft were due to fly past and land in turn. As Asad's formation wheeled to allow the planes behind to come in, it entered a dense cloud over Aleppo. Flying blind required skill which he did not yet possess, but he knew that he must watch his instruments and not trust to his senses. He noticed he was losing speed and opened the throttle: to his surprise the speedometer needle continued to fall. Any moment now the engine would stall and he would crash. He felt the engine vibrating and dust falling in his eyes. Only then did he realize he was flying upside down. He shot out of the cloud and found himself heading straight for earth. 'Just in time I managed to climb to safety, grazing the tops of the olive trees. Other cadets watching me said, "Has he gone mad?" They thought I was playing games but I wasn't.'[29] On the following day Asad graduated and collected his cup for aerobatics.

4

The Peasants' Revolt

School, the Ba'th and the air force were powerful shapers of Asad's attitudes. But there was another: the revolt of the peasantry. This awakening of rural society in the late 1940s and early 1950s was associated with the name of Akram al-Hawrani, a firebrand from Hama, the ancient city on the Orontes lying below the 'Alawi mountains in the central Syrian plain. What he accomplished in the plain had an immediate resonance in the mountain because many impoverished highlanders had been driven down there in search of a livelihood. More than the Damascene 'Aflaq, more even than Arsuzi and his anti-Turkish grievances, Hawrani provided a model for Asad and for the revolution of the country against the town which his generation was to accomplish.

Asad's own childhood in Qurdaha was not to be compared with the unrelieved misery of peasant families in the plains, but he was a country boy nonetheless and understood and shared rural grievances. Awakened to a sense of injustice by what he had seen at school in Latakia, his eyes were opened to the deprivation of the mountain poor. For years afterwards he remembered, for example, having seen a man from his own village, whose physical strength he had much admired, dying of an internal haemorrhage because he did not have the ten Syrian liras needed to see a doctor.

An educated young man like Asad, from the country yet no longer really of it, politicized as so many minority men were, with a sense of class grievance still unsatisfied by personal ascent, was well placed to become an agent of revolutionary change. He and men like him served as the vital bridge between the awakened countryside and the salaried lower middle classes of the towns which together provided the engine of the Ba'th. But the radical social and political changes which the Ba'thist state was to bring about in the 1960s, replacing an old order

41

with a new, could not have been effected had not the groundwork been laid a decade earlier.

In Asad's youth, Hama, at the heart of Syria, was the citadel of landed power and the capital of rural oppression. The first slap to the face of a landowner was delivered in 1952 in a village near the city, sounding a warning that the ancient edifice was coming under attack. The reason an anonymous peasant had the courage to strike his landlord was the campaign of agitation launched by Hawrani under the slogan of 'The land belongs to him who works it'. Born in 1914 into a once landowning but now impoverished Sunni family, Hawrani was both the product and the enemy of Hama, a small city, closed in on itself, and a byword for landlordism, conservatism, religious zealotry and xenophobia. Hawrani was to do a lot to change it.

By the late 1930s he had acquired a law degree and a circle of followers, his *shabab* or 'young men'. In 1941 he and a group of officers rushed to Iraq to lend a hand to Rashid 'Ali's revolt against the British; in 1943 he was first returned to parliament for Hama; in 1945 he and his friends seized the city's garrison from the French; in 1946 he founded a sports club with political overtones; and in early 1948 he fought in Palestine – one of only two deputies to do so although thirty had pledged they would. (The other was a young doctor and future novelist from Raqqa, 'Abd al-Salam al-'Ujayli.)[1] In 1950 Hawrani mobilized his followers into an Arab Socialist Party (ASP) with headquarters in Hama and branches in other centres.

In those days four families – the Barazis, the 'Azms, the Kaylanis and the Tayfurs – owned ninety-one of the 113 villages of the Hama region. Hawrani's effective tactic was to ally himself with the smallest of these families, the Tayfurs, and use them and their peasantry against the bigger landowners. A Tayfur son, Khalid, even became secretary of the ASP in Hama itself.[2] Hawrani released a rage fostered over generations.

Militants of his Arab Socialist Party incited villagers to harass landowning families and scare them off the land. A climax of the campaign was a three-day 'anti-feudalist' rally in Aleppo in mid-September 1951 attended by thousands of newly aroused peasants, the first gathering of so revolutionary a nature in the Arab world. Young people's clubs were started in many villages and party workers made promises to build roads and open schools and clinics.

Revolutionary tactics soon grew bolder. Rallies and festivities were organized in the villages and slogans became still more menacing as war was waged on 'feudalists' who had 'stolen' the land from the peasants. Agitation turned to violence. Crops were burned, shots fired at the houses of landowners, and threatening crowds made a number of villages too dangerous for their owners to enter. 'When we told the people "This land can be yours," there was a kind of explosion', Dr 'Aziz al-Saqr, then a party worker in the area, recalled. 'At that time the land we worked, the house we lived in, even the grave belonged to the landowner.'[3] (The son of a destitute 'Alawi peasant who had been driven down the mountain by adversity, Saqr took a doctorate at Moscow University and was in 1984 appointed governor of Latakia.)

Akram al-Hawrani was the first Syrian politician to grasp the dimension of the peasant problem, and the first to raise it in parliament and bring it to the forefront of national attention. His message and his tough, often brutal, ways with landowners shook the social and economic order in the Syrian heartlands.

Hawrani's activities in the plains were closely watched in the 'Alawi mountains and contributed to the climate in which Asad's generation threw off the yoke of their own local notables and saw the chance of revolutionary transformation in the country at large. On the coast, among Latakia's leading families, Hawrani became as notorious and as hated as he was by the higher reaches of Hama society. Landowners such as the Shrayta and Harun families of Latakia and the 'Ali Dib family of the coastal town of Jableh formed electoral alliances with mountain bosses in an attempt to check his rising power. But it was too late to reverse the trend. Hawrani's party established its own networks of patronage, helped school-leavers find places in the Military Academy, browbeat the old dignitaries and sent its own men to parliament. Hama returned seven deputies to parliament in Damascus. In 1949 six of these were landowners, with Hawrani alone representing the peasant opposition. At the next elections in 1954 the situation was reversed: only one landowner was elected, 'Abd al-Rahman al-'Azm, while Hawrani's list captured the other six, an index of the battles already won in the class war.

The land problem

As a student leader and pilot officer Asad began to see some of his country's problems at first hand. Student congresses took him to Aleppo, Homs, Hama, Damascus itself, journeys which taught him among much else that moving about in ramshackle buses on unmade roads was a slow, dusty and uncomfortable business. In the air force he heard from other cadets what their upbringing had been like, and from these travels, meetings and new acquaintances he grew more aware that the whole of Syria, and not just his corner of it, was a backward, socially repressive place.

Syria was a predominantly agricultural country, its backbone being two million peasants out of a then population of about 3.5 million, inhabiting some 5,500 villages built mostly of mud and mostly lacking piped water, sewerage, electricity, tarred roads or any other amenity of modern life. Because of overcrowding and poor sanitation the population was ravaged by disease: malaria was widespread, as were tuberculosis, diarrhoea and enteritis. In 1951–3, 36 per cent of registered deaths occurred among children under five. National income per head was a mere 440 Syrian *liras* (about US$ 157 at the rate of exchange at the time), although social disparities were such that most Syrians earned even less. Outside the two main cities of Damascus and Aleppo electricity was rare, serving fewer than three-quarters of a million people in the whole country. There were only some 13,000 motor vehicles, a single port, Latakia, and three small railways, all Ottoman-built and of different gauges.

The real bottleneck was on the land. Land, the main resource of the country, was mainly in the hands of absentee landlords who disposed at will of the peasantry as they had done since the pattern of land-holding was established under the impetus of capitalism in the nineteenth century. The French interlude between the wars had done little to change matters. When Asad was at school Jacques Weulersse, the French sociologist whose knowledge of Syria was unsurpassed, made a challenging prophecy.[4]

> The most profound determinant of the future is what happens to the peasant . . . One thing is certain: the problem of the peasantry will . . . become each year more pressing . . . The way it is solved will decide not only the shape and structure of tomorrow's Near East, but indeed the future of that Arab civilization that is struggling to be reborn.

The degraded peasantry was indeed Syria's most fundamental problem, and the worst conditions were to be found precisely on the central plain around Hama where uncertain rains made farmhands unusually dependent on their landowners. As the single crop of wheat or barley demanded no great farming skill, ploughing, sowing and harvesting were immutable routines carried out in unison on the estates, and thus easily policed by the owner or his bailiff. Even the peasant's chance to cheat his master out of a few bushels of grain was strictly limited.[5]

For many generations a sort of collective farming known as *musha'* had been practised. Land owned in common by a village was redistributed periodically to give each family a turn on the better plots. The system broke down, however, when first the Ottomans, then the Young Turks after 1909, and then the French attempted to draw up a land register, with the result that local notables and tribal shaykhs seized the chance to acquire legal title and expand their holdings at a time when Syrian crops were beginning to reach world markets. Powerful families came to own great latifundia, reducing the vast majority of peasants to the status of sharecroppers. Local despotisms took root in the countryside. After the 1858 Ottoman land code, the measure which set the process in motion, the family of the Ottoman Sultan 'Abd al-Hamid acquired no fewer than 110 villages in Syria, a model later emulated if on a more modest scale by such Syrian families as the 'Azms, the Barazis and the Kaylanis who, like their nineteenth-century Russian equivalents, computed their holdings not by the acreage but by the number of villages and men they possessed.

City merchants and moneylenders also bought their way in, while stronger village families secured more shares than their due, further eroding the principle of collective ownership. But collective work on the old model continued, with profits now being largely siphoned off to absentee owners. The land was neglected and starved of investment, while the city lived parasitically on the surplus extorted from the farm workers. Peasants, fearing the tax collector or simply unaware of what was going on, did not find their way on to the land register. When the sharecropper provided only his labour, he received between 25 and 30 per cent of the crop, a bare subsistence. If he also put up working capital, he could get as much as 70 to 75 per cent of the crop, and there were many variations of the split depending on whether the land was irrigated and on who supplied the water and the seed. Most peasants, however, had only their labour to sell.

Puffed up with wealth, the owner of a village demanded the same deference in town as was given him on the land. He was the candidate at elections, the spokesman for the community, the host when important guests passed through. On his estates he demanded total obedience and docility from his landless serfs. Those he needed he housed in his village, others he expelled. The sharecropper had no say, could appeal to no authority, had nowhere else to go, was despised by others and despised himself. One practice caused particular gall: the treatment of peasant women by the landowners. Hardly a girl could become engaged without the approval of the boss. Newly-weds could not build a house without his permission. If he wanted a girl and she resisted, she and her whole family risked being turned off the land. In Syria as in other Mediterranean societies a man's honour is inextricably bound up with the perceived virtue of his womenfolk, whether his mother, sister, wife, daughters or more distant female relatives. To defend this virtue or avenge it, a man will kill. The protection of women against abuse by landowners was a rallying cry which brought many young men in the Syrian countryside into the new political parties.

The colonels' rule

The Second World War and the years immediately after it had seen the creation of some new wealth in Syria. A handful of industrialists had started to manufacture cotton and rayon cloth, soap, cement, glass, and matches, financed mainly by wartime savings. At the same time, city merchants began putting uncultivated steppe in the north-east under the tractor to grow wheat in winter and cotton in summer – the boom crop of those years – with water pumped from the Euphrates. But such developments in town and country hardly made an impact on the life of the masses.[6] In the cities many lived on a pittance in wretched conditions, while in the countryside squalor and indigence were almost universal. Largely illiterate and with scarcely any possessions, in debt to urban usurers and in fear of the absentee owner, the peasants lived lives almost as miserable as those of Russian serfs under the Tsars. New money, like the old, was in very few hands and, as the state was weak and non-interventionist, wealth continued to mean power. In a country where transport was sketchy, mobility difficult and cash extremely scarce, the local notables, landowners and tribal shaykhs *were* the state. Their influence far outweighed that of any government official. In any event, provincial governorships, as well as top jobs in the judiciary, the police and the gendarmerie, were in their gift.

The military dictators who ruled Syria from 1949 to 1954 were ill-equipped to tackle the country's problems. They had served under the French and belonged to a pre-ideological generation which had not thought deeply about the postwar world. Of the three colonels who seized power[7] in quick succession in 1949 – Husni al-Za'im on 30 March, Sami al-Hinnawi on 14 August, and Adib al-Shishakli on 19 December – only the last was of real substance, remaining in power for over four years until he was in turn overthrown on 27 February 1954. But even Shishakli had no coherent social or economic philosophy with which to shape his policies, although he was a friend of Akram al-Hawrani and had flirted with the Greater Syria ideas of Antun Sa'ada. He was essentially a muscular nationalist who had won his spurs fighting the British in Iraq in 1941, the French in Syria in 1945 and the Zionists in Palestine in 1948.

The colonels' contribution to Syria from 1949 to 1954 was to let some fresh air into a system still slumbering in Ottoman stagnation and to preside over the country's first small steps towards modern statehood. A central bank was established; legal codes were revised and reformed; a start was made to the resettling of the nomadic bedouin population; religious labels were removed from identity cards; and literate women were given the vote. Above all, the colonels provided the time and opportunity for new forces to gather and prepare themselves for the greater transformations ahead.

Apart from mobilizing the peasants, Hawrani had been one of the first to recognize the political and revolutionary potential of Syria's new national army, and to cultivate friendships among the cadets at the Homs Military Academy. By 1949 he was able to pull the strings which resulted in the military coups of that year and then to bask in the limelight when his friend Shishakli emerged as Syria's strong man. In January 1952 he secured Shishakli's signature on a decree for the distribution of state lands, an early if not wholly successful attempt at land reform. But when Shishakli turned into a full-blown dictator, muzzling the press and arresting his opponents, Hawrani fled across the mountains to Lebanon.

He was joined there by the Ba'th founders, Michel 'Aflaq and Salah al-Din Bitar, themselves refugees from Shishakli's oppression. In exile in 1953 the three decided to merge the Ba'th and the ASP to form the Arab Socialist Ba'th Party, a coalition of the white-collar urban class, schoolteachers, government employees and the like, with revolutionary peasants. It was under the joint banner that they fought the 1954 elections after Shishakli's overthrow, carrying their alliance to the front of the political stage. Hawrani, as has been seen, swept the board in Hama, Dr Wahib al-Ghanim won in Latakia, and in Damascus Bitar defeated the secretary general of the pan-Syrian Social Nationalist Party.

The 1950s were an era in which the sense that radical social change was possible moved from the schools, party meetings and officers' clubs to the workplaces, homes and derelict farms of the country. Hawrani was an agent of change, a midwife of the new Syria over which Asad was to preside. No one did more than this astute, humorous, energetic man to shake the foundations of the old ruling class. He roused the peasants, politicized the army, and gave the theorists of the Ba'th a cutting edge. The anger of country boys, raging against the entrenched privilege of the cities, was given a sharper focus by his example. He showed rising young politicians like Asad what needed to, and what could, be done.

5

The Cairo Conspiracy

On graduation as a pilot officer Asad was posted to the Mezze air base near Damascus – and was inevitably plunged into the intrigues of the time, for the Syrian officer corps he joined in the early 1950s was the most politicized and faction-ridden in the Arab world. Since the first military coup of 1949 there had been no serious attempt to return the army to its barracks and it had become accepted that throughout the armed services men schemed and manoeuvred to place their friends and party comrades in key positions. With Shishakli overthrown and party life restored, the way was open for more active political infighting. Asad, a mere foot-soldier for the Ba'th, embarked on an attempt to win over brother officers and bring himself to the attention of party headquarters.

His first discovery was that the tensions and conflicts inside the officer corps mirrored the battles he had fought at school. Some so-called 'Independent' officers had links with leading city families and a handful of others flirted with Communism, but the main fault-line was between the Ba'th and Antun Sa'ada's pan-Syrian nationalists (generally known as the *Parti populaire syrien* or by its postwar name of the Syrian Social Nationalist Party). Whereas the Ba'th's homeland was the whole Arab world, for the SSNP it was 'Greater Syria', which pan-Syrians considered to be a 'nation' distinct from its Arab hinterland. This political cleavage, one of the most profound of Asad's youth, divided villages in the mountains and even individual families. Asad's aunt Sa'da had married into the Makhluf family of Bustan al-Basha, a village not far from Qurdaha just inland from the sea, whose sons were noted for their allegiance to the SSNP and who naturally viewed Asad's ties with the Ba'th with suspicion and hostility. Everyone in the mountains knew who was who.

Economic interests were also involved. The SSNP had managed to secure a hold over the management of the *Régie des Tabacs* in Latakia which it used to extend its influence over tobacco growers of the mountains. An SSNP tally clerk might, for example, give a fellow party member leave to declare only part of his crop, so giving him a chance to sell the balance on the black market at higher prices. The older generation denounced both the Ba'th and the SSNP as godless infidels and resented their inroads, but the young were not to be put off. With jobs and careers in their gift, the political parties seemed the wave of the future, the means of escape from the impoverished present. In the armed services, the Ba'th-SSNP conflict had graver political overtones. The SSNP was known to be pro-West, anti-Communist, and anti-Arab nationalist, whereas the Ba'th's ambition was to unite the Arabs so as to throw off Western domination.

Opposites exploded into violence in April 1955 when Colonel 'Adnan al-Malki, the leading Ba'thist officer in the army, was shot dead at a football match. His assassin, an 'Alawi military police sergeant, Yusuf 'Abd al-Rahim, was himself immediately gunned down by another 'Alawi. It was soon revealed that Yusuf 'Abd al-Rahim was a member of the SSNP, a connection which allowed the Ba'th and the Communists to mount a campaign against the SSNP and break it in a wave of arrests and treason trials. The witch-hunt was such that several prominent 'Alawis, mostly unconnected with the SSNP, fled to Lebanon to escape repression, among them the poet-politician Badawi al-Jabal, one of the first 'Alawis to hold office in a Syrian cabinet. A result of the purge was to tip the scales decisively in favour of the Ba'th. (Doubt was later cast on the circumstances of Malki's death, and it was even rumoured that Egyptian intelligence, said to be working through the Syrian Military Police chief of the day, Akram al-Dayri, had engineered the murder to provide a pretext to wipe out the SSNP.)

Malki's political murder was to have crucial consequences for Syria's modern history. With its principal rival eliminated, the Ba'th party found itself the strongest single force in the armed services. As a result Asad's career was advanced along with that of other Ba'thists. Singled out for promotion, he was recommended for further training and the base at Mezze provided plenty of scope for his natural competitiveness. He recalled how one morning a German instructor who was teaching him to fly the Fiat-59, a propellor-driven fighter, said to him: 'Hafiz, we've both had breakfast. Let's see who can make the other lose his first.' So they took off and, simulating a dog fight, chased one another across the sky.[1]

To his great satisfaction Asad was chosen in 1955 to go to Egypt for further instruction, a first trip abroad which involved moving up from ageing propellor-driven trainers to the excitement of jet aircraft. A year earlier his destination would have been England where Syria had been sending its pilots for combat training, but as Asad and his fellow graduates began their preparations, including a crash course in technical English, the arrangement with Britain suddenly collapsed. To the considerable annoyance of Anthony Eden's government Syria was edging into the orbit of Colonel Gamal Abd al-Nasser, the rising Egyptian leader whose Free Officers had overthrown the Egyptian monarchy in 1952 and whose challenge to imperial Britain was winning him an enthusiastic Arab following.

Cairo, the seat of Nasser's revolutionary government, was a stirring place to be heading for. To recapture Asad's mood at the time, it must be remembered that Arab society was still shaken by the defeat of 1948 and the loss of Palestine. The demoralized Arabs were at a loss to know how to defend themselves against the West and against Israel – until, that is, the charismatic Nasser emerged on the scene. The superhuman powers with which he was soon endowed showed how deep was the Arabs' need for a saviour to lead them out of the wilderness; and of all Arabs the Syrians, smarting from their treatment at the hands of the West and eager for unfettered independence, were the most susceptible to his appeal. The appeal became irresistible when he arranged for Soviet tanks, aircraft and artillery to flow into Egypt under the so-called 'Czech arms deal' of 1955. At a stroke Nasser had undermined the West's arms monopoly in the Middle East, invited the Soviet Union to leapfrog Western defence lines, and made the Baghdad Pact, a Western-sponsored regional alliance, an irrelevance.[2] His message of Arab self-assertion won immediate credibility and in Syria he rocketed to stardom.

Nasser then strengthened his hold on Syria with a defence treaty, but almost at once Israel attacked Syrian positions near the Sea of Galilee on 11 December 1955, inflicting scores of casualties, with the evident intention of demonstrating to Syria the futility of its new agreement with Egypt. Moshe Dayan, who had taken over as Israeli Chief of Staff in early 1952, had staked his reputation on reviving the confidence and fighting ability of the Israel Defence Forces after their lack-lustre performance in skirmishes against Syria's Golan fortifications, and the December 1955 raid was the high point of his endeavour. However, instead of driving Syria and Egypt apart, the attack convinced the Syrians that their only hope of security lay in still closer ties with Egypt and its Soviet arms supplier. Threatened by Israel, but also under pressure from Turkey and Iraq, the original members of the Baghdad Pact, Syria felt exceedingly vulnerable. It was in these circumstances that the Ba'th floated for the first time the heady idea of a union with Egypt.

In this spirit of commitment to Nasser a handful of Syrian pilots, Asad among them, flew to Cairo for a six-months course. They were detailed to start training on Spitfires, but as none of the Egyptian Spitfires had dual controls, they were soon sent up to fly solo. On the first day Asad took off and landed safely, as did his comrades. On the following day their Egyptian instructor decided to take the plane up for a test run while the trainees waited their turn. Asad was at the head of the queue: 'We saw the instructor perform some daring aerobatics and cheered him on. He went into a half-roll and dived. It looked terrific. But he didn't climb out of the dive, and it wasn't aerobatics.'[3] After the crash Egypt's poorly maintained Spitfires were grounded and the Syrian officers transferred to British-built Meteor-8s.

When on 26 July 1956 Nasser nationalized the Suez Canal Company in angry response to the West's withdrawal of aid promised for the Aswan High Dam, popular enthusiasm in the Arab world knew no bounds. The climax to the Suez crisis came three months later when Britain and France in secret collusion with Israel attacked Egypt in October. Alone among Arab states Syria offered to fight for Nasser, but knowing that militarily his cause was doomed he declined. His Syrian fans had to content themselves with blowing up a pipeline across their territory, a first if limited use of the 'oil weapon'.

Asad had a small part in the Suez drama. He had returned to Syria early in 1956 after finishing his course and was posted to an air base near Damascus, home of Syria's small and antiquated fighter force of Fiats and Meteors. When the Suez war broke out he was sent north to the Nayrab base near Aleppo to fly reconnaissance missions over northern and eastern Syria. Air defence was rudimentary, such early warning as existed being provided by police look-outs around the country who phoned in if they spotted an unfamiliar plane. By the time a policeman could reach a telephone, few and far between in those days, the plane was long gone.[4] Intruders were daily expected and indeed arrived, as Britain, which had bases in Iraq and Cyprus, was anxious to verify reports circulating at the time that the Russians had delivered MiG-17s to secret air strips in the Syrian desert. (As it happened, Syria had to wait until 1957 to receive its first Soviet warplanes.)

One day a call came through from a police station at Albukamal on the Euphrates to say that a British Canberra had been sighted flying in from Iraq. Asad was sent up to look for it and had the satisfaction of firing his cannon at it before it flew off towards Cyprus. By this time

Syria's pilots were practically living in their cockpits. Late one afternoon, some forty minutes before sundown, Asad was again ordered up to intercept an incoming aircraft. He tested his brakes at full throttle before take-off, and discovered they were faulty but he decided to risk it. After circling far and wide and finding nothing, with fuel running low and night falling he turned towards home, but Nayrab was not equipped for night flying. He could just pick out the runway, a black line in the surrounding near-blackness. It was too dark to check the wind direction from the wind-sock and when he asked for landing instructions he found his radio had gone dead. Unaware that the wind had changed during his flight, he came in down-wind, a serious matter in view of the Meteor-8's high tail-unit.

With poor brakes and a strong tail wind, he overshot the runway, raced across a field of small trees, and made for a stone wall. He straightened the craft with the rudder, opened the cockpit and gripped its sides to steady himself on impact. By a stroke of good fortune, the wheels butted against a water conduit causing the plane to vault over the wall and across a main road beyond, narrowly missing a tented camp of Palestinian refugees. The wheels flew off, the engine seized up, and the Meteor landed on its belly. Asad leaped out and threw himself into a ditch. Smoke was coming from the aircraft. With four Hispano-Suiza cannon and plenty of ammunition, he thought it might explode. After a while he heard people running among the trees looking for the pilot. 'No doubt they expected to find a corpse hanging from a branch.'[5] Once again Asad had had a lucky escape.

At the inquiry he admitted that he knew his brakes were defective: he was reprimanded, fined and given a suspended jail sentence. His crash landing was the talk of Syria's small air force. Some officers thought he was to blame but most felt he had done his duty and blamed the air base commander for sending him out on a mission which would bring him back at nightfall to a strip not equipped for night flying. Asad resented being punished for doing what he considered his patriotic duty and attributed the sanctions to prejudice against him on account of his Ba'thist allegiance or his 'Alawi background. He was a keen young officer, popular with his men but perhaps a touch too independent for his seniors. Less than a decade later he had risen to command the Syrian air force. It was noted to his credit that he bore no grudge against the officers who had passed judgment on him at the court of inquiry.[6]

Union with Egypt

On 1 February 1958 Syria and Egypt entered impulsively into a union. The initiative came from Syria, and more particularly from the dozen officers then running the armed services and whose feuding had reached the point where they needed an arbiter. The Syrian state had never felt secure. Quite apart from the threat from Israel, it had since independence been bullied, courted and pulled this way and that by rival Hashimite, Saudi and Egyptian designs. But such inter-Arab tussles were dwarfed by the fierce East-West contest in which Syria found itself caught up from the mid-1950s, subjecting its shaky political system to intolerable strains.

Impelled by the Ba'thists among them, the Syrian officers turned for help to Nasser, by now recognized as the greatest Arab of his generation. The Ba'th leaders had been campaigning for union with Egypt, but now they pressed for an immediate merger perhaps fearing that without Nasser's weight they would be outmanoeuvred by the Communists, who were then enjoying a moment of unprecedented popularity because of Soviet arms deliveries to Syria and promises of economic aid.

Nasser was not keen on an organic union with Syria. He had no ambition to run Syria's internal affairs or to inherit its problems. Rather he preached 'Arab solidarity', by which he meant that the Arabs should line up behind him against the great powers. In particular, he needed to control Syria's foreign policy in order to hold in check his Western and Arab enemies. This restricted notion of pan-Arabism was very different from the Ba'th's frontier-smashing unionism, but in the event Nasser could not have one without the other. Stampeded by the Syrians, he agreed to the creation of the United Arab Republic – and so ecstatic was the welcome he received and so savage his enemies' gnashing of teeth that his doubts were soon dispelled.

The union of Syria and Egypt in February 1958 was a profound shock to the Middle East power system: it brought Egypt into the heart of Arab Asia and upset the local balance of power. The Hashimites in Iraq, who had long hoped to bring Syria within their orbit, experienced the sharpest frustration as the creation of the UAR shut them out of the Levant. Saudi Arabia was overshadowed by the new colossus, and Jordan and Lebanon felt at risk. The remaining strongpoints of British power in Arabia braced themselves against the Nasserist tide.

Asad followed Nasser's moves and counter-moves with passionate attention, as did every politically minded Arab of the time. The Egyptian leader's style, his challenge to the great powers, his triumphs, his commitment to Arabism, aroused the most ardent fervour in Ba'thist breasts. Asad was soon to have the chance to see Nasser's regime at closer range. But before that he had some personal business to attend to.

Marriage

In 1958 Air Force Lieutenant Asad determined to marry Aniseh Makhluf, a girl he had known since childhood and whom he had singled out when he was in his early twenties. She was a distant relation as his Aunt Sa'da had married into the Makhluf family, a connection which allowed Asad to pay a number of exploratory visits to Aniseh's home village of Bustan al-Basha. He had fallen in love with her on his return from his training course in Egypt. She was a schoolteacher of demure good manners, a trim dark-haired young woman of about his own age who had been most respectably educated at the French-run Convent of the Sacred Heart at Banyas on the coast. But there were considerable obstacles to a marriage, which only sharpened Asad's resolve to overcome them.

The first hurdle was that, although Asad and Aniseh were related, her family was a good deal more affluent and prominent than his own. In an extended Arab family it was not uncommon to find one branch boasting, say, of a distinguished surgeon and another consisting of simple peasants scratching a living from the fields. The gap between the Makhlufs and the Asads was by no means so great, but it was real enough. Of peasant stock, Asad's family was neither large nor rich, although it had won respect in Qurdaha for standing up to the notables. But Aniseh's people were themselves notables, with a long-established reputation for that most prized of Arab virtues, generosity, and this in the most literal sense. When famine blighted the area in the First World War, many villagers came to Aniseh's prosperous grandfather to be fed and from that time on the family came to be called *makhluf*, meaning, in one of its senses, 'recompensed by God'. The tribute was retained as the family surname and with it the tradition of open-handedness. Both Aniseh's father and uncle kept open house where rooms were set aside to feed and lodge the poor. No one left their door hungry.

But there was a still more serious objection to the match: the Asads and the Makhlufs were politically at odds, the former boasting a prominent Ba'thist son, the latter known for their SSNP connections.

In fact Aniseh's first cousin, Badi' Makhluf, was the man who had shot down Malki's murderer, evidently on instructions from the party, an act for which he was subsequently tried, sentenced to death and hanged. The Makhluf family mourned their fallen son as a martyr to the SSNP cause, which did not help Asad to press his suit.

Aniseh's father Ahmad Makhluf set his face against the marriage. But luckily for Asad, he had allies in his Aunt Sa'da and in Aniseh's mother who was impressed by his qualities. Even as a bachelor he was a young man a mother could trust, with no record of wild escapades, rough behaviour or bad language. He had not courted anyone else or frequented cafés or cabarets, and even in Egypt where morals were looser he had been an exemplary cadet. Apparently uninterested in sexual experiment, he had from an early age seemed to be looking for a stable, intensely private marriage relationship which would free him for a life of professional achievement. It was significant that his choice fell on a quiet girl, herself of unblemished reputation. For her part Aniseh had a mind of her own and was a good judge of character. She was evidently taken by the intelligence of her suitor who had no touch of the village lout about him and whose ambition already set him apart from most 'Alawi young men of her acquaintance, still bounded by their rural environment. More surprisingly, he seemed different from other boys who like himself had broken free from village life through the channels of education, the ideological parties, and the army. Many of these seemed to think that their new status obliged them to laugh at their elders and the old way of life, throw off their religious beliefs, even scorn the white-domed tombs of saints which in the 'Alawi mountains were the only visible religious symbols.

The tug-of-war over Aniseh continued. Eventually Asad prevailed over the doubts of her family, carried her off to Damascus, and married her in front of a *qadi* or religious notary. They set up house in what was then the outlying and poor district of Mezze which for Aniseh was a considerable step down from the comforts and regard she had enjoyed as a notable's daughter. In the first years of their marriage Asad could not afford the standard of living she had been used to, but neither this nor the ups and downs of army and political life appear to have daunted her. She was to prove a devoted wife and mother and Asad's closest and most trusted confidante, providing him with a domestic environment of unquestioned respectability. Although it was a love match, marriage into the respected Makhluf clan also brought Asad worldly advantage, helping him to rise to a higher social level. It won him points in the 'Alawi community and contributed to his growing self-confidence.

Only weeks after their marriage, Asad and Aniseh had to endure nearly a year's separation. In mid-1958 Asad was one of a small group of Syrian pilot officers chosen to go to the Soviet Union for a course in night flying in MiG-15s and MiG-17s, newly delivered to Syria. He was given an emotional send-off by his family and friends for whom going to Moscow was like a journey to the moon: not so long before, to travel down the mountain from Qurdaha to Latakia had seemed a momentous leap. As he later recalled, 'In those days people said goodbye to you as if you would never return'.[7] Aniseh, already pregnant, went home to wait for him in Bustan al-Basha.

Like most Syrians Asad had viewed the Soviet Union with suspicion because of its atheism and because it had raced to recognize the State of Israel in 1948. Moreover, Ba'thists and Communists had always been rivals, competing for the same clients and only on occasion joining each other in the same trench against a common enemy. Ba'thists understood that Marxist internationalism was the enemy of Arab nationalism. But in the mid-1950s after Stalin's death, relations between the Arab world and the Soviet Union warmed up, with Moscow's public recognition of the legitimacy of Arab aspirations for unity. By the time of Asad's trip, with both Syria and Egypt at loggerheads with the West, the USSR had come to seem a valued friend.

The voyage to Russia was Asad's first contact with a country which was to be the principal ally of his presidency. Of course the Syrian trainees did not see much of the country or have a chance to meet ordinary Russians. They were first put through a few intensive weeks of technical Russian at a school near Moscow – which gave them the opportunity for occasional wide-eyed forays into the streets – and then sent to a remote wind-swept air base for their night-flying exercises. Nevertheless Asad's horizons widened, and in spite of the rigorous routine it was an unusual and mind-stretching experience. But after a few months the Syrians were pleading with their Soviet instructors to allow them to work overtime so as to finish their course early and return home. 'We were all ill with homesickness', Asad admitted later.[8] His heart and his ambitions lay in Syria and he was eager to get home.

Disillusion with the union

Returning from ten months in Russia in the spring of 1959, Asad hastened up the mountain to see his wife and the baby daughter born in his absence. The young aviator longed to breathe again the Mediterranean air of Qurdaha and savour home cooking after so many months of foreign diet, and he was feasted like a hero. But a shock awaited him when he reported for duty at air force headquarters in Damascus. Syria's marriage with Egypt was on the rocks. The Officers' Club, so lately the hub of politics in the city, had been shorn of all importance while the offices of the Ba'th party were deserted. The two ladders of his ambition had been kicked away from under him.

Before Asad left for the Soviet Union Nasser had been welcomed in Damascus like a new Saladin amid scenes of popular delirium unprecedented in modern times. But on Asad's return disenchantment had set in. Syrians felt they had much to complain of: unfair competition from Egyptian manufactures, stifling controls on banking and trade, the beavering of Egyptian spies and informers, even the rumoured influx of Egyptian peasants into the virgin lands of the Jazira which Syrians thought of as their own El Dorado. There was a further blow. To Nasser's ill luck, the union years were stricken by drought which brought misery to the countryside and helped undermine the land reform which Hawrani and his peasant followers had hoped would break the power of the landlords.

Nasser gutted Syrian politics. His conditions for uniting with Syria were that the Syrian army should withdraw from politics and the political parties be dissolved, but neither the officers nor the civilian Ba'th leaders truly understood that Nasser would exclude them from the union which they had created. Syrian officers were used to playing politics and fully expected to go on doing so, while the Ba'th's illusions were even greater: its leaders expected to be the ideological mentors of the UAR, providing Nasser with a corpus of doctrine and teaching Arabism to Egypt itself.

But these were daydreams. In place of the rich tumult of Syrian politics, Nasser erected a structure which was both authoritarian and rickety. All the decisions were taken in Cairo where he worked through a small group of officers and security men. In Damascus his power rested on a taciturn policeman, Colonel 'Abd al-Hamid Sarraj, whom he promoted Minister of the Interior.

A consequence of these arrangements was that Syria lost control of its affairs. Once a capital city, Damascus declined into the *chef lieu* of a province, a loss of importance illustrated by the closure of the foreign embassies. Union affairs, Nasser decreed, were to be in the hands of a central cabinet in which two Syrians, Hawrani and Bitar, were given office, while the affairs of Egypt and Syria, now renamed the Southern and Northern Regions of the United Arab Republic, were to be entrusted to local executive councils. The two regions sent delegates to a single National Assembly in Cairo composed of four hundred Egyptians and two hundred Syrians, each man handpicked by Nasser himself.

Union was not turning out as the Syrians had expected and, in their usual fractious way, they made their feelings plain. As his difficulties grew, Nasser cracked down on dissent, especially in the armed services. First to be purged were the Communists, and then any species of Ba'thist as well as any officer who fell foul of Sarraj and the Egyptian overlords. The more dangerous officers went to jail, the more fortunate to diplomatic missions abroad, but the majority of those of doubtful loyalty were simply posted to the Southern Region, that is to say to Egypt, where it was thought they could get up to no mischief. Asad found that the Aleppo air academy where he had won his spurs had been transferred to Egypt, together with part of the Homs military college, and that the Syrian officer corps was buzzing with stories of sackings, transfers, and slights suffered at the hands of the overbearing Egyptians. In October 1959, Nasser sent his closest aide, Marshal 'Amer, to rule in Damascus with full powers, a clear sign of the bankruptcy of the UAR's constitutional arrangements. By the end of the year the Ba'thist figureheads had resigned their sinecures and Hawrani, shaking the dust of Cairo from his feet, returned home to Hama disillusioned with the whole experiment of union with Egypt.

Such was the situation when, late in 1959, the axe fell on Asad himself: his squadron of night-flying MiG-19s was transferred to Egypt which he soon discovered was as depressed about union as was Syria. In 1958, with Nasser at the height of his glory, it had been widely expected that Cairo would soon be the capital of the entire Arab world: a group of Iraqi officers had overthrown the Hashimite monarchy in Baghdad and it was imagined that they would carry Iraq into the UAR, building it into a superstate from the Nile to the Euphrates. Jordan, Lebanon, and other lesser countries were not thought likely to resist for long the pull of the magnet. But events took another turn.

The main surprise was that Brigadier 'Abd al-Karim Qasim, who on 14 July 1958 had ushered in the Iraqi republic in a single blood-stained morning, turned out to be an 'Iraq firster' and not a pan-Arab nationalist at all (the fact that his mother was a Shi'i Kurd may have had something to do with it). When Nasserists tried to stampede him into union with Cairo, he looked for support to the powerful Communist party, and when in March 1959 nationalist officers rose against him in Mosul with Egyptian encouragement, Qasim turned the

Communists loose. They wrought a fearful massacre which put an end to relations between Qasim's Iraq and Nasser's UAR.[9] There could no longer be any question of Iraq joining the Syrian-Egyptian union, which was thereby doomed to remain a suffocating unequal partnership between Cairo and Damascus. The great Arab get-together which many had hoped would be cemented by Nasser's charisma was destined not to be.

The Military Committee

When Asad arrived in Cairo in 1959 a hint of collapsing expectations was already in the air. Syrian Ba'thists like himself were no longer seen by the Egyptians as partners in the greatest Arab enterprise of modern times but had instead become objects of suspicion, troublemakers if not yet enemies. The newcomers lived very much among themselves, drawing their pay, keeping in touch with each other, and collecting their tickets for home leave from a Liaison Office for Syrian officers' affairs in the Cairo suburb of Heliopolis. They spent much time lounging in Groppi's and Lappas, cafés where British officers before them had once whiled away off-duty hours. In the three and a half years that the Syrian-Egyptian union lasted, about a thousand Syrian officers were posted to Egypt, many against their will, and a further thousand Syrian cadets passed out of Egyptian military schools. Not all were unhappy with their lot: on double pay, in a government apartment, often with a car, life was not wholly disagreeable.

But the politically minded among them were disgruntled. Most evenings a group could be seen gathered round a café table where a senior man might hold forth to a circle of youngsters. The main topic was always the situation in Syria, and, for Ba'thists, the constantly rehearsed grievance was the suicide of their party. By bowing to Nasser's insistence that the party dissolve itself, 'Aflaq had left the Ba'th without leadership or defence. Meanwhile its enemies – merchants, landowners and city notables whom the Ba'thists had thought consigned to history – were climbing back to power. The country boys felt that their social and political ascent was threatened.

Exiled in Cairo, Asad and his friends felt a sense of shock, even of danger, damaging to the self-confidence which they had built up in the 1950s, and the angry, idle Cairo days brought to the boil a simmering resentment against 'Aflaq and Bitar whose sacrifice of the party, decided upon without consulting the rank and file, seemed criminal. 'We came to distrust their commitment to the Ba'thist ideals we had grown up with. We felt they had been trading in slogans', Asad later said.[10]

Rural raw-knuckled men like Asad, who had joined the party through the Arsuzi stream, had never much admired the middle-class Damascene theorists. Now, as the young officers pondered their plight, they persuaded themselves that 'Aflaq and Bitar had secretly welcomed the party's demise because it served to silence criticism welling up from more radical forces below. From this resentment the seed was sown of the great Ba'th schism which was to lead in 1966 to the bloody ousting of 'Aflaq and his friends, the triumph of Asad's group, and the long-running, violent, irreconcilable and, to outsiders, largely incomprehensible quarrel which ever since has separated the Syrian Ba'th from its cousin in Iraq where 'Aflaq eventually took refuge. In politics few enmities are so bitter as those which divide former comrades.

But was not Nasser to blame as well as 'Aflaq? As Asad recalled:[11]

> We sensed a tremendous hostility towards our party, filtering down from Nasser himself, and we started predicting that the union would end in catastrophe. Nasser suffered from a persistent paranoia about political parties, a seemingly incurable condition which no doubt stemmed from his experience of the corrupt parties of pre-revolutionary Egypt. He used to say – and his remarks would get back to us – 'I'm an honest and decent man, so what need have we of parties?'

The Syrian officers wanted to warn Nasser that he was putting the union at risk, but how were they to get past the courtiers surrounding him? They came to believe that Nasser, the towering symbol of Arabism, the undoubted patriot, was being manipulated by a clique as corrupt and reactionary as the old pashas whom he had ousted. In this atmosphere of gloom and doom, Asad and four fellow officers embarked on an enterprise which was to change the course of Syrian history.

Early in 1960 they founded a secret organization which they called the 'Military Committee'. Not for the first time in Arab affairs, young men in uniform saw themselves as saviours of their country, a precedent having been set in Syria with the three military coups of 1949. But the most spectacular example before them was, of course, that of Nasser himself, who with his Free Officers had seized power half a dozen years earlier, quickening the national pulse of his ancient country and galvanizing the politics of the whole region. Nasser was undoubtedly Asad's role model, but as the years wore on he provided lessons in mistakes to be avoided as much as in skills to be emulated. In Third World countries, when things go badly radically-minded soldiers cannot always keep their attention on purely military affairs.

Asad was thirty that year. His commitment to conspiracy marked the end of his carefree youth as a pilot and brought to the surface a strain of seriousness. Two clues to his character emerged at this time and were to be greatly developed in his later career. The first was his use of secrecy, a weapon he used to gain and hold the psychological initiative and to fog his decision-making. The second was his early realization that other players in the political game did not do their homework, had short memories, and acted impulsively – luxuries which he, coming up from nowhere, could not afford. Throughout his life the most consistent characteristic of Asad's moves was the cautious, patient planning which preceded them. He learned to examine the ground carefully before venturing out on it.

The beginnings of the Military Committee were modest indeed, involving just five men – Captains Asad and Jundi, Majors Jadid and Mir, and Lieut.-Colonel 'Umran. In fact at times they were even fewer. 'One or other of us might be posted away for a while or think it wise to lie low', Asad recounted.[12] Their first act was to swear each other to secrecy. Aged between 28 and 38, all had already had some experience of tortuous politics and shared the age-long instinct of dissimulation characteristic of the beleaguered and often persecuted minority communities of the Middle East. Three of the five were 'Alawis and two were members of another Shi'i offshoot, the Isma'ilis. Their cell was as hermetic as a Masonic lodge. But within a few years they were to rend and destroy each other on the journey to the top.

The oldest of them and the directing mind[13] was Lieut.-Colonel Muhammad 'Umran, born in 1922, a large, well-built man with the fresh complexion and blue eyes often found among 'Alawis. His family of smallholders belonged to the Khaiyatin tribe and hailed from the village of Mukharram on the eastern slopes of the mountains, facing inland. As a young man 'Umran had seen action in the Palestine War before being sucked into politics by the army coups which followed. Under the aegis of Akram al-Hawrani he had played a small role in the 1954 uprising against Shishakli. But 'Umran was not a typical soldier. Fond of reading and of argument, courteous and affable, he was something of an intellectual who impressed his colleagues by coming out with recondite pieces of information. Sent to France on a training course early in his career, he astonished his friends by preferring the public library to bars and bistros. But he lacked an edge of ruthlessness for which, as the going inside the group got tougher, he was to pay dearly.

In considerable contrast was the handsome, dark-haired figure of Major Salah Jadid. Stiff, silent and correct, he had the air of a Prussian staff officer and, being more inclined to listen than to talk, sometimes gave others the uncomfortable feeling that their words were being taken down for possible use against them. He was a clever, high-minded man with pronounced left-wing views and in the coming struggle for power was to be Asad's principal competitor. Jadid's birthplace in 1926 was the village of Duwayr B'abda, near the coastal town of Jableh, and his family were middle-ranking members of the Haddadin, the largest and most prestigious of the 'Alawi tribal confederations. As for his politics, Jadid's first allegiance was to the pan-Syrian SSNP – that is, until he switched camps to the Ba'th as a lieutenant in the 1950s. The story is that, falling foul one day of his commanding officer, he turned for help to Mustafa Hamdun, one of Hawrani's men then working for Military Intelligence. Hamdun sorted out his problem – and recruited him into the party, an example of how Hawrani and the Ba'th went about making useful military friends. Ideological parties managed to split mountain families right down the middle. Salah Jadid's brother, Ghassan Jadid, stayed on with the SSNP, rising to become one of its leaders. But in the aftermath of the Malki murder, when the SSNP faced a witch-hunt, he was shot down in a Beirut street in 1957, allegedly on orders from the then head of Syrian intelligence, Colonel Sarraj.

The smallholding backgrounds of Jadid and 'Umran put them socially a cut above Asad's poorer family, but all three men were rural 'intellectuals', sharing a commitment to revolution as well as the sharp 'Alawi hunger to get ahead. They formed the powerhouse of the secret Military Committee. 'Umran was the most cultivated, Jadid the most cunning and Asad the most careful, but by any standards they were an unusual trio and when they eventually fell out their internecine struggles were for several years what Syrian politics were mostly about.

Of the two Isma'ili members of the Committee, the most striking was 'Abd al-Karim al-Jundi, born in 1932 in the ancient Isma'ili centre of Salamiya, a fiery, emotionally unbalanced young man whose seething resentment against Sunni privilege was later to break out in acts of ferocious brutality. The other, Ahmad al-Mir, started life in 1922 in the high-perched Isma'ili settlement of Masyaf in the heart of the 'Alawi mountains, and became an honest if not very brilliant soldier who later had the ill luck to command the Syrian troops on the Golan Front during the Six-Day War.

At the start the Military Committee had no thought of seizing power in Damascus – undoubtedly an over-ambitious programme for a handful of junior officers many hundreds of miles from home. Their objectives were to rebuild their shattered party, protect the union, and overturn the old order in Syria, ensuring thereby their own continued ascent and that of their minority sects. Men from unfavoured communities stood to lose most if the Syrian political clock were turned back and the city elites recovered their lost influence.

To avoid attracting the attention of Egyptian Intelligence, the five conspirators took day trips out of Cairo or met in each other's homes as if for social reasons. Sometimes they held a meeting in a car or with apparent casualness over a cup of coffee at Groppi's where they must have seemed no more remarkable than other off-duty officers. As Asad recalled:[14]

> The Egyptian authorities kept watch on us: they knew we were former Ba'thists and that we were critical of what was going on, but they didn't think we were capable of doing anything. In fact we were not so worried about the Egyptians. Our real fear was that our own party leaders might get wind of our activities.

The Ba'th struggle to survive

These men were Ba'thists, imbued with the legalisms, procedures and jargon of the party that had suckled them. The Ba'th was the only political structure they knew and they saw no possibility of working outside it. This was reflected in the principles they agreed on as a basis for action. The first was that the party and its leadership no longer existed in Syria. The second was that, although orphaned, they must continue to consider themselves members of the Arab Socialist Ba'th Party and to act accordingly. Third, their duty was to keep the party's ideology alive, spread it among their fellows and seek to make secret contact with former civilian comrades. Their priority was to defend the union which in 1960–61 seemed truly threatened. News reached them from Damascus of the growing restiveness of the population under the hard hand of Marshal 'Amer and Colonel Sarraj. It seemed as if a tragedy was about to occur in which they could be no more than spectators. They begged the authorities to allow some Ba'thist officers to return to Syria and, increasingly desperate, contacted Egyptian officers on the edges of Nasser's circle, pleading with them to convey their fears to the president. But with Ba'thists sniping at him from outside the union government, Nasser had by this time come to regard the party as the main enemy of his burdensome Syrian venture.

'Umran and Jadid travelled to Syria and met secretly with some scattered party cadres but without revealing the existence of their own clandestine military organization, and the same discretion was observed in contacts with fellow exiles in Egypt. Asad later recounted:[15]

> The officers I spoke to knew I had a political past. They could see that my approach was not spontaneous, but they were not aware that there was an organization and a leadership. I was never asked, 'Who exactly are you and whom do you represent?' After a while enough trust was built up for them to keep to themselves whatever information I passed on – Ba'thists and especially the military among them have a feel for security problems.

In time and with great stealth the Military Committee built up a network of two or three dozen officers from whose ranks in the coming decade were to be drawn several key figures in Syrian public life. Like the five founder members, most hailed from rural backgrounds, with hardly any of them coming from Damascus or other cities; a good number were members of religious minorities.[16]

The loss of the Syrian base and the running battle with Nasser had greatly enfeebled the Ba'th throughout the Arab world. The danger was that it might sink altogether. 'Aflaq, the main object of the Military Committee's suspicions, struggled to function out of Beirut as head of the party's National (that is, pan-Arab) Command, in touch with younger party leaders such as Fu'ad Rikabi in Iraq, 'Abdallah Rimawi in Jordan and 'Ali Jabir in Lebanon, who fought to keep Ba'thist fortunes alive.[17]

It was a testing time, putting under strain the ill-cemented coalitions of which the Ba'th was made up. The founding congress in 1947 had joined the 'Aflaq and Arsuzi streams; the next congress in June 1954 had blessed the 'Aflaq-Hawrani marriage of schoolmasters and peasant agitators.[18] But then had come the destructive alliance with Nasser. The party's early ambition had been to build the first mass movement in the Arab world, and just when succees seemed in sight, the arrival of Nasser diverted the party from its original course. As Dr Munif al-Razzaz (who was to become secretary-general of the Ba'th's National Command in 1965) explained:[19]

> So great was the excitement he generated that it was supposed that he could realize all our aims at a stroke, by a decree from the top. Rather than struggling for twenty-five years, it was tempting to let an officer such as Nasser do the job overnight.

But Nasser forced the party to dissolve and then set about rooting out every vestige of it throughout the region.

In these trying circumstances two Ba'th congresses were held in Beirut, one in August 1959 and the other a year later, to take stock of the party's fortunes. The 1959 congress approved 'Aflaq's decision to dissolve, but the 1960 congress, which Jadid attended as a secret envoy of the Military Committee, reversed the decision, a pointer to the spirit of rebellion then beginning to stir.

The difficult decision facing the party was whether or not to seek an accommodation with Nasser despite all that had happened. He had done the party grave injury but there he was nevertheless, a pyramid in the Arab landscape which could not be ignored and to the common man the very symbol of Arab unity. At the 1960 congress it was decided to tone down criticism of the Egyptian leader and work to democratize the UAR from inside – a somewhat unrealistic objective. However, Akram al-Hawrani, Nasser's most forthright critic, could not go along with this policy. Instead, he blamed Nasser for all the ills of the unhappy union and called for an all-out breach with him. But such a step made the Ba'thist ideologues tremble. Whatever Nasser's mistakes and whatever their own sufferings, the union, that precious symbol of the pan-Arab dream, had to be preserved. They wished to reform, not to destroy, it.

Hawrani had personal reasons for bitterness, seeing that his own fortunes had been brought low by Nasser's rule. Before the union he had been Syria's king-maker: strong in the army, beloved by the peasantry, the first patron of the country boys. Nasser took all this from him, giving him in return an empty sinecure in the UAR government – until, that is, Hawrani threw it up in disgust. Hawrani attacked Nasser on the most sensitive issue for a self-proclaimed champion of Arabism – the issue of Palestine. Hawrani claimed that, for all the militant talk, Nasser was anxious to explore a peaceful settlement with Israel. Even at the height of his powers in the 1950s, Nasser had been prepared to accept the right of Israel to exist had it been less aggressive.[20] In contrast to this pragmatism, Hawrani tended to see the struggle between the Arabs and Zionism as an existential contest in which Arab survival itself was at stake. The debate about whether or not the Arabs could manage to co-exist with Israel, or rather whether Israel could ever give up what they saw as its aggressive religious racialism, was an important theme of Asad's political education. Much of his later life, the saga of wars and diplomacy, was a variation on it.

There were other divisive debates within the crippled party at that time. Iraqi members, for example, wanted party help against the Iraqi dictator, General Qasim, whom they held to be a greater enemy than Nasser.[21] The Jordanian party secretary, 'Abdallah Rimawi, decided that Nasser was right and the party wrong – and left the Ba'th. Some members turned to Marxism, others left politics altogether, but here and there across Syria a few Ba'th cells struggled to survive underground without direction or a unified line. With these isolated nuclei the Military Committee in Cairo tried to renew contact as it cast around for allies.

End of the UAR

Such was the Ba'th's pitiable situation when, much as the Military Committee had predicted, the United Arab Republic foundered. Syria was snatched out of the union on 28 September 1961 by a right-wing putsch led by a Damascus officer Lieut.-Colonel 'Abd al-Karim Nahlawi backed by Jordan and Saudi Arabia and by Syria's disgruntled business community. The immediate trigger was the panic among Syrian merchants provoked by Nasser's wide-ranging nationalization decrees of July 1961. No one in Syria fired a shot in defence of the union. Shaken by news of the Syrian mutiny, Nasser ordered a force of 2,000 Egyptian paratroopers to fly in and crush it, but when the Syrian army commands at Aleppo and Latakia rallied to the rebels, he sensibly countermanded his orders. An Egyptian advance party of 120 which had already landed was instructed to surrender. Nasser's 'viceroy', Field-Marshal 'Amer, was put on a plane to Cairo and many unwanted Egyptians were repatriated.

A breach on the scale of the Syrian-Egyptian divorce left a good deal of psychological damage in its wake. In both countries, many people were unclear where their loyalties lay or what Syria's secession would mean for their own lives. In Cairo, seat of the now defunct UAR government, there was a vast packing of bags and winding up of joint ventures, a bad-tempered unscrambling of claim and counter-claim, as Syrian civil servants, soldiers and businessmen were bundled back to Damascus. Some chose to defect and stay on. The break-up of the union changed the Middle East landscape as profoundly as its formation had done three and a half years earlier. Nasser's hold on Syria had paralysed the regional power system, but when his hold was loosed Syria recovered something of its old chaotic vigour. Parliamentary elections on 1 December 1961 brought back to life such veterans of the interwar independence struggle as the Aleppo leader, Nazim al-Qudsi, who now became president.

In revolutionary situations when the tide of events flows strongly, statements made in the heat of the moment can have unforeseen consequences. On 2 October 1961, a few days after the secessionist coup, sixteen leading Syrian politicians put their names to a manifesto denouncing Nasser and thanking the army for their 'blessed deliverance'. Among the signatories were not only Akram al-Hawrani, as might have been expected, but also to everyone's amazement the Ba'thist leader, Salah al-Din Bitar. An apostle of union now endorsed its destruction. The signatures were to have a profound effect on the careers of both men.

The scandal of Bitar's name on the secessionist manifesto was compared to the notorious black mark on the record of his colleague, Michel 'Aflaq. When the first Syrian dictator Colonel Husni al-Za'im seized power in 1949, 'Aflaq sent him a fawning letter almost certainly written under duress. It was said that 'Aflaq was made to stand in a barrel of excrement or, in another version, that he was forced to witness the torture of some of his disciples. Be that as it may, 'Aflaq's critics adduced the lapse as evidence of a lack of steel in his character. The same criticism was now directed at Bitar. He realized his mistake, withdrew his signature and proclaimed his continued attachment to the ideal of unity, but the damage was done.

Asad and his colleagues, having already written off 'Aflaq and Bitar, were far more affected by the misfortune which now befell Hawrani. Officers who had trusted and respected him were shocked when he nailed his banner to the secessionist mast. They were bewildered to see him side with the 'reactionaries'. His signature on the manifesto blighted his career, but it was a development which was to prove a godsend to the Military Committee. Had Hawrani condemned both Nasser *and* the secessionists, he might have stood a chance of climbing out of the chaos then engulfing Syria to take power for himself, becoming perhaps a Syrian Castro. His personality was magnetic, his socialism firmly rooted in rural realities, his group of officers among the strongest in the armed forces, and his wing of the Ba'th the most vital. But his disgrace left a space in which the Committee could nourish its own ambitions.

Back to civilian life

Not immediately, however. The break-up of the union found Asad and his colleagues still in Egypt where they were thrown into jail. Asad spent forty-four days in detention, entrusting to Mustafa Tlas, a friend from his days at the Homs Military Academy, the task of escorting his wife and baby daughter back to Syria by sea. This was, in fact, the Asads' second child. Their first whom they had taken to Egypt as an infant had fallen sick and died shortly afterwards. A brother officer recalled Asad kneeling by the child's bedside and weeping. But before the family returned home a second daughter was born in October 1960 whom they named, like their firstborn, Bushra, 'Glad Tidings'. Asad was eventually released and repatriated in exchange for a group of Egyptian officers detained in Syria.

Scarcely better treatment awaited him and his friends in Damascus where the new high command under Major-General Zahr al-Din[22] viewed them with the greatest suspicion. Asad was given indefinite leave. However, worried about his prospects, he hardly paused to embrace his family in Qurdaha before hurrying down to the capital to haunt the corridors of the air force headquarters. There he learned to his dismay that sixty-three Ba'thist officers (including all five members of the secret Military Committee) were to be cashiered and for the most part drafted into dead-end jobs in government ministries. Asad was sent to cool his heels in the Department of Maritime Transport in the Ministry of Economics. On his own testimony, he spent very little time at the ministry, only showing up at the end of each month to collect his pay. 'Why should I come to work when you owe me money?' he used to taunt his unhappy chief. The point was that his salary of 500 liras was less than the 600-lira flying officer's pension to which he was entitled, and he needed every lira to keep his young family whom he had lodged at a rent of 168 liras a month in a three-room apartment half-way up the mountain overlooking Damascus. (Following the 1963 revolution Asad made sure he was reimbursed.)[23]

The members of the Military Committee now set themselves the aim of overthrowing the secessionist government and began working in earnest to reconstitute and expand the clandestine organization they had started in Cairo. Their main targets for recruitment were lieutenants and captains of the classes of 1957, 1958 and 1959, who were now moving into useful positions. In spite of considerable success in bringing in sympathizers, they did not believe they could credibly make a bid for power on their own. They turned for help to officers of Nasserist persuasion – the most prominent being Colonel Jasim 'Alwan – whom the secessionist government had not dared to purge, not wishing to be accused of treachery to the Arab nationalist cause of which Nasser remained the great emblem.

But a fundamental problem soon arose. The Nasserists wanted to mount a putsch to bring their hero back in triumph to Damascus, while the Military Committee wanted a putsch merely to start talking to Nasser – a very different agenda. They hoped to engage him in a candid raking over of past mistakes so as to agree on a radically modified formula of government in which Nasser's powers would be limited and those of the Ba'th enhanced. These differences of aim produced predictable chaos.

In six crisis-packed days from 28 March to 2 April 1962, Syria was dragged on to a merry-go-round of coup and counter-coup which brought the faction-ridden officer corps to the brink of disintegration. It began when Colonel Nahlawi, the man who had destroyed the union six months earlier but who had been shunted off-stage, rounded up and jailed the government, including President Qudsi. Alarmed at being pre-empted, Asad's group and its Nasserist allies then rallied their friends against him, causing a despairing commander in chief to call the warring officers to an army congress at Homs on 1 April. The outcome of these discussions was that some officers were exiled and President Qudsi reinstated. More dissatisfied than ever, Ba'thists and Nasserists then mutinied again, storming the citadel at Aleppo on 2 April and killing the garrison commander. Asad, Jadid and 'Umran drove up in a taxi and were rewarded by the mutineers with the gift of a uniform and a kalashnikov rifle apiece.[24] But to their horror, Nasserist officers hoisted the UAR flag, declared unity restored and called on Egypt to send in paratroopers.

This was not at all what the Committee had told its sympathizers to expect. In some confusion it pulled out of the putsch which promptly collapsed. Asad hurriedly got rid of his rifle and uniform. Be it said in passing that in all these twists and turns, he and his colleagues had endeavoured to direct their army networks without the benefit of a telephone, a motorcar, or any other means of communication. Still civilians, they had no access to radios, guns or trucks, let alone tanks, and attempted to summon up these indispensable instruments of revolution through their recruits. So their failure was not greatly surprising.

Asad fled south to Lebanon via the Syrian coastal town of Tartus. But the Lebanese authorities picked him up and jailed him in Beirut for a week before returning him to Syria where he found himself in Mezze prison. He was interrogated, held for a few days and let off with a caution. Some of the lesser fry in the conspiracy faced trial and some were even sentenced to death, but the Qudsi regime was too weak to send them to the gallows. (They lingered on in prison until released by the Ba'th's successful revolution a year later.)

On the eve of these excitements, on 23 March 1962, Asad's wife Aniseh gave birth to their first son, Basil,[25] so all in all the Asads went through an anxious spell that spring. A few days after Asad's release from Mezze, the police, suspecting him of further plotting, raided his house at dawn frightening the whole family. One of his sisters was staying with them at the time to give Aniseh a hand with the baby, and it was she who inadvertently opened the front door at the first knock so that Asad was surprised in his bedroom which did not improve his temper. Nothing more incriminating was found than his service pistol. The next day a senior officer at headquarters called him in to smooth his ruffled feathers, even offering to return the pistol, but Asad declined to take it, remarking that it would be time enough to return it to him when he was back in the air force.[26] All knew that the boundary between being in and being out was a narrow one, shifting from one coup to the next.

Within the space of a few months Asad had contrived to get himself jailed in Egypt, Lebanon and Syria and had dabbled in a tangle of unsuccessful conspiracies. An ex-pilot officer, without money or prospects, he was living under a regime which had identified him as a troublemaker and which represented everything he detested. His career had been checked by the Syrian-Egyptian union and actually put into reverse by Syria's secession, leaving him stranded as a low-paid government clerk. Until these setbacks his life had been an almost unbroken success story: student leader, star pilot, highly regarded in his village, looked up to by his brothers, popular with other officers, the whole capped by a happy marriage into a socially well-placed 'Alawi family. He had given free rein to the robust side of his nature, showing dash in the air and forcefulness on the ground. He had become used to getting his own way. Now some of the exuberance seeped away to be replaced by an element of gritty doggedness as he and the Military Committee prepared to fight their way back up the slope.

6

Capturing the State

.Asad spent 1962 as a full-time conspirator. He and his colleagues on the Military Committee planned to take power in Syria by a conventional military coup – which meant stealthily putting together a junta of officers who on the day could deliver a punch strong enough to overthrow the government. Without a mass revolutionary movement at their command, they were forced to cast their conspiracy within the narrow bounds of the officers' club and the mutinous barracks which had been the arena of politics in the Syrian armed forces since 1949. There were accepted rituals for Syrian *coups d'état*. The plotters knew they had to seize control of Kisweh and Qatana, the two camps guarding the southern approaches to the capital; that the crack 70th Armoured Brigade was an essential instrument; that Homs, situated north of Damascus and home of the Military Academy, had to be stopped from interfering, and that from the very first hour the Damascus radio station had to be taken over to inform the populace that a new era had begun. Every self-respecting revolution needed a 'Communiqué No. 1' couched in suitably stirring language.

Although the conspirators were themselves outside the army, inexperienced and young – Asad was still only thirty-one – their objective was not out of reach. The secessionist regime they meant to topple rested on men and interests which had been greatly enfeebled by the violent events since independence: the Palestine War, the military coups that followed it, the rise of radical parties, and the shake-up of the marriage with Egypt. President Qudsi and the three prime ministers who served under him in the eighteen months the regime lasted – Dr Ma'ruf al-Dawalibi, Dr Bashir al-'Azmah and, finally, the aged and ailing Khalid al-'Azm – had largely lost the will to govern. 'It was a government without a people and without an army, the rule of a class which had had its day', Asad commented later.[1]

This was the last appearance in government of the city notables

72

who, under the Turks, then under the French and in the early years of independence, had been for so long the real masters of Syria. But by 1962 they could no longer control the apparatus of government, let alone the officer corps, nor did they have the strength to put down old enemies such as the Ba'th which was now beginning to organize again. Qudsi's secessionist government also had to bear the brunt of Nasser's fury. Unable to forgive Syria its defection, he turned his propaganda machine against Damascus, while Egyptian agents, funds and explosives poured into Syria across the permeable Lebanese frontier. Egyptian intervention became so flagrant that Syria complained to the Arab League, but Nasser's indignant threat to walk out of the League if the complaint against him were upheld quashed the matter and left the Qudsi regime helpless.

To push over this tottering structure seemed not unduly difficult, but the Military Committee had first to find suitable allies, and since its own networks were composed of junior officers, it was much in need of some top brass in command of large formations. The Syrian officer corps in 1962, in more than usual disarray, provided fertile ground for plotters. The collapse of the union and the mutinies which followed had taken their toll in purges and transfers. Many officers were locked up in Mezze prison, scores of others languished like Asad in petty government employment at home; others still were posted to distant embassies. Those who remained in service were so riven by feuds and surly with grievances that Beirut newspapers predicted a coup every other week.

The officers were split into five main factions: the so-called 'Damascus officers' who had destroyed the union and whose morale was crumbling along with that of the government they had put in power; Akram al-Hawrani's faction which had lost ground since the affair of Hawrani's signature on the secessionist manifesto; a sizeable group of Nasserist officers, some in important commands, but who suffered from the anomaly that the government they served was on the worst possible terms with the Egyptian leader; a faction of Independents who carried no one's banner; and finally the Ba'thists, among whom the Military Committee had already covertly recruited. Where in the other factions could more supporters be found?

The 'Damascus officers' were the enemy. The Hawranists were equally unapproachable, less because Hawrani had sided with the secessionists than because the Military Committee saw them as rivals. There remained the Nasserists and the Independents. In spite of their own reservations about Nasser and the mismanaged coup attempt of the spring of 1962, the Committee turned again to the Nasserists, making secret contact with two key officers, the head of Military Intelligence, Colonel Rashid al-Qutayni, and the commander of the Homs brigade, Colonel Muhammad al-Sufi, with the proposal that they combine in an assault on the government. After a good deal of bargaining both were won over.

But this was not sufficient. On orders from the Committee, a group of Ba'thist junior officers then asked for an interview with the leading Independent in the army, Colonel Ziad al-Hariri, commander of the front facing Israel, and offered him the leadership of their movement. 'If we succeed, you can become chief of staff. If we fail, you can disown us', was their argument.[2] The offer came at a timely moment. Prime Minister Khalid al-'Azm, a staunch opponent of officers meddling in politics, was about to strip Hariri of his prestigious command and post him as military attaché to Baghdad. So Hariri joined the conspiracy.

As a result of these secret negotiations, a six-man junta was assembled late in 1962 – the Military Committee trio, Asad, 'Umran and Jadid together with Hariri, Qutayni, Sufi – but with very mixed objectives. Hariri wanted to save his own career, the Nasserists simply wanted Nasser back, while the aims of the Military Committee were more complex and ambitious. Alone among the various factions it had a tightly knit structure, a unified leadership, and a programme. This was, first, to return the Ba'th to power in Syria; second, to set themselves on the ascent once again; and only then to promote the cause of Arab unity.

Knowing what they wanted was an enormous advantage, but it could not entirely compensate for the fact that, insofar as the public was concerned, they were obscure young men, from an unfavoured community, cashiered from the army. They were not very welcome even in civilian Ba'thist circles. The party had recruited military supporters, as had other ideological parties, because the army had become too important to neglect, but also for self-protection. Arab politics was no tea party. Ba'thists had been massacred in large numbers in Iraq in 1959 and had suffered imprisonment and torture in several other countries. When the prospect was one of being killed or jailed, qualms about soldiers in politics seemed overly fussy. Nevertheless soldiers were not brought into the party leadership, where civilians still hoped to keep control.

This was part of the background to the Military Committee's relations with 'Aflaq at this time. Asad and his friends did not like 'Aflaq and he was suspicious of them, but they needed each other. The officers needed 'Aflaq's name, which for the world at large still personified the Ba'th, as well as what remained of the party apparatus to match any pro-Nasser show of strength in the streets. 'Aflaq in turn knew that without army backing he had no chance of a come-back.

In the spring of 1962, struggling to re-enter Syrian politics after four miserable years, 'Aflaq convened a National Congress at Homs – the first on Syrian soil since the dissolution of the party in 1958. Akram al-Hawrani was not invited, nor were Ba'thists who had defected to Nasser, nor those cadres who, against 'Aflaq's orders, had tried to keep their branches alive during the union years. The Military Committee sent Muhammad 'Umran to take a quiet note of the proceedings. The congress put 'Aflaq precariously back in the party saddle. Backed by a combative delegation of Iraqi Ba'thists, who sensed that their moment was coming in Baghdad, he was able to get the congress to pass a resolution to re-form the Syrian party and, in a gesture to party ideals, to issue a somewhat hypocritical call to Egypt for a new union 'far removed from one-man rule, from police state rule' – hardly a friendly overture to Nasser.[3]

In the wake of the congress, 'Aflaq and the Military Committee made contact with each other and, without letting the old leader into their secret or briefing him in detail about their plans, the officers won a pledge of his support for a coup. There was a good deal of humbug on both sides. But what bound them together was the unspoken understanding that once they had made use of the Nasserists to get rid of the secessionists, they would not repeat the mistake of surrendering power to the Egyptian leader. How power was to be shared between them was left unsettled.

The March coup

On 8 February 1963, Asad and his friends woke up to the heart-warming news that their party comrades in Baghdad had brought down and killed the Iraqi dictator, 'Abd al-Karim Qasim. The bloody drama in Baghdad opened the way for success in Damascus.

Qasim was a much more formidable opponent than the mild bespectacled Qudsi presiding over Syria. To dislodge Qasim the underground Ba'th party in Iraq, led by a rough-hewn young man of poor background, 'Ali Salih al-Sa'di, had recruited and armed an underground militia two thousand-strong, forged alliances with Arab nationalist officers in the Iraqi army, and won over the professional associations of lawyers, doctors and engineers which formed the backbone of the Iraqi middle class. They had brought the students out on strike, seized the Al-Rashid air base, and shot dead the air force commander, Jalal al-Awqati, at the front door of his house an hour before zero hour at 9.30 a.m. Fighter planes were then sent to strafe the Defence Ministry where Qasim, who worked at night, had just gone to bed. Twenty-four hours later the insurgents had flushed him out and taken him to the broadcasting station where he was summarily executed. (Reuters cabled the revolutionaries with an offer of $40,000 for a film clip showing Qasim dead, but was refused.)

The events in Baghdad changed the rules of Arab politics. Iraq, which Qasim's isolationism had kept out of play, re-entered the mainstream, and the Ba'th party was transformed. From being a divided and enfeebled rump of a party it suddenly looked a major radical and pan-Arab force on a par with Nasser himself. This change in the party's fortunes was greatly to the advantage of the Syrian comrades, and to none more than to Asad and his friends. It was a more than welcome boost because, unlike the Iraqi Ba'th, the Syrians had no party militia, indeed hardly a party, only a sketchy military network, and very little support among the professional and middle classes. Indeed, conscious of weakness, 'Aflaq cautioned the officers against acting hastily – but was ignored.[4] The Military Committee was on its mettle to match the Iraqi example.

Syria's six-man secret junta decided to mount their coup on 7 March, just a month after the Iraqis. But at the eleventh hour Military Intelligence raided the apartment where the planners were assembling. Some officers were arrested and others went into hiding. Struggling with inadequate communications, Asad had the unnerving task of getting a message to units about to move that the coup had been put back by twenty-four hours.[5]

On the night of 7–8 March tanks and infantry began to move on Damascus. Colonel Ziad al-Hariri led a brigade from the Israeli front while in Suwayda, capital of the Jabal al-Duruz, Ba'thist officers seized command of a second brigade and headed for the capital. Caught in a pincer movement between these two units, the crack 70th Armoured Brigade at Kisweh under Lieut.-Colonel 'Abd al-Karim 'Abid surrendered. Muhammad 'Umran promptly took it over: the Military Committee's chief strategist was back in uniform and at the head of one of the army's most prestigious units. A potentially hostile brigade stationed at Qatana on the south-western approach to the capital did not intervene, very probably because Widad Bashir, a Ba'thist who had been in Egypt at the same time as Asad but had escaped being cashiered, took control of army communications in the Damascus area. With Kisweh invested and Qatana neutralized, Hariri's force marched on Damascus, setting up road-blocks in the city and throwing cordons around the central post office and other sensitive points. Captain Salim Hatum, a hot-headed Druze party man, captured the radio station. The Ministry of Defence was occupied without a fight and the commander-in-chief, General Zahr al-Din, placed under arrest. Also apprehended were President Qudsi, Akram al-Hawrani and a number of other secessionist personalities. That morning Salah Jadid bicycled into the city to take over the crucial Bureau of Officers' Affairs which controlled transfers and promotions throughout the armed forces. Thus another member of the Military Committee slipped quietly into a key job.

Asad's moment of glory was the capture of the Dumayr air base east of Damascus where the entire air force was concentrated and which offered the only serious resistance to the putsch. Some planes had been sent up to bomb the rebels. The plan was for him to move against Dumayr at the head of a company from Hariri's brigade, aiming to arrive before dawn to avoid being attacked from the air. But there was a hitch. The parleying at Kisweh, which led to the surrender of the 70th Armoured Brigade, took longer than expected and it was broad daylight when Asad, still in civilian clothes, halted his small force some three kilometres from the base around which tanks had been deployed. He later related:[6]

> I sent someone forward with a warning that I would start shelling if there was any resistance. After a few minutes two of their officers drove up to propose a negotiation. I went at once to the base commander. 'It's all over for you', I said. 'We don't want to kill anyone but unless you surrender we will have to use force.' I advised him to bring down the planes.
>
> 'Do you think we will surrender to Nasserists?' one of the officers shouted. The man who put this question had been jailed with me in Cairo at the break-up of the union. 'Only yesterday', I answered, 'we were in prison together. You know I am a Ba'thist not a Nasserist.' The atmosphere became very tense, but after a good deal of shouting they gave in. They could have resisted – the forces at their command were stronger than my small unit. But they were cowards. When my troops entered the base, they would have killed the secessionist officers had I not intervened to protect them.'

Later that morning the coup-makers assembled at army headquarters to celebrate their lightning victory. The coup had been a walkover, completed in a not too strenuous and almost bloodless morning, and greeted with indifference by the population. A week earlier Asad and the others had been living the shadowy and precarious life of obscure plotters with hardly a telephone or a motorcar between them. Now they were the strongest force in Syrian politics. They had actually brought it off, their revolution had succeeded. The first communiqués of the new regime were written and broadcast by Dr Saber Falhut, an ebullient Druze man of letters, who became known as 'the poet of the revolution'. (For many years he was to head Syria's national news agency, SANA.) The ninth communiqué broadcast at 8.40 that morning was of special interest to the Military Committee: it reinstated its five members in the armed services together with some thirty other officers. Air Force Captain Asad, promoted lieutenant-colonel, was named commander of the Dumayr air base. Asad was the youngest and most junior member of the trio – 'Umran, Jadid and himself – which dominated the Military Committee, so, in planning the coup, he had to some extent deferred to the other two. But he alone had aviation expertise as well as friends and followers in the air force, assets which won him the command of the base and boosted his status in the Committee. In due course the air force became his fief and his springboard for greater things.

After the coup exhilaration was intense but so was anxiety. Without much experience or any sort of training, the new rulers faced the task of running not just the army but the state itself. Their first act was to invest power in a secret twenty-man National Council for the Revolutionary Command (NCRC), composed of twelve Ba'thists and eight Nasserists and Independents – reflecting the factions which had come together to overthrow President Qudsi. Its exact membership was for months to be a matter of puzzled speculation among the public. On the day after the coup the NCRC instructed the Ba'thist leader Salah al-Din Bitar to head a government to implement its policies, and a few days later still, largely for form's sake, six civilians – three Ba'thists, 'Aflaq, Bitar and Mansur al-Atrash, and the leaders of three Nasserist splinter groups – were brought into the Command. But from the start power lay with the officers.

How the civilians chafed at the secretive ways of the officers! Atrash, son of the Druze chieftain Sultan Pasha and a Sorbonne-educated party veteran, recalled the NCRC's early workings:[7]

> The officers let us do the talking although, as we later discovered, they had agreed beforehand among themselves what the decisions were to be. One day I lost my temper: 'Why don't these gentlemen speak? May I suggest they appoint a liaison officer to communicate their views to us?' Eventually Colonel 'Umran deigned to give us civilians some vague notions of what they were planning.

In the Military Committee there was as yet no hint of the quarrels which were later to destroy it. As in Cairo, decisions were taken jointly and in secret. The members were buoyed up and bound together by a sense of destiny, by the will to transform their country, by the shared exhilaration of knowing that their conspiracy was the motor of the new Syria. The consciousness of being an instrument of history was to remain part of Asad's armoury. Visibly aware of his responsibilities, he projected an air of great seriousness, but now as later his sense of power was disguised by restrained behaviour and affable good manners.

Politics inside the NCRC in the early days of the revolution was mainly a matter of bargaining for jobs between the various rival factions, often in night-long sessions. As their chairman and commander-in-chief, they chose a popular officer, Colonel Lu'ayy al-Atasi, whom they released from prison on the morning of 8 March and promoted lieutenant-general. He posed no threat to them and had taken no part in the coup. Advanced to the same rank was the principal coup-maker Ziad al-Hariri who took over the coveted post of chief of staff. But as neither Atasi nor Hariri had a personal or political power base in the forces, the real contest inside the NCRC was between Ba'thists and Nasserists.

Nasserist officers took eye-catching jobs: Muhammad al-Sufi became defence minister and Rashid al-Qutayni deputy chief of staff, but the Military Committee, which by now had coopted five other officers,[8] ensured that Ba'thists held the real levers of power. The Military Committee was henceforth a 'junta within the junta', placing its men where it mattered and deciding on its line before NCRC meetings. 'Umran was given command of the Fifth Brigade at Homs (switching in June to the 70th Armoured, the brigade he had briefly taken over during the coup). Jadid at Officers' Affairs deftly set about promoting friends, purging enemies, and drafting back into active service large numbers of Ba'thist reserve officers. Ahmad Suwaydani, one of the Military Committee's co-opted members, took over Military Intelligence, while Mazyad Hunaydi, an early Cairo associate, was put in charge of the Military Police. The Homs Military Academy, a nursery for fostering party power, was placed in Ba'thist hands and that summer admitted hundreds of Ba'thist students from modest backgrounds – Asad's youngest brother, Rif'at, among them. They were given a crash course and commissioned to fill commands which had been held by their class enemies.

Asad became in all but name the real boss of the air force, which, even in a country with small and poorly equipped armed forces, was a dizzying promotion for a man in his early thirties, a mere captain only the day before. But Asad, with his assurance and ambition freshly fired, was not in the least daunted, and vigorously set about consolidating his fief, putting his mates where he needed them and building up a personal power base by looking after the people around him and seeing to their welfare. He did not neglect self-improvement: it was noticed that he kept a volume of Arabic philology on his desk at the air base.[9]

Steadily Asad and his friends built a fortress which they hoped to make impregnable to outside attack. But still they lacked a front man. They were all too junior, too little known, to present themselves credibly to the public as Syria's real rulers. In the circumstances their masterstroke was to appoint Colonel Amin al-Hafiz, a bluff, tough, no-nonsense soldier, to the critical post of minister of the interior. The Military Committee had made his acquaintance in Cairo during the union years when he was a staff college instructor. He was not a party member but they felt he was a friend. However, aware of surveillance by Egyptian Intelligence, he had kept his distance from the young conspirators. Hafiz was a Sunni, the son of an Aleppo policeman, who like other schoolboys threw stones at the French during the Mandate before volunteering for service in the 1948 Palestine war. In 1954 he joined the uprising against Shishakli and was promoted to command the Eastern Front at Dayr al-Zur and then to be commandant of the Homs academy, before being posted to Cairo. When Syria broke with Egypt in September 1961 Hafiz was shipped home to Damascus – where he was promptly contacted again by the Committee's leader, Muhammad 'Umran. He later recalled:[10]

'Umran wanted to know my opinion about the chances of a coup. He showed me a position paper in which he had outlined the overall political situation, the strength of the regime, the Ba'th's assets and those of their principal rivals. 'We think of you as one of us', he said. But I was not tempted.

In December 1961 the Qudsi regime exiled Amin al-Hafiz to Buenos Aires as military attaché, and it was from there that he was summoned back to Syria by the victorious officers after the 8 March coup. Somewhat bemused, he found himself promoted lieutenant-general and entrusted with the Ministry of the Interior, although he had had nothing to do with either the party or the Military Committee. The Military Committee wanted him to front for them and pulled the necessary strings.[11]

Struggle with the Nasserists

The victory of the Ba'th in both Damascus and Baghdad threatened to trap Nasser, as he put it, 'between the hammer and the anvil'. If Damascus and Baghdad were to unite, Nasser's influence would be forced out of Arab Asia, a disagreeable prospect for a leader whose dominance right across the Arab world had been recognized even by his enemies. For the Ba'th the stakes were just as high: after twenty years of political struggle, it now had a chance to rule. Nasser and the Ba'th were destined to be adversaries.

To begin with, the underlying savagery of their relations was cloaked in make-believe. On the surface they shared a pan-Arab philosophy, belonged to the 'liberated' Arab world in contrast to the kings and princes 'shackled to imperialism', and together had worked to overthrow the 'secessionists' in Damascus and the 'isolationists' in Baghdad. Under the pressure of popular expectations 'unity talks'[12] between Cairo, Baghdad and Damascus were started within a week of the Syrian coup with the declared aim of setting up a pan-Arab federation. But it was a hollow exercise. The talks were no more than a smokescreen hiding profound differences from view. Even as the leaders talked, Nasserists and Ba'thists fought it out on the streets of Syria and Iraq. Michel 'Aflaq and the officers of the Military Committee were privately agreed in regarding the Cairo proceedings as a charade. In fact the Committee members mostly stayed at home to guard the fort, sending 'Umran to listen in at the last sessions.

Nasser adopted a patronizing, bullying tone towards the Syrian Ba'thists and pressed for a merger of political forces in all three countries into a single party structure under central leadership – his own. In an attempt to force the Syrians into submission he warned that he would publish a record of the talks and so awaken the 'anger of the masses' – a threat later carried out to the discomfiture of 'Aflaq and Bitar who, as the transcript showed, were poor, even fumbling, negotiators. On 17 April 1963, after a month of on-off talks, a draft constitution was published which purported to provide for a new, tripartite United Arab Republic to come into being in May 1965. None of the negotiators believed for an instant that the scheme had a future.

Nasser had a strong antipathy for the Ba'th leaders, feelings which were amply reciprocated. He resented their claim to have pioneered Arab nationalist ideas which he subsequently adopted, and disliked being reminded that the Ba'th had played a part in persuading him to adopt Arabism as Egypt's official policy. He had dismissed 'Aflaq and

Bitar as ineffectual theorists but their party's success in Iraq and Syria now forced him to take them seriously. They would have to be smashed. After the Cairo talks Nasser's tactics became rougher. He launched a propaganda campaign against the Syrian Ba'thists, encouraged his supporters to demonstrate in Damascus, and threatened to withdraw the Nasserists from the Syrian government. Michel 'Aflaq became the butt of savage sarcasms, scoffed at as a tin-pot 'Roman emperor' or a 'Cypriot Christian' of doubtful Arab credentials who had the effrontery to aspire to Arab leadership. The Ba'th leaders understood that to save themselves they had to eliminate Nasser's instruments in Syria and Iraq. At closed party meetings 'Aflaq voiced violently anti-Nasser sentiments, falling out with his colleague Bitar who still thought that a formula might yet be found for co-operation with Egypt.[13]

Nasserist power in Syria was based on a few dozen officers and three civilian political groupings of which the most formidable was the Movement of Arab Nationalists (MAN),[14] a pan-Arab party which believed in the indispensability of Nasser's leadership and which had grown with such speed over the previous eighteen months that by 1963 it was able to bring large numbers of young militants on to the streets. The MAN – recruiting mainly right-of-centre Sunni middle-class nationalists – was the Ba'th's most dangerous rival in Syria, Iraq, and indeed most Arab countries.

So alarmed were Asad and his friends at the dangerous stirrings of Nasser's supporters that they mounted what was in effect another coup. Between 28 April and 2 May 1963 over fifty pro-Egyptian officers and NCOs were purged from the Syrian armed forces, causing the two leading Nasserists on the NCRC, Defence Minister Muhammad al-Sufi and Deputy Chief of Staff Rashid al-Qutayni, to resign in protest. They were followed by the five Nasserist cabinet ministers. The Nasserists struck back on the street, sparking vast riots in Damascus and Aleppo on 8 and 9 May. The Military Committee called on Interior Minister Amin al-Hafiz to restore order: fifty rioters were shot dead; MAN's offices and newspaper were closed down and those of its leaders who did not escape were put on trial and given long prison terms. Nasser loyalists were purged from every sector of public life and their place taken by Ba'thists. The grim jest in Damascus was that Amin al-Hafiz had learned his techniques of policing during his stay in Argentina. When the Iraqi Ba'th in turn moved against the Nasserists, no one was left in doubt that the party's programme in both Syria and Iraq was to hold undivided power. Any accommodation with Nasser was ruled out. It was kill or be killed.

On 18 July 1963 Nasserists led by Colonel Jasim 'Alwan, backed by the MAN and underpinned by Egyptian Intelligence, mounted a daylight assault on the Damascus radio station and army headquarters. Sub-machinegun in hand, the stalwart Amin al-Hafiz directed the defence. Hundreds of people were killed and wounded, many caught in the crossfire, before Ba'thist tanks and the party's new National Guard regained control. 'Alwan made his getaway, but within hours twenty-seven officers were hauled before military courts and shot there and then, in breach of the time-honoured tradition whereby losers were banished to embassies abroad. On 22 July Nasser denounced the Syrian Ba'thists as fascists and murderers and formally withdrew from the 17 April union agreement. This was the final breach.

Some basic questions

Did the Military Committee foresee that it would come to this? That the affair with Nasser ended in a welter of blood was a sobering baptism. It seemed that power could be held only at the price of slaughter such as Syria had not known since the struggle against the French. In their years in Egypt the five members of the Committee had professed themselves to be fervent unionists. The declared aim of their Committee, its very *raison d'être*, had been to defend the union. Yet now, faced with the choice of reviving the union or keeping power for themselves, they had no hesitation in choosing the latter.

Asad was considered less bitterly hostile to Nasser than 'Umran and Jadid, his fellow 'Alawis in the leadership, and less prepared to make the final break with Egypt. Part of the evidence concerns the treatment of Nasserist officers in the wake of Jasim 'Alwan's rebellion. A number of prisoners taken during the fighting were interrogated, and in some cases tortured, at Asad's Dumayr air base. Asad found time to visit their families to ask whether they wished to send anything to their sons. Several of the lesser conspirators were eventually released on his initiative and taken back into the army.

The Syrian-Egyptian relationship was to be a persistent preoccupation of Asad's life. He was to have occasion to ponder long and hard on the dilemma that Syria could do little with Egypt and little without it. At the time of the union in 1958, Nasser hoisted Ba'th hopes to the skies, then dashed them in an ill-fated enterprise which was to put in doubt the very core of Ba'thist doctrine and raise difficult questions. If a union of Syria and Egypt could not work, was pan-Arabism itself a mirage? And if Syria's destiny lay not with Egypt but with its immediate neighbours in the Levant, was this not a vindication of the Ba'th's pan-Syrian rivals and of their 'Greater Syria' theories? These queries about Syria's proper place within the Arab family were long to puzzle Asad and their roots lay in those turbulent years of the 1950s and 1960s when, in common with his fellow Ba'thists, he first ardently held Nasser's banner aloft, then trampled on it.

Consolidation of power

Having routed the Nasserists, the Military Committee's considerably easier target was the group of Independent officers around General Ziad al-Hariri, now Defence Minister as well as Chief of Staff. When Hariri was rash enough to lead a delegation to Algeria on 23 June 1963, the Committee used his absence to purge, demote and transfer some twenty-five of his key supporters. As a consolation prize Hariri himself was offered the post of military attaché in Washington, but he chose to drop out of politics and retire to Paris. Hariri's ousting brought new titles and responsibilities to Amin al-Hafiz, who now became Minister both of Defence and of the Interior, deputy military governor and acting Chief of Staff. At the same time, to protect it from any new street uprising, the Syrian Ba'th formed a paramilitary National Guard on 30 June, on the model of the Iraqi party militia, and entrusted its command to Hamad 'Ubayd, a co-opted member of the Military Committee.

This brutal jockeying was evidently too much for the last remaining Independent in a position of power, the mild-mannered General Lu'ayy al-Atasi, chairman of the NCRC and commander-in-chief. Anxious to keep itself out of the limelight and still shy of showing the Syrians who were their real masters, the Military Committee urged him to stay on,[15] but he insisted on resigning, and again the Committee chose to promote the already much titled Amin al-Hafiz to the vacant posts and brought him on to the Military Committee, the real command centre of Syrian politics. 'We organised him at that time', Asad later related. 'We got him to join our Committee not because he was important, but because when we discussed military affairs the army commander had to be there.'[16] But the all-purpose Sunni front man who now held half a dozen of the highest offices in the land was not wholly docile. Exposed to the public and accumulating so many jobs, Hafiz began to be seen, and what is more to see himself, as an influential figure in his own right. It was a prescription for future trouble.

In four crowded and blood-stained months from March 1963, Asad,

'Umran, Jadid, and their colleagues on the Committee eliminated all organized resistance to their still behind-the-scenes rule. But they paid a heavy price as, almost from the start, they had to govern by force rather than consent. They were a fraction of what was itself a minority, a military splinter group of a semi-defunct party without a popular base. The experience of those early days affected their attitudes for years to come: even when the party grew strong and secure, it never rid itself of habits of wariness and repression.

On the regional stage Asad and his comrades broke fresh ground. Although they could not have foreseen it at the time, their coup inaugurated a new era in Arab affairs in which Egyptian-led unionism was never again to seem credible. Nasser was not to regain the initiative. Indeed so damaging was his rivalry with the Ba'th that his last years were dogged by it, and it was to play a part in the sequence of miscalculations which engulfed the Arabs in the Six Day War. The old pattern of inter-Arab relations in which Syria had for so long been a political football kicked back and forth between more powerful neighbours was shattered. Damascus now took in hand its own destinies for the first time since independence, and from these confused and violent beginnings it was in due course to grow into a leading regional player.

7

Capturing the Party

The years immediately following the 1963 coup were Asad's apprenticeship for power. They were a tough, instructive interlude in which one rival after another fell, or was pushed, leaving him to breast the tape alone. In the course of them he made lasting friendships as well as permanent enmities. Without this training in survival his tenure at the top might not have been so prolonged nor have made such a mark.

But such judgments were for the future.

The coup threw Asad into the deep end of politics. He and the other young Ba'thists who had seized power in Damascus and Baghdad that spring faced the task of translating their leftist instincts into practical policies. Their energies had gone into preparing their coups, not into thinking out a detailed programme. The Iraqi Ba'th provided a striking example of unpreparedness for government. After the takeover, it was found necessary to broadcast some sort of a policy statement to the Iraqi people who were understandably anxious to know what was in store for them. But who was to write it and what was it to contain? Hurriedly two Ba'thist intellectuals from neighbouring countries, Dr Munif al-Razzaz from Jordan and Dr 'Abdallah 'Abd al-Da'im from Syria, were called to Baghdad to put something together. 'We got lost in government', the proletarian coup-maker 'Ali Salih al-Sa'di later lamented.[1]

The Syrians floundered just as badly as they cast about for 'theoretical guidance'. The Military Committee could hardly go for help to 'Aflaq and Bitar whose middle-class reformism they despised. So with little intellectual baggage of their own to match their radical inclinations, they turned to a Marxist faction which some Ba'thists had formed after the party's dissolution. This group of 'thinkers' was led by Hammud al-Shufi, a Druze schoolteacher of thirty-six whom voracious reading of socialist literature and harsh jail experience during the union

86

years had converted into an out-and-out left-winger. Against great odds Shufi had kept a clandestine Ba'th cell alive in Suwayda,[2] capital of the Druze governorate, and had become something of a local firebrand. He was much influenced by the Iraqi Ba'thist revolutionary 'Ali Salih al-Sa'di and by Yasin al-Hafiz, a Marxist theorist from Dayr al-Zur which, despite its remoteness on the Euphrates, furnished Syrian politics with an unusual amount of talent. Evidently believing they had much in common, the Military Committee and Shufi's Marxists joined forces and together dominated the Ba'th party's Regional Congress of September 1963 at which Shufi was elected secretary and Asad a member of a new eight-man Regional Command.[3] Neither 'Aflaq nor Bitar nor any of their supporters was included.

'Aflaq had conceived of his party as a pyramid with a National Command at its apex under a secretary-general – himself since the foundation – directing the party's affairs throughout the entire Arab nation. In each separate country, or 'region' in Ba'th jargon, party matters were in the hands of a Regional Command which enjoyed some autonomy from the National Command but was in the last resort subject to it. What now happened was that the officers on the Regional Command claimed greater freedom than 'Aflaq had intended.

For Asad, election to the highest body of the party's structure in Syria meant his first exposure to the public. It did not yet mean real power: 'Umran and Jadid were in front and Amin al-Hafiz even more in the public eye. To much of the party, to government servants, to political circles in Damascus, Asad was still an unknown quantity who had barely emerged from anonymity. He was not prepared for government, knew nothing of administration and hardly anything of statecraft, and had little familiarity with Syria's problems or those of the region. Nevertheless he now sat on the party's Regional Command with the Marxists, debating policies and theories and taking decisions, and no doubt it was an enriching experience. He situated himself 'on the left' in his determination to overthrow privilege, but this was more a gut feeling than a theoretical commitment. 'Alawis like himself, downtrodden sectarians at odds with the Sunni establishment, had been in opposition for a millennium.

In Arab society where institutions are sketchy, men in power need to make themselves personally accessible in order to get things done. People come to them for favours of all sorts. A single phone call can sometimes break a bottleneck. As a member of the new junta Asad had his share of visitors and problems to sort out. Khalid al-Fahum, a Palestinian who was to achieve prominence on the pro-Syrian side of PLO politics, remembered calling on young Colonel Asad in a small bare office at Air Force Headquarters on Baghdad Street. Fahum was anxious to learn where the new rulers stood, more particularly on Palestine. Asad, he concluded, was certainly 'left' in hating the city bosses and their rural allies and made no bones about it. He sided unreservedly with the peasantry of his home province. But he was clearly not a Communist. Fahum noted with relief that this 'Alawi officer saw no difference between a Syrian and a Palestinian and seemed a committed Arab nationalist.[4]

The first post-coup congress of September 1963 gave a clear signal that the officers were rebelling as much against 'Aflaq as against the old social and economic order. They privately rejected him and his ideas and were determined to take from him the party he had founded, arguing that they were rescuing their party from hands which had grown feeble and corrupt. 'Aflaq was well aware of the threat to him. (Some students of Syria have claimed that the subsequent takeover was so thorough that the party thereafter bore no relation to 'Aflaq's creation and should therefore be renamed the 'Neo-Ba'th'.)[5]

The Regional Congress at which 'Aflaq was defeated was a dress rehearsal for the party's sixth National Congress, held in Damascus in October 1963, when 'Aflaq just managed to retain his post of secretary-general but was otherwise swamped by an alliance of the Syrian and Iraqi delegations led by the radicals Shufi and Sa'di. The National Command elected at that time revealed, much as the Regional Command had done, the changing balance of power between the factions. Bitar was dropped altogether, while for the first time military Ba'thists – the Syrians Salah Jadid and Amin al-Hafiz and the Iraqis Ahmad Hasan al-Bakr and Salih Mahdi 'Ammash – moved in.

New to power in Baghdad and Damascus, the Ba'th was keen to assert itself in Arab affairs as a fount of doctrine whose recipes were valid for the region as a whole. It sought to rival Nasser who a year earlier had published his own ideological blueprint, Egypt's 'National Charter', and to match Ahmad Ben Bella who was projecting Algeria as a model for the Third World. The Ba'th too wanted to have its say. This was the significance of a sixty-page keynote document adopted at the congress. Drafted by the officers' Marxist allies, by Yasin al-Hafiz in particular, it was titled somewhat pompously 'Some Theoretical Propositions'.[6] Not surprisingly the officers of the Military Committee had tinkered with the passages dealing with army-party relations. Sensitive to the charge of hijacking 'Aflaq's party, they argued that the army's intervention in politics had been providential: 'The organic fusion of the military and civilian vanguard sectors is an urgent prerequisite for ... socialist reconstruction', the document declared.

Political indoctrination of the troops was held to be no less important than military training.

In 'Some Theoretical Propositions', the Ba'th was given official status as 'the leading party' in Syrian public life around which lesser but like-minded political forces were to gather. Ba'th-affiliated 'popular organizations' of workers, peasants, students, writers, women, youth, and the like, were seen as components of a genuine 'popular democracy', in contrast with Western-style parliamentary democracy which was denounced as a front for 'feudalism' and the *grande bourgeoisie*, incapable of ushering in socialist transformation. Thus the seed was sown for the later institutions of the Ba'thist state and an underpinning of theory was provided for the harsh warfare which the newcomers were soon to wage on the urban propertied classes.

Bowing to the new forces dominating the Regional and National Congresses, Bitar resigned as prime minister, and in his place Lieut-General Amin al-Hafiz formed a government – although the Military Committee placed Muhammad 'Umran as deputy premier to keep an eye on him. Salah Jadid, the Committee's number two, promoted from lieutenant-colonel to major-general, became Chief of Staff. The officers were now in key slots: 'Umran oversaw the government machine, Jadid ran the army, while Asad's brief was to extend the Committee's networks in the armed forces.

Asad's comrades had entrusted him with the most important security job of the regime. The officers realized that the only way to protect the army from the factionalism which had been its bane since independence was to make it a Ba'th monopoly. This was the prerequisite for establishing durable rule in an inherently unstable country. As Asad saw it, the aim was to create an 'ideological army' in stark contrast with the 'army in politics' of the past. He therefore set about building inside the armed services and on the model of the civilian organization[7] a hierarchical structure of party cells, divisions, sections and branches, a task which took him on visits to units all over the country.

For ideological guidance in this job he sought the help of 'Aflaq's early rival, the philosopher Zaki al-Arsuzi, who through the channel of Dr Wahib al-Ghanim had inspired Asad's first steps in student politics. Arsuzi had long since retired but Asad brought him out and took him on tours of army camps, getting him to lecture to the men and meet the officers. Delighted by Asad's attentions, the older man contributed frequent editorials to the party and army press[8] and gave Asad himself ideological insights which were important to his development at this time. In due course Asad arranged for Arsuzi to receive a pension which he kept until his death in Damascus on 2 July 1968. 'He lived a poor man and died as one, but he was respected by all who knew him', was Asad's epitaph.[9] Meanwhile Asad went about his work of bringing every unit under the close control of the Military Committee by ensuring that loyalists occupied the sensitive commands and that the political education of the troops was not neglected. In performing this task, he showed a mastery of detail and a bent for patient planning which suggested the mind of an intelligence officer. His grassroots knowledge of the armed services was to contribute to his later ascendancy.

The late summer and autumn of 1963 were the high point of Ba'th fortunes when everything seemed to be going its way. The violent breach with Nasser in July appeared to have bred a new confidence. A blueprint was dreamed up of a Ba'thist Fertile Crescent formed by a federation of Syria and Iraq which would overturn Egypt's long hegemony and carry the tide of pure doctrine into Jordan, the Gulf, Saudi Arabia and down to Aden where the party was in contact with 'Abdallah al-Asnag, head of the Aden Trades Union Council, and then along the North African seaboard to Morocco where the opposition leader Mehdi Ben Baraka was a friend. Underground cells sprang up in Libya, in Sudan, even it was rumoured under Nasser's nose in Egypt. The horizon was unlimited and the party's enthusiasm knew no bounds. To the outside world, ignorant of the internal feuding, Michel 'Aflaq, party founder, ideologue and visionary, had come into his kingdom. The Tunisian paper *L'Action* ran a picture of him above the caption, 'The philosopher who made two coups in a month'.

The Iraqi débâcle

The fractious reality of Syria and Iraq soon put such visions to flight. Before the year was out the Iraqi Ba'th had fallen, while Asad and his friends in Syria were under siege. The Iraqi comrades made the first mistake, and as so often in the history of modern Iraq, it had to do with the Kurds, the mountain people of the north who, straddling the borders of Turkey, Iran, Iraq and Syria, aspire to a homeland of their own. When in February 1963 the Ba'th seized power in Baghdad with the help of Arab nationalist officers, its first act was to slaughter the Communists to avenge the Mosul massacre of 1959. But after this had been done (with the Central Intelligence Agency supplying names and addresses of party cadres), it was feared that some Communists had escaped to the northern mountains where the Kurdish leader, Mullah Mustafa Barzani, was rallying his forces. So, in a show of militant

'Arabism', the young Ba'th leaders went to war against the Kurds in June 1963.

The Iraqi army quickly won control of towns and roads but, after burning several villages and killing a good many peasants, it failed to pacify the wild countryside. Syria sent a brigade to join in the burning and killing, but in the unfamiliar terrain it suffered many casualties. It was a discouraging intervention.

Worse was to follow. The Kurdish war sharpened differences in Iraq between the army and the party and in particular between 'Abd al-Salam 'Arif, the leading Arab nationalist officer, and the intemperate Ba'thist leader 'Ali Salih al-Sa'di. Sa'di's party militia, the National Guard, had become a lawless rabble which terrorized the population and was detested by the officer corps. Even a general was not safe from being stopped on the street by a gun-toting irregular. On 11 November 1963 exasperated Iraqi officers, acting in collusion with Foreign Minister Talib Shabib and other 'moderate' Ba'thists, seized Sa'di and bundled him without possessions or a passport on to a plane for Madrid. Immediately Sa'di's National Guard as well as the party rank and file rioted in support of their leader, splitting the party and threatening its very existence.

An anxious 'Aflaq came hurrying to Baghdad with five members of the National Command to rescue what he could. Seeking to placate Sa'di's followers without offending the officers, he dissolved the Regional Command, deported Talib Shabib and his friends to Beirut, and declared that, until fresh party elections could be held, he and the National Command would direct Iraq's affairs.

That a Christian philosopher from Damascus should presume to rule Iraq provoked angry hilarity in officers' messes where the idea was considered offensive to Iraqi patriotism, to Muslim sentiment, to the pride of the Iraqi army, and even to common sense. Brushing 'Aflaq aside, an army junta led by 'Arif took power on 18 November. More damaging still from the Ba'th's point of view, 'Arif at once made it up with Nasser and declared himself faithful to the 17 April unity project. The Ba'th was out. Ahmad Sa'id, the hell-raiser of Cairo's 'Voice of the Arabs' radio station, called for the slaughter of 'Aflaq and his colleagues before they left Baghdad; and such was the temper of the city that they had to make an undignified run for it. Sheer survival rather than Arab conquest was now the Ba'th's priority, and the fantasy of cornering Nasser gave way to the unpleasant truth that the Syrian Ba'th itself was cornered.

The disaster in Iraq came as a chastening shock to the Military Committee, forcing it to have second thoughts about the alliance with the Marxists with whom Asad and 'Umran sat on the Regional Command. Homegrown Syrian radicals like Shufi could not be allowed to wreak the havoc which Sa'di had wrought in Iraq. Accusations flew back and forth about who was responsible for the Iraqi débâcle, and the tendency was to blame the far left. The sudden slump in the party's fortunes caused 'Aflaq and the officers to forget their quarrels and brought them into a tactical alliance against the Marxists. In February 1964 Sa'di and his Syrian disciple Shufi were expelled from the party together with their supporters at emergency Regional and National congresses. Asad's natural pragmatism was reinforced. His commitment to the left was not undermined, but the lesson he learned from the crisis was that the ready-made solutions of the Marxists were not for him – nor for the country either. Rejected in Damascus, Syria's Marxist philosopher, Yasin al-Hafiz, left to seek the socialist dawn in the freer air of Beirut. In Iraq a new provisional leadership was appointed to rebuild the party in clandestinity under a young man who had not been involved in the fiasco, Saddam Husayn al-Takriti.

The Hama riots of 1964

Dropping the Marxists did not win the Ba'th points in Syria. On the contrary, its enemies rose against it, seeing in the party's infighting hope that it could be brought down in Damascus as it had been in Baghdad. The challenge was even tougher than that posed by the Nasserists the previous July.

The troubles began in the early spring of 1964 with a campaign of agitation in Syrian cities in which prayer-leaders, preaching inflammatory sermons against the secular, socialist Ba'th, whipped up street riots and closed the souks. Egyptian and Iraqi embassies in neighbouring countries disbursed funds to fan the flames, but there was in any event plenty of combustible material around: the Syrian economy was stagnant; merchants, dreading the inroads of Ba'thist radicalism, sat on their money; city and country notables resented the rise of the minority upstarts and their humble Sunni allies; while the common people were greatly frustrated at being kept in ignorance of what the new rulers were up to behind closed doors.

Wholly absorbed in its internal struggles, the Ba'th had not given Syria good government, or indeed much government at all, with the result that instead of celebrating the first anniversary of its revolution in self-congratulatory triumph, it had to put down a popular uprising. Hardly a city escaped serious disorders, but the centre of the insurrection, was Hama, stronghold of landed conservatism and of the Muslim Brothers. Hostility between the Ba'th and the Brotherhood was not new: they had been clashing everywhere in Syria since the 1940s. In Hama the once great landowners of the central Syrian plain, who had paid the price of Hawrani's peasant revolt, bore the Ba'th a special grudge and saw in the Brothers' shock troops a means of hitting back at their tormentors.

In April 1964, as rioting flared into something like a religious war, firearms were used for the first time. Funded by the old families and the merchants and egged on by Shaykh Mahmud al-Hamid from the pulpit of the Sultan mosque, the Muslim rebels threw up roadblocks, stockpiled food and weapons, ransacked wine shops to spill the offending liquor into the gutters, and beat up any party man they could find. A young militiaman of the Ba'th's National Guard, an Isma'ili called Munzir al-Shimali, was caught, killed, and mutilated, an atrocity which set off a full-scale assault on every vestige of the party in Hama. The National Guard commander, Hamad 'Ubayd, called up army support and used tank-fire against the densely populated warrens of the city. After two days of street fighting, the insurgents took cover in the Sultan mosque which they had made their principal weapons store, whereupon the Prime Minister, General Amin al-Hafiz, gave the order to flush them out. The mosque was shelled and the minaret from which the rebels had been firing collapsed, killing many of them. In all some seventy Muslim Brothers died. Many others were wounded or captured, but many more disappeared underground.

Among the prisoners was a tall, red-bearded fanatic called Marwan Hadid who had some years earlier attracted attention as an extremist. Like Asad himself, he had spent some time in Egypt during the union years studying agricultural engineering, and had fought the Ba'th for control of the Syrian students' society at Cairo University where he was remembered as a diehard religious fundamentalist.[10] On his return to Syria in 1962, Hadid, whose heart was in the fusion of religion and politics, took up *shari'a* law at Damascus University, moving from there into clandestine work in the Muslim cause in his native Hama. To a man like him – and there were many in the same mould – government by the secular Ba'th was an offence against God and nature; Ba'thists were infidels spurning the holy law who had to be exterminated for the health of society. Yet in spite of these incendiary opinions Hadid got off lightly in the aftermath of the 1964 battles. Held for a few months, he was released in the hope that he had learned his lesson, but he returned at once to recruiting and preparing for the next round.

For Syria's new rulers, the bloody events in Hama were a formative experience not to be forgotten. The city had long been a symbol of oppression for the rural poor – the background of so many of them – and a stronghold of Sunni conservatism, but now they came to loathe it as a centre of malevolent reaction, an irredeemable enemy of everything they stood for.

On the party's Regional Command Asad joined in the decisions to put down the troubles and prove to Hama who was in charge. (It foreshadowed his crushing of the city eighteen years later, the greatest act of internal violence of his presidency.) Two of his close friends were directly affected: 'Abd al-Halim Khaddam, the former schoolboy activist from Banyas, and Mustafa Tlas, the one-time Ba'thist scout leader from Rastan. At the time of the 1964 Hama insurrection, Khaddam, who had qualified as a lawyer, was the hard-pressed governor of the city, while Tlas was appointed head of the field tribunal set up to deal with the insurgents. A tank corps officer, he had been in Egypt with Asad and the others and was brought into the Military Committee after the 1963 coup.

The shelling of the Sultan mosque outraged Muslim opinion, igniting a fever of strikes and demonstrations across the country and bringing professional men out together with shopkeepers, craftsmen and manual workers in a call for civil liberties, for the freeing of political prisoners, for an end to the state of emergency which the Ba'th had imposed after its coup and still not lifted. Ba'thists had expected hostility from men of property and from the old political and religious elites, but they were taken aback by the wide range of opposition which included not just their predictable middle-class enemies but Sunni working people of the cities as well. Syria's rulers were able to measure the extent of their unpopularity. To cool popular tempers, General Amin al-Hafiz, associated in the public mind with the repression, gave up the premiership to Bitar, himself a respectable conciliatory figure from the Damascene Sunni middle class, who broadcast a pledge to protect personal and public freedoms. A provisional constitution was hastily promulgated. Evidently the regime felt the need to win time.

It was clear to 'Aflaq that civilian Ba'thists could exercise very little influence over the course of events. Dispirited at what he saw as the sorry record of the Ba'thist revolution, he left Syria in June 1964 to spend several months with a brother in West Germany. His apprehensions were well-founded: by the end of September Amin al-Hafiz had resumed the premiership.

Fall of 'Umran

In its first eighteen months of rule, the Military Committee had weathered three crises: the gory clash with the Nasserists, the rout of the Iraqi comrades, and the Hama insurrection. These violent events took their toll in quarrels between the officers as they struggled to stay afloat. Muhammad 'Umran, the senior member of the Cairo conspiracy, had little taste for the harsh struggle for survival. He had wanted a reconciliation with the Nasserists and had opposed the use of tanks at Hama. He resented General Hafiz's prominence which he felt eroded his own leadership. Hailing from the Hama side of the 'Alawi mountains, 'Umran knew the city well, and argued that the local people could be won over rather than bludgeoned. The problem of how to govern now became paramount in the Committee. Could a vast overturning of Syria's power structures, such as the country boys wanted, be accomplished by conciliation? Would men who held capital and influence give up without a fight? Believing there was no escape from coercion, Salah Jadid approved General Hafiz's strong-arm methods. He saw the Hama events as a reason to press ahead with the destruction of class enemies before the Committee was itself cut down. 'Umran was perhaps less committed to a radical programme and flinched from bloodletting. Jadid's relations with him suffered and the cohesion of the conspirators, who since 1960 had kept each other's secrets, was shaken.

Asad listened to the disputes between the two older men and bided his time. When the Military Committee was first set up, its members had had an equal voice, but rank counted nonetheless and Asad was junior to both Jadid and 'Umran. He was not yet a candidate for the top job. In the autumn of 1964 he went from one to the other in an attempt to bridge the gap between them: the Committee was the centrepiece of his life and his instinct was to preserve it. But in the end he was forced to take sides. He chose to ally himself with Salah Jadid against 'Umran – a choice which, as it turned out, proved to be prescient. Just why he did so cannot be exactly determined. Perhaps it was because he shared Jadid's view that Hafiz, their bluff front man who had been forced by the pressure of events to take unpopular measures, could still play a useful role in screening the Committee from public view. Perhaps he recognized Jadid as the tougher character. Perhaps it was their common origin which influenced him, because like Jadid he was a coastal 'Alawi. Moreover, Asad at this time was still a natural radical, still primarily motivated by the age-old grievances of his country background. Jadid's programme of widespread national-izations may therefore have been more to his liking than 'Umran's instinct to conciliate the Sunni business community (although in later years it was the 'Umran model which Asad was to follow). Whatever the weight of these various reasons, Asad threw in his lot with Jadid, and in December 1964, in a further step up the ladder of advancement, was appointed to command the Syrian air force with the rank of major-general.

The fall of 'Umran was engineered with ruthless speed. At odds with his comrades on the Military Committee, he turned for support to the party's National Command – a move which brought 'Aflaq hurrying back from Germany that November, no doubt in the hope of turning the tables on his officer detractors. Breaking his oath of secrecy, 'Umran revealed to 'Aflaq and his group the inner workings of the Committee, the plans laid long ago in Cairo, the caucus tactics, the stealthy capture of the party's rank and file. 'Aflaq must have suspected much of this, but to the others, and especially to non-Syrian members of the National Command, 'Umran's candid outpourings came as a great shock. Insofar as his own career was concerned, it was a false move: he was immediately punished by his former colleagues who, exacting a rough justice of their own, stripped him of his party and government jobs and despatched him without more ado to 'serve the revolution' as ambassador to Spain, a country by now familiar to other Syrians and Iraqis who had fallen from favour. 'Umran's humiliation was also that of 'Aflaq, a patent demonstration of his lack of authority. Invoking his title of secretary-general of the party, he called on his National Command to dissolve the Regional Command now dominated by the officers, but the party rose against him in the country and he was forced to withdraw his request. It was at about this time that an old-guard Ba'thist tauntingly asked 'Aflaq how big a role his party still played in government. 'About one-thousandth of one per cent', the Ba'th founder replied.[11]

'Umran's fall from grace brought an extra bonus to the Asad family. Some months earlier, when facing domestic insurrection, the Military Committee had formed a small strike force to protect its wing of the party and manned entirely by its own loyalists. It was commanded by 'Umran. But when he was exiled, it was entrusted to Asad's younger brother, Rif'at. This was the embryo from which grew the praetorian guards of Asad's presidency – Rif'at's famous, some would say infamous, Defence Companies.

With 'Umran exiled and 'Aflaq silenced, the radical officers moved to destroy the economic power of the city bourgeoisie. They were determined, in Asad's words, 'to end the exploitation by a handful of families',[12] which they saw as the necessary precondition for the building of a new, more equitable order. In the first week of January 1965 about a hundred companies, many of them mere workshops, employing in all some 12,000 workers were nationalized. Critics scoffed that the names of the companies had been taken from the telephone book. State ownership was then extended to electricity generation, oil distribution, cotton ginning and to about 70 per cent of foreign trade. Threatened with ruin, the Damascus merchants again gathered their forces, pulled down the metal shutters of their shops and, again with the help of Muslim preachers, called out the populace in their traditional gesture of defiance against the government. But this time they faced the party's National Guard and a newly formed Workers' Militia: shopfronts were broken down by gangs of Ba'thists and scores of businesses summarily confiscated, while, to neutralize the mosques, the state assumed powers to appoint and dismiss prayer-leaders and took over the administration of religious property (*awqaf*), the main source of funds of the Muslim establishment.

The contest with 'Aflaq

The civilian party leadership had an even harder time of it once 'Umran was banished. With enemies threatening at home and abroad, Asad and Jadid had no patience with the civilians' anti-army bias and were in a hurry to elbow aside what they considered a muddled and discredited party leadership. The overriding question was: whose party was it to be?

Although 'Aflaq's National Command wrestled to keep the Military Committee in check, invoking party rules and regulations against the officers, it was plain that the initiative lay with the anti-'Aflaq forces. In this contest the officers found valuable allies in a civilian faction called the 'Regionalists', grassroots Ba'thist cadres from outlying districts like Dayr al-Zur on the Euphrates, Hawran in the south, and Latakia on the coast, who had secretly kept their local party branches alive during the union and whose allegiance 'Aflaq had failed to win back once the party was re-formed. Their dislike of 'Aflaq was so great that they would not join in party activities even after the coup of 8 March 1963. Asad called them the 'true cells of the party', and it was with them that the Military Committee had tried to make contact when it was building its networks. Asad set out to woo them and they proved valuable allies of the Military Committee in the coming duel with the old guard.[13]

What lay at the heart of the officers' quarrel with 'Aflaq? Many years later, long after he had won the battle, Asad displayed a visceral distaste for the party founder, a strength of feeling pointing to the unbridgeable distance between 'Aflaq and the officers. They condemned him for being a remote autocrat, for having ditched the party, for his 'rightist' views, but there was also a gulf of generation, education and style separating them. City born and bred, steeped in the graces and formalities of old Damascus, 'Aflaq and Bitar were already well into their fifties, whereas the officers, some twenty years younger, were sons of peasants with the earth scarcely out from under their fingernails. The older men had studied at the Sorbonne where they had read European literature and philosophy and grown to be at ease with abstract ideas, whereas, apart from military training, the soldiers had hardly gone beyond the basic curriculum of a provincial secondary school. Men so different could not hold each other in esteem.

There were other important differences to do with the nature of the party and the government. 'Aflaq's Ba'th was a debating society, a seedbed of ideas at a time of Arab intellectual poverty: this was its great appeal to students, schoolteachers and aspiring *petits fonctionnaires* in the early years, and which for decades afterwards evoked nostalgia among all those whose lives it had touched. 'Aflaq preached a message of Arab pride which fired young people with the vision that their backward and colonized countries could take their place in the modern world. His conception of the party was of a mobilizing agent closer to the people than to any regime, a pressure group outside government whose role was to keep the rulers on the straight and narrow. The officers, in contrast, saw the Ba'th as an instrument of government, as a ruling party, as the central institution of their state.

'Aflaq was a thinker not a party manager, and although the Ba'th set up branches outside its Syrian birthplace – in Jordan in 1948, Lebanon in 1949, Iraq in 1950, Libya in 1954, Kuwait in 1955, Yemen and Aden in 1955–6 – he had failed to weld them into a coherent pan-Arab movement. Instead of convening annual congresses, he convened none between 1947 when the party was founded and 1954. Then four years later, in 1958, he disbanded the Syrian party, the heart of the whole movement, without putting the matter to a congress. His life had been spent in opposition, he was not used to power and perhaps was not temperamentally suited to cross the line into government. The attitude of the officers was very different. They believed they had rescued the Ba'th from 'Aflaq's mistakes and, by fighting off all challengers at the risk of their lives, now deserved to rule.

The contest between them was fought out within the framework of the party. In challenging 'Aflaq the officers turned his pyramid on its head, removing ultimate authority from the hands of his National Command and putting it into those of the Regional Command – that is to say, their own. They convened a Regional Congress in March 1965 to endorse the principle that the government was entirely subject to the party and that the secretary of the Regional Command would *ex officio* be head of state. The Regional Command would also have the power to appoint the prime minister, the cabinet, the chief of staff and the top military commanders. Very little in this schema was left to 'Aflaq and his National Command.

'Aflaq was greatly perturbed by the way the current was moving. He itched for a showdown with the men who he considered were stealing his party from him, and in May 1965 called a National Congress to denounce his military challengers. But at this critical moment several of the non-Syrian members of the National Command – the Lebanese Jibran Majdalani, the Saudi 'Ali Ghannam – advised caution, fearing that if the officers were pushed too hard they might, as in Iraq, sweep the civilians aside altogether. For these party veterans Ba'thist Syria was a precious haven in a generally hostile Arab world. So 'Aflaq kept quiet. To his distress, he was forced to step down from the post of secretary-general he had occupied for eighteen years and was replaced by the 46-year-old Dr Munif al-Razzaz, a doctor and writer of Jordanian nationality but Syrian origin. However, Razzaz, who had joined the Ba'th in 1950 and had won his party spurs in King Husayn's prisons, was not rooted strongly enough in Syrian affairs to bridge the gap between the old Ba'th and the new. In vain that summer he summoned joint meetings of the National and Regional Commands but the deadlock continued. It was no help to the civilians that Asad was elected to the National Command as the officers' eyes and ears: Atrash remembered him as 'aggressive, opinionated and not willing to come to terms'.[14]

At this point in the struggle between 'Aflaq and the officers, the cards were unexpectedly reshuffled by no less a person than General Amin al-Hafiz. To the outside world he was Syria's strong man – prime minister, commander-in-chief, secretary of the party's Regional Command, chairman of the Presidential Council – but to the Military Committee he was a man of straw without political base or party background. Behind the scenes they kept him on a short rein. 'He could not transfer a single soldier without our permission', Asad later recounted.[15]

This treatment no longer accorded with the view Hafiz had of himself. Knowing the civilian old guard was sorely in need of a military ally, and not at ease in the radical company of the Military Committee, he changed sides, abandoning the Committee and joining the veterans – a move which brought him into immediate confrontation with the regime's real strong man, Salah Jadid, the supreme arbiter of Syrian affairs from the late summer of 1965, powers which he disguised behind the unprepossessing title of assistant secretary-general of the Regional Command. Jadid had built up a considerable personal power base. He controlled the government machine through his friend, the socialist Dr Yusuf Zu'ayyin, whom he appointed Prime Minister that August at the age of thirty-four. He controlled army transfers and promotions through the Defence Minister, Hamad 'Ubayd. And through Asad and his party machine in the armed forces he was assured of the loyalty of the troops.

In November 1965 about eighty of 'Aflaq's party faithful, not an officer among them, met to review their prospects over an *al fresco* lunch in the village of Surghaya in the hills north-west of Damascus. Half a dozen sheep were slaughtered for the meal which was to be almost the last time these men were to feel truly at home in their own country. Emboldened by this gathering, the National Command passed a resolution in December forbidding the Regional Command to transfer or dismiss officers without its authority. Jadid rebelled at once against this direct challenge, instructing Colonel Mustafa Tlas to arrest the commander of the Homs garrison and his deputy, both known to favour the National Command.

The veterans then played their hand with the bravado of men who knew they were doomed. Dr Razzaz, the new secretary-general, called the National Command into emergency session and decreed the dissolution of the rebellious Regional Command. In its place, and on paper at least, he installed a whole new leadership for Syria: Bitar was brought back to the premiership; General Hafiz chaired a new hand-picked Presidential Council; Muhammad 'Umran, the disgraced member of the Military Committee, was flown in from Madrid and appointed Minister of Defence and commander-in-chief; and Atrash was made chairman of an expanded National Revolutionary Council from which members of the Military Committee were dropped. Needless to say, Jadid and his friends paid not a whit of attention to these appointments. The two sides were now at war and only force could decide the outcome.

Although Asad had neither liking nor sympathy for the old guard, he was not happy with the drift towards a showdown. True to his careful instincts, he preferred to try and patch things up or, if that were not possible, for the party to 'purge itself' through its own machinery. As the dénouement of the officers' conflict with the National

Command approached, Asad hung back, from caution or distaste. For some such reason he took leave that summer from his duties as air force commander and went to London for three months accompanied by another senior air force officer, Naji Jamil, the head of the Military Police, Husayn Mulhim, and a doctor, Yusuf Sayigh. It was his first and at the time of writing last visit to Britain. The four men put up in a flat in Kensington and, so far as is known, Asad's only contact with British officialdom was a call at the Foreign Office to see George Thomson, then Minister of State for Foreign Affairs. Britain had had a brief contact with the Syrian air force, supplying planes and training between 1953 and 1955, but the relationship was interrupted when Syria allied itself to Nasser's Egypt and was not renewed. The ostensible motive for Asad's journey was to obtain treatment for a back and neck complaint, the result of a crash landing as a trainee pilot. But his aches and pains may have been something of a diplomatic illness.

The 1966 coup

Warfare between 'Aflaq and the officers began on 21 February 1966 when General 'Umran, testing his new powers as Defence Minister, ordered the transfer from their commands of three of Jadid's key supporters. They were Major-General Ahmad Suwaydani, former head of Military Intelligence and now of Officers' Administration; Colonel 'Izzad Jadid of the tanks corps; and Major Salim Hatum whose commando unit stood guard over the radio and television station, the presidential palace, and other important buildings. The Military Committee struck back the following day – but first it staged a diversion to throw its opponents off-balance.

As a ruse, the commander of the front facing Israel, the 'Alawi officer 'Abd al-Ghani Ibrahim, reported to headquarters in Damascus that a quarrel had broken out among frontline officers and that guns had been drawn. The news brought 'Umran, Hafiz and the Chief of Staff hurrying to the Golan for lengthy discussions with officers manning the front. They returned exhausted to Damascus at about 3 a.m. on 23 February. Two hours later they were rudely roused by the sound of gunfire.

General Hafiz's private residence was under armed attack by a commando force led by Salim Hatum backed by Rif'at al-Asad's party unit. In support of the assault was a squadron of tanks under 'Izzat Jadid. From inside the villa, the general and his bodyguard put up a spirited defence. Shooting in central Damascus continued until noon as wave after wave of commandos hurled themselves into the fray. At last, with his ammunition spent and his bodyguard slaughtered, his villa shattered by tank fire and his children wounded (a daughter afterwards lost an eye), Hafiz surrendered. (The commander of his bodyguard, Lieutenant Mahmud Musa, was taken to hospital where 'Izzat Jadid pursued him to finish him off. But Musa had been a commando and Hatum intervened to save him, eventually smuggling him out to Beirut.) The morning's fighting had taken about fifty lives.

Braving the curfew people picked their way through the rubble to stare at the gutted residence, its furniture leaning from sagging floors awash with water from burst pipes. Smaller clashes took place in other cities. In Hama officers loyal to the National Command held out until subdued by Mustafa Tlas at the head of a force sent up from Homs. In Aleppo 'Aflaq loyalists briefly held the radio station, while token resistance was also reported from Latakia and Dayr al-Zur.

Asad had returned from London in time for the battle, but his air force did not intervene. Perhaps there was no need, or perhaps he opposed its use in such a sensitive intra-party conflict. As the fighting raged he spent the morning on the telephone, cajoling and threatening officers in units around the country to bring them over to the Committee's side.

The battle was followed by an instant and thorough purge of army, party and government, involving some four hundred officers and officials. General Hafiz, 'Umran, and commanders loyal to them were carted off to Mezze prison, the grim old hill-top fortress in Damascus where star political prisoners are confined. Some thirty veteran Ba'thists, including Bitar, Atrash, Shibli al-'Aysami as well as Lebanese, Saudi and Jordanian members of the National Command, were rounded up and interned in a guest-house on the Baghdad Road. Of the top leaders only Dr Munif al-Razzaz put up some token resistance, issuing statements attacking the putsch from his various hiding-places. He was too sick and lame to attempt the hazardous journey over the mountains into Lebanon made by others in those days.

After the battle and the round up of his supporters, Michel 'Aflaq sat at home waiting to be arrested, but the new regime resisted the temptation. In due course he travelled to Lebanon, and from there to Brazil. Ultimately he made his home in Iraq where Ba'thists loyal to him gave him a respectful haven after their seizure of power in 1968. But he never saw his native land again. A quarter of a century of teaching and struggle, the life's work of the Arab world's most celebrated political theorist, ended in exile and disgrace.

One of the first acts of the new regime was to appoint Asad Minister of Defence. In his courteous way he called on Mansur al-Atrash, Jubran Majdalani and other former party comrades on the National Command in their place of detention, to inquire after their health and talk over recent events. Atrash remembered Asad's elation. He must surely have been relieved that the paralysing party feud had at last been resolved, but on his own testimony he did not approve the methods used. His tendency thereafter was to blame the goriness of the coup on the impetuous commando leader Salim Hatum, which in itself was a pointer to his feelings. A few months later he told a correspondent of *Le Monde* that the army's intervention had been regrettable: the Ba'th, he claimed, was essentially a democratic party, but it had been necessary to end the dictatorship of the National Command.[16] Later still, in 1969, he told a party congress that he had hesitated to take part in the February 1966 events and had initially refused the Defence Ministry.[17] But whatever his qualms, Asad was now very close to the top.

8

Blindly to the Brink

The bloody intra-party shoot out of 23 February 1966 gave the thirty-five year old Asad his first seat in a Syrian cabinet. He got the defence portfolio, which thrust him at once into the forefront of the Syrian-Israeli confrontation, from then on the major preoccupation of his life.

The government of which he became a member was to prove the most extreme Syria had ever known, rash abroad, radical at home, engulfing the country in war, and attempting to refashion society from top to bottom. It earned a reputation for repressing the population and brutally disposing of its challengers. How powerful a figure was Asad in this government and what role did he play in these developments? Certainly he wholeheartedly supported the broad aim to overturn Syria's social, political and economic structures and bring to the fore men and communities hitherto on the margin, and it can be said with even greater conviction that, having won power, he was determined to hold on to it. But the doctrinaire temper of the government was at variance with his own cautious instincts which recoiled from his colleagues' headlong rush for change. In spite of his standing as a minister, this was not a happy period for Asad and his was not a dominant voice in the new regime.

The regime had emerged from three years of power struggles following the 1963 coup, but now that Nasserist rivals had been defeated, the right-wing and religious opposition put down in Hama, and the Ba'thist older generation seen off, the Military Committee at last had the elbow room to rule. This brought about a change in the instruments of power. Up to that moment the Military Committee itself had been the central institution through which the officers imposed their will. Now the Committee, already weakened by 'Umran's defection, withered further, in fact lost much of its *raison d'être*, as the officers secured a monopoly over the state apparatus. There was no longer any need for a secret caucus.

A consequence of the move to more conventional government was the promotion of Salah Jadid as Syria's ruler. He did not proclaim himself head of state and, perhaps because of an 'Alawi reluctance to claim a post traditionally reserved for Sunnis, he preferred to govern with the modest title of assistant secretary of the Ba'th's Regional Command. But he was number one nevertheless, he packed the Command and the government with his followers and friends, he put his stamp on events, while a gap opened up between him and Asad.

In terms of the future, this was not altogether to Asad's disadvantage, for such was Jadid's absorption with running the country that he gave Asad a good deal of scope to run the armed services. A conspirator of Jadid's experience understood very well the importance of control of the army. His first care after the 1963 coup had been to take over the Bureau of Officers' Affairs in order to oversee all postings, moving up from there to become Chief of Staff. But in 1966 he had to concentrate on civilian government and relied on Asad to keep the army loyal. Asad had backed him against 'Umran, was his stalwart comrade of many years, and seemed to present no threat.

In 1966 Jadid was a goodlooking man of forty, polite, soft-spoken and usually dressed in civilian clothes. He was by nature discreet. He seemed not to like human contact, and rarely appeared in public or made speeches. He was known to be a man of high personal morality who was not interested in wealth or even comfort, and who lived in a simple apartment whose furniture was said to be worth less than £100 sterling. Such austerity and seclusion somewhat alarmed his fellow citizens who found him an enigma. The new leader was not to be seen playing backgammon or sipping Turkish coffee in the leafy open-air cafés of Damascus, like some of his colleagues. He came early to the office, a modest four-storey building on the edge of a residential suburb, and left late. It was learned that he had for a long time been supporting the destitute families of two of his brothers both of whom had been heavily involved with the pan-Syrian SSNP outlawed by the Ba'th in 1955 after the Malki murder. One of his brothers, Ghassan, had been killed by Syrian Intelligence in 1957 and another, Fuad, had spent seven years in jail, gaining his freedom only in 1963. Not unnaturally the public suspected Jadid of secret SSNP sympathies, and because he was an 'Alawi it was whispered that he unduly favoured his own community.

Jadid was further to the left than Asad and the team he picked reflected his proclivities. Three young doctors of fiery socialist views were catapulted into the three main offices of state. Dr Nur al-Din al-Atasi, a rebellious scion of the Atasi landowning family which once dominated the Homs countryside, became Head of State. To reassure Syrian public opinion and especially the Sunni majority, it was useful to have an Atasi out front. Dr Yusuf Zu'ayyin, the socialist son of a rich merchant from the Euphrates town of Albukamal, continued as Prime Minister. And Dr Ibrahim Makhus, became Foreign Minister. He was something of a fanatical idealist, the son of an 'Alawi religious family rich enough to afford to send him to medical school at a time when poorer lads like Asad had no choice but the army. All three were rebels from relatively privileged backgrounds. 'Syria is ruled by three doctors. It must be sick', quipped the French-language Beirut daily, *L'Orient*.

Atasi, Zu'ayyin and Makhus were Jadid's appointees. They had held various ministerial posts since 1963 but nothing to prepare them for their present prominence. The formative event of their lives was the Algerian war against France (1954–62) when they served for a spell as volunteer medics with Houari Boumédienne's forces. Undoubtedly their Algerian experience encouraged them in the belief that Israel like France could be made to yield, a powerful strand in their radicalism. Their rawness in office showed in a lack of moderation. Zu'ayyin was a clever and determined man but he had a violent nature, often shouting at his officials and banging his desk (on one occasion breaking its glass top and overturning an inkwell), while Makhus's extreme nervousness sometimes rendered his speech almost unintelligible. The three doctors' overheated views affected their style of dress. On a visit to Paris Zu'ayyin, sporting a Mao-style jacket, was told that General de Gaulle could not receive him in such attire. He kicked against the protocol – but eventually donned a tie and was admitted to the Elysée palace.

On the whole they were a comradely bunch, men in their mid-thirties, self-consciously belonging to a new Ba'th generation and united in a vision of the changes they hoped to bring about. They also shared the special Syrian characteristics of defiance and combativeness, compounded by prickliness and suspicion. Many Arabs have a sense of unfair treatment by more powerful nations, but Syrians have one skin less than most and feel the wrongs done them more acutely. The new rulers bore the burden of a whole catalogue of frustrations: the European carve-up of their country, Zionist colonization of Arab land, disillusion with Nasser, the failed union, the failed party, a fear of foreign plots. These were Asad's disconcerting colleagues in the first cabinet of which he was a member.

Jadid did not altogether neglect the security side of things, and here too his left-wing bias was evident. As his Chief of Staff he brought in Ahmad al-Suwaydani, and promoted him to the rank of major-general. A Sunni country boy from the southern border town of Dar'a, Suwaydani had served as military attaché in Peking where he had absorbed a powerful dose of Maoist doctrine. Asad was not keen on his new Chief of Staff who, as Jadid's man, was a check on his own powers. Behind the scenes there were also disagreements about a delicate subject then beginning to loom large – how much aid, and above all how much freedom, Syria should give the Palestinian groups harassing Israel. Asad believed in helping the guerrillas, but the Maoist Suwaydani wanted to give them a freer rein than his Defence Minister judged wise.

Another radical officer appointed by Jadid was Colonel Muhammad Rabah al-Tawil, a Sunni from Latakia, who was made Minister of Labour as well as head of the newly formed Popular Resistance Forces. But, for the public in town and country, the most radical appointment was that of the impetuous Isma'ili officer Colonel 'Abd al-Karim al-Jundi. A founder member of the Military Committee and one of Jadid's main supporters, he became Minister of Agrarian Reform before taking control of all the internal security services, a post in which he acquired a fearsome reputation for cruelty.

Such were the main personalities of the new-look Ba'th government which took over Syrian affairs just fifteen months before the Six Day War, but its competence to rule, still less to wage war, was hardly striking. The team over which Jadid presided was made up of middle-ranking officers bumped up to generals overnight and of inexperienced medical practitioners whom the excitements of the times had brought into politics, underpinned by droves of provincial schoolteachers of Ba'thist inclination drafted into government offices as the cadres of the new system. All these men were unknown to the public. With the exception of Atasi, their names had no resonance, their families were obscure, they commanded no automatic respect, in a state of affairs departing fundamentally from Syrian tradition in which networks of patronage stemming from men in public life provided the foundation of government. Asad, without wealth or connections, was as much a puzzling newcomer as the others. Nevertheless, for all their failings and inexperience, these men completed the rout of the old order by means of nationalizations and land reform, and replaced it with a new political elite stemming from the alliance of educated country boys and lower middle-class urbanites which underpinned their revolution.

The Jadid regime set about stamping society with its puritan imprint. Salaries of the head of state, of ministers, senior officers and top bureaucrats were slashed, and their black Mercedes limousines replaced with humble Volkswagens and Peugeot 404s. Corruption was spurned with contempt, while 'class struggle' became both petty and vindictive. Anyone, however blameless, who was remotely connected with the old influential families, was purged from government service, to the extent that people became afraid to reveal their surnames for fear of reprisals. In the Foreign Ministry only a handful of senior career diplomats managed to retain their jobs, mainly on account of their ability and their lack of political affiliation.[1] As ownership of more than one house was a liability because of the risk of confiscation, there was a rush to sell and prices collapsed. Those who could afford it fled the country. Government control was extended to private schools, many of them run by religious foundations, and those which refused to accept state management were closed down. Meanwhile the rural poor, the minorities, the underprivileged of all sorts, sensing a change in their favour, began to flood into the cities and to alter the look and tone of urban life. It seemed that this at last was the government of the landless and deprived, the triumph of the windswept plains over the bright lights of the towns. In mobilizing society for what seemed like a Leninist party state, the population was classified as friend or foe, within each of which were a number of sub-categories: 'workers', 'soldiers', 'peasants', 'students', 'women' were friends, while 'feudalists' and 'reactionaries' were unmitigated foes, although a certain tolerance was allowed to 'harmless reactionaries'. It was as if simply being a Syrian conferred no rights. In the pursuit of its programmes the regime seemed excessively doctrinaire, as if attempting nothing less than to transform the Syrian character.

There was, of course, a positive side. Jadid and his team were by and large honest men and their achievements were not discreditable. An attempt was made at systematic economic planning. Work was begun on major infrastructural and industrial projects, such as road and rail networks, the great dam on the Euphrates which had been a Syrian ambition since 1945, and the opening up of newly discovered oil fields in the northeast. Most of these projects were set in train with Soviet help, for within eight weeks of taking office Prime Minister Zu'ayyin had won the promise of Soviet co-operation.

Moscow had initially hesitated to give Jadid's team its support but had soon come round, causing some Western chancelleries to fear that Syria was becoming a pawn in Soviet designs, and was even in danger of falling to the Communists. Although Syria had been buying Soviet arms and sending officers to Soviet academies for training since the mid-1950s, a change in the relationship appeared to be taking place.

Khalid Bakdash, the veteran leader of the Syrian Communist Party, was allowed home after eight years of exile, while for the first time in Syrian history a Communist, Samih 'Atiyya, entered the government as Minister of Communications. Jadid and some of his colleagues toyed with the idea of 'scientific socialism' but for all their radicalism they had not lost the old Ba'thist suspicion of Communism, nor the resolve to rule alone. Bakdash came home on stringent terms, forbidden to hold meetings or make speeches, while, as Asad made plain in an interview with *Le Monde*, the Communist in the cabinet was there in an individual not a party capacity.[2] On the Soviet side of the account, the record suggests that the Russians obtained little leverage over Syria in return for their largesse. The leftism of the new team was homegrown and had little to do with Soviet inspiration. It was the result of local conditions, not global politics. Right up to the Six Day War a year later the keys to the conduct of Syria's rulers were revolution at home, continued competition with Nasser, frustration about Israel, the powerful foe across the frontier whom they regarded with angry but ineffectual defiance, and nervousness about domestic enemies.

The Hatum conspiracy

There were still plenty of enemies around. Akram al-Hawrani's group, remnants of 'Aflaq's movement, and various species of Nasserist continued to exist on the political scene and had not given up hope of a comeback. All had to be watched, but, by a paradox, the most serious threat developed from inside the regime itself – from Colonel Salim Hatum[3] whose commandos had forced General Hafiz's surrender on 23 February 1966. The regime owed him its existence, but Hatum felt the debt had not been paid. This was to be the cause of much trouble.

Hatum was an early Ba'thist and an energetic and ambitious officer. Brave, even rash, he was not politically astute. Born in 1928 into a poor family from the Druze village of Dhibin, he had elbowed his way into a role in the 8 March 1963 revolution and been rewarded by a seat on the expanded Military Committee. But that was as far as he got. He was not elected to the party's Regional Command, nor given high rank or a big job like some others. Instead his commando battalion was sent back to the humdrum task of guarding the radio station. His vanity wounded and his ambition unsatisfied, he came to believe that his colleagues wanted to unload on to him the full blame for the killings of 23 February. He was heard to voice the suspicion that they planned to do away with him, and then erect a statue to his name. The restless Hatum became a focus of dissidence.

Hatum's sense of grievance was shared by the Druze community as a whole, which was beginning to feel hard done by under the Ba'th. Some prominent Druzes had been axed: Hammud al-Shufi, leader of the party's Marxist wing, had been dropped in 1964; Hamad 'Ubayd, defence minister briefly in 1965, had to his indignation landed in jail after the 23 February coup. (He had backed Jadid against General Hafiz and expected to regain the defence ministry, but Jadid gave the job to Asad who was closer to him. 'Ubayd rebelled and was arrested.) These falls from grace alarmed the Druzes, prompting them to complain that 'Alawis were getting all the top jobs. Vexed by these accusations, the Regional Command charged that the Druzes were themselves kindling sectarian strife.

Hatum's frustrations became threatening when he linked up with 'Aflaq's ousted supporters, then looking for military allies. Dr Munif al-Razzaz, still underground in Damascus and encouraged from abroad by those members of his National Command who had managed to escape to Beirut, began to gather followers including some in the armed services. He formed a clandestine military committee of his own headed by another Druze officer, Maj.-General Fahd al-Sha'ir, a man of independent mind and 'Aflaqi sympathies who had served as Deputy Chief of Staff and commander of the front facing Israel. But Sha'ir had no talent for political intrigue and the conspiracy made heavy weather – until, that is, it received support from an unexpected quarter. Sha'ir was approached by officers close to Hatum with the suggestion that they unite against Asad and Jadid. Hatum and Sha'ir were both Druze officers of about the same age, but that is as far as the resemblance went. For a steady professional soldier like Sha'ir, a graduate of a Soviet military academy, the reckless and resentful Hatum was an alarming partner. But an offer of help from such a proven fighter whose commandos still guarded key installations seemed a godsend. Moreover, Hatum talked of rounding up and killing the key figures of the regime, a task for which Sha'ir himself had no stomach.

Plans for a coup were made, but each time that a date was fixed something went wrong. It was planned for 1 June 1966, on a Thursday night when many officers went home to their families, but last-minute fears of intervention by the armoured brigade at Homs caused it to be called off. Hatum then went to Cuba on a month-long mission at the head of a delegation, childishly warning that if the coup went ahead without him, he would reveal all to the authorities. He did not return until 4 August, when the coup was rescheduled for 3 September. But before it could be mounted, the authorities uncovered it. The manner in which this came about spoke volumes about the state of the Syrian officer corps in the months before the great contest with Israel.

One of Hatum's cronies was another Druze, Colonel Talal Abu 'Asali, then commander of the northern section of the Israeli front, a jovial figure who liked the company of junior officers. One evening that August a group of them invited him to a party. As the drink flowed tongues were loosened: some young men, secret supporters of Razzaz and Sha'ir, began attacking Jadid and Asad, while others sprang to their defence. Eventually they came to blows. Next morning the Jadidists sent word to headquarters of what had happened and the Chief of Staff, General Suwaydani, came down to investigate. Half a dozen revellers were put under arrest and brought before a court of inquiry – on which sat none other than Salim Hatum. The conspirator now acted out the part of inquisitor. In a pantomime of an interrogation, he made great play of striking the officers while at the same time whispering to them, 'I'll kill anyone who talks'. Not content with thus protecting Sha'ir's supporters, he ordered the posting away from the front of a prominent Jadidist who had been involved in the brawl.

Salah Jadid had kept an eye on the affair from Damascus and smelled a rat. He named a new committee of inquiry which this time included the ruthless 'Abd al-Karim al-Jundi, head of National Security. It went about its job more thoroughly. The young officers were badly beaten and one of them, Major Muhammad al-Nu'aymi, a simple young man from a bedouin background, broke down on 20 August and confessed. He gave away half a dozen officers in Sha'ir's conspiracy. These in turn betrayed others and in all some two hundred were detained, many of them Druzes. This was not a witch-hunt against the Druzes, but because Sha'ir had for security reasons recruited within his own tightly-knit community.

General Sha'ir went into hiding. Civilian Ba'thists fled for their lives. Bitar managed to escape to Beirut from the guest-house on the Baghdad Road where he had been held since the February shoot-out. Dr Munif al-Razzaz was also smuggled over the mountains to Lebanon, but his period in hiding had unsettled him, a state of mind reflected in the rancour of his attack on Syria's new leaders in his book, *Tajruba al-murra* (The Bitter Experience), which nevertheless became an important source on inner Ba'thist politics.[4]

A veteran civilian Ba'thist who went to ground in Syria was Ahmad Rustum, who had played host at the *al fresco* lunch for the party's old guard in the village of Surghaya in November 1965. (While on the run he managed to write a couple of school textbooks which had been commissioned by the Ministry of Education!) From his hiding place Rustum put through a telephone call to security chief 'Abd al-Karim al-Jundi to give him a piece of his mind. 'I've got 55 tanks', Jundi shouted back. 'If you've got 56, come out and fight!'[5]

But there was a sequel to the affair which put Jadid, Asad and the whole regime in danger. The purging of large numbers of Druzes from the army caused feelings to run high in the Druze capital of Suwayda, so much so that the local party branch sent a heated memorandum to Salah Jadid requesting the officers' reinstatement. To calm things down Salah Jadid announced that he would himself visit Suwayda on 8 September, accompanied by the Head of State, Dr Atasi, and Jamil Shayya, the only Druze member of the Regional Command.

This was Hatum's opportunity. As his wing of the conspiracy had not yet been blown, he and his friends decided to entrap Jadid in the Druze city and overthrow the regime. He alerted Talal Abu 'Asali to control the front with a squadron of tanks; he instructed another associate, the Military Intelligence chief Mustafa al-Hajj 'Ali, to take over his own commando battalion and ensure that the important Qatana camp was in friendly hands; and he then set off for Suwayda ahead of Jadid, calling in on a tank unit on the way to urge its commander, Ibrahim Nur al-Din, to cut the Suwayda road once Jadid and his party had passed through. Accordingly, on 8 September when Jadid had assembled a large number of local dignitaries at the party offices in Suwayda, Hatum suddenly burst in gun in hand and threatened to kill them all. In the uproar that followed, he was restrained by Druze religious elders who could not accept that guests enjoying their protection should be harmed. Jadid and the others were locked up in the house of a party member, while Hatum took over the garrison, arresting 'Alawi officers and stripping them of their rank.

But the triumphant Hatum had not taken Asad into account. While the drama was unfolding, word of the mutiny reached Asad at the Defence Ministry in Damascus. Acting swiftly to save Jadid and the regime itself, he sent air force jets to buzz the Suwayda citadel and ordered the crack 70th Armoured Brigade to rush south to the Jabal al-Duruz. Angry negotiations over the telephone followed between Asad in Damascus and Hatum in Suwayda, with the latter demanding a purge of Jadidists and the re-entry into the Regional Command of the Marxist Hammud al-Shufi, a Druze like Hatum himself. But as soon as Hatum heard the planes he knew his cause was doomed. Whatever the outcome of the contest, Suwayda would be exposed to aerial bombardment and his Druze community would suffer. He took the only way out — the road south to Jordan where King Husayn, no friend to the Damascus regime, gave him political asylum together with some two dozen of his comrades. From the safety of Amman over the next few days Hatum and Abu 'Asali fed the flames in a series of newspaper interviews denouncing 'Alawi ambitions which, they claimed, had brought Syria to the verge of civil war.

The puzzle remains how Asad in Damascus heard of Jadid's plight in time to rescue him. One story has it that Jadid's driver, on the pretext of fetching a packet of cigarettes from the car, drove off and raised the alarm. But it is doubtful that he could have got past the tank roadblock. Another suggestion is that Mustafa al-Hajj 'Ali betrayed the conspirators and alerted Asad by telephone. Certainly he failed to take over Hatum's commando battalion as instructed or to ensure that Qatana was on Hatum's side. At all events, if Asad had had any inhibitions about using the air force against 'Aflaq and Hafiz in February 1966, he had none about sending it against Hatum in September.

Asad's prompt action saved the day, earning Jadid's gratitude and trust. He and Jadid now embarked on yet another massive purge of the Syrian officer corps, and among those thrown out were no fewer than eighty-nine members of the Ba'th party's military organization which Asad had himself built up but of whose loyalty he now had doubts. Scores more were arrested, with the purge continuing into 1967. The Druze community, already disgruntled before these events, was beside itself. Party activity in the Druze mountains was brought to a standstill for several months and Sultan Pasha al-Atrash, the grand old man of the Druzes, was moved to write an open letter of protest to the General Staff in December 1966.[6] As Minister of Defence Asad sanctioned the dismissal of some 400 officers, the biggest shake-up the Syrian army had ever known. He and Jadid were determined to put an end to factionalism once and for all. But if to the 400 were added the Nasserist and secessionist officers cashiered or arrested in the various upsets since 1963, Syria would clearly be seen to have stumbled into war in 1967 without an officer corps or at any rate with a greatly depleted one.

Eventually General Sha'ir was himself captured and, according to some reports, badly treated. It is said that he was made to get down on all fours like an animal and was ridden by his tormentors through dirty water. In March 1967 a large number of defendants were brought before a military court presided over by Lieut.-Colonel Mustafa Tlas, Asad's friend who had already distinguished himself in a similar capacity after the Hama disturbances of 1964. Fahd al-Sha'ir was sentenced to death on charges of plotting to overthrow the regime, together with Salim Hatum and Talal Abu 'Asali – the last two *in absentia*. Sha'ir made a stir in court by his contemptuous retort to Tlas: 'You are a junior officer and your tribunal has no basis in law.' In the event, the death sentence on him was not carried out.

A couple of months later Syria was at war. Among its many horrors, the Six Day War provided a grim postscript to Salim Hatum's story. On the sixth day he announced that he was returning to Syria to fight and travelled up from Jordan with a group of supporters. Perhaps he imagined that war would have wiped the slate clean, or perhaps, as his detractors alleged, he was hoping to profit from the devastation of the conflict. But he was met by intelligence officers, driven to Damascus, and hauled before Tlas's military court which confirmed his death sentence. Jundi broke his ribs before having him shot while only half alive at 5 a.m. on 26 June 1967. This savagery may have been Jundi's revenge for the insults Hatum had thrown at him. When Hatum was slandering the Syrian government from Amman, he had impudently telephoned Jundi to demand that his wife be sent to join him and when Jundi refused had lashed out abusively. Before dying his last request was that his wife be allowed to keep her teaching job so as to raise their children. Asad had played a crucial role in thwarting Hatum's conspiracy and in the massive purge which followed, but he did not approve of the brutal dénouement. Three years later, on becoming president of Syria, he received Hatum's widow and gave her a pension.

The eve of war

By the eve of the Six Day War Syria's leaders were in a state of high emotion – part righteous indignation, part exhaustion, and part panic. They saw themselves as the victims of plots hatched by rival officers, by religious fanatics, by the propertied classes, all backed in various ways by reactionary monarchs and the Central Intelligence Agency. Above all, they were convinced that Israel had been assigned a special role to destroy their revolution. Some of this paranoia was well-founded. Although they did not know it, Israel had cracked their codes and was routinely monitoring their communications: it was therefore well aware of the parlous state in which the Syrian government and army found themselves. An Israeli spy, Elie Cohen, had operated at the very centre of Syrian affairs and had given Israel details and photographs of the Golan defences before his capture and execution in 1965.[7] As for indigenous enemies, Salim Hatum's conspiracy was real enough, as were the subversive stirrings of the Ba'thist old guard. The Damascus leadership was forced to spend anxious weeks smoking out its enemies.

It was true too that King Husayn and King Faysal rejoiced in the hope that the Ba'th's days were numbered. In the four years since the party had come to power, thousands of disaffected Syrians had fled to Jordan, Saudi Arabia and Lebanon where they influenced opinion against Damascus. Jordan in particular became the centre of much anti-Syrian plotting. A clandestine radio station called on Syrians to rise against their rulers and it was from Jordan that Hatum had rallied friends and funds for his conspiracy. His colleague Abu 'Asali later claimed in the Egyptian press that Jordan, Saudi Arabia and the United States had conspired with Hatum against the Syrian government. Syria felt beleaguered and its denunciations of its neighbours took on a hysterical edge. It struck back with terror of its own: on 21 May 1967 a Syrian car bomb blew up at the Ramtha border post killing twenty-one Jordanians. Two days later Jordan closed the Syrian embassy in Amman and sent the ambassador packing.

But foreign plots were not the worst of Syria's afflictions. Just when the regime was waking up to the possibility of an Israeli attack – trenches were dug in Damascus, youths were herded into defence squads, and small arms handed out to the People's Militia – it was rocked by a rebellion of outraged citizens. The trouble started on 25 April when the army magazine, *Jaysh al-Sha'b* (The People's Army), published an article scoffing at religion and dismissing God as 'an embalmed toy in the museum of history'. The most senior of Syria's religious dignitaries, Shaykh Hasan Habannaka, led 20,000 people on a protest march through the capital. He was immediately arrested, whereupon the souk struck in his support. The regime expropriated shopkeepers and expelled two Saudi diplomats who were accused of funding the disturbance. The author of the offending article, which was inevitably blamed on the CIA, was sentenced to hard labour for life – and in due course released.

As if these were not troubles enough, Syria was at the time absorbed in negotiations with the Iraq Petroleum Company (IPC) over oil transit fees, financial haggling which took place in a fevered atmosphere since, to slogan-fed youngsters, the 'battle of petroleum' was seen as yet another phase in the Arabs' struggle for independence from the West. By December 1966 the talks were deadlocked and the government had seized IPC property, stopped the oil flow across its territory, and was urging the Iraq government to nationalize the industry. The campaign to wrest £40 million in back payments from the IPC was so hard fought that the secretary of the Syrian delegation (who was responsible for interpreting as well as taking the minutes) fainted twice – and was brought round by the Prime Minister and sometime physician, Dr Yusuf Zu'ayyin. By March 1967 the IPC had agreed to a 50 per cent increase in transit dues, a victory for Syria which won its rulers some respect. But the bargaining continued right up to 5 June. Zu'ayyin was in fact on his way to a meeting with the IPC team when he was told that Syria was at war.[8]

Such was the state of the country when the Israeli thunderbolt struck.

9

The Six Day Walkover

Fifteen months after becoming Defence Minister Asad was to play a part in precipitating a great international crisis, the Six Day War of 1967, which was to change him as profoundly as it did the Arab environment. The shock woke him up as nothing else could and transformed the parochial putschist into a student of strategy and international politics.

The army Asad inherited in 1966 was as ill-prepared for war as he was himself. It was a poorly-trained, under-officered force some 50,000-strong which had been equipped 'on the cheap' by the Soviet Union with weapons being phased out of the Red Army. Syria did not have the resources to buy anything better. It had about 500 tanks, only half of them operational, supported by about 100 MiG-17s, but with no air defence missiles and no navy to speak of. Its gravest weakness lay in the fractured officer corps crippled by the great purge put in hand by Asad himself in the wake of the military conspiracies of late 1966. Even after this bloodletting, the army command was by no means united, and Asad as Defence Minister was still far from being its sole boss. His Chief of Staff, Ahmad al-Suwaydani, was not his man but owed allegiance to Salah Jadid, as did several other key officers. Syria's conduct of the coming war undoubtedly suffered from this divided chain of command. It was as titular chief of a ragged company that Asad faced an Israeli war machine tuned to a high state of readiness.

In the decade since the Suez campaign Israel had built up forces that could move fast and hit hard: mobile armoured units able to cover long distances, mechanized infantry, heliborne and naval paratroopers for use behind enemy lines, and above all an air force of Mirage and Super-Mystère interceptors and Mystère fighter-bombers of unchallenged superiority. The main lesson Israel had learned from the Suez war was the importance of air dominance not only to neutralize Arab air forces but also for use as flying artillery against infantry and tanks. Whereas

117

the Arab states had no coherent doctrine or strategy for either offence or defence, Israel's forces were shaped by a military doctrine designed to make up for the country's small size and population. It had devised a pre-emptive strategy to ensure that fighting took place on Arab rather than Israeli soil. Its key asset was a well-practised system for calling up reservists, put in place in the early 1950s, which dispensed with the burden of a large standing army and allowed it by 1967 to mobilize up to half a milion men at speed. As it was assumed that Israel would probably have to fight every few years to keep the Arabs weak, the idea was accepted that it should use such conflicts to secure better strategic frontiers.

In 1966–7 Israel's armed forces were led by a large and able officer corps, whose stars were Chief of Staff Yitzhak Rabin, his deputy Chaim Bar Lev, Chief of Operations Ezer Weizman, Air Force Commander Mordechai Hod, Military Intelligence chief Aharon Yaariv, and Mossad director Meir Amit. War was their profession. Most of them had been soldiers for more than two decades dating back to Second World War service with the British forces. Whereas since 1948 Syria had undergone a sort of unruly permanent revolution, Israel had been robustly fashioned by the bulldog will of David Ben Gurion. Whereas Syria was isolated even in the Arab world, Israel had warm friends on every continent. To procure high-technology weapons Shimon Peres had forged close ties with France in the 1950s, but by the 1960s Yitzhak Rabin was overseeing a switch to a more generous partner, the United States. Syria was supplied by the Soviet Union, but in a relationship characterized on both sides by a good deal of bewilderment.

When Asad took over the Defence Ministry he knew that Syria was dwarfed by its more powerful neighbour: the fact of Israel had overshadowed Syria's entire experience of independence since the Second World War, and on the very day of his appointment, Syrian and Israeli guns exchanged fire across the frontier in the latest of a series of bruising engagements. But he had no inkling of just how dangerous a moment the early summer of 1967 was nor that Israel would use him as a decoy to bag the greater enemy, Nasser. In June Syria was to serve as the sprat to catch the Egyptian mackerel.

Border incidents

The Six Day War grew out of something small and local: a low-level, long-running border dispute between Syria and Israel. Ever since 1949 there had been armed friction on the border. At issue were three patches of ground located respectively on the eastern shore of the Sea of Galilee, near the Hula marshes north of it, and further north still at the tip of the so-called Galilee Finger. The 1947 UN Partition Plan had put these pockets on the Israeli side of the line, but the Syrian army had taken and held them in the 1948 war. However, under the Syrian-Israeli 1949 armistice agreement Syrian troops were withdrawn and the salients demilitarized, but sovereignty over the three demilitarized zones (DMZs), as they were then named, remained by common accord undecided. Israel was determined to possess them. It sent in soldiers disguised as farmers to establish occupation; these moves attracted Syrian fire, which in turn gave Israel a reason to hit back. In other words, whenever Syria attempted to check Israel's advance, retaliation was immediate. General Carl Von Horn, head of the United Nations Truce Supervision Organization, came to believe that Israel deliberately provoked Syrian attacks.[1] A landmark in Israel's creeping annexation of the DMZs was a raid against Syrian positions in December 1955 in which fifty Syrian troops were killed, as well as two others in February 1960 and March 1962. But, to Syria's vast frustration, Israeli strikes were accepted by international opinion as legitimate self-defence.

All three DMZs were of strategic and economic importance, but the one along the Sea of Galilee was of special interest because it was close to the intake of Israel's National Water Carrier, an ambitious project, begun in the 1950s, to divert water from the Jordan to the northern Negev desert. This irrigation programme was thought to hold the key to Israel's capacity to absorb future immigrants, and as such aroused intense Arab alarm. It was seen as a theft of Arab resources – 77 per cent of the Jordan's waters came from tributaries arising in Arab countries – which would consolidate Israel and doom the Palestinians to permanent exile. So the battle for the DMZs became entangled with the ownership of water, always an emotional issue in the Middle East, and with the wider issues of the Arab-Israeli dispute.

By escalating the conflict and by the greater use of artillery, tanks and aircraft, Israel had by the early 1960s seized most of the disputed salients, drained the Hula marshes, won exclusive control of the Sea of Galilee, and by 1964 completed its National Water Carrier.[2] Syria responded to the seizure by shelling Israeli settlements in the Hula valley, only to draw on its head further air strikes. It also encouraged Palestinian guerrilla attacks on the water carrier: Fatah's very first (unsuccessful) attempt at sabotage on 31 December 1964 was directed at this target.

Such was the thankless task which landed in Asad's lap when he became air force commander that month, and by the time he was appointed Defence Minister in February 1966, it had grown even more acute. How might Syria resist a stronger enemy which escalated the conflict on every occasion, resorted to force as a matter of routine, and pursued its national interest regardless of the interests of others? It was a formidable dilemma: to do battle was to invite defeat; yet to lie low meant to surrender, in effect to concede to Israel supremacy on the ground and in the air. This was not an option which Asad and his colleagues could contemplate.

As Defence Minister Asad was concerned with the border on a daily basis. In 1966 incidents grew more frequent and more violent, sometimes owing to his own stubbornness, sometimes to Israel's determination to teach the new Ba'th team a lesson. There were whole nights of sporadic firing, land and air clashes, with the forced evacuation of Syrian border villages, and frequent shuttles by General Odd Bull, the UN's chief truce observer, between Asad in Damascus and Yitzhak Rabin in Tel Aviv. Protests by Syria to the ambassadors of the great powers proved totally ineffective. The lessons of weakness and friendlessness were soon brought home. When Syria attempted a water diversion of its own, Rabin used long-range tank fire against Syrian equipment and then closed down the project altogether with an air raid on the engineering works on 14 July 1966, using means which Asad could not employ in reverse. Syria took the matter to the Security Council where Israel claimed that it had been attacked by Syrian-backed guerrillas. To Syria's bitter disappointment the Council failed to condemn Israel.

Outgunned in the field, outvoted at the United Nations, the Syrian government then began to trumpet a new if somewhat unrealistic doctrine: it would no longer waste time at the Security Council but would respond to every Israeli move by striking at targets inside that country. In addition, inspired by the examples of Algeria and Vietnam, it proclaimed its confidence in a 'people's liberation war': as Damascus Radio put it, 'Arab Damascus is no less heroic than Hanoi'. Defiance was soon put to the test. On 15 August an Israeli gunboat ran aground on the Syrian side of the Sea of Galilee, breaching a tacit agreement that Israeli boats would come no closer than 250 metres to the Syrian shore. Asad sent his air force into action, losing two aircraft, one brought down by Israeli ground fire, another by a Mirage. This would not be the last time he sent his pilots into battle on what were virtually suicide missions.

Such was the pattern of Asad's first six months in office. Israel bashed Syria at will, trampling on its rights – and then posed as the injured party. Before the Six Day War Asad's whole experience of battle was of this tit-for-tat on the border. His forces got a bloody nose from time to time but it was a level of punishment he appeared ready to take to make his point. What he did not foresee was that Israel, leaping a few rungs up the escalation ladder, would seize the chance to administer a knockout blow.

The Egyptian factor

Three factors turned the grumbling complaint on the Syrian-Israeli border into a fever. The first was Nasser's state of mind in 1966–7, unnerved by problems on many fronts; the second, the introduction of Palestinian guerrillas into the conflict; and the third, Israel's shrewd assessment that these two elements could be combined to its advantage.

Having survived the trap set for him in 1956 by Britain, France and Israel, Nasser in 1966 was a bogeyman to his enemies and a superman to his fans as the living embodiment of Arab aspirations. But, although few could see it, he was already past his peak and losing control of the environment he had dominated for so long. In particular, he was facing a wounding challenge from a rising and vocal Arab *avant-garde*.

Nasser had won the admiration of the Arabs by defying the West in the 1950s, but the price he paid was to be burdened with the general expectation that he would deal decisively with Israel, if necessary by war. It was an uncomfortable position. He knew that war was beyond his means and he did everything in his power to steer the Arabs away from it. The clearest indication of his true policies came when the Ba'th regime that emerged in Syria after the 1963 coup raucously demanded a forceful Arab response to the National Water Carrier which Israel was due to complete at the end of that year. Nasser summoned the Arab kings and presidents to a summit meeting in Cairo in January 1964 – the first ever – to muzzle the Syrian hotheads in an anti-war consensus; and for nearly three years thereafter he used the mechanism of successive summits to rein in the Syrians and impose on the Arab world a defensive, not to say passive, policy towards Israel.

As a sop to the Palestinians, the Cairo summit created the Palestine Liberation Organization. Its name was deceptive. Far from a call to arms, the PLO was a sort of corral in which the Palestinians could charge about harmlessly letting off steam. The whole idea was to placate nationalist sentiment while denying Israel a pretext for war.[3]

By 1966, however, Nasser's containment strategy was wearing thin.

And, as it became clear that he had no plans to challenge Israel, Arab opinion was plunged, amid much floundering and questioning of old certainties, into a crisis of confidence. Who was going to liberate Palestine, young Arabs asked, if Nasser could not do the job? Was he after all just a bankrupt dictator, perhaps even an American agent? An index of Nasser's decline was the defection from his camp in the mid-1960s of the political movement which for a decade had been his most ardent supporter: the Movement of Arab Nationalists (MAN), the nearest thing to a Nasserist party to exist outside Egypt and a tool he had used in many a political battle, especially against the Ba'th. To lose MAN was to lose the core of his Arab constituency. Men who would once have followed Nasser to the ends of the earth now openly questioned his leadership and, looking for a way out of their wilderness, turned sharply left.

Perhaps in the hope of winning back the defectors and certainly because he discerned a gathering imperialist conspiracy against him, Nasser himself also turned left. The immediate cause of his anxiety lay in the mountains of Yemen where his forces were engaged in a messy guerrilla war against royalist tribesmen backed by Saudi Arabia. He had sent an army to prop up the young Yemen republic after the 1962 revolution against the Imamate and had since been trapped there in a conflict which sapped his resources, demoralized his troops and robbed him of freedom of manoeuvre on other fronts. Nasser's duel with King Faysal, the Saudi monarch, came to obsess him as he saw his regional leadership slipping away. So desperate was he to get Faysal to drop the Yemeni royalists that in mid-1966 he threatened to invade Saudi Arabia itself, a move which understandably alarmed Faysal's American allies for whom the rich Saudi oil-fields were a vital interest. In Nasser's mind the Arabian struggle was part of a world-wide imperialist offensive against the movement of national liberation in Asia and Africa of which he was a champion. His friend Ahmad Ben Bella of Algeria had been overthrown; Mehdi Ben Baraka, the Moroccan opposition leader, had been kidnapped in France by Moroccan, French and Israeli agents – and murdered; Sukarno of Indonesia had fallen; the 'West' had driven down the price of cocoa to oust Nkrumah of Ghana. Convinced he too was on a Western hit-list, Nasser veered towards the Soviet Union, and in May 1966 invited the Viet Cong to open an office in Cairo. What he failed to realize in these defiant yet defensive moves was that by alienating the United States (for whom the invitation to the Viet Cong was a red rag to a bull) he removed whatever restraint America might have exercised on Israel in the Middle East arena. Indeed, Washington came to regard Nasser as a pro-Soviet troublemaker whose disciplining would be to everyone's advantage. Israel was happy to concur.

A beleaguered Nasser, casting anxiously around for a means to restore his fortunes, was part of the dangerous regional scene on to which Asad stepped as Syrian Defence Minister in 1966. It is doubtful whether he, or anyone else in the Syrian leadership, understood how vulnerable the Egyptian leader then felt himself to be. At the forefront of their minds was the knowledge that, holding them responsible for the crushing of his supporters in Syria, Nasser would punish them if he could. They viewed him with reluctant respect but also with the greatest suspicion. They suspected him of plotting their overthrow, of defeatism over Palestine, of creating the PLO as an instrument of Egyptian policy. They had not forgotten his contacts with the United States in the 1950s and did not trust his rapprochement with Moscow. In a general way, they felt Nasser held himself safely distant from the battle with Israel which was their daily preoccupation and was not overly troubled to see them suffer. These were as much Asad's attitudes as those of his colleagues, blinding him to the dangers ahead. He was still a beginner in Middle East politics. The ambivalent Syrian-Egyptian relationship greatly contributed to the coming crisis.

The Palestinian factor

The Palestinian factor then intervened to give further impetus to the crisis. From the early 1960s a handful of Palestinian militants, exasperated by the Arab states' fear of war, looked for ways of taking affairs into their own hands. The creation of the PLO, so patently a device to shackle them under its chairman, Ahmad Shuqairy, a wordy lawyer who had never held a gun, spurred them to set up organizations of their own. Had the summit strategy survived, these little movements would no doubt have been contained, but Syria broke ranks, helping the Palestinian guerrillas to burst out of the Arab box and develop momentum to the excitement of the Arab public. For Arab regimes to lock them up again came to seem politically more costly than the Israeli retaliation which might now be provoked. Taking note of these trends, Nasser abandoned his policy of crisis containment in the summer of 1966 and refused to attend any further summits.

Yasir 'Arafat and George Habash were the most vigorous exponents of Palestinian frustration. 'Arafat's Fatah announced its début in the guerrilla struggle on 1 January 1965, while some months earlier Habash, who had been a founder of MAN, hived off MAN's

Palestinian members into a separate organisation which was to grow into the Popular Front for the Liberation of Palestine. It mounted its first (unsuccessful) incursion into Israel in October 1964. Not to be outdone, Shuqairy of the PLO, hitherto noted as an orator with a gift for curdling rather than spilling blood, prepared to enter the guerrilla business on his own account.

Without Syrian backing these pinpricks would have caused Israel little concern, as Jordan and Lebanon were doing their utmost to prevent the guerrillas mounting raids from their territories. Indeed up to the war of June 1967 more Palestinians were killed by soldiers of these states while attempting to enter Israel than by the Israelis themselves.[4] But Syria was another matter. The temper of Jadid's government was militant and the deeply felt Palestinian cause occupied a central place in Ba'thist ideology. The concept of a 'people's war' attracted party radicals. Moreover, the fact that Shuqairy's PLO was backed by Egypt was good reason for Syria to promote Palestinian groups of its own, such was the competition between Damascus and Cairo. But, and this was the determining issue at that moment, Syria also came to see the Palestinian guerrillas as useful instruments in its exasperating and unequal struggle with Israel over possession of the demilitarized zones.

From 1964 to 1966, as head of air force armaments and then as air force commander, Asad gave some help to the first small bands of Palestinian guerrillas. 'It was in Syria that the lungs of the Resistance were filled with oxygen', he was grandly to claim.[5] About 100,000 Palestinian refugees had found refuge in Syria after the 1948 war and were treated, as far as the law was concerned, as Syrians: given places in schools and universities, allowed to join labour unions, admitted into government service and drafted into the army. And when the militias emerged the Jadid regime welcomed them as revolutionaries. But as a career officer Asad did not see the Resistance in such heroic terms or consider it a major player: attaching Palestinians to Syrian army intelligence, he entrusted them with small sabotage operations,[6] giving them the use of two training camps and passing on to them a plane-load of arms donated by Houari Boumédienne after he had displaced Ahmad Ben Bella as ruler of Algeria.[7] (Algeria was in fact the first Arab country to recognize and aid 'Arafat's Fatah; Syria was next.)

When Israel destroyed Syrian engineering works in July 1966 and shot down two Syrian MiGs in August, Asad decided to riposte with Palestinian querrilla raids which in the autumn in 1966 become more frequent and effective. Did he believe that Israel could be driven out of the DMZs by such means? A few dreamers in the Syrian cabinet may have imagined that under pressure the Israelis would pack up and leave as the French had from Algeria. But the Syrian leaders had clearly not thought through the implications of introducing the guerrillas into their contest with Israel. Their politics were gestural rather than reasoned: they were looking for relief from the frustrations of impotence. The emotional equation was simple: they could not contemplate surrendering to Israel, but neither could they match it in conventional battle. The guerrillas seemed to offer an honourable way out. Sharing the region's mood of mounting impatience and deriding other Arab governments as defeatist, Asad and his colleagues began to see the cross-frontier forays of the commandos as a way of keeping up the fight. Jadid's team had not yet grasped that Israel's policy of deterrence rested on a readiness to escalate without limit. But whereas, in bringing in the guerrillas, Syria escalated from weakness, Israel was able in response to escalate from strength.

Syria and the Palestinians had different strategies, however. 'Arafat seemed anxious to ignite a general Arab-Israeli war as quickly as possible on the ground that Jewish immigration and atomic weapons development would soon put Israel beyond reach. Asad neither sought a war nor expected one to break out. His colleagues promoted the notion of a 'people's war' as a substitute for conventional warfare, not as a prelude to it. When in the summer of 1966 'Arafat attempted to throw off Syrian restraint, Asad had him and a number of his associates locked up in Mezze prison for over a month. 'Arafat was already suspect to the Syrians because of his early allegiance to the Muslim Brothers and also because of an accusation made against him at this time. One of his principal rivals, Yusuf 'Arabi, then head of al-'Asifa, Fatah's military wing, was wounded in an operation against Israel in 1966 and died in hospital at Qunaytra. The story circulating in Damascus was that on his deathbed he had told the Syrian commander of the front, 'Abd al-Ghani Ibrahim, that 'Arafat had betrayed him. Such accusations were not uncommon between rival guerrilla leaders, but they were perhaps a factor in landing 'Arafat in jail. The episode marked the beginning of the intense mutual antipathy between 'Arafat and Asad. Faruq Qaddumi, an ex-Ba'thist and later the PLO's 'foreign minister', went to negotiate 'Arafat's release with Asad,[8] and by all accounts had a hard time of it.

The Israelis observed the uneven course of the Syrian-Palestinian relationship with some interest, as General Aharon Yaariv, head of Military Intelligence, revealed to foreign correspondents in Tel Aviv three weeks before the war:[9]

The Syrians use this weapon of guerrilla activity because they cannot face us in open battle, because they are militarily very weak, and they know we are bent upon establishing ... certain facts along the border.

Such was the tinder waiting to be ignited: Nasser at bay, casting about for some bold stroke to raise him up again, an increasingly active Palestinian movement, and Syria, smarting over the loss of the DMZs and putting the guerrillas to use.

Raising the temperature

From the autumn of 1966, Nasser watched the Syrian-Israeli escalation with growing concern. No longer able to restrain the Syrians through the mechanism of Arab summits, he signed a bilateral defence pact with them on 7 November, pledging to come to their aid if attacked. It was an attempt to regain some control over policy-making in Damascus: the two countries exchanged ambassadors – for the first time since Syria's secession in 1961 – and set up a joint high command. But the pact only papered over years of distrust. Nasser suspected the Syrians of wanting to see him destroyed in battle, while the Syrians suspected him of wanting them to go down alone. King Husayn was the most apprehensive onlooker. He judged that in signing the defence pact Nasser had fallen into a trap locking him into Syria's escalation, and, moreover, that the Syrians would applaud if his own throne were toppled in war.

Israel chose this moment to raise the regional temperature. On 13 November, six days after the conclusion of the Syrian-Egyptian pact, it launched its largest military action since Suez: a brigade of over 3,000 men and forty tanks, with cover from two Mirage squadrons, invaded Jordan on a five-mile front and smashed the undefended West Bank village of Samu' in the Hebron hills. The raid was said to be a reprisal for guerrilla action, but, curiously enough, Israel had not attacked Syria which promoted the guerrillas, but Jordan which had done its utmost to control them. The effect was to provoke riots in Jordan so violent that Husayn was very nearly overthrown. Bombs went off in Amman and troops were called out to quell the disturbances. Husayn's Palestinian subjects demanded a radical change of policy: what was the point of protecting Israel rather than letting loose the guerrillas, when you were punished for it? Why was Jordan at odds with Syria, Egypt and the PLO? Why did it cold-shoulder the Soviet Union? Shuqairi called on Jordan's Arab Legion to turn its guns on the 'traitor Husayn'. Dr Atasi, the Syrian Head of State, encouraged by the fact that Israeli retaliation had been directed at Jordan rather than at Syria, proclaimed a 'holy war against the throne of treason'. And Cairo Radio led the pack. Hitting back, Husayn taunted Nasser with hiding from Israel behind the screen of United Nations forces in Sinai.

By its raid on Samu' Israel, as it no doubt calculated, sharpened Arab divisions, radicalized opinion, and set its lamentably weak and hopelessly quarrelsome neighbours lurching amid mutual plots and accusations, to the very edge of the precipice.

The point to be borne in mind is that, well into 1967, Asad and his colleagues conceived of the struggle with Israel in terms of greater or lesser border clashes. Their gaze remained focused on the three DMZs which, to their indignation, Israel had by this time swallowed up. A wider conflict was wholly outside their experience and therefore unimaginable. Thus renewed border clashes occurred in the early weeks of 1967, punctuated by appeals for restraint from the UN Secretary-General, U Thant, and by fruitless sessions of the Syrian-Israeli Mixed Armistice Commission. Syria demanded that Israel withdraw to the 1949 armistice line, remove its fortifications and paramilitary farmers from the DMZs, and allow Arab farmers back. But Israel, which had won control of the zones in fifteen years of strength and stealth, had no intention whatsoever of retreating.

It then gave events a decisive push. Following a well rehearsed and fully predictable pattern, it sent an armoured tractor into the DMZ on the shores of the Sea of Galilee on 7 April 1967, provoking Syrian fire. The Israeli air force went into action to silence the Syrian guns; Asad ordered his planes up to meet it and in the ensuing air battle six Syrian MiGs were lost. Israeli war planes roared cock-a-hoop over Damascus. This was the most serious military reverse Syria had suffered since 1948. It was no consolation that several Arab countries came verbally to Syria's defence, for Asad's old dilemma remained intact: how to defend Syria's rights without getting thrashed? Yet even after this large-scale engagement the Syrian leaders failed to look beyond the disputed border salients, as if they could not see where events were leading. In a Note to the Security Council Syria charged that the crisis was due to 'the determination of the Israeli authorities to liquidate once and for all the Arab rights in the demilitarized zones'. But as with previous appeals to the Council, Syria obtained no satisfaction. Israel, ignoring Syria's claim to rights in the DMZs, based its defence on the charge that Syria harassed border settlements and sent guerrillas against it.

Israel's aims and Nasser's response

What was Israel doing in drawing Syria's fire in the DMZs and then punishing it when it rose to the bait? Did it want Syria to give up all hope of the salients? Was it ramming home the message that Arab governments must keep their frontiers quiet or take the consequences? Was it worried that Syria's use of the guerrillas might endow the Resistance with a political status? Yet another explanation is that Israel was seeking to frighten Egypt into disciplining Syria, its new treaty partner. Nasser had worked hard from 1964 to hold back the Syrians lest they drag him into war, so by hitting Syria Israel was signalling Egypt to try harder and do better. An Israeli spokesman said as much at the time. 'We must use force', General Yaariv told the press in the interview already quoted, 'in order to have the Egyptians convince the Syrians it doesn't pay.'[10]

But some Israeli leaders seemed to have still wider objectives. The sheer magnitude of the attack on Samu' in November and the way Asad had been drawn into the April dogfight suggested that some Israelis were not seeking merely to punish or deter. Ever since the 1950s a strong lobby in the Israeli Defence Forces had pressed for bigger and more frequent retaliatory raids against the Arabs to heighten tension and even court war in order to push forward Israel's frontiers to more defensible lines.[11] This lobby was very active in 1966–7, but improved frontiers were no longer its only objective.

Political leaders such as Prime Minister Eshkol did not want war, and the intelligence appraisal was that the Arabs would not be ready to fight for at least another four years. But Israeli activists, with no inhibitions about being provocative or raising the temperature, seemed deliberately to want to escalate hostilities.

In baiting Syria, their real aim seems to have been to destroy Nasser. This was what the IDF had trained for. Nasser was the old enemy who, turning defeat into victory in 1956, had come to symbolize Israel's ultimate bogey: Arab independence and Arab unity. It seemed a golden moment to strike. He was psychologically rattled, over-close to the Russians, on bad terms with the Americans, at the mercy of the reckless Syrians. What can be asserted with confidence is that the guerrilla pinpricks, of which Israeli leaders made so much at the time, were not at the forefront of their minds. Terrorist harassment, General Moshe Dayan said dismissively on 8 June, was 'a nuisance but not a cause of war'.[12]

Once the time-clock of the crisis was set in motion, the explosion became inevitable. In early May Palestinian guerrillas planted a few mines near the Sea of Galilee, drawing on Syria's head a series of ever more explicit Israeli threats; on 12 May an Israeli military spokesman said that Israel's options ranged from conducting its own guerrilla warfare inside Syria to 'the invasion and conquest of Damascus'; on the same day Prime Minister Levi Eshkol warned there could be no immunity for a state aiding saboteurs; on the 13th Eshkol said that Israel 'may have to teach Syria a sharper lesson than that of 7 April'; on the 14th Chief of Staff Rabin warned that if Syrian sabotage continued, Israel's 'reaction will be far different from the reprisals against Jordan in the past'.[13] Israeli journalists and many Arabs interpreted this strong language to mean that Israel was intent on overthrowing the Syrian regime by force. Word reached Nasser from the Russians and from the Syrians, as well as from his own intelligence, that Israel was in fact preparing to attack. Whether troops were massed or not became a subject of subsequent debate, but, given Israel's repeated recourse to force, the reports were readily believable. It is possible that Moscow's warnings were based on information leaked by Israel itself,[14] with the intention of making Nasser believe an attack on Syria was imminent.

The Egyptian leader found himself in an embarrassing situation. He had been scorned for not coming to Syria's aid in the 7 April air battle, the Saudis speculating publicly about why he had not bombed Eilat or fired missiles over the heads of the UN force in Sinai. 'Anyone who imagines that Egypt will wage any kind of battle against Israel, to defend Syria or anyone else, will wait a long time', Jidda Radio mocked. Jordan's propaganda played the same needling tune, harping on Nasser's duplicity in posing as the Arabs' champion while letting Israeli shipping on its way to Eilat pass freely through Egyptian waters in the Straits of Tiran.

Nasser could not stay out of the crisis. His battered reputation would not have survived: a champion loses his title if he does not enter the lists. He could afford to ignore a Syrian-Israeli border clash but not the threat of war, for if Syria were invaded, Egypt's own strategic position would be gravely compromised. As Nasser himself put it: 'Who starts with Syria will finish with Egypt'.[15] Mohamed Heikal, Nasser's confidant, later explained:[16]

> We found Syria's regime unattractive, but there was a sense in which Egypt and Syria were natural allies. It was unimaginable for us to allow Israel to make war on one front alone.

Also weighing on Nasser's mind was his undoubted awareness that if Syria went down undefended Arab morale, Arab security, Arab nationalism itself, the whole movement of Third World emancipation to which he was devoted would suffer a crippling blow.

Anxious to avoid war, yet not trusting the Syrians to handle the explosive situation alone, Nasser moved to take the management of the crisis into his own hands. In Heikal's words, 'The Egyptian view was that if the frightened Syrians made a wrong move, they could get us all into serious trouble'.[17] So to take command and reassure the Syrians, Nasser, in answer to Rabin's fierce warnings to Syria, sent Egyptian troops across the Suez Canal into Sinai. He wished to shift the epicentre of the crisis away from the Syrian border which he could not control, to the Egyptian border which he thought he could. And with this intention, a day or two later, on 16 May, he called for the withdrawal of the UN Emergency Force from the positions on the Sinai border between Egypt and Israel which it had manned since the Suez war. Significantly, he did not ask the UNEF to withdraw from the most sensitive point of Sharm al-Shaykh, overlooking the Tiran Straits, or from the Gaza Strip. But when UN Secretary-General U Thant replied that a partial withdrawal was not possible, Nasser, unable to climb down, had little option but to ask on 18 May for a total pull-out. Egyptian advance units then took over the UNEF posts on the Sinai border – but still not the post at Sharm al-Shaykh. The Straits remained open and unmined. Quite clearly Nasser hoped to avoid complications over Tiran and the Gulf of Aqaba which Israel had prised open to its shipping in the 1956 campaign and whose closure, it had often declared, would be a *casus belli*.

For three days Nasser made no further move. In his own eyes he had already achieved a lot: he had retaken the initiative from his volatile Syrian partners and had temporarily silenced those Arab critics who had accused him of hiding behind the UNEF. But some segments of Arab opinion and even some of his own officers were urging him to go for higher stakes. While they egged him on, there was at this crucial moment little countervailing pressure from either Israel or the United States. Neither Lyndon Johnson nor Levi Eshkol warned him to go no further, and their silence may have prompted his next gamble. On 21 May Egyptian troops were at last sent to occupy Sharm al-Shaykh and on the night of the 22nd, in a fighting speech at a Sinai air base, Nasser closed the Straits to Israeli ships as well as to strategic cargoes bound for Eilat.

The nature of the conflict immediately changed. What had begun as an attempt to manage Syria's crisis became an Egyptian-Israeli crisis of far greater dimensions. Asad, along with the rest of the Syrian regime, had been shunted to the sidelines. For the next several days they were to be no more than anxious spectators.

Nasser was basically a cautious man. Yet here, in the middle of a highly publicized crisis, he behaved with uncharacteristic rashness. Why? At work was a psychological motivation of a sort that has made other seasoned politicians overplay their hand. Nasser longed to turn the clock back to before 1956. It rankled with him that Israel had wrested from him in its Suez aggression the right of passage to Eilat through Egyptian waters. Now an opportunity seemed to present itself for him to regain by diplomacy what had been taken from him by force. Such was the prize for which he gambled. And once he had closed the Straits, his main concern was to hang on to this gain without actually having to fight. An immediate bonus was the wild applause of his fans: seeing its champion step back into the ring, the Arab world cheered Nasser as it had not done for years.

Nasser's strategy was to attempt to frighten Israel into prudence, while making it clear that he would not attack first. This was what he promised U Thant in Cairo on 23 May and subsequently in reassuring messages to both Washington and Moscow. Indeed, the Russians insisted on it: the Soviet ambassador called on him at 2.30 a.m. on 26 May to warn him that Egypt must on no account fire first. So more troops were posted to Sinai, to take up defensive positions (and not a very good defence at that). Behind the muscular rhetoric, Nasser's speeches spelt out the same message. Israel was promised a horrible fate only in the event of its starting a war.[18]

> If Israel embarks on an aggression against Syria or Egypt, the battle against Israel will be a general one . . . and our basic objective will be to destroy Israel.

Or again:[19]

> We have regained the rights which were ours in 1965 . . . We have left the next move to Israel . . . If Israel chooses war, then it is welcome to it.

He claimed to be ready for a confrontation and must have envisaged that military force might actually be used, but in his mind it was force to deter Israel, not to attack it. And even this must have seemed to him a remote possibility, as nothing else can explain Egypt's unpreparedness for war.

In the same spirit of deterrence, Nasser welcomed his old enemy, King Husayn, to Cairo on 30 May and signed with him a defence pact similar to the one with Syria. These pacts between antagonists had no military value whatsoever, but, with Arab opinion inflamed, the stark choice for Husayn was to rally publicly to Cairo or risk falling to the mob. Even Husayn, less deluded than others about the enemy's strength, imagined that an Arab show of solidarity might give Israel pause. Of course, in retrospect the folly of the Arab leaders was to allow their public to be infected with war fever – to which the posturing of PLO leader Shuqairy at the head of a puny Palestinian militia contributed not a little.

The next day, 31 May, in talks with Robert Anderson, President Johnson's special envoy, Nasser agreed to send Vice-President Zakariya Muhieddin to Washington on 7 June, in the evident expectation that the beginning of a process of negotiation would rule out the possibility of war. To head off a conflict Nasser was ready to make a substantial concession to Israel – if this could be done quietly and without causing him political embarrassment. Ever since 1957 Israeli ships passing through the Straits of Tiran on their way to Eilat had engaged in an elaborate reflagging exercise. On approaching the Straits the Israeli flag was lowered and the flag of another country, say Liberia, was raised in a fig-leaf gesture to Egyptian national sensitivities. Once through the Straits and approaching Eilat, the Israeli flag was rehoisted. This verbally agreed arrangement was for a decade a closely guarded secret which both sides had an interest in keeping. Egypt had no wish to publicize a cosmetic compromise, while Israel's Labour government feared to furnish ammunition to the right. Wishing to defuse the crisis in early June 1967, Egyptian diplomats at the United Nations told the secretariat that Egypt would be ready to revive the old tacit formula so long as Israel did not insist on spelling out the terms. In other words, Nasser was signalling that he was ready to compromise on the crucial question of the Straits.

In the meantime, his policy of deterrence seemed to be working: he doubted that Israel would dare to take on the combined Arab armies and, on the wider stage, he trusted the Soviet Union to hold the United States in check. But deterrence ultimately rested on Egypt's armed strength, and for this Nasser relied on Marshal 'Amer's appraisal that Egypt could handle anything Israel might send against it in Sinai.

International reconnaissance

The argument in Israel was never whether or not to fight. Everyone in the leadership was agreed that Nasser, having made the blunder of handing Israel an internationally recognized *casus belli*, must not be let off the hook. The anxiety of the Israeli government and high command was that the opportunity to destroy him might be missed. This was the appalling risk Israel would run if it allowed the problem of the Straits to fall into the hands of the United Nations, or would-be mediators, or, as was proposed at the time, if it left the problem of challenging Nasser's blockade to a group of maritime powers. When Nasser indicated privately, through the UN, that he was prepared to reopen the Straits under the old unwritten reflagging arrangement, the Israeli response was to demand a public and formal Egyptian commitment, in effect a total climbdown. Clearly Israel's fear was that Nasser's offer would rob it of its grounds for going to war.

The debate in Israel was between those who advocated immediate war and those who wanted a little time in which to secure prior international, and especially American, understanding. There was no wish to repeat the 1956 experience when the superpowers had insisted that Israel give up its Suez campaign conquests. Israel also had to be sure that any Soviet intervention, admittedly a remote eventuality, would be neutralized by the United States. Accordingly those who argued for a delay won the day, and so began the two-week countdown to war which in Israel came to be known as the 'Waiting Period'.

Foreign Minister Abba Eban was sent to Paris, London and Washington to go through the motions of testing what the world would do to break the blockade. General de Gaulle cautioned him against starting hostilities, but Israel, which was switching its arms procurement from Paris to Washington, could afford to ignore him. French Intelligence knew that Israel's war machine was unbeatable by any line-up of Arab states, which explained de Gaulle's warning to Eban that, if Israel attacked, it would forfeit French goodwill. In London Eban found more sympathy. Indeed the diaries of British Labour cabinet ministers – Harold Wilson, Richard Crossman, Barbara Castle[20] – reflect the widely felt anxiety of the time that Israel was facing disaster. This raises the important question about what British Intelligence was reporting to the politicians. Is it possible that MI6 was unaware of the true balance of power, in spite of its links with the CIA? Did the CIA collude in concealing the facts of Israeli strength and Arab feebleness? From British political memoirs of the period it would appear that no one in the British government knew the truth.

By demonstrating that the great powers would not reopen the Straits for Israel, Eban's trip was designed to get international sanction for what Israel intended to do itself. However, the impatience of the Israeli activists to go to war revealed the true purpose of Eban's journey rather sooner than he expected. On his arrival in Washington, he found a new brief from the Israeli cabinet awaiting him: the blockade of the Straits was to take second place in his discussions with the Administration; instead he was instructed to inform President Johnson that Israel was in grave and imminent danger of a general attack by Egypt and Syria. In the circumstances it requested a public pledge that any attack on Israel would be equivalent to an attack on the United States. Specifically, Israel asked that US forces in the Mediterranean join up with the IDF to face the threat of an Arab assault.[21]

Eban and his colleagues back in Israel knew that they were asking Johnson for something which he was constitutionally unable to deliver:[22] Congressional approval was needed for such a far-reaching commitment. Moreover, the Vietnam war had so absorbed American energies that there was no readiness for further military burdens. The fact was that the bogey raised by Israel of an Arab attack was a fabrication. By invoking the threat in this peremptory and pressing fashion, Israel was presenting the United States with just two options: act with us or we act alone – and that was indeed the intention behind Eban's instructions. If Johnson refused the first, it could be taken that he was sanctioning the second.

Lyndon Johnson did not like being pushed around by the Israelis, and would give them neither a pledge to fight alongside them nor an official green light. On hearing Eban's alarmist claim that Israel was in imminent danger of an Arab assault, he ordered the American intelligence community to check the evidence. The analysts laboured through the night of 25–26 May sifting and evaluating the data and reached the conclusion that Egypt was not preparing to attack. Worse still for the hawks in Israel, the American judgment was that Israel could trounce the Arabs within a week, whoever fired the first shot.[23]

Johnson reminded Eban of the restraints on him from both Congress and public opinion. He stressed the need to work through the United Nations. He promised to try to put together an international maritime force to open the Straits. And when advising Israel not to start hostilities, he used and repeated a curious phrase: 'Israel will not be alone unless it decides to go alone'. According to William Quandt, whose analysis of American-Israeli relations at this period is the most authoritative so far published, the meaning of Johnson's sibylline utterance was that Israel should not count on the United States if, contrary to all reasonable expectations, it got itself into trouble.[24] Although Johnson's top advisers were unanimous in believing Israel would win, the president could not afford to ignore the remote possibility that something might go wrong, or that the Soviet Union might intervene and Israel call on him for assistance. However, Johnson made up for his official caution, giving the Israelis through private back channels[25] the encouragement they were so eager for, and after the war his support was generous and immediate. Even in the few days before it, US arms shipments were already on their way.[26]

A few Americans and Israelis professed to believe that the Soviet Union, wishing to exploit America's involvement in Vietnam, had instigated the whole crisis in the hope of gaining some advantage for itself in the Middle East.[27] This is without foundation. Moscow had no significant leverage on the radicals in Damascus whose defiant behaviour made it nervous, and Nasser did not consult his Soviet friends before his decision to close the Straits.

The countdown

In Israel the tense countdown to war precipitated a long-brewing political crisis between Mapai, the party which had dominated Israeli plitics since the creation of the state, and a group of impatient younger men, several of them disgruntled generals, who, two years earlier in 1965, had split from Mapai to form their own party, Rafi. Disciples of David Ben Gurion, they included such men as Moshe Dayan, Shimon Peres, Haim Herzog and Yitzhak Navon. Distrustful of accommodations with the Arabs and with a taste for strong-arm methods derived from their defence backgrounds, these young Turks criticized the Mapai old guard, and especially Levi Eshkol who had replaced Ben Gurion as prime minister and defence minister in 1963, for failing to assert military supremacy over the Arabs. They saw in the crisis of May 1967 a moment of enormous potential for Israel if it struck out with speed, strength and resolve. They were desperately worried that Eshkol would defuse the crisis, as he had others in the past, by 'talking it out' and delaying action. They felt he was a 'non-doer', a 'watcher'. They longed to get back into positions of power where they could shape events. Dayan, for example, had been Chief of Staff for nearly five years and Peres director-general of the Defence Ministry.

To fend off his critics Eshkol agreed to go to war but only once the Americans had been won over and their approval secured. However, this only provided Rafi with further reasons to portray him as vacillating. In late May Rafi harassed him by invoking the authority of Ben Gurion and by winning over the left-wing Mapam, then part of the government coalition, to its point of view. Demonstrators outside Mapai headquarters carried banners with such slogans, aimed at

Eshkol, as, 'Never a soldier, how can you command soldiers?' Without pressure from Rafi the 1967 war might never have been fought.

The decisive event was almost an army putsch: straining at the leash, a claque of generals led by Ezer Weizman, chief of operations, and Aharon Yaariv, head of intelligence, held a stormy meeting with the Prime Minister on 28 May demanding immediate war. A day or two later, Weizman had another angry interview with Eshkol in which he is said to have ripped off his badges of rank, and thrown them on the desk saying, 'If you do not give the order to go to war, Jewish history will never forgive you.'[28]

Egypt's deployments in Sinai, the TV pictures of war fever in Cairo and especially King Husayn's pact with Nasser all played into the Israeli generals' hands. Yielding to these political and military pressures, Eshkol agreed to form a new National Unity Coalition in which he surrendered the key defence portfolio to Moshe Dayan. This was the man Rafi and the generals wanted, in the belief that he would find a way to satisfy or bypass Eshkol's insistence on overt American support.

Bent on war, the generals put in place a defence minister who would promptly unleash it. But along with Rafi came Gahal, an amalgam of the Liberals and Menachem Begin's right-wing nationalist Herut. By bringing Begin into the government – the Revisionist outcast now admitted for the first time to the heart of affairs – the generals ensured a cabinet which would not only wage war but wage it for territorial gains, especially on the West Bank.[29] Some commanders and politicians considered that Israel's War of Independence had been incomplete and wished to extend the state's frontiers to the Jordan. Sole control of a united Jerusalem had also long been an Israeli dream.

On 30 May Meir Amit, the director of Mossad, was sent to Washington under an assumed name to get an American 'green light'. Calling on CIA director Richard Helms, he learned what he had come to find out – that no one in Washington would be very upset if Israel went to war and won. Johnson had not been in a position to be quite so candid as his aides. From the time Egyptian forces started pouring into the wastes of Sinai, the Israeli high command knew that the Egyptians had walked into a trap. It read Egyptian radio traffic, noted the plaintive cries for water and fuel, and observed the traffic jams and the supply columns going astray. The Egyptians seemed so disorganized that, if they were given a breathing space, they could only get better and might yet turn into a fighting force. It was because the situation on the ground in Sinai was so beckoning that the Israeli generals could barely restrain themselves. They wanted to attack at once. Their great fear was that a leak might reveal just how promising the prospects were and so rob them of a unique chance to smash the Egyptians.[30] The CIA knew that Israel could not be held back.

In contrast to Israeli eagerness, Arab governments neither wanted war nor were ready for it. A third of the Egyptian army was in Yemen, while the force sent to Sinai had had, as the Israelis could see, virtually no training in attack or manoeuvre, and little in defence. The Syrian army was crippled by politics and purges. When in early June Prime Minister Zu'ayyin woke up to the possibility of war, General Suwaydani, the Chief of Staff, went to the front to pass the message on. 'How can we fight without officers?' a senior officer, Colonel Michel Khury, cried. 'Promote the officer cadets', Suwaydani retorted. As for Jordan, its soldiers were competent fighters but starved of modern weapons, especially aircraft. Egypt, Syria and Jordan, politically at loggerheads, had no joint operational plans, either for defence or offence. The eleventh-hour pacts concluded between them were a military liability. Anything further from the popular belief of an Arab 'ring of steel' tightening around Israel would be hard to imagine. But this was not a fact which Israel's leaders wished to share with the Arabs or the world at large or even their own people. On the contrary, it was a cunning ruse of war to convince opinion that the Jewish state was in danger of extinction and deserved sympathy in its unequal struggle.

It can be seen with hindsight that Israel's preparation of opinion was as brilliantly managed as the war itself. It amounted to one of the most extensive and remarkable exercises in psychological warfare ever attempted. So successful was this manipulation of the public that while the unwitting Arab masses clamoured for war, ordinary Israelis and Israel's friends abroad suffered quite unnecessary anxiety. Informed Israelis have long since conceded that their state had not been in any real danger since the Palestine War − or to be precise, since the rearming and consolidation of the Jewish state which took place between the first and second truces of 1948.[31]

Arab disarray

By destroying the Egyptian air force on the ground on the morning of 5 June 1967, Israel brought the Arab world to its knees. Photographic reconnaissance early that morning had shown the Egyptian air force to be totally unprepared. Aircraft at its major bases, lined up in pre-1939 parade style, were sitting targets. The strategy of a simultaneous blitz on all Egyptian airbases derived from a 1953 contingency plan codenamed 'Egg-basket'. Stripped of air cover, the Egyptian army in Sinai was routed, losing in four dreadful days over 10,000 killed, 13,000 captured, and many hundreds of tanks and guns smashed. As a fighting force, it ceased to exist. Unaware of the early disaster which had befallen its ally and acting on misleading orders from the Egyptian high command, Jordan opened up that morning with small arms and light artillery against Israeli positions. King Husayn's handful of Hawker Hunters tried to bomb Israeli airfields but, when refuelling at noon, they were wiped out on the ground by Israeli Mirages. Fifteen minutes later, after an ineffectual sortie over Israel, much of Asad's air force, along with two Iraqi air squadrons which had moved up to the Jordanian border, suffered the same fate. It was Asad's first devastating experience of modern war.

Once the air forces of Egypt and its allies had been dealt these death-blows, Israel went all out for the acquisition of territory: in the minds of some, to trade later for peace; in the minds of others, to secure impregnable frontiers; and for nationalists like Begin, so as to 'liberate' the whole of Eretz Israel. On 7 June Arab East Jerusalem was taken and the West Bank overrun. The Sinai passes were seized as well as Sharm al-Shaykh overlooking the Straits of Tiran. On 8 June Israeli aircraft and torpedo boats attacked and crippled an American electronic surveillance ship, USS *Liberty*, off the coast of Gaza, no doubt to keep Washington in the dark about the objectives of Israel's headlong race. That Israel was prepared to kill American sailors said much about the lengths to which it would go in its land-hunger. The territories were not acquired in a moment of absent-mindedness nor by the unforeseen fortunes of war. Early on 9 June, Israeli advance forces reached the Suez Canal although, with the road to Cairo now open, Egypt had already accepted an unconditional ceasefire.

For the first four days of war, Asad had remained virtually passive, contenting himself with sporadic shelling of Israeli border settlements as he had so often done in the past. One or two Syrian patrols ventured across the frontier, to which Israel responded with heavy bombardments. Syrian inertness may seem surprising in a country whose border conflict with Israel had been the detonator of the whole conflagration. Asad had defied Israel over the DMZs, had sent Palestinian guerrillas against it when more conventional means were lacking, had forced Nasser to throw down the gauntlet – and then more or less sat tight when war came. Syrian inaction was to cause much ill-feeling among its allies and to attract the charge that it had let them down.

The truth is that the scale and speed of the war caught all the Syrian leaders, Asad included, off-balance. They were mentally unprepared for Israel's all-out, highly mobile blitzkrieg. They had no clear sense of Israel's strength, will and designs, nor were they able to comprehend that the border tussle over the DMZs which had so absorbed them had been totally swallowed up in Israel's ambitious restructuring of the region. Even Nasser and Husayn, more seasoned players than Asad, had believed that the great powers would not allow Israel to redraw the map. For Asad there was another cause for consternation. His beloved air force had been wiped out in a morning and it took him time to recover from the shock. He was thereafter a crippled minister of defence, and to move troops without air cover would have been foolhardy. In any event, the Syrian army was not capable of mobile combat, having been trained only for positional defence in the Maginot-like fortifications of the Golan Heights.

Further confusion was caused by the Egyptian commander of the Eastern Front, General 'Abd al-Mun'im Riad, who had taken over his command in Amman on the signature of the Egyptian-Jordanian pact six days before the war. On the outbreak of hostilities, believing a fictional report from Marshal 'Amer that Egyptian forces were advancing into the Negev, he ordered Jordan's two armoured brigades to move south out of their well prepared positions in support of the supposed Egyptian offensive. Jordanian officers bitterly disputed the move which in fact facilitated Israel's capture of the West Bank. And to relieve the Jordanian troops he had moved south, Riad requested Syria to send a brigade into Jordan. Asad complied – but at his leisure. By the time the Syrian troops arrived on the evening of 8 June, the West Bank had been lost. A few days later, after verbal skirmishings with Riad, Asad called his brigade home. It will be recalled that Jordan had for months been plotting with Syrian renegades to overthrow the Ba'th regime and just three weeks before the war Syria had struck back with its car bomb at the border post of Ramtha. These were hardly circumstances in which Jadid, Asad and the others would hasten to risk their own safety to defend Jordan. Similarly, their long feud with Egypt did not predispose them to obey the orders of the unfortunate General Riad.

The attack on Syria

On the eve of war Syria had been the target of Israel's fiercest threats, but when war actually came, Israel seemed extraordinarily reluctant to move against it. Yitzhak Rabin, then Chief of Staff, records in his memoirs that on 8 June the Ministerial Committee on Defence decided *against* attacking Syria altogether.[32] Syria's sponsorship of Palestinian guerrillas, which Israel had vowed to punish, appeared suddenly to have been forgotten, lending support to the argument advanced here that the crisis-mongering on Syria's frontier was no more than a pretext to entrap Nasser, annex Arab Jerusalem and the West Bank, and otherwise radically reshape Israel's regional environment.

However, at dawn on 9 June, a few hours after Syria's request for a ceasefire, Defence Minister Dayan ordered an immediate attack. Earlier he had been a strong advocate of leaving Syria alone. As early as 1951, when skirmishing over the DMZs, he had acquired the conviction that to scale the Golan Heights and expel the Syrians would be a costly exercise. He may also have been worried that an Israeli move against Damascus might trigger a Soviet intervention:[33] the Syrian Head of State, Dr Atasi, and Foreign Minister Makhus had been in Moscow as recently as 30 May-1 June to solicit Soviet support. In fact, the visit was unsuccessful and Syria was promised nothing. It may be that, getting wind of this, Israeli fears of the Soviets faded. On 9 June, once the Northern Front had been reinforced with two brigade groups switched from Sinai, Dayan, acting on his sole authority without consulting Rabin or Prime Minister Eshkol, changed his mind about leaving Syria alone. His second thoughts seem to have been prompted by pleas from Israeli settlers in the border region and by pressure from David Elazar, whose Northern Command had so far been denied its share of glory. In any event, victory had its own impetus, and the temptation to add Syria's scalp to those of Egypt and Jordan must have been great.

A three-pronged Israeli force with close air support moved to assault the Golan plateau. With neither air cover nor air defence, Asad's infantry put up a stalwart resistance in hand-to-hand fighting. Israel lost 160 tanks against Syria's 86. Six hundred Syrian soldiers fought and died in place[34] under continuous bombing, napalming and strafing. At this stage Israel, whose own troops were battle-weary, was inclined to halt and consolidate its gains. But in the course of the night of 9–10 June Chief of Staff Suwaydani, advised by Ahmad al-Mir, commander of the front, that the Syrian defences were in danger of being outflanked and the army trapped, gave the order to fall back north of Qunaytra, the principal town of the Golan, and join in the defence of the capital some forty miles away. At 08.45 on 10 June, while this redeployment was taking place under bombardment but in reasonably good order, Damascus Radio broadcast a Defence Ministry announcement that Qunaytra had fallen. Whatever the source of this report, it was false, but it stood for over two hours until Asad ordered the broadcast of a correction. In the meantime the Syrian withdrawal turned into a rout as soldiers on the wrong side of the town ran to save their skins. Exploiting the mistake, Israel promptly resumed its advance and took Qunaytra. Ahmad al-Mir escaped on horseback to the Hawran when his armoured column came under fire, and runaway Syrian soldiers were later found herding goats in the mountains.

The road to Damascus lay open, but under American pressure the Israelis did not go down it. Moscow had made clear to Washington that it would not tolerate the destruction of a friendly regime.[35] Acting on the suggestion of President Tito of Yugoslavia at a Warsaw Pact meeting on 8 June, the Soviet Union also broke off relations with Israel as a means of bringing pressure on it to accept a ceasefire.[36] This may have saved Asad more troubles, but it is probable that by this time the Israelis had taken about as much territory as they could handle. A ceasefire went into effect on the afternoon of 10 June, which did not inhibit Israel two days later from seizing a strongpoint on Mount Hermon which the Syrians had abandoned, and which was to become a prime Israeli electronic listening post.

Was the false Syrian report about Qunaytra a deliberate mistake? By announcing its premature fall and thus advertising the threat to Damascus, the government may have been hoping to prompt the Security Council into enforcing an early ceasefire. But a more plausible explanation was probably the chaos, even panic, which then swamped the Syrian leaders. In this sorry muddle as well as in the handling of the campaign as a whole, Asad had to bear his share of responsibility – especially for the loss of the air force – but in the conduct of the war he had not been the sole or even the principal decision-maker. There was little joy in being a defence minister in wartime without full powers.

Israel sacked Qunaytra – once a city of 17,000 inhabitants (30 per cent of them Circassians). It also cleared the surrounding villages and, over the next six months, forcibly drove some 90,000 people, stripped of everything they owned, off the Golan to join in open fields and tented encampments some 30,000 others who had fled during the fighting. Only about 7,000, mainly Druzes, stayed on in their old homes, and only 400, again mainly Druzes, were allowed back. Israeli military settlements took root on the farms of the displaced Syrians.[37] Qunaytra was thereafter to be the badge of Syria's defeat, an emblem of hatred between Syria and Israel and a cross Asad had to bear.

10

The Fight to the Top

The June 1967 war was a week-long nightmare for Syria's Defence Minister. On 5 June Asad lost his air force, on the 10th the Golan, and on the 12th the strongpoint high on Mount Hermon from which Israel could then monitor every movement in the Damascus plain. The Syrian capital, now virtually under siege, was swarming with tens of thousands of refugees. Unable to sleep, he fainted with fatigue at the Defence Ministry, and when the immediate danger was over, went home and brooded over the catastrophe for three days, refusing to see anyone.

The stress of war took its toll on victor as well as vanquished. Israel's Chief of Staff, Yitzhak Rabin, collapsed on 23 May under the pressures of the 'waiting period' and on recovering saw Moshe Dayan promoted Defence Minister to reap the glory for the campaign Rabin himself had planned. In Cairo it was a darker story. Nasser came near to nervous and physical breakdown and suffered intense grief when his friend and army chief, Marshal 'Amer, committed suicide. Haggard, he told an aide, 'I see his face in every file I read and in every plate of food they put before me'.[1] In Amman Jordanian and Egyptian officers stormed and flung insults at each other as King Husayn bitterly contemplated his now much reduced kingdom.

In Syria too the post-mortem on the war provoked furious quarrels among the leaders. The party, the high command and the government were racked by mutual recriminations. The officers blamed the civilians for precipitating the conflict, while the civilians denounced the officers for incompetence. Several party members demanded Asad's immediate resignation from the Defence Ministry and an attempt was made to oust him from the Regional Command. It was defeated by only one vote, that of the regime's security chief, 'Abd al-Karim al-Jundi, whose own name had been put forward to succeed Asad but who, in a comradely gesture, supported his rival.

What put a temporary end to the quarrelling was the realization that, if ranks were not closed, the whole regime could be in danger, as the war had not only gravely discredited the Ba'th but had brought back into circulation some old contenders for power. On 5 June forty Syrian officers who had been exiled to Beirut resolved to return home to fight Israel. They informed the authorities of their intention but were arrested on arrival by a regime too nervous to accept such offers of help. In Mezze prison, General Sha'ir, who had led the old guard's abortive coup eight months earlier, banged on his cell door imploring to be sent to the front. But again, the regime thought him too dangerous to be put at liberty. A handful of former opponents were let out, however, among them Muhammad 'Umran, the first head of the Military Committee, and Amin al-Hafiz, the head of state overthrown in February 1966. They were released on 9 June, the day Israel stormed the Golan. It was characteristic of the unstable temper of the time that Hafiz was immediately approached by dissident officers and invited to lead a coup but sensibly declined: 'I didn't want history to say I helped Israel by creating chaos at home', he said later.[2] The veteran 'Aflaq loyalist Mansur al-Atrash, also freed at this time, sourly recalled, 'It was not agreeable to know that we owed our freedom to defeat'.[3]

The Ba'thist regime had never been popular, but now, in the wake of the defeat, it was execrated. Ill-wishers said that it had not sent the best units to the front because it was more concerned with its own survival than with that of the country. No one was prepared to give the soldiers credit for the brave if brief defence of the Golan. Syria's three doctors whose bellicose speeches had fuelled the crisis were seen to be children in the international arena, living in a make-believe world where slogans and taunts were substitutes for real power. To make matters worse, after the rout on the Golan the official Syrian media fatuously claimed that Israel had not achieved its war aims since it had failed to topple the regime – a consoling notion borrowed from a Soviet commentary of the period to the effect that the 'imperialists and Zionists' had been unable to bring down Syria's 'progressive government'. Public opinion was not impressed.

The importance of this moment of national ruin in Asad's career cannot be overestimated. Without a doubt, the defeat was the decisive turning point in his life, jolting him into political maturity and spurring the ambition to rule Syria free from the constraints of colleagues and rivals who he felt had led the country to disaster.

Before the war, Asad had not given an impression of driving ambition. Perhaps his greatest asset was his ability not to arouse suspicion. Although he had grown steadily in importance since the

Ba'th takeover of 1963, he had always been somewhat overshadowed by 'Umran, Hafiz and Jadid. He had not been at the front of the political stage, apparently content to be a solid member of the team without the aspiration to become number one. Projecting an air of sincerity, he did not inspire fear in the upper echelons of the party, nor was he thought of as deep or scheming. It is likely that Salah Jadid had no notion that every time he took a step up the ladder, Asad was only a rung behind. Indeed, Jadid was slow to see a threat in the robust, forthright, good-natured fellow Asad then seemed. But after the war, as the lessons of the defeat sank in, Asad's good nature gave way to something more steely, and it was from this time on that he set about in earnest building a personal power base in the armed services. In the manner of a tribal leader, he forged loyalty to himself by distributing favours and rendering services, and assiduously furthered the careers of friends like the tank officer Mustafa Tlas.

Resentment was the original fuel of Asad's resolve. He did not consider himself responsible for the catastrophe. The policies which had led to it had been the work of Jadid and of the government and the Regional Command which Jadid had packed with his appointees. Yet accusing fingers were pointed at Asad for the loss of the Golan, accusations which aroused in him an imperious spirit: if he were made to take the blame, he might as well henceforth take the decisions. But there were more substantial reasons for his resolve to become master of Syria: the attitudes and policies of Jadid's regime had lost all appeal for him.

First of all, there was the matter of the guerrillas. After the defeat the Jadid government continued to glorify them and affirm its commitment to a 'people's war', whereas for Asad the war had proved that the Palestinians could not be allowed to freewheel as they pleased: their raids had played into Israel's hands, giving it a pretext to threaten Syria and suck Egypt into the crisis. Then there was the question of the 'class struggle' which the Jadid regime was intent on waging at home and abroad. Internally the bourgeoisie was still seen as the enemy, while externally the government declared it would have no truck with 'reactionary' Arab regimes, refusing even to attend the Khartoum summit of August 1967, the Arab world's postwar stock-taking. The summit pledged aid to the battered economies of Egypt and Jordan to the tune of £135 million a year, but the absent Syria got nothing. In contrast to this exclusiveness, Asad wanted to close ranks at home and to seek greater military co-operation between Arab states, whatever their ideological differences.

Again, the Syrian government refused to accept Security Council

Resolution 242 of 22 November 1967 which proposed that Israel should trade territories seized in the war for peace. It denounced as a betrayal of Palestinian rights any compromise or peaceful settlement with Israel. Asad was no less resolute than others in denying Israel its conquests: in fact, the war convinced him that expansionism was in Israel's very nature and that an immense Arab effort would be required to contain it. But he had no patience with bluster which served to isolate Syria from much of the rest of the world.

Internal disputes

The disagreement between Asad and his colleagues which began in 1967 became acute the following year, and at the heart of it was a dispute over priorities. Asad's attention was fixed on the military contest with Israel, whereas for Jadid and the doctors the internal revolution still came first. In shorthand terms, Asad's 'nationalist' objectives were at odds with their 'socialist' ones. More than ever his view was directed outwards towards the lost province, theirs inwards to the further transformation of Syria – a difference of perspective which coloured attitudes on a whole range of issues. It was not only a matter of Syria's relations with the Palestinians and the position it should adopt towards neighbouring states and the great powers. It also affected domestic choices. How should the country's limited resources be spent? Should a truce be called in class warfare? What sort of party should the Ba'th be, and what should be its relations with the public and with other left-wing groups? In party conclaves the arguments grew in venom and at the Fourth Regional Congress of September 1968 became irreconcilable.

In traditional Ba'thist fashion there was a torrent of talk and much theorizing until the outcome was settled by Asad's greater armed strength. There may have been a hint of wisdom after the event in Asad's later account of his side of the argument, but the views he then put forward prefigured the policies he applied once in power, and must therefore be taken to reflect his genuine convictions at the time. The war and the great unpopularity the regime incurred caused him to part company with his more radical colleagues. In effect, he was moving to the right.

As he related:[4]

We differed about the party and how to build it. We debated at great length and our discussions could overflow into books. A crucial question was this: some of my colleagues believed the party should close in on itself to protect party militants from the infiltration of opportunists. Men who had suffered prison and torture in the party's cause believed they had won the right to rule. 'We are in power', they used to say, implying that people who had not taken part in the struggle should be kept out of the party.

My view was the very opposite. I did not think that prison and torture were absolutely essential in the formation of a good party man: the experience of government could also be a test of a man's qualities. Of course, opportunists were a danger but not one to be exaggerated. If we were to admit a thousand new members, two hundred among them might be undesirable, but the party would still have gained eight hundred good members. I believed that shutting the party in on itself would make it like stagnant water in a ditch, unable to cope with the flow of change. In fact a party closed in on itself would give free rein to opportunists in its midst. Party members would start to believe they were a class apart.

The dispute about whether the party should open its doors or remain a tight far-left coterie spilled over into the related questions of the Ba'th's dealings with rival political parties and with the public at large. Asad wanted a more liberal approach:

There was no quarrel between us about the need for the Ba'th to be the main source of organized power in the state. But we had not seized power on our own in 1963: there were other currents in the country which had much in common with us. We dealt with their leaders as individuals and even included some of them in the cabinet, but we didn't recognize them as organized political groups. I was for doing so. I believed we should form a front with them.

My colleagues objected that if we gave these groups a place, we would have to share with them what we had won. But I felt that even if they were to benefit, we who had led the revolution would benefit still more since our basic political aims would be advanced. A front would strengthen the revolution rather than enfeeble it. And it would have the great advantage of recognizing political facts in the country as they were.

Not only did Asad recommend opening up the party to new members and bringing in political allies, he also wanted to devise ways to include the people in the political system, at least at the local level. There were at the time no local government in the Syrian provinces and no institutions in the capital, save a Council of Ministers which exercised both legislative and executive authority under the direction of the Regional Command.

> It was hard to pretend that this was any sort of a democratic system, or that we were involving the people in our forward march. I used to argue that we should have an opening outwards, an *infitah*, although I came to dislike the term when Sadat used it later before going to Jerusalem. But I used to say at the time that we should open up and give the people institutions through which they could play their part and help to build a dynamic economy. Otherwise we would soon go hungry.

In foreign relations too, Asad argued for a more pragmatic approach.

> Before 1970 there was an almost total breach between us and the other Arabs. We used to say that the Cause was an Arab one yet we didn't give the Arabs a chance to join in. Some of my colleagues denounced other countries with great fanaticism. I strongly believed that we should encourage other Arabs to play their part and not be the ones to obstruct a joint Arab effort. Whatever the conflicts between regimes, the Arabs faced a common danger.

The issue of Syria's relations with one at least of its Arab neighbours became a burning one when on 17 July 1968 the Iraqi Ba'th party, underground since 1963, regained power in Baghdad. Asad's colleagues were not overjoyed: the Iraqi Ba'th supported 'Aflaq whom the Syrians had defeated and expelled in 1966. So the Syrian party newspaper *Al-Ba'th* reported the news briefly and frostily under the headline 'Radio Baghdad announces a military coup'.[5] And Baghdad soon became a haven for old guard Ba'thists and other opponents of Damascus, such as the former Syrian head of state, Amin al-Hafiz, who moved there from Beirut. But Asad, although hostile to 'Aflaq, recommended closer ties with the Iraqis with a view to putting together an 'Eastern Front' against Israel.

A further subject of disagreement was about how to deal with Moscow. As Asad later recalled:

> Our relationship with the Soviet Union was not satisfactory. It appeared that our government was in accord neither with the socialist countries nor with the non-socialist ones. We were in accord with no-one. This was not a practical way to confront our problems. When a country is exposed to danger, as we were, it must mobilize support wherever it can.

The Soviet leaders resented their lack of influence over Jadid's government and were at best lukewarm about the 'leftist' policies which had, after all, helped trigger the 1967 war. The Soviet media had spoken of Syrian 'hotheads'. Moreover, there was little sympathy in Soviet circles for Jadid's contention – which he had advanced on a visit to Moscow in February 1967 – that his regime should be considered to be practising 'scientific socialism' although it refused to co-operate with the Syrian Communist Party. Asad could see that Jadid's policies had failed to win Syria the backing it needed. After talks in Moscow with his Soviet opposite number, Marshal Andrei Grechko, in August 1967, he resolved to put relations with the Soviet Union on a businesslike basis, free from doctrinal or emotional ups and downs. Only Moscow could supply the arms for the new-style army he planned to build, but the Russians were not just arms merchants: for their aid to be effective, a framework of trust and consultation was needed. Arms transfers had to be set within the context of a sensible political relationship.[6]

Building up support

The growing acrimony between Asad and Jadid was soon the talk of the army and the party. Everyone had to choose to stand with one or the other, so that insiders began to speak of a 'duality of power' at the heart of Syrian affairs. Step by step Asad started evicting Jadid's men from positions of influence in the armed services, the most spectacular example being the ousting of the Chief of Staff, Ahmad al-Suwaydani, in February 1968 and his replacement by Asad's close friend Mustafa Tlas. Suwaydani's relations with Jadid had in fact been strained by the disastrous 1967 war, which perhaps made his removal easier to accomplish. Moreover, like other Sunnis from Hawran in southern Syria, Suwaydani was beginning to grumble at what he saw as undue 'Alawi influence in the army, reason enough to get rid of him. (He was suspected of involvement in an abortive coup in August 1968 but fled the country. In July 1969, when a plane on which he was travelling made a stopover in Damascus, he was arrested.)[7] His replacement by Tlas was crucial for Asad.

Mustafa Tlas had been Asad's firm friend since they met at the Homs Military Academy in 1951. Both had been schoolboy Ba'thists, both loved poetry, and both ended up as regular officers *faute de mieux*: Asad had wanted to be a doctor while Tlas dreamed of studying literature and philosophy at the Sorbonne. Debonair and quick-witted, Tlas was an amusing companion, and a dependable one, celebrated in the army for seeming unruffled whatever the crisis. He had been with Asad in Egypt during the union, and after the 1963 coup was co-opted on to the Military Committee. Then, in the wake of the Hama troubles of 1964, he presided over *ad hoc* tribunals set up to try political opponents, and in February 1966 moved his brigade in support of the assault on 'Aflaq. Now promoted deputy defence minister, Tlas helped Asad tighten his grip on the armed forces, bringing back 'good elements' – that is, men loyal to them – who had fallen out with the government, and slowly purging men loyal to Jadid, 'one by one, as one might take the leaves off an artichoke'.[8]

Another of Jadid's supporters to be axed was the unfortunate Ahmad al-Mir who had commanded the Golan front during the Six Day War. He was retired from the army after the débâcle but, no doubt because he had been a founding member of the Military Committee, was given a seat on the party's National Command. In October 1968 Asad was able to shunt him abroad to the Syrian embassy in Madrid, the traditional haven for political failures. But the most telling blow Asad struck at Jadid was the removal of Colonel 'Izzat Jadid, his relation and key supporter, from command of the crack 70th Armoured Brigade, the country's main strike force.

An anecdote from this period throws light on Asad's obsession with loyalty as he worked to bring back into the air force pilots and technicians whom he felt had been unfairly purged. General Fu'ad Kallas, whom Asad had appointed to command the Air College, recalled:[9]

> At a meeting someone raised the case of X. Should he not be brought back? Asad gave the questioner a hard look but said nothing. A little later the subject came up again and this time Asad said: 'I've heard something disagreeable about this officer. When he was on a course in England in 1954, his brother wrote asking for help for their sick mother. X took a £5 note out of his pocket, held it up and said he wouldn't part with it to save her life. Anyone who can't be loyal to his mother is not going to be loyal to the air force.'

Steadily Asad extended his grip on the army, but Jadid still dominated the party apparatus. At the Regional and National Party Congresses of September and October 1968, Asad was outvoted on most issues and his arguments rejected. He managed to secure the dismissal of two of the socialist doctors, Premier Zu'ayyin and Foreign Minister Makhus, but his own future on the party Command remained in the balance as military interference in party affairs was unpopular with the rank and file. As his breach with Jadid widened, Asad's high-handed strategy was to sever the army and its own internal party apparatus from the civilian leadership and apparatus headed by Jadid. He forbade army officers to have any contact with the civilian party and in turn denied civilians access to party branches in the army. He even banned the distribution of Regional Command circulars to army units, and although himself still a member, he stopped attending its meetings. Henceforth there were in effect two Ba'th party structures co-existing uneasily in Syria, the one military and the other civilian.

By the end of 1968 Asad had already outstripped Jadid in the accumulation of power. His manoeuvrings in the army – postings, transfers, sackings, re-recruitment – threw Jadid on the defensive. Having once led the Military Committee against 'Aflaq, he now was himself confronting an army challenger, and having devoted his time to civilian matters, it was too late to re-establish his supremacy over the army. 'Jadid's fatal mistake was to attempt to govern the army through the party', Dr Munif al-Razzaz, the civilian party leader who had himself been deposed by Jadid in 1966, wryly commented. 'It was a mistake with which we were familiar.'[10]

The overthrow of Jundi

Although by now weak in the armed forces, Jadid still controlled the security and intelligence services through 'Abd al-Karim al-Jundi who, as head of the party's Bureau of National Security from September 1967, greatly expanded the state's apparatus of repression. An army of petty informers was recruited, arbitrary arrests became frequent, and tales of torture, not hitherto common in Syria, contributed to an atmosphere of terror. Few dared to go about in the capital after dark for fear of being stopped by the security police and taken away. People were even reluctant to leave the country because security agencies were known to confiscate empty houses. Much of this nastiness was linked with the name of Jundi.

In 1968 he was a clever man of thirty-six but with something not quite normal in his make-up, a penchant for cruelty which suggested that he was more of a nihilist than a radical socialist. It was said that his wife, with whom he was on bad terms, was his only boss. Jundi treated jokes about himself as criminal offences. When he heard that a group of lawyers and other professional men had gossiped about him at a private gathering, he moved to arrest them, forcing several to flee on foot to Lebanon where they remained out of harm's way until his downfall.

In February 1969 the conflict between Asad and Jadid erupted into violent clashes, or rather, while the two rivals still chose to pitch their dispute in policy terms, their respective bully boys came to blows. On the level of gun and fist the contest was waged between Asad's combative younger brother, Rif'at, and Jadid's security chief Jundi.

Rif'at was a man of action who sometimes appeared impatient with his elder brother's careful and deliberate approach. After joining the Ba'th in 1952 at the age of fifteen, he had started his military service under the union government in 1959 but, on Syria's secession, had transferred to the Ministry of the Interior. During the troubled months of intra-party strife in 1965 Rif'at was appointed deputy commander of a special party security force which, it will be recalled, was first commanded by Muhammad 'Umran but which Rif'at inherited once 'Umran split with the Military Committee. This unit, which had played a role in the February 1966 coup against General Hafiz, now waged war on Jundi.

Hostilities broke out when Rif'at came to believe that Jadid was planning an attack on Asad's life. A car was seen prowling near Asad's house and its driver confessed under interrogation that he had been sent by Jundi to assassinate him. The evidence could not be checked, and the way it had been extracted tended to discredit it, but it was enough for Rif'at to urge his brother to act without delay. He argued that unless Jundi was disarmed, the Asad brothers were themselves at risk.

In the four days, 25–28 February 1969, the two brothers carried out something just short of a coup of their own: tanks were moved to key points in Damascus; the editors of *al-Thawra* and *al-Ba'th*, the government and party newspapers, who were loyal to Jadid, were ousted and replaced by Asad's men, and the same fate befell the staffs at the Damascus and Aleppo radio stations. In Latakia and Tartus, main centres of 'Alawi affairs, fierce scuffles took place as Asad's followers drove out the Jadidists from party and government offices. But the decisive event was Rif'at's squeeze on Jundi in Damascus.

Vehicles of Jundi's security service were in the habit of filling up with petrol in the Ministry of Defence compound – which gave Rif'at the idea of arresting each driver as he came in. In this way Jundi was stripped of his fleet of jeeps, but only when his own chauffeur was taken did he realize his time was up. He had been cornered by the Asads. In the night of 1–2 March, after a violent telephone altercation with 'Ali Dhadha, the head of Military Intelligence, he blew his brains out. No doubt he knew that, if he were arrested, he would be held responsible for many crimes and perhaps feared that he would suffer the fate of Salim Hatum, the comrade he had tortured before having him shot two years earlier. Jundi was an arrogant man and probably could not tolerate the prospect of facing interrogation, trial and judgment. As events closed in on him, he must have felt lonely and exceedingly vulnerable: few members of his own Isma'ili community, his ultimate safety net, remained in positions of power in the army or the party, and, without funds or friends or the will to make a life for himself outside Syria, he did not have the option of fleeing abroad. His wife killed herself a few weeks after his suicide. Jadid, flanked by Nur al-Din Atasi, the Head of State, and Prime Minister Zu'ayyin, led the funeral cortège in Jundi's home town of Salamiya. Although the Ministry of Defence sent a wreath, Asad did not attend. But it was reported on good authority that, on hearing of Jundi's violent end, he wept. Asad had engineered Jundi's downfall, yet he seemed to abhor violent confrontations, all the more so when the victims were his comrades.

The change in the balance of power which followed Jundi's death consecrated the young Rif'at as Asad's strong right arm in internal conflicts. A handsome, well-built man, Rif'at had perhaps more than his share of the Asad family's heritage of confidence and daring. Eager for power and the good life, he did not much mind how he got them. His ascent was now beginning.

Among Jadidists, Jundi's death caused great despondency as it was immediately recognized that a vital asset had been lost. A witness of these events recalled:[11]

> One night when Dr Zu'ayyin was visiting me, I received a telephone call with the news that Jundi had been shot or had shot himself. He had been taken to the Italian Hospital which is very close to my house. I went to have a look and found him already dead. When I told Zu'ayyin the news, he broke down and started crying. He let out a curious phrase, something like 'We are all orphaned now', by which he must have meant that with Jundi's death he and his group had lost a protector.

Asad had won an important round but over the next eighteen months he seemed extraordinarily hesitant to press his advantage. There could be no question of reconciliation with Jadid, yet he allowed Jadid's Regional Command to continue to function, although forcing it to give ground on policy issues. Class struggle was toned down, criticism of other Arab regimes was muted, some political prisoners were released, a more broadly-based government was formed, and the beginnings of an 'Eastern Front' were stitched together with Jordan and Iraq. Syria emerged from its isolation and started attending Arab summits. In early March 1969 envoys came to Damascus from President Nasser, from President Boumédienne of Algeria and even from the new Ba'thist regime in Iraq to offer to mediate in the Asad-Jadid struggle which was by now the talk of Arab governments.

At about this time Asad and Nur al-Din Atasi called on Nasser in Cairo. At the best of times the Egyptian leader had mixed feelings about Syria and Syrians. They had clamoured for union with Egypt and then seceded, dealing him a body-blow. They had sucked him into the catastrophic Six Day War from which he never recovered. But now, in the last months of his life, all venom spent, he wearily asked his visitors about other Syrian Ba'thists whom he had known. He learned that one had been killed, another languished in jail, a third was in exile. 'Ah, you Ba'thists', he exclaimed. 'You're so harsh with each other! When we in Egypt formed our Free Officers movement we agreed that if we ever fell out, each of us would be free to return to private life.' In this as in so much else, the Syrians were not ready to follow Egypt's example.

Of the five founder members of the Military Committee, 'Umran was in exile in Lebanon, Mir banished to Madrid and Jundi dead. The remaining two, Asad and Jadid, were locked in mortal combat for the lonely peak of power.

11

The Black September Fiasco

Even as Asad battled with Jadid for control of Syria in 1969–70, turbulent events in the region forced him to raise his sights from the narrow internal power struggle. While this was as yet undecided, the 'Black September' crisis in Jordan into which he was drawn provided the still inexperienced Syrian soldier with a brutal introduction to regional and international politics. At the very outset of his career as Syria's leader it brought him up against the formidable US-Israeli combination with which he was to do battle for much of his presidency.

In February 1969 Jundi's suicide had given Asad a decisive advantage over Jadid, but that was not the only or even the most important event of that month in determining the subsequent course of his life. That February Israel's Prime Minister, Levi Eshkol, died and was replaced by Golda Meir who, ably assisted by her ambassador in Washington Yitzhak Rabin, carried Israel into an increasingly intimate relationship with the United States from which Asad and the Arabs were to suffer greatly. Newly installed in the White House, Richard Nixon made his first foray into Middle East diplomacy which, although it fizzled out in the Rogers Plan of 1969–70, brought Dr Henry Kissinger on to the stage as the most forceful manipulator of the region's destinies since Europe carved up the former Ottoman provinces after the First World War. In February too Yasir 'Arafat, the 39-year-old leader of Fatah, took over the Palestine Liberation Organization, turning it from a talking shop into a fighting movement. In March the stricken Nasser began his defiant 'War of Attrition' against Israel which grew into a prolonged and bloody duel across the Suez Canal between the Israeli air force and Egypt's Soviet-supplied air defences in which more than a million Egyptians were driven from their homes. And in April the turbulence spread to Lebanon where an enfeebled government embarked on a long, destructive battle with

154

Palestinian guerrillas encamped in strength on its territory.

Asad saw most of these developments as immensely threatening. No more than Egypt had Syria yet recovered from the Six Day War. Asad was struggling to rebuild his army, to cope with the refugees, and to take stock of Israel's new dimension as, standing astride occupied Arab territories from Sinai to the Jordan, it grew ever stronger with unstinting American aid. As Asad saw it, two major dilemmas were inherent in the postwar situation. The first was posed by America's peace initiatives which appeared designed to draw Nasser, now humbled in war, and an all too willing King Husayn into separate settlements with Israel – settlements which offered little to the Palestinians and nothing to Syria, leaving it exposed to Israeli power and unable to recover its lost territory on the Golan. The second dilemma for Syria's defence minister was posed by the guerrilla organizations which, now flush with funds and swollen with recruits, were riding high in popular esteem on the Arab states' humiliation.

On both these difficult questions of peace and the guerrillas, Asad and Jadid were at odds. Jadid and his faction were out-and-out 'rejectionists', reflecting as they did the view widely held in the Arab world that any settlement with Israel would legalize the 'theft' of Palestine. Arab opinion was not ready for a compromise which it saw as surrender to Zionism. The Arab sense of outrage after the war was still sharp and the West's evident admiration for Israel's military prowess helped keep the wound open. In July 1970 a joint session of the Syrian Ba'th party's Regional and National Commands reaffirmed Syria's rejection of UN Resolution 242. Nasser and Husayn were taken to task for imagining that American brokerage could be fair in seeking what *al-Ba'th* described derisively as the 'peace of the tomb'.

Asad was no less critical than his colleagues of the Rogers Plan, named after Nixon's Secretary of State. As much as any man he wanted justice for the Palestinians. But he was not a rejectionist, nor was he in principle opposed to a settlement, only to a dishonourable and partial one – and this was to be a consistent theme of his life. He had considerable sympathy for President Nasser who, in spite of waging the punishing War of Attrition, was still viewed askance by some Arabs for his readiness to contemplate a negotiated peace. He recalled:[1]

> Whenever Nasser spoke about peace, my colleagues objected. It was not just the Rogers Plan or the Jarring mission [a UN peace initiative] – they disagreed with the underlying premise. They were against

anything he said about peace. Any remark he made about Resolution 242 counted against him.

Clearly Asad found such blanket rejectionism unreasonable.

Disagreement was sharper still over the guerrillas. Whereas Jadid saw them not just as future liberators of Palestine but as instruments of Arab revolution, Asad's enthusiasm for them had by now evaporated. He had grasped that the squabbling irregulars could not alter the military balance with Israel and were in fact a military liability, in that they gave Israel a pretext to strike when it chose. Meanwhile, in those Arab countries where the Palestinians had taken to arms their presence was destabilizing. Before 1967 the dispossessed refugees had waited for the Arab states to return Palestine to them, but now they would wait no longer, directing their new-found militancy as much against their Arab hosts as against Israel. Wholly dependent on the Arab states for money, arms and training, they yet expected to be allowed to pursue an independent strategy. In 1969–70 the Palestinians posed an especially acute problem for a defence minister such as Asad who, with the Israeli army camped just down the road from his capital, saw the Resistance less as a source of inspiration for a demoralized Arab public than as a security risk. The 'people's war' which the guerrillas hoped to wage seemed a delusion and their independent strategy an intolerable threat. He saw clearly that the contest with Israel was one between conventional armies in which irregulars were a dangerous nuisance, concluding that the Palestinians should refrain from interference in the internal affairs of the countries in which they lived and, even more crucially, should fall in behind Arab state strategies. These views were to bring him into conflict with Palestinian leaders, and especially with Yasir 'Arafat.

Very early on, then, when the Palestinians emerged as a challenge after the Six Day War, Asad recognized the difficulty of reconciling their militancy with the security of Arab states. So, while remaining an unshakeable supporter of the Palestine cause, he kept a tight grip on the several thousand commandos then living in Syria. For example, in a directive of May 1969 he laid down that only certain groups would be allowed into the country, that they could not carry arms in public, could not march or demonstrate without a permit, and could not set up training camps and shooting ranges except in specified areas. Above all, they could not raid Israeli-occupied territory from Syria without written approval from the Ministry of Defence.[2] There was another sense in which the guerrillas sharpened the conflict between Asad and Jadid. The Syrian Ba'th had set up its own Palestinian commando group, Sa'iqa, which as it grew to a force of some 5,000 Jadid came to use in the internal struggle as a counterweight to Asad's army support.

On a visit to Jordan in 1969 Asad saw at first hand the nature of the challenge the guerrillas posed to established Arab authority. To his surprise and distaste, he found the capital, Amman, plastered with slogans – such as 'All power to the Resistance' – while *fidayin* swaggered in the streets, often picking fights with soldiers of Husayn's bedouin army. They were said to have arrested Jordanian officers and made them walk barefoot. Asad had a high regard for the profession of arms and was confirmed in the belief that such disorderly forces could not be tolerated.[3] He commented later:[4]

> Never in my life have I been for anarchy nor will I ever be. Anarchy leads only to suffering and never reaps results. I would have wished the Palestinian resistance to remain pure and free from involvement in the internal affairs of Arab states. But while I opposed Palestinian anarchy in Jordan and in Lebanon, I also believed in the Palestinians' right to find a suitable base from which to conduct their struggle – whether from Syria, Jordan, Lebanon, Egypt, or any other place. That was my opinion from the very beginning and it remains so today.

It was not a dilemma which he was easily to resolve.

The Jordan crisis

Asad's ambivalence about the Palestinians was put harshly to the test during the Jordan crisis of 1970. A confrontation between the king and the guerrillas had been brewing for months. Some Palestinian factions, and notably George Habash's Popular Front for the Liberation of Palestine, wanted a showdown in the belief that they could topple Husayn. To precipitate a clash the PFLP hijacked four civilian airliners on 6 and 9 September, taking hundreds of hostages, including Americans and Israelis, and stampeding 'Arafat's Fatah into joining their insurrection. But Husayn refused to be intimidated. Forming a military government on the 15th, he went to war against the guerrillas and inflicted terrible damage on their refugee camps.

When fighting first broke out the Palestinians begged Asad for help and he rushed arms to them – including guns taken from the guard unit at the Syrian Defence Ministry. Then as the Jordanian army continued to pound the guerrillas a stream of further anguished appeals reached Asad in response to which he sent still more arms together with some volunteers. He also telephoned Hardan al-Takriti, Iraq's Defence Minister, who since the 1967 war had kept some 15,000 troops stationed in Jordan, to enlist his help in easing Husayn's pressure on the embattled Palestinians. When these moves proved of no avail and when the Palestinians' situation became desperate, Asad decided to intervene more forcefully in what was to become known as Jordan's 'Black September'.

The interpretation of these events and their impact on Asad's power struggle with Salah Jadid have been the subject of much controversy. It is the received wisdom that Jadid ordered the Syrian army into Jordan but that Asad refused to commit the air force to battle, so dooming the venture to failure. The resulting clash between the two men is said to have driven Asad to take power in Damascus. But there is much that is inaccurate about this account.

Before the Jordan crisis broke out Asad was already master of Syria in all but name: the officer corps was almost wholly in his hands, as were Rif'at's elite strike force and the Palestine Liberation Army brigades stationed in Syria. He had taken control of the national security services formerly run by Jundi as well as the People's Army, a civil defence force, Sa'iqa, the one armed force Jadid disposed of, had been neutralized: its offices were closed and tanks surrounded its camps. There could have been no armed intervention in Jordan of which Asad did not approve: in fact intervention was his policy and on this score he was not in dispute with Jadid.[5]

On 18 September Syrian armour crossed the frontier in support of the guerrillas, taking the town of Irbid in northern Jordan the following morning. Asad directed operations from his advance headquarters in the officers' club at Dar'a on the Syrian-Jordanian border. What were his objectives? From his own testimony and that of others intimately involved, his intention was not to help overthrow Husayn, as the guerrillas evidently hoped, but simply to protect the Palestinians from massacre,[6] and as a result his intervention was from the start both reluctant and circumscribed. He had some hope that with Syrian help the guerrillas could establish a safe haven in northern Jordan from which they could negotiate terms with the king. But the plan never came to fruition. On 22 September Husayn ordered Jordan's 40th Armoured Brigade, with air support, to engage the Syrian tanks. Large numbers were knocked out, and by that afternoon Syrian units had turned tail and were on their way home. Asad later admitted with some embarrassment:[7]

It was a difficult predicament. I was distressed to be fighting the

Jordanians whom we did not think of as the enemy. I didn't bring up our own much stronger air force because I wanted to prevent escalation. My feeling was that as long as we could achieve our goal of protecting the guerrillas without committing the air force, there was no need to do so.

The brief unhappy campaign was a striking illustration of the conflict between Asad's state interests and the interests of the Palestinian guerrillas. He sided with the Resistance, yet had no sympathy for its aim of marching on Amman. His half-hearted intervention drew abuse from the guerrillas who felt betrayed, as well as understandable hostility from Husayn which debarred co-operation between them for years to come.

But Asad, Husayn and the guerrillas were not the only actors in the drama. In Washington Syria's move into Jordan was perceived by President Nixon and his National Security Adviser Henry Kissinger in quite a different light from the tentative, limited operation Asad had in mind. Nixon and Kissinger were persuaded that Moscow was using its Syrian client and the *fidayin* revolutionaries to bring down Jordan's pro-Western government and so expand its own influence. 'If we failed to act', Kissinger wrote in his memoirs, 'the Middle East crisis would deepen as radicals and their Soviet sponsors seized the initiative.'[8] American suspicions of Soviet intentions had been aroused a year or so earlier by Brezhnev's supply of combat aircraft and military advisers to Egypt during its War of Attrition with Israel of 1969–70. Washington had seen this development as evidence of Soviet designs on the Nile, whereas in fact the Russians were merely trying to shore up Nasser against Israel's evident attempts to bring him down with its deep-penetration raids that year into the Egyptian heartlands. Having misread the situation in Egypt, Washington compounded its error by rearming Israel on the argument that this was the best way to check what was seen as the growing Soviet presence. And now that Moscow's hand was again discerned behind Syria's intervention in Jordan, Kissinger turned to Israel to contain what was perceived as a new Soviet threat.

Hard pressed by the guerrillas and unsure of Syrian intentions, King Husayn on 20 September called on his American friends for help. At this moment of grave anxiety, even of panic, he went further still: he let Washington know that if the United States could not itself provide the protection he needed, he was ready to accept an Israeli intervention against the Syrians.[9] Husayn was in effect recognizing that his survival depended on a local balance of power: if Syria pressed too hard on him, Israeli pressure from the opposite direction was needed to keep him on the throne. But in acquiescing in such an Israeli role in inter-Arab affairs, Husayn departed from the Arab consensus, taking a step which was to affect much of his subsequent career. It was not a move which endeared him to Asad in Damascus.

On 21 September, on the morrow of Husayn's cry for help, Henry Kissinger and Yitzhak Rabin, Israel's ambassador in Washington, agreed a plan for Israel to launch air and armoured strikes against Syrian forces the next day. The plan was then approved by Nixon and Husayn. And in preparation for the strikes Israel made much publicized military deployments in the direction of Jordan. Washington also put airborne troops on the alert and an American armada headed for the eastern Mediterranean. Emboldened by these preparations, Husayn's own armour and air force then engaged the Syrians on 22 September, as already described. Asad took the heavy hint. He had no intention of committing himself to unequal combat with Israel, let alone with the United States – and above all he was uncomfortable fighting Jordan. So on 22 September, before Israel attacked, he withdrew to his side of the border.

In Washington the Syrian retreat was greeted with jubilation and Israel was given full credit for what was considered a resounding success. A grateful Kissinger telephoned Rabin on 25 September with a fulsome message from the president to Golda Meir:[10]

> The President will never forget Israel's role in preventing the deterioration in Jordan and in blocking the attempt to overturn the regime there. He said that the United States is fortunate in having an ally like Israel in the Middle East. These events will be taken into account in all future developments.

Rabin was moved to write in his memoirs that he had 'never heard anything like it'. In fact Israel had been only too happy to play the part allocated to it: it was a constant of its policy to keep Husayn in power so that he might quell the Palestinians, and as a possible partner in eventual peace talks. For years thereafter the often canvassed but elusive 'Jordan option' spared Israel the need to face up to the Palestine problem.[11]

From the start, Nixon and Kissinger viewed the Jordan crisis of 1970 through the narrow binoculars of the East-West contest and gave little thought to the stresses and strains in the Arab camp in the wake of Israel's 1967 victory or to the problems posed for Arab regimes by Palestinian impatience. America's worldwide ambition to keep on top of the Russians was confused with Israel's regional ambition to keep on top of the Arabs. Israel was promoted to a privileged place on the US side of the superpower struggle for having, in Washington's perception, faced down not just the Syrians but the Russians as well. In the words of the historian William Quandt, Israel came to be regarded 'as the helpful junior partner in the successful management of a grave global test of superpower wills'.[12] Not only was Israel thereafter entrusted with keeping the peace in the Middle East on America's behalf, but the crisis served to launch the 'strategic relationship' between the two countries which was to have consequences extending far beyond the Middle East into Central America, Africa, and East-West relations. In these far-flung theatres, Israel was to lend a discreet hand in defence of US interests and be rewarded with US support for its own regional ambitions.

But was the Jordan crisis really a 'test of superpower wills' as it was portrayed, or was this itself a misjudgment? The designs attributed by Nixon and Kissinger to the Soviet Union are hard to substantiate. Moscow had seen its Arab friends go down to humiliating defeat in 1967, and since then had been wrestling with the costly and thankless task of keeping an enfeebled Nasser afloat. It was not looking for fresh Middle East adventures. Its leverage over the shaky and divided Syrian junta was negligible and, insofar as it had any, it used it to restrain Asad rather than encourage him to intervene in Jordan. Furthering the Soviet Union's Middle East ambitions was not among Asad's motives for action. Indeed, 'Black September' had little if anything to do with East-West rivalries. It was rather a result of the fraught triangular relationship between the Arab states, Israel and the dispossessed Palestinians. The guerrillas precipitated the crisis, with 'Arafat being dragged along by the more extreme elements in his movement in a bid to take over Jordan. But by challenging Husayn the Palestinians brought disaster down on their own heads. Moreover, having got themselves into trouble, they pleaded for Syrian help, but when Asad's assistance fell short of their expectations, they turned against Syria as well.

So was established a pattern which was to be repeated on several occasions, notably in Lebanon, in the following years. The Palestinians found it hard to grasp that their cause was not advanced by pursuing policies in collision with the interests of their host countries. Hard pressed by the guerrilla onslaught backed, or so it seemed to him, by Syrian armed strength, Husayn gave a hostage to fortune: he consented to Israeli protection, a move which breached any semblance of Arab solidarity but which also established Jordan's tacit dependence on

Israel, shackling Husayn's diplomacy for years to come and undermining his credibility with other Arab leaders.

And what of Asad's role in the imbroglio? His intervention was ill-considered, half-hearted, and unsuccessful. He accomplished nothing of benefit to himself, to Syria, or to the Palestinians whom he was trying to help. He did not prevent their slaughter by Husayn's troops. His feelings for the PLO had already cooled, but the Jordan crisis introduced a note of angry exasperation into his relations with 'Arafat which, under future trials, was to develop into outright hostility. Asad's relations with Husayn were also to be greatly complicated by the crisis. Before it Syria and Jordan had feuded vigorously, abusing each other and harbouring each other's enemies, but always within the bounds of Arab family quarrels. Now the Israeli outsider had intruded. And after Husayn's flirtation with Israel, Asad's instinct was alternately to punish him for his infidelity and to seek to woo him back to the Arab ranks.

At the end of the day, all that Asad accomplished by sending his army to protect the guerrillas was to give Israel an opportunity to draw Jordan under its wing and to promote itself in American eyes as an indispensable regional partner – hardly an outcome of which Asad could be proud. Asad, Husayn and the guerrilla leaders had all made false moves which were to muddy their future relations and weaken them to Israel's advantage. Such was the uncomfortable prelude to Asad's assumption of power.

The seizure of power

But the Jordan crisis had little to do with Asad's struggle with Jadid on the internal Syrian scene. As it happened, a veteran Algerian diplomat, Lakhdar Brahimi, on a visit to Syria at this time, was dining in Damascus with the Head of State, Dr Atasi. 'Don't discuss serious matters with me', Atasi said plaintively, 'Asad is in charge. Go and see him.'[13] Brahimi understood that by September 1970 Asad had in an informal way already taken over in Syria. But he cautiously waited several more weeks before advancing to the front of the stage.

A week after Asad withdrew his tanks from Jordan, President Nasser of Egypt, the father figure of Arab politics, died on 28 September 1970. It is very probable that this event helped resolve the long-running struggle for power in Damascus. As long as Nasser lived other Arab rulers, even those who opposed him, surrendered to him something of their responsibility, but once he was no longer there each had to fend for himself in a lonelier world. With the substance of power already in his hands, Asad may have felt that he could not further delay putting an end to the uneasy interregnum in Syria created by the contest between himself and Jadid. Asad attended Nasser's funeral in Cairo on 1 October and witnessed the vast outpouring of Egyptian grief. But on his return to Damascus he found a yawning vacuum of authority. Syria was without a government and the party was split beyond repair: he and Jadid and their respective supporters, no longer on speaking terms, confronted each other with undisguised venom.

Asad had the backing of the army but Jadid still dominated the party apparatus and, in a last-ditch attempt to regain control, called an emergency National Congress on 30 October: its first act was to order the Defence Minister to desist from any further army transfers so long as the congress remained in session – an instruction Asad peremptorily rejected. For a dozen days the policy debate raged on in true Ba'th fashion. Asad derided his radical critics, scathingly pointing out that, with Nasser dead, they could no longer hide behind him in making their empty gestures of defiance at Israel. 'It would have been better', he lectured, 'to refrain from gratuitous provocation which the enemy can exploit to trap us into a battle our army is in no state to fight, let alone win'[14] – remarks which aroused a storm of protest from the Jadidists. They charged him with accepting defeatist settlements and bowing to the imperialists. Inside the congress Jadid still commanded a majority among top party cadres, which he used to push through resolutions stripping Asad and his faithful aide, Mustafa Tlas, of their army commands and government jobs, and denouncing the 'duality of power' which their 'indiscipline' had created.[15] But Asad had taken the precaution of deploying troops around the conference hall, so the resolutions were no more than rhetoric, the vain gestures of men who knew they were already defeated.

As the congress drew to a close, Jadid's supporters, fearing that Asad would move to arrest them, became increasingly distraught. Dr Yusuf Zu'ayyin, the former premier, was afraid to sleep at home and sought shelter in the house of As'ad Kamil Elyas, then head of the prime minister's press department. Elyas later recalled:[16]

Coming home late from the office, I noticed a car parked outside my gate. There was a man in the back seat wearing a hat and dark glasses. As I approached he called out my name and I recognized Zu'ayyin's voice. To my surprise, he asked if he could come and live with us, so I gave him a room slightly apart from the rest of the house where he could be served alone. He used the bathroom at night to avoid disturbing the children.

When the party congress broke up in acrimonious confusion on 12 November 1970, Asad wasted no time: the arrest of his opponents followed the next day. Some were offered posts in Syrian embassies abroad, the traditional haven for losers, but Salah Jadid is said to have angrily refused. 'If I ever take power', he is believed to have told Asad defiantly, 'you will be dragged through the streets until you die.' Angered by such unsporting bitterness, Asad consigned Jadid to the grim fortress of Mezze prison, where, at the time of writing eighteen years later, he still languished. No doubt keeping Jadid locked up for so long reflected Asad's enduring fear that if freed he and his numerous relations would seek revenge. Dr Ibrahim Makhus, Jadid's Foreign Minister, escaped to Algeria where in due course he found employment as a surgeon in the Mustafa Basha hospital. Zu'ayyin fled to his home town of Albukamal on the Euphrates, but was arrested a few months later and spent a decade in jail before being released on grounds of ill health in 1981, when he went to live in Hungary where his brother had settled. Like Jadid himself, Dr Nur al-Din Atasi, the former head of state, remained incarcerated in Mezze.

Most of Asad's closest associates lent a hand in the seizure of power. His brother Rif'at took charge of security in the capital. Mustafa Tlas and another friend, Colonel Naji Jamil, chief of air operations, made sure that there was no resistance from within the armed forces. Colonel Muhammad al-Khuly, chief of air force intelligence, was given the task of rounding up Jadid's men in the party, the army and in government ministries. Asad gave Khuly eight hours to complete the job but Khuly did it in two. 'Did you shed any blood?' Asad asked him. 'Not a drop. We trapped them like rabbits in their beds.' The manhunt spread to all the major cities. It was a bloodless coup − not a coup at all, only a 'corrective movement', Asad was to say − which barely ruffled the surface calm of the capital: shops continued to trade; road and telephone links with Lebanon remained open; there were no tanks on the streets. But the official dailies did not appear and the radio and TV maintained a discreet silence on these turbulent happenings, and for three long days the world, sensing that something was up in Damascus, waited and speculated on the outcome. In his thorough, unhurried way Asad tied up loose ends, took soundings at all levels of the party, and, anxious to respect the forms of party legality, put together a new Provisional Regional Command. These were busy days: standing on the top rung of the ladder in such a country and in such a situation, Asad had to see to everything himself.

On 16 November, just when he had put the finishing touches to a communiqué ushering in the new era, word reached Asad that the Libyan leader Mu'ammar al-Qadhafi had landed unannounced at Damascus airport and was waiting in the VIP lounge for someone of suitable rank to receive him. Rumours of the Damascus power struggle had been circulating in the Arab world for months and Qadhafi, who had a keen nose for a political drama, had dropped in to see for himself what was going on. Asad went out to meet him at the airport. 'It's a good thing you didn't arrive half an hour earlier', he joked.[17] News of his accession to power was made public that evening. Hot on Qadhafi's heels came the Iraqi Foreign Minister, 'Abd al-Karim Shaykhli, with congratulations from Iraq's Ba'thist regime. The Iraqis, who detested Jadid, had been encouraging Asad to take over, although Syrian exiles in Baghdad, such as Michel 'Aflaq and Amin al-Hafiz, would have preferred to see all members of the hated Military Committee consigned to oblivion.[18]

A day or two earlier, Asad's wife had a dream. He had come home late after a stormy session at the party congress and had told Aniseh that the situation was critical. She urged him to get some sleep. On waking she told him that she had dreamt she was in the street in the middle of a large crowd of people all looking in the same direction. Following their gaze she saw in the distance a square object which, as she came closer, turned out to be a box with a peep-hole in one side of it.

She put her eye to the hole: there was the Aqsa Mosque in Jerusalem, one of Islam's holiest shrines. She picked up the box, turned round and, finding her husband standing behind her, handed it to him. 'It means', she told Asad that morning, 'that you will triumph over your enemies and become the strongest of all the Arab leaders.'

PART TWO

The Leader

12

Asad's State

Asad's rule in Syria began with an immediate and considerable advantage: the regime he displaced was so detested that any alternative came as a relief. As it was an open secret that he was more liberal than Salah Jadid, his victory ushered in a political honeymoon. People were longing to breathe more freely.

From the beginning Asad projected a different level of seriousness in state-building from anyone who had gone before. Undoubtedly he was influenced by the model of Nasser, the most prestigious Arab ruler of his generation whose regime he had observed at first hand, and from Egypt he borrowed a sense of the dignity and the panoply of government in contrast to the somewhat makeshift Syrian tradition of administration struggling to escape from bad Ottoman habits. Syrian Ba'thist rule as Asad developed it was a hybrid animal: from Jadid he inherited Soviet-style *étatisme* and a commitment to promote unfavoured classes. But anxious to throw off the unpopularity the radicals had earned, he dropped class warfare and set about broadening the base of his support by wooing the disaffected social classes with economic and political liberalization. His ambition was, above all, to establish his rule on a firm footing.

Asad was not an impulsive man. As he demonstrated in the months of manoeuvring preceding his capture of power, his habit was to weigh his moves carefully, to study the ground, to brood over possible consequences, before venturing forward. And as with his takeover, so now in his state-building he showed a surprising measure of forethought. The 1963 coup had been mounted with little or no anticipation of the problems of government, and Asad had in the subsequent years pondered the lessons of this unpreparedness. Now he came to power with detailed blueprints of how he intended to proceed.

His keynote in 1970 was the need for reconciliation and national unity after the divisive years, and in those early days he was on his feet from morning till night receiving delegations from all over the country who came to offer their congratulations to the *Fariq*, the General who had delivered them from their tribulations. To dispel the old view of Syria's rulers as a harsh, anonymous and inward-looking caucus, he set off on tours of the provinces, showing himself to the people and bringing back to Damascus sackfuls of petitions and complaints which it took his hard-pressed staff weeks to sort through. Whole villages turned out to greet him, in contrast with the sullen indifference of the past when coups and counter-coups in the capital were often met with resignation. This time there was a real sense of a fresh start.

One of his more striking encounters was in Suwayda, capital of the Jabal al-Duruz, where he paid tribute to Sultan Pasha al-Atrash, the old nationalist warrior then in his late eighties who had led the revolt against the French in the 1920s. According to Druze tradition, Sultan Pasha was marked out for glory from his birth, as it occurred (in 1885) not just on a Friday but on the 27th day of Ramadan, the Night of Destiny – two portents of exceptional promise. An angel had appeared to his mother in a dream saying, 'Name your son Sultan and he will be a Sultan'. The Druze say that in seventy years of warfare, which began when the Turks hanged his father, Sultan Pasha was never wounded or captured, nor was his horse ever killed under him, clear evidence of divine protection.[1] But in spite of this glorious past Sultan Pasha had in the postwar years been on cool and sometimes hostile terms with Damascus. So when Asad came to honour this early nationalist and claimed continuity with his generation, he moved out from the narrow exclusiveness which had come to mark the Ba'th under Jadid. On Sultan Pasha's death in 1982 at the age of ninety-seven, about a million people attended his funeral. Asad came again to pay his respects and issued a personal message of mourning for the 'Commander in Chief of the Great Arab Revolution'.

Another overture in a somewhat different direction took the form of a directive to the board of the Writers' Union instructing it to rehabilitate members of the pre-revolutionary intelligentsia who, when the Ba'th first came to power in 1963, had been generally ill-considered in the party's campaign to destroy the power of the old ruling class. Now Asad turned the page. The novelist Colette Khury, granddaughter of the Protestant statesman Faris Bey al-Khury, recalled that in a message to these forgiven writers, Asad declared, 'I am determined that you shall no longer feel strangers in your own country'.[2]

By 1971, an index of the more liberal climate was the staging of a play in Damascus by Sa'dallah Wannus, an 'Alawi playwright, debunking the official version of the Six Day War. Called 'An

Entertainment for the Anniversary of 5 June', it attempted to tell the disagreeable truth about the war in a form which was nevertheless palatable. In the play government functionaries made windy victory speeches at an official commemoration of the war, but their rhetoric was interrupted by shouts of protest from the public on the lines of 'It wasn't like that!', 'It was my village the Israelis took', 'I remember what happened!' These interventions came from actors seated offstage and were part of the play, but this was not evident to some members of the audience who tried to join in and had to be restrained. The play was a great success.[3]

Ordinary people soon had reasons to be thankful for Asad's accession. The price of basic foods was cut by 15 per cent. The hated security services were purged and curbed, while responsibility for dealing with a number of crimes was transferred from the army to the police. Detention orders and many confiscations of property were revoked. Restrictions on travel and trade with Lebanon were lifted, restoring to Syrians their natural space. Assurances were given to the private sector, and exiles and emigrants were encouraged to bring home their money and their skills. When the Ba'th first seized power Asad had been in the forefront of the drive to break the city's hold over the countryside. But by 1970, and with ambitious economic and military plans in mind, he knew he needed allies in the urban middle class, so, breaking with his political past, he tried to win over the shopkeepers, businessmen and artisans of the towns as well as the many citizens who had fled Syria since 1963, mainly Sunnis from the former leading families.

Asad also set about courting the various layers of former Ba'thists who over the years had left the party or been pushed out. Relatively few of his party opponents were locked up in 1970 at the time of what he termed his 'Corrective Movement' – mainly Salah Jadid himself and his immediate supporters – while the less important were soon freed. Using the familiar tactics of carrot and stick, Asad urged the Jadidists to co-operate but warned them that there would be no second chance if they misbehaved. Short of party cadres, he also tried to lure back men of 'Aflaq's persuasion, differing in this from his former Military Committee colleagues who had had nothing but rancour for 'Aflaq's generation. 'Let us rebuild together', Asad appealed to the old members, 'and if we fail our heads will all be on the block together.' Some two thousand accepted his invitation. Among them were such party ideologues as Georges Saddiqni, who was to be Minister of Information during the October War, and Dr Shakir al-Fahham, a scholarly Ba'thist who had been secretary of the party's historic founding congress in 1947 and had risen to become Rector of Damascus University. Now he was entrusted with, first, the Ministry of Higher Education, and then the Ministry of Education for the whole decade of the 1970s – positions to which Asad attributed great importance.

In these efforts of national and party reconciliation Asad displayed moderation and a skill for getting people of different characters and backgrounds to work together. It was noticed that he did not pass on bad opinions of men but kept them to himself. As a conciliator, he always strove to balance things out, whether discordant personalities or discordant ideas. In the Arab tradition of leadership, men in power tended to gather around them devoted followers, their *zilm*, and this was indeed how Asad had built up his own military power base. But now, in what seemed like a conscious departure from this somewhat primitive system, he set about trying to form state cadres and state institutions.

Restoring national unity

From the start of Asad's presidency two ideas about how to govern Syria were held in somewhat uneasy balance in his mind: the first was that he would allow no challenge to his rule, the second that wide popular backing for his policies was nevertheless necessary. He wanted to restore national unity but, his temperament being authoritarian rather than democratic, without taking undue risks. He seems to have had no ambition to create a pluralist society or to return to the chaotic democracy of 1955–8 which had brought Syria to the brink of disintegration. Rather he wished to mobilize Syrian energies for the battles ahead, seeking a national consensus cemented by his leadership. On the domestic front his key idea was that, unless Syria were itself united, there could be no hope of joint Arab action and therefore no hope of recovering the territories lost to Israel.[4]

When pictures of Asad appeared on the hoardings they were welcomed by the common people who had distrusted the faceless collegiality of the previous regime. Yet, for an 'Alawi to rule Syria, and to do so openly in defiance of the centuries-old tradition that power belonged in Sunni hands, demanded political courage. Salah Jadid had not been so bold. He had chosen the Sunni Atasi to front for him, in tacit admission that membership of a heterodox sect on the outer limits of Shi'ism was a political handicap. On overthrowing Jadid, Asad in turn seemed to hesitate on the threshold of the top job, contenting himself at first with the title of prime minister and putting forward as head of state a little known Sunni schoolteacher of thirty-nine, Ahmad al-Khatib. But his early doubts were not in keeping with his character and convictions, as from boyhood he had tried to free himself from sectarian complexes. On 22 February 1971, he assumed 'presidential powers' and on 12 March a plebiscite confirmed him as president for a seven-year term. His intention from the start was to rule not just without a front man but without serious curbs of any sort; and in this too he broke with the model of Salah Jadid's 'collective' regime, which had abolished the title of 'president' and replaced it with that of 'head of state' stripped of any real power. Asad restored the presidential title and assumed it, thereby making clear that he would be boss in fact as well as name and that there would be nothing collective about his rule.

When Syria's new constitution was published on 31 January 1973, protests erupted, in Hama especially, because this document of 156 articles omitted to stipulate that the president of the republic should be a Muslim. It was a matter which exercised Syrian opinion because, since the 1930s, Syrian constitutions had laid down that the religion of the head of state had to be Islam. Soft-pedalling the Ba'th's traditional secularism in order to avoid confrontation, Asad instructed his newly formed People's Assembly to add the desired clause. But he seized the chance to give vent to his liberal view of Islam which, he said, should be 'far removed from the detestable face of fanaticism . . . Islam is a religion of love, of progress and social justice, of equality for all, a religion which protects both the small and the great, the weak and the strong, a religion in tune with the spirit of the age.'[5]

The question was then posed whether as an 'Alawi he could legitimately be called a Muslim. To resolve this dilemma, Asad appealed to an influential Shi'i cleric, the Imam Musa al-Sadr, head of the Higher Shi'i Council in Lebanon, who issued a *fatwa* or religious ruling that the 'Alawis were indeed a community of Shi'i Islam. A religious barrier to Asad's presidency was thus removed. When the still unsatisfied opposition then rioted to demand that Islam be declared the state religion (something which had not featured in the constitutions of 1930, 1953 or 1964), Asad stood firm and secured massive endorsement for his constitution in a referendum on 12 March 1973.

The institutional basis

While retaining the essentials of power in his own hands, Asad was anxious to give his state formal institutions, if of a somewhat ceremonial nature. 'I have always been a man of institutions', he liked to say,[6] and in explaining what he meant he often evoked his early days as a student politician in Latakia when he rose to be chairman of his school's students' committee and then chairman of the nation-wide Union of Syrian Students. 'I did not impose myself on those committees. The students elected me, and I earned their respect because I worked within their institutions.' Whatever element of self-justification, even defensiveness, this recollection suggests, there was in Asad's mind an unbroken link between the student leader of the late 1940s and the state builder of the 1970s.

The bedrock institution of Asad's state was, of course, the party. As secretary-general of the Ba'th, his control over the party was unchallenged, but this did not mean that the party itself had no influence. In fact its power stemmed from Asad's respect for it: he understood that to weaken the party was to weaken his own rule. A stickler for the forms of legitimacy, one of his first acts on overthrowing Jadid had been to secure the appointment of a fourteen-man Provisional Regional Command. At the apex of power, the Regional Command, soon expanded to twenty-one members, became under Asad's chairmanship the principal forum where the country's internal and external policies were debated and decided – even if Asad invariably had the last word. It was the only group of men with whom throughout his presidency he was to meet regularly.

In 1970 one of the first acts of the Provisional Regional Command was to nominate 173 members of a People's Assembly drawn from a wide range of political tendencies,[7] which set about drafting a permanent constitution. (Two years later the Assembly was elected by universal suffrage.) By mid-April 1971, party elections were held throughout Syria to select delegates to a Fifth Regional Congress (8–14 May) and an Eleventh National Congress (23–31 August) – which in turn elected new Regional and National Commands.

Party congresses were to play an important role in Asad's state. Meeting every four years or so, these get-togethers assembled several hundred delegates representing the divisions, sections and branches of the party's vertical command structure throughout the country. Closed to the public, they were occasions for the presentation and lively discussion of reports and also gave a chance for rising Young Turks to challenge their elders in a robust atmosphere of 'party democracy'. The congresses laid down policy guidelines and established a sort of national pecking order by electing from among their number a Central Committee made up of party elites – provincial governors, party secretaries at governorate level, generals in the armed forces and security agencies, ministers, members of the People's Assembly, leading academics, representatives of women's organizations – in fact Syria's top people.

All the balloting and debating revitalized the party but also consolidated Asad's hold over it. No longer 'Aflaq's opposition party of high-minded idealists, it became a ruling party, providing the backbone of the country's establishment, in fact a ladder of advancement for a new breed of careerists. Swollen with new recruits as well as seasoned cadres, the party took shape as an instrument of government, soon extending its tentacles to every corner of the country.

Having won back some old party members, Asad set about destroying any remaining support for Michel 'Aflaq or for the former head of state, Amin al-Hafiz, both of whom had found refuge in Baghdad after the Ba'th's recapture of power there in 1968. This he did by staging a treason trial in 1971 of the party founder and a hard core of about a hundred of his followers, most of them *in absentia*, on charges that they had conspired to overthrow the Syrian government in 1970 (before Asad's takeover) with financial and military help from Iraq. 'Aflaq, Hafiz and three others were sentenced to death and ninety-nine others to terms of imprisonment. Although Asad remitted the death sentences a few months later and released most of the defendants who had been caught in Syria, the trial was the clearest possible warning that he would brook no interference from Iraq and would tolerate no loyalty to 'Aflaq within the Syrian party.

At the same time as Asad revitalized the party congresses and Commands, he expanded and gave more authority to the party-controlled Popular Organizations created by Jadid's regime in order to mobilize support among the main social categories of the Ba'thist state – workers, peasants, students, women, youth and so forth. These grassroots mass movements were made into the building blocks of Asad's system, and the men who ran them were given considerable powers.[8]

Yet another development on which Asad set great store – and which had been a subject of dispute between him and Jadid – was the formation of a National Progressive Front in which political groupings other than the Ba'th could also make a showing. The Front was inaugurated on 7 March 1972 after several months of haggling over the terms of its charter and the respective powers of the members. Besides the Ba'th, which necessarily dominated the Front, its other members were the Communist Party, the Arab Socialist Union (a Nasserist relic of UAR days), the Arab Socialist Movement (the rump of Akram al-Hawrani's party), and the Organization of Socialist Unionists (ex-Ba'thist Nasserists). But these four parties were not allowed to canvass for supporters in the army or the student body, which were reserved exclusively for the Ba'th. The Front was something more than theatre, however: it reflected the divided loyalties in the radical camp caused by the upheavals of earlier years. The base of Asad's regime was correspondingly broadened. Several leaders of the Front were given seats in the cabinet. (A paradoxical consequence of the Front's formation was to bring about a split in the Communist Party and the Nasserist ASU, to the Ba'th's advantage. So at the end of the day, rather than introducing a measure of plurality, the Front served only to confirm the Ba'th's dominance.)

Probably more effective than the People's Assembly or the National Progressive Front in giving the population a say was the system of local government which Asad put in place, like so much else, in the first year of his presidency. The process was started by elections to local councils in each of Syria's fourteen governorates on 3 March 1972. Candidates for seats on these councils were not limited to Ba'thists but included members of other parties in the Front as well as independents who came to represent the conservative opposition to the regime. By statute, 51 per cent of the council members had to be peasants or workers, and the balance merchants, members of the professions or intellectuals. At the March elections independents won a majority in both Damascus and Homs.

The councils' role was to assist the governor in the performance of his executive duties. In the main cities of Damascus and Aleppo, the council was about 100-strong, and from this number was chosen a ten-man executive board, who shared among themselves the different areas of administration such as education, housing, health, transport and so forth. Whereas in each of the governorates the councils assembled every three months, the executive boards met daily with the governors. At the local level these men had real power. Before this system of local government was introduced, Syria was extravagantly centralized: the smallest matter from the most distant province tended to land on the prime minister's desk. Asad strengthened central planning and made it more sophisticated, but to an extent he decentralized implementation. Councils were even given the power to raise some local taxes in order to finance projects outside the Five-Year Plans.

These new structures of local government were matched by a parallel party structure. In each governorate a Ba'th party secretary kept an eye on the governor, while members of the local party command supervised their opposite numbers on the governor's executive board. In day-to-day affairs, therefore, the party served as a watchdog overseeing the work of the elected representatives.

A traveller in the Syrian provinces would have discovered three men of importance in each provincial capital: first in terms of protocol was the party secretary who, at the apex of the local party organization, was the instrument of the Regional Command and hence of Asad, its secretary-general; second came the governor who, like a French *préfet*, was the representative of the central government and hence of the president; and third was the head of political security, as often as not an 'Alawi colonel, whose role was to uncover and deal with any seditious activity and whose chain of command also led ultimately to Asad. For the system to work smoothly these three men had to get on together, but their relative importance differed from place to place. In a border region, for example, where security problems might loom large, the security chief would take precedence, but in the fast-growing Euphrates development area the governor's weight would be greater. Inevitably, the personalities of the men involved also determined the power balance between them.

Throughout Syrian society something like a two-tier system was installed: at the base was the security bedrock of the regime, an infrastructure of control in which 'Alawis were often but not exclusively to be found. Although Asad was not an 'Alawi sectarian, as the choice of his closest associates made clear – his prime minister, defence minister, foreign minister, private secretary, speech writer, personal bodyguard were all non-'Alawis – he still depended on his own community for security of tenure and ultimate survival. On this foundation a second tier was erected of administration, of economic activity, of semi-representative institutions, of public office and private gain which could afford to be more diverse and more open to all the talents.

The power base

In less than three years Asad summoned Syrians no fewer than five times to the ballot box: to confirm him as president, to elect representatives to the People's Assembly, to approve the constitution, to elect the governorate councils, and in foreign affairs to pronounce on Syria's proposed, but never realized, federation with Egypt and Libya. These ballots, each preceded by strenuous attempts to explain the issues and engage popular support, and the institutions which went with them, were a considerable improvement on the arbitrary and unstructured state of affairs which Asad had inherited. But there was an unresolved contradiction between the forms of participation which he so sedulously cultivated and the reality of his own ultimate control. To say he was an autocrat *malgré lui* is to do him more than justice because he had a powerful sense of knowing best. Yet he seemed also to have a hunger for democratic structures and gave a great deal of care to his new-born institutions. Perhaps what came to tilt the balance towards autocracy was the dangerous times he lived in and the nature of Arab politics, essentially brutal joustings between individual leaders each enjoying something like absolute power in his own country. On the specific matter of political repression things were plainly better under Asad, at the start at least, although even then the regime never gave up its prerogative to hit hard, unhampered by the courts, whenever it thought it necessary.

There was an enormous accumulation of power at the centre. Yet Asad's rule was not based on force alone, nor would it have survived had it been so. Most thinking Syrians accepted that he had come to heal the wounds in their society caused by the policies of his predecessors. The factor of public approval was not negligible. Arab regimes such as his, so often derided as oriental despotisms, in fact required a measure of popular consent, and the importance of public opinion could be gauged by the strenuous efforts made to mobilize it, by the repeated exercises in public self-justification, and by the strident media campaigns which rival Arab states waged against each other. Both the leaders and the led sensed that once popular consent was withdrawn, the substance went out of a regime.

In governing Syria Asad, at the start, consulted at enormous length; he listened, he went into detail, he turned problems inside out with laborious thoroughness, but in the end he alone decided. In spite of the new institutions his rule was personal. For all its innovations and improvements, the state Asad forged was imposed on society, not derived from it.[9]

What did his power rest on? In spite of the plebiscite and the popular welcome he had received it could not be said to rest on the will of the people: in no significant sense was he voted into office. His was a government which grew out of seven years of bloody struggle, and its foundations were and would remain the army, the security services and the party and government machines. But these largely closed worlds were not monolithic. Inside them ambitious men jockeyed for influence and intrigued against each other as in any political system, although all looked to the president to arbitrate between them. It was here, away from public view, that the cut and thrust of politics in Asad's Syria took place.

Asad did not wholly stifle political activity but confined it to in-groups such as the higher echelons of the party, the army commanders, and the security chiefs, all ultimately dependent on himself. Those outside these privileged circles soon learned they could go about their business without undue fear or constraint so long as they accepted that politics was not their domain. In such circumstances the only recourse of his opponents was silence or, in the case of last-ditch enemies like the Muslim Brothers, riot, revolt and assassination.

The team

In 1970 Asad began a long innings. His first day in office saw the final eclipse of the military officer and the emergence of the stubborn yet prudent ruler who, unwilling or unable to delegate, drove himself thereafter for fourteen hours a day. He was forty, married to a self-effacing wife, and surrounded by a young family of five, a daughter and four sons – of whom from now on he saw very little. There were to be no more family holidays, no weekends together, scarcely any family meals at which he presided. By nature Asad was a worker, and now, at the centre of his system and with dangers threatening from enemies on all sides, meticulous control of every detail became an obsession, unending desk-work became his fate. Interviewed many years later, his eldest son, Basil, could hardly remember an occasion in his youth when his father at home was not reading official papers.[10]

In his first year Asad put his team together, assembling the men who in many cases were to serve him for fifteen years and more. Just as he was consistent in his political principles, so he seemed extraordinarily reluctant to change the faces around him: it was in Asad's temperament to put a high price on loyalty. His personal staff at the presidency, even the clerks and coffee makers, remained unchanged year after year and repaid his trust with devotion. For the general public and for foreigners Asad might have seemed to lack charisma, but in those who worked closely with him he appeared to inspire deep affection and respect. Part of this was perhaps due to his man-management, his relaxed warmth with his staff and his personal knowledge of their situations. On one occasion the head of Syrian television inadvertently broadcast a programme about Faysal I (the Hashimite monarch who was briefly king of Syria in 1920) at a time when Asad was quarrelling with the Hashimite King Husayn of Jordan. Asad's secretary telephoned for an explanation of this political gaffe. The television chief had none: his father had suffered a stroke and he had been too busy to vet the programme before transmission.

Frostily he was told to go home and await sentence. But he had scarcely arrived there when he received another call from the secretary. There was no word of reproach. 'The president sends you his greetings. He wants to know where you wish your father to be sent for treatment.'[11]

The secretary in question was none other than Muhammad Dib Da'bul, universally known as Abu Salim, who, as the guardian of Asad's door and the keeper of his appointments book, was a central figure of the new regime. A Sunni from the small town of Dayr 'Atiya near Aleppo, Da'bul like his master seemed to spend most hours of the day and night at his desk, and even slept by the scrambler telephone in his office when Asad was abroad. In a system in which the president was all, the man who controlled access to him became himself very powerful, indeed a good deal more powerful than most ministers. One of Da'bul's functions was to sift the president's mail and forward important matters to Asad for his instructions. Asad would annotate letters in his own hand, often writing witty comments in the margin.

Asad's speech writer, interpreter and head of his press office was a Palestinian Christian, the mild and dedicated As'ad Kamil Elyas, who in the early years doubled as foreign policy adviser and general presidential factotum. Asad was a demanding taskmaster, insisting on a high standard of Arabic prose in all statements or letters issued under his signature, and himself making time to read classical Arabic. In the Arab world a care for the classical language was the mark of a true nationalist. One of Elyas's assistants in the presidential press department was Intisar Adhami, a young woman from a respectable Damascene Sunni family, who, like Elyas and Abu Salim, was still at her post nearly two decades later. Asad had found these three on the prime minister's staff when he first assumed the post in November 1970 and simply took them with him to the presidency where they remained. (It was not until the mid-1980s that Elyas, grown old in the job, gave up directing the press office to Jubran Kurriyeh, a Syrian Protestant.)

An even longer-serving but more ceremonial fixture was the *chef de protocole*, Khalil Sa'dawi, who had been at the palace in one job or another since the Second World War. On April Fools' Day 1979, Sa'dawi's mischievous colleagues presented him with a (forged) decree terminating his appointment. Tearfully Sa'dawi, a small grey-haired man with a ramrod back, protested that he would die rather than leave the president's service. Hearing of the prank Asad assured him that he could stay, which he did. Another faithful servant was the president's personal bodyguard, a Palestinian soldier, Colonel Khalid Husayn, who had taken care of Asad since the 1960s and was to win fame in June 1980 when he shielded him from the exploding grenade of a would-be assassin.

Equally unchanging were the important personalities of the regime. Asad's closest military ally in his struggles with Jadid was Mustafa Tlas, his friend from their days together as officer cadets. Tlas had become Chief of Staff in 1968, had helped Asad defeat Jadid and was rewarded by being appointed Defence Minister in March 1972, a post he still occupied in the late 1980s. (Tlas's promotion to a place in the military hierarchy second only to Asad's raised a small problem of rank. Asad was a *fariq*, a lieutenant-general, a rank he retained on becoming president and which none could thereafter surpass. So, to distinguish Tlas from the leader above him and from the major-generals (*liwa'*) below him, a special rank of *'imad* was created which he alone held for several years, until Hikmat al-Shihabi also acceded to it on becoming Chief of Staff, followed in 1984 by his deputy, 'Ali 'Aslan.)

It was natural that Asad should pay particular attention to the armed forces, the principal underpinning of his state. A country such as he aspired to run could not live under the threat of the putsches which had afflicted Syria for so long. Long before coming to power Asad had worked to strengthen the Ba'th apparatus within the armed forces so as to build what he termed an 'ideological army', politically educated and free from factionalism. Now he carried these trends further. The Ba'th's political monopoly in the army was confirmed and reinforced; all paramilitary forces such as the Palestinian Sa'iqa were brought firmly under army control; the army itself was expanded to the point where no single unit could hope on its own to carry out a coup; its officers were given monetary and other privileges. And Asad himself as commander-in-chief struck a balance between rival army commanders, a practice he extended to the competing security and intelligence services. He alone held all the strings.

In security matters Asad's most trusted henchman and a principal prop of his regime was the 'Alawi officer, Muhammad al-Khuly, head of Air Force Intelligence since 1963, who after 1970 built up what was in effect a presidential intelligence service answerable only to Asad. In a post so close to the centre of power Khuly came to be much hated and plotted against precisely because other men resented his unrivalled access to the president. (He was to hold this position until October 1987 when, in the wake of the Hindawi affair, he was shunted out of intelligence and into the administrative post of deputy commander of the air force.)

From the start Asad's principal preoccupation lay in foreign affairs – a presidential *domaine réservé* – and as his principal executant in this field he chose his friend from their militant schooldays, 'Abd al-Halim Khaddam. A Sunni from the coastal town of Banyas, Khaddam had worked as a lawyer and schoolmaster before entering government service as a provincial governor under the Ba'th in the 1960s, first in Hama, then in Qunaytra (where he was serving when the city was lost to Israel in the Six Day War) and finally in the District of Damascus. In the late 1960s he was promoted minister of economics and foreign trade and is thought to have been Asad's spy in Jadid's rival camp. Asad rewarded him with the foreign ministry where, with great displays of energy and combativeness, he was to grow over the years into the front man of Syrian diplomacy, offending many by his brusque and hectoring manner but recognized as an effective instrument of Asad's will.

Inside the civilian party apparatus Asad's chief aide was 'Abdullah al-'Ahmar, a Sunni from the village of Tal near Damascus, who like Khaddam was trained as a lawyer and owed his promotion to provincial governor, first at Idlib and later at Hama, to the 23 February 1966 coup. Following Asad's accession, 'Ahmar rose to become assistant secretary-general of the party's National Command, in effect Asad's chief party assistant, and the passing years saw him grow into an ever more influential Ba'thist bureaucrat.

Asad's first three prime ministers, all Sunnis from Damascus, did not stay in office as long as some of his other colleagues but they were there long enough to oversee the great restructuring of the Syrian economy associated with the third and fourth Five Year Plans, 1971–81. First came Major-General 'Abd al-Rahman Khulayfawi, an able army administrator, then Mahmud al-Ayyubi, who made his name as director-general of the Euphrates dam project, and then Muhammad 'Ali Halabi. He in turn was succeeded by the town planner and professor, Dr 'Abd al-Ra'uf al-Kasm, who remained in office for over seven years, from 1980 to 1987. He was replaced as premier by the Speaker of the People's Assembly, Muhammad al-Zu'bi, who, to the scandal of Damascenes accustomed to the prime minister being chosen from among their number, was a country boy from the Hawran.

A feature of Asad's character was his dogged, somewhat obstinate consistency. He was not a man easily moved. Tactically he could show flexibility and catch his enemies by surprise, but on fundamentals he was almost wholly predictable. His key ideas, his methods of work, and his principal associates were very largely determined from the beginning of his rule and remained substantially unaltered thereafter.

There was, of course, some wear and tear of ideals as well as of persons, especially in moments of crisis, and some correction of aim, but continuity was to be his hallmark.

The end of 'Umran

Asad was quickly very firmly in the saddle, but there was one man who posed something of a threat so long as he was at large. Muhammad 'Umran, first leader of the Military Committee, started plotting against the new regime from Lebanon where he had lived since being released from Mezze during the Six Day War. (It will be recalled that 'Umran had broken with Jadid and Asad in 1965 to side with 'Aflaq and Hafiz, only to be routed with them in February 1966.)

In spite of the ups and downs in his fortunes and his present distance from the scene, 'Umran had not given up political ambition in Syria. He had retained links with old-guard Ba'thists like Salah al-Din Bitar and perhaps dreamed that Bitar might one day front for him as Amin al-Hafiz had done for the Military Committee. More to the point, 'Umran still had friends in the officer corps, friends who had helped Asad oust Jadid and, 'Umran believed, might now help him oust Asad. He believed they would rally to him if he showed his hand.

'Umran had set up house in the Lebanese port of Tripoli where the 'Alawi community was in frequent contact with 'Alawis across the border in Syria. Through such channels he thought he detected in early 1972 a current of opinion in his favour, and waited upon events. To help plan his return he set up a small 'brains trust' of which the most prominent members were Jubran Majdalani, a Lebanese lawyer and former member of 'Aflaq's National Command; Nabil Chuwayri, an early Ba'thist; and Raja Sidawi, an expatriate Syrian financier.

In a foolhardy gesture of defiance 'Umran then sent Asad a letter informing him of his intention to return home – in effect daring Asad to arrest him. He may have calculated that his army friends, who had tolerated his banishment, would not now stand for his imprisonment. But this was a misjudgement. 'Alawi officers in key commands were not ready to risk their gains in another round of musical chairs at the top.

'Umran's ambitions were soon brought to an abrupt end. On 4 March 1972, about a week before his planned return, he was murdered at his home in Tripoli by two assailants, one of them a woman, who were said to be Palestinians. Some sources claimed the assassins were sent by Nazih Zirayr of Homs Intelligence (later promoted head of

General Intelligence, *Mukhabarat al-'ama*), under the direct orders of General Naji Jamil, head of the party's bureau of state security, *Maktab al-amn al-qawmi*. Zirayr publicly denied the charge. Yet Jamil and 'Umran were known to be at daggers drawn, and Jamil, who had an air force background, was also Asad's personal friend. It was widely believed that Jamil, possibly encouraged by Rif'at al-Asad, planned the killing to promote Asad's interests but without consulting him. Other sources maintained that the intention was not to kill 'Umran but only to kidnap him, and that he was shot in a scuffle. In the event, 'Umran's family did not blame Asad for his death and 'Umran's son, Najih, called on Asad some six months later and wept in his arms. The exact circumstances of 'Umran's murder were never cleared up to the public's satisfaction, but after it most of his officer faction, with the exception of relatives and close friends, fell in behind Asad and were suitably rewarded.

Of the five comrades who had banded together in Cairo twelve years earlier he now stood alone.

13

Sadat, the Unsound Ally

From the moment of coming to power Asad was in the grip of an obsession. He was convinced that Israel had won the Six Day War by ruse, catching the Arabs napping, but that it was not inherently unbeatable. He longed to wipe away the stain of defeat which had affected him personally and profoundly, restore the confidence of his troops, recover the land, and show the world that, given a chance, the Arabs could acquit themselves honourably. The need to fight another round was his obsession. Without first redressing the balance with Israel, he saw no hope of a negotiated settlement. Israel was simply too well-placed to be inclined to disgorge the vast tracts of Arab territory it had seized, much of which in any event it hoped to retain on a permanent basis. In December 1970, very shortly after coming to power, Asad reaffirmed Syria's rejection of Security Council Resolution 242 of 1967 on the grounds that it meant the 'liquidation of the Palestine question'. War, not UN resolutions, was the only way to make Israel yield.

Asad differed from most Arab leaders in daring to contemplate an attack on Israel – an Arab 'first' he was to share with Sadat. Not in the least defeatist, he genuinely believed the Arabs could snatch back and hold some if not all their lost land. By changing the balance of power, another round would allow them to deal with Israel from something like equality, and no longer from weakness and humiliation.

This grim assessment that war was a necessity was peculiarly Syrian, stemming from the frustrations of twenty years of border tussles with Israel, from Syria's passionate attachment to the Palestine cause and, more generally, from the perception that Syria and Israel, face to face and competing for primacy in the Levant, were doomed to be antagonists. Any gain for the one must be a loss to the other. Syria could expect no favours from Israel and would grant none. No other Arab state sensed as acutely as Syria that the contest with Israel involved nothing less than the Arabs' national existence. From 1970, and even earlier, Egypt and Jordan had in their different fashions attempted to find a *modus vivendi* with Israel, reaching out a hand to it and offering real concessions, but Syria wanted to put the clock back to before Israel's conquests in the Six Day War. In this Asad was merely reflecting what his public demanded. Hardly reconciled to Israel's existence within its prewar frontiers, Syrians were outraged by its wartime expansion and believed that what had been taken by force could only be regained by force.

Asad was an ardent nationalist who had come to power at the very moment when Nasser's death left the pan-Arab movement leaderless. The temptation to see himself as a possible successor must have been very great and undoubtedly he had a high opinion of himself. Still largely unknown and without Nasser's personal charisma, he could not realistically aspire to fill the gap left by the Egyptian leader, yet he seems to have felt that destiny had chosen him to rescue the Arabs from some of the consequences of Nasser's 1967 blunders – to which Syria, admittedly, and Asad himself had contributed: the Golan in particular weighed on his mind. So, with the stubborn patience which was the hallmark of his character, he set about preparing for war, not talking too freely or bragging about what he hoped to do but working quietly for the opportunity to hit back.

The search for allies

Even to consider waging war Asad needed first of all to break out of the regional and international isolation to which Syria had been condemned by the extremist policies of the Salah Jadid regime. Ten days after his seizure of power he flew to Egypt for a meeting with Nasser's successor, Anwar al-Sadat, at which he announced that Syria would join the proposed federation of Egypt, Libya and Sudan; and very quickly doors were flung open in other directions – towards Lebanon, towards Tunisia and Morocco with which relations were restored, towards Saudi Arabia then at odds with Syria because the pipeline carrying Saudi oil across Syrian territory to the Mediterranean had lain damaged since May 1970. It was now reopened and a Damascus-based radio station which had been preaching subversion in the Arabian peninsula was closed down.

But an overture to the Soviet Union was even more indispensable. In February 1971, ten weeks after his coup, Asad paid his first visit to Moscow as Syrian ruler, knowing full well that nowhere else in the world could he hope to obtain the weapons required for the enterprise he had in mind. By this time Syria had a fifteen-year-old military and economic relationship with the Soviet Union, so there was a solid base on which to build, and indeed as Defence Minister Asad had himself made several journeys to the Soviet bloc when, in the immediate aftermath of the Six Day War, he had struggled to rebuild his shattered army. He had visited Czech armaments factories and struck up an acquaintance with Marshal Grechko, the Soviet Defence Minister. But in 1970 the circumstances were delicate and the Kremlin more wary. It viewed Asad's seizure of power with a certain reserve, fearing it might presage a swerve towards the West which could undercut Soviet interests. It had not been particularly happy with the left-wing 'adventurism' of Jadid and the fiery doctors but, from Moscow's point of view, there had at least been no danger that that regime would fall into the Western orbit. A non-doctrinaire nationalist such as Asad could prove dangerously independent, however.

Asad moved fast to put relations with the Kremlin on a hard-headed basis. His former colleagues had expressed their sympathy for the Soviet Union in slogans, posturings and the mouthing of half-baked and ill-digested socialist ideology, expecting in exchange total Soviet support which to their disappointment they did not always get. Asad dropped the rhetoric but tightened the bond. His earlier dealings with Moscow and his own sceptical and pragmatic nature had taught him that solid relations could be built only on mutual interests. The Russians were not in the habit of making gifts: he could not expect something for nothing. In particular, he grasped early on that the Soviet Union's friendship for the Arabs would never match the United States' generous, sentimental and open-handed commitment to Israel: whatever he secured from Moscow would have to be paid for, and if he could not raise the cash, payment would have to be in some other coin.

The essence of his policy towards the Soviet Union, for which he had argued in the leadership before 1970 and which he now put into practice, was that arms in sufficient volume and of the right quality could be acquired only within the context of Soviet regional interests. What did the Russians want? Asad knew their Middle East priorities well: a stable presence and listening post in the heart of the Middle East, access to friendly air and naval facilities, a lever on the peace process, and above all the curtailment of American influence. Soviet interests had to be understood and addressed. Only by showing the Russians trust and by giving them something of value could their confidence be won and the flow of arms assured. In practical terms this meant that Asad agreed to a measure of co-ordination with Moscow, although at this stage and for another decade he resisted formalizing the tie in a Treaty of Friendship and Co-operation as Moscow would have liked.

It was far from being a cloudless relationship and it was to take Asad several years, in fact the best part of the 1970s, to get the Soviets to recognize him as their indispensable regional partner. As Syrian officials privately conceded, Soviet attitudes were often patronizing or even downright scornful of the Arabs' will to fight, and Arab disunity was routinely cited as a pretext for withholding supplies. Another source of tension was Asad's candid and forceful insistence that he would tolerate no meddling in his internal affairs by the Soviet embassy in Damascus, and that relations had to be based on strict mutual non-interference. In the end Asad's tactics got him much of what he wanted and once they had taken his measure, the Russians were at some pains to keep him happy.

The obverse of his efforts to woo the Soviet Union in the interests of his war strategy was a neglect of the West, especially of the United States: for nearly seven years, from 1967 to 1974, Syria had no relations with Washington. Other Arab states – Egypt, Algeria, Sudan and Iraq among them – had also broken with Washington at the time of the Six Day War but there had been a drift back, if not to diplomatic relations then at least to something like business as usual often under the cover of consular or commercial sections. Syria remained adamantly closed to the United States, and not only because of Asad's Moscow diplomacy. There were personal factors as well. Like many Syrians he viewed the United States with mistrust, even with animosity. No one in his entourage understood how the Arab case might be put to the West, nor how Western public opinion and governments might be won over. As the United States was equally ignorant of and hostile to Syria, the gulf between the two countries was very deep, which was to prove a grave disability for Syria in the political bargaining which followed the October War.

But in 1971 it did not seem to matter. Asad's overriding concern was armaments, not diplomatic manoeuvring. Appreciating his business-like approach, the Soviets indicated that they were ready for a long-term relationship and started treating him with a certain regard. Between February 1971 and October 1973 he was accorded the privilege of several meetings with General Secretary Leonid Brezhnev on the half dozen visits he paid to the Soviet Union, some of them unreported. On the longer stays the Russians took him on tour to Leningrad and Kiev, Georgia and Armenia, Uzbekistan and Azerbayjan.

In Moscow he was always given apartments in the Kremlin itself where the hospitality was gargantuan. The poor boy from the 'Alawi mountains could not but be impressed by the magnificence of the place, the immense dining halls and reception rooms, the golden domes and cut-glass chandeliers – and by the power of a state that could afford such luxury for its rulers.

Dealings with Egypt

If the Soviet Union was Syria's only possible armourer, Egypt was the obvious ally. Asad's earlier dealings with Egypt – his exile in Cairo as a young man and the bloody struggle with Nasser's Syrian supporters in the early months of Ba'th rule – had left a sour taste, but unpleasant personal memories were of little account when weighed against the geopolitical necessity of a Syrian-Egyptian alliance. Asad's Ba'thist upbringing had taught him that the success of the Arab cause depended on a Syrian tie with Egypt. Damascus and Cairo were the two pivots of Arab history: when they were at one the Arabs triumphed, and when they were apart the Arabs became weak and vulnerable. If Syria had not seceded from the United Arab Republic in 1961, the catastrophe of 1967 when Israel played on Syrian-Egyptian differences would not have happened. Of all the Arabs, the Syrian Ba'thists had been the first to cheer when Nasser proclaimed 'Arabism' to be Egypt's official policy in 1955, and then the first to weep when the Syrian-Egyptian union ran into trouble. Asad understood the premises of Nasser's Arab policy which gave Syria a central role: Nasser had been able to dominate the region and confront Israel and the great powers once he had brought Syria under his control and, conversely, he was thrown on the defensive once Syria broke free. Clearly Syria and Egypt stood and fell together. It was such thoughts which carried Asad to Cairo within days of his coup.

In military terms he knew that a two-front strategy against Israel was the essential prerequisite for victory. In 1967 Egypt, Jordan and Syria, suspicious of each other and at odds, had fought separate, unco-ordinated wars, allowing Israel to defeat each of them in turn. Next time Asad was determined that Israel would be forced to fight on two fronts simultaneously, an analysis Soviet defence planners endorsed.

Asad could not consider King Husayn a fighting partner, as Syria and Jordan had been on poor terms for years. The débâcle of the Six Day War, when Jordan accused Syria of failing to defend the West Bank, had envenomed relations further, as did Husayn's subsequent secret meetings with Israeli leaders. The Black September crisis of 1970 which had brought Jordan and Israel together had driven Jordan and Syria still further apart. Asad knew well that Husayn could not contemplate hostile action against Israel, nor would he welcome such action by others for fear that war would shake the tightrope between the Arabs and Israel on which he was precariously balanced. In the 1972–3 run-up to the October War Asad saw Husayn more as an enemy than an ally.

So Egypt was Syria's only choice as war partner: a two-front strategy with Egypt was in fact the bedrock of the secret planning which Asad and Anwar al-Sadat began early in 1971. Asad had full confidence in his Egyptian ally. Although Sadat had yet to establish himself on the world stage, and had been overshadowed by Nasser for much of his life, to the Syrians he was already a familiar figure as one of Nasser's principal lieutenants with a nationalist aura all his own. It was well known that as a young man during the Second World War he had trafficked with German spies and spent time in jail for plotting to kill pro-British collaborators, and he had been the one to announce to the world the Free Officers' revolution of 1952, emerging in 1970 as Nasser's chosen successor. He had experience, style, political sophistication and, aged fifty-three in 1971, a certain mature, pipe-smoking calm.

At this stage Asad was more inclined to stress his affinities with Sadat than any difference between them. Their careers seemed to march in step: Sadat was confirmed as president of Egypt on 15 October 1970, just a month before Asad seized power, and, in turn, Asad's presidential plebiscite on 12 March 1971 took place only a few weeks before Sadat in early May locked up his principal left-wing challengers in 'Ali Sabri's so-called 'power centre' and made himself uncontested master of Egypt. Asad's confidence was not just in Sadat but in Egypt itself, which with its size and strength was evidently the senior partner in the relationship. The War of Attrition which Egypt had waged against Israel from March 1969 to July 1970 had shown how far Nasser had managed to rebuild the Egyptian army in both armaments and morale. Moreover, opinion in Egypt seemed as anxious as in Syria to join battle with Israel and force it to return the territory it had seized.

At the start Asad's alliance with Sadat was forged under the cover of the proposed Federation of Arab Republics embracing Egypt, Syria, Libya and Sudan. As well as providing a bonanza for constitutional lawyers, this ambitious plan announced in April 1971 led to much to-ing and fro-ing between the member states. Although Sudan soon dropped out and the project withered within two years to an empty husk, the frequent federal summits provided Asad and Sadat with occasions for secret meetings. By the end of 1971 the two leaders had taken soundings in Moscow, had appointed Egypt's war minister, General Muhammad Sadiq, supreme commander of both armies, and had reached agreement on broad strategy. They also decided to exclude the intemperate Colonel Qadhafi from their counsels. What they knew they needed above all was huge quantities of armaments, and it was to filling their arsenals and training their troops that they devoted much of 1972 and 1973. The pattern of those years was of ever closer Syrian-Egyptian co-operation. Asad and Sadat made further visits to each other's capitals and to Moscow as did their defence ministers and teams of senior officers. So frequent were these contacts that with hindsight it seems astonishing that the alarm was not sounded. Instead, the outside world ridiculed Sadat for repeatedly promising a 'year of decision' in his conflict with Israel – a contest which he was regularly obliged to defer. 'It was a good thing no one believed him', Asad later remarked.[1]

One reason the signals were not read correctly was that the world was watching Sadat rather than Asad, and Sadat was sending out contradictory messages which left observers more bemused than alarmed. The Israelis for their part concluded that he was an Egyptian leader with no pan-Arab ambitions, who had turned his back on war – in fact that he was the very antithesis of Nasser. What was not widely realized was that Sadat had come to think that the Arab-Israeli stalemate, as well as the Russians themselves, whose scepticism about his warlike intentions exasperated him, needed a salutary jolt. His predilection for shock tactics – the belief that political change could be brought about by individual actions of a startling nature – was perhaps a late outgrowth of his youthful terrorism.[2] So he quarrelled spectacularly with Moscow, while flirting discreetly with Washington.

The row between Cairo and Moscow dominated 1972, reaching a climax in July with Sadat's abrupt expulsion of Russian personnel from Egypt – a total of 7,752 advisers, weapons experts, field troops and dependants.[3] He justified his *coup de théâtre* on the grounds that the Soviet authorities were not only being impossibly slow in making promised arms deliveries but were sacrificing Arab interests on the altar of détente with the United States. He professed to believe that Moscow wanted to prevent Egypt from fighting and that he needed to call its bluff.[4] But it later emerged that Sadat's anti-Soviet move was more connected with the feelers he was then putting out to Washington.

As it happened, Asad was in Moscow on 8 July 1972 when Sadat told Ambassador Vladimir Vinogradov that the Soviet experts in Egypt had to go. Asad was having his own small tiff with the Soviet leaders at the time, as he was coming under more than usual pressure to sign a Treaty of Friendship and was adamantly refusing to do so. 'Friendship needs no treaty', he liked to say.[5] The deadlock was such in his Kremlin talks that he ordered his delegation to pack their bags, whereupon Brezhnev called on him in his suite to propose that the talks should resume without further mention of a treaty. It was at this juncture, on the last day of Asad's visit, that news of Sadat's bombshell reached Moscow. Brezhnev made his way to Asad's Kremlin suite for a second time: 'I know you will tell me', he said ruefully, 'that our treaty with Egypt has not saved us from embarrassment there. But we would like you to help us with Egypt if you can.' Asad agreed to fly directly from Moscow to Cairo to try and patch things up. He was as startled and perturbed as the Russians themselves by Sadat's impulsive gesture so alien to his own temperament. Like Sadat he wanted Soviet arms transfers to be larger and faster, but he was aghast at Sadat's recklessness in endangering a relationship with Moscow which was so vital to the Syrian-Egyptian war effort. When Sadat urged him to expel his own Soviet advisers (then between 2,500 and 3,000) he refused, declaring publicly that 'they are here for our own good'.[6] Pursuing his mediation efforts, he went to see Brezhnev again in September, and in October persuaded Sadat to send Prime Minister 'Aziz Sidqi to Moscow to repair the damage. In the autumn of 1972 the flow of Soviet arms and experts to Cairo was resumed.

Sadat threw out the Russians although he had signed a Treaty of Friendship with them a year earlier, whereas Asad kept the experts while declining a treaty. Sadat grumbled a great deal that the Soviet Union was trying to dictate issues of war and peace in the Middle East, whereas Asad made a point of asserting that no outside power could prevent him fighting if he chose to do so: 'As far as we in Syria are concerned, a decision on war cannot be made in Moscow'.[7]

Perhaps Asad should have been alerted by these early signs of Sadat's waywardness. But Sadat could claim, and Asad had to concede, that shock tactics had worked: after the 1972 quarrel, Soviet aid to both Egypt and Syria rose to unprecedented levels. The whole episode was not to the cautious Asad's liking but in the end he was reassured and went forward with his partner beyond the point of no return.

On 23 April 1973 he flew secretly to Cairo and from there Husni Mubarak, then Egypt's air force commander, escorted Sadat and Asad to the presidential rest-house at Burj al-'Arab, west of Alexandria, for two days of detailed discussions in which they agreed the main lines of their campaign.[8] The pace then quickened. In early May Asad was off again to Moscow in search of more aircraft and air defences. Given Israel's air superiority, he needed a dense net of low- and high-level anti-aircraft systems – AA guns and SAMs with their supporting electronics. He returned home accompanied by no less a person than the Soviet air force commander, Marshal P.S. Kotakhov – a clear sign of Soviet commitment to his war. With Soviet help Syria built up a force of 300 combat aircraft, more than a hundred SAM batteries with between 400 and 500 launchers, and at least 400 anti-aircraft guns.[9]

But in spite of – or perhaps because of – their differences with Sadat, the Russians were still giving Egypt priority, with Syria trailing several months behind in acquiring the latest equipment. In 1970 Egypt had been the first to receive ZSU-23 radar-guided anti-aircraft guns and the first to be shown the advanced MiG-21 MF only then being introduced into the Soviet air force, for which Syria had to wait until 1972–3. In 1972 Egypt was again ahead in getting the mobile SAM-6 and the T-62 battle tank, the Soviet Union's latest at the time.

Did the Soviet authorities know that the October War was coming? Obviously, yes. Did they help in its planning? The answer must also be yes, to the extent that Arab arms requirements were worked out with Soviet experts on the basis of specific military plans.[10] But they were not told officially that Syria and Egypt would attack until 4 October, two days before the outbreak of war. Did they then approve? They must clearly have had doubts. The Soviet Union's dilemma was that, to retain influence with both Syria and Egypt, it had to supply them with weapons for the recovery of their territory lost in 1967 – their most urgent national priority. But the Soviet Union was also anxious to dispel the threat of war because it feared a regional confrontation with the United States. In seeking a way out of this dilemma it tried to persuade Washington to impose a political settlement on Israel. For example, when Brezhnev and his Foreign Minister, Andrei Gromyko, met Nixon and Kissinger at San Clemente, California, on 23 June 1973, Brezhnev proposed that Israel withdraw to its pre-1967 borders in return for an end to the state of belligerency, with final peace to follow after negotiations with the Palestinians.[11] Kissinger did not hesitate to reject terms which he considered pro-Arab as well as likely to consolidate Soviet influence. A chance to avert war was missed.

The next decisive step in the run-up to the October War was a top secret meeting of the Syrian-Egyptian Armed Forces Supreme Council from 21 to 23 August 1973. Wearing casual clothes as if going on holiday, Syria's six most senior officers – Defence Minister Mustafa

Tlas, Chief of Staff Yusuf Shakkur, Air Force and Air Defence Commander Naji Jamil, Chief of Operations 'Abd al-Razzaq al-Dardari, Military Intelligence chief Hikmat al-Shihabi, and Navy Commander Fadl Husayn – boarded a Soviet passenger liner at Latakia on its regular run to Alexandria, where they held two days of discussions with their Egyptian opposite numbers at Naval Headquarters at Ras al-Tin. This was the final review of war plans by the men who would conduct the battle. Close attention was given to an elaborate deception intended to fool Israel and the United States into believing that the massing of men and equipment on the Syrian and Egyptian fronts was no more than routine autumn manoeuvres.

The two chiefs of staff, the Syrian Yusuf Shakkur and the Egyptian Sa'd al-Shazly, then signed a formal document enshrining their joint intent to go to war and recommending a choice of possible dates to their political masters. The battle could start on a date between 7 and 11 September or between 5 and 10 October at a time when Suez Canal tides and hours of moonlight were favourable. A two-week countdown was requested, whichever D-Day was chosen.[12]

From Alexandria Mustafa Tlas and Husni Mubarak flew to Syria to brief Asad and Sadat who were holding a summit meeting of their own on 26–27 August in the mountain resort of Bludan, west of Damascus, where they had gone to avoid the summer heat. It was then that the decision to fight in October was taken. Asad recalled later that Sadat, who faced student trouble at home, was anxious to go to war before the autumn term brought mutineers thronging back to the campuses. Asad saw the point but felt that their great venture could not be made to depend on an academic timetable.[13]

D-Day was finally decided upon at a secret meeting of Asad and Sadat in Cairo on 12 September (held in the wings of a tripartite summit with King Husayn of Jordan). On 22 September the fifteen-day countdown began and at Asad's house in Damascus on 3 October, he and Egypt's war minister, General Isma'il, agreed on H-Hour. The Syrians wanted to attack at dawn with the sun behind them; the Egyptians preferred dusk to allow for a night crossing of the Canal free from Israeli air attack. The compromise reached was that the attack would be launched on both fronts at 14.05 hours on 6 October.

Divergence of aims

Although Asad did not know it, his enterprise with Sadat was flawed from the start, because behind the impressive facade of co-operation there was no unity of mind, and on this hidden reef the Arabs' great hopes were to founder. The points of divergence could scarcely have been more fundamental: the two leaders were not at one on the reasons for fighting. Asad went to war because he believed there could be no satisfactory negotiation with Israel until the Arabs had snatched back some at least of their lost land. Peace-making, he believed, could be a product of war, but not a substitute for it. Sadat went to war because the peace diplomacy he was already conducting, covertly as well as overtly, had faltered. He thought a shock would revive it.

As early as December 1970, very shortly after succeeding Nasser, Sadat sent private word to Washington that he was interested in peace. On 4 February 1971 he offered to reopen the Suez Canal, blocked since 1967, in exchange for a partial Israeli withdrawal linked to a timetable for a comprehensive settlement. On 15 February he assured the UN negotiator, Gunnar Jarring, that Egypt was ready for peace with Israel if it withdrew from Sinai. Israel refused. In early March he appealed in vain to Nixon to support his 4 February proposal. Then, when he signed his friendship treaty with the Soviet Union on 27 May, he hastened to inform Washington that this did not diminish his interest in a peace settlement.

When in late 1971 Henry Kissinger, Nixon's National Security Adviser, displaced Secretary of State William Rogers as America's key foreign policy-maker, Sadat was quick to open a 'back channel' to him to communicate the same peace message. In response Kissinger made it amply clear, directly and through go-betweens such as King Faysal's brother-in-law, the Saudi intelligence chief Kamal Adham, that he would not act on the peace process so long as Soviet influence in Egypt remained strong.[14] So to meet what he took to be Kissinger's conditions, Sadat expelled the Russian experts in July 1972. But even this dramatic move failed to draw Washington and its Israeli ally into talks. Although understandably upset, Sadat still did not give up, sending his national security adviser, Hafiz Isma'il, to repeat to Kissinger in two days of secret discussions in Connecticut on 24–25 February 1973, and yet again at another unpublicized meeting outside Paris on 20 May, that if Israel undertook to withdraw from the occupied territories, normalization and peace were on offer.[15] No one could say he did not try. Indeed, these were only the high points of a continuous, but increasingly despairing, Egyptian endeavour to get peace talks with Israel started between 1971 and 1973 and thereby preclude the need to go to war. These efforts came to nothing largely because it was Kissinger's deliberate policy to stall and prolong the Arab-Israeli stalemate.[16]

Husayn of Jordan was as eager as Sadat for peace talks. Fearful of war, he watched Syrian and Egyptian preparations with mounting anxiety. The 1967 war had cost him half his kingdom, another conflict could cost him the throne itself. In an attempt to pre-empt this danger, he went twice to Washington in February 1973 to try to enlist Nixon's and Kissinger's backing for the proposals which he had already and repeatedly put to Israeli leaders face to face:[17] if Israel gave up the idea of annexation, he would make peace; he would agree to border changes as well as to Israeli military outposts, even settlements, along the Jordan river. But Kissinger would waste no time on proposals which Israel had already rejected. In May 1973 Husayn warned Washington that the Syrian and Egyptian build-up was too realistic to be considered simply manoeuvres,[18] and on receipt of this warning Kissinger called for a high-level review of the possible threat. Israel's Defence Minister, Dayan, went so far as to order a partial mobilization, but the alarm proved false, or at least premature.

Israel and the United States were convinced that the Arabs would not dare start a war they had no hope of winning. The view was that Israel's superiority, especially in the air, robbed the Arabs of any rational military option. Indeed, so lamentable had been earlier attempts at Arab co-operation that the notion that Egypt and Syria, historically at odds, could effectively combine was utterly discounted. In both Israel and the United States complacency bred of the 1967 walkover remained unshaken and was if anything reinforced by Sadat's expulsion of the Russians and by the vast strength Israel had acquired with American help.

Kissinger's overweening confidence in his own powers of persuasion also led him to dismiss Husayn's warning. He had let it be known that he would be ready to begin preliminary talks on the Middle East problem following the Israeli elections of 30 October, and he felt sure that the prospect of a possible diplomatic settlement would be enough to keep the Arabs quiet until then. It need hardly be added that Kissinger had no sympathy for the Arabs' acute sense of frustration over Israel's continued occupation of their territory and over the ever more explicitly annexationist tone of Israeli leaders. In fact, he deliberately sharpened the Arabs' frustrations in the belief that this would make them more pliant. Sadat's vacillations from peace plea to war threat were laughed at, while the unknown Asad was ignored.

Asad had taken note of Sadat's public peace proposals, such as the offer of a conditional reopening of the Suez Canal of February 1971, but read their failure as reassuring proof that Sadat shared his view that nothing of substance could be regained from Israel without a war.

But he knew nothing of Sadat's 'back channel' to Kissinger, failed to grasp how strenuously his Egyptian ally and his Jordanian neighbour sought talks, and did not realize the extent to which Sadat saw war as no more than a shock to awaken the dormant peace process.

Thus while Asad planned to regain territory, Sadat hoped merely to unblock a process of diplomacy. Asad's was a war of liberation, Sadat's an essentially political war. Of course, there was a certain overlap in their positions. Asad did not imagine that a war, however much territory was regained in the course of it, could of itself settle the complex Arab-Israeli conflict: political negotiations would have to follow. But the weight given by each to the political and military aspects of the campaign was very different.

Sadat told his generals that he wanted to wage a 'limited war' – repeatedly making the point, as recorded by Mohamed Heikal, that if he could win back only ten millimetres of ground on the Canal's east bank, this would immeasurably strengthen his negotiating hand.[19] Asad in contrast envisaged the Syrian army retaking the Golan, the Egyptian army retaking Sinai, and Israel being forced under pressure to give up in subsequent negotiations the rest of its 1967 conquests – the Palestinian territory on the West Bank of the Jordan and in the Gaza Strip. This was Asad's understanding of his agreement with Sadat. As he insisted later:[20]

> The goal was the retrieval of territory which Israel occupied in 1967. Each country was free to plan its offensive on its own front, but it was agreed that Syria's aim was the recovery of the Golan while the Egyptian objective was to reach the Sinai passes in the first stage before regrouping for the reconquest of the whole peninsula. This was what Sadat and I decided and it was on this principle that we went to war.

Why did the crucial difference in war aims not become plain at the many prewar meetings? The explanation is that Sadat lied to Asad, deliberately deceiving him about his intentions and leading him to believe that the offensive Egypt would launch would be wider in scope than was ever intended. The deception was not a mere verbal misunderstanding: the Syrians were actually fed false war plans.

Egypt's Chief of Staff, General Sa'd al-Shazly, was from the start convinced that Egypt could mount only a limited attack across the Suez Canal to capture and hold a narrow strip of land on the eastern bank. He judged that a larger offensive to drive Israel beyond the Sinai passes, let alone out of Sinai and the Gaza Strip altogether, was wholly beyond Egypt's powers: its air force was too weak and its SAM air defences too few and too static to support any substantial advance east of the Canal. To move into Sinai beyond the SAM umbrella would in his view be suicidal folly, as the Egyptian ground forces would then be annihilated by the Israeli air force as they had been in 1967. Accordingly he prepared a plan, code-named High Minarets, for the limited cross-Canal attack which he believed was the only one feasible.

But such a restricted objective was unavowable. National honour demanded a military plan to liberate the whole territory seized by Israel. Securing arms in quantity from the Russians, always the subject of hard bargaining, also required setting one's objectives high. When Sadat and his war minister of the time, General Sadiq, went to Moscow to plead for arms in October 1971, the plan on which they based their requests was not the modest High Minarets but the more ambitious 'Operation 41' which envisaged seizing the key Giddi and Mitla passes some forty to fifty kilometres east of the Canal. An element of double-dealing was therefore built into Egyptian war planning from 1971 onwards: while the Chief of Staff and a handful of planners worked secretly on High Minarets, Egypt's Soviet advisers and the Syrians were led to believe that the objectives set out in Operation 41, renamed Granite Two, were the real ones. But as Shazly was later to explain, 'Granite Two remained a paper plan, impossible with the means at hand'.[21]

Deceiving the Soviet authorities was one thing and might possibly have been justified to get the weapons flowing. In any event the Egyptians believed it was only prudent to be less than candid with Moscow as they were never sure how much information it might share with Washington in the context of détente. An element of mis-representation could even be passed off as part of a necessary deception plan.[22] But it was quite another thing for Sadat to deceive his Syrian ally, and so expose him to dangers far greater than those he had anticipated.

The fraud began at the Sadat-Asad summit at Burj al-'Arab in April 1973 when the two leaders agreed on the overall shape of the campaign. Sadat knew that Asad would not fight alongside him unless the joint aim was the liberation of both Sinai and Golan, to be pursued by putting maximum simultaneous pressure on Israel on both fronts. So he sold him Granite Two. At this meeting Asad was unhappy about deficiencies he detected in Egypt's preparations for so big an operation and, overcoming Sadat's reluctance, he insisted on questioning Egypt's new war minister, General Ahmad Isma'il, who was summoned from

Cairo for the purpose. As a result of this interview the war was put back from the spring to the autumn of 1973 to allow time for more equipment to be acquired.[23]

General Shazly reveals in his memoirs how Asad was hoodwinked. On Sadat's instructions, Isma'il ordered Shazly to revive Granite Two shortly before Asad was due at Burj al-'Arab, and when Shazly protested that the plan was no more militarily feasible in 1973 than it had been in 1971, Isma'il confessed that it was a political manoeuvre to keep the Syrians in line. The Egyptians had no real qualms about deceiving the Syrians because of their deep dislike of them: Egypt still bore the wounds of the Syrian secession and there was a widely shared feeling that the fractious, thankless Syrians had bitten the hand that fed them. So great was the distaste for Syria that Shazly even argued, in the privacy of the Egyptian General Staff, that Egypt would be better off fighting the war alone. But Sadat wanted his Syrian ally on board. Isma'il's solution to the problem of satisfying Asad was simple: work on the two plans – the limited High Minarets and the more ambitious Granite Two – would proceed together but whereas the first was the real one, the second which provided for the seizure of the Sinai passes would be presented to Asad, but 'would never be implemented except under the most favourable conditions'. 'I was sickened by the duplicity', Shazly wrote.[24]

Sadat's bad faith was by no means Asad's only problem. His precious war plans were betrayed to the enemy but, such was Israeli and American complacency, with no effect on the course of the battle. In late August or early September 1973 an Arab intelligence service received a coded message from a Syrian agent – a major-general in the Syrian army who had been recruited by this service two years earlier – requesting an immediate meeting. The Syrian brought with him a complete set of plans for the October War as drawn up by the Egyptian and Syrian high commands, copies of which were promptly conveyed by trusted emissaries to just two recipients: Henry Kissinger and Moshe Dayan.

But the documents were simply not taken seriously. Dayan and Kissinger were certain this was an Arab exercise in disinformation, designed to cause Israel the expense and disruption of yet another pointless mobilization and to induce the United States to press Israel to be more flexible in its response to the peace proposals Egypt and Jordan had advanced. When war came on 6 October the plans forwarded to Dayan and Kissinger were found to be exact in every particular, except for an eight-hour discrepancy over H-Hour which was given as 6 a.m. The plans had evidently not yet been amended by the˜compromise, reached by Asad and General Isma'il on 3 October, which fixed H-Hour at 2.05 in the afternoon.

Kissinger never revealed, and would doubtless categorically deny, that he had any precise foreknowledge of the October War. Dayan was privately more candid. When the war was over he made contact with the Arab spymaster whose astonishing intelligence scoop had gone unheeded. His message said in effect:[25]

> I am aware that you have me at your mercy. If you reveal what you know, my career will be over. In the meantime please be kind enough to receive with our deepest gratitude the highest military decoration Israel can award to a foreign national.

Perhaps it was just as well that Asad had no inkling of how shaky his position was when he went to war or how far his strategic environment had been impaired. Not only was he bamboozled by his Egyptian ally into believing it would deliver a bigger military punch than it ever intended, but his war plans were in enemy hands. These were not auspicious circumstances for the campaign he had dreamed of since 1967.

The immediate prelude to the war

At a summit meeting in Cairo on 10–12 September 1973 Asad and Sadat welcomed Husayn back to the Arab fold, in a replay of the eleventh-hour Arab reconciliation of 1967. Egypt and Syria agreed to resume diplomatic relations with Jordan on the occasion of the king's decision to release from detention hundreds of Palestinian guerrillas who had survived the Black September butchery. But as usual the new-found cordiality in Cairo covered up much private chicanery. Husayn knew well enough that if he joined Egypt and Syria, when war came he would expose himself to devastating Israeli punishment, but that if he remained aloof he would face an Arab charge of treachery. So in Cairo he publicly mended his fences with the Arab warmongers while giving private assurances to the United States and Israel that, if war broke out, he would do as little fighting as he decently could.[26] Asad's feelings were equally ambivalent: he needed Husayn to plug a gap in his defences, while detesting the king's contacts with Israel. Sadat befriended Husayn for similarly mixed motives: anticipating a bout of postwar peace diplomacy, he wanted to make sure that Jordan would not upstage him in the United States. To complete the triangle, neither Sadat nor Husayn had any trust in Asad: memories of Ba'thist intrigues against them were still too fresh. Such was the state of Arab harmony on the eve of the October War.

As Husayn had feared, when war came Arab pressures mounted on him to join in, and he quietly sought Israeli permission to move a brigade to the Syrian front, in a plea passed to Kissinger through the British Prime Minister, Edward Heath. In Washington, Kissinger and Simcha Dinitz, the Israeli ambassador, enjoyed the joke. 'Only in the Middle East', Kissinger wrote in his memoirs, 'is it conceivable that a belligerent would ask its adversary's approval for engaging in an act of war against it.'[27] What Kissinger did not add was that, by inviting Israel to protect Jordan when Husayn called for American help in 1970, he had himself created the uncomfortable situation in which Husayn now found himself.

In spite of his conspiratorial youth, the Asad of these early years of power appears to have been outclassed in deviousness by Sadat and Husayn, both of them more experienced in the rough game of Arab politics. Against his two years as president of Syria, Husayn had by 1973 already clocked up two decades on his exposed throne while Sadat had served as long at Nasser's side. Asad's relative innocence was reflected in his war aims, which were quite simply the military reconquest of territory without any clear view of what would follow and without a fallback position in case of failure. On any objective assessment, success was not impossible but hindsight suggests that the odds were heavily stacked against it. It is probable that Asad's enthusiasm for the war which he had seized power to wage and which absorbed all his emotions gave him a blind spot, blotting out any doubts a less committed man might have had about his 'Arab brothers'. Perhaps he lacked the imagination to grasp that, seen from Cairo or Amman, the Arab-Israeli conflict did not have the clear-cut, black and white, good-versus-evil quality which was the traditional view from Damascus.

14

The October Illusion

The October War of 1973 was the Arabs' most considerable military undertaking of modern times. But far from realizing the extravagant hopes they placed in it, the conflict was to prove politically catastrophic, setting them on a course of disintegration and heightened vulnerability. For Asad it was an occasion of the sharpest disappointment, yet paradoxically it was also the beginning of his regional importance.

In the first twenty-four hours of their surprise attack, launched at 14.05 hours on Saturday 6 October, Egypt and Syria stormed formidable Israeli defence barriers on both the Sinai and Golan fronts. In what the American military historian, Colonel Trevor Dupuy, described as 'one of the most memorable water crossings in the annals of warfare',[1] 100,000 Egyptian troops and over 1,000 tanks were put across the Suez Canal where they overwhelmed Israel's Bar-Lev Line and established five defensive bridgeheads of their own. Meanwhile, Syria flung 35,000 troops and 800 tanks against Israel's fortifications on the Golan Heights, bursting through at several points and almost reaching the rim of the escarpment which overlooks the Sea of Galilee, the Jordan River and northern Israel beyond.

These developments caused great elation in the Arab camp as it was evident that Israel's ascendancy was being challenged for the first time since 1948. After living with the shame of the resounding defeats of 1948, 1956 and especially 1967, not to mention countless painful skirmishes in between, the Arabs had now dared to attack – and had proved they could win. The age of impotence seemed to be over. Whatever the outcome of the war, one of its aims, the recovery of self-respect, had been achieved on the first morning.

That morning, several hours before H-Hour, Asad had installed himself in the underground War Room at Damascus GHQ, waiting for the campaign to open with the roar of heavy guns along the whole length of the 65-kilometre front. This was the battle he had dreamed of for years. He was so excited and preoccupied that he quite forgot that 6 October was his forty-third birthday. 'You're right!' he cried when someone reminded him of it, 'I hadn't noticed.'[2]

For Asad and Sadat, as for the whole Arab world, it was a moment of immense satisfaction, balm for the wounds of the past. The brio, style and courage of the blows struck at the very start were to give both leaders something like a blank cheque on a fund of political capital allowing them much freedom of action thereafter. Early success also gave wide currency in both countries to myths about the war which, by exaggerating triumphs and minimizing setbacks, bore little relation to the final balance sheet.

The story of Egypt's crossing of the Suez Canal is familiar, as are the feats of staff work, engineering, and commando daring which preceded it. At precisely the same minute as the barrage began on the Golan, some 4,000 Egyptian guns and 250 aircraft pounded Israeli forces in Sinai. Under cover of this fire, hundreds of rubber dinghies ferried waves of infantry and their personal missiles across the Canal. The thirty-five forts of the Bar-Lev Line were attacked and in most cases overrun; a forward perimeter was quickly established to deal with Israeli armoured counter-attacks, while high-velocity water jets blasted some eighty passages through the 60-foot-high sand barrier piled up along the eastern bank. Heavy-duty bridges were then thrown across the Canal to carry tanks and mechanized infantry through the gaps and into Sinai.

By the morning of 7 October Israel had lost 300 tanks. It rushed reinforcements south and on Monday, 8 October, three armoured divisions under Generals Sharon, Adan and Mendler, supported by scores of aircraft, counter-attacked the Egyptian bridgeheads. They were driven off with further heavy losses of some 260 tanks. These running battles, in which Israeli forces were frittered away in considerable confusion, constituted in the judgment of the American military historian already quoted, 'the worst defeat in the history of the Israeli Army'.[3]

On the Golan the Syrians faced an obstacle only slightly less daunting than that overcome by their Egyptian partners. Along the entire length of the so-called Purple Line – the 1967 ceasefire line – Israel had dug an anti-tank ditch four metres deep and four to six metres wide, flanked by a high earth embankment and protected by minefields on all sides. Electronic devices, monitored from an observation post 2,000 metres up on Mount Hermon, kept these defences under permanent surveillance. Behind the tank trap was a network of 112 fortified blockhouses, and behind these the tanks, artillery batteries and infantry of the Golan garrisons. The Syrians knew what they were up against. General Gabriel Bitar, director of military intelligence, had drawn up detailed maps of each section of the front by sending combat patrols to scout out Israeli deployments. For months Syrian commandos had rehearsed an assault on a full-scale model of the Hermon strongpoint seized by Israel after the ceasefire in the Six Day War and which Syria was determined to recover. It was to change hands a few times yet.

The Golan is a basalt plateau strewn with rocks of lava from extinct volcanoes whose conical mounds dot the desolate landscape. This strategic battleground wedged between Lebanon to the north and Jordan to the south overlooks Israel on one side and the plain of Damascus on the other. Here on the narrow front Asad had massed a field army 60,000-strong in two echelons, one forward, the other in reserve. It was armed with some 1,300 tanks, almost 600 artillery pieces, 400 anti-aircraft guns and more than 100 batteries of SAM missiles of different varieties.

On 6 October three Syrian infantry divisions, the 5th, 7th and 9th, each with an attached armoured brigade, were thrown across the Purple Line, butting in serried ranks against Israel's defensive screen. At the same time in their well-practised move, helicopter-borne commandos seized the Mount Hermon observation post in hand-to-hand combat, a bold stroke which deprived the Israelis of gunnery spotting and enabled Syrian artillery to target in on Israeli tank formations.

Although fighting along the whole front was intense, the Syrian armoured spearheads made uneven progress: in the north and in the centre opposite Qunaytra, where Israeli defences were stiffer, the 7th and 9th Divisions suffered heavy losses as they crossed the anti-tank ditch, but they still managed to smash their way forward to modest gains. In the south, however, General 'Ali 'Aslan's 5th Division broke clean through the Israeli line and, fanning out swiftly in three columns, drove the outnumbered defenders from much of southern and central Golan. Only the hurried arrival of Israeli tank reservists, pitched piecemeal into battle as soon as they reached the plateau, prevented a total collapse on the morning of 7 October.

Two Syrian armoured divisions, the 1st and 3rd, had been held back in reserve to take advantage of any breakthrough. When in the Damascus War Room Asad and his Chief of Staff Shakkur saw the spectacular progress of the 5th Division, they ordered the 1st Armoured to slice through the centre of the front, just north of the

5th's axis of advance, and attack Israel's key Golan command post at Naffaq, an abandoned village astride the road from Qunaytra to the Jordan.

By the night of 7–8 October, then, two Syrian thrusts, by the 5th Division and the 1st Armoured, were within striking distance of the eastern shore of the Sea of Galilee and the Jordan bridges. It seemed as if one more desperate push would get them there, opening up the prospect of the recapture of Syria's territory. Victory, Asad felt, was within his grasp.

The going had been hard, hundreds of tanks lay smashed, but the two-front strategy was working. In Sinai and on the Golan Israel had been dealt severe blows and was giving ground.

The troops the Arabs fielded were new-style armies, very different from the ill-led, ill-trained, under-equipped men whom Israel had routed in 1967. Then the Arabs had stumbled into war without forethought or preparation, whereas the 1973 campaign was preceded by years of meticulous planning and elaborate annual rehearsals. In a sort of backhanded tribute to the enemy, a real effort had been made to recruit better educated and technically more proficient officers and NCOs, chosen on the basis of competence rather than political allegiance. In Syria Asad had put an end to the factionalism which had paralysed and almost wiped out the officer corps, while in Egypt commanders like Chief of Staff Shazly and Chief of Operations Gamasy had thoroughly overhauled the demoralized armed forces inherited from Marshal 'Amer. In both countries the profession of arms enjoyed new status.

Both armies had acquired and mastered advanced Soviet weapons: not only tanks, artillery batteries and aircraft in profusion but also innovations such as man-portable missiles, the anti-tank 'Sagger' and anti-aircraft 'Strella', and, most important of all, SAM-6s mounted on mobile launchers which were used in combat in October 1973 for the first time. These weapons went some way to neutralizing Israel's armour and air supremacy.

Taking a leaf, or rather several, from Israel's 1967 book, Egypt and Syria struck first, caught their enemy off-balance – and announced to the world that it was Israel which had attacked them. Surprise accounted for a good part of the Arabs' initial success. Not only did Israel and the United States simply not believe the Arab war plans they had received, but they misread Arab intentions by misreading Sadat himself whom they thought a buffoon. Israel was foxed by the tight secrecy observed by both Syria and Egypt; by the Arabs' more secure communications (aided by a Swedish-Swiss device known as 'Cryptovox' purchased by the Syrian armed forces in 1972); and by an active deception plan which may have included the Palestinian attack on the Schoenau transit camp in Austria used by Soviet Jews on their way to Israel. The uproar in Israel when the camp was closed was such that Prime Minister Golda Meir flew to Vienna on 1 October to remonstrate with Chancellor Bruno Kreisky. Israel was much distracted by this affair on the very eve of the conflict. Also effective was the Arab decision to go to war on the Jewish Day of Atonement and during the Islamic fast of Ramadan. Asad kept the date of D-Day very secret, sharing it only with Chief of Staff Shakkur and a handful of senior officers. Foreign Minister Khaddam did not know it, and the war caught him unawares at the UN General Assembly in New York. With Syrian airports closed, he was forced to fly to Turkey and from there embark by car on a long and arduous journey home. One man close to Asad who was let into the secret was the head of his press office, As'ad Kamil Elyas. He was summoned three days before the attack and, in Asad's thorough way, given a series of texts to draft – the first speech to the nation after the outbreak of hostilities, letters to foreign leaders, and so forth – texts which were kept under lock and key and brought out when needed.

Some weeks before the attack an Israeli air reconnaissance mission led by Aviem Sella (an air force officer who was later to gain fame in the 1981 raid on Iraq's nuclear facility and notoriety in 1986 as the handler of Jonathan Jay Pollard, an American spy for Israel in the United States) detected that Syria had acquired mobile SAM-6s. To test these defences, the Israelis entered Syrian air space on 13 September and, when the Syrian air force rose to meet them, shot down twelve Syrian MiGs. But in spite of these heavy losses Asad did not retaliate as some Israelis thought he would, nor did he expose the electronics of his dense SAM network. He was careful to keep his powder dry for the big assault. So successful was Arab dissimulation that as late as the night of 5–6 October the CIA reported that 'neither side appears bent on initiating hostilities. For Egypt a military initiative makes little sense ... For the Syrian president, a military adventure now would be suicidal.'[4]

But perhaps the Arabs' greatest coup was to deny Israel the chance of attacking first. When in the early hours of 6 October it finally became obvious to the Israelis that an Arab attack was coming, Chief of Staff David Elazar recommended a pre-emptive strike against Syrian air bases, but Defence Minister Dayan and Golda Meir herself ruled it out on political grounds. The 1967 blitz had been preceded by three busy weeks spent in persuading international opinion and especially the United States that Israel was the victim, not the aggressor. These efforts, in the Israeli view, had borne fruit in that they had helped Israel retain the Arab territories it had seized in the war.[5] But in 1973, with the Arabs already at the gate, it was too late to prepare opinion for another muscular demonstration. So the option of pre-emption was rejected and the Arabs managed to get their blow in first, dominating the battlefield for nearly forty-eight hours. 'We were not used to a campaign where the initiative was in the hands of the enemy', Dayan later conceded.[6]

The campaign

What, then, went wrong with the Arab war effort? Briefly, the two-front strategy broke down: Egypt did not advance from the Canal as Syria had expected, Syria fought alone for a long week, and Israel got the better of them one after the other.

Egypt's 'operational pause' from 7 to 14 October lies at the heart of the controversy surrounding the October War. After crossing the Canal, storming the Bar-Lev Line and routing the Israeli tank units defending it, the massive Egyptian force simply dug in. With its back to the Canal, its five divisional bridgeheads were merged into two army bridgeheads defending a strip of desert a mere ten kilometres deep. One or two raiding parties were sent forward but no attempt was made to race in strength for the key Sinai passes controlling the only east-west routes across the peninsula. On 7 October after winning the 'battle of the crossing', and on the 8th after repelling Israel's counter-attack, the Egyptian armies sat tight in their defensive positions. And this was just the moment when Israel, under severe pressure on the Golan, would have been hard put to it to spare the aircraft or the tanks to prevent Egypt from establishing a new line at the passes.

The Russians who had provided the weapons for the campaign were puzzled. 'I don't see why your troops are not advancing', Ambassador Vinogradov objected to Mohamed Heikal, Sadat's confidant. 'Why haven't you consolidated your gains and begun to push on to the passes?' According to the ambassador, an impatient General Secretary Brezhnev had himself asked, 'What is the limit of their limited objectives?' Heikal was one of many Egyptians who felt that an opportunity had been missed:[7]

> It is my belief that had the passes been reached and occupied the whole of Sinai would have been liberated with the incalculable political consequences that would have flowed from such a victory.

But the Egyptians had no intention of moving. The men who mattered were all against it. As has been seen, Sadat's aim was to give the immobile peace process a jolt, not to embark upon large-scale reconquest. The flawless success of the crossing had surprised the Egyptians themselves and their cautious War Minister, General Isma'il, recoiled from further operations which might expose the Egyptian army yet again to destruction in the Sinai wastes. The Chief of Staff, General Shazly, had for two years lavished all his energies on planning to get the army across the Canal – and no further. He passionately opposed advancing beyond the SAM cover and exposing his troops to the superior Israeli air force.[8]

But they had told the Syrians otherwise.

In Damascus Asad and his generals waited from hour to hour for the Egyptians to move and found it utterly incomprehensible that they did not. They constantly expected that the next telegram, or the one after, would bring news of an Egyptian offensive. Heart and soul in their own war and under enormous stress, the Syrian high command had little time to ponder what was happening on the Sinai front. At first their instinct was to explain away Egyptian inactivity as due to some yet undivulged military consideration. Gradually, however, the alarming truth dawned on them that Egypt would not advance and that they were fighting alone. There was as yet no suspicion of Egyptian motives, no thought that they had been betrayed, but bewilderment turned to anguish. 'It was the worst disappointment of the war', Asad recalled.[9]

Israel was very soon aware of Egypt's modest intentions. Its air reconnaissance showed that the troops were digging in, the mobile SAMs were not being moved forward, the deployments were wholly defensive. The Americans were able to confirm these Israeli conclusions with evidence from the horse's mouth. On 7 October, less than twenty-four hours after the start of hostilities, Sadat sent a 'back-channel' message to Kissinger stating his peace terms and adding, 'we do not intend to deepen the engagements or widen the confrontation'. Kissinger promptly shared with Israel's ambassador, Simcha Dinitz, his judgment that Sadat would not extend the war beyond the territory already gained.[10]

Early that morning Dayan ordered the air force into 'immediate, continuous action' against the Syrians. It was, he considered, 'the only force that could stop them'.[11] Given Egyptian inactivity, Dayan realised that nothing needed to be spared for Sinai. With Israel's defences in the southern Golan collapsing, the Israeli high command knew that if Syria's armoured spearheads reached the descent to the

Jordan River it would be very difficult to repel them. Already in Israeli minds Syria was identified as an adversary quite different from either Egypt or Jordan, a view summarized by a Dayan aphorism:[12]

On the Jordanian border we have civilian settlements but no enemy. On the Egyptian border we have an enemy but no settlements. On the Syrian border we have both. If the Syrians get to our settlements it will be calamitous.

For three days, 7, 8 and 9 October, Syrian troops on the Golan faced the full fury of the Israeli air force as, from first light to nightfall, wave after wave of aircraft swooped down to bomb, strafe and napalm their tank concentrations and their fuel and ammunition carriers right back to the Purple Line. The front was turned into an inferno. With the Syrian air force unable to compete, Israel dominated the Golan skies but it lost many planes to Syrian ground fire. According to Asad, the Syrian Operations Room reported that Israel flew an average of 1,000 sorties a day against the Golan and fewer than 50 against the Egyptians in Sinai. (Colonel Dupuy has calculated Israeli sorties against Syria as averaging 500 a day, rising to 600 on 9 October, and has suggested that higher estimates were due to multiple sighting reports.)[13]

While Syrian forces in southern and central Golan were taking the fiercest punishment, the 7th Division in the north, which had been badly hammered in the first two days, now regrouped on the evening of 8 October and prepared for a night advance, protected by darkness from air attack and taking advantage of superior Syrian night-vision equipment. A decisive Syrian push through the exhausted Israeli ranks could still have swung the battle. But the 7th's able commander, Brigadier-General 'Umar Abrash, a graduate of the US Army staff college at Fort Leavenworth, was killed when his command tank was hit. As a result the Syrian offensive was delayed until the morning of 9 October; and although it then made progress, it was halted by massive IAF intervention. Another Israeli disaster was narrowly averted.

Military historians have long debated why the Syrians were stopped. Among the reasons which have been advanced were the greater skill and co-ordination of Israeli tank crews and the fact that the Syrians, often unwilling to yield an inch of hard-won ground even for the purposes of manoeuvre, were imprudently brave. But there is little doubt that the deciding factors were Israel's air superiority over Syria as well as the freedom of the Israeli Air Force to devote its *undivided* attention to the Syrian front. Syrian supply convoys and reinforcements were disrupted and often almost wiped out by air harassment, while Israeli lines of communication winding up to the Golan were largely undisturbed, the Syrian air force being unable to reach them. The IAF commander, Major-General Binyamin Peled, later claimed that from 5.30 a.m. to 10.30 a.m. on 7 October, when Syrian advance units were poised above the Sea of Galilee, no Israeli ground forces were there to oppose them and they were held only by the IAF.[14]

The Syrian advance was blunted, stopped and then turned. By the evening of 9 October, in spite of repeated and fierce Syrian counter-attacks, Israeli units were back at several points on the Purple Line. That same day Israel widened its air attacks to economic targets deep inside Syria – the oil refinery at Homs, Mediterranean ports, power plants, storage depots – allegedly in retaliation for Syrian ground-to-ground missile firings on Galilee air bases. On 10 October the air force headquarters in Damascus and several civilian buildings came under rocket fire. At this stage civilian morale was high with the euphoria of the first few days still intact and, despite the civilian casualties, the inhabitants of the city were more inclined to race up to the rooftops to watch the air battles than to take shelter in basements. On 11 October reinforced Israeli units with strong air support struck across the Purple Line, fighting their way into the maze of tank traps, minefields and concrete pillboxes which were the forward defences of Damascus. By this time the IAF had wreaked great damage on Syria's SAM net but the Syrian air force was still in action and, although short of tanks, Syrian infantry made lethal use of anti-tank weapons in their retreat.

As the tide turned, Asad's mood remained outwardly serene, earning him a reputation for strong nerves, but his impatience with the Egyptians mounted. Communications between the two high commands lost the brotherly warmth of the prewar period. Syrian prodding became sharper as Egypt was reminded of the commitment it had made to a co-ordinated plan. Following Israel's in-depth raids, Asad called on Sadat to send his bombers against Israeli cities, but, reluctant to escalate the conflict, Sadat demurred. Relations between the allies were not improved. To relieve the pressure which Syria was still bearing alone, its high command then sent a senior officer to Cairo to plead for an immediate Egyptian offensive, an appeal which embarrassed the Egyptians and set in train a debate within the general staff for and against a forward push. But still Egypt did not move. By 13 October, when on the Syrian front Israel was finally held just short of the village of Sa'sa' on the road to Damascus, relations between Syria and Egypt were barely civil.

In those few days from 8 to 13 October 1973 Asad's hopes

evaporated of liberating the Golan and of upsetting by force the regional balance of power. It was a bitter blow. Eight hundred tanks, hundreds of other armoured vehicles, 6,000 men, and much else besides had been lost. The war damage was to be estimated at some $3.5 billion.[15] He could not help a pang of regret for what might have been. 'Had I known', he said later with measured understatement, 'that the Egyptian army was going to settle down a few kilometres beyond the Canal, I would have set my own army less ambitious objectives.'[16]

The Syrian army had fought its way forward and now as stubbornly fought its way back. But instead of being able to threaten Israel, Syria found its own capital coming within range of Israeli artillery. Nevertheless it was not like 1967. There was no shame in what had happened, nothing to conceal from the public or to lie about. The army was neither broken nor defeated. Israel had not destroyed it as a fighting force. On Asad's orders Syrian radio and television provided factual coverage of the war, reporting setbacks as well as successes. The Syrians had been a match for the Israelis whose losses had also been enormous and Asad took comfort in the belief that the cream of the Israeli pilots had fallen to Syria's air defences. His troops had acquitted themselves well and the enemy, having pushed a salient into Syria, had now made itself vulnerable to counter-attack. Asad suspected that on his front the Israelis had had enough. They were not keen to take on his powerful second defence line, far less to attempt to enter Damascus. The outcome was not what he had hoped for but, on the surface at least, Asad took the reverses with composure and faced the Israeli advance with defiance.

After days and nights in the War Room he came above ground about this time and called on his brother-in-law, Muhammad Makhluf whom he found alone, their wives and children having been sent to the 'Alawi mountains. Although the mood in the city had changed with the fortunes of war and people were now nervous and downhearted, Makhluf was surprised to find Asad in good spirits and still optimistic about the future. But not having eaten properly for several days, he was also very hungry. He opened the refrigerator and helped himself to some cheese.

The Egyptian offensive

On Sunday, 14 October, Sadat finally launched an attack into Sinai. After resisting for a whole week all pressure to move from the Canal bridgeheads, he now abruptly changed his mind. What brought this about? No doubt Egypt's military achievements of the previous week had given him confidence, perhaps even a momentary sense of immunity. The brilliant crossing of the Canal on the 6th, the defeat of the Israeli counter-attack on the 8th, the consolidation of a seemingly impregnable Egyptian defence line on the east bank, all created in his mind the psychological springboard for further action. But Asad was undoubtedly the main reason. The pressure he was applying could no longer be ignored without endangering the Syrian-Egyptian relationship. Sadat had no love for Asad or for the Syrians, nor, as his duplicity over the war plans revealed, would he allow his diplomacy to be derailed by Asad's eagerness to liberate territory. In his eyes the Syrian leader was a provincial soldier of limited experience and political sophistication who lacked his own grasp of high strategy. Yet at this stage of the war Sadat could not afford an open breach with Damascus which might have brought his double-dealing to public attention, and with it an inevitable accusation of betrayal. He needed to maintain his alliance with Syria, both to reinforce the peace diplomacy he was planning and, in the shorter term, to fragment Israeli strength. By 13 October Israeli forces were half way to Damascus and, from Sadat's point of view, a Syrian collapse seemed imminent, which would allow Israel to switch all its forces to his front, putting his own precious gains at risk. For the Canal bridgeheads he had won were all-important to Sadat: in his mind they were his lever on the peace process, his claim to the attention of callous and indifferent foreign statesmen who had disregarded his calls for peace in the prewar years but who could ignore him no longer.

Whatever the exact balance of Sadat's motives, his offensive into the wastes of Sinai on 14 October, like the decision to go to war itself, was dictated by political not military considerations. His top commanders were to a man against it. Chief of Staff Shazly pleaded that this folly, as he saw it, be called off. Third Army Commander General Wasil talked of resignation, while Second Army Commander General Ma'mun first threatened to rebel against his orders, then had a nervous breakdown. War Minister Isma'il overruled all these objections, but admitted the decision to attack was political.

Militarily the Egyptian offensive was grossly ill-conceived. For one thing it was a week late and Israel, which had by this time mobilized its reserves and fought Syria to a standstill, was ready to meet it. In Israeli minds the centre of gravity of the conflict had already moved from the Golan to Sinai.[17] But Egypt's attack was not only late, it was also half-hearted. Instead of punching in strength towards the passes, a move which even at this late stage still had a slim chance of success, Egyptian armour made four separate thrusts dispersed across a front 150 kilometres wide,[18] and fielding a mere 400 tanks against Israel's 900.[19] In open country, without adequate SAM cover or the support of missile-carrying infantry, these armoured columns were easy game for Israeli anti-tank fire – and for the deadly Israeli air force. By midday it was all over and the mauled remnants crawled back to the bridgeheads: Egypt had lost more than 250 tanks.

News of the long-delayed Egyptian offensive gave Asad and the Syrian high command a brief moment of hope that the fortunes of war might still be reversed and that Egypt might after all redeem its pledges. But its rapid defeat brought gloom even denser than before. Asad was determined that Syria and Egypt should fight on, but now the only prospect was of a stubborn back-to-the-wall defensive war, not the swift splendid campaign he had dreamed of. Not only had Sadat's empty but costly gesture done nothing for the Syrians, but worse still, it laid Egypt open to the manoeuvre which Israel had planned from the beginning and which the Egyptian General Staff had in fact anticipated – that is to say, a reverse crossing of the Canal by Israeli forces to take the Egyptian bridgeheads from the rear. On the night of 15–16 October, Israeli armour slipped through a gap between the Egyptian Second and Third Armies and crossed the waterway at Deversoir at the northern end of the Bitter Lakes. Moving fast and strongly reinforced over the next few days, the Israelis mopped up Egyptian SAM batteries, ambushed convoys, attacked rear headquarters and created general havoc.

Sadat was slow to react to this deadly threat to his whole campaign. He was enormously reluctant to admit a setback, and for several vital days the Israeli crossing was publicly dismissed as no more than a handful of enemy tanks lurking in the Deversoir bushes. No general alert was given for fear of causing panic, although, with the bulk of its armour in Sinai, the Egyptian high command knew that the small strategic reserve west of the Canal could not hold the marauders. The fatal flaw at this critical moment was Sadat's adamant refusal to bring troops and tanks home from the Canal front. When on the 16th Shazly recommended such action, Sadat threatened to court-martial him. Three days later, when the situation had further worsened, Shazly again pleaded for partial withdrawal, but Sadat ruled, 'We will not withdraw a single soldier from the east to the west'.[20] Clearly his obsession to hold on to what he thought was his political ace on the Canal blinded him to the grim reality of his military situation at home. By 22 October Egypt was at Israel's mercy. Encircled by Israeli forces, cut off from their home base and an open prey to the IAF, without food, water or ammunition, 45,000 men of Egypt's Third Army were helplessly marooned in their Canal bridgehead.

Defence of Damascus

Sadat's deception of Asad went beyond the sabotage of their two-front strategy, which his calamitous eleventh-hour offensive did nothing to restore: it extended to the peace diplomacy which he secretly conducted throughout the conflict. As Asad had understood it, the basis of the Syrian-Egyptian alliance was that the two countries would be as one in war as in peace, keeping each other fully informed, in step so as to prevent the enemy exploiting breaches between them. To go to war had been a joint decision; to make peace must, he thought, be equally co-ordinated. It was only after the war, and to his considerable distress, that Asad discovered that Sadat had been engaged in political activities during the fighting which he had not disclosed to his ally,[21] a situation which perhaps says as much about Asad's relative innocence at the time as about Sadat's craftiness. The Egyptian leader did not feel under any obligation to share with Asad his grand design. As he was something of a fantasist, he believed he was personally, on behalf of all the Arabs, engineering a dramatic breakthrough in the peace process which he had no intention of letting his junior partner disturb.

Only later did Asad learn that Sadat had been in secret communication with Kissinger on almost every day of the war, and had even, on 15 October, on the morrow of his ill-fated Sinai offensive, taken the startling initiative of inviting him to Cairo. And there were many other such overtures. Before the war, from 1970 to 1973, the main thrust of Sadat's diplomacy, as has been seen, was to express his readiness for peace if Israel withdrew to its 1967 frontiers. Eliciting no response, he went to war to break the logjam and then immediately set about attempting to link a ceasefire to an Israeli withdrawal. Such was the tenor of his secret wartime signals to Washington. Asad was kept in the dark. Indeed, he was scarcely aware of the manoeuvrings going on in world capitals and the Security Council. When the Russians broached the subject of a ceasefire, he felt he would have time enough to consider the matter once a resolution was tabled.[22] Equally, he had no wartime contact whatsoever with the United States. Preoccupied with the fighting, he neglected diplomacy.

From 9 October, once Israel had pushed Syria back to the Purple Line, Asad's mind was wholly taken up with the defence of Damascus – and with burgeoning hopes of regaining the initiative. Thanks to a

Soviet airlift, his battered troops were being re-equipped, and a fresh division, the 3rd Armoured, was moved up to man the second-line defences at Sa'sa'. Arab allies were pressed to join the fray, and especially Iraq, the first Arab country Asad had told of his intention to go to war. In fact, shortly before H-Hour on 6 October he had asked the Iraqi ambassador to carry a request for help to President Hasan al-Bakr, and a couple of days later a prominent government minister, Muhammad Haydar, had flown to Baghdad with a more urgent plea. Iraq joined the war on the 10th, committing 100 aircraft, over 300 tanks and some 18,000 men. (Before sending troops to Syria's aid, Iraq felt obliged to ask Moscow to request Iran, Israel's ally, to ease its pressure on Iraq's eastern frontier[23] – an illuminating sidelight on the intricacy of Middle East relationships.) Although the Iraqis suffered heavy losses in their first engagement with the Israelis on 13 October, they and a Jordanian brigade which entered the line on the 14th played a role in strengthening the Syrian ring around the salient which Israel had pushed across the Purple Line towards Damascus. King Faysal of Saudi Arabia also sent some 2,000 troops in a gesture of solidarity, while a Moroccan brigade made a token showing in the foothills of Mount Hermon (a squadron of F-5s which King Hasan had promised to the Arab war effort failed to turn up when its pilots were jailed for an attempted coup against their monarch).

By 20 October, in spite of continued Israeli strategic bombing and artillery shelling of Mezze military airport, Asad felt strong enough to consider a counter-attack against the Israeli salient threatening his capital. But by this time he was beginning to be aware that he faced an even more acute threat from his ally's diplomacy.

US and Soviet factors

In angling for American support in favour of Israel's withdrawal from occupied territory, Sadat was several years behind the times. He had no means of knowing that Henry Kissinger had swung the United States decisively behind Israel with the result that the comprehensive settlement Egypt and Syria were seeking was pie in the sky. The whole war was based on an illusion. Sadat duped Asad and in turn was duped himself.

As early as August 1967, two months after the Six Day War, the Israeli cabinet privately decided that there would be no full withdrawal from Sinai or the Golan but that Israel would instead insist on border changes to be determined in direct negotiations with Egypt and Syria.[24]

As for the West Bank, the seizure of which had been a prime war aim, Israel's ambitions there were greater, varying from a partial to a complete takeover. Such a programme needed American support – in advanced weapons, in credits with which to pay for them, and also in political backing, because large-scale annexation such as was contemplated was frowned on by much of the international community. To win over the United States was Yitzhak Rabin's mission during his five-year stint as ambassador in Washington from February 1968 to March 1973, and he was brilliantly successful. The colourless but clear-sighted Rabin was the architect of his country's alliance with the United States, to which Golda Meir added a powerful dose of emotional advocacy when she became prime minister in March 1969. Rabin and Mrs Meir had a great deal to build on since Israel, after a brief flirtation with neutrality, had consciously chosen to align itself with the West as early as the outbreak of the Korean war in 1950. The trend to seek security treaties with the West reached a climax of sorts in Israel's collusion with Britain and France in the Suez campaign of 1956, and its military skills were then spectacularly confirmed in 1967, inevitably attracting American attention. But in the early 1970s a more formal US-Israeli link was forged – largely due to the efforts of Dr Henry Kissinger.

Ever conscious of his background as a Jewish refugee from Nazi Germany, members of whose family had died in concentration camps, Kissinger never tried to disguise his deep attachment to Israel nor his friendship and affection for its leaders.[25] But to win support from President Nixon and leading members of the Administration whose commitment to Israel was less fervent than his own, Kissinger portrayed Israel as a US strategic asset in the global struggle against the Soviet Union. Israel's interest in holding on to Arab territory and in retaining ascendancy over the Arabs was presented as an American interest to exclude Soviet influence from the Middle East. Thus Kissinger married America's global concerns to Israel's local ambitions. Such was the fundamental premise of his Middle East thinking when he took control of US foreign policy as National Security Adviser, then also as Secretary of State, rising as Nixon sank into the Watergate scandal to become the tsar of Washington's diplomacy with almost presidential powers.

The growing US-Israeli intimacy was reflected in ever larger credits and arms deliveries. In 1970 Israel received $30 million; in 1971 after the Jordan crisis, in which Kissinger called on Israel to help protect King Husayn, the aid rose to $545 million. And during the October War of 1973 Kissinger called for a $3 billion aid bill (subsequently scaled down to $2.2 billion) to pay for the flood of arms airlifted to

Israel: 33,000 tons of arms and equipment from mid-October to mid-November and an extensive sea-lift after that, far outstripping the Soviet Union's resupply of Syria and Egypt. In 1972 the United States financed 28 per cent of Israel's defence budget; by 1973 this had risen to 42 per cent,[26] and it was to rise a good deal further.

Among the unpublicized landmarks on the road to America's alignment with Israel were Nixon's letter to Golda Meir on 23 July 1970 (promising that the United States would not insist on Israel's accepting the Arab definition of Security Council Resolution 242); a memorandum of understanding of 1 November 1971 (in which the US agreed to supply the engine for the Kfir fighter, itself modelled on French Mirage blueprints obtained by Israeli agents); another memorandum of understanding of 2 February 1972 (in which the US conceded that Israel need not commit itself to full withdrawal from the occupied territories as part of any interim agreement). Most significant of all, the United States undertook to make no move in the Middle East peace process without first discussing it with the Israelis.[27] These secret commitments directed against the Arabs were to become a permanent feature of the Israeli-US relationship.

Kissinger adopted as America's own the main theses of Israeli policy: that Israel had to be stronger than any possible combination of Arab states if it were to consider making concessions; that the Arabs' aspiration to recover territories they had lost in 1967 was 'unrealistic', 'unattainable', indeed a dangerous aim of pro-Soviet 'radicals'. He ruled out the search for a 'comprehensive settlement' between Israel and its neighbours, arguing instead for limited agreements reached in bilateral negotiations between Israel and individual Arab states, in which Israel stood a better chance of retaining territory; above all, he espoused the Israeli view that the PLO could not and should not be considered an interlocutor. In his own dismissive phrase, 'The idea of a Palestinian state run by the PLO was not a subject for serious discourse'.[28] And this was not the end of it. Kissinger argued that making the Arabs wait – in other words frustrating their hopes of a settlement by a 'prolonged stalemate' – was a desirable aim of American diplomacy which would teach the Arabs to moderate their 'impossible' demands and show them the futility of relying on the Soviet Union.[29] He strove to put the United States in sole control of the peace process by excluding not just the Soviet Union but also Western Europe which he judged too friendly to the Arabs.

Yet, at the same time – and it was this aspect of his diplomacy which was later to seem duplicitous – Kissinger encouraged the Arabs to look to the United States for a settlement and to him personally as the man who could deliver it. Arab leaders who came to rely on him, even Asad to an extent, did not at first realize that he was a dangerous opponent. Not only were they ignorant of the extensive and confidential American-Israeli co-ordination of policies and strategies, but they were slow to grasp that Kissinger was determined to frustrate their aspirations. They did not know that he opposed the widely accepted interpretation of Resolution 242, held by the State Department itself − that Israel should trade 'territory' for 'peace', retreating with only minor adjustments to the 1967 lines. Only much later were they to learn that their central objectives − the recovery of their territory and a fair deal for the Palestinians − had been struck off Kissinger's agenda before he even embarked on his famous Middle East shuttles. Kissinger gave them hints, as in the phrase he often used to Arab envoys − that he would not promise what he could not deliver but would deliver everything he promised. But in the end he hoaxed them. Washington insiders saw what was going on at a relatively early stage, but the enlightenment of the rest of the world, above all of the Arabs, the victims of his diplomacy, had to wait for America's Middle East architecture to be completed in the late 1970s, and they did not learn the full story until the publication in 1979 and 1982 of the two volumes of Kissinger's memoirs.

Given this background, Sadat's prewar and wartime diplomacy could not but fail. By his secret overtures to Kissinger, his expulsion of the Russians to please him, and his double-dealing with Asad, he only weakened what was already a feeble Arab hand.

The US-Israeli alliance was not matched by anything comparable on the other side. Soviet-Egyptian relations were distinctly uneasy and marked by mutual suspicion, while Asad's dealings with Moscow were largely about armaments. The Soviet Union supported the Arab case for full Israeli withdrawal to the 1967 lines and self-determination for the Palestinians, but there was little co-ordination of strategy, as was illustrated by a political muddle early in the war. On the evening of 6 October, when the Syrian and Egyptian armies were bursting across Israel's defence lines, the Soviet ambassador in Cairo told Sadat that Asad had asked Moscow to work for a ceasefire. Sadat was astounded and rang Damascus for confirmation. Asad vehemently denied the report, and a ceasefire at this point would indeed have made nonsense of his whole war strategy. How did the confusion come about?[30]

The initiative came from the Russians, who favoured an early ceasefire because they wished to avoid a confrontation with the United States and because they feared that their Arab friends could not keep up the early momentum for long. It is also possible that Moscow may have been misled by its man in Damascus, Ambassador Nurieddin Muhieddinov, who had had an exploratory talk with Asad before the war about the Soviet support Syria could expect in the Security Council when the fighting stopped. A report of this interview, once it had made its way through the Soviet bureaucracy, may have been the basis for the Soviet ambassador's mistaken remark to Sadat on 6 October about Asad wanting a ceasefire. Whatever the origins of this tangled affair, it illustrated how little co-ordination or even plain speaking there was between Arabs and Russians. A few days later on 10 October there was another muddle when the Russians, after what they claimed were 'not easy' discussions with Egypt and Syria, proposed to Kissinger a 'ceasefire in place'. But Sadat and Asad were still not ready to stop fighting, and the episode was just a further example of their poor liaison with Moscow.

In contrast, Kissinger's co-ordination with Tel Aviv, by way of Ambassador Dinitz, embraced goals as well as tactics: he was as determined as Israel's leaders that Israel should end the war without territorial loss and preferably with territorial gain – to rub the Arabs' noses in the folly of attempting to impose a military solution.[31] And in the meantime, as the battle raged, he used ceasefire diplomacy and a massive American airlift to give Israel the time and the means to turn the tables on its opponents.[32] Later he congratulated himself on having held up a Soviet ceasefire proposal for seventy-two hours 'to help the Israeli offensive in Syria'.[33] The Arabs were up against greater odds than they knew.

Ceasefire

When on 16 October, two days after his ill-fated Sinai offensive, Sadat addressed an 'open letter to President Nixon' in the course of a speech in the People's Assembly, Asad was unpleasantly surprised: Sadat was proposing no less than a ceasefire to be followed by a UN-sponsored peace conference. Admittedly Sadat linked his offer to the recovery of the occupied territories and the defence of Palestinian rights, but what was shocking to Asad was Sadat's evident readiness to end the fighting, trusting to American goodwill for a satisfactory aftermath. Asad remained convinced that Israel would yield only if some form of military pressure were kept up. Moreover, Sadat had not consulted him on this important departure from their agreed position. 'I would have preferred' he wrote to Sadat, 'to have seen the proposals outlined by you to the People's Assembly before they were made public . . . It gives me no pleasure to write these words, but I wish to hide none of my thoughts and opinions from you since we are engaged together in a battle of life and death.' Sadat replied in conciliatory fashion, justifying his initiative by 'my conviction that we must conduct the political and the military battle side by side'. He promised to consult Asad if anything new arose.[34]

Soon, however, he had more urgent things on his mind. As Israeli armour rampaged on the west bank of the Canal, Soviet Premier Kosygin rushed to Cairo on 16 October to urge Sadat to accept a ceasefire in place, without any Israeli commitment to withdraw. Two days later he showed Sadat satellite evidence that no fewer than 300 Israeli tanks and armoured vehicles were behind Egyptian lines. Israel, rearmed by airlifted American weapons, some flown straight to the Sinai battle zone, was now threatening Egypt's Third Army, the port of Suez, and the road to Cairo, indeed raising the spectre of a general Egyptian collapse. The blow to Sadat's morale was terrible. Despairingly he cabled Asad on 19 October:[35]

> We have fought Israel to the fifteenth day. In the first four days Israel was alone . . . but during the last ten days I have, on the Egyptian front, been fighting the United States as well, through the arms it is sending. To put it bluntly, I cannot fight the United States or accept the responsibility before history for the destruction of our armed forces for a second time . . .
> My heart bleeds to tell you this . . .

Asad saw at once that this defeatist message signified the end of the Arabs' military pressure on Israel and the abandonment of their common strategy. Usually a man of calm and restraint, he now raged within the privacy of his office at Sadat's broken nerve. His fighting alliance with Egypt was collapsing. In a last effort to salvage it, he asked an aide to draft a reply[36] to which he put the finishing touches:[37]

> I received your message yesterday with deep emotion. I beg you to look again at the military situation on the northern front and on both sides of the Canal. We see no cause for pessimism. We can continue the struggle against enemy forces, whether they have crossed the Canal or are still fighting east of the Canal. I am convinced that by continuing and intensifying the battle, it will be possible to ensure the destruction of those enemy units that have crossed the Canal.

My brother Sadat, for the sake of the morale of the fighting troops, it is necessary to emphasize that although the enemy has as a result of an accident been able to break our front, this does not mean it will be able to achieve victory.

The enemy succeeded in penetrating the northern front several days ago, but the stand we then made and the subsequent heavy fighting have given us greater grounds for optimism. Most points of enemy penetration have been sealed off and I am confident that we shall be able to deal with those remaining in the course of the next few days. I consider it imperative that our armies should maintain their fighting spirit.

I am sure you appreciate that I have weighed my words with the utmost care and with full realization that we now face the most difficult period of our history . . .

God be with you.

To this plea Asad received no reply.

The irony was that, although Sadat was by now more than ready for a ceasefire, Kissinger was not. On Brezhnev's urgent invitation he set out for Moscow on 20 October with the ostensible purpose of concerting a superpower formula for bringing the war to a close. But just as he had stalled earlier to give Israel time to threaten Damascus, so, with Egypt in dire straits, he now stalled again to give Israel time to tighten the noose around the Third Army. Even so, he thought he had perhaps moved too fast. 'Possibly I could have delayed my departure [for Moscow] another twenty-four hours – and strengthened Israel's military position still further', he wrote later.[38] While he did not want the Third Army destroyed, which some Israeli generals were pressing for, his diplomacy required an Egypt so enfeebled as to offer little resistance to his postwar plans.

The text he finally agreed with Brezhnev called for a ceasefire in place followed by direct negotiations between the parties under appropriate auspices, to implement Security Council Resolution 242. It was adopted by the Security Council at 12.52 a.m., New York time, on 22 October 1973 as Resolution 338 and was intended to go into effect twelve hours later. Halting the fighting where the armies found themselves left Israel holding new bargaining counters in both Syria and Egypt. The word 'withdrawal', so central to Arab demands, did not appear in the resolution, nor did the word 'Palestine'. Resolution 242 was not spelled out but was left in all its ambiguity, to be determined by face-to-face talks as Israel had always wanted.

Egypt and Israel promptly accepted the ceasefire, but Syria did not. Asad knew very well that he could not hold out alone, but he was outraged that Sadat had taken him for granted. Nor did he appreciate the two superpowers striking a deal over his head without bothering to consult him. If there was one trait which came to the fore in a crisis, it was his dislike of being pushed around. So he took his time over the UN resolution, striking a defiant pose for a couple of days and trying to salvage some dignity from a profoundly humiliating outcome.

Sadat knew that Asad's feelings were affronted and belatedly tried to conciliate him with a telephone call on the afternoon of 22 October in which he explained that the ceasefire was the result of a superpower agreement. Asad's recollection of the conversation was as follows:

'I know nothing about any agreement', Asad said.

'I thought they had informed you. That's why I didn't do so myself', Sadat lamely replied.

'But *we* are the ones fighting! We are your associates in the war! It was your responsibility to inform me', Asad protested.

'I've explained everything in a letter which my prime minister, 'Aziz Sidqi, is bringing you.'

'I suspend judgment then', Asad replied.[39]

Later that evening, when the ceasefire had come into effect at 18.52 hours Middle East time, Sadat rang Asad again, obviously perturbed that his disgruntled ally had still not publicly complied with it.

'You haven't announced your acceptance of the ceasefire', he complained.

'On what basis do you propose that I should cease fire?' Asad queried. He had already called off his planned counter-offensive against the Israeli salient but was in no mood to make things comfortable for Sadat.

'They have offered to return the territories to us', Sadat assured him.

'I have seen no evidence of that.'

Sadat was exasperated. He could see that Asad was going to hold out, which put him at a disadvantage with the Arab public. 'All right', he said curtly before hanging up. 'You will be seeing Sidqi.'[40]

Asad's temper was not improved by Israel's recapture that day of the Mount Hermon observation post dominating the Golan. After seizing it on the first day of the war Syria had fought off repeated Israeli assaults, but on the night of 22–23 October Israeli helicopter-borne commandos, with air and artillery support, overran the fortress in one of the fiercest engagements of the war. Israel did not believe that its acceptance of the ceasefire inhibited it from operations on the Syrian front, a view not wholly unjustified since Syria had not yet announced its own acceptance.

That same evening Sidqi flew in to Damascus to a chilly reception in the president's office. He apologized for not keeping Asad better informed of the various steps, beginning with Kosygin's visit, which had led Egypt to the ceasefire. His difficult brief was to convince Asad of Sadat's threadbare claim to have won a major Israeli concession, and he began by repeating the very words of Sadat's letter: Egypt had accepted the ceasefire because Israel was going to withdraw from the territories it had occupied in 1967.

'Who promised you that?' Asad asked.

'The Americans and the Soviets.'

'On what guarantee?'

'We are quite sure of it! In any event, if they don't keep their promise, we can return to war. Our troops are still in place.'

'How long will this return of territories take?' Asad enquired.

Sidqi was confident. 'It will start immediately, immediately! And at the latest it will be completed within six months.'

Asad did not believe a word of it. Faced with such ill-founded optimism which offended against his whole reading of the situation, he could only respond gloomily, 'I have heard what you have to say'.[41]

Asad spent 23 October pondering the few choices open to him. At seven a.m. that day his foreign minister, Khaddam, summoned the Arab ambassadors in Damascus to an urgent meeting. He informed them that Syria intended to reject the Security Council Resolution but, seeing that the Palestine problem concerned them all, it wished to know their governments' opinions of the Syrian position, and what contribution their governments could make to Syria's war effort. Answers from Arab capitals started reaching Damascus late that evening, some expressing approval of Syria's rejection of the resolution. But on the request for help there was silence. Khaddam then asked the ambassadors to contact their governments again, whereupon all the Arab countries concurred that Syria had no choice but to accept the resolution.

While these exchanges were in progress, Asad took direct soundings by telephone with a number of Arab leaders – Faysal of Saudi Arabia, Hasan of Morocco, Boumédienne and Qadhafi, Hasan al-Bakr of Iraq and some Gulf rulers. They all sympathized with his predicament and, now that Egypt had pulled out, expressed concern on Syria's behalf. Well into the evening he consulted with the Ba'th party Commands and with the leaders of the National Progressive Front.

Finally he summoned his generals. Sadat's behaviour was still a mystery to them and they were not yet ready to condemn him, but they had to face the facts. The two-front strategy with which they had gone to war had collapsed. If they wished to fight on, they would have to set themselves an independent strategy and take up the struggle at another time. The consensus was to accept the ceasefire and this was done late on the 23rd. But in a last gesture of defiance, Syria's message of acceptance to the UN Secretary-General spelled out its understanding that Resolution 338 called for total Israeli withdrawal from the occupied territories and the safeguard of Palestinian rights. Israel protested that this formulation changed the sense of the resolution and meant that Syria had not accepted the ceasefire, but to what he took to be an Israeli threat to renew hostilities Asad did not react.

Sadat's more pliant attitude did not serve him well. Paying no regard to the 22 October ceasefire, Israel went all out in the next few days to try to force the surrender of the Third Army and lay siege to the town of Suez. By continuing to hit Egypt hard it seemed not merely to wish to improve its bargaining position but to bring down Sadat himself. It appeared that Golda Meir and her generals thirsted to punish him for catching them napping on 6 October. Nor were they deterred from further assaults by two more Security Council resolutions, 339 on 23 October and 340 two days later, demanding immediate implementation of the ceasefire.

As Sadat's screams for help grew more and more desperate, Brezhnev's anger mounted at Kissinger's apparent tolerance of Israeli violations of a ceasefire which he and Kissinger had worked out together. He suggested the urgent despatch of Soviet and US troops to implement the resolutions, failing which he threatened to act alone. For Kissinger this message from the Kremlin conjured up two spectres: the reinforcement of Soviet forces in an area from which he was determined to expel them, and the horrid thought that Moscow might seek to impose a comprehensive Middle East peace settlement, an outcome which both he and the Israelis were determined to oppose.[42] To heighten the drama to his own advantage and win domestic support, Kissinger chose to portray Brezhnev's impatient message as an 'ultimatum', an unacceptable challenge which the United States could not but take up. He ordered a worldwide alert of US forces to face down the Russians. Israel's local misdemeanours and ceasefire violations were swallowed up in an East-West crisis largely of Kissinger's devising.

In the end he did with some difficulty rein in the vengeful Golda Meir. She wanted Sadat's head, whereas he wanted Sadat's survival because he grasped that the moderate Egyptian would be more useful to Israel in power than out of it. So their dispute was not really, as it was presented, about honouring ceasefires or treating opponents justly, but about which of them better understood Israel's long-term interests. Kissinger glimpsed the postwar opportunity of setting Egypt on the road to a separate peace – which was to be Asad's biggest nightmare.

15

Duel with Henry Kissinger

The great tug-of-war between Asad and Kissinger for the body and
soul of Egypt began even before the October War came messily to an
end in a welter of ceasefire violations. Asad knew in his bones that if he
and Sadat were to salvage a peace even half-way to their liking, they
had to stay together despite the collapse of their war strategy: he could
not afford to let Sadat drift off on a path of his own. Their alliance was
the only defence of Arab interests he could envisage in the hazardous
postwar era. Meanwhile, Kissinger was just as clear-headed about the
need to steer Sadat away from Syria and into a new relationship with
Israel and the United States. There was therefore something inevitable
about the struggle between the still unknown leader of a modest Third
World country and the superstar of the international scene. Behind the
diplomatic manoeuvrings of the time – the Secretary of State's eye-
catching shuttles, the disengagement of the warring armies, the
preparations for a Geneva conference – lay a trial of will and strength.
Whoever won the tug-of-war for Egypt would win the peace and
restructure the region to his advantage.

Asad's first postwar meeting with Sadat took place at Kuwait
airport on 1 November 1973, a week after the ceasefire. Gone was the
euphoria of their prewar planning. With their relationship overshadowed by Egypt's failure to exploit the Canal crossing, the two men
were not at ease. Privately Asad held Sadat to blame for the
breakdown of the two-front strategy but he made no public accusation,
as he still attributed Sadat's caution in battle to fear or to some
military circumstance of which he was unaware. Above all he wanted
to keep the spirit of co-operation alive. But Sadat too nursed a
grievance. Had his 'Syrian brothers' not got themselves into trouble
and called for help, he would not have attacked into Sinai on 14
October, opening the way for Israel's devastating Deversoir crossing.
At the meeting there was a certain amount of haughty bluster in his

demeanour which even extended to his hosts, the Amir of Kuwait and members of the royal family who had come to the airport to salute the leaders of the wartime coalition. As Asad and Sadat talked, an Egyptian functionary came to remind them that the Kuwaiti dignitaries were waiting to entertain them at a lunch in their honour, but Sadat ordered him out of the room: 'Let them wait!'[1]

Convinced of the wisdom of his strategy, Sadat was determined to lead the Arabs in peace as he had in war. His head was full of the great things he expected from Henry Kissinger, who was due to pay his first visit to Cairo on 7 November, and from the friendship he meant to forge with the United States. It was agreed that Asad would stop off in Cairo later in the month, on the way to a summit in Algiers where he and Sadat would brief their fellow Arab leaders about the war.

What Sadat did not discuss with Asad, because it was too humiliating, was that Israel had him by the throat. The Egyptian Third Army was on the brink of collapse and the besieged town of Suez was desperately short of food, water and medicines. In the circumstances, Israel was able to extort from him a whole string of concessions: the return of Israeli prisoners of war, the lifting of the blockade of the Bab al-Mandab Straits, and above all direct talks in which a defeated Egypt would be the supplicant. To loosen Israel's hold, Sadat tried to insist that it pull back its forces to the positions it had occupied at the time of the 22 October ceasefire – a ceasefire which Israel had subsequently and repeatedly violated. But Golda Meir would have none of it. So to break the deadlock Kissinger proposed that both sides commit themselves to a more ambitious disengagement of forces in which the 22 October lines, which were the subject of the immediate controversy, would cease to be relevant. Accordingly, on 16 November, an Egyptian and an Israeli general, Gamasy and Yariv, met in a tent under UN auspices at a point known as Kilometre 101 on the Cairo-Suez road to discuss a separation of forces.

While the generals were talking, Asad, en route for the Algiers summit, arrived on 24 November in Cairo where at the Tahra Palace he found Sadat waiting for him in the full dress uniform of a field-marshal. The Egyptian leader at once launched into a long monologue about the problems of troop disengagement on the Sinai front: the Israelis were to pull back so many kilometres and the Egyptians so many, they had demanded such and such and he had countered with such and such. Asad was quite bewildered. This was the first time he had heard the word 'disengagement', a term which had not figured before in Arab military or political discourse.

'What are you doing?' he exclaimed. 'What is this disengagement?

How can you disengage your forces from Israel's when Israel is still facing Syria in combat? Did we go to war to arrive at this? Do you have the right to act alone?' Clearly he did not appreciate how the plight of the Third Army weighed on Sadat's mind.

'Don't you trust me?' Sadat exclaimed. 'Are you accusing me of acting unilaterally?'

Asad soon learned that Sadat was proposing to negotiate a bilateral agreement with Israel to separate their armies, even though nothing of the sort had been foreseen in the prewar planning. It was a painful awakening. As Sadat spoke of the benefits of disengagement, Asad's anger mounted. He recalled 'Aziz Sidqi's assurance that with the ceasefire the great powers had promised the return of the occupied territories.

'Is this a *joint* decision?' he cried. 'You have already gone three-quarters of the way to an agreement with Israel.'

'Surely there is trust between us?' Sadat asked.

'There are actions which belie trust.'

'All right, then!' Sadat said with characteristic impetuousness. 'I'll cancel everything!'

The next day the two men travelled in separate planes to Algiers. When Asad landed, Houari Boumédienne, the Algerian President, took him aside to say that Sadat had flown in a little while earlier complaining of Asad's accusations of unilateral action. 'What do you think is going on?' Asad inquired. 'He is obviously looking after himself', the Algerian drily replied.[2]

Shortly after the Algiers summit, on 29 November, Sadat did indeed cancel the Gamasy-Yariv talks at Kilometre 101 – but not to please Asad. In fact, the initiative to break off the negotiations came from none other than Kissinger. In their tent the generals had made remarkable progress towards separating their respective armies and, by 26 November, had seemed on the point of reaching an ambitious agreement. The terms had been proposed by Yariv: if Egypt withdrew most of its tanks from Sinai, Israel would pull back to the east of the Sinai passes. But rather than welcoming this great stride towards Egyptian-Israeli harmony, Kissinger privately urged the Israelis to go slow,[3] and on his prompting Yariv dropped all further mention of the Sinai passes from his proposals and instead offered Gamasy a straight exchange of Israel's latest conquests on the west bank of the Canal for Egypt's east bank bridgeheads. Angered by this change, which would have done no more than restore the prewar *status quo*, the Egyptians broke off the talks.

Why did Kissinger intervene? He could not allow the generals at

Kilometre 101 to upset his grand design of an Egyptian-Israeli accord sanctioned and endorsed by a UN-sponsored peace conference at Geneva and presided over by the two superpowers. He saw that if Israel were rash enough to agree to a large-scale disengagement in Sinai before a Geneva conference convened, Syria would demand equal treatment on the Golan. But as Israel was unlikely to budge from there, Israeli-Syrian talks would soon be deadlocked, and this would jeopardize Israel's chance of an accord with Egypt. So, to protect Israeli-Egyptian progress from possible Syrian obstruction, Kissinger advised Israel not to give too much away too quickly. Disengagement before Geneva risked giving Syria a veto on Egypt's moves. Kissinger wanted the Russians to attend a Geneva conference, but he had no intention of sharing the peace-brokering with them: they were to be given a role just big enough to prevent them obstructing his plan. To his way of thinking, the sole purpose of Geneva was to give international respectability to the nascent Israeli-Egyptian peace process. Once Israel had struck a deal with Egypt in such a forum, Syria and the other Arabs could do nothing more effectual than howl. Thus he skilfully played his end of the tug-of-war rope.

On 10 December Asad returned to Cairo to attempt to regain some control over his wayward Egyptian partner. Sadat called on him in the imposing but somewhat seedy Qubba Palace, the habitual residence of visiting heads of state, and to quell Asad's fears that he was moving forward on his own, pledged not to attend the Geneva conference unless Kissinger promised substantial Israeli withdrawals on both the Egyptian and Syrian fronts. Sadat argued that the opening session of the conference was likely to be brief and formal because of the forthcoming Israeli elections — due to be held in December 1973 — and negotiations would drag on into the new year, so it would be best for Egypt and Syria to try to recover as much territory as possible before even going to Geneva. As if to set his pledge on record, he summoned Foreign Minister Fahmy to witness it (although, as Asad recalled, Fahmy was not invited to sit down to receive the presidential instructions):[4]

> Tell Kissinger when he comes that I have agreed with President Asad that disengagement lines must be drawn clearly on the map before the Geneva conference. If this does not happen, we are not going to Geneva.

Syria and Egypt, Asad thought with some relief, were now back in tandem. But he was soon to know better.

Three days after Asad's visit Kissinger was at Sadat's side and by the time he left Egypt nothing remained of these promises. Sadat was soon persuaded that there could at this stage be no lines on maps, only a statement of general principles.[5] In other words, there would be no Israeli pullback before Geneva, nor a detailed commitment to withdraw. Far from defending a common Egyptian-Syrian position, Sadat assured Kissinger that, if necessary, he would go to Geneva without Asad. In fact, eager to escape from any Syrian or Soviet control, he welcomed Kissinger's idea of breaking the conference up into bilateral negotiating subgroups. On the latter's urging, Sadat made a further crucial concession: he agreed to the omission from the letter of invitation to the conference of any mention of the Palestinians and he promised that he would not raise the Palestine problem during the negotiations. Kissinger had managed to distance Sadat from his wartime ally and from the displaced Palestinians whose grievance lay at the heart of the Arab-Israeli dispute.

Round one to Kissinger

The first Asad-Kissinger encounter took place in Asad's office in Damascus at 4 p.m. on 15 December 1973 and lasted for six and a half hours. For Kissinger this was the enemy, the most militant of Israel's neighbours, the closest to Moscow, the only substantial obstacle to his plans for the region. Sadat was already half-way out of the Russian orbit and falling over himself for America's friendship; King Husayn, a long-time Western protégé, already had a tacit relationship with Israel; Saudi Arabia was being wooed with American arms and technology. Only Asad held out and was presumed to be radical, intransigent, hostile. Kissinger came to this first meeting with neither goodwill nor good intentions. Since 1967 Syria and the United States had hardly seemed to inhabit the same planet. The country was *terra incognita*. 'Flying into Damascus after six years of no relations was like going to China. We weren't quite sure what we were going to find', Harold Saunders, a Middle East specialist on the National Security Council, remembered.[6]

Asad was just as uninformed about the United States and indeed about the Western world as a whole. The negotiation with Kissinger was his initiation into the great game of international diplomacy which was henceforth to occupy much of his presidency. But although he had already been in power for three years, it was a field in which he was inexperienced: his energies and thoughts had been absorbed by domestic problems and by preparations for the war. Now he found himself fighting a different sort ᵓf battle on unfamiliar ground. Still a novice, he did not realize that Kissinger cast him as the enemy, nor did he have a clear grasp of what the Secretary of State was after. He was resentful of America's overt support for Israel – the massive wartime airlift had especially angered him – but he saw in Kissinger's sudden focusing on the Middle East a sign of hope: perhaps the United States wanted a settlement after all. Although the Soviet Union had supplied Egypt and Syria with the arms to fight the October War, few Arabs believed that Moscow had the means to deliver peace. Convinced that it could not, Sadat had turned decisively towards Washington, and even Asad was tempted. Only the United States had leverage over Israel, and Kissinger, now in Damascus, was the world-acclaimed magician of diplomacy. Flattered and intrigued by his presence, Asad was ready to place considerable trust in him.

A few hours before Kissinger's arrival, Asad had received a special envoy from Sadat. This was Ashraf Marwan, Nasser's son-in-law and one of the men to whom Sadat entrusted delicate missions. A lanky, baby-faced intellectual famous for his hyper-volubility, Marwan brought splendid news. He reported that Sadat had the previous day settled with Kissinger everything Asad had discussed in the Qubba Palace: disengagement in both Sinai and the Golan would be agreed before the Geneva conference which was due to open less than a week hence on 21 December. The Sinai line had already been drawn and it was up to Asad to waste no time in drawing the Golan line during Kissinger's visit. There was just one trivial change of plan, Marwan said. Actual implementation of Israel's withdrawal would have to be postponed until early in the new year. Reassured by this report, Asad was reasonably confident that both Syria and Egypt would regain a substantial slice of territory before going to Geneva, that they would not go without it, and that the main purpose of Kissinger's present visit to Damascus was in fact to fix the new line on the Golan. As he waited for the Secretary in his office, he brought out a map and spread it out.

Kissinger arrived at the presidential palace, jovial and affable, grasping Asad by the elbow as he shook his hand warmly, and hailing the new era of friendship between the United States and Syria. Asad stiffened. 'There can be no friendship for the moment', he replied, 'since you have taken sides. But at least we can work to eliminate differences.'[7] Kissinger was not used to Arab leaders who resisted his charm. The duel between the two men began in earnest as an exercise in verbal staying-power. Kissinger, in professorial style, opened with an hour-long presentation intended, it would seem, to establish his intellectual ascendancy, to which Asad listened impassively before remarking with a small smile that roles in life were sometimes reversed. A professor could turn statesman, a president become a professor. Whereupon he launched into an hour-long speech of his own outlining the premises and principles of Syria's foreign policy, a statement which Kissinger subsequently wryly referred to as Asad's first 'lesson'.[8]

Undoubtedly there was something didactic in Asad's manner: he wanted to be quite sure that Kissinger understood the necessary historical background to the issues at stake, and he did not mind taking plenty of time to explain himself. In any event, he was by nature digressive and was accustomed to meetings lasting several hours, having been brought up on interminable Ba'th party discussions. But long-windedness was also a negotiating technique, instinctive at this early point in his diplomatic career but later perfected and deliberate. The aim of the wearisome preliminaries became the wearing down of his interlocutor so as to gain the psychological advantage and eventually control him. Over the years more than one American envoy was to wilt under the relentless lectures to which he compelled them to listen. But in Kissinger Asad had met his match.

After the early jousting at their first meeting Kissinger was anxious to move to the practical details of convening the Geneva conference. He spoke of the problem of drafting a letter of invitation to suit everyone, and suggested that it would be wiser to postpone the difficult question of Palestinian participation; he explained his preference for negotiations in subgroups rather than in plenary session; he tried to probe the extent of Asad's commitment to a Soviet role.

Asad put three direct questions which were to him the heart of the matter: Did the United States agree that Syria could not surrender any territory? Did it agree that there could be no peace without the Palestinians? Would the Geneva conference address these central questions or would it be a time-wasting exercise?

Faced with questions he had no intention of answering, Kissinger took refuge in 'constructive ambiguity':[9] the answers to Asad's questions, he explained, would emerge only in negotiations. But with disengagement and the recovery of territory at the front of his mind, Asad found this most unsatisfactory and, turning to a map of the Golan, he tried there and then to draw the reluctant Kissinger into a discussion of Syrian claims. Israel should withdraw, he declared, not only from the salient captured in October but also from much of the Golan seized in 1967. Kissinger backed sharply away.

The following is Asad's recollection of their exchange:

'What then did you agree with Sadat?' he asked, suddenly uneasy.

'We agreed about the Geneva conference', Kissinger replied.

'Is that all? I was in Cairo a few days ago and Sadat assured me he would reach an agreement with you about disengagement before we went to Geneva.'

'Nothing of the sort took place', Kissinger said.

'But just two hours ago Ashraf Marwan was here to say that you and Sadat had agreed on that.'

'Well', said Kissinger, 'We did briefly discuss the Egyptian front, but we did not discuss the Syrian front at all. And we did not link progress on disengagement to the Geneva conference.'

'Sadat informed me otherwise. He insisted to me that we would not go to Geneva unless disengagement on both fronts was agreed.'

'Nothing of the sort took place', Kissinger repeated.

Asad was still not ready to give in. 'But what I agreed with Sadat was at Sadat's own suggestion. Unless disengagement lines are drawn, Syria will not go to Geneva and neither will Egypt.'[10]

In spite of his brave words, Asad had suffered a shock. Clearly Sadat's pledges meant nothing. He was saying one thing to Kissinger and another to Asad and under these circumstances, with the Arabs at odds, it would be extremely dangerous to go to Geneva. Asad took an instant mental decision not to attend the conference. If he stayed away, Sadat might not go either, or, if he did, he would surely not dare to venture too far ahead in Syria's absence.

So Asad let Kissinger continue discussing the conference, raising no objection to the proposed date or to the suggested phrasing of the invitation. Eventually Kissinger asked him which day he planned to travel and who would be accompanying him.

'Nobody is going', Asad said calmly.

'What do you mean, nobody is going? Didn't we agree a date just now?'

'You asked my opinion about the date and about the letter. I raised no objection because these matters are no longer my concern.' Asad was pleased to have sprung a small surprise.[11]

He felt that by this tactic he had at least put some check on Sadat and that nothing irretrievable had been lost. But what he did not realize was that he had played straight into Kissinger's hands for, far from regretting Asad's decision to stay away, Kissinger was positively gleeful. He had engineered the breakdown of the overly successful talks at Kilometre 101 precisely to keep Syria out of the picture. Now he was only too happy to lock Egypt into a solitary embrace with Israel at Geneva. This was the bilateral relationship he wanted to nourish. If Jordan came as well, it could cause no trouble, but Syria was another matter.

Kissinger reported to President Nixon a day or two later:[12]

The Syrian non-participation decision is very satisfactory for us – a blessing in disguise . . . We should let Asad stew in his own juice . . . As I look ahead, I believe there is a real chance of an Egyptian-Israeli agreement on disengagement.

The United States, he continued, should make clear to the Soviet Union that supplying Syria with arms could contribute to another Middle East war, which would have a serious effect on US-Soviet relations. As for supplying Israel, 'our continuing sea pipeline of arms is absolutely essential'.

There could be no clearer statement of Kissinger's aims and sympathies. He could congratulate himself on his performance in the tug-of-war so far.

Conflicting perceptions

The Arabs and the Israelis had fundamentally different perceptions of the meaning of the October War. With characteristic hyperbole, the Arabs believed it had changed the world, broken the stalemate, avenged the 1967 defeat, and restored their self-respect. They felt they had earned the right to be taken seriously and were ready to exchange 'peace' for 'land' in accordance with the provisions of Resolution 242, putting an end to a conflict which had absorbed their energies for over thirty years. Their initial victories were trumpeted by the official Arab media and the later setbacks glossed over as if they did not matter. Their message to Israel was: you have seen what we can do. Settle now or we will in due course have to fight again.

The October War was no less of a watershed for Israel but the conclusions it drew were very different. Its leaders were outraged that the Arabs had dared commit the *lèse-majesté* of attacking them. Indignation was salted with a touch of alarm, for the war had made a dent in Israel's perception of itself after 1967 as a mini-superpower. The early Arab successes had caused deep despondency, plunging Dayan into pessimism and indecision. He called the war an earthqake, and his reputation never fully recovered from it. So, having plucked victory from what had, for a moment, looked like defeat, Israel's instinct was to punish the Arabs, not reward them, and there was no inclination to seek a comprehensive settlement involving the return of territory on all fronts. On the contrary, Israel's priorities were to deny the Arabs the fruits of war, prevent them from ever again developing a two-front strategy, reassert Israeli military supremacy and dismiss Palestinian claims, preferably for ever. Above all, Israel was anxious to exploit to the full its new leverage over Egypt.

Where did Kissinger stand between these rival perceptions? As has been seen, he first ensured a free hand for himself by elbowing aside the Soviets, the Europeans, the non-aligned and the UN Secretary-General. Then he sold the United States to the Arabs as the one power which could get Israel to withdraw, and himself – the architect of détente, of the opening to China, and of the Vietnam settlement – as the diplomatic wizard who alone could deliver such an outcome. Early in November 1973 he gave an interview to the Arab world's leading journalist, Mohamed Heikal of Cairo's *al-Ahram*, an interview which reverberated round the region. 'The Soviet Union can give you arms, but the United States can give you a fair solution by which your lands will be returned to you.'[13] The irony was that, by and large and in the crucial months from October 1973 to early 1975, Arab leaders believed him. It was their ignorance of the Nixon Administration's record, to which their long breach with Washington contributed, which led them to nourish hopes of Kissinger's diplomacy. They did not know that he had undermined the Rogers Plan for a comprehensive settlement; that he had deliberately ignored Sadat's peace overtures before the war; that he had dismissed the Palestinian case out of hand; and that he had pressed for a full US alliance with Israel backed by arms and funds on an unprecedented scale. Evidently his post-October War strategy was directed to securing Israel's objectives and undermining those of the Arabs. Paradoxically, the vociferous right in Israel was far from happy with his performance, believing he could have done still more, and holding him responsible for 'saving' the Egyptian Third Army.

The Geneva conference, and Sinai one

A week after his visit to Damascus Kissinger stage-managed the Geneva conference which opened at the Palais des Nations on 21 December 1973, only to adjourn after ceremonial speeches that same afternoon – and not so far to meet again.

The host was the UN Secretary-General, Kurt Waldheim, the co-chairmen were Kissinger and Gromyko, and the only participants were the foreign ministers of Israel, Egypt and Jordan. Syria was represented by a nameplate and an empty chair. Was this brief gathering a non-event? Kissinger did not think so. In the eyes of the world the conference was the forum in which was to be negotiated the implementation of Security Council Resolution 242. This was the burden of the speeches by Gromyko, Isma'il Fahmy of Egypt and Zayd Rifa'i of Jordan who all spoke of the need for a total Israeli withdrawal, for Palestinian self-determination and the dawning of peace. Kissinger let them speak, confident that his real objective of an Egyptian-Israeli agreement would now have international sanction. The multilateral forum was a fig-leaf for the bilateral deal he had in mind. Geneva *legitimized* his secret diplomacy, giving it respectable endorsement. Everyone was fooled – the Russians who thought they had a role to play, the Egyptians and Jordanians who accepted Kissinger's assurances that this was a first step towards the full implementation of Resolution 242, even the absent Asad who allowed Syria's name to remain on the table.

Less than a month later, on 18 January 1974, Egypt and Israel signed an agreement to disengage their forces in Sinai. It would have come sooner but for the interruption of the Israeli elections on 31 December which returned Golda Meir's Labour Alignment to power with a smaller majority. 'Sinai One', as the agreement came to be known, was stitched together by Kissinger in a seven-day shuttle between Jerusalem and the oasis of Aswan on the Upper Nile where Sadat had gone to enjoy what is perhaps the best winter climate in the world. Here Sadat, at Kissinger's prompting, began making the concessions which were to undermine the Arabs' strategic position for years to come. There were extenuating circumstances. Suez and the Third Army were still at Israel's mercy and he was desperate to bring them relief. Yet his poor hand was partly of his own making, seeing that he had thrown away whatever leverage Soviet support might have provided and squandered Arab strength by dissolving his wartime bond with Syria. He stood alone and defenceless, and Israel with Kissinger's help made a meal of him.

Sadat had hoped Israel would pull back east of the Sinai passes and that Egypt would be able to retain a force of some two divisions and 200 tanks on the east bank of the Canal, a deal which would have gone some way to justify the vast sacrifices of the war. But it was not to be. Instead, in one climbdown after another, he left the passes in Israel's hands, whittled down his own strength on the east bank to a trivial 7,000 men and thirty tanks – and even these few tanks he seemed prepared to give up. Heikal described the scene:[14]

> General Gamasy, the Director of Operations, could not believe his
> ears. 'What a heavy price we paid to get our tanks into Sinai,' he

said . . . He went over to the window and I saw that he was in tears. Kissinger . . . noticed Gamasy's emotion and was irritated by it. 'Is anything the matter, General?' he asked.

What Gamasy found most difficult to stomach was a ban on SAMs and on long-range artillery in a 30-kilometre zone each side of the Egyptian and Israeli front lines, between which had been squeezed a UNEF-patrolled buffer zone. Egypt had now to withdraw its anti-aircraft defences not just from the Sinai bank of the Canal but from the west bank as well, re-siting them deeper into Egypt. There were many other concessions: the Bab al-Mandab Straits and the Suez Canal would be open to Israeli shipping; as a warrant of Egyptian good intentions, an immediate start would be made to rebuild the devastated cities along the Canal; Egypt would not allow Palestinian raids into Israeli-occupied territory or conduct hostile propaganda against Israel; US reconnaissance aircraft would monitor the agreement. Israel had pressed for a formal Egyptian declaration of non-belligerency which at this stage it did not get, but with Sinai One Egypt took a big step out of the Arab-Israeli conflict. In return Egypt was at last able to supply its hard-pressed Third Army.

But Egypt had to swallow another bitter pill. Before pulling back across the Canal the Israelis dismantled and shipped home plant from the Suez oil refinery and from a neighbouring fertilizer factory as well as cranes and harbour machinery from Adabiya. What they could not take they blew up. They bulldozed thousands of tons of earth and sand into the conduit bringing fresh water to Suez, blocking it over a five-mile stretch. Contemplating the pillage and destruction, General Shazly wondered whether in some perverse way Israel liked living in a climate of hatred.[15]

Reporting to Asad

'Do you understand the meaning of what you are doing?' Asad in Damascus shouted down the telephone to Sadat in Aswan. 'It means that Israel will move to our front every tank and gun it has in Sinai.' He had heard that the very next day, 18 January 1974, the Chiefs of Staff of Egypt and Israel were to sign the disengagement agreement at Kilometre 101 and this was his futile, eleventh-hour attempt to stop it. Sadat tried to calm him down. He was about to set off on a Middle East tour to explain his policies to Arab leaders. 'Don't worry!' he cried, 'I'll come to see you tomorrow.'

'All right, *ahlan wa sahlan*! But you should understand the danger of signing such an agreement.'[16]

Gone were the days of the comradely têtes-à-têtes. When Sadat and his party flew in to Damascus on 19 January they faced a Syrian delegation headed by an icy Asad across a table in an airport conference room. As Asad recalled, Sadat opened the nine-hour encounter in defiant mood.

'What do you mean by saying that I am entering into a purely bilateral arrangement?'

'I mean that Egypt is leaving the battle', Asad said bluntly. 'Israeli troops opposite you will now be moved to the Golan.'

'But I'm committed to Syria! I always will be!'

Asad first invited members of the Syrian delegation to speak, then when his turn came launched into an impassioned exposition of his notion of commitment. Several countries were 'committed' to Syria in that they condemned Israeli occupation and aggression. Now Egypt with its disengagement agreement would become just another state offering little more than sympathy. Such lukewarm support was unacceptable: the Egyptian army had to stay in the field. 'We committed ourselves jointly to the war, we fought together, how have things now changed?'

After long and inconclusive discussions Sadat suggested that their delegations withdraw, leaving Asad and himself alone. The altercation continued. Was it true, Asad enquired, that the Suez Canal was to be reopened and that Israel would be allowed to use it? 'Do you believe what you read in the newspapers?' Sadat laughed. 'I want to fool Israel. I'm not going to open the Canal.'

Asad returned to his main worry. 'If you think I want you to stay in the field because I'm afraid to fight alone, you are wrong. The issue is not one of fear. The point is I will not be able to justify your move to Arab opinion, and this will certainly cause a loss of confidence. Why are you in such a hurry to disengage? Can't you leave just one point of confrontation? Perhaps just a single unit at the front? This will at least signal to the Israelis – and to the Arabs – that the Egyptian army is still facing Israel and that war could flare up at any moment. Israel would not then be able to relax completely.'

'All right, all right. Put your mind at rest', Sadat said finally. 'I will keep a unit engaged against the Israelis.' But by this time Asad had little faith in such promises.[17] Well before the expiry of the forty-day deadline for Sinai One, the process of mutual withdrawal on the Egyptian front was complete and not a single Egyptian unit remained engaged.

Isolating Asad

Asad and Kissinger then began to circle each other as attention shifted to a possible disengagement on the Syrian front. Kissinger knew that Israel was determined not to give up the Golan: it had not been inclined to surrender these strategic heights before the war, still less after Syria's breakthrough in October. Golda Meir's view was that the Syrians should be given not an inch for their temerity. But Kissinger's interest – and he argued to Mrs Meir, Israel's interest as well – was to protect Sadat and the Egypt-Israel agreement, and for this a token movement on the Syrian front was necessary however difficult it might be for Israel to swallow. Without a Syrian disengagement agreement Sadat would be isolated in the Arab world and he might then be unable to take further his new relationship with Israel. His first disengagement step might itself be at risk. So Kissinger needed something cosmetic on the Golan to allow the Egyptian-Israeli relationship to flourish.

Asad saw the disengagement process in quite another light, believing optimistically that it would lead in stages to the liberation of the whole of the Golan. This is what his war had been for. In the belief that he was being accommodating, he therefore trimmed his opening demand to the recovery of half the territory – and of course the whole of the salient seized by Israel in October. The contradiction between what Asad expected and what Kissinger intended for him lay at the heart of their struggle in the second round of the prolonged tug-of-war.

At this time Asad still believed that the United States wanted Arab friendship and an honourable settlement. He was attracted, even won over, by the Secretary of State's warmth, wit and apparent sincerity, and the fact that Kissinger was a Jew, in Arab eyes a sort of cousin, was if anything disarming. Sinai One had left Asad in an uncharted landscape. He realized that he was under threat from Egypt's disengagement but not what the precise dangers were or where the next blow would fall. His immediate emotion was anger with Sadat for breaking ranks. When on the morrow of his wrangle with Sadat at Damascus airport, Kissinger came to see him, Asad treated him to an hour and a half's tirade on the subject of Sadat's duplicity, 'its controlled fury [as Kissinger later recalled] all the more impressive for his eerily cold, seemingly unemotional demeanour'.[18] Directed at Sadat but sparing his American Svengali, the outburst showed how far Asad was from suspecting the true objectives of Kissinger's strategy.

Asad's whole nature rebelled against Sadat's way of doing business with Israel. Sadat was volatile, rashly trustful, impetuous and expansive in negotiation, sweeping quibbles aside in favour of the big picture. Asad was stolid, niggardly, essentially wary. Kissinger was later ruefully to remark that the Syrians and the Israelis were more alike than either cared to admit. But anger was not a useful emotion in Asad's predicament. As he saw it, the fundamental difference between himself and Sadat was that Sadat seemed to think he could get what he wanted by 'taking off [his] uniform', as he promised Golda Meir he would do after the disengagement agreement, whereas Asad was convinced that Israel would give ground only under continued military pressure. The question he now had to ask himself − and ask his generals − was whether Syria dare exert pressure on its own. Did Syria still have a military option?

Syria's circumstances were by no means hopeless. Israel did not have Asad by the throat as it had Sadat; no beleaguered Syrian army depended for its very survival on Israel's mercy; the salient which Israel had pushed forward towards Damascus was itself exposed to harassment and Syria could always mount raids, use its artillery and generally make life uncomfortable. 'We could still wage a war of attrition', Asad concluded, perhaps with more optimism than the situation warranted. 'So long as fighting continued, Israel had not won, and if it had not won that meant it had lost.'[19] Throughout the spring of 1974, as each side prepared for the Golan haggle, the guns were rarely silent at the front. It was Asad's way of signalling that he was not a Sadat and that his interests would have to be seriously addressed. But he had few other assets. He was holding some Israeli prisoners, a useful card but one which Mrs Meir insisted he play before she would even start negotiations. He also hoped to derive some leverage from the oil embargo which the Arab oil states had imposed during the October War and which was still holding in the early weeks of 1974.

On 12 February he flew to Algiers to confer with Boumédienne, Sadat and King Faysal of Saudi Arabia on what the next move should be. As might be expected, Sadat defended his conciliatory strategy as the right way to peace while Asad expressed strong reservations. But the other leaders urged him to proceed with disengagement and, to get things started, they recommended that Syria should give Kissinger a list of the Israeli prisoners it was holding. The POW list written in Arabic was accordingly carried by special messenger from Damascus to Washington where Dr Sabah Kabbani, head of the newly opened Syrian interests section, handed it to Kissinger on 20 February. Asad was well aware of the emotional and political importance of the POWs to Golda Meir and, by giving her the list, was attempting to send her a signal. He thought that the Israelis would understand his gesture and might reciprocate with a positive one of their own. When Dr Kabbani gave the list to Kissinger, he urged that before translating it the Israelis should be made to understand its meaning: it meant that the October War had created a new situation in which Syria was able to take positive steps towards a comprehensive settlement. Kissinger told Kabbani that he would not let the Israelis know that he had the list until he reached Israel on 27 February because, as he claimed, he wanted to use it to extract in exchange an Israeli pledge to comply with Syrian demands concerning the disengagement lines. However, he did not keep that promise. As soon as Kabbani left him, Kissinger contacted Simcha Dinitz and asked him to pass on to Golda Meir the news that the names of the Israeli prisoners were safely in his keeping.[20]

The Arabs' 'oil weapon' was the other big subject for debate at the Algiers summit. Unsheathed in late October, it provided for a ban on some oil shipments to the United States and the Netherlands as well as production cutbacks ranging from 5 to 10 per cent. Even though its effect was more psychological than real, Kissinger was nevertheless resolved to strip Asad ahead of the Golan negotiations of any benefits he might derive from it. So he recruited Sadat to argue for the lifting of the embargo against Asad's view that it should hold long enough to help him in the coming talks. Asad secured such a pledge at Algiers but events were to prove that it was an uncertain commitment as Arab leaders bent over backwards to show goodwill to Kissinger.

The Saudi and Egyptian Foreign Ministers, 'Umar al-Saqqaf and Isma'il Fahmy, were sent to brief Kissinger in Washington on the Algiers resolutions, and immediately fell victim to a characteristic Kissinger ploy. He went personally to the airport to greet them, in itself a rare attention, and embraced them in the Arab manner. Perhaps not distinguishing between personal and official relations, they did not imagine that a man who treated them so warmly could be working to undermine their national interests. But after the affectionate greeting came the bad news: Kissinger told them the president would not receive them under the threat of the oil embargo, and lifting it had to be kept quite separate from the Syrian-Israeli negotiations. After consulting their governments, Saqqaf and Fahmy caved in and the embargo was eventually scrapped on 18 March 1974.

Asad had lost both his cards, the POW list and the oil weapon. But Kissinger was still not satisfied that Asad was as weak as he might be before the start of the negotiations, and did his utmost to shut off any potential source of support for him, either in the Arab world or in Moscow. He realized that if Boumédienne of Algeria, a radical leader born of a colonial war, could be persuaded of the merits of step-by-step diplomacy, he could be used to put pressure on Asad. So, on several of his Middle East forays, Kissinger found time to call in at Algiers. Then, to sow suspicion between Syria and the Soviet Union, he gave Brezhnev in Moscow on 26 March the startling news that Asad had asked the United States for arms. Between set teeth Brezhnev inquired why the United States had not complied, to which Kissinger replied with a straight face that he was anxious not to fuel the arms race.[21]

The slender basis for this piece of mischief was a teasing exchange which had taken place in Damascus a few weeks earlier. Remembering that Kissinger had justified the airlift of arms to Israel by saying that he could not allow US arms to be defeated by Soviet arms, Asad had jokingly tried to overturn the axiom: what if Syria were to acquire US arms? It would then be US arms versus US arms. Would not Kissinger's argument collapse? In these remarks Asad was not asking for American weapons, but was making a serious point. He wanted to puncture the view, which Kissinger had made official US policy, that the Soviet Union could be kept out of the Middle East by making Israel overwhelmingly strong. 'Let there be no more talk about American weapons versus Soviet weapons', he told the Secretary of State. 'The problem should be pictured not as the US versus the USSR but as Arab against Israeli.'[22] Kissinger got the point all right, but it did not prevent his misquoting Asad in Moscow in the evident hope of stirring things up between the two allies. When the Syrian leader went there himself in April 1974, to talk things over with Brezhnev and Gromyko on the eve of his Golan negotiations, he found he had a certain amount of explaining to do.

These stratagems were reasonably legitimate compared to the one Kissinger used to strip Asad of any possible military option. Kissinger knew that if fighting were to break out again, Sadat might feel obliged to join in, the oil embargo would be revived, the Russians might return to centre stage, and his own diplomacy would be subject to unwelcome constraints. Kissinger's fear was that Iraq, the one Arab state which had given Asad useful military support in the October War, might now come to Syria's aid again, allowing it to resume hostilities or threaten to do so. Determined to prevent this happening, Kissinger, in collusion with the Shah of Iran and the Israelis, fanned into flames in the spring of 1974 a long-smouldering conflict between the Iraqi Kurds and the Baghdad government, so pinning down the Iraqi army at home. Stirring up the Kurds was a well-rehearsed scenario as Israel had been giving the Iraqi Kurds intermittent help for two decades in the belief

that destabilizing Arab states, even those a long way off, was always to
its advantage. A first group of Kurds had come to an Israeli base near
Ramleh in the mid-1950s for sabotage training, and Rafael Eitan, later
Israel's Chief of Staff, had himself paid a clandestine visit to Iraqi
Kurdistan. By the mid-1960s Israel had become one of the Kurds' main
props.[23]

This murky affair was among the subjects investigated in the wake
of the Watergate scandal by a Congressional committee on CIA
clandestine operations, under the chairmanship of Congressman Otis
Pike (Democrat, New York). The Pike Report completed in January
1976 was considered too sensitive to be released, but was leaked to the
Village Voice[24] in February and then published by the Bertrand Russell
Peace Foundation in 1977. In it Kissinger was reported as explaining
the arming and financing of the Kurds as a means to dissuade Iraq
from any 'international adventurism' – that is to say, coming to the aid
of Syria. The Kurds were never intended to win, merely to sap Iraq's
strength. The report continued:

> Our clients [the Kurds], who were encouraged to fight, were not told
> of this policy. It was a cynical enterprise, even in the context of a
> clandestine aid operation.

The closest Kissinger came to an admission of such dirty tricks was
when he wrote, 'Iran was our ally and was keeping Iraq's armed forces
occupied on its eastern frontier, far away from Syria'.[25] But the Kurds
paid a heavy price for the Secretary's meddling.

Believing that the United States was helping him realize his national
aspirations, the trusting Kurdish leader, Mullah Mustafa Barzani, sent
Kissinger a present of rugs and then of a gold and pearl necklace for
his bride on the occasion of his wedding in March 1974. But having
served the purpose of weakening Iraq, and thereby ensuring that it
could not come to Syria's aid, the Kurds were abandoned in a trade-off
between Iraq and Iran formalized in the Algiers agreement of 13 June
1975. Iran sealed its frontier to the Kurds, whereupon many were
slaughtered by Iraq and tens of thousands displaced from the border
areas. In exchange Iraq ceded to Iran joint control of the Shatt al-Arab
waterway at the head of the Gulf. By this time a thoroughly
disillusioned Barzani had come to realize that he had been cruelly used.
There were to be longer-term and still more fateful consequences. The
Algiers agreement, wrung out of Iraq under pressure of the Kurdish
war, continued to rankle and one reason why the Iraqi ruler, Saddam
Husayn, went to war against Iran in 1980 was to tear it up.

So much for the later conseqences of Kissinger's diplomacy, but in the meantime Asad was now isolated and enfeebled, just as the Secretary of State wanted.

Disengagement agreement

Kissinger's month-long Syrian shuttle, 29 April to 29 May 1974, brought Asad for the first time into the blaze of world publicity. There is little doubt that he relished the battle of wits for which both he and Kissinger were well endowed. Harold Saunders, then one of the Secretary's aides, calculated that the protracted duel involved 130 hours of face-to-face talks and no fewer than twenty-six arrivals and departures at Damascus airport.[26] Kissinger made it a habit, and Asad came to expect, that each session began with a 'seminar' on the policies and personalities of world leaders, or on some weighty political topic such as China and the Vietnam negotiations, or the relations between Congress and the executive branch of the American government. Asad was eager to learn about the world and found in Kissinger a ready mentor. As there was something pedagogic in both their natures, the discussions were usually lengthy, and they came to admire, even to like, each other. The well-publicized contest made Asad's reputation as a dogged champion of Syrian interests and as an independent actor in Arab affairs. But if his prestige rose, his gains on the ground were meagre and the whole drama of the shuttle was no more than a classic example of Kissingerian hocus-pocus.

When disengagement was first proposed the Syrian and Israeli positions were far apart. So to narrow the gap Kissinger invited the two countries to send representatives to Washington with new proposals. Moshe Dayan came in late March and was told that Syria would at the very least have to recover the town of Qunaytra as well as a symbolic sliver of land west of the old ceasefire line. The Syrian emissary, General Hikmat al-Shihabi, head of Military Intelligence – who touchingly arrived bearing gifts of inlaid furniture and brassware for the Secretary which were consigned to the State Department basement – was told that Qunaytra was at this stage all Syria could hope to recover. Kissinger won Shihabi's approval of the principle of a three-zone disengagement schema, as in Sinai – that is to say, a UN buffer area flanked by Syrian and Israeli zones of restricted forces and weapons. The stage was thus set for Kissinger's month-long shuttle between Damascus and Jerusalem.

Putting flesh on the bones of the schema was not easy. There were hiccups over where exactly the Syrian and Israeli forward lines would be drawn, over the size of the UN force in the buffer area, over the depth of the limited force zones, and especially over who was to control the hills overlooking Qunaytra – once, that is, Israel had agreed to give it up. Twice the negotiations were about to collapse altogether, with Kissinger's luggage already on the plane, before Asad called him back. An obstacle which held them up for tedious hours was the matter of Palestinian guerrillas. Israel wanted Asad to promise to prevent *fidayin* raids, but he was equally firm in refusing any such commitment. He was determined not to be lured into becoming Israel's frontier policeman. When the Palestinian issue was first discussed, Kissinger tried to disguise it with a euphemism which he had used successfully in the Sinai accord. Then Egypt and Israel had agreed to refrain from all 'paramilitary' as well as 'military' actions against each other – the former referred to the guerrillas. 'What is this paramilitary action?' Asad asked, pretending puzzlement. He would not accept the term, and for a day or two they played semantic games. At last Asad said, 'Let's speak frankly: you mean the Palestinian resistance. I cannot accept any limitation on their activities in the agreement.' To stop Kissinger pressing the point, he had had published in the Syrian press that day a statement saying that *fidayin* operations would not be included in the proposed separation of forces.[27]

Kissinger understood that the matter was of political rather than practical importance, as Asad had in any event never allowed guerrilla raids against Israel from the Golan. To break the impasse he suggested that the United States inform Israel that it interpreted the Syria-Israel ceasefire to exclude guerrilla raids and that it recognized Israel's right to hit back if it came under guerrilla attack. Kissinger tested this formula on Asad who remarked that what the United States chose to do was no concern of his.[28] The obstacle had been neatly turned. As they talked the heavy guns thundered at the front just down the road. Asad noted that at sticky moments the shelling would intensify, and he recalled that during the Vietnam negotiations Kissinger was said to have strengthened his negotiating hand with bombing raids.

Finally Israel agreed to give up the salient captured in October as well as a narrow ribbon of territory which looped around Qunaytra, symbol of Asad's 1967 defeat. Though it lay in the UN buffer zone and remained out of bounds to his troops, the city was returned to Syrian hands. But before evacuating it the Israelis blew up and bulldozed buildings, water storage tanks and communication lines, as they had done in the Suez area, and were duly condemned for this at the United Nations. The destruction of the town confirmed the Syrians in their view of the Israelis as latter-day Vandals. But apart from the recovery of Qunaytra, Syria had little to show for the treasure and the 6,000 men lost in the war.

The Israelis gained some satisfaction from an expanded UN force 1,250-strong and from retaining control of the Mount Hermon observation post as well as of the hills immediately west of Qunaytra. Syria and Israel agreed to limit forces and armaments within twenty kilometres of their front lines and not to position SAMs within twenty-five kilometres. The disengagement agreement was signed by military representatives of both countries in Geneva on 31 May 1974.

The substance of the hard-fought bargaining was often trivial – a kilometre here or there – but the time and media exposure invested Asad's encounter with Kissinger with wider significance. Syria won back very little but Asad conducted himself well, fighting for every inch and not falling for flattery as Sadat had done. While accepting US mediation, he did not throw away his friendship with the Soviet Union. Personally and politically he came out of the experience a bigger man.

But herein lay the essence of Kissinger's confidence trick. By the attention he lavished on him, Kissinger persuaded Asad that a process for the recovery of his territory had begun and that a step had been taken towards peace – a peace for which Asad explicitly declared himself to be ready.[29] But Kissinger's aim was not a Syrian-Israeli peace, still less a comprehensive settlement on all fronts; it was an Egyptian-Israeli peace which, by removing Egypt from the military equation, would leave the Syrians, Palestinians and Jordanians at Israel's mercy. The modest Syrian step was a device to allow Kissinger to draw Sadat into more far-reaching commitments.

Kissinger was as assiduous in helping Israel as he was in dividing and undercutting the Arabs. He turned on its head the State Department argument that US support for Israel would alienate the Arabs, asserting the contrary thesis that a strong Israeli-US alliance would force the Arabs to come begging. 'The Arabs may . . . loathe us . . . but . . . they have to come to us'.[30] The strategic relationship forged during the 1970 Jordan crisis was deepened during the October War with the massive arms air and sea lift and a ten-fold increase in funding. Political co-ordination, aimed at protecting Israel from having to negotiate with the Palestinians and from pulling back to the pre-1967 frontiers, became more than ever a part of the relationship. Kissinger understood, and had to teach the Israelis, that disengagement need not be a step towards full withdrawal but could be a substitute for negotiations on final borders.[31]

As before, the Secretary of State acted on the assumption that he usually knew better than Israel's own leaders what was good for them. It was he who persuaded the Israelis that it was not to their advantage to destroy the Egyptian Third Army; he again who explained that Syrian disengagement was a 'political imperative' to achieve the much-wanted peace with Egypt; he who urged Mrs Meir not to tie the question of Israeli POWs in Syria to Egypt's disengagement as she had wanted to do: this, he explained, would play into Asad's hands and allow him to block Sinai One. It was he who told Dayan to be tougher, advising him that the Arabs should not get the idea that the United States could easily influence Israel. And it was he who counselled Israel not to give up any Golan settlements in the deal with Asad.

These tactical tips were reinforced by secret commitments. Kissinger fell in with Mrs Meir's view that the Palestinians should not figure in the invitations to Geneva and that no other parties would be invited to future meetings 'without the agreement of the initial participants' – in effect giving Israel a veto on future Syrian or PLO participation.[32] Sinai One had been accompanied by a confidential US-Israeli Memorandum of Understanding in which the United States pledged that it would 'make every effort to be fully responsive on a continuing and long-term basis to Israel's military equipment requirements'.[33] Now the Golan agreement was accompanied by another secret Memorandum in which the United States promised to co-ordinate with Israel any future peace initiatives with Syria.[34] On the eve of his Syrian shuttle and to encourage the Israelis to do what was in any event very much to their advantage, Kissinger persuaded President Nixon to waive repayment on $1 billion of the $2.2 billion credit granted to Israel for arms purchases in the October War. A couple of months later a further $500 million was waived. Commenting on these achievements, a leading American academic, Professor Stanley Hoffman, was moved to describe Kissinger as 'in a way the most important political personality of Israel'.[35]

The Arabs also did not go away empty-handed. They too got secret pledges. To Sadat the United States promised to work for full implementation of Resolution 242, and to Asad for full implementation of Resolution 338. But these pledges had been gutted of meaning by Kissinger's contrary and more specific undertakings to Israel.

Epilogue

There was a bizarre epilogue to this phase of Asad's duel with Kissinger. In June 1974 Richard Nixon, by then afflicted by phlebitis and his Watergate miseries, made a swing round the Middle East to celebrate America's new standing in the region. Between 12 and 18 June he called in on Sadat, Faysal, Asad, Rabin (who had replaced Mrs Meir as premier in April) and Husayn. Nixon wanted acclaim abroad to offset disgrace at home, but the Arabs, who did not understand about Watergate, saw his visit in terms of their own concerns. For them it meant reconciliation with the United States after a long estrangement and American support at the highest level for the honourable peace they longed for. Everywhere, even in Syria, large and friendly crowds turned out to welcome the American President.

Kissinger did not find it a comfortable trip, because the chief seemed to have little insight into his Secretary of State's strategy and kept departing from the script. Nixon pledged to Sadat that he would work for the restoration of Egypt's international frontier in Sinai and spoke of the need to bring the Palestinians into the negotiations – precisely what Kissinger had promised the Israelis he would not do.

Kissinger was to face even greater embarrassment in Syria where the party arrived on 16 June. After the ceremonial niceties – the resumption of diplomatic relations and a promise of a (modest) American aid programme – Asad drew Nixon into his study. This was the moment he had waited for. He began by making an explicit statement of his acceptance of Resolutions 242 and 338 and of his readiness for peace with Israel provided it withdrew to its pre-1967 lines and restored Palestinian rights. He wanted to believe in American good intentions but by this time he needed reassurance. Throughout Kissinger's shuttle, Asad had pressed him for a written undertaking that the United States would support Syria's right to regain the whole of the Golan – but in vain. Now he sought the same pledge, and more, from Nixon. What was America's interpretation of the UN resolutions? Did step-by-step mean making progress on only one front at a time? Did the United States intend Israel to hand back the Golan when it withdrew from Sinai? And how did Nixon envisage Israel's final borders?

Kissinger had built his whole Middle East diplomacy on evading these questions: it was essential for the Arabs to believe one thing while Israel was promised quite another. So Asad's probing created a problem, particularly as Nixon, in the same expansive vein as in Cairo, edged perilously close to giving Asad the assurances he asked for. In a real sense Kissinger was saved by the bell: the American party had that afternoon to catch a plane for Israel. As Nixon moved still closer to Asad's position, Kissinger broke in. 'Mr President', he cried, 'We have to leave. Our time is up. The plane is waiting.' The luckless Nixon made another attempt to answer Asad, and again found himself interrupted by his Secretary of State. Nixon flushed and said, 'Henry, don't you want me to speak?' Unperturbed, and with affable assertions that the matter could best be dealt with when the president returned to Washington, Kissinger drew the meeting to a close and ushered his chief out to safety.[36]

Reflecting on this curious episode, Asad and his colleagues came to believe that Nixon was ready to commit the United States to the search for a comprehensive settlement, but that Kissinger torpedoed the president's intentions. On 8 August, under threat of impeachment, Nixon resigned and the inexperienced Gerald Ford took over the presidency. Kissinger was more than ever in control. Although he did not then realize it, Asad had lost his duel.

16

1975: The Year Things Fell Apart

Asad was in cheerful mood when, on the signing of the Golan disengagement agreement, he gave a long interview to Arnaud de Borchgrave of *Newsweek*.[1]

> Israel now faces the same problem I had when my doctor told me I had to give up smoking or face a dangerous health hazard. Continued occupation has become injurious to Israel's health . . . As when I gave up smoking, Israel will have withdrawal symptoms, but they will get over it.

The burden of his remarks was that now that Israel had started to withdraw, peace was at last in prospect. He made it absolutely clear that he was ready for 'real peace' with Israel, and that once it was achieved there would be no need for demilitarized zones such as Kissinger had so laboriously contrived. He looked forward to negotiating with Israel at Geneva within the framework of Security Council Resolutions 242 and 338. His conditions for peace were, as they were to remain, Israeli withdrawal from the territories occupied in 1967 and the restoration of Palestinian rights.

De Borchgrave pressed him: 'Even if the decision is to dismantle the State of Israel?'

'I would imagine that what the PLO decides will not exceed the spirit of the UN resolutions. And these do not call for the dismantling of Israel', Asad replied.

These conciliatory words from a man thought to be the hawk among Israel's neighbours reflected Asad's commitment to a settlement in the wake of the October War and his confidence in Henry Kissinger's ability to deliver it. His quarrel with Sadat and the meagre pickings from the Golan agreement had still not seriously dampened his expectations. Moreover, the summer of 1974 was the high watermark of Syria's new relationship with the United States, and Asad shared the general Arab relief that Washington was at last addressing the area's problems. Arab leaders pressed Kissinger and Nixon to reveal the American peace plan: did they favour complete Israeli withdrawal? Where would the final boundaries lie? Could an American-Palestinian dialogue be arranged? At this stage the Arabs' only real anxieties sprang from their inability to obtain clear answers. Their hopes remained more or less intact.

With his dramatic shuttles, Kissinger had achieved a separation of warring forces in Sinai and on the Golan. But this was only the beginning. As he never tired of reassuring the Arabs,[2] these steps were not ends in themselves but were meant to start a process which, as confidence grew, would lead on to the fundamental problems of Palestinian aspirations, final frontiers and regional security. Asad and Sadat drew great satisfaction from Nixon's pledge that he would work to implement the Security Council resolutions. What then was the next step to be? Symmetry seemed to demand that after Sinai and Golan the disengagement process move to the West Bank. If an Israeli-Jordanian agreement could be reached, providing for a partial Israeli pullback from the Jordan river, this could pave the way for another round – Sinai, Golan, West Bank, and so on – until all the territories had been recovered and a framework agreed for Arab-Israeli coexistence. So great was the eagerness for peace that for some this incremental method seemed too slow. Impatient souls argued that the time had come to abandon step-by-step altogether in favour of one big leap towards peace on all fronts at a reconvened Geneva conference. The Arabs hoped that they had earned the right to peace with honour.

These rosy visions which Asad shared in the summer of 1974 were far removed from political reality, given the very different objectives which Israel and the United States had quietly agreed upon over the previous four years. Israel wished to restore the *status quo* of 1967–73 by which, in ever closer alliance with the United States, it had reigned supreme over the area. It wanted to make quite sure that the Arabs could never again mount a challenge as they had in 1973. The dispute between Arabs and Israelis was really about the shape of the postwar Middle East. There was a great deal of naiveté in the Arabs' faith in the United States at this time and of self-deception in the nature of the 'lesson' they thought they had administered in the October War. They had meant to impress the world, but had managed only to alarm it. Their war had sparked off a great superpower crisis, conjuring up the spectre of a nuclear exchange, and helped to trigger an explosion in oil prices. The trend towards greater control by oil producers over their industry had in fact started in 1970, but the conflict speeded it up, and the price rises were so steep that they fuelled an anti-Arab backlash which served to erode sympathy for what were legitimate political grievances.

The record suggests, however, that the Arabs' biggest mistake was to be seduced by Kissinger, and they were to pay dearly for their innocence. They failed to grasp that the main American champion of the US-Israeli alliance could not but throw his formidable weight behind their enemy. The pursuit of his design to separate Egypt from Syria by fostering an Egyptian-Israeli relationship under US protection released a host of local demons which were to plague Asad and many others. The vast reordering of the area which Kissinger effected, the reversal of alliances and the consequent breakdown of security, wove a thread of tragedy into Asad's life. A political career which until then had been largely confident and optimistic grew sombre as, with the collapse of his hopes for an honourable postwar settlement, Asad's world became a hostile place. The crucial turning-point came in 1975 when, with the signature of the second Egyptian-Israeli disengagement agreement, a great chasm opened up in Arab affairs.

Instead of bringing peace, Henry Kissinger's diplomacy plunged the region into unprecedented turbulence, spreading violent disorders which more than a decade later had not abated. Kissinger's achievements in the Middle East have been widely admired, but on examination they proved no less destructive than the havoc he wrought in Chile, where the assassination of Salvador Allende opened the door to the Pinochet dictatorship, or in Cambodia where the extension of the Vietnam war led to the still more terrible dictatorship of the Khmer Rouge.[3] Small countries were sacrificed to ill-considered strategic designs. So it was in the Middle East.

Husayn and the Palestinians

Kissinger started working for a second, more extensive Egyptian-Israeli agreement almost as soon as the ink was dry on the Golan accord. In fact, the main purpose of the Syrian accord was, as has been seen, to give Sadat room to move deeper into a relationship with Israel. But before concluding 'Sinai Two' – as the second Sinai disengagement agreement came to be called – Kissinger had to clear away a few obstacles, and of these the most considerable were what to do about Jordan and, looming behind Jordan, the complex and contentious issue of the Palestinians. Could these somehow be finessed out of the way to allow Sadat to move forward?

King Husayn was understandably anxious not to be left out of Kissinger's diplomacy, but he could not press for a 'separation of forces' on the West Bank as he had scrupulously *not* opened a front against Israel in October 1973. Yet, whatever name was given to the process, he too wanted to begin recovering territory and thought that he had amply earned the right to US support by his long friendship with the West, his crushing of the Palestinian guerrillas, and the risks he had run in his secret contacts with Israel and in his efforts to avoid war.

Kissinger could not ignore Husayn's claims but his efforts to meet them were half-hearted. He made a brief attempt to persuade the Israelis to negotiate with Husayn, arguing that it was in their interest to treat with the king today rather than tomorrow or the day after with 'Arafat and the PLO, who were after all the enemies to be kept out at all costs. He had often won past arguments with Israeli leaders about who was the best judge of Israel's interests, but this time he could not get his way. The Rabin government refused to make even a token withdrawal from the Jordan valley or to slacken in any way Israel's physical hold over the West Bank. It was prepared to offer Husayn a sort of housekeeper's role: he could help run the place under Israeli military occupation. But Husayn could not afford to appear an Israeli vassal, so the Jordan shuttle never got off the ground and Husayn was left to reflect, not for the last time, that in a conflict between his interests and Israel's his voice was scarcely heard in Washington.

The Palestinians were more firmly ruled out of account. Kissinger's shortcomings as a mediator were nowhere more evident than in his attitude towards the Palestinians whose dispossession was the central element of the Arab-Israeli dispute which he was allegedly seeking to defuse. Far from looking for a solution to their plight, he endorsed the Israeli view that no role or recognition should be given them and deliberately turned a deaf ear to their signals. The PLO sent four messages to Kissinger between July and October 1973 calling for a dialogue with the United States. In response General Vernon Walters, then deputy director of the CIA, was sent to meet one of Yasir 'Arafat's aides in Rabat, Morocco, in November but his brief from Kissinger was that 'the United States has no proposals to make'.[4] On 'Arafat's pleading, a second meeting was arranged in March 1974, but once again the Secretary of State stonewalled. He also shied brusquely away when Sadat suggested that he should meet 'Arafat. For Kissinger the PLO was not the advocate of a legitimate national claim but a 'disruptive force', a 'terrorist group', 'unacceptable as a negotiating partner', 'overtly anti-American', 'dedicated to the destruction of two important friends of the United States': Israel and Jordan. A PLO-run state was 'certain to be irrendentist' and, with Soviet help, was bound to develop into a radical hotbed like Libya or South Yemen, from which operations against Israel would inevitably be mounted.[5]

Holding highly coloured views such as these, indistinguishable from those of Israeli hard-liners, Kissinger encouraged Israel to exclude the PLO from the postwar settlement. Indeed, a prime aim of his step-by-step technique was to ensure that the Palestine question was for ever pushed beyond the horizon. Kissinger's inhibitions may not have derived solely from an understandable reluctance to tackle a difficult subject: he seemed also to suffer from a psychological block, shared by many Jews, about how to treat the losers in Israel's success story. To admit a Palestinian claim to nationhood was seen as undermining the moral and political legitimacy of Israel's own nation-building. Uncomfortable with the Palestinians, Kissinger accepted Israel's strategy of seeing them as a security problem to be dealt with by tough physical means, rather than as a political problem to be solved by negotiation and compromise.

As for the Palestinian leaders' own behaviour, the tragic irony of much that passed for resistance politics was their total irrelevance. They canvassed for support around the world, squabbled among themselves and with Arab hosts, engaged in obscure debates over the wording of revolutionary texts and tried from time to time, usually in vain, to slip a punch through Israel's defences. But Israel was determined to offer them nothing but the sword. The more Arab and international endorsement the PLO received, the more firmly Israel and Kissinger refused to treat with it.

In the autumn of 1974 the Palestinians won unprecedented backing for their national aspirations when on 20 October an Arab summit at Rabat declared the PLO to be the 'sole legitimate representative of the Palestinian people'. This decision transferred responsibility for the recovery of the West Bank from King Husayn to the PLO. Chief advocates for the change were Asad and King Faysal who did not wish Husayn to benefit from acting as spokesman for the Palestinians and who hoped to promote the PLO to a negotiating role in Kissinger's diplomacy – such was the extent of Arab wishful thinking. Fresh from this Arab success, Yasir 'Arafat climbed to still greater heights when he addressed the General Assembly of the United Nations on 13 November, winning a standing ovation and observer status for his movement. One memorable line in his hour-long speech was: 'I have come bearing an olive branch and a freedom fighter's gun. Do not let the olive branch fall from my hand.' So just as the Palestinians thought they were getting somewhere, Kissinger dropped the West Bank from his agenda, aligning himself yet again with Israel. In the words of Israel's representative at the UN, Ambassador Yosef Tekoah: 'The PLO will remain what it is and where it is – outside the law and outside Palestine'.

'Arafat's efforts to edge his unwieldy movement into a negotiating posture had the effect of causing Kissinger and the Israeli leaders to work all-out for what the Palestinians feared most of all, a separate Egyptian-Israeli deal.

Sinai Two

Asad lost hope in the possibility of a comprehensive settlement early in 1975. His optimism evaporated as with growing alarm he began to see that Kissinger had got the better of him and that American pledges to implement Resolution 242 were worthless. Already in the latter months of 1974 evidence was piling up of Kissinger's true intentions as he tried to narrow the gap between Egypt and Israel in preparation for a second step on the Sinai front, but by the turn of the year the facts were too blatant to be ignored. On 3 December 1974 Rabin candidly stated that the aim of the deal he hoped to strike with Egypt was to isolate Syria.

Not surprisingly, Asad's confidence in Kissinger's step-by-step tactics crumbled, as did his remaining trust in Sadat. Asad angrily warned Sadat that another partial withdrawal in Sinai would only prejudice Syria's chances of recovering the Golan, to which Sadat answered with windy statements that he would accept nothing less than a full Israeli withdrawal from Sinai, the Golan, the West Bank and Jerusalem – all within three months – and moreover that he was confident the United States would ensure it. Such fantasies, flagrantly at odds with what Sadat was himself quietly negotiating with Kissinger, only served to make Asad angrier still.

Battle lines were soon drawn. In mid-January 1975 King Faysal of Saudi Arabia, the Arab world's most respected leader, was given an ecstatic welcome in Damascus where, after endorsing Asad's insistence on a comprehensive Israeli withdrawal and guarantees for Palestinian rights, he promised Syria $350 million in aid. The Egyptian journalist Mohamed Heikal, who was in Damascus for the king's visit, was one of the first Arabs, perhaps the first commentator in any country, to pronounce that Kissinger had no overall plan to solve the Middle East crisis but intended merely to split the Arabs.[6] Soviet Foreign Minister Gromyko hurried to Damascus in early February to share with Asad his alarm that Kissinger was not only dividing the Arabs but also undercutting the Soviets. To counter these dangers Gromyko and Asad called for the immediate resumption of the Geneva conference with the participation of all the parties including the PLO. But this was as much a pipedream as Sadat's vision of an all-round Israeli retreat.

The last phase of the Asad-Kissinger duel was now at hand as the Secretary of State, who had been working behind the scenes on Sinai Two, now pressed forward in spite of cries of concern from all over the Arab world. Taking Egypt out of the Arab military equation ruled out the possibility of war: this was Kissinger's ambition. But to Asad it sounded more like a death sentence for Syria, Jordan and the Palestinians who would then be unable to present any credible check upon Israel's ambitions. The Secretary saw it as stabilizing the region, Asad as overturning the region's balance.

Kissinger paid an exploratory visit to the Middle East in mid-February, three weeks before embarking on 7 March on what he hoped would be his last Egypt-Israel shuttle. Between these visits Asad, in a last-minute attempt to deflect him from his course, again spelled out his views on Middle East peace through Arnaud de Borchgrave of *Newsweek*.

Asad: 'If the Israelis return to the 1967 frontier – and the West Bank and Gaza become a Palestinian state – the last obstacle to a final settlement will have been removed.'

De Borchgrave: 'Could this be a peace treaty with Israel?'

Asad: 'Yes, it could. When everything is settled it will have to be formalized with a formal peace treaty. This is not propaganda. We mean it – seriously and explicitly. You look so surprised from the expression on your face. This is not a new logic in Syria's policy; it is our fundamental position, decided by party leaders.'[7]

A couple of days later Asad returned to these themes in a speech in Damascus:[8]

> For our part we look upon peace in its true sense . . . a peace without occupation, without destitute peoples, and without citizens whose homeland is denied to them . . . Anyone who imagines that the peace process can be piecemeal is mistaken . . . We way now as we have always said – that peace should be based on complete withdrawal from the lands occupied in 1967 and on the full restoration of the rights of the Palestinian Arab people.
>
> It is being said – and we might ask – what are these rights? Our answer is: let the PLO be asked. It is the PLO which will answer and we will support it in its reply.'

This emphasis on the PLO meant two things. First, Asad wanted to promote the PLO as a party in the peace process and was anxious to help 'Arafat in the battle he was then waging with George Habash's rejectionists. Secondly, Asad was aware of the need for Syria and the PLO to stand together as Egypt slipped further out of the Arab camp. He was already looking to his defences. On 8 March, with Kissinger back in the Middle East for the Sinai Two shuttle, Asad announced his readiness to establish a joint military and political command with the PLO, and 'Arafat welcomed the idea.

The next day Kissinger spent four hours with Asad in Damascus. There was real poignancy in an encounter between two men who by this time recognized the irreconcilability of their positions and yet retained a measure of respect for each other. Had Asad liked Kissinger less, he would no doubt have been rougher with the man who was threatening to turn his whole environment upside down. Kissinger's aide Harold Saunders was struck by the Syrian leader's politeness. 'I profoundly disagree with your strategy', he remembered Asad saying, 'But I don't want it to affect our personal relations.' Saunders had rarely seen such civil behaviour between political enemies.[9]

Asad protested to Kissinger at his customary length that a further step in Sinai would be an act of immense significance, destroying Arab solidarity and isolating Syria – precisely what Kissinger had in mind. The latter explained that his policies were dictated by the circumstances of the time: President Ford was still finding his feet and could not risk offending domestic opinion by putting pressure on Israel; Premier Rabin, newly in office with the slimmest of Knesset majorities and contending with fierce right-wing opposition, could advance only cautiously; the PLO successes at Rabat and at the UN were to many alarming rather than reassuring. And once again Kissinger tried to convince Asad that a fresh step in Sinai did not preclude progress on other fronts. But the contradictions between them were total, and from then on the row was out in the open. Asad's mounting anxiety was reflected in numerous statements to the Western media. To the *Washington Post*, for example, he declared that peace could be achieved only 'by a collective Arab movement on all fronts', and not by Kissinger's 'tiny acrobatic movements'.[10] On French television a few days later he asserted:[11]

Individual, partial or small steps do not spell peace . . . The Americans are clearly aware of our opinion. These steps aim at creating new contradictions from which Israel will benefit . . . To be serious, the movement towards peace must be a collective movement.

Asad's pleas and objections were all swept aside, as they had to be, for Kissinger had by this time accepted the Israeli view that there could be no further concessions of any importance either on the Golan or on the West Bank. Yet Kissinger's mediation between Egypt and Israel was not plain sailing either, and was even suspended for a couple of months at the end of March, as Israel insisted that it would not withdraw from the Sinai passes and oilfields unless Egypt explicitly renounced belligerency. Kissinger would have wished the Israelis to be more flexible, seeing that Sadat was ready to give them the substance of what they wanted, if not yet the politically sensitive words. Once again he claimed to know better than the Israelis. 'If we wanted the 1967 borders', he railed privately against Rabin and his colleagues, 'we could do it with all of world opinion behind us. The strategy was designed to protect you from this. We've avoided drawing up an overall plan for a global settlement.'[12] The Israelis remained unmoved.

But this was only a hiccup and during the summer the process of taking Egypt out was swiftly completed. The landmarks were a meeting in Austria at Salzburg between Presidents Ford and Sadat on 1–2 June and, more to the point, a private haggle between Kissinger and Simcha Dinitz, Israel's ambassador to Washington, early in July in the Virgin Islands where Kissinger was on vacation. Here the deal was struck which finally opened the way for the bilateral Egyptian-Israeli agreement which, despite their tough negotiating tactics, the Israeli leaders had longed for all along. Following a last shuttle in August, Sinai Two, a package of three published and four secret agreements, was initialled on 1 September 1975 and signed in Geneva on 4 September. As the United States was a party to these accords, they were in effect trilateral arrangements establishing a precedent for Camp David three years later. The Soviet Union boycotted the ceremony on the grounds that Kissinger's diplomacy had 'frozen' the Middle East in Israel's favour.

Under the terms of the published agreements[13] Egypt and Israel undertook to resolve their conflict by peaceful means and to proceed towards 'a final and just peace settlement'; they renounced the threat or use of force; non-military cargoes going to or from Israel would be allowed through the Suez Canal; the disengagement of forces was continued with an Israeli pullback of between twenty and forty kilometres to provide a wider UN buffer zone; the Mitla and Giddi passes were demilitarized, although Israel retained a surveillance station near the eastern end of the Giddi pass and continued to control the main route leading down to the Gulf of Suez; Egypt recovered the Abu Rudais oilfields on condition that it shared the road to them with Israel. A major innovation was the stationing in the passes of some two hundred American technicians to oversee the Egyptian and Israeli early-warning systems.

The American presence, together with that of UNEF and the substantial demilitarization of the whole area from the Canal to the passes, meant that Egypt lost once and for all any ability to put military pressure on Israel. Its role as a combatant in the Arab cause was over.

The United States' secret agreements – one with Egypt, three with Israel – have been extensively leaked.[14] The United States promised Egypt to consult with it on any Israeli violations of the agreement, to help it build an early-warning system in Sinai, and to *attempt* to get new talks going between Syria and Israel. But these crumbs for Sadat were sparse compared to the banquet Kissinger set before Rabin.

The commitments he made to Israel on behalf of the United States were lavish to a degree never seen before. Israel got a promise of $2.5 billion for 1975–6 and further payments to compensate for the loss of Egyptian oil; a guarantee of oil supplies from Iran or, failing that, directly from the United States; and an open-ended undertaking to maintain Israel's military strength. The political engagements were still more far-reaching. The United States pledged that it would not recognize or negotiate with the PLO so long as it did not recognize Israel's right to exist and did not accept Security Council Resolutions 242 and 338. This clause, which was to cramp American policy-making thereafter, formalized the veto Kissinger had already given Israel on Palestinian participation in the peace process. The Palestinians found themselves in a Catch 22 situation. To start a dialogue with Washington they had to recognize Israel's national claim while abandoning their own (because 242, and by extension 338, referred to Palestinians only as refugees). More than a decade later the Palestinians were still caught in this impasse.

On the subject of Syria, Kissinger had already agreed with Dinitz in the Virgin Islands that only 'cosmetic' changes need be contemplated on the Golan. Now he got Ford to write the Israelis a letter saying that, in any Golan talks, the United States would take into account Israel's position that it should not return to the 1967 borders. The United States further pledged that Israel would not be pressured to negotiate with Syria, Jordan and Egypt all together, but only with each of them bilaterally. Insofar as Egypt and Jordan were concerned, the United States agreed that there would be no further 'interim steps' before the conclusion of final peace treaties. In other words, these countries had to accept peace on Israel's terms or resign themselves to the continued occupation of their territory.

More generally the United States promised to co-ordinate its peace strategy with Israel, to make no proposals without first consulting it, and to seek to prevent the adoption of proposals made by others if they seemed contrary to Israel's interest. Israel also wanted a firm US commitment to protect it in the event of Soviet military intervention in the Middle East, but it had to be content with a promise to 'consult' – one of the rare occasions when fear of Congressional objections checked Kissinger's generous hand.

With this elaborate package of agreements, understandings and commitments, Israel secured virtual control over the Middle East policy of the United States. Kissinger had tied the hands of his successors as well as his own. To the nationalist right in Israel, unsatisfied with his achievements, Kissinger was a typical assimilated Jew, anxious to 'find favour' with the Gentile world. Yet in service to the Jewish state, he may one day be seen to rank only behind Theodor Herzl and David Ben Gurion.

Some three weeks after the signing of Sinai Two, Kissinger gave a dinner for Arab delegates to the United Nations who still knew little of his secret agreements. Blandly he assured them that close relations between the United States and the Arab world were 'irreversible', adding that in the days ahead the United States would 'refine its thinking on how the legitimate interests of the Palestinian people can be met in an overall peace'.[15] He was even ready, he said, to work for a second Golan accord. Asad was one Arab who was no longer duped.

Kissinger, who lacked neither courage nor confidence, came to see Asad for the last time on 3 September 1975, on the eve of the signature of Sinai Two. It was a briefer meeting than usual, lasting a little over an hour, and more than a little chilly. Kissinger dangled the bait of further talks on the Golan but Asad had no time to waste on empty charades. By now he felt thoroughly betrayed and was angry with himself for having given even brief credence to Kissinger's assurance that disengagement would proceed in step on both the Egyptian and Syrian fronts and that the United States did not mean to divide the Arabs. Real peace, he told Kissinger wearily, could not be achieved by showering arms on Israel nor by introducing early-warning systems and US technicians, but only by Israeli withdrawal and satisfaction for the Palestinians.

Although he had been outwitted, it was not in Asad's nature to indulge in self-pity. Grimly he faced the truth that, with his environment falling apart, he was compelled to protect himself and his country from the tidal wave of disturbance which swept across the Middle East as a result of Sinai Two. For the Egyptian-Israeli agreement was profoundly destabilizing. The removal of Egypt, the largest and strongest of the Arab states, left the rest of the Arab world with a sharply heightened sense of insecurity. Who would now defend it? Who could act as a brake on Israel's expansion or deter it from striking at will? Ferocious feuds broke out. Egypt quarrelled violently not only with Syria but with Libya and with the Palestinians. Syria and Iraq crossed swords. Feeling that every man's hand was against it, the Palestinian movement became even more fragmented, and in Lebanon was sucked into a murderous war with the Maronites which in length and savagery made the PLO's earlier clash with Husayn seem tame.

The spectre of Israeli hegemony, so humiliating to the Arabs after 1967, now returned to haunt them as hopes awakened by the 1973 war proved vain. For years the Arabs had yearned for a great leader or an Arab coalition or a friendly external power to impose a new regional order so as to even things up between themselves and Israel. Now they found themselves back in the old unhappy stalemate, only matters were far worse than before because Egypt, the linchpin of the Arab system, was no longer Egypt.

All these emotions could be seen reflected in the sombre statement which Asad and the Ba'th party's National Command issued on the day of Kissinger's farewell visit to Damascus. Calling on the Arabs to mobilize in the face of the Zionist enemy, it expressed 'great anxiety' at the 'serious setback' which the Arabs had suffered. It was painfully obvious to Asad and to every thinking Arab that Egypt's pan-Arab phase, which had begun twenty years earlier, was over, at least for the time being. Kissinger had, of course, not done the job single-handed: the knocks Egypt had suffered from Syria's secession, from the Yemen War and the 1967 disaster, and from its economic exhaustion, had helped prepare the ground for its retreat from Arab commitments, for its switch of alliances from Moscow to Washington, and its readiness for dialogue with Israel. But whatever the causes, Sadat's ideological somersault was so complete that it seemed a sort of 'anti-Suez', setting in reverse everything Nasser had stood for.

Quarrel with Iraq

Security considerations were uppermost in Asad's mind as he contemplated the ruin of his relations with Egypt and the final collapse of the wartime alliance. He had always been faithful to Nasser's doctrine that in defence of the region Arabs should unite only with Arabs — a scheme of things in which the Egyptian-Syrian alliance was central. Now Sadat had abandoned Syria and taken Egypt into the orbit of the United States, Israel and the Shah's Iran. The slanging match which at once erupted between Damascus and Cairo formed one pole of Asad's world in 1975; the other was an equally bitter quarrel with Iraq. Sinai Two did not create the feud between Syria and Iraq, but it exacerbated a rumbling conflict of which the root cause was the gory split in the Ba'th party on 23 February 1966 when 'Aflaq's old guard was put down in blood by the Military Committee in Damascus. Two years later, in 1968, 'Aflaq's Iraqi supporters seized power in Baghdad which immediately became a haven for Syrian exiles. From then on, the two capitals traded plots, accusations and rival claims to party legitimacy. On Asad's accession in 1970 differences were papered over and correct if not wholly amicable relations were restored to the extent that, when Syria went to war in 1973, Iraq lent it valuable aid.

Kissinger's diplomacy tore up this fragile entente. Unable to resist an opportunity to attack a party rival, Iraq's leaders taunted Asad with defeatism over his Golan agreement with Israel, using against him the very accusations he was himself levelling at Sadat: was he not also betraying the Arab cause by courting Kissinger, accepting Resolution 242 and contemplating a peaceful settlement? A long way from the front line and having lost no territory to Israel, Iraq could afford to refuse all truck with the enemy, align itself with Habash's Rejection Front and strike holier-than-thou poses. Asad dismissed such sniping as the bile of men 'who had not fought and who never would fight'. He counter-attacked by charging that Iraq's 1975 accord with Iran over the Shatt al-Arab was a collusion with imperialism, a 'surrender of Arab land' and a betrayal of the 'revolution in Arabistan' – the Arabs' name for Iran's border province of Khuzistan whose population was partly Arabic-speaking and whose 'liberation' was later to figure as an Iraqi war aim in the Gulf War. So envenomed did relations become that even Iraq's aid to Syria in the 1973 war provided a subject of dispute, with Damascus deriding Iraq's help as too little and too late while Baghdad, with self-serving hyperbole, accused Syria of gross ingratitude in not acknowledging that Iraq had saved the day.

If Damascus and Baghdad had not been so much at odds, they might perhaps have been able to resolve their long-standing dispute over the division of Euphrates waters. Rising in Turkey, the Euphrates flows through Syria and Iraq before merging with the Tigris to swell the great Shatt which debouches into the northern Gulf. Dam-building and irrigation projects in all three countries from the 1960s onwards caused a row to break out over the volume of water each was entitled to – a dispute which at the time of writing was far from settled. Iraq's charge in April 1975 was that Syria's great Euphrates dam at Tabqa, built with Soviet help, and Lake Asad which rose behind it in the 1970s threatened the livelihood of three million Iraqi peasants downstream in the Euphrates basin. The squabble over water rights grew into a vast bone of contention, not to be assuaged by mediation attempts, most notably Saudi efforts. From 1975 onwards the two countries began abusing each other over the airwaves – 'fascist right-wing criminal' was standard invective – arresting each other's sympathizers, moving troops threateningly to the border, and setting off explosions in each other's capitals.

Caught between the fires of Cairo and Baghdad, Asad felt lonely and exposed – and lonelier still when King Faysal of Saudi Arabia was assassinated on 25 March 1975 by an apparently deranged, American-educated member of the royal family. The austere Faysal, a stalwart nationalist, had been a staunch Asad supporter during and after the October War. It was he who took the lead among Arab producers in pumping money into Syria's war-ravaged economy. The oil money, more than capital-starved Syria had ever previously dreamed of, was a sort of consolation prize, feeding an investment and consumer boom and obscuring the disastrous consequences of the October War.

Faysal had first approved of Kissinger's step-by-step diplomacy on the understanding that it would lead to a comprehensive peace, but when this proved a delusion he shared Asad's anger and would undoubtedly have been a powerful ally in the troubled times ahead. So his disappearance from the scene was sorely felt. His successor, King Khalid, was a weaker personality and more susceptible to Washington's arguments. Devotees of conspiracy theories saw in Faysal's murder, preceded by the sudden deaths in the United States of his Foreign Minister, 'Umar al-Saqqaf, and of the governor of the Saudi Arabian Monetary Agency, Anwar 'Ali, within days of each other in November 1974, a US-Israeli plot against the Arabs.

Apart from the dissensions it fuelled, Kissinger's peace diplomacy stimulated an unprecedented arms race. Feeling intensely vulnerable, Asad turned for yet more weapons to the Eastern bloc, the only source available to him. He could not hope to fight Israel alone, but could he at least aspire to become strong enough to deter an Israeli attack? This was a puzzle with which he was to wrestle for the rest of his presidency. Thus an immediate result of Sinai Two was to upgrade relations between Damascus and Moscow. In early September, within days of its signature, Asad set off for Czechoslovakia and a few weeks later, on 9 October, arrived in Moscow to review with all the top leaders – President Podgorny, General Secretary Brezhnev, Premier Kosygin, Foreign Minister Gromyko and Defence Minister Grechko –

the dangerous situation in which he now found himself. Asad was grateful for the Soviet arms airlift during the October War – no fewer than 934 return flights – but politically the Russians had been inept, allowing Kissinger to cut them out of postwar diplomacy to Syria's disadvantage. As both Asad and the Soviet leaders saw themselves as victims of the Secretary's of State's scheming, they drew closer together. The great progress made in Syria's infrastructure from the mid-1970s onwards and in the growth of its armed services stemmed from this tighter bond.

The reverse of the coin was a distancing from Washington after the brief honeymoon which began with the restoration of relations in June 1974. Asad did not break with the United States as his hot-tempered predecessors might in the circumstances have done. Whatever the ill it had done him, he accepted that it was the reigning great power which had to be dealt with, so he kept the channel open – for some years in the person of Richard Murphy, US ambassador in Damascus. But from then on Asad never wholly trusted the United States again.

Lost opportunity

Was an opportunity for peace missed after the October War? One of the big 'ifs' of contemporary Middle East history concerns the two years in which Kissinger was in charge. Had the United States wanted a settlement it was uniquely well placed to achieve one: Israel was dependent on its arms and aid, the Arabs welcomed its mediation, and the Soviet Union, Europe and Japan were all out of the picture. So receptive was the Arab mood that Israel could no doubt have secured some territorial adjustments on all fronts, extensive demilitarization and international guarantees, quite apart from the more enduring security which normal relations with its neighbours would have provided.

But the Arabs' case was flawed by their unrealistic belief that their war effort entitled them to a settlement, an expectation further boosted by the oil price explosion – the very factors which alarmed Israel into resisting concessions. The gravest Arab weakness lay as ever in disunity. Built largely on distrust, the Egyptian-Syrian alliance could not resist the battering of war and fell apart. Jordan and the PLO were rivals, each scheming against the other. The Arabs could not easily agree on how to dispose of Palestinian territory, even if Israel had withdrawn from it. Tensions divided oil-rich and oil-poor countries.

Yet beyond such quarrels, which were the very stuff of Arab politics, the eagerness for peace was widely shared.

Israel, however, was not ready for a comprehensive settlement, wanting neither to withdraw to its pre-1967 frontiers nor to treat with the Palestinians. The October War had dented Israel's complacency but failed to persuade it of the need for a radically new approach to its neighbours. The instinct was still to dominate the Arabs, to deter them by overwhelming strength, to break up the Arab front at all costs rather than to seek a stable peace through compromise. Israeli thinking about the Arabs became trapped in the rut of military security. The equation was a simple one: Palestinian terrorism posed no significant threat; the only real danger came from a combined attack by the conventional armies of Egypt and Syria; but once Egypt was removed, Syria alone presented no military problem.[16] That this policy nourished frustrations and hatreds seemed of little account compared to the benefits it conferred. The call for 'defensible frontiers', which meant staying on the Jordan river and the Golan, now melded with an annexationist tendency which had long existed in Zionism.

Into this context Kissinger appeared like a *diabolus ex machina*, enjoying unfettered scope because Nixon's last year and Ford's first were a time of unusual presidential weakness. Devoted to the Israeli cause and endowed through charm, quick wits and tactical skill with extraordinary personal authority, he was able to sweep aside dissenting views whether from the Pentagon, from leading figures of the foreign policy establishment, prominent academics or American ambassadors to key Arab countries. Kissinger even managed to steer two presidents away from the global settlement both appeared to want.

There was perhaps a more particular reason why the opportunity for peace was missed in 1973–5, and this was the manipulative attitude towards the region which Israel had long had but which took root in Washington also as the two countries embarked on their strategic relationship from 1970 onwards. For good reasons of self-defence Israel had early sought close, if usually tacit, relations with the non-Arab states of the region, such as Iran and Ethiopia, in the hope of containing the Arabs by a 'periphery' strategy. It also intervened covertly where and when it could to undermine Arab societies – in the 1960s, for example, by helping the southern Sudanese in their struggle against Khartoum, by helping Iran arm the Yemeni tribes against Nasser during the Yemen civil war, or by arming and funding Iraqi Kurds against Baghdad.

The Israel-Iranian relationship, close from the mid-1950s, grew still more intimate in the 1970s when, under the Nixon Doctrine, these two proxies were built up with US aid in order to protect America's regional interests. But what they really shared was hostility to the Arabs and it was through them that the United States was drawn into murky waters. The resort to 'dirty tricks' proved addictive. Just as Kissinger made use of the Israeli-Iranian relationship for his Middle East diplomacy, so in southern Africa he put the Israeli-South African relationship to work against African regimes he considered undesirable, such as the left-wing government of Angola which took power in the wake of the Portuguese revolution of 1974. It was not long before Israel was contributing ideas, intelligence and operational capabilities to American strategy in many parts of the world.

Given this wider picture, it was perhaps unreasonable to expect Kissinger's Middle East arrangements to be anything but biased.

17

The Lebanese Trap

With Sinai Two Henry Kissinger and Israel shaped an Arab order to suit their convenience – an order Asad was determined to contest. To accept the *diktat* of Sinai Two would have meant Syria's declining into just another weak state on Israel's borders, another Jordan perhaps, living on sufferance, projecting no power, and devoting much of its military energies to protecting Israel from Palestinian raiding. Such an inglorious fate was utterly repugnant to a man of Asad's touchy nationalism. The slogan of 'steadfastness' that he then launched conveyed the will to fight back and not simply accept an environment in which, with Egypt neutralized, Israeli supremacy was unchallengeable.

With this defiance Asad's Syria took its first steps towards becoming a substantial regional power and Israel's only remaining Arab opponent of any stature. The notion that Damascus is to be reckoned with in Middle East affairs has in recent years become a commonplace. But it was not always so. Memories have faded of its subordinate role in the first decades of independence, when it was a good deal less important than either Cairo or Baghdad and often seemed little more than a political football kicked back and forth between them. In 1955 Syria fell into Egypt's orbit, and spent the next twenty years in the toils of that relationship, whether wedded or divorced, whether allied in war or at odds in peace. Egypt then lay at the centre of the regional power system, the magnetic pole alternately attracting and repelling Syria. This was the world Nasser had made and which shaped Asad's adult thinking. But 1975 shattered the familiar pattern, forcing Asad to forge a new system of power relationships.

Survival was uppermost in his mind as he came to understand that Kissinger had outfoxed him. Sadat had betrayed him, Iraq was hostile, Saudi Arabia after Faysal's death was uncertain. In the exposed middle ground, under the immediate shadow of Israel, lay Syria, with around it Jordan, Lebanon and the mass of volatile and desperate Palestinians.

Vulnerable to Israeli power and manipulation, these fragile societies were now in the firing line. Under this threat Asad's attention was forced to shift away from peace diplomacy and the duel with Kissinger towards his immediate neighbourhood, which became his prime arena of interest. To resist, Syria needed weight, strategic depth, allies. And so was revived an old idea, predating the Anglo-French carve-up of the region, of the essential unity of the Arab Levant with Damascus as its focus. Both his protective envelope and his area of potential weakness, the Levant was the strategic terrain which Asad now struggled to bring under control.

From 1975, therefore, dated Asad's intense interest in every twist of Palestinian politics, in every shift in King Husayn's nimble footwork and, of course, in every chapter of Lebanon's long torment which was to absorb him for the next decade and beyond. Put in bald military terms, his anxiety was that Israel might attack on one of his exposed flanks: a left hook through Lebanon or a right hook through Jordan. But the threat was not only military. Israel might turn his flank politically by gaining a preponderant influence over either of these neighbours, or it might entrap him by escalating its conflict with the Palestinians. What was at stake in the confrontation with Israel was not just Syria's security, although that peril was real enough, but also its nationalist reputation, its regional stature.

Asad's first defensive move was a rare sortie to Lebanon in January 1975 for a meeting with President Sulayman Franjiya. Given huge publicity, this encounter in the sleepy town of Shtura in the Biqa' valley was meant to signal the closer bond Syria wanted with its neighbour at this dangerous time. Syria's interest in Lebanese affairs did not arouse surprise in either country, for in the general perception Syria and Lebanon were members of the same body. Within living memory, the French had enlarged autonomous Mount Lebanon, the home of Maronite Christians and Druzes, to create the Republic of Lebanon by the addition of territories inhabited, as it happened, mainly by Sunni and Shi'i Muslims. The inhabitants of the coastal cities – Tripoli and its hinterland, Beirut itself, Tyre and Sidon – as well as the Biqa' valley and the south thought of themselves as belonging to a larger entity which they called Syria. In culture, religious diversity, ethnic background, spoken dialect, even in what they ate and drank, Syrians and Lebanese were much of a piece. The populations of the two countries were thoroughly intermingled, with countless families straddling the French-drawn frontier. Intimacy did not, however, preclude a certain measure of suspicion and rivalry, even extending to the relative value of the Lebanese and Syrian *lira*, with the

Lebanese currency at that time invariably ahead. Lebanese Christians feared Syrian irredentism, while Syria in turn was wary of Christian Lebanon's traditional ties with the West and its wavering commitment to the Arab cause. But by and large Syrians and Lebanese knew that they belonged together.

As the overspill in both directions was so immediate, each was highly sensitive to developments in the other's country. The mountain frontier was notoriously permeable to smugglers, to political refugees, to troublemakers, to ideas. A coup in Damascus was always the subject of anxious speculation in Beirut, while Damascus tried to make sure of a say in the composition of Lebanese governments and especially in the choice of president as well as of intelligence and security chiefs. The two countries were like connecting vessels: the political temperature of the one could not but affect that of the other.

Syria's involvement with Jordan and the Palestinians was only slightly less intimate. Three months after his meeting with President Franjiya, on the very day in March that Kissinger began the Sinai Two process, Asad invited Yasir 'Arafat's PLO to join Syria in a 'united command' and in June, as Kissinger's wooing of Sadat intensified, Asad responded by proposing a second 'united command', this time to King Husayn of Jordan. On 10 June Asad paid a visit to Jordan, the first by a Syrian ruler since 1957, and declared in the newly revived spirit of regional solidarity that Syria and Jordan were 'one entity and one country'.[1] Even more exposed than Syria to Israeli power and disgruntled at being left out of Kissinger's peace plans, Husayn echoed these sentiments on a return visit to Damascus in August. A long honeymoon between Syria and Jordan followed.

Asad had no illusion about the military value of links with Lebanon, the Palestinians and Jordan: they were political accords, which reflected his concern to protect himself by exerting some control over his immediate environment. Nor was there any great trust between Asad, 'Arafat and Husayn. The three were thrown together in self-defence, in the shared if threadbare hope that, if they closed ranks, Israel could be held.

Civil war

The immediate challenge came from Lebanon.

Civil war broke out in the spring of 1975 and, the fire spreading by leaps and bounds, had by the end of the year claimed thousands of lives, inflicted massive physical damage, partitioned the country between armed gangs, and destroyed the authority of the state. First and foremost, the warfare in Lebanon posed a security problem for Syria: in Asad's own words at the time, the security of the two countries was indivisible.[2] He reacted to the threat by repeated attempts to stop the fighting and check the drift towards partition. Three trusted subordinates, the energetic, rough-spoken Foreign Minister Khaddam, Chief of Staff Shihabi and Air Force Commander Jamil, were his chosen instruments, making numerous journeys across the mountains to the Lebanese capital to bring the warring parties together. (Lebanon was to engross Khaddam to such an extent over the coming decade that the Lebanese nicknamed him the *wali*, or the governor. Lebanese politicians, however, sometimes complained that life under his thumb was worse than it had been under the French.) The traffic was as heavy in the other direction, as Lebanese and Palestinian leaders of all factions flocked to consult Asad. In 1975 alone he met the PLO fourteen times.

At the heart of the conflict lay the Palestinians. Over 150,000 of them had taken refuge in Lebanon after the 1948 war, a total swollen mainly by natural increase to about 400,000 by the mid-1970s. A considerable number were assimilated into Lebanese life but most of this stateless and wretched population lived on the outskirts of the principal cities in camps which had become part slum, part fortress. Following the PLO's violent showdown with King Husayn in 1970–71 many guerrillas took refuge in Lebanon, turning the hilly 'Arqub region in the southeast of the country, which had been largely neglected by the government, into their stronghold. But the Palestinians' presence was felt far beyond the camps and the remote 'Arqub. As Muslim Lebanon provided a supportive environment, the Palestinians were soon woven into the fabric of life, particularly in West Beirut where the various militias set up their headquarters and where their leaders came to exercise great influence. The *dolce vita* of the capital was more agreeable than the rigours of Fatahland, but there was more to it than that: Lebanon was the only country where Palestinians enjoyed any freedom of movement. Efforts were made to regulate them – notably the Cairo Agreement of 1969 – but paper promises were soon forgotten. When Israeli raids showed that they could expect no protection from the Lebanese army, the Palestinians moved heavy weapons into the refugee camps in a clear breach of the Agreement. Soon the encroachments on Lebanese sovereignty became blatant and beyond counting.

Politically, the Palestinians found allies in the Muslim establishment and, significantly for the future, they also forged alliances with, and helped arm, radical movements which sprang up at that time in Lebanon's permissive climate. Because of this local backing and their own strength, the Palestinians came to throw their weight about, resisting attempts to control them by the weak Lebanese state.

For a decade, from the mid-1960s, the expanding Palestinian presence served increasingly to polarize Lebanese opinion. Muslims, sharing Arab nationalist sentiments, were committed to their cause, but Christians on the whole were not, and the more importunate the Palestinians became, the wider grew the Muslim-Christian cleavage. Most Christians wanted to keep their country out of the Arab-Israeli dispute. In their view Lebanon's *raison d'être* was to provide a refuge for Christians, distinct and separate from the Islamic Arab hinterland. They feared the Palestinians whom they came to see as dangerous agents of change, threatening their preponderance, trampling on Lebanese sovereignty, encouraging malcontents to wage class warfare, and above all dragging neutral Lebanon into conflict with Israel.

The Christian front-runner was Pierre Jumayil's Kata'ib (or Phalanges) Party, the oldest, best organized and best armed of the Maronite vigilante groups and increasingly seen by Christian opinion as the only effective champion of 'Christian Lebanon'. Ranged against it was the 'National Movement', a motley collection of radical parties and private armies which came together in 1973 under the banner of Kamal Junblatt, an intriguing figure, part Gandhian socialist, part ambitious politician, part feudal Druze chieftain. His National Movement fronted for the Palestinian militias without whose strength he could not have challenged the Maronites. As battle lines were drawn, most of the country's politicians took sides. President Sulayman Franjiya and ex-President Kamil Sham'un, both with strong-arm gangs of their own, fell in behind the Kata'ib, while leading Sunni politicians like Rashid Karami of Tripoli and Sa'ib Salam of Beirut became spokesmen for the Palestinian cause.

The Palestinians were not the only source of tension in Lebanon. From the birth of the republic Muslims and Christians differed on the political culture to which they felt they belonged, the former tending to identify with the Arab world and the latter with the West. Within both Christian and Muslim camps were further fissures and antagonisms: Lebanon was, after all, a patchwork of clans, creeds and ethnic groups living in uneasy balance, a state of affairs recognized in the elaborate sharing out of public offices and perks on the basis of sectarian identity. The most striking features of the Lebanese system were first the enduring political influence of a handful of notables, then the sectarian schisms, and finally the control of economic life by a network of trading and banking families more concerned with profit than with public good. These arrangements were a recipe for nepotism and resistance to reform. As a result, Muslims came to resent the Christians' built-in privileges and to press for change. Druzes and Shi'a in particular grew disgruntled with a political system founded in essence on a pact between Maronites and Sunnis, which relegated them to lesser status. The underdogs and the poor of all sects began to challenge the fat living of the rich, whether Christian or Muslim. The most potent development was the mobilization of hundreds of thousands of Shi'a, victims of government neglect, Israeli bombing and Palestinian high-handedness, by the remarkable Iranian-Lebanese cleric, the Imam Musa al-Sadr, whose Movement of the Disinherited was founded in 1974 and its military wing, Amal (Hope), in 1975.

Other forces competed for the backing of the underprivileged as well as of all those dissatisfied with the closed, often corrupt circle of the establishment. In the Lebanese free-for-all, in which fifty daily newspapers were published among countless other periodicals, raucous extra-parliamentary pressure groups flourished, importing into the country the various currents and quarrels of the wider Arab world. Communists, Socialists, Ba'thists, Nasserists, pan-Syrians, and rival sub-sects of each, campaigned against each other and against Lebanon's unreformed political machine. So fragmented a society laid itself open to penetration and manipulation by agents from the surrounding countries and beyond. In this 'centre' of the Arab world, where money, ideologies and politics were traded, tussles for influence raged between Israel and its neighbours; between Syria and its Arab opponents, Egypt and Iraq; between Britain and France; between France and the United States; and between the Soviet Union and the West, to the great disturbance of the local scene.

The system might have survived such indigenous and imported stresses, however, had it not been for the added disruption of the Palestine problem. It had been clear from the Six Day War of 1967 when Israel took over the whole of former Palestine, that Lebanon could enjoy no stability in the absence of a political settlement for those who had been dispossessed. Unsatisfied Palestinian frustrations could not but overturn the unsteady Lebanese equilibrium. It was not by chance that the long rumbling tensions erupted into civil war in 1975. Serious disturbances broke out in the spring, precisely at the time when Secretary of State Kissinger started his Sinai Two shuttle, and the conflagration raged out of control in the autumn just as Egypt and Israel concluded their agreement. The Lebanese civil war ran parallel with Kissinger's Middle East diplomacy and can be seen as the gravest of the regional conflicts provoked by his step-by-step advance to Arab disunity.

For when it became clear that Kissinger's objective was not a comprehensive settlement but merely to take Egypt out of play, two powerful currents of alarm and frustration were released in Lebanon. The Christians felt that they would never be quit of the hated and hostile Palestinians, while the Palestinians, deserted by the most powerful Arab state, trembled for their future. It was this insecurity which drove both sides to war. On a flying visit during his early shuttles, Kissinger met Lebanese politicians who pleaded with him to save their country by doing something for the refugees.[3] But he did nothing. After ten years of mounting fear Lebanon in the mid-1970s could have been saved only by a comprehensive Middle East settlement in which the Palestinians were accommodated. Such was the devout hope of Lebanese of all complexions, of neighbouring Arab states and of the mass of Palestinians. But Kissinger and Israel decided otherwise. Sinai Two gave Lebanon its *coup de grâce*.

Israeli reprisals

Israel's part in the tragedy predated Kissinger's. It had long been Israel's policy to make its neighbours pay heavily for Palestinian raids from their territory. Massive retaliation was designed to oblige host governments to control the guerrillas, and on most fronts it worked. But when the Palestinians started operating out of southern Lebanon in 1968, the puny Lebanese army was too weak to bottle them up. Its attempts to do so resulted in clashes which themselves sharpened Lebanon's tensions, sparking off a violent internal debate about the role of the army: should it protect the guerrillas from Israeli strikes (as Arab nationalists demanded) or punish the Palestinians (as the Maronites preferred)?

As it happened, Palestinian attacks on northern Israel from Lebanon were small-scale and ineffective between the 1967 and 1973 wars, largely limited to cross-border sorties into the occupied Golan Heights. But Israel hit the hapless Lebanese in response to Palestinian operations anywhere in the world, or sometimes simply because Lebanon gave the guerrillas house-room. The aim of Israeli retaliation went beyond punishing or deterring the Palestinian enemy: it was evidently designed to provoke dissension inside Lebanon.[4]

For example, when an Israeli airliner was attacked at Athens airport in December 1968 by guerrillas of George Habash's PFLP, Israeli commandos raided Beirut airport and blew up thirteen Lebanese airliners, sparking off a cycle of strikes, demonstrations, and the fall of the government. Israeli attacks against southern Lebanon became particularly brutal following the influx of Palestinians from Jordan in 1970–71. There were several large-scale armoured sweeps through villages, in which houses were bulldozed, prisoners taken, and resisters shot. The increasing use of Israeli air power made parts of the south uninhabitable and accelerated the flight of Shi'i peasantry to slums around Beirut where inevitably they upset the community balance and were soon to change the character of the capital altogether. Following the brutal murder of Israeli athletes at the Munich Olympic Games in 1972, a two-day Israeli rampage along Lebanon's Mediterranean coast dynamited bridges, flattened scores of houses and left a trail of death and devastation in sixteen villages.

These attacks set the Lebanese against each other as well as Christians against the guerrillas. The Palestinian presence gave Israel a mechanism with which to provoke violent confrontations between Maronites and Palestinians, and a handle over Arab peace in general. On the night of 9–10 April 1973 Israeli commandos raided central Beirut and murdered three Fatah leaders in their beds, immediately precipitating huge anti-government demonstrations, a clash between the Muslim prime minister Sa'ib Salam and the Maronite president Sulayman Franjiya, and more than two weeks of fierce fighting between the Lebanese army and Palestinian militias.

When in the spring of 1974 groups of Palestinians started striking into Israel proper, Israeli reprisals duly escalated, with further damage to the fabric of Lebanon. On 15 May, in an attempt to secure the release of some of their fighters held in Israeli jails, Palestinian guerrillas took hostage a schoolroom of children in the Israeli border town of Maalot. The unit responsible called itself 'Kamal Nasser' after one of the Fatah leaders assassinated by Israel in Beirut in April 1973. When Israel refused to trade and stormed the building, sixteen children were killed in the crossfire before the guerrillas themselves were killed. The Maalot killings triggered off several days of ferocious, widespread and systematic Israeli attacks by aircraft, gunboats and ground forces against Palestinian camps and Lebanese villages, in which whole settlements were flattened and between 300 and 400 people killed and wounded.

These violent events took place when Kissinger was in the Middle East, in fact at the height of his Syrian shuttle. He asked Asad for his reaction to Maalot. 'Asad was icily aloof', Kissinger wrote later. 'Why wouldn't Israel give up twenty prisoners and save its children?' he inquired,[5] but even then Asad was worried that Israeli retaliation against Lebanon might sooner or later suck Syria in.

In all, there were some forty-four major Israeli attacks on Lebanon between mid-1968 and mid-1974, resulting in the deaths of about 880 Lebanese and Palestinian civilians.[6] But beyond these casualties and the material damage, the attacks undermined the coherence of Lebanese society and tore the country apart. From 1973 onwards both sides of the Lebanese divide, sensing that they faced physical annihilation, stepped up their efforts to arm themselves and scrambled for allies.

As the fighting in Lebanon spread in tandem with the final phase of Kissinger's diplomacy, Asad became convinced that the conflict was being manipulated from outside. In his analysis, the Lebanese civil war had been fanned into flame to distract the Arab world from what Kissinger was cooking up between Egypt and Israel: it was a cover for Sinai Two, drowning it in blood. Secondly, he saw it as a plot to draw the Palestinian Resistance into war in order to destroy it. And thirdly, he believed the goal was to partition Lebanon, the 'old Zionist aim', as he put it.[7] If the Christians were driven by Palestinian and Muslim pressure to set up a sectarian statelet of their own, Arab nationalism as a bond between Arabs would be discredited, Islam would be made to seem intolerant, the Palestinian programme for a 'secular democratic state' embracing Muslims, Christians and Jews would appear hollow, and Israel would reign supreme over a balkanized Levant.

Asad was obsessed by the precedent of the Jordan crisis of 1970. 'Black September' had blooded him when he was on the very threshold of power, and there too Palestinian militias had challenged the state. He had intervened half-heartedly to try to protect the guerrillas, but had balked at outright war with Jordan and withdrawn his troops within days. Yet even his ineffectual show of force had at the time been enough to give Israel the chance to threaten intervention and thereafter, as Husayn's protector, to extend its influence over Jordan and manoeuvre the king into a covert, equivocal relationship. Was the Jordan nightmare to be repeated in Lebanon, allowing Israel to spread its tentacles up Syria's western flank?

In Asad's view, Syria and Israel were engaged in a contest for the Levant as a whole. Just as they jousted over Lebanon, so they were also engaged in a struggle for Jordan, with Asad endeavouring to bind the king to him and Israel trying to prise him away. As Syrian-Jordanian ties grew closer, Israel's Prime Minister Rabin warned the king in February 1976 to beware of the 'Syrian bear'.[8] Syria was 'playing with fire', he declared, in attempting to build an eastern front.[9] And on the day in March when Husayn called on Asad in Damascus, Moshe

Dayan tried to throw a spanner in the works by revealing Husayn's many secret talks with Israeli leaders since the Six Day War.[10] Right across the Levant chessboard Syria and Israel were jockeying for position.

Asad was by this time persuaded that Israel and the United States were acting in collusion, concerting their diplomatic strategies at the United Nations and elsewhere, as well as their covert operations on the ground in Jordan and Lebanon where he suspected them of inciting the Christians against the Palestinians. Whenever a laboriously negotiated ceasefire seemed to be holding, some outrage would set the place ablaze again, discharging a fresh spate of tit-for-tat kidnappings or killings, as if *agents-provocateurs* were determined to fuel the spiral of violence. He knew that Israel, whose alliance with the Maronites became public in 1976, had a strong intelligence presence in Lebanon, while American agencies were not absent. A former employee of the US National Security Agency was one American official to allege that the Athens station of the CIA had been used to activate the Kata'ib and 'kindle the war'.[11]

Asad felt his environment bristling with perils. He could not allow the Lebanese crisis to rot. If necessary, he would have to intervene and he felt no qualms about doing so. His gut conviction was that Syria's concern with Lebanon was in the very nature of things, whereas interference by Israel, a state alien to the region, could only be illegitimate and malign. Of one thing Asad was certain: if the American-Israeli 'conspiracy' against him was to be thwarted, the fighting in Lebanon had to be stopped. The longer it continued, the greater Israel's opportunities. In his mind it was as clear as a mathematical formula.[12]

The violence grows

From December 1975 onwards a number of developments in Lebanon caused Asad extreme alarm. As the violence grew he envisaged two possible outcomes, both equally horrendous: either the Maronites would set up a separate state, which would bring Israel in as its protector, or the radicals with Palestinian backing would beat the Maronites, which would bring Israel in as punisher. If Syria intervened, it faced defeat; if it remained on the sidelines, Lebanon would fall to the enemy.

Abductions, random killings and other acts of savagery had already become depressingly familiar, but the massacre on 'Black Saturday', 6 December 1975, of some 200 Muslim civilians, rounded up and butchered in Beirut by Christian militiamen simply because of their religion, touched new depths of barbarism which seemed to rule out any hope of reconciliation. The massacre and the revenge killings that followed stampeded populations back and forth to the security of their co-religionaries, as whole neighbourhoods in hostile territory were blotted out. Each side took further cruel and decisive action in January to 'clean' its patch of alien elements and secure its lines. The Christians overran and razed the Shi'i slum of Karantina in Beirut's port area and the nearby Palestinian camp of Dbaya, because they lay astride roads from Christian East Beirut to the Christian heartlands in the mountains. At the same time the National Movement and its Palestinian allies overwhelmed and ravaged the Christian localities of Damur, Jiyah and Kamil Sham'un's fief of Sa'diyat lying astride the roads linking Muslim West Beirut to the south. Partition was becoming a reality.

To head off a Lebanese collapse, Asad had tried to persuade the warring camps to agree on reforms. In February he encouraged President Franjiya to issue a Constitutional Document giving the Muslims some of the key concessions they had campaigned for: equal parliamentary representation with the Christians; more powers for the Sunni prime minister who was to be chosen by parliament rather than by the Maronite president and whose signature would be required on all decrees and laws; equal access to top civil service posts; and a reference to Lebanon as 'an Arab country'. A year or two earlier these adjustments might have kept the peace, but in the charnel-house which Lebanon had become by the spring of 1976 they were woefully inadequate.

In March 1976 came the knockout blow to the Lebanese state: the disintegration of the army into its religious components, with mutinies by Muslim officers in favour of the left while Christian officers flocked to the Kata'ib. Then, with support from the mutineers, the radicals went on the offensive: they drove Christian forces out of downtown Beirut and bombarded the presidential palace, sending Franjiya fleeing for his life. They began moving against the Christian mountain, herding the Maronites back into a 'Little Lebanon' with the port of Junieh as its main centre.

Asad's dilemma in the spring of 1976 was that those in Lebanon most intent on pursuing the fight were his presumed friends and protégés – Kamal Junblatt's radicals and the Palestinians. So worried was he that in mid-March 1976 he cancelled at short notice a state visit he was due to make to France, his first ever as Syrian president to a Western country.

The red-line agreement

The Lebanese crisis was Henry Kissinger's swansong, the last occasion on which he exercised his manipulative skills in the Middle East before President Carter's election removed him from office. As the civil war grew more menacing in the spring of 1976, Kissinger's concern was how to break the tidal wave of radicals and Palestinians which was carrying all before it. He had until then been largely indifferent to the Lebanese predicament, but the victories of the left could no longer be ignored. The Soviet Union which was backing the winning side looked like gaining valuable ground. A more immediate worry was what Syria and Israel would do. Both saw Lebanon as crucial to their security, but, if they clashed, a new Middle East war might be the consequence, putting at risk Kissinger's achievements and in particular the Israel-Egypt relationship.

For Kissinger, as indeed for Asad and Rabin, events in Lebanon seemed a replay of the Jordan crisis of 1970. Then Asad had sent in his armour until forced out by the spectre of an Israeli strike. Was not this the model for Lebanon in 1976? Once again the Palestinians were at war, and once again Israel was flexing its muscles to keep Syria out. Israeli warnings had been conveyed to Syria through the United States whose ambassador in Damascus, Richard Murphy, told Asad that Israel would view any Syrian entry into Lebanon as 'a very grave threat' to itself. Murphy's ultimatum – do not intervene, or Israel will[13] – was given added force by his caution that the United States might not be able to hold Israel back. It was a classic expression of Israel's traditional position that the presence of other Arab troops in either Lebanon or Jordan would be considered a *casus belli*.

Then Henry Kissinger had a cleverer idea. It may have dawned on him when he went to the airport in Washington on 29 March 1976 to greet King Husayn of Jordan. The two men shared many secrets from the 1970 crisis. In the receiving line at the airport the king and Kissinger came upon L. Dean Brown, the former US ambassador to Amman who had been their go-between in the critical days of Black September. It was perhaps this chance encounter as well as his conversations with Husayn at this time which planted the seed of a characteristically byzantine scheme in Kissinger's fertile mind. Within twenty-four hours he brought Dean Brown out of retirement and sent him on a special mission to Beirut.

Until that moment, the received wisdom in both Washington and Jerusalem was to scare Asad into keeping out of Lebanon as Christians

1. Hafiz al-Asad was born in 1930 in this rough-hewn village house in the 'Alawi mountains where he grew up. From an early age Asad attempted to transcend his sectarian 'Alawi background.

2. Asad's father, 'Ali Sulayman, a peasant who rose to become a minor notable, and his strong-minded mother Na'isa.

3. Asad won a cup for aerobatics and dreamed of politics while he was at the Aleppo Flying School in the early 1950s.

4. As a disgruntled Air Force officer in Cairo in 1960-61 Asad founded a secret Military Committee which became the instrument of the later seizure of power.

5. (top) Asad became Defence Minister in 1966. He was eventually to topple Dr Nur al-Din Atasi, the Head of State, with whom he is pictured here.

6. (centre) Crowds turned out in Damascus to acclaim the new leader after the 'Corrective Movement' of November 1970, Asad's coup which finally brought stability to the Syrian leadership.

7. (bottom) Asad's friendship with his long-serving Defence Minister, the Sunni officer Mustafa Tlas, was typical of his concern to forge alliances across the Sunni-'Alawi divide in Syria.

8. Asad's great military gamble turned sour during the 1973 War, as Israeli guns pounded Syrian positions on the Golan Heights, which the Syrians were forced to abandon. (Christian Simonpietri/Sygma.)

9. The mood at the Arab Summit in Algiers in November 1973 was grim when Asad and Foreign Minister Khaddam gathered with other Arab leaders to take stock after the October War. (Michel Laurent.)

10. Immediately after the October War Kissinger was in Cairo to woo Sadat into a separate peace with Israel. (Sobi/Sygma.)

11. Asad's faith in evenhanded American mediation led him to welcome President Nixon and Henry Kissinger to Damascus on 16 June 1974 when diplomatic relations with the US were resumed. (Azad.)

12. The two important women in Asad's life have been his wife, Aniseh, and his daughter, Bushra, pictured here in June 1974. Asad has tried to maintain the privacy of his wife and children, away from the glare of publicity. (Alexandra de Borchgrave.)

13. (left) Kissinger's public relations gestures disguised his lack of sympathy for Arab aspirations in their struggle with Israel. (Claude Salhani/Sygma.)

14. (right) A guiding principle of Kissinger's Middle East diplomacy was close policy coordination with Israel, whose Prime Minister, Golda Meir, he held in special esteem. (Henri Bureau.)

15. (top left)   Meeting President Carter in Geneva on 9 May 1977, Asad's hopes in American diplomacy revived. (Wide World Photos.)

16. (top right)   Hardpressed by his enemies, Asad turned for help to Moscow in October 1980 and signed a Treaty of Friendship with General Secretary Leonid Brezhnev. (SANA.)

17. (bottom left)   A pugnacious Menachem Begin came to Washington to defend Israeli policies to his worried ally Ronald Reagan two weeks after Israel's invasion of Lebanon in 1982. US-Israeli relations seemed to be spinning out of control. (Jean-Louis Atlan/Sygma.)

18. (bottom right)   Yasser Arafat and King Husayn, adversary-partners, whom Asad struggled to control, made a vain attempt in April 1983 to sink their own differences. (A. de Wildenberg/Sygma.)

19. Worried by Soviet-American detente, Asad visited Moscow in 1987 to press Gorbachev not to waver in his support of Syria.

20. By 1988, Asad, already the master of Syria, had striven to establish himself, as the Arab world's dominant personality.

and Palestinians battled it out. This was Israel's instinct and to begin with it was Kissinger's too. His brainwave was to turn the received wisdom on its head. Surely the right policy was not to scare Asad off the scene, but rather to scare him on to it? Instead of saying to him, 'If you go in, so will Israel', the shrewder message was, 'If you *don't* go in, Israel certainly will'.

Kissinger was not feeling well-disposed towards the Syrian leader: his initial appreciation had long since given way to something cooler as Asad proved the sharpest and most obstructive critic of his diplomacy. He was aware that Asad's overriding fear was of an Israeli intervention in Lebanon to save the Christians, a fear which was causing him to attempt to restrain Junblatt and 'Arafat from pressing the Christians too hard. Kissinger grasped that Asad's anxieties could be turned to advantage: instead of protecting the Palestinians, Asad might be induced to crush them in order to prevent them from triggering off what he most feared – an Israeli invasion.

The benefits for the United States and Israel could be great indeed: the Palestinians would be humbled, the left reined in, Moscow thwarted, and Asad himself tarnished by a deed heinous in Arab eyes. How much of this Kissinger worked out and how much was just 'feel' must be a matter of speculation.

To ensure the desired outcome required the pulling of a few strings. Syria had to be told that the United States would not disapprove of an intervention in Lebanon and that Israel would not contest it by force; Israel in turn had to be persuaded – against its natural instinct – to accept the entry of a Syrian army into Lebanon; and in Lebanon itself the fighting between Christians and Palestinians would have to be kept going because if it stopped Syria would have no further cause to intervene.

Israel was not easily convinced of the wisdom of letting Syrian troops in, seeing that it was an axiom of Israel's policy that Syria had to be contained, not encouraged to expand. But on this occasion too Kissinger was able to argue that he knew best what was good for Israel. He won unexpected support from Chief of Staff Mordechai Gur and chief of Military Intelligence Shlomo Gazit, who both asserted that the entry of Syrian forces into Lebanon would actually weaken the Syrian army and divert its attention from the Golan Heights. Rabin was eventually converted.

Everything was in place for the secret US-Syrian-Israeli understanding which came to be known as the 'red-line' agreement – an unwritten, unsigned and by the Syrians unavowed accord whereby Israel agreed to the entry of Syrian troops into parts of Lebanon.[14] The Israelis hedged their acceptance by insisting that Syrian troops south of the Damascus-Beirut road could not exceed one brigade and could not bring in SAMs. Israel also insisted on limiting Syrian air and naval deployment. This interpretation of the 'red-line' agreement was contained in a letter from Israel's then Foreign Minister Yigal Allon to Kissinger, the terms of which he passed on to Damascus.[15] But, these restrictions apart, the fact remained that the red-line agreement was an invitation to Syria to come in, not a warning to it to stay out. Syria could now move against the Palestinians in Lebanon with the assurance that Israel would not interfere.

The turnabout was heralded by a dramatic change of tune from Washington. Right up to the end of March the State Department publicly warned Damascus against intervention, but suddenly thereafter the White House, Kissinger himself, L. Dean Brown and the Damascus embassy started issuing expressions of approval for Syria's 'constructive' role. Never did red light change more rapidly to green.

L. Dean Brown, Kissinger's envoy, handled the Lebanese end of the affair. Visiting Junblatt in his castle of Mukhtara, he expressed gloom about the future of co-existence between Druzes and Maronites which Junblatt took to mean American sanction for partition – and therefore for a continuation of the war.[16] To the three principal Christian leaders, Franjiya, Jumayil and Sham'un, holed up in their mountain fortresses, Brown made plain that they could not expect rescue from the Marines as in 1958, but that their salvation lay in strengthening themselves through closer ties with Israel.[17] Thus the Lebanese war machine was primed.

Threats from Junblatt and 'Arafat

In 1976 Asad felt compelled to intervene militarily in the civil war. His move was not impulsive. It had been long pondered and debated within the Ba'th party leadership. The writing had been on the wall for months. As early as December 1975 Asad had sent into Lebanon units of the Palestine Liberation Army and of Sa'iqa to rein in the radical alliance and separate the combatants. He had warned bluntly that Syria would strike at anyone who broke the peace, but his words had gone unheeded.

On 27 March 1976 he had a stormy seven-hour meeting with Kamal Junblatt, the uncontested leader of the Lebanese left. Junblatt had just announced the formation of a 'Fakhreddin Army' (named after a seventeenth century Druze hero) to unite all Muslim and leftist forces and wage 'total and irreversible' war on the Christian forces.[18] But to Asad Junblatt's war policy seemed utter folly, playing straight into Israel's hands and exposing Syria itself to untold peril. 'Why are you escalating the fighting?' he asked. 'The reforms in the Constitutional Document give you 95 per cent of what you want. What else are you after?' Junblatt replied that he wanted to get rid of the Christians 'who have been on top of us for 140 years'. The problem was that, as a Druze, Junblatt was constitutionally debarred from the presidency which was reserved for Maronites alone. To rule Lebanon as he aspired to do, he had to smash the confessional system, but smashing the system meant smashing the Christians or at least subjugating them. In spite of his inherited position as a Druze baron, Junblatt was a genuine man of the left. Since the founding of his Progressive Socialist Party in 1949, he had campaigned for reform, coming to stand as a champion of the have-nots of Lebanese society. He had early befriended the Palestinians, proclaimed himself a Nasserist, enjoyed cordial relations with Moscow, and from the late 1960s onwards had gathered together a vast constituency of Arab nationalists and radicals of all sorts. And by the spring of 1976, as his allies besieged the strongholds of his old Maronite rivals, he scented victory.[19]

But Asad was filled with horror at the prospect of a radical, adventurist Lebanon on his flank, provoking Israel and alarming the West by giving free rein to Palestinian militants. And this was precisely where Junblatt's ambition was leading. For if Junblatt could not seize the whole of Lebanon, he evidently had his eye on the 'leftist' half – the south, the Shuf, Sidon and West Beirut – where he saw himself running a sort of Mediterranean Cuba which he imagined Soviet support would make invulnerable.[20] The steering committee of his National Movement was already posing as the cabinet of this future 'people's republic', with as its 'prime minister' a radical Shi'i pamphleteer, Muhsin Ibrahim, who had travelled from MAN to Marxism. Asad had little taste for the upheaval Junblatt was seeking to bring about. He was not averse to reform in Lebanon: he had in fact inspired Franjiya's Constitutional Document and when that failed had forced through the premature election of Ilyas Sarkis in the hope that a new untarnished leader would stabilize the situation. But he was a man of order and he did not want the Maronite establishment deposed.

Junblatt stormed out of the meeting with Asad totally unpersuaded of the need to stop his war. Returning to Beirut, his attacks on Syria and its leader became more strident and, to Asad's dismay, his commitment to battle still more wholehearted. In Asad's view Junblatt's ambition blinded him to the big picture, but he held the

Palestinian leaders still more culpable as their troops alone made Junblatt's warlike strategy credible. 'Arafat, Abu Iyad, George Habash and the others had evidently not learned the lesson of their disastrous confrontation with King Husayn in 1970.

Asad's relations with the Palestinian Resistance had long been highly ambivalent: in theory he was with it heart and soul, in practice it was a constant source of trouble. A passionate advocate of the Palestine cause, Asad could claim that no Arab leader had fought for it more consistently or had more firmly linked his own future to the recovery of Palestinian rights. First to arm the guerrillas in the 1960s, Syria had been the only Arab state to attempt to protect them against King Husayn in 1970. In 1971, when Husayn was finishing them off in the wilds of northern Jordan, Asad had sent Mustafa Tlas to negotiate a deal which would have given the militias sanctuaries overlooking the Jordan valley but, obsessed by hatred of the king, the Fatah leadership had shortsightedly refused to compromise, making the move to Lebanon inevitable. In 1971–3 Syria had housed the fighters and kept them supplied as they took over the hill country of 'Arqub – their 'Fatahland'. From 1972 Syrian anti-aircraft gunners had even been posted secretly to Palestinian camps in Lebanon to protect them against Israeli air attack. Again in April-May 1973, when the Palestinians were fighting the Lebanese army, Asad had sent Syrian commandos to their aid and closed the frontier with Lebanon in their support. Asad was even to claim later that the thirteen Syrian planes shot down by Israel on the eve of the October War had been defending Palestinians in the 'Arqub.[21]

But when all was said and done, Asad had no confidence in the guerrillas, and considered their operations a dangerous nuisance in that, for trifling results, they allowed Israel to mobilize international sympathy and exposed Arab states to attack. Asad would not prevent anyone going off to fight Israel if they wished to do so, but in Syria at least any such operation had to be firmly controlled and subordinated to national policy.

The war in Lebanon brought to the surface the essential irreconcilability of the interests of the Arab states and those of the guerrillas. The Palestinians yearned for freedom to decide their own strategies, but such independence could be had only at the expense of the security of Arab states. In 1975–6 Asad woke up to the fact that the Palestinians held the key to Lebanon's sovereignty: the power of decision over peace and war. This was the crux of his conflict with them.[22]

'Arafat came three times to Damascus that spring, in March, April and May but, just as Asad's encounter with Junblatt had been a dialogue of the deaf, so his encounters with 'Arafat simply widened the chasm between them. The cautious Syrian leader, a strategist with an iron grasp of the possible, wrestled with the mercurial Palestinian whose temperament inclined him to the taking of impossible risks. Asad warned 'Arafat to keep out of the war. Disturbance in Lebanon was not in the interests of the Resistance. There could be no possible connection, he argued, between fighting the Christians in the Lebanese mountains and recovering Palestine. In a major speech on 12 April he declared:[23]

> We are against those who insist on continuing the fighting. A great conspiracy is being hatched against the Arab nation . . . Our brothers in the Palestinian leadership must understand and be aware of the gravity of this conspiracy. They are the prime targets.

But 'Arafat dreamed of autonomy for his movement free from Arab tutelage. Both Iraq and Egypt were pressing him to resist Asad's influence. Half the Lebanese population was on his side, leading him to believe that his position there was both legitimate and unassailable. He would not be dictated to by Syria. Just as Junblatt yearned to rule Lebanon, so 'Arafat saw a leftist Lebanon in which he held the real power as the best haven and the most effective springboard for his homeless people. So he made the fateful decision to continue the war against the Christians. It was to be a war against Syria.

Syrian intervention

Asad sent an army into Lebanon to teach the Palestinians sense and to keep the Christians Arab. On the night of 31 May to 1 June 1976 Syrian armoured columns crossed the border in strength and immediately broke the Palestinian and leftist siege on several Christian settlements, notably the important town of Zahla in the Biqa' valley. Once reasoning, persuasion and threats had failed Asad felt he had no choice. This was his first major use of force since the October War, but whereas that campaign had expressed the deepest Arab yearnings and won him enthusiastic applause, his Lebanon action was widely misunderstood, was shot through with mixed motives and unnatural alliances, and proved profoundly unpopular. It was an altogether awkward and thankless venture which was to cost Asad friends abroad and generate at home one of the worst crises of his presidency.

At first his intervention was low-key, even tentative, each advance preceded by calls on the Palestinians and their allies to lay down their arms and withdraw from Christian areas. Asad was clearly anxious to avoid large-scale clashes or casualties to either side. As in Jordan in 1970, his tanks were given no air cover. But when the Palestinian command rejected his ultimatums, Asad brought in artillery and aircraft in support of thrusts deeper into Lebanon. Sharp engagements were fought along the Damascus-Beirut highway, in and around the southern port of Sidon, in Fatahland, in the foothills of Mount Hermon, and around the northern port of Tripoli. By late June Syrian forces were blockading Palestinian and leftist strongpoints and supply lines by land and sea and controlled some two-thirds of the country, although not the populated coastal strip.

The battle in the Sidon area was to be of traumatic significance. Not expecting to meet resistance, a Syrian tank unit ran into a Palestinian ambush in which at least two tanks were destroyed and four others captured. Some Syrian officers and crews were killed. Rumours spread that they had been beheaded and their heads kicked about like footballs, although this was almost certainly untrue. Reports also reached Asad that Syrian soldiers who had been manning anti-aircraft guns in Palestinian camps had been beaten up and in some cases killed. He was outraged by these incidents and his heart hardened against the Palestinians. The fools were digging their own graves by sucking him deeper into a conflict he longed to avoid. With all the indignation of a man convinced of his own rectitude, he wrote off the Palestinian leaders not just as reckless adventurers but as thankless wretches who bit the hand that fed them. The extraordinary personal animus between Asad and 'Arafat probably dates from the Sidon ambush.[24]

Syria's intervention turned the tide of the civil war, throwing the Palestinians and leftists on the defensive and allowing the Christians to move to the attack against hostile enclaves in their territory, and in particular against the great sprawling camp of Tal al-Za'tar in Beirut's eastern suburbs to which they now laid siege. After a fifty-two-day blockade of savage intensity, this slum, inhabited by some 30,000 Palestinian and Shi'i refugees, fell to Christian forces on 12 August. About 3,000 civilians died, many of them slaughtered after the camp had fallen to Kamil Sham'un's private army, the so-called 'Tigers', commanded by his son Dany.

The merciless carnage at Tal al-Za'tar was the first of many massacres of Palestinian civilians by other Arabs, prefiguring the Sabra and Shatila killings of 1982 perpetrated by Christian militiamen with Israeli encouragement, and the 'war of the camps' of 1986–7, in which the Palestinians' tormentors were Shi'a allied to Syria. But by illustrating the switch in Syria's friendships, Tal al-Za'tar dug a trench of hatred and suspicion between Asad and the Palestinians.

Asad's war on the Palestinians and his defence of the Christians were seen as an astonishing, and to many a profoundly shocking, reversal of alliances. The lion of Arabism was slaughtering Arabism's sacred cow. For the rest of his presidency Asad was to bear the burden of a policy which was as unpopular with the Arab masses as it was misunderstood. Israel meanwhile watched him thrashing about in the Lebanese quagmire with undisguised satisfaction. Prime Minister Rabin observed sardonically that he saw no need to disturb the Syrian army in its killing of 'Arafat's terrorists'.[25] Kissinger's calculations had proved correct: his discreet string-pulling had caused Syria, of all countries, to bash Palestinians and dash Soviet hopes.

The outcry against Asad's war in Lebanon was heard from one end of the Arab world to the other. Sadat broke off relations and his foreign minister accused Asad of genocide.[26] Iraq's strong man Saddam Husayn sent troops to the Syrian border, calling Asad a megalomaniac whose mad ambitions had immersed him in a bloodbath of his own making.[27] Junblatt denounced the Syrian government as a fascist military regime, and both he and Palestinian leaders called for all-out war against Damascus. For Asad's military intervention had put an abrupt end to Junblatt's daydreams. And the paradox was that once Asad had robbed him of everything he had struggled for, Junblatt really did revert to being a narrowly vindictive, lord of the Druzes. This normally non-violent man, this Gandhian, became very violent indeed, seeing himself at last as the frustrated instrument of a historic Druze revenge on the Maronites. With his vision of a socialist Lebanon shattered, he seemed to be taken over by the ancient feuds of his ancestors.[28] The now beleaguered National Movement appealed for the despatch of Algerian, Tunisian, Libyan or Iraqi troops, for UN or French intervention, or indeed for help against Syria from any quarter. At the same time Syrian embassies in various countries came under attack from pro-PLO Arab demonstrators. More ominously for Asad, there were persistent reports that the oil states, which had so generously funded Syria's boom after 1973, were now cutting back their subsidies.

In the closed world of Ba'thist politics, another painful shaft was fired at him: Salah al-Din Bitar, co-founder of the party and now in exile in Paris, asked in an article in *Le Monde* how it was that Syria, 'the beating heart of Arabism', could have joined Christian isolationists on a course so foreign to its traditions. The answer, he said damagingly, lay in the nature of power in Damascus: lonely, cut off from the people, stifling all democracy.[29]

Two other charges, widely circulated at the time, did Asad much harm. The first was that he was acting in collusion with the United States to crush the Palestinians in order to pave the way for an American peace plan. He took this hard, seeing that he had reason to consider himself the main obstacle to, and main victim of, American and Israeli scheming. The second slur was that he was playing minority politics – hastening to the relief of the Maronites because he was himself a minority man. Anti-Syrian demonstrators in Beirut chanted: 'Asad, we can stomach you as an Alawite but not as a Maronite!'[30] Insight into the feelings of threatened minorities was indeed part of Asad's inheritance, but, in all fairness, his Lebanese adventure was motivated by geo-strategic reasons, by the need to head off an Israeli intervention, and not by narrow sectarian sentiments. When still a schoolboy, he had self-consciously climbed out of the minority trap in order to embrace the Arab cause. Now, angrily warning his enemies not to push him too far, he declared that 'nothing embarrasses us in this country. We have gone beyond complexes and have been free for a long time.'[31] It was a personal *cri de coeur*.

Although he put a brave face on it, at home his regime was shaken and there were frequent reports of disturbance and disaffection that summer, amplified by his enemies but real nonetheless. In September three Palestinians were hanged in public for seizing a Damascus hotel and taking hostages. In the face of such violence, Asad felt the need for more protection: a Presidential Guard was set up under his wife's kinsman, 'Adnan Makhluf, while his brother Rif'at was promoted to the rank of full colonel and his Defence Companies, the praetorian guard of the regime, were reinforced.

Among the casualties of Asad's armed foray into Lebanon were good relations with the Soviet Union. The Soviet leadership was alarmed at the turn of events in the spring of 1976 and sent Premier Kosygin to the area, first to Iraq and then to Syria. In Baghdad, where he arrived in late May, Kosygin publicly cautioned Syria against intervention in Lebanon, but by the time he reached Damascus on 1 June it was too late. Asad had overnight thrust his troops and his Russian armour across the border. In spite of Asad's lengthy explanations, the Soviet premier was angry[32] and Tass commented sourly that Syria's intervention had done nothing to staunch the 'ever-swelling river of blood'.[33] The reasons for Soviet displeasure were easy to divine. The Russians admired Junblatt (he was one of only a few

Arabs to be awarded the Lenin Peace Prize); they had close ties with the PLO; loath to have to choose between Asad and the Lebanese left, they were embarrassed to see them fighting each other. Above all, they had expected great political gains in Lebanon, perhaps hoping to turn it into a unique relay station for their regional influence once their friends had triumphed. By destroying these expectations Asad seemed to be putting the clock back to a Western-dominated Lebanon, thereby annulling ten years of hard work by the left.

As the Syrians advanced into Lebanon, Junblatt and the Palestinians waited for the Soviet Union to save them, and Kosygin in Damascus was bombarded with appeals. Some deluded souls even imagined Soviet paratroopers would drop out of the skies. Moscow had indeed told the Lebanese Communist Party and other friends on the left that it disapproved of Syria's intervention, and this was locally misunderstood to mean that Moscow would do something to stop it.[34] In fact, the Kremlin intended not a breach with Syria but merely a cooling of relations. Brezhnev sent a message to Asad urging him to withdraw and Moscow made repeated pleas to all three parties – Syria, the Lebanese left and the Palestinians – to close ranks.

For Asad the practical consequences of Soviet displeasure were severe enough: new arms contracts were postponed and, at a time when Israel seemed particularly threatening, he was largely deprived of a superpower prop. Recalling the crisis a decade later he said with characteristic understatement,[35]

> There was a setback in our relations with the Soviet Union. Certain commitments between us came to an end. It was difficult for them to understand the nature of our relations with Lebanon.

Advanced Soviet weaponry did not again reach Syria until 1978 when, in the wake of Sadat's trip to Jerusalem, Asad was back in favour as the Russians' friend in the Middle East.

The opprobrium heaped upon him from all quarters did not divert Asad from his objectives of removing the Palestinians from the Christian heartlands, separating them from the leftist National Movement, and taming both in the interests of his wider anti-Israeli strategy.

The summer of 1976 was spent in low-level military operations alternating with renewed appeals and ultimatums. Then, in late September and October, Asad launched a number of major offensives which ended in the near-rout of the Palestinians and their allies. He was now ready to accept a Saudi invitation to a peace-making summit in Riyadh on 16 October which consecrated his Pyrrhic victory. His presence in Lebanon was legitimized. His troops were recognized as the major contingent in a proposed 'Arab Deterrent Force' which Saudi Arabia and Kuwait agreed to fund. The Palestinians were returned to their camps after promises had been extracted from them (and soon broken) to abide by the Cairo Agreement. Asad's venomous quarrels with Sadat and 'Arafat were for the moment papered over, and all this was endorsed at a wider Arab gathering in Cairo on 25 October. In mid-November Syrian troops marched into West Beirut, the leftist private armies vanished from the streets and the civil war was declared over.

But Asad's victory was partial and compromised. From then on he had to bear the burden of having pursued a course which the majority of Arabs saw as profoundly anti-Arab. He defended himself, then and later, eloquently and repeatedly, tracing in public the whole history of his relations with Junblatt and 'Arafat. From first to last Asad remained convinced that, whatever the outside pressures on him, his intervention had been tactically and morally correct and that he had been impelled by the highest principles.[36] He had been forced to act by the blindness and ambition of men who could not grasp the nature of his life-and-death struggle with Israel. But the shadow remained. Whatever his justifications, he was never wholly believed, and in some important way he was seen to have departed from the Arab mainstream.

Israel and the Maronites

The men whose war had forced his intervention continued to plague him, the one in life and the other in death. It was widely believed at the time that Asad not only wished to tame the Palestinian movement but also to depose Yasir 'Arafat and name in his stead Syria's man, Khalid al-Fahum, a Damascus-based former teacher of chemistry who was then chairman of the Palestine National Council. But 'Arafat, both then and in the coming years, proved remarkably resistant to Syrian pressures.

'Arafat's civil war ally, Kamal Junblatt, was assassinated on 16 March 1977 when on his way from his castle, Mukhtara, to B'aqlin, the largest Druze village in the Shuf. His car was intercepted, two men got in, ordered his bodyguards out, and blew off the top of his head before making their getaway. Kamal Junblatt's son, Walid, who succeeded him as head of the Junblatt clan, was one of many to hold the Syrians responsible. As he later explained: 'My father was badly advised. He was informed that a coup was in preparation in Syria and that by attacking the 'Alawi leadership there he could upset the regime. All he did was sign his death warrant.' Walid Junblatt called on Asad at the end of the forty-day period of mourning for his father. He had to choose between Syria and Israel and, notwithstanding his suspicions of its complicity in his father's murder, he chose Syria. It was nevertheless disconcerting to be greeted by Asad with the words: 'How closely you resemble your father!'[37] Whether or not Asad willed Junblatt's death, he was blamed for it throughout the Arab world and his reputation suffered. There was, however, some benefit to be derived: with Junblatt's disappearance, the anti-Syrian coalition he led fell apart.

Nevertheless, Asad's fundamental objective in Lebanon eluded him. He had fought against the Palestinians and protected the Christians in order to deny Israel a pretext for intervention. But his controversial and costly move proved vain: by the end of 1976 Israel was more deeply involved in Lebanese affairs than ever and was flaunting its intimate relationship with the Maronites to the shock and horror of Arab opinion which for three decades had sought to put the 'Zionist entity' into quarantine. The Christians had accepted Syria's help but to Asad's fury they had also reinsured with Israel. Israeli weapons, advisers and cash flowed into the Maronite heartlands through the port of Junieh while southern Lebanon was restructured to Israel's advantage. As early as July 1976, barely a month after Syria entered Lebanon, Defence Minister Shimon Peres announced the 'good fence programme' whereby the frontier security barriers which Israel had erected in 1974 were opened to traffic, offering Lebanese residents of the border villages employment, medical care and markets for their produce in Israel, and thereby giving Israel a chance to turn them into collaborators against the Palestinians. Israeli armoured patrols now penetrated freely into Lebanon and, by October, a pro-Israeli militia led by Major Sa'd Haddad, a Christian officer of the defunct Lebanese Army, was functioning as Israel's early-warning system along the whole border.[38]

The Christians were thankless, the Druzes bitter, radicals of all shades vengeful, the Palestinians hostile and still in arms, and Israel, now as much part of the Lebanese scene as Syria itself, able to tweak Asad's tail at will. In defence of his strategic environment, Asad had fallen into the Lebanese quagmire.

18

Jimmy Carter's False Dawn

The all-important question for Asad on Jimmy Carter's election to the presidency in November 1976 was whether his Administration would follow in Kissinger's pro-Israeli footsteps or revert to a more balanced Middle East policy. Like much of the world, Asad knew next to nothing about the Southern Baptist peanut farmer who had captured the White House, and had gloomily watched Carter vying with Gerald Ford for the Jewish vote during the campaign. Carter in turn had never met an Arab, except once at a racecourse in Florida.[1] Grown sceptical, Asad was doubtful whether America's bias could be reversed after the thorough job Kissinger had done in robbing the Arabs of the fruits of the October War and giving Israel a decisive edge. But prudently he sent the president-elect a congratulatory telegram in which he called for 'a fair US attitude' towards the Arab-Israeli conflict and spelled out his peace terms. These were the familiar duo: an Israeli withdrawal from Arab territories occupied in 1967 and the restoration of the 'legitimate rights' of the Palestinians.[2]

This formality completed, Asad did not press the point. Like other Arab leaders, he was slow to grasp how radically Carter was proposing to depart from the assumptions and procedures of the Kissinger era, and how much help he would need from the Arabs if he were to succeed. When Carter began to expound his ideas, the Arabs reacted with less excitement than might have been expected. His programme, and especially his concern for the Palestinians, struck them as no more than simple justice. Unlike the Israelis, the Arabs had no experience of intervening in US domestic politics and were inclined to sit back and see what Carter could deliver.

In the light of the US-Israeli intimacy which had grown up since 1967, Carter's programme was revolutionary indeed. Having made human rights a central tenet of his foreign policy, he saw the wrongs done to the Palestinians as somewhat akin to those suffered by the blacks in the United States which, for moral as well as political reasons, he could not ignore. Steeped in the scriptures from childhood, he revered the lands of the Bible and cherished the ambition to make peace there. He, and even more so his Secretary of State Cyrus Vance, were critical of Kissinger's inclination to see the world in terms of geopolitical competition with the Soviet Union. Discontents existed in the Third World which they perceived to have little or nothing to do with Soviet ambitions. Vance was scathing about the way Kissinger's obsession with the global contest had damaged rather than advanced US interests in places like Angola, where misguided American moves in 1975 had driven the main nationalist movement into Soviet and Cuban arms.[3] In the Middle East, US neglect of Arab concerns, at a time when the rise of OPEC signalled the post-colonial awakening of the developing world, risked opening rather than closing doors to the Russians. It was all very well arming Israel to the teeth as a 'strategic asset' against the Soviet Union, but one had to take on board the frustrations which this policy aroused among Israel's Arab neighbours.

Another influential advocate for a 'constructive US relationship with the Arab world'[4] was Carter's National Security Adviser, Dr Zbigniew Brzezinski, a Polish-born professor of international politics who, just when Kissinger in 1975 was shaping the Middle East to Israel's advantage, was helping draft a set of very different proposals in a celebrated Brookings report.[5] This was a sort of 'counter-Kissinger', in which the traditional concern for Israel's wellbeing was balanced by an awareness of Arab interests.

All this then – the Bible and Brookings, the fear of another war and another energy crisis, a sense that Kissinger had left the peacemaking job half done, pity for the Palestinians under Israeli occupation – promoted the Middle East to the top of Carter's foreign policy priorities. He called boldly for a comprehensive settlement to be negotiated before the end of 1977 at a new session of the Geneva conference at which he envisaged that, in exchange for peace, Israel would withdraw to the 1967 borders with only minor adjustments. Most strikingly of all, he proposed a new deal for the Palestinians – no longer defined as refugees as in Resolution 242 or as terrorists as Israel wanted the world to see them, but as a people deprived of basic rights who needed a homeland of their own. Carter believed the Palestinians had to be involved in the negotiations and hoped that the United States would be able to start talking to the PLO.

Operationally there was also a significant correction of aim. Kissinger's habitual practice had been to reach prior, usually secret, agreement with Israel before facing the Arabs;[6] Carter believed in consulting closely with Israel but was not prepared to concert with it against its Arab foes.[7] Carter was by no means anti-Israeli but nor did he view the Middle East solely in the perspective of Israeli interests and security. The Arabs also existed, suffered, hoped and feared. After years of ever closer US-Israeli relations, which blossomed under Lyndon Johnson and reached their full flowering with Henry Kissinger, this return to 'even-handedness' amounted to a considerable U-turn.

Not altogether surprisingly, the Israeli leaders were horrified by Carter. Every one of his ideas, save for his declared objective of seeking 'real peace', was anathema to them. He seemed to be tearing up all the secret pledges, commitments and Memoranda of Understanding which they had extracted from Washington over a decade. Not only did his programme seem to imply giving back the West Bank, acquiescing in what would almost certainly become an Arab Republic of Palestine, and returning the strategic Golan Heights to Syria; it also signified a crucial change of course for the 'peace process'. Kissinger's bid to wean Egypt from the Arab camp, now so near fruition, was, it would seem, to be abandoned in favour of Carter's pan-Arab free-for-all, in which Israel's regional supremacy, hard won in the 1967 and 1973 wars, risked being thrown away. Faced with this threat – far deadlier than any the Arabs had presented – Israel resolved to fight, and mobilized every asset including its powerful American lobby.

When Prime Minister Rabin paid his first visit to President Carter in March 1977, Carter found him timid, stubborn and ill at ease.[8] This was a misjudgment. Rabin was seething with suppressed rage. Himself a Washington insider for nine years, he viewed Carter as a dangerously inexperienced outsider who looked like giving Israel a lot of trouble before he learned 'political maturity'.[9] To Rabin Carter seemed to be breaking all the rules of the US-Israeli relationship: he took Middle East initiatives without first clearing them with Jerusalem, dared to air disagreements with Israel in public as if to rally American opinion to his side of the argument, and on arms deliveries seemed inclined to demote Israel from its privileged position above that of America's NATO allies. The Israelis were especially put out by Carter's efforts to befriend Asad – so very different from Kissinger's policy of 'letting Asad stew'. Eager to meet Middle East leaders at first hand, Carter in his first weeks in office invited them to Washington. Sadat, Husayn, Rabin and Crown Prince Fahd made the journey, but Asad, no doubt wishing to demonstrate his greater independence, refused the chance to state his views in the White House. 'No thank you', he replied, when Vance brought him the invitation. 'Has the United States still not understood our position after thirty years?'[10] Yet he was delighted when Carter agreed to meet him in neutral Geneva. The Israelis were upset by this deference and Asad's Arab rivals were less than overjoyed.

Middle East rivalries

Jimmy Carter understood that Syria had to be a major player if a comprehensive negotiation were to get under way. But he did not wholly grasp how far the peace process was bound up with regional tussles for power, not just between Israel and individual Arab states but between Arab states themselves. An enduring feature of Middle East politics is a network of inter-state rivalries, which underlie the moves of the principal players irrespective of their ideological colouring. If one of them acquires greater influence it is felt as a loss by the others. Failure to give due weight to this latent competition is often to misunderstand the dynamics of the regional system.

What Asad looked for from the new US Administration was recognition, even political reward. If he was to be a player, his vital interests would have to be addressed, and of these, the most immediate was the need to extend his influence over his neighbours – Lebanon, Jordan and the Palestinians – in order to protect his flanks and create some sort of counterweight to Israel now that Sinai Two had removed Egypt from the scene. For a start he had pacified Lebanon, dousing the fires of civil war and putting a stop to the adventurist ambitions of the Lebanese left and its Palestinian allies – at considerable cost to his Arab standing and to his relations with the Soviet Union. He now wanted the extension of Syria's writ in the Levant endorsed. His implicit message to Carter was: Recognize me as the regional man of influence and I will deliver peace and stability.

But there were great difficulties for Carter, or indeed for any American leader, to see things this way. For one, there was no sympathy for Syria's assumption of a right to a say in the affairs of its neighbours, and especially Jordan whose friendship with the West was of long standing. For another, Israel, whose voice was always heard in Washington, was totally opposed to the emergence of a Syria strong enough to challenge its own claim to dominance in the Levant. Indeed, much of the reasoning behind Israel's agreements with Egypt, its support for the Lebanese Maronites, and its numerous contacts with King Husayn was to isolate and enfeeble Syria. Israel was particularly aware that if Syria were unchecked it could prove a dangerously effective sponsor of the Palestinians. But the prospect of a regionally influential Syria was also a bogey to Asad's Arab brothers. His attempts to extend his writ over Jordan, Lebanon and the Palestinians was resented by these players, but it also aroused the fears and jealousies of Egypt, Iraq and Saudi Arabia, all nervous of the added prominence Damascus might get if these efforts were to succeed. Suspicion was voiced that Asad was bent on resurrecting a 'Greater Syria' of hegemonic ambitions.

Egypt had no greater liking than Israel for a strong Syria. The fear of a powerful rival on its north-eastern approaches was deeply rooted in Egyptian history: Nasser, King Faruq, Muhammad 'Ali, and indeed the pharaohs had experienced it. Sadat's anger at Asad's criticisms after the October War stemmed not just from wounded vanity or hurt at being accused of abandoning the Arab front, but was also in part an expression of this traditional worry. Iraq, the other hostile pole of Syria's political geography, was equally uneasy at the rise of Damascus as a centre of regional importance – a knee-jerk geopolitical instinct on the part of Baghdad which was sharpened by the long-running feud between the Syrian and Iraqi Ba'th parties. And Saudi wariness of Syrian power was just as persistent. The Saudis were happy to see Syria containing Israel but were less happy at the prospect of Ba'thist power extending through Jordan to their own northern frontier. The Saudis' concern to contain Asad could be seen in their advice to King Husayn to draw back from too close ties with him, in their efforts to supplant him as the arbiter between Maronites and Palestinians, and in the scaling down of their financial aid. Legend has it that on his deathbed the founder of the modern Saudi state, King 'Abd al-'Aziz ibn Sa'ud, advised his sons to 'keep your eye on Syria', because, he explained, any expansion of Syrian influence, particularly if it meant a Syrian link with either Iraq or Egypt, was a threat to Saudi interests.

Beyond inter-Arab rivalries lay the profound issue of whose order was to prevail in the Middle East, a question which had remained open ever since the end of the Ottoman era in 1918. The supremacy of Britain and France between the world wars had provided only a temporary answer. With the rise of Nasser in the 1950s there was for a few brief years the possibility of an indigenous 'Arab nationalist' order in which Arabs would shape their own environment, but these hopes were extinguished by Israel in the Six Day War and were only partially revived by Arab efforts in the October War. The order implicit in Kissinger's post-1973 diplomacy was the very antithesis of Arab nationalism, as in breaking up the Egyptian-Syrian alliance he resolutely ruled out any effective Arab combination. His vision was of an American-sponsored system, in which Israel would be the cornerstone in a new partnership with a tamed and neutered Egypt. Kissinger and Israel presented the new arrangements as the best way to safeguard Western interests from Soviet encroachments, but behind this smokescreen the real point was whether an Arab or an Israeli order would prevail. Under Nasser Egypt had been the linchpin of an Arab system, but under Sadat Egypt changed camps, with grim consequences for lesser Arab states.

Asad had won greater visibility and attention for himself and for his country in the three years since the October War, but his overall strategic position was far from solid. Kissinger, Israel and his Arab rivals had seen to that. He was at a turning-point: either his ascent would continue by way of a new phase in the peace process, or his hard-won gains risked being taken from him, reducing him to insignificance.

Some of these complexities may have escaped Jimmy Carter when, full of good intentions, he sought to probe what sort of man Asad was and what he had to say about the knotty problem of the Palestinians. Certainly Carter had little inkling of Asad's hopes and ambitions or of his resentment at the way American policy had all too often thwarted him.

Meeting with Carter

Asad's seven hours with Carter at the Geneva Intercontinental on 9 May 1977,[11] in a blaze of world attention, carried the Syrian leader to the highest peak he had yet scaled and seemed to assure him a place in a revitalized peace process. He could not resist opening the meeting with an hour-long history lesson on the reality of Arab insecurity and Israeli expansionism, and on the long record of Western high-handedness in the region. He was gratified to see an attentive Carter nodding and taking notes. Asad felt that the new American president grasped the essence of the Arab-Israeli problem, in itself an enormous step forward from his standpoint. The two men got on well: as Carter disarmingly remarked, they were both country boys made good, and they were soon at ease with each other. Asad was taken by Carter's warmth, by his serious interest in the area, and by his readiness to seek advice on the complex problems it presented, whereas Carter for his part was glad to discover that Asad had a sense of humour. He summed him up as a self-confident leader of independent mind whose sense of the past endowed him with patience to confront the present.

Asad was encouraged to find that the American president had an open mind on the two critical issues of Palestinian rights and Israeli withdrawal. In front of the press, and with Asad beside him, Carter repeated his support for a Palestinian homeland, and later, in face-to-face talks, hinted that he would work to convince Israel to pull back to its pre-1967 borders. Carter in turn was reassured to find that Asad seemed ready for peace and was willing to consider concrete steps – such as ending the state of belligerency, setting up demilitarized areas and buffer zones patrolled by peace-keeping forces, securing guarantees, and pressing ahead with economic reconstruction – to help bring it about.

But the friendly atmosphere obscured the vast chasm between them. On the boundaries question Asad made clear to Carter that no Arab leader could agree to give up territory no matter how great his desire for peace. He ridiculed the concept of 'secure borders' in an age of modern weapons, and mocked the Israeli view that it could win security by taking other people's land. 'The Israelis claim that they took the Golan to protect their settlements', he said, 'but then they built new settlements on the Golan, some of them only three hundred metres from our positions!' What, he wanted to know, was the American view on permanent boundaries, seeing that Israel would take Damascus if it could? Carter would make no promises.

The problem which took up most of their time was what to do about the Palestinians and, in spite of Carter's patent goodwill and his references to a 'homeland', here too the obstacles were fearsome. Kissinger had thrown up two roadblocks to keep the Palestinians out of the peace process. He had given Israel the right to veto any new participants in the Geneva conference, and he had pledged that the United States would not talk to the PLO unless it accepted Resolution 242 and Israel's right to exist. Carter sought Asad's help in overcoming these obstacles: was there a way, he asked, to get to talk to 'Arafat? Could the PLO be induced to make a statement accepting 242, perhaps with a reservation about the Resolution's depiction of the Palestinians as refugees? Carter saw Kissinger's pledge as a procedural hurdle to be cleared in order to allow the Palestinians to be drawn into the negotiations.

Asad, however, was more concerned with substance than procedure. What could Carter offer the Palestinians, he asked. How did he define their rights? How could they be expected to accept Resolution 242 or recognize Israel before they had been assured of the recovery of the West Bank and Gaza? King Husayn had told him that Israel had offered Jordan a mere ten kilometres of the West Bank in final settlement! But, Asad continued, the return of the West Bank and Gaza would not in itself be enough to solve the problem. The hundreds of thousands of dispossessed refugees had also to be given the choice, in accordance with the UN resolutions, of returning to their country or of receiving compensation.

The gulf between procedure and substance was clearly revealed. In the following weeks Carter and Vance made repeated attempts to get the PLO to issue a statement which would open the way to a dialogue with Washington. To Israel's indignation, Vance even went so far as to suggest an acceptable form of words.[12] But the United States could not promise the PLO a seat at the Geneva negotiating table – Israel's veto prevented that – still less a Palestinian state. Faced with this negative prospect, 'Arafat's Executive Committee refused to give up what it considered its 'last card' – recognition of Israel.

The PLO undoubtedly wanted a dialogue with the United States: it made many gestures of goodwill, providing bodyguards for Americans in Lebanon in 1976, helping arrange the evacuation of American civilians from the civil war, and even supplying intelligence which saved the lives of US diplomats.[13] But it could not bring itself to utter the words Carter wanted. In the years that followed it was endlessly debated whether or not the Palestinians had missed a unique opportunity. The truth was that the Israeli-Kissinger roadblocks proved extraordinarily effective and, as Vance wrote, were 'to make our task of finding a way to deal with the PLO close to impossible'.[14]

Did Carter and Vance give too much weight to Kissinger's pledge to Israel? At least one American diplomat, Ambassador Talcott Seelye, believed that Carter was wrong to interpret it as ruling out even exploratory contacts with the PLO. He recalled being told by the author of the pledge, Henry Kissinger himself, that had the Republicans won the 1976 election, he would have engaged the Palestinians in a dialogue.[15] If it was all right for Kissinger to consider talking to the PLO, should Carter have been inhibited from doing so? In the event, no US-PLO dialogue was started and no Palestinian took part in negotiations. The Palestinians remained condemned to continued occupation or dispossession.

These frustrations were in the future: in May 1977 there was a moment of keen optimism. After taking leave of Carter in Geneva, Asad told his staff of his great hope in the new president and indicated that he looked forward to further meetings with him. But the promise of that first encounter was never realized and Asad did not see Carter again – until the latter visited him in Damascus some years later as a private citizen. Syria was to be cut out of the peace process as swiftly and decisively as the Palestinians.

What went wrong? At Geneva Asad's approach was perhaps too leisurely, too maximalist, too concerned with principles and the legacy of history and too little with the operational nuts and bolts of getting a negotiation started. In counting on Carter to impose a settlement on Israel, Asad may have succumbed to the Arab failing of overlooking the severe domestic pressures to which any American president is subject when dealing with the Middle East. Moreover, there was no co-ordination on peace-making in the Arab camp but on the contrary the familiar rivalries and suspicions: Sadat had no intention of letting Asad dictate his peace diplomacy; Husayn shared Israel's alarm at Carter's courtship of the PLO; while the Palestinians, eager to control their own destinies, distrusted all Arab governments almost as much as they hated Israel. Even Asad's small triumph in getting the American president to meet him in Switzerland was hollow, in the judgment of a senior US official:[16] he would have made more impact had he gone to Washington. If his intention was to influence the US Administration, there was no virtue in staying away.

But none of this would have mattered had Israel not skilfully seized the initiative from both Carter and Asad.

Enter the Likud

The task of subverting Jimmy Carter's Middle East policy and of removing Asad and the Palestinians from the peace process fell to Menachem Begin and his Foreign Minister, Moshe Dayan. Begin, the great outsider of Israeli politics since the foundation of the state, startled the world by defeating the long-serving Labour Party at the Israeli elections of May 1977. He brought to the premiership most of the ideas of his mentor, the Russian-born agitator Vladimir Jabotinsky (1880–1944) whose muscular 'Revisionist Zionism' had taken shape in opposition to the gradualist strategy of mainstream Socialist Zionism. Strong on rhetoric, Jabotinsky had between the world wars called for mass Jewish settlement in Palestine and the unabashed use of force against the Arabs to establish full Jewish sovereignty on both banks of the Jordan. He argued that a Zionist state could not be secured by compromises with the Arabs but needed the protection of an 'iron wall'. War was not simply a measure of last resort but a legitimate means of national conquest.

Born in 1913 in the then Polish town of Brest-Litovsk, Begin had risen through Betar, Jabotinsky's brown-shirted youth movement, becoming its leader shortly before the Second World War. When the Russians invaded Poland in 1939 he was sent to a Siberian prison camp and on being freed in 1941 joined the Polish army in exile and was posted to Palestine in 1942 as an English-language translator. He deserted and in 1943 took over the local Revisionist militia, the Irgun, which used terror tactics against the British, the Arabs and also against the Hagana, the Labour-controlled Jewish underground army. Among Irgun operations were the attack on the British army headquarters at the King David Hotel in Jerusalem in June 1946, the massacre of Arab villagers at Dayr Yasin in April 1948, and the suicidal voyage two months later of the illegal arms ship *Altalena* which brought Irgun into direct military conflict with David Ben Gurion, Israel's first Prime Minister, who was to remain Begin's life-long enemy. In the wake of the *Altalena* incident, the Irgun was forced to disarm. So, to continue the Revisionist struggle for a Jewish homeland on *both* sides of the Jordan, Begin founded the 'Freedom Movement', Herut – denounced by such prominent Jews as Albert Einstein and Hannah Arendt (in a celebrated letter to the *New York Times* on 4 December 1948) as 'closely akin in its organization, methods, political philosophy and social appeal to the Nazi and Fascist parties'.

For nearly twenty years Begin was to remain on the extremist fringe of Israeli politics. But his political fortunes brightened in 1965 with the formation of Gahal, a parliamentary bloc, under his leadership, of Herut and the businessmen's Liberal Party. Full respectability followed when he was brought into the National Unity cabinet on the eve of the 1967 war by generals who shared his view that Labour had blundered in leaving the West Bank in Arab hands in 1948 and that the opportunity for 'liberating' it must not now be missed. To celebrate his appointment, Begin climbed Mount Herzl the next day to salute the grave of Jabotinsky.

The conquests of the Six Day War turned Begin's Revisionist ideology into practical politics. Now his all-absorbing cause became to prevent the return of the West Bank to the Arabs. When in 1970 Golda Meir accepted the Rogers Plan with its implication that Israel might consider trading land for peace, Begin resigned from the government. In 1973 he joined General Ariel Sharon, the personification of Israeli militarism, in forming the Likud, a coalition of right-wing parties which in 1977 put an end to twenty-nine years of Labour rule, whereupon he promptly hung a portrait of his revered Jabotinsky in the prime minister's office.

Begin's immediate objective was to destroy Carter's Middle East policy which threatened to push Israel back to its pre-Six Day War frontiers and open the door to Palestinian nationalism, and to this task he brought a good deal of guile and zeal.

It took Begin and his Foreign Minister, Dayan, from July to October

1977 to force Carter to abandon what they considered his dangerous policies. Success was achieved with a two-track strategy. The first consisted of a concerted campaign against Carter's declared objectives, ranging from harassment to stonewalling and open defiance, with special focus on Carter's proposed Geneva conference which Begin was resolved would be held on his terms if it was held at all. The second was to bypass the Geneva conference altogether and lure Egypt into a bilateral agreement. These two tracks were pursued simultaneously, no doubt on the view that, if the second failed, the first could provide a tolerable fallback position.

So far as Geneva was concerned, Carter wanted Palestinian participation, Begin would have none of it. Carter wanted Israel to acknowledge that Resolution 242 meant withdrawal on all fronts, Begin never tired of affirming that the West Bank was 'liberated', not occupied, and that he would never give it up. Carter wanted a moratorium on Jewish settlements to allay Arab fears, whereupon Begin promptly founded new ones. He repeatedly reminded Carter of the commitments Kissinger had entered into and pressed him and Secretary Vance to refrain from publicly airing views at variance with Israel's. After his first encounter with Carter in July 1977, Begin was alleged to have privately described the president as a 'cream puff'.[17] The formidable resources of the American Israel Public Affairs Committee were mobilized against him to such effect that Carter, bruised and defensive, was soon back-tracking on all the major issues.

The high point of Israel's subversion of Carter's objectives was reached following the publication on 1 October 1977 of a joint US-Soviet communiqué on the Middle East. The two superpowers, co-chairmen of the first Geneva conference, called for its early reconvening to negotiate 'a fundamental solution to all aspects of the Middle East problem in its entirety'. The settlement was to include 'withdrawal of Israeli Armed Forces from territories occupied in the 1967 conflict; the resolution of the Palestinian question, including ensuring the legitimate rights of the Palestinian people; termination of the state of war and establishment of normal peaceful relations . . .' Dayan had been given a draft of the communiqué two days earlier, time enough to alert the lobby: the uproar among Israel's friends in and out of Congress was tremendous. It was not only the references to Israeli withdrawal and Palestinian rights which outraged the lobby, but also the reappearance on the scene of the Soviet Union, seen as the Arabs' chief support. The barrage of protest took the Administration aback.

As it happened, the Syrians were slow to grasp the significance of the joint communiqué and did little to advance their own interests at this crucial moment. At a meeting at the UN Plaza Hotel the day after the statement was published, Vance asked Foreign Minister Khaddam for his reactions. 'When the Americans and the Soviets agree about something, we Arabs tend to be suspicious', Khaddam joked. It was the wrong signal, suggesting to Vance that the Arabs were scarcely more enthusiastic about the joint US-Soviet initiative than the Israelis.

At this point Dayan moved in for the kill. On the night of 4–5 October, he confronted Carter, Vance and Brzezinski in more than five hours of bargaining at the US mission to the United Nations. Dayan's tactics were rough. The statement was totally unacceptable to Israel, he said, and he asked Carter to state publicly that he stood by all past understandings and secret agreements between the United States and Israel – if not, Israel might publish them. He wanted Carter to proclaim his opposition to any form of Palestinian state. When Carter demurred, Dayan threatened to announce that he had asked for such an assurance and that Carter had refused to give it – a ploy Brzezinski later described as blackmail.[18] Dayan correctly judged that Carter, already shaken by clashes with American Jewish leaders, would not relish a showdown and would draw back from putting the quarrel before the American public.

The turning-point of the night's negotiations came when, in an admission that he needed Dayan's help to get the troublesome Jewish lobby off his back, Carter said to Dayan, 'Let's talk politics'.[19] Dayan seized the opening to press his advantage, and from that moment on the president's need to placate Israel's friends in the United States won precedence over his commitment to a comprehensive settlement in the Middle East.

That night he instructed Vance to work out an agreed position with Dayan. By the early hours of 5 October the US-Soviet communiqué was gutted and the rules for Geneva rewritten in a US-Israeli Working Paper. A short statement issued after the night's labours stated that acceptance of the US-Soviet communiqué of 1 October was 'not a prerequisite for the reconvening and conduct of the Geneva Conference'. Carter had climbed down.

Asad's regional needs and ambitions were simply disregarded. To check Egypt from making a separate agreement with Israel, he had been pressing for a unified Arab delegation to do the actual negotiating at Geneva. He also wanted Syria to participate in the discussion of the Palestine problem. The US-Israeli Working Paper denied him both. It provided that after an opening plenary session, the conference would break up into bilateral committees to negotiate bilateral peace treaties. In other words, Asad would lose all control over Sadat. Moreover,

Syria was the one interested party excluded from the working group on the West Bank and Gaza – a group which the Working Paper specified would consist of Israel, Egypt, Jordan and the Palestinian Arabs.

Dayan secured the exclusion of Syria – his principal aim – by making a tactical concession over Palestinian participation. To Carter's relief, even gratitude, he agreed that some Palestinians such as West Bank mayors could participate in the opening session and in the West Bank working group, provided Israel could weed out known PLO members. Candidly he spelled out the long-held Israeli argument for sidestepping Syria and making peace with Egypt alone. If one wheel were removed, he argued, the car could not run again. Peace with Egypt was the way to stabilize the region and rule out the possibility of war.

Asad was dismayed at the outcome of Dayan's efforts: Israel had managed to strip him of all control over other Arab parties and to keep out the PLO. Bilateral committees meant that Israel could deal with a fragmented Arab world. Worse still, Carter now saw Asad as an obstacle and charged him with going back on his earlier promise of co-operation. In recalling this period a decade later, Cyrus Vance still held to the view that Asad had 'cut himself out'. By insisting on control of the whole Arab side, 'he missed the chance to participate in a broad conference in which everything could have been discussed including the return of the Golan Heights. This was not only unwise, it was self-defeating. Asad shot himself in the foot.'[20] But in the opinion of another American, Talcott Seelye, who became ambassador to Syria in August 1978, 'Israel was determined to cut Syria out and do a deal with Egypt alone. Even had Syria moved faster and been more flexible, it is doubtful whether it would have got any satisfaction.'[21] The record appears to support this latter interpretation.

Asad's case may have gone by default. He did not fight his corner strongly enough. He sent no envoy to Washington to protest about the neglect of his interests in the US-Israeli Working Paper, although it must be said that, unlike Dayan, he was in no position to intervene at the top. Instead he attempted to put pressure where he could, sending Foreign Minister Khaddam and Deputy Defence Minister Naji Jamil on tours of the Arab states to ask them to intervene with Sadat to reject the US-Israeli proposals. General Jamil even went to Cairo on 22 October to lecture the Egyptian leader on his duties to the Arab cause, only managing to exasperate Sadat and prompt him to throw off Syrian fetters once and for all.

The wooing of Sadat

The Israeli government had meanwhile made considerable progress towards its aim of a direct dialogue with Sadat, the second track of its campaign to scuttle Carter's Middle East policy. It is widely supposed that Sadat himself, by his dramatic journey to Jerusalem in November 1977, launched the process leading to Egyptian-Israeli peace. But the first moves were in fact made by the Israelis. It was they who covertly importuned Sadat to deal bilaterally. This necessarily involved a certain deception of their American ally, seeing that Carter was still wedded to the objective of a comprehensive, multilateral settlement. To embark on so significant a political initiative without consulting Washington and at variance with Washington's declared aims represented a major departure from the close political and operational co-ordination with the United States which Israel had hitherto pressed for. But as Begin was scheming to entrap Sadat, he needed freedom from American constraints.[22]

In wooing Sadat, Israel sought the help of three leaders who were well-placed to act as intermediaries. Nicolae Ceausescu of Romania had for several years been involved in attempts at Middle East peacemaking; the Shah of Iran, Israel's main regional ally, was also on good terms with Sadat, as was King Hasan of Morocco who also maintained discreet but long-standing contacts with Israel, largely by way of the Moroccan Jewish community. Begin began his seduction of Sadat by asking Ceausescu whom he called on in Bucharest at the end of August 1977 to help arrange a meeting between himself and the Egyptian President.[23] Also that August, Dayan called on the Shah in Tehran with the same request,[24] and in the first week of September he flew secretly to Morocco to enlist the good offices of King Hasan as well.[25] This three-pronged diplomatic effort bore fruit on 16 September when Sadat's confidant, Deputy Premier Hasan al-Tuhami, came stealthily to Tangier to hear Dayan argue the case for an Egyptian-Israeli summit.

Sadat was intrigued by these overtures and he was certainly attracted by Dayan's promise that the whole of Sinai could be restored. This was the big prize, but there were other arguments. Sadat shared the Israelis' dislike of negotiating in an open forum at Geneva under the eye of suspicious, even hostile, parties such as the Soviet Union and Syria. Again like Israel, he was unimpressed with Carter's vision of a settlement to satisfy everyone, so at odds with Kissinger's scheme of a tripartite partnership of the United States, Israel and Egypt which would direct the affairs of the region and keep troublemakers down. As an added inducement to deal direct, Israel provided Sadat with intelligence warnings of a Libyan-backed plot to overthrow him.[26]

To help him assess Israeli motives, Sadat himself went to Bucharest and Tehran in late October to consult Ceausescu and the Shah. He wanted to hear from them what Begin and Dayan had said. And, according to his own testimony, it was on this journey that the idea of going to Jerusalem first came to him.[27]

Such was the background to Sadat's shock announcement on 9 November that he was ready to go to the end of the world in search of peace, even 'to the Knesset itself', and when he arrived at Jerusalem's Ben Gurion Airport ten days later, it was evident that Israel's second track had proved brilliantly successful, killing the Geneva conference stone dead. All the disputes about who should be invited and about how negotiations should be conducted were suddenly rendered meaningless. Thoroughly upstaged, the Carter Administration had no alternative but to ditch its own policies and join the Israeli-Egyptian bandwagon.

Last meeting with Sadat

Asad's last great duel with Sadat took place in Damascus on the night of 16–17 November 1977 when for seven hours the two men argued, pleaded with and stormed at each other, but in the end it was a dialogue of the deaf which left them more at loggerheads than ever and intent on pursuing their separate paths. Sadat had come in a last-ditch attempt to get Asad to approve his direct dealings with Israel – or at least to win his silence. The long bitter night was the climax of four years of growing estrangement rooted in the disappointments of the October War, but which was greatly envenomed by Sadat's moves towards a separate relationship with Israel. This was to be their last meeting.

At one point in their long argument, Sadat exclaimed: 'Let us go together to Jerusalem! Or, if you cannot come, then please keep silent. Don't condemn me. If I fail, I will admit I was wrong and tell my people to give you the leadership.'[28] Asad was baffled by such histrionics. Sadat was always in a hurry – in a hurry to end the October War, in a hurry to disengage, in a hurry to go to Jerusalem and so destroy the chances of a comprehensive settlement. Now he was about to jump into recognition of Israel before bargaining had even started. He was proposing to begin at the point where a wise man might after long negotiation hope to end up. So great was Asad's exasperation that for a moment he thought of locking up the Egyptian leader and preventing him leaving Damascus.[29]

But beyond the confrontation between the two leaders lay the stubborn facts of divergent national trajectories. Egypt and Syria were heading in different directions, and not surprisingly viewed the problem of how to deal with Israel from opposite standpoints. Asad had been totally opposed to Sadat's contacts with Israel from the moment of Egypt's unilateral ceasefire in October 1973, and his alarm had grown sharper following Egypt's disengagement agreements, especially Sinai Two which in his view robbed the Arabs of what little advantage they had won in the October War. Asad was by now obsessed with the geopolitical equation: it was blindingly obvious to him, yet apparently not at all clear to Sadat, that the formal removal of Egypt from the Arab camp would leave the rest of the Arab world a prey to Israeli designs. In language more highly charged than he customarily used, he warned Sadat of the catastrophic consequences of his journey. It would be the gravest setback in Arab history. It would produce such a strategic imbalance that Israel would be able to hit one defenceless Arab country after another, beginning with Lebanon and the Palestinians. Far from bringing peace, it would banish it. Indeed anything short of a comprehensive peace was not worth having.[30] As he expounded these passionate arguments, Asad was unaware – and this lent irony to the occasion – that Sadat's secret contacts with Israel had already taken him beyond the point of no return.

Asad's doom-laden gloom was in sharp contrast to Sadat's ebullient confidence on the eve of his great adventure. The Egyptian leader had a showman's instinct for the dramatic happening. He had decided to brazen out his incipient love-affair with Israel and fly in person to the enemy's capital where he would preach his message of reconciliation from the Knesset itself, changing the course of history in a single breath-taking act. Psychological barriers thrown up by long years of conflict would come tumbling down and Israel would grasp his outstretched hand. He hoped that Begin would respond to his own grand gesture with a pledge to withdraw from all the occupied territory. He had not grasped that Begin intended to return Egyptian territory alone precisely in order to retain the rest. In Begin's mind, peace with Egypt was the key not to dismantling Eretz Israel but to making it impregnable.

By the morning of 17 November, Asad and Sadat were too angry with each other even to hold a joint press conference, and Sadat faced the press alone. He acknowledged Asad's opposition but confirmed his own decision to go to Jerusalem. Later that night, on his return to Cairo, it was announced that the journey would take place two days hence, on 19 November. Asad waited for his guest to leave before speaking out.[31]

> I am extremely sad that I could not convince Sadat of the gravity of this visit and of its far-reaching consequences for our Arab cause. Peace is our aim in Syria, as it is in Egypt and in the whole Arab world. But a successful strategy cannot be pursued through unsuccessful tactics.

The 19th of November was declared a day of national mourning.

Given everything that was at stake, it was a low-key reaction. Asad hoped to avoid a total breach with Egypt and the increased vulnerability it would bring him. Even after Sadat's visit to Jerusalem he denied that there was a 'divorce' between Syria and Egypt, to allow for the slim chance that Israel's niggardliness might yet cause Sadat to draw back.

Later, when it became evident that Asad's pessimism was more realistic than Sadat's hopes, it was commonly said that Sadat had pursued a personal and impetuous course without popular backing. In fact, though the manner of his diplomacy was indubitably his own, he was in many ways faithfully reflecting the national grievances and aspirations of his countrymen. In the mind of many Egyptians, a move towards peace with Israel was not a retreat into isolation but, on the contrary, an affirmation of Egyptian leadership. Sadat was determined to lead the Arabs in peace as in war, believing that where he blazed a trail, others would have to follow. Anti-Syrian feeling ran strongly in Egypt. Cut to the quick by Asad's accusations of treachery after the October War, nursing a whole catalogue of grievances against the Ba'th party, some of them dating back to the unhappy union, Sadat was anxious to put Damascus in its place. He gave a clue to his thinking when he urged Herman Eilts, the US ambassador in Cairo, to remind Asad that Cairo was the capital of the Arab world. In bursting out of the Geneva framework, he was freeing himself from unwelcome Syrian shackles.

In the last days of October, Carter wrote two letters to Sadat confessing that he could not get all the parties to agree the procedures for Geneva laid down in the US-Israeli Working Paper – meaning principally Syria. He proposed joining with the Soviet Union in calling on the UN Secretary-General to convene the conference, counting on the Soviets to bring Asad along. To Sadat this meant giving Asad a hold over his diplomacy: Carter's letters may have precipitated his decision to bypass Geneva. For, as the Saudis told Washington on 28 October, Asad was about to agree to attend the conference if the co-chairmen put Palestinian rights and an Israeli withdrawal on the agenda.[32]

Syria was not Sadat's only bugbear. Like many Egyptians, he also bore a grudge against the plutocrats of the Gulf who owed their oil billions to Egypt's sacrifices in the October War and yet were terribly reluctant to share their wealth. On one of his fund-raising trips to the Gulf Sadat to his great humiliation overheard someone say, 'Here comes the beggar'. In January 1977, after Cairo had been shaken by food riots, a high-level Saudi delegation promised massive financial aid – but failed to come up to Sadat's expectations. All these were reasons for wanting to break out of the cycle of war and poverty. Driven by economic need, Sadat was lured by the thought of tapping American wealth in an Egyptian 'Marshall Plan', an idea which Kissinger had first planted in his head.[33]

But whatever the exact balance of Sadat's motives Asad's unshakeable view thereafter was that Sadat destroyed the chances for a comprehensive settlement at Geneva by going it alone. His tone against the Egyptian leader hardened. The Syrian media compared Sadat to the Nazi collaborators Quisling and Pétain and his visit was described as treachery and capitulation. The thread which had snapped during the confrontation in Damascus in November 1977 was never mended.

Camp David accords

Ten months were to elapse before Begin, Sadat and Carter put their names to the Camp David accords of September 1978, and a further six months before the signature of the Egypt-Israel peace treaty of 26 March 1979. This was the time it took Menachem Begin to bend Sadat and Carter to his will.

To succeed in its designs, Israel had first to whittle down Sadat's expectations expressed in his Knesset speech of 20 November 1977. He had offered Israel peace, security, normal relations with its neighbours and whatever international guarantees it chose, provided it withdrew from the territories occupied in 1967 and allowed the Palestinians to establish their own state. Neither of these preconditions survived the grinding months of negotiation.

Carter's high ambitions were also disappointed. He had wanted to be the architect of an overall settlement, but instead found himself realizing what by now was Begin's blueprint. A mere couple of months after Sadat's Jerusalem visit, Carter set about promoting an Egyptian-Israeli agreement only loosely connected to the Palestine problem: a dialogue with the PLO was removed from his agenda, Syria no longer seemed a necessary player and the Soviet Union was ignored.

This remarkable reversal of policy owed much to Begin's unshakeable refusal to budge from the West Bank, to Sadat's uncertain commitment to the Palestinians and to the Syrians, to Carter's domestic weakness in the face of Israel's friends, and to the Administration's weary need to get an agreement of some sort. At the end of the day Washington accepted Israel's argument that an Egyptian-Israeli peace ruled out the threat of war and was therefore in America's interest.

The scaling down of the peace process from its original multilateral aims to its bilateral outcome was a two-stage affair: Dayan masterminded the first and Begin the second. It was essentially Dayan's achievement to detach Egypt from Syria by his secret courting of Sadat; and it was then Begin's achievement to unlink Egypt from the West Bank, a coup he pulled off at Camp David by playing on his own fearsome reputation. When the discussion came to focus on the future of the West Bank, Begin delivered an emotional tirade: 'I, Menachem Begin, steward of four thousand years of Jewish history, cannot be the one to give up the historic claim to the Biblical lands.' But privately he added to Vance, 'I won't be prime minister five years from now' – hinting, in effect, that further progress could be made when he was gone. By this stratagem he won Carter's and Sadat's agreement to defer the question of ultimate sovereignty over the West Bank until after a transition period in which the Palestinians would enjoy a limited form of autonomy, so uncoupling its fate from the Egypt-Israel accord.[34]

In the end Sadat made peace on the basis of two accords with no formal link between them: one was a strictly bilateral deal providing for the return of Egyptian territory alone, and the other was a set of vague provisions for Palestinian autonomy. All along Begin had intended to give up Sinai in order to have *carte blanche* on the West Bank – which, under the subterfuge of his Palestinian home rule proposals, is what he got.

The Camp David negotiations from 6 to 17 September 1978 ended with another Begin coup – a muddle over settlements in the occupied territories.[35] Carter thought he had secured a pledge from Begin to freeze settlements until the negotiations on West Bank autonomy were completed, and with this assurance he got Sadat to approve the two accords. But there was no written pledge from Begin to support Carter's understanding. Instead Begin claimed that he had agreed to no more than a three-month suspension, and it was then the sorry task of Ambassador Herman Eilts to tell Sadat that there had been a 'misunderstanding' over settlements. 'You are sending me home naked', Sadat grimly replied.[36] Khaddam, Syria's Foreign Minister, had predicted that Camp David would be 'Sadat's last striptease'.[37] The fact that Carter chose not to confront Begin on this crucial matter but let the Israeli version stand, was perhaps the clearest indication of the supremacy Begin had won over his negotiating partners.

Alienation

A week after Camp David, Cyrus Vance called on Asad in Damascus for sad but courteous farewells – something of a leave-taking between Syria and the United States. Kissinger had visited Asad in similar circumstances at the time of Sinai Two, but for Vance, a liberal lawyer of enlightened views who had genuinely hoped for a comprehensive settlement, it was a more uncomfortable occasion. Vance liked Asad and considered him one of the most intelligent of the Arab leaders, but he knew the United States had achieved nothing for Syria.[38]

> I remember Asad said something to me along the lines that he was weary and was now going to sit on the side of the road and observe events. If circumstances changed, he would not hesitate to change his position, although as in the past he would always be guided by the paramount interests of Syria.

Asad had suffered many disappointments at the hands of the United States, but Carter's betrayal, as he saw it, was particularly painful because he had expected so much from the new Administration. Although he continued to keep open a channel to Washington, by 1979 his alienation from the United States was almost total as he felt his vital interests had not only been disregarded but deliberately undercut. He never visited the United States nor rid himself of a deep distrust of US intentions towards him. Nevertheless, in September 1979, on a flight to Cuba to attend a non-aligned summit, his aircraft strayed into US air space and he found himself obliged to radio a polite greeting to Jimmy Carter.

But Asad's alienation from Egypt was if anything more profound. On coming to power he had joined with Egypt to wrest the occupied territories back from Israel. And he had failed. The Golan and the West Bank were more firmly than ever in Israeli control and Egypt, his partner in war, was now Israel's partner in peace. His struggle to hold Sadat back had been in vain and the Syrian-Egyptian axis, backbone of Arab strength, was broken. As a Ba'thist, as an Arab nationalist and as a Syrian, Asad took it hard. It was a profoundly gloomy moment.

To what extent was Asad himself responsible for what had happened? Could it have been otherwise? Would greater tact and deference have held Sadat in the Arab camp? There is no evidence that Asad asked himself these questions. Perhaps after all there was something irreconcilable about wanting to keep Egypt as a partner and yet being resolved to make Damascus a regional centre of power in its own right. Asad had given Syria a strength and importance it had never had before, he had endowed it with the will and the means to project influence beyond its borders. As such it had become a rival of Egypt which, even though enfeebled and disillusioned by thankless wars, had been accustomed to primacy in Arab affairs. It was perhaps inevitable that Asad and Sadat should fall out.

Searching for help

Sadat's overtures to Israel from 1977 to the peace treaty of March 1979 exposed Asad to two distinct perils: physical destruction by means of a surprise Israeli attack, or political destruction – the marginalization of Syria and even his own downfall – if Sadat were to draw other Arab states in Egypt's wake. So Asad's immediate priorities were, first, military protection and, second, the isolation of Egypt to prevent the general 'capitulation' he feared.

Among Arab countries Iraq seemed the only possible military counterweight to Israel. It was a measure of Asad's need that, although he was at daggers drawn with the Iraqi leaders, he appealed to them on 20 November 1977 – the day of Sadat's Knesset speech – to bury the hatchet and 'face our pan-Arab responsibilities'.[39] His call for help was all the more remarkable because it came amid a welter of tit-for-tat plots, frontier closures and explosions in each other's capitals. Barely a month earlier, on 25 October, Asad's Foreign Minister Khaddam had narrowly escaped death at the hands of a pro-Iraqi Palestinian gunman in Abu Dhabi. But Iraq turned a deaf ear to Asad's pleas, no doubt gleeful at his difficulties. So there was no help to be had from that quarter.

Asad then rallied what Arab friends he had in a high-sounding 'Front of Steadfastness and Resistance' which met in Qadhafi's capital, Tripoli, on 5 December 1977 to condemn Sadat. But the front gave him little real comfort: Algeria, its most substantial component, was by now locked in conflict with Morocco over the Western Sahara; the People's Democratic Republic of Yemen was weak and far away; 'Arafat's PLO was as much adversary as partner; while Libya was both too erratic and too 'rejectionist' for Asad's sober taste. All this was shadow-boxing with no real substance to it.

Asad came to feel that only the Soviet Union could protect him against a possible Israeli blow to finish him off. But unfortunately his relations with Moscow left much to be desired. Egypt's switch from East to West, robbing Moscow of a strategic foothold and cutting it out of peace diplomacy, had made the Russians sceptical of Arab friendship. Nor had they yet forgiven Asad his Lebanon intervention of 1976 when he routed their leftist friends. At the time they expressed their displeasure by refusing to replace ammunition expended in that campaign and by dragging their feat on new arms deliveries. But now Asad needed arms more desperately than at any time since 1973, so it was with cap in hand that Khaddam rushed to Moscow a week after Sadat's Knesset appearance and that Chief of Staff Shihabi followed him a month later. Asad himself went in February 1978 to put his case for new tanks and aircraft, and especially for an air defence system, and won the satisfaction of a reference in the final communiqué to 'raising the level of [Syria's] defensive capability'.[40] But the pledge was painfully slow in being honoured.

Clearly the Russians took some persuading that Asad was worth bailing out. They needed concrete evidence. In June 1978 he allowed a Soviet naval squadron to call in at the port of Latakia, a facility he had denied them following the row over Lebanon. But it was to take two visits to Moscow by Shihabi, a further visit by Asad in October 1978, public Syrian complaints of Soviet dilatoriness, a five-day stay by Defence Minister Tlas in January 1979 and finally a visit to Damascus by Soviet Foreign Minister Gromyko on 26 March 1979 – the day of the signature of the Egypt-Israel treaty – before the Soviets threw themselves behind Syria's defence effort. So, as Begin drew Sadat's teeth, Asad spent sixteen nail-biting months, from November 1977 to March 1979, pleading with the Soviet Union to give him a minimum of deterrence.

In these months the moment of maximum danger came when Israel invaded Lebanon in March 1978, seizing the whole of south Lebanon up to the Litani river and sending a panic-stricken population fleeing northwards. 'Operation Litani' was portrayed as a response to the Palestinian hijack of an Israeli bus on the coast south of Haifa on 11 March when more than thirty Israeli civilians were killed in the subsequent shoot-out. But in scope and destructiveness, the Israeli invasion dwarfed the incident which had provoked it. Some 2,000 Lebanese and Palestinians were killed and an estimated 200,000 displaced from their homes. Angry at what he saw as Israel's disproportionate violence, Carter told Begin to pull his troops out and lent American backing to the despatch of a UN force, UNIFIL, as a buffer in south Lebanon between Israel and the PLO. After three months the Israelis did depart, but not before establishing a buffer zone of their own along the border under a Lebanese proxy, Major Sa'd Haddad, and greatly expanding their contacts with the Maronites of Mount Lebanon to the North. Israeli arms flowed into the Lebanese port of Junieh and Israel's relations with the rising militia leader, Bashir Jumayil, grew closer.

Asad feared that Israel's Litani Operation was the prelude to an attack on Syria itself. He had some 30,000 troops in Lebanon, but he was in no shape to take on the invaders as his army, sucked into smuggling and other misbehaviour, was already suffering from the insidious ills of exposure to an increasingly anarchic society. His Golan front was depleted, his men ill-equipped, his air defences negligible, and his air force less of a match than ever for the Israeli air force. More ominously, in 1978 Syrian forces were clashing fiercely with Christian militiamen of the Lebanese Front armed by Israel. Asad could not risk a general conflict, so, at considerable political cost to himself, he kept out of the fight. Instead, he concentrated on defending the approaches to Damascus, vital to his security – in other words, the Biqa' valley, now seen more than ever as Syria's forward defence line. But the experience of passivity was a humiliating one and a reminder of the leverage Israel had over him in Lebanon.

Reconciliation with Iraq

The Camp David accords threatened both Syria and Iraq with isolation if Sadat managed to draw the rest of the Arab world after him. In the face of this common danger the two countries joined forces to prevent Saudi Arabia and Jordan from joining the peace process. Reversing its earlier policy of decrying Asad, Iraq appealed to him on 1 October to attend an Arab summit in Baghdad to decide what to do about Egypt.

A wary dialogue followed. Tariq 'Aziz, a leading member of Iraq's Revolutionary Command Council, came twice to Damascus to warm up relations between the two warring wings of the Ba'th party. 'Aziz was well-known in Syria since he had taken refuge there after the overthrow of the Iraqi Ba'th in 1963 and had worked on the party newspaper. At a dinner given for him by veteran Ba'thist Mansur al-Atrash, it seemed as if the gory schism of 1966 could be bridged. Asad's faithful aide Mustafa Tlas was there, as was Ahmad Iskandar Ahmad, Syria's dynamic Information Minister.[41] A truce was called between two Arab regimes which had hated one another for a decade and more.

The entente was sealed by Asad himself on a three-day visit to Baghdad on 24–26 October 1978 when he made it up with President Ahmad Hasan al-Bakr and with Iraq's rising star, the formidable Saddam Husayn. At this meeting of old enemies, Ba'thist pan-Arab dogmas were duly paraded. A Charter for Joint National Action was signed, hailed as ushering in an 'important qualitative change in relations' between Syria and Iraq – a euphemism for an end to plotting and killing. When men have drunk from the same doctrinal fount they speak a common language which turns easily to sanctimoniousness: 'I would rather be a private soldier in a united Arab world than a general in a secessionist state', Asad told his hosts. 'My brothers, I have no personal ambition to satisfy: it is the same to me if our capital is Baṣra or Mosul or Homs.' But he added a word of caution. 'The road to union between us is not carpeted with flowers.'[42]

Within a week Asad was back in Iraq for the Baghdad summit of 2–5 November called to condemn Egypt and attended by every other member of the Arab League. As a warning to Sadat to go no further, sanctions were agreed in the event of Egypt's signing a peace treaty. Meanwhile, it was decided to suspend further meetings of the League Council in Cairo and to set up a support fund for front-line states: Syria was promised $1.8 billion a year for ten years, Jordan $1.2 billion, the PLO $150 million, the occupied territories another $150 million, and Lebanon $100 million – promises only partially kept and which were later to lead to much wrangling. In an eleventh-hour bid to draw Egypt back from the brink, a delegation was sent to Cairo to offer Sadat $5 billion a year for ten years, or so it was rumoured, if he renounced Camp David. Sadat refused to receive the envoys.

The reconciliation between Iraq and Syria set Israeli planners totting up Syrian and Iraqi tank forces. They need not have worried. For Asad and Saddam Husayn the important achievement of their new alliance was that it forced the Saudis, privately reluctant to censure Egypt or antagonize Washington, to fall into line behind them. Camp David was checked and Sadat denied the Pied Piper role of which he had dreamed. When on 26 March 1979 he signed his lonely treaty with Israel, he was immediately punished: relations were broken off, Egypt was expelled from the Arab League and the League's headquarters were moved out of Cairo where they had been since 1945. A short while later Egypt was suspended from the Islamic Conference Organization. Sadat had become an outcast.

Forged to bring about these results, the Syrian-Iraqi tactical alliance survived a few more weeks. In January 1979 Saddam Husayn paid a visit to Damascus and Asad made a return trip to Baghdad in June – but almost immediately thereafter relations reverted to the familiar pattern of intrigue and subversion.

Stocktaking

Camp David and the peace treaty transformed Israel's strategic environment. Always more than a match for all the Arabs combined, Israel had now neutralized the largest and most powerful Arab state and had become wholly unchallengeable. Freed from the threat of a two-front war, it faced no pressure to solve the Palestine problem nor to heed the angry clamour from Syria and other Arab states. To those who regarded peace between Egypt and Israel as a welcome breakthrough, Asad's fears were simply not comprehensible. Far from correcting Kissinger's work President Carter had ended up completing it. And just as Sinai Two had cost the American taxpayer billions of dollars, so Carter now pledged further billions to secure the peace treaty, paying Israel to do what it desperately wanted to do anyhow. 'We bought the sands of the Sinai for an exorbitant price from Israel, then paid Egypt a large price to take them back', was the sardonic summing up of the veteran American statesman George Ball.[43] There was a failure to grasp how the achievement of Israeli objectives since the October War, abetted by Kissinger and acquiesced in by Carter, had broken the Arab system and ensured Israeli supremacy. (For example, in September 1978 while the Camp David talks were in progress, Asad on a state visit to West Germany seized the occasion of a banquet in Bonn to attack Sadat's policies: to his dismay President Walter Scheel made an impromptu reply registering dissent.) But the incomprehension was not only in the West. Among some Arab leaders there was also a good deal of confusion about the significance of Sadat's initiative. Anxious to bring the Saudis in on his side, Sadat sent Nasser's son-in-law, Ashraf Marwan, to explain to King Khalid why he had gone to Jerusalem. To the envoy's surprise, the pious king seemed unconcerned about the political or strategic consequences: his objections were solely religious.[44]

Why did Sadat have to go to the holy city of Jerusalem? He could have met Begin anywhere in the world. And why did he have to go on 'Id al-Adha [the feast-day closing the pilgrimage season] when all good Muslims should be turning their thoughts to Mecca?

As time passed it came to be seen that Sadat's journey to Jerusalem was less a historic breakthrough towards peace than a fracture in the peace process, which over a decade later had not been repaired.

19

The Enemy Within

Just when Asad was facing defeat in his long struggle against Israel and the United States, his home base blew up in his face. The chain of external events which was so catastrophic for him, from Sadat's visit to Jerusalem to the Egypt-Israel peace treaty, coincided with an internal terror campaign of unparalleled ferocity. The removal of Egypt from the Arab line-up had left Syria especially vulnerable externally, and it was at precisely this moment that the country was engulfed in violence. Inevitably, when everything he had fought for − indeed his life itself − was at risk, Asad came to see himself as the victim of a great conspiracy in which his enemies at home and abroad had joined forces to bring him down. In 1977 he was in a situation not unlike that of Nasser in 1967: stripped of defences, driven into a corner, and brooding over the sombre conclusion that the West in collusion with Israel and his Arab opponents was out to destroy him.

One of the worst outrages occurred on 16 June 1979 when terrorists slaughtered large numbers of 'Alawi officer cadets at the Aleppo Artillery School. A member of staff, Captain Ibrahim Yusuf, assembled the cadets in the dining-hall and then let in the gunmen who opened fire indiscriminately. Thirty-two young men were killed outright according to the official report,[1] and another fifty-four wounded, but other sources say the death toll was as high as eighty-three.[2] It was a declaration of war.

Hit-and-run terrorism had jolted Syrian city life since Asad's intervention in Lebanon in the summer of 1976, but there had been nothing on the scale of the Aleppo massacre. Rather the pattern had been one of random explosions and assassinations, somewhat mystifying to public opinion as no one could be sure who was behind them. Some of the victims were prominent officers and government servants but others were professional men, doctors, teachers and the like, who were not involved with the regime and were therefore undefended.

Most of them were 'Alawis which suggested that the assassins had targeted the community and were deliberately setting out to sharpen sectarian differences, and in this they were successful. Every 'Alawi came to feel he was a potential target and the community as a whole trembled.

Among the two or three dozen victims in the years before the outrage at the Artillery School, the better known were the commander of the Hama garrison, Colonel 'Ali Haydar, killed in October 1976; the rector of Damascus University, Dr Muhammad al-Fadl, killed in February 1977; the commander of the missile corps, Brigadier 'Abd al-Hamid Ruzzuq, killed in June 1977; Professor 'Ali Ibn 'Abid al-'Ali of Aleppo University, killed in November 1977; the doyen of Syrian dentists, Dr Ibrahim Na'ama, killed in March 1978; the director of police affairs at the Ministry of the Interior, Colonel Ahmad Khalil, killed in August 1978; and Public Prosecutor 'Adil Mini of the Supreme State Security Court, killed in April 1979. Asad's own doctor, the neurologist Dr Muhammad Shahada Khalil, was killed in August 1979. It was shocking and wounding to Asad that some of the best and brightest men of the society he was fashioning, especially professional men from his own community, were falling to the assassins.

The economic boom

These acts of terror did not erupt in a vacuum. They were the most extreme expression of a general malaise spreading through Syrian society as Asad's Corrective Movement, welcomed with relief at the beginning of the decade, began to look tarnished. Not only had the economic boom which followed the October War run out of steam, but new inequalities had been created, in many ways as flagrant as those which the Ba'th revolution of the 1960s had sought to correct. A lucky few with access to the government cornucopia were acquiring vast wealth, fortunes such as Syrians had never known before, and thereby arousing the fierce resentment of all those without such access. The ruling Ba'th party as well as the higher echelons of the military and the government were packed with careerists and profiteers, and Asad himself, once so popular, was beginning to be viewed more critically. People complained that his preoccupation with foreign affairs had led him to neglect the domestic scene and to turn a blind eye to the abuses of some of his associates. There was a sense that the hero who had fought the October War, waged the battle against Camp David and given Syria international stature was now heading for trouble. Asad in 1977–8 looked weak indeed.

Yet he had accomplished a great deal at home in the 1970s. The country had been transformed in almost every statistic. Stability and relative freedom, combined with the vast inflow of capital after the October War, had resulted in unprecedented economic expansion. Before the war foreign aid, mainly from Arab and socialist countries, had barely totalled $50 million a year; in 1974 it leaped to an annual average of $600 million.[3] The Arab oil producers were the big donors, but as international confidence in Syria grew loans and grants came in from the United Nations, the World Bank, West Germany, France, and even the United States. Syrians working in Arab oil countries, now awash with funds following the oil price explosion, started to remit several hundred million dollars a year, while Syria's own oil exports, which had brought in a mere $70 million in 1973, rocketed to ten times that sum in 1974, for the first time outstripping revenues from cotton, the country's traditional export earner.

The boom years widened Syria's horizons, as could be seen in the increasingly ambitious targets of the five-year plans. The first plan, 1961–5, envisaged total investment, both public and private, of about $600 million in local currency, and the second, 1966–70, increased this to $1.2 billion. But after Asad came to power the third plan, 1971–5, provided for investment of $2 billion, rising in the fourth plan, 1976–80, drafted in the full euphoria of the boom, to $13.5 billion – about 54 billion Syrian *lire*, an astronomical figure by Syrian standards and reflecting the excitement of the times.[4] The affluent years released a dynamism in Syrian society which made it a very different place from the poor, inward-looking, over-controlled country which Asad had taken over from Salah Jadid. There were by the mid-1970s twice as many Syrians, 7.5 million of them, as when Asad graduated from the air force academy twenty years earlier, and the armed services, the bedrock of his regime, had grown to over 225,000. Undoubtedly the new numbers and the new prosperity contributed to the robustness with which Asad had risen to meet the challenges of Sadat, Kissinger, Nixon and Carter.

As Syrian budgets swelled, development projects proliferated and consumption soared – at least for some. In 1963 there were only 55 millionaires in Syria – millionaires, that is, in Syrian *lire*; in 1973 there were 1,000; in 1976, 3,500, of whom 10 per cent owned more than 100 million Syrian *lire* each (about $25 million at the exchange rate of the time).[5] Instant millionaires constituted the core of a new bourgeoisie, many enriched by commissions, kickbacks and even theft made possible by the dozens of government-financed projects. Before the October War government and business had been largely separate, interacting perhaps but not interpenetrating. After the war it was hard to say where the sphere of government stopped and that of business took over, so intertwined had they grown. It became virtually impossible to do deals of any size without government connections and handouts to officials. Partnerships grew up between businessmen and the military and political barons of the regime, spawning networks of patronage, corruption and cronyism. All too often, by submitting projects to the government and pushing them through without adequate study, middlemen rather than government planners determined the shape of the economy, with the motor being the lure of private gain rather than the public interest.

It was in this period, 1974–6, that such prominent people as the Vice-premier for Economic Affairs, Muhammad Haydar ('Mister Five Per Cent'), began to amass considerable wealth. Haydar was seen as the archetype of the startling improvement in 'Alawi fortunes resulting from the community's political ascent. His native village of Wadi 'Ayyun high in the 'Alawi mountains was in his youth ten kilometres from the nearest made-up road and lived, without school, hospital or government authority, on tobacco smuggling and the pay of a handful of boys in the army. In the 1950s the local Ba'th party, of which Haydar became secretary, press-ganged young men to build a track linking the village to the outside world. Haydar rose in the party, was elected to the Regional and National Commands, and then for nearly a decade lorded it over the Syrian economy, in which position he was well placed to look after himself.

Others on the way to becoming super-rich included Asad's brother-in-law Muhammad Makhluf and his youngest brother Rif'at, who in those affluent years travelled abroad, explored foreign capitals, acquired a taste for Western luxuries and made contact on equal terms with other top people in the region. It was a time when Syrians, and especially once underprivileged minorities and classes, broke out of the straitjacket of poverty and rural parochialism to glimpse that they and their country could join the modern world.

At this time Rif'at, self-consciously the shield of his brother's regime, built up his Defence Companies, turning them into the best armed, best trained and best paid units in the Syrian army. In financing and equipping this praetorian guard, Rif'at put to good use his friendship with Prince 'Abdallah ibn Sa'ud, the commander of the Saudi National Guard. Military matters were not his only interest. At the party's Sixth Regional Congress of April 1975 he was elected to the Regional Command and given responsibility for youth affairs, whereupon he enthusiastically set about pushing young people, particularly 'Alawis, into university courses and into parachute training, girls as well as boys. To be Asad's brother, to have access to large and unaudited budgets, and to be operating in an Arab environment where personal contacts were all-important was to be able to do almost anything one liked, and Rif'at was at times above the law.

For the first time since the Ba'th takeover in 1963, Asad and the ruling group of officers and party functionaries, overwhelmingly from country or small town backgrounds, stood on a foundation of real wealth. They were no longer mere putchists, nor simply a junta of ex-peasant officers who had captured the city. Money, economic development, a strong leader, the raising up of neglected classes and not just the 'Alawi element in them, all these seemed to be consolidating Asad's regime. The new class in the making was building a new Syria – but it was also indulging in city comforts, enjoying perks and abusing its new-found powers. Before the boom hardly any of the newcomers had owned a car or lived in anything grander than a two-bedroom apartment, but now they took to wealth and luxury as to the manner born. In 1960 Damascus had been a quiet town of around half a million people; by the mid-1970s its population had tripled and it was a thriving building-site bursting at the seams. The benefits of prosperity were even beginning to take the edge off the resentments of the old families who had been shunted aside by the revolutionary upstarts. For a moment, and until the Lebanese crisis of mid-1976, Ba'th rule had never seemed more stable.

The Muslim opposition

By 1976–7, however, shadows were beginning to darken the edges of the picture. The Syrian economy lost momentum as Saudi Arabia and other Gulf states, bowing to public outrage at Asad's assault on the Palestinians in Lebanon, reduced the petro-dollar flow. Keeping a large expeditionary force abroad was a burden, as was the daunting task of absorbing into Syria hundreds of thousands of Lebanese refugees, not to mention Syrian expatriate workers fleeing the civil war. Not everyone benefited from the fat years. The rough influx of peasants into the cities disquieted the urban lower middle classes, while inflation brought new hardships to lowly civil servants and to artisans on subsistence wages. There was an explosion in the cost of living and in land and property values. A small apartment in central Damascus, which might have cost 50,000 *lire* in 1970, had by 1977 increased seven or eight times in value (and was to increase a further ten-fold in the next decade). Workers were forced out to mean rooms in outlying villages which were themselves being sucked into the expanding metropolis. Men whose self-esteem was rooted in the old quarters of the cities where life had not changed for generations found themselves devalued and uprooted. Children of old notable families stripped of political influence, merchants outclassed by new money, religious families downgraded by the secular climate of the times all seethed with resentment.

Asad may not have grasped how much discontent was created by the dramatic changes of those years and by the upsets to the social order resulting from the Ba'th's revolution which had hoisted some to the skies and brought others low. To deal with a groundswell of complaint about corruption and unfairness, he brought back as prime minister in August 1976 the well-liked army administrator General Khulayfawi who had been his first premier. But this did not stem the increasingly vocal grumbles about ill-gotten gains inside and outside government. The have-nots were beginning to stir. In response Asad announced in August 1977 the formation of a 'Committee for the Investigation of Illegal Profits', which began vigorously enough by arresting a score of top businessmen and government servants but then backed away when it found itself tangling with personalities close to the regime. Asad's brother Rif'at, a prime example of private enrichment, could not be touched because he was at the pinnacle of the pyramid and because his Defence Companies were by this time increasingly needed in the battle against the terrorists.

When the assassinations started the government blamed them on the old enemy Iraq, and the fact that a six-month lull in the killings followed Asad's truce with Baghdad in October 1978 seemed to lend credence to the allegation. But the Aleppo massacre of June 1979 changed the picture. It was now evident that, whatever external forces were at work – and neighbouring countries certainly lent a hand – Asad had to recognize that he faced a dangerous internal opposition which would stop at nothing to overthrow him. It seemed to him a bitter irony that, having consciously tried to soften the class warfare of his predecessors and preach national reconciliation, he yet had to wrestle with domestic enemies more ferocious than any which had confronted Salah Jadid. It seemed that, whatever benefits he brought, his enemies would not disarm.

As the violence became an almost daily worry, the authorities identified the terrorists as 'the Muslim Brothers', a blanket phrase they were to use throughout the five-year crisis to describe the Muslim or

Muslim-spearheaded opposition which manifested itself in a variety of guerrilla groups with different leaders and histories and operating in different parts of Syria. The movement of dissent was wider than the guerrillas, but they were the sharp end of the grave internal challenge Asad faced from 1977 to 1982.

From his youth he had come up against the Muslim Brothers, engaging them in fist fights in the schoolyard in Latakia. In fact, a current of organized Muslim activism had existed in Syrian public life since the 1930s. Pockets of Islamic resistance to French rule had sprung up in several Syrian cities in the latter part of that decade. Paradoxically it was the French who in 1938 caused these isolated groups[6] to merge by insisting on discussing the then contentious issue of Islamic teaching in schools with a single nation-wide organization. This had provided the impetus for the birth of the *Shabab Muhammad* (Young Men of Muhammad).[7]

Just at this time a young Syrian, Mustafa al-Siba'i, returned home to Damascus from studies in Cairo where he had fallen under the spell of the founder of the Muslim Brotherhood, Hasan al-Banna, who from small beginnings in 1928 had built up a vast popular movement in Egypt dedicated to ending British rule and replacing it by an Islamic state. Egyptian ferment spilled over into other Arab countries and, with Siba'i's help, into Syria. Taking in hand the *Shabab Muhammad*, Siba'i linked them to the Egyptian Muslim Brothers and by 1943 had forged a political force strong enough to send him to parliament in Damascus. From then on, political Islam remained a sturdy actor on the Syrian scene, as Asad discovered as a schoolboy, but neither powerful enough to dominate nor so weak as to be stamped out. It was a sort of fever that rose and fell according to conditions at home and manipulation from abroad.

The rise to prominence of the Ba'th from 1955 onwards was a bitter blow to Muslim activists, who grew angry and restive as traditional Sunni society was overturned by secular radicals. When the Ba'th captured the state in 1963, small bands of Islamic militants went underground in Aleppo and Hama to organize armed resistance. For example, in Aleppo in 1963 Shaykh 'Abd al-Rahman Abu Ghidda founded a clandestine Movement of Islamic Liberation, and in Hama in 1965 Marwan Hadid – a long-time activist who, it will be recalled, had been briefly jailed for taking part in the 1964 armed rising against the Ba'th – began recruiting a secret strike force which he called *Kata'ib Muhammad* (Phalanxes of Muhammad). Absorbed by its own party infighting, the Ba'th in those years did not detect that Islamic militants were forming cells, stockpiling weapons, adopting *noms de guerre*, making foreign contacts and training their cadres in urban warfare. By drafting large numbers of Ba'thist schoolteachers into government service after the 1963 revolution, the Ba'th had itself given the Muslim Brotherhood a chance to implant itself in the schools and influence the young.

Mosque study circles where boys went in the holidays to study Arabic and the Quran became places of recruitment for the terrorists. A potential recruit would be asked to hide a weapon, then to return it, then to take it again and learn to strip and assemble it. The next stage might be to involve him in the surveillance of a Ba'th party official or the reconnoitring of a government building. 'Now you are one of us', his Islamic mentor would say. 'Your neck is on the block like ours.' A brutal method used to harden young men was to get them to gun down unprotected workers like street-sweepers who because of their job had to be out early. Several were killed in this way.[8]

Not all Muslim political activity was underground. The leading light of the Syrian branch of the Muslim Brothers was 'Isam al-'Attar, an outspoken critic of the Ba'th who, not being allowed to return to Syria after making the pilgrimage to Mecca in 1964, set up headquarters at Aachen in West Germany whence from 1968 onwards he waged a war of words against Damascus in his magazine, *al-Ra'id* (The Guide). More abusive was another Muslim newssheet, *al-Nadhir* (The Warner), which reflected the views of the guerrilla groups inside Syria. Money and supplies were channelled in through international networks such as the Federation of Muslim Students in Europe, run from 'Attar's Aachen base and from branches of the Brotherhood in neighbouring countries, notably Jordan.

The outbreak of terror

Asad's domestic troubles in 1977–8, and the growing importance of Rif'at, produced the first serious rift in the regime's power elite. Major-General Naji Jamil, a Sunni from Dayr al-Zur, had been Asad's friend and companion since their early flying days. He played a role in the 1963 coup, accompanied Asad to London in 1965, and took over from him as head of the air force in 1970. By 1978 he was also deputy defence minister and head of the Bureau of State Security. As intelligence supremo he was perhaps the major prop of the regime. Quite suddenly in March 1978 Jamil fell from grace and was sent into discreet retirement (although he retained a seat on the party's National Command, a purely face-saving appointment). Jamil was replaced in the key state security job by another of Asad's close associates who had made his career in air force intelligence, the 'Alawi officer, Major-General Muhammad al-Khuly.

Jamil's fall appears to have been triggered by three factors: the most obvious was the deteriorating security situation with which he was failing to cope; more particularly, the stresses of the times brought him up against Rif'at who aspired to be in sole charge of anti-terrorist operations; but Jamil's fatal error was to express disrespect for Asad in the inner councils of the regime. It was rumoured that he had dared to hint that, having made Asad, they could unmake him. He seemed to be challenging the ascendancy which Asad, though now beleaguered, had acquired over the group of men with whom he came to power. Jamil paid the price. His successors were soon to have their hands full.

Early in the terrorist campaign the opposition acquired a martyr in the person of the Hama fanatic, Marwan Hadid, who had been fighting the Ba'th in one way or another since his campus days in Cairo in the 1950s and who was now the imam or prayer leader of the Barudiya mosque where he delivered anti-Ba'th sermons. Of Albanian origin, the Hadid family were merchants, one of whose sons, Marwan, was a Muslim Brother, another, 'Adnan, a Communist, and a third, Kan'an, a Ba'thist – illustrating the classic fault-lines in Syrian political life. Arrested in 1976 and jailed, Marwan went on hunger strike. Asad sent Kan'an, then a Syrian diplomat in Tehran, to try to persuade him to break his fast, but to no avail.[9] Marwan died in June 1976 in the Harasta military hospital east of Damascus, immediately becoming a source of inspiration for his followers who vowed to avenge him. But it was to be another three years before the Artillery School massacre of June 1979 marked the start of full-scale urban warfare against 'Alawis, against Ba'th party officials, party offices, police posts, military vehicles, barracks, factories and any other target the guerrillas could attack. Russian technicians in Syria were also not spared: ten were killed or wounded in a rash of incidents in January 1980.

From mid-1979 to mid-1980 the underground held the initiative and Asad seemed in greatest danger. From their safe haven deep in the ancient warrens of northern cities like Aleppo and Hama where cars could not enter, the guerrillas emerged to bomb and kill. They set fire to buildings, closed shops, whipped up anti-government demonstrations and strove to control the streets. When cornered, they often blew themselves up with grenades strapped round their waists. They sent hit teams to kill party members in their beds, such as 'Abd al-'Aziz al-'Adi, a member of the Hama party leadership who was murdered in front of his wife and children and his body thrown into the street. The Hama party secretary, Ahmad al-As'ad, had several narrow escapes, in one of which a grenade rolled by a terrorist down the pavement towards his front door was providentially trapped in a pile of jasmine clippings left by a neighbour after an evening's pruning.[10] Gunmen twice attacked his house at night but were fought off. Other Ba'thists had a similar tale to tell, among them 'Ali Badawi, a member of the Aleppo governor's executive council. In June 1980 his house was besieged by guerrillas who killed one of his brothers. Another, shot in the stomach, was saved when a British surgeon transplanted a kidney from Badawi's sixteen year-old sister.[11]

Such incidents illustrated the trials party workers suffered in those years. In Aleppo between 1979 and 1981 terrorists killed over 300 people,[12] mainly Ba'thists and 'Alawis but including a dozen Islamic clergy who had denounced the murders. Of these the most prominent was Shaykh Muhammad al-Shami slain in his own mosque, the Sulaymaniya, on 2 February 1980. This was the climax of an extremely violent few weeks which opened with the arrest in November 1979 of the prayer leader of Aleppo's Great Mosque, Shaykh Zayn al-Din Khayrallah, an event which provoked massive demonstrations, numerous assassinations and the boycott, on orders of the Muslim Brothers, of the feast of al-Adha which ends the pilgrimage season. Khayrallah's son-in-law, Husni 'Abo, turned out to be the underground's military commander in the Aleppo region. He was seized, brought to trial and executed. He was succeeded as commander of the *Tali'a al-muqatila* (Fighting Vanguard), one of the most effective of the guerrilla groups, by a young engineer from Qunaytra, 'Adnan 'Uqla, who had helped plan the massacre of the Aleppo cadets[13] and who was to die in turn in 1982. Several terrorist leaders arose in those terrible times, only to be hunted down. As against their 300 victims must be set a toll of some 2,000 Muslim opponents killed by the security forces in Aleppo, as well as thousands more rounded up and thrown into jail where they were often beaten and tortured.

In March 1980, having failed to bring down the government by assassinations, the Muslim Brothers tried the bolder strategy of swamping it with large-scale urban uprisings. By intimidating shop-keepers, they got the business quarter of Aleppo to shut down for two weeks. Open defiance spread to Hama, Homs, Idlib, Dayr al-Zur and even to the distant town of Hasaka beyond the Euphrates. Would Damascus, Asad's capital, follow the trend? Anonymous leaflets circulated calling on merchants in the Hamidiyah, the capital's principal bazaar, to close in solidarity with the northern cities. At this critical juncture when the government seemed in imminent danger of losing control Asad found an ally in Badr al-Din al-Shallah, the influential chairman of the Federation of Syrian Chambers of Commerce, a patriarch in his eighties who rallied prominent shopkeepers and urged them to stay open, turning the tide in favour of the regime.[14] Damascus merchants had benefited more than their colleagues in other cities from the new wealth of the 1970s. Their proximity to the centre of power gave them opportunities for contacts and alliances with officers and officials of the regime to everyone's mutual benefit. Asad had learned from Jadid's difficulties that to give his regime a stable base he must conciliate, or at least not wholly alienate, the Damascus commercial class. This policy now paid off. His greater liking for Damascus than for Aleppo or Hama dated from this moment of averted danger.

Bloodthirsty retribution

Between 1977 and early 1980 Asad seemed slow to react to the internal crisis, as if reluctant to admit that profound fissures existed in his society. To some extent his natural caution may have been responsible for what looked almost like passivity, but it was also difficult for him to admit that his efforts to unite the country around his person had not merely failed but were collapsing into virtual civil war. The man who on coming to power had disciplined the arbitrary security services and tried to restore confidence in the rule of law now found himself under pressure to resort to the most savage methods simply to stay afloat. The conciliator was under force of circumstance turning into a despot, and it was not a transformation that Asad enjoyed.

In January 1980 as the crisis deepened Asad appointed a new prime minister, Dr 'Abd al-Ra'uf al-Kasm, a city planner and university professor who had served for a brief spell as governor of Damascus City and who had a reputation for honesty. He was the son of a Damascene religious figure, a *mufti*, and was a student acquaintance of Asad. Kasm increased the salaries of state employees, made a further attempt to crack down on corruption and allowed some measure of public criticism. Yet the violence continued, stimulating an anguished debate inside the party about the causes of the revolt. Where had the party gone wrong? Who was to blame? Was terrorism a response to corruption or did its roots lie deeper? Had mass recruitment allowed unprincipled elements to infiltrate the party? There was great alarm at the top when it was discovered that air force intelligence, run by Asad's new security supremo, General Muhammad al-Khuly, had harboured an agent of the Islamic underground who before his capture and execution leaked to the Muslim Brothers the car registration numbers of most of the state's top intelligence officers.

A tougher mood prevailed at the party's Seventh Regional Congress (23 December 1979–6 January 1980) when Asad's forceful younger brother Rif'at led a drive to wage all-out war against the terrorists. The government was losing control, he argued; the bureaucracy was corrupt and the party torn by useless ideological debate; citizens showed no sense of responsibility. What was demanded was absolute loyalty: those who were not with the regime must now be considered against it. The Ba'thist state had to be defended, in blood if necessary. Stalin had sacrificed ten million to preserve the Bolshevik revolution and Syria should be prepared to do likewise.[15] He asked for a free hand. Seeing that the Islamic terrorists had sworn to kill every infidel, he pledged his readiness to fight 'a hundred wars, demolish a million strongholds, and sacrifice a million martyrs'.[16] It was not a programme inviting restraint. The Congress marked the rise of Rif'at to a position second only to Asad's in the state. The iron-fist methods he put into practice probably saved the regime, but also changed its character.

Resolving to match the brutality of their enemies, the authorities now made more use of military units equipped with heavy weapons to root out urban guerrillas. But the real innovation was the arming of the party and its sympathizers. In every city, citizen militias were formed and weapons distributed to Ba'th-affiliated Popular Organizations. The neutrality of the street had earlier given the insurgents an advantage, but now, as the population was pressed to choose between fighting for or against the government, many chose the government side, less perhaps out of conviction than from exasperation with the disruptions – the strikes in the souk, the bombs in schools and supermarkets, and the constant fear of death.

On 9 March helicopter-borne troops were sent against Jisr al-Shughur, a town between Aleppo and Latakia where demonstrators had attacked barracks and party offices. A ferocious search-and-destroy operation left some two hundred dead. Scores of prisoners were hauled before field tribunals. A few days later the entire Third Division, some 10,000 men and 250 armoured vehicles, was sent north to bring Aleppo in line. It was joined by men of Rif'at's Defence Companies. After parleying failed to restore order, the troops were sent in at the beginning of April to seal off whole quarters and carry out house-to-house searches, often preceded by tank-fire. Hundreds of suspects were rounded up and carried away. Standing in the turret of his tank, the divisional commander, General Shafiq Fayadh, told the townspeople that he was prepared to kill a thousand men a day to rid the city of the vermin of the Muslim Brothers. His division stayed in Aleppo for a whole year, with a tank in almost every street. In Aleppo as elsewhere the military were backed up by armed party irregulars. According to Anwar Ahmadov, a Soviet consul who lived through the Aleppo crisis, 'It would have been a very different story if the population, who were by this time sick of violence, had not co-operated with the authorities and informed on the Islamic guerrillas'.[17] Hama experienced much the same cycle of terrorism and repression in the years before the great showdown in 1982.

At last in the spring of 1980 Asad threw himself into the fray. He seemed to free himself from the distaste for contact with the crowd which with the passing years was becoming more pronounced, from that undoubted reserve which even at the height of his acclaim had caused him to be something less than a populist leader. Hitherto his speeches, delivered on predictable occasions such as the anniversary of the revolution or the opening of parliament, tended to be reasoned and literary discourses. But now an orator appeared, theatrical in his anger and defiance, able to set large audiences alight and to do so night after night. On 8 March 1980, the revolution's seventeenth anniversary, Asad made a ringing declaration of Islamic faith, clearly hoping to steal the opposition's clothes:[18]

> Yes! I believe in God and in the message of Islam . . . I was, I am and I will remain a Muslim, just as Syria will remain a proud citadel flying high the flag of Islam! But the enemies of Islam who traffic in religion will be swept away!

Against all precedent he harangued the nation again on the 10th, 11th, 17th, 22nd, 23rd, 24th and on into April at clamorous, overheated congresses of the various Popular Organizations – of workers, peasants, craftsmen, youth, women, teachers, writers, students, sports-men. Preaching the use of 'armed revolutionary violence' against the 'reactionary violence' of the guerrillas, he brought tens of thousands of young men and women cheering to their feet.[19] Lukewarm about 'revolutionary violence', the Syrian Bar Association and the federations of doctors and engineers were dissolved and their officers taken into custody, some never to reappear.

On 26 June 1980 Asad, now himself at the forefront of the battle, narrowly escaped death at the hands of his Islamic opponents. Terrorists threw two grenades and fired machine gun bursts at him as he waited to welcome an African visitor at the gate of the Guest Palace. He kicked one grenade out of harm's way while a guard threw himself on the other and was killed instantly. Asad's personal bodyguard, Khalid al-Husayn, thrust the president to the ground and shielded him with his body.

A wave of fury swept through the 'Alawi community, and with it a thirst for revenge. Asad's brother Rif'at vowed to raze Damascus. 'Why do they want to kill us? We can kill too!' was the mood. Deflected from the capital, he spent his fury elsewhere. At 3 o'clock the next morning, 27 June, two units of Rif'at's Defence Companies were wakened and told to assemble in combat dress. Briefed by Major Mu'in Nasif, Rif'at's deputy and son-in-law, they were told that their mission was to attack a prison in Palmyra, deep in the desert, where Muslim Brothers were being held. The men were trucked to Mezze airport and flown in ten helicopters to Palmyra. At 6.30 a.m. half the force, about sixty men, were driven to the desert prison, split up into six or seven squads and let loose on the prison dormitories with orders to kill everyone inside. Some five hundred inmates died in cells echoing to the fearful din of automatic weapons, exploding grenades, and dying shrieks of 'God is great!'[20] In an attempt to pull a veil of legality over the massacre, it was later said that the prisoners had been condemned to death by a field tribunal with emergency powers. In any event, the war went on. On 8 July membership of the Muslim Brothers became a capital offence, although a grace period of a month was given to those who wished to give themselves up. Hundreds of the smaller fry came forward, but the hard core remained unmoved.

Particularly bloody retribution for further terrorist acts was wreaked on Aleppo in August 1980 and on Hama the following April when scores of males over the age of fourteen were rounded up almost at random and shot out of hand.[21] The drive to silence opponents spilled across frontiers. Syrian commandos raided a Muslim Brothers' training camp in Jordan in late July 1980. Hostile journalists in Lebanon were killed: Salim al-Lawzi, publisher of *al-Hawadith*, in March, and Riad Taha, head of the journalists' union in Beirut, in July. The following year, in March 1981, assassins went looking as far afield as Aachen for the Muslim Brothers' 'guide', 'Isam al-'Attar, killing his wife, Bayan al-Tantawi, when she opened the front door. But the murder which caused the greatest disquiet was that of the veteran Ba'thist leader, Salah al-Din Bitar, in Paris on 21 July 1980. The Syrian hand behind these killings was not proved but was widely suspected.

Co-founder of the party with Michel 'Aflaq, Bitar belonged to the civilian Ba'thist generation ousted by the Military Committee's coup of

1966. Condemned to death *in absentia* in 1969, he had been pardoned by Asad in 1970 and had returned briefly to Syria in an attempt at a reconciliation. Asad no doubt hoped he would settle in Damascus as a counterweight to 'Aflaq in Baghdad. But five hours of talks in January 1978 failed to heal the breach between them. Returning to his Paris exile Bitar, aided by some Gulf money, published a periodical called *al-Ihya' al-'Arabi* (Arab Revival), an echo of the name he and 'Aflaq had first given their little knot of disciples in the 1940s. In its columns he campaigned for democratic freedoms and human rights in Syria. For example, in February 1980 he published the Syrian Bar Association's demand for the restoration of the rule of law. He also harped woundingly on the sectarian, in other words 'Alawi, basis of the regime, a crime in the eyes of Damascus. It was rumoured that he was pressing the Saudis to cut off aid to Syria. Worse still, he was said to have made contact with Asad's foes in Baghdad, with Akram al-Hawrani, with General Amin al-Hafiz, the soldier who had fronted for the Military Committee until 1966, with Hammud al-Shufi, a former Syrian ambassador to the United Nations who had broken with the regime in 1979, and with other fading names from the past, becoming a rallying point for widely different strands of the Syrian opposition. For a moment it must have seemed that Bitar could present a real danger and some such fear may have contributed to the decision to put an end to him. After his death his widow, Malak, took his body for burial to Baghdad where among Asad's bitter enemies she herself sought refuge.

Men like Bitar probably posed no physical threat to Asad but their criticisms touched a raw nerve, because they were directed at sensitive areas where he seemed to depart from Arab nationalist orthodoxy. Bitar and others like him charged Asad with ambivalence regarding American peace plans: had he not negotiated a Golan disengagement with Kissinger? And was this not, after all, the opening which had allowed Sadat to conclude his separate peace? How could he claim to champion the Palestine cause while crushing the PLO? Was not his 'army of occupation' in Lebanon implementing a tacit agreement with Israel to divide the country between them? Did he not bear some responsibility for the estrangement with Egypt and for the collapse of the entente with Iraq? These were just the accusations which all those who did not understand Asad's policies, or did not wish to understand them, commonly made. He could make reasoned answers to do with the overriding need to hold Israel in check, defend his corner, yet seek an honourable peace or live to fight another day. But he remained exposed to the shafts of unconvinced critics.

Asad's long war with the Islamic underground was approaching its dénouement. In the autumn of 1980 his enemies regrouped for yet another campaign. Assassinations of prominent men were resumed, and Asad lost two friends, a heart specialist, Dr Yusuf Sayigh, and a National Progressive Front leader, Darwish al-Zuni, both killed in December 1980. At the same time the formation of an 'Islamic Front' was announced, which in a seductively phrased manifesto attempted to group the opposition within a single anti-Asad National Alliance. The Front promised free speech, free elections, an independent judiciary, land reform, and much else, under the banner of Islam. It was led from a base outside the Middle East by a three-man high command: 'Adnan Sa'd al-Din originally from Homs, Muhammad al-Bayanuni[22] from Aleppo, and the Hama-born pamphleteer Sa'id Hawwa. Alarming to Asad was the publicity these men won in Arab countries and in the West and the support they appeared to be getting from sympathizers in Egypt, Jordan and Saudi Arabia.

The Islamic Front's biggest success was to carry the terrorist war to Damascus itself. Eluding the security forces, the guerrillas exploded a car bomb outside the prime minister's office in August 1981, another outside air force headquarters in September, a third outside a Soviet experts' centre in October, and in their bloodiest operation yet killed and wounded hundreds of passers-by on 29 November with a massive explosion in the Azbakiya district of central Damascus where a complex of intelligence agencies was located. Stiff with troops, the city was turned into an armed camp. Checkpoints were everywhere, body searches became routine. Private and family life was much disturbed and when terrorists set fire to government food stores, as they often did, it was not easy to fill the larder. Hardly anyone dared stir after dark and even during the day few party members ventured out on foot. Some even stayed away from work until warned that they risked expulsion from the party. Asad was little seen in those months. When on his fifty-first birthday, 6 October 1981, Islamic terrorists in Egypt killed Anwar al-Sadat, leaflets in Damascus threatened him with the same fate. In 1976 Asad had acquired his first armoured Cadillac, now he became one of the best guarded men in the world. But his family did their utmost to live a normal life. As Basil, aged nineteen in 1981, recalled:[23]

> Because of the random killing people advised me not to go out but I felt I could defend myself. All of us children were convinced that if anything should happen to one of us, it would have no political impact on our father.

The Hama uprising

Hama, the conservative city in the central Syrian plains, had long been a redoubtable opponent of the Ba'thist state. By early 1982 relations between the city and the authorities in Damascus were inflamed, to say the least. The ruin of the local notables, the rise of the 'Alawis and the prolonged terror and counter-terror of the Islamic insurrection had brought this citadel of traditional landed power and Sunni puritanism to the end of its tether.

At 2 a.m. on the night of 2–3 February 1982 an army unit combing the old city fell into an ambush.[24] Roof-top snipers killed perhaps a score of soldiers. The troops had stumbled on the hideout of the local guerrilla commander, 'Umar Jawwad, better known by his *nom de guerre* of Abu Bakr, whose command post deep in the warren was linked by radio to a network of cells. At once government forces were rushed in. Besieged on all sides, Abu Bakr gave the order for a general uprising. Lights were switched on in the city's mosques and the chilling cry of *jihad* against the Ba'th rang out over the loudspeakers used for the call to prayer. At this signal hundreds of Islamic fighters rose from their hiding places. Killing and looting, they burst into the homes of officials and party leaders, overran police posts and ransacked armouries in a bid to seize power in the city. (Two girl parachutists, the special butt of Islamic conservatives, were slain in their beds by assassins who came in over the rooftops.)[25]

A strong guerrilla force set siege to the residence of Governor Muhammad Harba, a local man who had gained a doctorate in France for a study of Syrian agriculture and whom Asad had appointed to his post in January 1980. The terrorists shouted to him through loudhailers to come out with his hands up. But like others on the government side he had stockpiled arms and ammunition, and with his brother and four bodyguards kept the assailants at bay for five hours until security forces fought their way through to him. By the morning of 3 February some seventy leading Ba'thists had been slaughtered and the triumphant guerrillas declared the city 'liberated'. Governor Harba, party secretary Ahmad al-As'ad, intelligence and army chiefs and those members of the local leadership who had survived the night met, bleary-eyed and in arms, at party headquarters to take stock of their desperate situation. They faced defeat by a full-scale urban insurrection such as had never before occurred under Asad's rule.

In Damascus there was a moment of something like panic when Hama rose. The regime itself shook. After battling for five long years it had failed to stamp out an underground which had killed the flower of the 'Alawi professional class and had tarred Asad's presidency with the charge of illegitimacy. Fear, loathing and a river of spilt blood ruled out any thought of a truce. Hama was a last-ditch battle which one side or the other had to win and which, one way or the other, would decide the fate of the country. Every party worker, every paratrooper sent to Hama knew that this time Islamic militancy had to be torn out of the city, whatever the cost. Some such understanding that this was the final act of a long-drawn-out struggle may serve to explain the terrible savagery of the punishment inflicted on the city. Behind the immediate contest lay the old multi-layered hostility between Islam and the Ba'th, between Sunni and 'Alawi, between town and country.

The battle for Hama raged for three grim weeks: the first was spent by the government in regaining control of the town and the last two in hunting down the insurgents. Heliborne troops were sent to help the local garrison seal off the town before going in for the kill. Altogether Hama was besieged by some 12,000 men,[26] but this was no ordinary military operation: it was more of a civil war, testing soldiers' loyalties to the limit. Some deserted to join the insurgents.

As the tide turned slowly in the government's favour, the guerrillas fell back on the old quarters, especially the strongholds of the Barudi and Kaylani districts which they had prepared for a long siege. On the banks of the Orontes river the old mansions of the Kaylani family were smashed by shell-fire or brought down by the mines of army engineers. But the common people living deeper in the maze of streets were the main victims as, without food, water or fuel in the cruel winter weather, they were all too often buried in the ruins of their homes. After heavy shelling, commandos and party irregulars supported by tanks moved in to subdue the acres of mud-and-wattle houses whose interconnecting roof-tops and courtyards were the guerrillas' habitat. Many civilians were slaughtered in the prolonged mopping up, whole districts razed, and numerous acts of savagery reported, many of them after the government had regained control of the town. Entire families were taken from their homes and shot. Some guerrillas escaped into underground canals, whereupon an enraged Asad ordered the exits to be blocked up. Scores of mosques, churches and other ancient monuments were damaged and looted, including the celebrated eighteenth century 'Azm palace museum. In nearly a month of fighting about a third of the historic inner city was demolished.

Government forces too suffered heavy losses to snipers, and many armoured vehicles were hit by grenades in the rubble-strewn streets. But the price of the rebellion was paid by Hama as a whole: large numbers died in the hunt for the gunmen. Just how many lives were lost in Hama must remain a matter of conjecture, with government sympathizers estimating a mere 3,000 and critics as many as 20,000 and more. Complicating an accurate count was the fact that many women and children fled through the cordon of troops ringing the city and were at first presumed to be among the casualties. But whatever the toll – and a figure of between 5,000 and 10,000 could be close to the truth – the impact of the battle on the Arab and international perception of Asad's regime was very great indeed.

In 1961, twenty years before, a busload of students on a day's outing from Damascus University had stopped at Hama for a cup of coffee, but they were not welcome in that fiercely conservative place. An angry crowd drove them back into their bus because some of the girls were in trousers. Apart from killing a lot of people, the pounding of the town in 1982 was designed to banish such puritanism once and for all. In rebuilding the shattered society a conscious effort was made not just to erase the past but to change attitudes, and a great deal of public money was spent.

Heavily damaged old quarters were bulldozed away, roads were cut through where once no car could pass, squares and gardens were laid out. The whole of Hama was reshaped on a grand scale, with ring roads and roundabouts serving entirely new quarters furnished with schools, clinics, playgrounds and shopping malls. Among major public buildings put up after the rising were a 230-bed hospital, a cultural centre, a girls' sports institute and teacher training college, a central market of oriental design, headquarter buildings for the Peasants' Union and the federations of teachers and engineers, and a sports centre of outrageously ambitious proportions complete with Olympic-sized swimming pool. On Asad's orders, the state funded the construction of two large mosques to make up for those destroyed in the fighting as well as a Catholic church as large as a cathedral. Among the revolutionary changes was the introduction of mixed bathing in 1983 and the first college dormitory block in the whole of Syria to house both male and female students. By then the Sporting Club had some eighty girl members and in 1985 Hama girls were the national ping-pong champions. But all this could not erase the name of Hama as the byword for a massacre.

The disillusioning decade

The war against the terrorists convinced Asad that he was wrestling not just with internal dissent but with a large-scale conspiracy to unseat him, abetted by Iraq, Jordan, Lebanon, Israel and the United States.[27]

> We were not just dealing with killers inside Syria, but with those who masterminded their plans. The plot thickened after Sadat's visit to Jerusalem and many foreign intelligence services became involved. Those who took part in Camp David used the Muslim Brothers against us.

He saw himself as the victim of a 'terrible alliance' of external and internal enemies.[28]

As early as March 1980 he publicly accused the Central Intelligence Agency of encouraging 'sabotage and subversion' in Syria so as to bring 'the entire Arab world under joint US-Israeli domination.'[29] And when on 10 February 1982, in simultaneous statements, the State Department in Washington and the Muslim Brothers in West Germany broke the news of the then still unreported Hama insurrection, already a week old, Asad saw it as clear proof of collusion. By announcing that fierce fighting was taking place the United States, in his view, was attempting to encourage the uprising. The US ambassador, Robert Paganelli, was summoned to the Ministry of Foreign Affairs at 1.30 a.m. to be told of Syria's displeasure.

Asad's fears were not paranoiac. He was indeed surrounded by enemies. He had exasperated Washington by his attacks on the Egypt-Israel peace treaty. He had broken with Iraq and after the emergence of Ayatollah Khomayni had sided with revolutionary Iran. He was on the worst possible terms with King Husayn of Jordan. He had tangled dangerously with Israel in Lebanon. Another centre of hostility to him was the Syrian expatriate community in Saudi Arabia and the Gulf where over the years thousands of Syrian exiles had settled, many of them members of former landowning or political families. They had no love for Islamic fundamentalism but saw the guerrillas as a battering ram which might bring Asad down. All these had an interest in his overthrow, enough of a motive to arm and fund the guerrillas on the time-honoured Syrian precept that, for an internal opposition to get anywhere, it had to have external support.

The guerrillas were formidable opponents. They had a fortune in foreign money, sophisticated communications equipment and large arms dumps – no fewer than 15,000 machine guns were captured.[30] And as soldiers they were not novices. About half of those captured had been trained in Arab countries, mainly in Jordan. When Asad and Husayn met at Tito's funeral in May 1980, Asad furiously accused the king of having a hand in 'the blood being shed in Syria',[31] a charge

Husayn was publicly to admit five years later when he was once more on good terms with Asad.[32] Evidence of Iraqi complicity was also overwhelming. Many of those arrested confessed under interrogation to links with liaison officers in Baghdad, and many of their weapons and vehicles were of Iraqi origin. Trucks smuggling arms across the desert from Iraq were repeatedly spotted by Syrian military helicopters and intercepted. Asad's fiercest sarcasms were directed at his arch-enemy Saddam Husayn:[33]

> The hangman of Iraq was not content to kill tens of thousands of his own people. He came to Syria to carry out his favourite hobbies of killing, assassination and sabotage. That man has been sending arms for the criminals in Syria ever since he took power.

The Syrian government also seized weapons supplied to the guerrillas by Lebanese Christian militias, especially the ultra-nationalist Guardians of the Cedars who were closely linked to Israel. Asad was convinced that Israel used these groups to destabilize him and on at least one occasion Syrian agents snatched guerrillas from Lebanon where they had taken refuge with the Phalanges.[34] In any event, the mountain frontier with Lebanon and the desert frontier with Iraq made it virtually impossible to staunch the flow of arms.

In Asad's mind one of the most telling pieces of evidence implicating the United States was the discovery of US equipment in the hands of the guerrillas, and especially sophisticated communications equipment of a kind, he claimed, that could only be sold to a third party with US government permission. Syrian intelligence was convinced that an American manufacturer had, with the US government's blessing, arranged for consignments to reach the guerrillas through Israel, East Beirut and Amman. Asad later recounted:[35]

> We told the Americans that we had proof and they asked us to produce it, which we did. They denied giving the Muslim Brothers this equipment. 'All right, then', we said, 'here are the serial numbers. Perhaps you can tell us to whom you did sell it.' The Americans refused to say. Finally I said to them, 'Your involvement is clear and nothing can prove your innocence, but I'm prepared to let the matter rest'.

But despite their funding, weapons, sophisticated matériel, and their proven ability to disrupt the state, the guerrillas were political simpletons. They spoke of establishing an Islamic republic in Syria, but advanced no coherent programme. No one truly knew what life would be like under their rule, and although they had the sympathy of religious conservatives, and of some merchants, former landowners and other victims of Ba'th rule, the weight of opinion was against them. Their long campaign of terror was political insanity. At the end of the day Ba'thist Syria, a state ruled by an armed party and resting on a broad coalition of the countryside and the swelling public sector, proved robust enough to defeat the challenge.

After Hama immense relief was felt in Syria – at least on the winning side. It was possible for normal life to resume, for officials to walk about without fear of the gunman, and for their wives and families to emerge from their hiding places. Asad himself, who had been virtually invisible for months, made a dramatic appearance on the streets of Damascus on 7 March 1982, the eve of the nineteenth anniversary of the Ba'th's revolution, when for two full hours he was carried shoulder-high by a tumultuous crowd from the Guest Palace to parliament. That day it was a new Asad, brutal and vengeful, who roared:[36]

> Brothers and sons, death to the criminal Muslim Brothers! Death to the hired Muslim Brothers who tried to play havoc with the homeland! Death to the Muslim Brothers who were hired by US intelligence, reaction and Zionism!

The passage from the 1970s to the 1980s brought significant changes in the style and thinking of Syria's ruler. Optimism faded. A certain trust in the future gave way to a harsher, more cynical judgement of men and affairs as the world showed itself a complex and cruel place. Asad's nature became tougher, harder, more suspicious about scheming enemies at home and abroad.

The Muslim Brothers' terror campaign set the seal on an enormously disillusioning decade. It must be recalled that it followed immediately on the long unsuccessful struggle with Israel and the United States over the nature of the post-October War settlement. In Asad's mind the physical battle with the guerrillas was an extension of the diplomatic one which had ended with the disastrous US-sponsored Camp David accords, only the latest as he saw it in a long string of Western conspiracies, dating back over fifty years to the First World War, to divide and enfeeble the Arabs. The insurrection was just another instalment in the plot: he was being punished for his refusal to surrender. He grew to believe that he was rejected by the West, that the West did not approve of him, that Washington and Jerusalem, let alone his Arab rivals, were bent on his destruction, and moreover, that far from encouraging Israel to be reasonable the West threw its weight behind Israel's expansionism and its dreams of hegemony. At home the lesson he drew from the terrorist war was that the Right had not disarmed but during all the years since the Ba'th revolution had merely lain low waiting for the moment to pounce. A vengeful Asad turned left, imposing tighter controls over private business and reducing still further the acreage of individual land-holdings. For a while in the wake of the emergency there was a return to something like the class warfare of the 1960s.

The disillusioning decade took a heavy toll. The regime which Asad had intended to be humane was brutalized. Habits of arbitrary rule acquired in the struggle for survival proved addictive, and the relatively liberal atmosphere of the beginning of his presidency could not easily flourish again in the shadow of the powerful instruments of repression which had grown up.

Asad did not revel in killing, but resorted to it only for *raisons d'état* or in what might laxly be called self-defence. Faced with the gravity of the threat from the terrorists, he sacrificed many of the principles of his Corrective Movement. Unleashing Special Forces on whole communities, using tank fire against residential quarters, slaughtering prisoners, arming civilian supporters, shooting suspects or, what was scarcely better, hauling them in batches before field courts – this slide into brutality swept aside any semblance of the due process of law. Intelligence agencies, much used in the Middle East as instruments of state power by Arab regimes, by Israel, and by interested foreign states, loomed larger than ever. They had been virtually unknown in Syria before the 1950s, but were introduced in their all-pervasive form by Nasser's union regime. The big expansion occurred, however, with the struggle against the Muslim Brothers. It was then that intelligence agencies infiltrated many Syrian institutions, including the diplomatic service which was to be a source of later headaches. As for the Ba'th party, its mood turned triumphalist after the crushing of the underground. Ba'thists saw the ordeal as conferring on them an unchallenged right to rule and a free hand with the spoils.

Asad was by nature solitary and authoritarian. These aspects of his temperament now grew more pronounced. In 1970 he was popular, by 1982 he was feared.

20

Standing Alone

In the 1980s Asad became more remote and more an object of orchestrated adulation than he had been in the 1970s, but how much of this was a reaction to the events he had lived through and how much a development of his own personality was open to question. He had never seemed to enjoy contact with the crowd, but security worries made him something of a recluse, rarely travelling round the country and even in Damascus seldom seen outside the highly guarded short length of street linking his house to the presidential office. He became known to his subjects only on television.

Years of absolutism resulted in Asad's image becoming somewhat larger than life, while that of his colleagues shrank, a state of affairs with which he did not seem unduly unhappy. By the 1980s the honest nationalist who had won world attention as one of the toughest of Arab leaders was carried aloft on the wings of a personality cult which endowed him with the stature of a superman. This unhealthy ascent was another product of the Muslim Brotherhood crisis. In the boom years of the 1970s when employment was buoyant and money plentiful, such inflation of the leader was unnecessary: the country's prosperity spoke for itself. But when recession started to bite and the Islamic guerrillas shattered the peace, a public relations campaign was mounted in which he was praised more fulsomely than anyone before in modern Syria.

The inventor of the cult was Ahmad Iskandar Ahmad, Asad's Minister of Information from 1 September 1974 until his untimely death of brain cancer on 29 December 1983, one of the longest serving ministers in Asad's presidency and one of the closest to his master. A talented and lively 'Alawi journalist from Homs, Ahmad had caught Asad's eye during the October War when he brought out a twice daily newssheet in which he wrote morale-boosting editorials. Promoted minister, he streamlined Syria's media by welding into a team the seven

339

men concerned with information (the heads of radio-television; the three dailies, *Al-Ba'th*, *Al-Thawra* and *Tishrin*; the state news agency SANA; advertising; and press distribution) – all to the greater glory of Asad. The key to his success was his ability to catch the trend of Asad's thinking and prepare opinion for changes of policy. In the rage and fury of Arab politics, ministers of information are very important, and much as Mohamed Hasanein Heikal had been to Nasser – publicist, sounding-box and image-maker – so Ahmad Iskandar Ahmad was to Asad. Evidence of the personality cult was the constant recital of his name by all and sundry, the immense portraits of him hung from prominent buildings and the numerous statues erected to him up and down the country, such as the massive bronze figure in pensive pose seated at the entrance to the new Asad Library opened in Damascus in 1985.

But the man who was thus adulated had aged in the crisis years. Eating irregularly, rarely going out for fresh air, closeted in his heavily-curtained office for fourteen hours at a time, he undermined his health and grew haggard. He slept little and developed the disconcerting habit of summoning an aide or a friendly ambassador to his residence in the middle of the night for a chat which was likely to last until 3 a.m. when, with the household long since in bed, Asad would call in one of the guards to make his guest a cup of coffee. In 1977 he had built a large villa on the Mediterranean coast north of Latakia which became known rather grandly as his summer palace. Here during the difficult years he would go from time to time by himself to think things out and ponder his response to events. He liked to focus in solitude on a single problem, wrestle with every aspect of it, sleep on it, and wake up to fresh ideas.

Fear of the gunman was perhaps not the only, or even the main, reason for his seclusion. Perhaps, in accordance with Machiavelli's dictum that to lead men you must turn your back on them, he made remoteness a principle of government.

Access to the president, the rarest of commodities which Asad measured out with minute care, became the touchstone of influence. He maintained tension between his subordinates by making himself more or less approachable to them, by seeming at times to listen to one more than his fellows, to give his favour first to one then to another. Cabinet ministers might see him only twice in their term of duty, on being sworn in and on leaving office. A very big gap separated Asad at the pinnacle of the system from the next man down, whom he changed from time to time, and then a further but smaller gap separated the current favourite from the rest of the ruling group.

From his early days of authority, even when he was still minister of defence in the late 1960s, Asad's relations with his colleagues had tended to be formal. Even his oldest army comrade, Mustafa Tlas, then Chief of Staff, knocked politely before entering his office. But with presidential power came ever greater formality. In the 1980s there was no socializing between him and his colleagues, no invitations to each other's houses, not even courtesy visits on feast days. Asad's wife might on occasion receive the wives of leading personages, but as she herself led a life of great discretion (appearing in public only briefly once a year at the Martyrs' Orphanage), this was as near as anyone got to friendly relations with the presidential couple.

For his staff Asad's inaccessibility was reinforced by the fact that he did not keep regular hours. He had an office at home and another in the presidency, and no one knew which he would use on any given morning nor when he would come to work. His day was lengthy but extraordinarily free from routine or fixed appointments. Over breakfast he read the briefings prepared by his security chiefs and his staff of news-gatherers. He structured the rest of the day in his own unhurried way. It could mean that foreign ambassadors had to wait for months to present their credentials, important visitors were sometimes kept cooling their heels for days on end, and state papers piled up awaiting his signature. His week was as unstructured as his day: Asad did not take a weekend break and no one could remember when he had last gone on holiday. Fridays, the Muslim day of rest, saw some slackening of work but his staff would be at their posts as on any other day and he would expect to be able to reach key subordinates on the telephone.

Asad's preferred instrument of government was the telephone. In the early 1970s he had ruled by chairing meetings, by reconciling opposing views, by being physically at the centre of things. By the 1980s he had become for most people a disembodied voice on the telephone. He scarcely ever attended meetings, but his officials were always aware that he was watching and would pick up the telephone if their performance fell short. He seemed to spend the best part of the day on the telephone but the calls always originated with him: only a handful of people, perhaps no more than three or four security chiefs, had the right to ring him. Others – including the highest in the land – had to content themselves with passing messages and receiving instructions through Abu Salim, the presidential private secretary. The prime minister, the top generals, the party bosses, the heads of state enterprises lived on the *qui vive* in anticipation of a call from the boss. He might demand an explanation or need a figure and require it immediately. Many found such interrogation by telephone difficult to handle. He left them in no doubt when he was displeased. His crisp manner in these exchanges contrasted with the leisurely discursiveness of his conversations with foreign visitors. He was known never to forget or forgive disloyalty or disobedience.

Asad's intimidating manner meant that his colleagues were reluctant to offer him unsolicited advice, preferring to puzzle out what was on his mind. Yet in dominating others Asad did not resort to fits of temper or banging the table but, always civil, relied rather on his greater experience and also on the fact, that having made them, he could also break them. His associates respected him as a great man, while never forgetting that it was he who had promoted them out of the ranks and that their future and that of their families depended entirely on his favour.

All too often, and with good reason, people were frightened of making mistakes and would not dare take the initiative, with the result that Asad's desk was weighed down with trivial matters. 'This is not the business of a president', he would sometimes grumble, yet in such a personal system a ruling by him might be needed to arbitrate quite small issues. For example, two medical students wrote a book, secured a foreword by a prominent physician, and submitted it for publication – but without first clearing it with the university medical faculty as regulations demanded. The faculty head wanted to expel them, the minister of higher education wanted to defer their final examinations by a year, and it required the president's intervention to sort things out.[1]

Asad professed to dislike giving orders. He urged his ministers, deputy ministers, army chiefs, directors-general of public enterprises and the prime minister himself to act on their own initiative. Dr Kasm, who served Asad as prime minister for nearly eight years, skilfully trod the fine line between deference and independence, owing his long tenure of office to his understanding of the boss's complex personality.[2]

> One could argue with him and he would listen, but you had to be sure you had a good case. It wasn't always easy. He didn't give orders, in fact he refused to do so. Even if I were to say to him, 'What would you think if I did such-and-such?' he would answer, 'You are the prime minister, not me. Do it, and then we shall see. If it turns out well, I shall say bravo, and if not . . .'

Nor did Asad seem to need advice. By the standards of most modern states, his presidential offices were grossly understaffed. His principal aides were a private secretary and a general who handled his dealings with the army. One of the most important departments of the presidency was the news and information office, which monitored Arab and foreign press and broadcasts and compiled thrice daily digests for him. It also handled anything concerning him in the media. From the early 1980s this key news department was headed by a Syrian Protestant, the hard-headed, no-nonsense Jubran Kurriyeh who had taken over from the Palestinian As'ad Kamil Elyas, for years Asad's chief interpreter, note-taker and speech-writer. But however able and hard-working these men were, the presidency seemed to be run on antique lines, with no proper archives, no proper research or secretarial back-up, no word-processors visible, no apparatus commensurate with the role and image Syria had achieved in the world. There were no facilities for typing letters in English, and it might take two or three days to find a document. A nasty incident occurred in 1984 when a greetings cable from President Reagan on the occasion of Ramadan was mislaid and reached Asad only some ten days after it was sent!

Asad saw himself as the guardian of Syria's institutions and the arbiter between competing interests. 'I am the head of the country, not of the government', he would say.[3] He claimed that Syria was ruled by a collective leadership and that his generals, party colleagues and ministers deferred to him only as they might to an elder brother. But his authority was so vast and his control of detail so tight that he was without question the ultimate decision-maker on matters big and small.

The final defeat of the Muslim Brothers brought a certain change in the lifestyle of the Asad family. After the emergency the villa where he lived with his wife and five children was extensively remodelled, expanded and refurbished, although when the decorator put in gilt Louis XIV-style furniture Asad had it removed. The new setting was spacious and comfortable enough to receive heads of state and other important visitors, but it was still no more than the home of a successful professional man with none of the Arabian Nights splendour of the palaces of kings and presidents in other states of the region. Even so, it was a far cry from the simplicities of the Asad household in the early 1970s. A contractor recalled building a bomb shelter in Asad's house in 1973 with its entrance leading off the laundry room. When the workmen arrived at six a.m. they used to drink a cup of coffee with the president who was already up. His wife would bring down the laundry to the washing machine and prepare her husband's meals in the kitchen. By the 1980s a cook and a maid were in evidence, but Asad kept the bed he had slept on as defence minister fifteen years earlier and the chair he used when he first took power. He was more interested in power than its trappings.

The sobriety of the Asad household was relaxed in the 1980s as their children grew up and started having friends of their own. The eldest child and only daughter, Bushra, was her father's favourite. She was a tall elegant young woman with a lively face framed in cascading light brown hair. She qualified as a pharmacist at Damascus University where her four brothers followed her in due course. Basil, Asad's eldest son, studied civil engineering. He was a serious, determined youngster, interested in computers and a sportsman good at horseriding, sailing, shooting and parachuting. As for the three younger boys, Bashar studied medicine, Mahir business studies and Majd, the youngest, electrical engineering. Asad insisted that they complete their education in Syria, unlike the children of some grandees who preferred foreign universities. At college the Asad children, aware of their duty to set a good example, worked hard, wore the prescribed military-style uniform and were noted for their good manners, unlike some of the *jeunesse dorée* of the regime who wore fashionable clothes, quarrelled with their teachers, and whose wild driving was a hazard on the streets of the capital. The daughter of one security chief turned up for her examination with a posse of bodyguards and insisted that the professor help her write her papers.

The ethos of the Asad family was rather self-consciously puritanical. The children were intensely loyal to their father yet as they grew up they saw very little of him. Basil recalled:[4]

> We saw our father at home but he was so busy that three days might pass without our talking to him. We never had breakfast together, or dinner and I can't remember our ever lunching together as a family, or only once or twice, on formal occasions. As a family we might spend a day or two together in Latakia in the summer, but even there he worked in his office and we didn't see much of him.

The security doctrine

The harsher and more redoubtable Asad of the 1980s was, it could be said, the creation of Henry Kissinger and the Israelis. It was Kissinger's manipulation of the Middle East in Israel's interest which destroyed Asad's hopes of the possibility of an honourable settlement and brought out the Saladin in him.

Asad had come to power with the notion that if only the Arabs could rise from their knees after the 1967 defeat and show their valour, the justice of their case would be manifest and the world and Israel itself would see the wisdom of a fair deal. Such hopeful thinking produced the October War, conceived as an effort to recover lost territory and open the way for negotiations. Although the war was a military disappointment, in its wake Asad was ready for peace with Israel and a new relationship with the United States which he thought genuinely wanted a comprehensive settlement. This was the age of innocence.

Then began the slow erosion of hope, the steady dispelling of illusion. The first shock was Kissinger's removal of Egypt from the battlefield with the second Sinai disengagement agreement of 1975. Even so, and particularly with Jimmy Carter's arrival on the scene, Asad still entertained the hope that peace could be made at an international conference of all the parties under superpower sponsorship.

By 1978 the mood had changed. Israel's subversion of Carter's Middle East policy, culminating in the Egypt-Israel peace treaty, marked Asad's loss of trust in American good intentions. Israel's belligerent behaviour thereafter convinced him that it was not ready for co-existence with its neighbours. His perception of Israel darkened. Menachem Begin's election, the settlement of the West Bank, the destruction of Iraq's nuclear reactor, the annexation of the Syrian Golan, the US-Israeli agreement on strategic co-operation, and the invasion of Lebanon were evidence in his eyes that Israel was irredeemably aggressive and expansionist, seeking nothing less than regional mastery and Arab capitulation. With such a neighbour peace could no longer be realistically envisaged. Asad was careful never to close the door to a settlement, but Israel's maximalism brought out a maximalism of his own. The latent Arab view of Israel as a foreign body in Arab Asia, the product of an outdated Western colonialism which could not live in an Arab environment, was revived.

He could not forgive the United States its role in the worsening climate. He particularly resented Washington's encouraging Israel to make separate arrangements with individual Arab countries, rightly judging that this policy gave Israel the advantage, undermined Arab security, and ignored the profound sentiment of common destiny uniting the Arab peoples.

After these disappointments he threw himself defiantly into the anti-American camp. When, for example, in November 1979 revolutionary students took over the American embassy in Tehran and held its staff hostage, Asad came out in support of Iran. And a month later when Soviet troops marched into Afghanistan, he was one of the very few leaders outside the Soviet bloc not to condemn the invasion. Syria abstained at the UN in January 1980 when a vote was taken on the

Afghan crisis. Asad was signalling to whoever cared to notice that, faced with Washington's bias, he had no option but to turn to the Soviet Union. Then on 8 October 1980 he signed a twenty-year Treaty of Friendship and Co-operation with Brezhnev in Moscow. He had long resisted such a tie but now, significantly, the initiative for it came from him. As long as he still had faith in the equity of American diplomacy, he had balked at such an alliance, but, with Carter's collapse to Israeli pressure, he saw the Soviets as providing his only credible deterrent against Begin's dangerously overweening Israel. Another pointer to his anti-Western mood was his friendship for the combative Colonel Qadhafi. He travelled to Libya for the tenth anniversary celebrations of Qadhafi's revolution on 1 September 1979 and within a few months revived the militant 'Steadfastness Front' of Syria, Libya, Algeria, South Yemen and the PLO originally formed in response to Sadat's 1977 visit to Jerusalem. From Tripoli, in another snub to Washington, Asad went on to Cuba for a non-aligned conference.

After the loss of Egypt in 1978, Asad had hoped to redress the regional balance by an alliance with Iraq, the one Arab country which had given Syria effective military help in the October War. Although the two ruling parties were at odds, popular pressure for closer ties made a Syrian-Iraqi axis seem a credible option – at least for a few months. The collapse of these expectations in 1979 and Iraq's total immersion in its struggle with Iran resulted in a fundamental redrawing of Asad's map of the Middle East. He had lost Sadat, broken with Saddam Husayn, and found himself confronting a dangerous Begin buoyed up by an uncritical Ronald Reagan. The challenge forced him to rethink his regional strategy and produced the policies and ideas which then became associated with his name.

Asad had always been a patient man, able to take the long view in conflicts with Arab rivals and in the contest with Israel. Believing that time was on the Arabs' side, he counselled other leaders not to hurry, not to negotiate impulsively, not to make concessions from weakness. He felt the Arabs were too inclined to worry about how to solve Israel's problems rather than their own. He urged them to stand up and be steadfast.

These ideas became the basis of a security doctrine: Syria had to keep up the fight – with Soviet help, with whatever Arab help it could muster, but above all with self-help. As the only remaining barrier to Israeli domination, it must if necessary stand alone. Two corollaries sprang from this doctrine: the first was the imperative need to protect the core Levant area with Syria at its centre, the second the ambition to achieve parity with Israel, what Asad liked to call 'comprehensive strategic balance'. The former was essentially defensive, the latter more of a springboard for future action, whether in war or peace.

It was Asad's sense of increased vulnerability which compelled him to seek to extend his influence over his immediate environment so as to prevent Israel turning his flank. The defence of Damascus demanded that neither Lebanon nor Jordan, nor indeed the Palestinians, be allowed to enter into bilateral negotiations or to conclude separate deals with Israel, as Sadat had done. Any such contacts would provide Israel with a point of entry into the Arab Levant, enabling it to fragment and control it, neutralizing Syrian power in the process. Asad's own security and what he took to be Arab security in general caused him to insist that Beirut, Amman and the PLO pursue policies in harmony with his own.

For example, when King Husayn convened an Arab summit in Amman in November 1980 to win support for his vision of negotiations with Israel leading to a Jordan-West Bank federation, Asad boycotted the meeting, then moved troops to the Jordan frontier. He did not question that Syria had the right to intervene militarily against Jordan to prevent it threatening Syrian, or more generally Arab national, interests.[5]

In Asad's vision of how to cope with Israel the notion of parity was even more central than the defence of the Levant. This was his most radical break with the somewhat defeatist Arab consensus which had hitherto prevailed, and Asad came to it from his gloomy observation of the course of Sadat's peace diplomacy. In his view, Sadat had not made peace with Israel, he had capitulated: Sinai had not been liberated, Egypt itself had been fettered. Peace, he concluded, was not for the weak, and it was a maxim to which he returned time and time again.[6] Parity was not just a matter of striking a military balance with Israel but of matching it right across the board, in education, technology, social progress and external alliances, as well as in purely armed strength. The conclusion in late 1981 of the US-Israeli agreement on strategic co-operation gave a further impetus to his way of thinking.[7]

Asad had an acute awareness of the many slights the Arabs had suffered at Israel's hands since 1948 as a result of their weakness. Unless they could pull themselves up to Israel's level, they could neither wage war nor negotiate peace: however it was dressed up, the flagrant imbalance could lead only to capitulation. The *status quo* of 'no peace, no war' was preferable to either an unwinnable war or an imposed peace. He refused to attend the first Fez summit of November 1981 at which Crown Prince Fahd (later king) of Saudi Arabia tabled a peace plan which Asad considered premature.

The heart of his argument was that a genuine settlement went beyond the return of territory to a revision of the entire power relationship between Israel and the Arabs. Whose will was to prevail in the region? The Arabs might get land back only to live in fear of what Israel might do next. What was the good of Egypt regaining Sinai if the price was toothlessness and loss of regional importance, or of Jordan recovering the West Bank if it were to become an Israeli vassal, or even of Syria winning back the Golan if it meant abandoning its Arab vocation and its championship of Palestinian rights?

In Asad's scheme of things, the Palestine problem was too important to be left to the Palestinians. It was much bigger than a disputed land or the fate of a few hundred thousand refugees. It was the rightful concern of all the Arabs, and the way it was settled would determine under whose order the Arabs would live and what meaning was to be given to their independence. A 'wrong' settlement – for example, the proposal for Palestinian 'autonomy' under an Israeli umbrella or any sort of Israel-Jordan deal over the West Bank – would perpetuate Israel's hegemony and put the Arabs at a permanent strategic disadvantage. Even more than the need for defence, this lofty view of Arab national imperatives was the crux of Asad's long quarrels with Sadat, Husayn and 'Arafat, all tempted at different times by partial solutions.

Asad ruled out a regional settlement imposed by Israeli military force as he believed the Egypt-Israel treaty to have been, and indeed any peace made in return for a recognition of Israeli superior power. In conversations with American envoys he sought to convince them that the key to Middle East peace lay not in Israeli supremacy but in an Arab-Israeli balance of power on the model of the East-West balance. Viewing the problem exactly as the Israelis did, he aspired to be a guarantor of the peace, to be strong enough to make the enemy keep it. He dismissed as unstable and humiliating any peace resting on Israeli power alone.

Containing Israel, checking what he saw as its inherent expansionism, forcing it to abandon aggression by a system of mutual deterrence – these were the constants of Asad's thinking in the years after Camp David. But in demanding parity, he challenged Israel's cherished dogma of the need to be stronger than any possible Arab combination. And, as Israel showed no inclination to give up its military edge or the United States to falter in its commitment to it, Asad's programme seemed a touch unrealistic. His determination to stand up for himself sometimes attracted the charge that he was an obstacle to peace. Moreover, the closer Syria seemed to get to parity, the more it was perceived in Israel as an unacceptable threat which would have to be dealt with. Israel fought Asad in Lebanon in 1982, and further war scares waxed and waned throughout the 1980s, but Asad's resolve did not weaken and over the years he had the satisfaction of seeing much of the Arab world come round to his way of thinking.

'Greater Syria'

Asad's focus on the Levant led inevitably to the accusation that he was trying to put together a 'Greater Syria', a concept of considerable local resonance which aroused apprehensions among his Arab rivals, not to mention Israel and the West. When he began to press Lebanon, Jordan and the Palestinians into his orbit, the question was asked whether, under Ba'thist camouflage, he was not in fact harbouring pan-Syrian ambitions. He had at various times in his career made statements of a pan-Syrian flavour. For example, when Golda Meir claimed the Golan as Israeli, Asad retorted on 8 March 1974 that Palestine itself was 'a principal part of southern Syria'. In April 1975, at the Ba'th's Sixth Regional Congress, he argued that there was no contradiction between the unity of natural Syria and the aspiration to Arab unity. When he sent his army into Lebanon as if by right in 1976, pan-Syrians applauded this overt challenge to the colonial carve-up of the 'Syrian homeland'. It was at about this time that the Syrian Ba'th made contact with the Syrian Social Nationalist Party after a twenty-year breach between them following the assassination of 'Adnan al-Malki in 1955, the first step in a partial public reconciliation. The suggestion was that the objectives of these old rivals were no longer so far apart. Asad's 'national strategy' of resisting Israel in Lebanon seemed to overlap with the SSNP's 'national ideology' of a reconstituted natural Syria.[8] (It was perhaps no accident that in the 1980s Syria's defence minister, General Mustafa Tlas, who also ran a publishing house, reprinted *Nushu' al-umam* (The Rise of Nations), the seminal work first published in 1938 by the SSNP founder Antun Sa'ada (1904–49), in which the case for a unique Syrian identity was argued.)

But these pointers did not amount to a convincing case. There was, in fact, a good deal of contrary evidence to show that Asad was no convert to pan-Syrian romanticism. For example, he disagreed with the pan-Syrians over Egypt. Whereas he had strained every nerve to preserve the bond with Egypt until it was snapped by Camp David, they opposed Syrian-Egyptian links in the belief that Syrian nationalism – the unity of the land and its people – was something quite distinct from the wider Arab world.

A committed Arab nationalist since his boyhood, Asad forged his Levant security doctrine as a means to contain Israel. At odds with both Cairo and Baghdad, he could find no comfort in pan-Arab unionism and fell back *faute de mieux* on his Syrian environment. While his rhetoric about his neighbours was sometimes proprietorial – as when he ridiculed King Husayn as the 'marshal of East Jordan' who presumed to rule a territory carved out of Syria by the British[9] – his design was not annexationist. He was even careful to deny such an ambition regarding Lebanon, where it might seem most natural and where his security was most at risk. 'The Ba'thist regime', he declared on 29 December 1985, 'was the first to recognize Lebanon's sovereignty, independence and unity It is true that we are one people, but we are two states.'[10] In sum, his 'Greater Syria' was a product of strategic need, not ideological conviction.

Yet, such disclaimers apart, Asad evidently had a deep-rooted sense of the greatness of Syria, its centrality, its leading role in Arab politics – and indeed of the dignity of its leader. Under his rule it had ceased to be the plaything of more powerful neighbours to become a star player in its own right – in his view Israel's only effective challenger. To Syria's reputation as the fountainhead of Arab nationalism and the motor of the Arab revolution of modern times he added strength, stability and a coherent if often contested strategy.

In the mid-1980s the massive honey-coloured walls of the Damascus citadel, last reconditioned in the mid-thirteenth century by Baybars, the first Mamluk sultan, were cleared of the mud-and-wattle clutter obscuring them and repair work was begun by teams of stonemasons. The restoration of this political monument at the heart of the old city was no travel-brochure promotion dreamed up by the Ministry of Tourism but a political act by the president expressing the will to resist of the ancient capital of *bilad al-sham*.

21

Ally of the Ayatollah

The most daring feature of Asad's foreign policy, reshaped to confront the world of Camp David, was undoubtedly his alliance with revolutionary Iran, which led to something quite new in the region – a Shi'i axis from Tehran through Damascus to South Lebanon. From the moment Ayatollah Ruhollah Khomayni took power in early 1979 Asad judged it a supreme Arab interest to befriend him. It was not a perception shared by many in the region, least of all by Iran's Arab neighbours. Nasser had preached that Arabs should unite only with Arabs and here was Asad, a latter-day champion of the Arab cause, aligning himself with a major non-Arab power then threatening Arab states across the Gulf.

To Arab opinion, even to Asad's own domestic opinion, his decision to back Iran was perplexing and controversial. The choice set him at odds with much of the Arab world, introducing an element of unease and apprehension into other leaders' estimates of him, for the alliance with Iran served to underline what they saw as the atypical, somewhat menacing character of the Syrian regime. Once again, as when he intervened against the Palestinians in Lebanon in 1976, Asad seemed to be stepping outside the Arab nationalist mainstream. Yet, unmoved by the worries of others and convinced as ever of his own rectitude, he stuck to his guns through the ups and downs of the Gulf War. By joining hands with a state outside the Arab family and with a revolutionary Islamic movement challenging the Sunni establishments, Asad displayed uncommon freedom from convention and rewrote the rules of the Middle East power system. There were important strategic reasons for his move, but it was also rooted in his own background as a member of a community derived from Shi'ism and in the fellow feeling of a man of rural and minority origins for people, and especially the deprived Shi'a of Lebanon, who had themselves long been oppressed.

The Iranian mullahs whom Asad befriended triumphed over the

Peacock Throne after a prolonged trial of strength. Throughout 1978 Shah Muhammad Reza Pahlavi had fought a running battle against mutinous mobs until, his will sapped by cancer and American indecision, he threw in his hand, leaving the country on 16 January 1979. Two weeks later on 1 February, the 76-year-old Khomayni returned home to claim his inheritance.

Asad, then in the throes of his life-and-death struggle with the Muslim Brothers, watched Khomayni's Islamic assault on the Shah with close attention. The Shi'ism of the Ayatollah was a very different sort of militant Islam from the Sunni fundamentalism of the Syrian guerrillas. In fact, Asad's rage at the guerrillas and at the Sunni establishments in the Arab world which lent them overt or covert support may have been a factor in his decision to reach out towards Tehran. Far from being disturbed by the Iranian revolution, he cheered it on.

Even while the Shah was still in power he gave a helping hand to some of Khomayni's lieutenants — men like Ibrahim Yazdi, Mustafa Chamran and Sadeq Qotbzadeh who were later to serve as ministers of the Islamic Republic. Qotbzadeh, for example, was given a Syrian passport which allowed him to conduct his anti-Shah activities in the disguise of Paris correspondent of the Damascus daily, *al-Thawra*.

Asad's main contact with the Shah's opponents in the 1970s was the Imam Musa al-Sadr, head of the Lebanese Shi'i Supreme Council, the remarkable religious leader of Iranian origin who had established himself in Lebanon in 1959 and who in nineteen years of pastoral and political work gave the downtrodden Shi'a of Lebanon unprecedented cohesion and self-esteem.[1] On frequent visits to Damascus Sadr became Asad's confidant, political ally and friend: he was the man who in 1973 helped Asad confront his Sunni critics in Damascus by proclaiming in a celebrated *fatwa* that the 'Alawis were an authentic part of Shi'i Islam. In the difficult summer of 1976, a crucially delicate moment of Asad's career, he did him an important service by keeping the Lebanese Shi'a community out of Kamal Junblatt's leftist coalition which Syria was at the time trying to rein in. As Asad's go-between with the Khomayni camp in the 1970s, Sadr was the harbinger of the Damascus-Tehran axis of the 1980s although Sadr himself did not live to see it. In August 1978 he vanished mysteriously on a visit to Libya; in fact, the news of his disappearance and presumed death broke during the Camp David talks that September and Asad mourned him as bitterly as he mourned Sadat's defection.

Asad welcomed the Ayatollah's takeover in Tehran with a telegram of warm congratulations and, a few weeks later, sent him a gift of an illuminated Quran carried to Qum by Syria's Information Minister, Ahmad Iskandar Ahmad. After kissing the holy book, the Ayatollah thanked Syria for the offer of asylum it had made him in October 1978[2] when, having been expelled from Iraq and not yet settled at Neuphle-le-Château, near Paris, he needed a base from which to mount his final attack on the Shah. Syrian-Iranian relations developed rapidly after the revolution. Asad's Foreign Minister, Khaddam, visited Tehran in August 1979, and rather extravagantly proclaimed the Iranian revolution to be 'the most important event in our contemporary history'. Syria, he boasted, had supported it 'prior to its outbreak, during it and after its triumph'.[3]

One reason Asad chose to back revolutionary Iran was that he disliked the Shah's anti-Arab partnership with Israel and his subservience to the United States. The two men had met in December 1975 when Asad went to Tehran in the hope of persuading the Shah to press Washington to be more even-handed in the Arab-Israeli dispute.[4] But nothing came of it and to Asad's anger the Shah lent a hand in Begin's scheming to entrap Sadat. So Asad shed no tears over his downfall and determined to put the change of regime in Tehran to his advantage.

He was at pains to convince his fellow Arabs that the Ayatollah's Iran should be seen in a totally new light – no longer the Shah's Iran, the friend of Israel, the agent of America, but an Iran committed to anti-Zionism and anti-imperialism. He argued that the Ayatollah had broken the vice in which Israel and the Shah had held the Arabs for three decades. Much like the Israelis, Asad saw the Middle East as a single whole, his geostrategic view extending beyond the Arab heart to include peripheral countries. From this standpoint he welcomed the change which Iran made in the regional balance of power, sensing that, at a time when Israel was more dangerous than ever, he could find strength in this new dynamic force. Iran, he argued, was a natural counterweight to Egypt; Israel had gained Egypt by the peace treaty, but lost Iran to the revolution.

From his own vantage point Asad was right to see an asset in the new-style Iran. The fall of the Shah was a blow to Israeli and Western interests as great as that dealt twenty-five years earlier by Nasser's emergence on the Middle East scene. Like Nasser's Arab nationalism, Khomayni's Islamic internationalism was an indigenous movement determined to affirm itself against outsiders. Denouncing the United States as the 'Great Satan' Khomayni tore up the Shah's agreements with it, broke off diplomatic relations with Israel, stopped the flow of oil to it, withdrew from the Central Treaty Organization (CENTO), and, in a symbolic gesture, turned over the Israeli embassy in Tehran to

'Arafat's PLO. So while many shuddered at the rise of the Ayatollah, Asad sided with him in a striking demonstration of political foresight and strategic flexibility.

Relations with Saddam Husayn

But in claiming the Ayatollah as a friend, Asad was also seeking help against his most dangerous Arab neighbour, Iraq. Khomayni's Iran was well placed to provide it.

Syria and Iraq were divided by party schism, by geopolitical rivalry and by the personal animosity of their leaders. They also quarrelled over economic matters, over the division of the Euphrates waters and over oil pipelines, one of which, to Iraq's regret, crossed Syrian territory and was controlled by Asad and another which to Syria's anger, Iraq had built across Turkey.[5] For years the two countries had played host to each other's exiles, shadowy figures who opposed reconciliation between Damascus and Baghdad because they feared that they would be sacrificed to it. Incestuously involved with each other, the Iraqi and Syrian Ba'th parties were riven by mutual distrust as each was convinced that the other had planted a Trojan horse in its ranks. Yet in spite of this background of hostility, Syria and Iraq buried the hatchet in 1978 following Sadat's entente with Israel in a common effort to contain and punish him. Better relations between Damascus and Baghdad seemed on the way.

On 28 July 1979, however, Iraq's strong man, Saddam Husayn al-Takriti, announced the uncovering of a plot against him hatched by some of his closest colleagues – in league, as he alleged, with a 'foreign side' soon identified as Syria.[6] More than fifty of the accused were brought before a special court and a score of them including some of the most prominent men in Iraq were gunned down by their party comrades, Saddam Husayn himself to the fore.

Twelve days before announcing the plot Saddam had taken over as president of Iraq from Ahmad Hasan al-Bakr, at which time he also assumed the functions of secretary-general of the Ba'th party, commander-in-chief, head of the government and chairman of the Revolutionary Command Council. All power was his. It appeared that the elimination of his rivals was linked to his accusations against Syria. In any event, talk of reconciliation between Baghdad and Damascus now abruptly ended.

Asad protested innocence and asked Saddam for evidence of Syrian complicity. He sent Foreign Minister Khaddam and Chief of Staff

Shihabi to Baghdad to assure him that if Iraq had any proof of Syrian wrongdoing those responsible would be punished. All they brought back was a tape-recording of rambling confessions by one of the accused. Asad then proposed that Iraq's allegations be examined by an Arab League committee but Iraq did not pursue the idea. Nevertheless, despite Asad's protestations, there may have been something of a Syrian connection, if only an indirect one on the following lines. A number of Saddam's associates[7] favoured a loose federation with Syria as a means of checking Saddam's rise to absolute power: a proposal then being canvassed in Damascus and Baghdad was that Bakr might be the federation's head, Asad his deputy and Saddam number three. Suspecting that a tie with Syria would limit his power, Saddam set about torpedoing the federal idea. When Asad came to Baghdad on 16 June 1979 to take the union idea further Saddam in a clear snub did not trouble to go to the airport to meet him. Very probably those Iraqis who feared Saddam secretly discussed with Damascus how best to check his rise, arguing that he posed as much of a problem to Asad as to themselves. Bakr for one sent Asad a private plea to speed up union negotiations because 'there is a current here which is anxious to kill the union in the bud before it bears fruit'.[8] Getting wind of these soundings Saddam ousted Bakr, killed off the waverers, and broke with Syria: it was the only certain way of becoming number one.

The emergence of the Islamic Republic put paid once and for all to any hope of a Syrian-Iraqi entente and in fact greatly sharpened their antagonisms, for just as Asad welcomed the Ayatollah so the Iraqi leader feared him. On almost every aspect of the Iranian situation – the Shah, the Ayatollah, Shi'ism, or whether or not the Arabs could live in good neighbourly relations with Iran – Syria and Iraq held opposing views. And of these the awakening of the Shi'a across the region was the main underlying issue. A community which Asad had come to value, Saddam saw as a deadly danger to the integrity of his country.

Iraq had never been a homogeneous state. Carved out of three ex-Ottoman provinces by Britain in 1921, it included rebellious Kurds in the northern mountains, unfavoured Shi'i Arab tribes in the south, and in between a Sunni Arab minority virtually monopolizing political power. Under-represented at the centre, Kurds and Shi'a were always centrifugal forces of great disruptiveness. In the 1960s and 1970s the Kurds took to arms against Baghdad, but the Shi'a were also a security threat, if a less overt one. They had begun to stir after the overthrow of the monarchy in 1958 and moved into something like outright opposition ten years later when the Ba'th seized power in 1968. To keep the Shi'a down the Iraqi Ba'th accused their 'highest authority',

Ayatollah Muhsin al-Hakim, of being a CIA agent, causing him to flee for his life shortly before his death in 1970.

Khomayni, himself exiled for opposition to a repressive ruler, came in 1965 to the Iraqi holy city of Najaf, a centre of Shi'i piety and scholarship where he spent the next thirteen years. In Najaf, in a Shi'i community smouldering with discontent, he was one of a group of influential *'ulama* – divines like the Iraqi Baqir al-Sadr and the Lebanese Muhammad Husayn Fadlallah and Muhammad Mahdi Shamseddin – who were to formulate and spread the Islamic revolutionary message. From the 1960s there also took shadowy shape in Iraq an underground extremist Shi'i party, the *Da'wa al-Islamiya* (The Islamic Call), not directly connected with these *'ulama* but feeding on the revivalism they inspired.

In October 1978 Saddam Husayn made the fatal mistake of expelling Khomayni from Iraq – less than four months before he was to triumph in Tehran. The *Da'wa* now began to stage demonstrations and throw bombs. On 1 April 1980 its terrorists nearly killed Deputy Premier Tariq 'Aziz at a student gathering in Baghdad, a prelude to a rash of assaults on government officials. Saddam's immediate response was to crush the *Da'wa* and indeed any expression of Shi'i dissent in a campaign of arrests, torture, executions and forced deportations. On 8 April all members of the *Da'wa* were retroactively condemned to death and on the same day the scholarly Ayatollah Baqir al-Sadr (who had been under arrest since June 1979) was hanged together with his sister, the novelist and Islamic feminist Bint al-Huda.[9] Tens of thousands of others whose loyalty was suspect were simply dumped across the frontier with Iran, in what in restrospect might be seen as the opening shots of the Gulf War. To Saddam Husayn, Shi'i dissidence raised the spectre that the south of Iraq, with the great port of Basra and the Shi'i holy places of Najaf and Karbala, might break away from the Iraqi state.

Asad's view of the world of Shi'i Islam was altogether more favourable than Saddam's. The Shi'a in Asad's Levant environment were overwhelmingly the deprived peasants of South Lebanon who for generations had worked the tobacco fields of absentee landowning families – very much as the 'Alawis had done in his youth. The struggle of rural Shi'a for a greater stake in a Lebanese state dominated by Christian and Sunni notables was a replica of his own struggle in Syria. On one occasion in the early 1980s a deputation of Beirut Sunni leaders asked Asad for help against the invading hordes of Shi'i peasants who were changing the character of their city. Asad was unsympathetic: he reminded his visitors that he was himself a peasant who had overturned the power of urban notables.

His friendship with the Lebanese Shi'i leader, the Imam Musa al-Sadr, added a personal reason for siding with the Shi'a, and this Musa al-Sadr was none other than the cousin and brother-in-law of Baqir al-Sadr whom Saddam Husayn hanged in 1980. It was hardly surprising therefore that the Shi'i question hung like a poisoned sword between Damascus and Baghdad.

The 'wrong war'

All these contentions apart, at the end of the day Asad and Saddam broke with each other because they were totally at odds over who was the Arabs' main enemy. Asad's attention was fixed on the threat from Israel, while Saddam was totally preoccupied with Iran. Facing in different directions, one towards the Mediterranean and the other towards the Gulf, Syria and Iraq inevitably had different perceptions of the dangers threatening them.

Asad was aghast when on 22 September 1980 Iraqi forces crossed in strength into Iran, launching the Gulf War on its murderous course. There was no clean start to hostilities, seeing that in the previous eight months some eighty skirmishes had been reported up and down the frontier, with loss of life and damage to property on both sides.[10] The propaganda battle over the air waves had started up almost immediately after the triumph of the Iranian revolution in early 1979. These messy beginnings were to make it difficult to apportion blame for starting the conflict – as it turned out, an important issue in ending it – although few could dispute that Iraq's invasion in late September marked the escalation into all-out war of what had been a mere border conflict.

From the very first Asad condemned Saddam's war as the wrong war against the wrong enemy at the wrong time. To fight Iran was folly: it would exhaust the Arabs, fragment their ranks and divert them from 'the holy battle in Palestine'.[11] Instead of making an enemy of revolutionary Iran, the Arabs should do all they could to prevent it falling back into Israel's clutches. In contacts with the kings of Saudi Arabia and Jordan, Asad tried to bring pressure on Saddam to stop the conflict. This was and remained his public position. He detested the war on principle, but if it had to happen his private worry was that Iraq might win a quick victory, as most observers were then predicting – a terrible outcome which would trap him between a triumphant Israel and a triumphant Iraq, both of them hostile to him. So, anxious to avert an Iraqi victory which could complete his encirclement, Asad took the plunge. It had been daring enough to welcome Khomayni's Iran before the war – a move which had required much explaining to the Saudis and others – but now he decided to go further and back Iran's war effort.

On a visit to Moscow shortly after the outbreak of war he issued a joint statement with Brezhnev supporting 'Iran's inalienable right to determine its destiny independently and without any foreign influence'.[12] The Russians, happy to see the United States expelled from Iran, which for them was the big bonus of the revolution, gave Syria and Libya permission to sell on Soviet weapons to Iran. There were immediate reports of an arms airlift from Syria by way of Greece, Bulgaria and the Soviet Union and from Libya over the Black Sea, using as carriers the Shah's large fleet of Boeing 747, 727 and 707 aircraft.[13] In January 1981, Iran established scheduled air links with Damascus, Tripoli and Algiers, a more than symbolic switch from the daily El Al flights which had connected Israel to Iran before the revolution.

Links of another sort were also developing between Syria and Iran. From mid-1979 onwards Iranian volunteers began passing through Syria on their way to Lebanon, where they proposed fighting Israel and its proxies. Syria thus became the staging post between the fount of militant Shi'ism in Iran and the now aroused Shi'i community in Lebanon. Moreover, as Asad was convinced that Iraq was lending covert aid to the Muslim Brothers challenging him in Syria, he instructed his intelligence services to join Iran in mounting subversive missions against Iraq. One way or another – in arms supply, intelligence sharing, irregular operations and propaganda – Syria soon found itself up to its neck in the Gulf War on the Iranian side.

Saddam Husayn's response was not slow in coming. In August 1980 Iraqi forces stormed the Syrian embassy in Baghdad and expelled most of its staff on the charge that they were smuggling guns and explosives to Saddam's Shi'i enemies, and on 12 October Baghdad broke off relations with Damascus in a torrent of denunciation. Saddam then trumpeted in his media every damaging charge made by Asad's enemies: that he had surrendered Qunaytra to Israel without a fight in 1967, that he had cravenly asked for a ceasefire on the second day of the 1973 war, that he had intervened in Lebanon in 1976 in collusion with Washington and Jerusalem, that he bore on his conscience the massacre of Palestinians at Tal al-Za'tar, and that he had conspired to destroy the projected union between Syria and Iraq in 1979. Syria replied in kind in the familiar currency of Arab invective.

The more hostile Saddam became, the more Asad relied on Iran to make sure that the Iraqi leader he had come to hate did not survive the war. Asad's attitude to the war was thus ambivalent: it was the 'wrong war' and yet, as his feud with Saddam deepened, he could not welcome a settlement which left Saddam in place. In other words, he was against the war but wanted it to continue until it produced an outcome to his satisfaction – a position not unlike that of some other countries. In 1982 Asad closed the border with Iraq as well as the pipeline carrying Iraqi oil across his territory and signed with Iran an extensive trade pact which for several years thereafter secured oil for Syria at preferential rates.

As the Gulf War ground on, large numbers of black-shrouded Iranian women were to be seen in Damascus, many of them widows or mothers of fallen men who were given a package tour to Syria to ease their suffering. Most journeyed to the Shi'i shrine of Sayidah Zaynab outside Damascus to say a prayer at the tomb of the Prophet's granddaughter. In preparation for closer ties, Iran's Foreign Minister, Dr 'Ali Akbar Velayati, came to Damascus on New Year's eve, 1981. In his hotel room that night he was shocked to observe that Syrian television took its viewers on a tour of the city's floor shows, celebrating with suitable revelry the end of one year and the beginning of another. To the faint embarrassment of Syrian officials, Velayati opened the official proceedings the next morning with a tirade against the flimsily clad dancers he had seen on television. It was an early lesson in the susceptibilities of their new ally, for by this time Syria and Iran were strategic partners.

The role of Israel

Israel watched developments in the relationship between Iran and the Arabs as closely as Syria did – and with much the same motives if from the opposite point of view. Just as Asad sought support from Iran, so Begin worried that he might get it. A perennial Israeli concern was to prevent a concentration of Arab strength, in particular to break up any sort of Arab 'eastern front' such as Asad was constantly trying to put together. Much of the rationale for Israel's friendship with the Shah had been precisely to neutralize Iraq, dissuade it from joining up with Syria and divert its growing military capability away from Israel. In the Shah's day Israel supplied Iran with agricultural expertise and more importantly with weapons and training for the armed services and for SAVAK, the Shah's secret police, in exchange for oil. Israel also joined Iran in covert operations against Arab targets. For example, from the mid-1960s onwards it helped arm and train Kurdish guerrillas to harass the Baghdad government on the argument that if Iraq was pinned down at home, it would have no energy to spare to help Syria against Israel. So the bond with Iran was of strategic importance to Israel and Israeli leaders over the years from Ben Gurion to Begin paid numerous secret visits to Tehran.[14] The 70,000 strong Iranian Jewish community also helped provide a bridge between the two countries in much the same way as the influential Moroccan Jewish community helped forge discreet links between Israel and King Hasan.

The Shah's troubles in 1978 were therefore cause for alarm in Israel, an alarm compounded by the Syrian-Iraqi reconciliation of November that year effected as a riposte to Camp David. Just when Israel's Iranian ally was collapsing, the dreaded Arab eastern front seemed to be taking shape. In the event, it was soon evident that Israel had little to fear on this score, but the fall of the Shah was nevertheless a major setback and was further aggravated by Asad's prompt moves to supplant Israel as Iran's regional ally.

However, from Israel's point of view these unfavourable developments were soon offset by the growing tension between Iran and Iraq, and the opening this presented for Israeli action. Revolutionary Iran needed arms and, no longer able to get them from the United States, was looking for alternative supplies. Israel was happy to oblige, seeing in the arms trade an opportunity to establish a secret relationship with the mullahs. In 1980 Begin quietly resumed sales of military equipment to Iran beginning with spares for F-4 fighter planes.[15] The *demi-monde* of the arms bazaar provided intermediaries for this sensitive traffic between two ostensible enemies. Begin was aware that, with American hostages still held in the Tehran embassy, Washington would not look kindly on such trade, but the attraction of restoring the old Israel-Iran alliance was very great. When the Carter Administration got wind of Israel's arms sales it protested vigorously,[16] whereupon they were halted for a few months. But in November 1980 after Reagan's election they were resumed.

Anxious to fend off American anger, Israel got Morris Amitay of the American Israel Public Affairs Committee to ask Richard Allen, shortly to be named Reagan's national security adviser, how the incoming Administration would view Israel's shipment of US-made aircraft parts to Iran.[17] And a few weeks later on Reagan's inauguration, the director general of Israel's Foreign Ministry, David Kimche, hurried to Washington to persuade the Administration of the benefits of selling arms to Iran – or at least of letting Israel do so. Arms sales, he argued, were a means of making contact with the Iranian military in preparation for the post-Khomayni era,[18] they would strengthen Iranian 'moderates' and weaken Soviet influence in Iran – arguments used by Israel to conceal its own motives and which were a few years later to suck the United States into the 'Irangate' scandal. Before the end of January 1981 the new Secretary of State, Alexander Haig, privately gave Israel the permission it sought.[19] And once the hostages were out, Israel's covert arms transfers to Iran mushroomed in 1981 to include tank and artillery ammunition, spare parts for US-built M-48 tanks, refurbished jet engines and other systems for the F-4s, the F-5s and the F-14 Tomcats, a trade of tens of millions of dollars which was to grow to billions over the coming years, shrugging off all Washington's attempts to staunch it.

Israel's self-interest was to stoke the fires of the Iran-Iraq War. The conflict exhausted two potential adversaries, drained Arab oil wealth and provided Israel's arms trade with valuable export outlets. But all along Begin had Asad's Syria in his sights. This was the main regional enemy to be neutralized. From his point of view, the Gulf War and the Egypt-Israel peace treaty served the same purpose of ensuring Israel's supremacy over Syria and the whole Levant. The peace treaty had removed Egypt from the confrontation, the Gulf War removed Iraq.

Israel not only primed the pump of the Gulf conflict but appears to have had a hand in getting it started – for the same self-serving reasons. Much of the information which led Saddam Husayn to invade very probably came by indirect routes from Israel. In deciding to attack Saddam Husayn was influenced by intelligence estimates of Iran's weakness reaching him by way of Saudi Arabia and the United States and from Iranian exiles in Paris and Baghdad, many of them ex-officials of the Shah who dreamed only of ousting the mullahs and returning home in triumph. Reports circulating at the time spoke, for example, of total chaos in Iran's armed services and in the officer corps in particular. About a hundred senior officers had been shot, hundreds more had been jailed, and over ten thousand had been dismissed. Elite formations such as the Imperial Guard and the Immortals Brigade had been disbanded, while what remained of the regular army was locked in conflict with the new Revolutionary Guard Corps. The army was said to be down to six under-strength divisions, little more than brigades, while the air force had lost half its pilots and was running out of spares – and what spares there were could not be located because the American-supplied computers had broken down.

So parlous did Iran's situation seem that Saddam was convinced he could overthrow Khomayni within a week. He sent word to the ruler of Kuwait that General Gholam 'Ali Oveysi, the former martial law

Governor of Tehran then in exile in Baghdad, could be in Tehran within days.[20] Saddam did not know that some of these over-confident estimates of Iran's weakness were of Israeli origin.

Exiles such as Oveysi had close ties with Israel dating from before the revolution, while the United States at this time relied almost exclusively on Israel to monitor the unfolding drama in Iran. As Carter's CIA chief Admiral Stansfield Turner was to admit, US intelligence assets in Iran had atrophied in the Shah's last years.[21] After the Shah's fall 'we had nothing in Iran. We had no idea of what was going on', Major-General Richard Secord, who had been in charge of US arms sales to the Iranian air force, was to tell the Iran-Contra congressional hearings in 1987.[22] Although Israel's own networks were disrupted by the revolution – 25,000 Iranian Jews had left the country in the early weeks – its information was still better than anyone else's. In assessing the Iranian situation, it was natural that Washington should turn for help to its Israeli ally. Such was the dependence that, in planning the rescue of the American hostages in Tehran, the chairman of the Joint Chiefs of Staff, General David Jones, sought the advice of Israel's Chief of Staff, General Rafael Eitan.[23] Israel was thus in a strong position to feed information which suited its purpose to Baghdad.

The Iranians had an inkling of Israeli involvement in the run-up to the war. President Bani-Sadr told Eric Rouleau of *Le Monde* that Iran had been forewarned of the Iraqi attack by an intelligence report of secret talks in Paris in the summer of 1980 in which Israeli and US military experts, Iranian exiles and Iraqis had taken part.[24]

Interests in the war

A lot of people had an interest in stirring up the Gulf War. While Israel was largely concerned with its long-term security, the United States was preoccupied with the American captives held in Tehran since November 1979. With every passing day exasperation grew in Washington and the idea took root among the more belligerent members of the Administration such as Zbigniew Brzezinski, Jimmy Carter's national security adviser, that they would be released only by military means. First, brushing aside the qualms of Secretary Vance, Brzezinski forced through the American rescue mission which ended in fiasco at Tabas in the Iranian desert in April 1980. Then, undeterred by failure and by Vance's resignation, he set about planning a second round,[25] but, seeing that the United States could not itself do the job, he came to believe that an Iraqi attack provided the best means of prising the hostages free. There were several pointers to Brzezinski's preference for military action over negotiation. When the hostages were first seized two Iranian brothers, Cyrus and Muhammad 'Ali Hashemi, hammered out an arms-for-hostages deal with the State Department which Assistant Secretary Harold Saunders thought promising enough to recommend to Cyrus Vance. But Brzezinski kept raising so many fresh issues that when news broke of the rescue mission, the Hashemi brothers came to believe he had been playing for time. The same thing happened in the weeks before the outbreak of the Gulf War: Brzezinski appeared to lose interest in negotiations, leading the Hashemis to conclude that he had foreknowledge of the war and had placed his hopes in it.[26]

In going to war Saddam Husayn was also spurred on by Arab friends. Alarmed at the impact of the Iranian revolution on the Gulf and badly shaken by the seizure of the Grand Mosque at Mecca by Muslim extremists in November 1979, the Saudi royal house looked to Iraq to contain Khomayni's Iran. Equally King Husayn of Jordan, anxious to protect his close ties with the Gulf rulers, saw Iran as a deadly threat[27] and urged Iraq to stand firm. From the moment war was declared Husayn opened his port of Aqaba to Iraqi war supplies and depleted his arms stocks on Iraq's behalf.

But whatever foreign hands were at work, Saddam had his own reasons for challenging the Ayatollah. His most pressing motive was almost certainly defensive and his war might best be described as pre-emptive: Khomayni's Shi'i *revanchisme* was so threatening to the integrity of his country that the temptation to strike a quick blow while Iran was dizzy with revolutionary turmoil was probably irresistible. Saddam's second motive was to tear up the 1975 Algiers Agreement which, extorted from him under the pressure of the Kurdish war, had forced him to yield to the Shah partial control of the Shatt al-Arab waterway. Now he resolved to return the Shatt to exclusive Iraqi control: as the Shah had found it intolerable for Iranian vessels to have to fly the Iraqi flag as they came up the Shatt to the Iranian ports of Abadan and Khorramshahr, so Saddam longed to make Iran again acknowledge his sovereignty over the whole waterway. Behind Saddam's obsession with the Shatt was a sense of grievance at Iraq's minuscule Gulf frontage compared to Iran's sprawl along the whole of the opposite shore.

Ambition also played a part in Saddam's war. Iraq's oil and water resources, its fertile land and the benefits of his own strong leadership seemed to mark it out for greatness at a time when its rivals were enfeebled: Syria paralysed by internal terrorism, Egypt out of the Arab game, Turkey in the hands of a military junta after years of anarchy. Was this not Iraq's moment? When Saddam demanded that Iran grant autonomy to the Arabs of Khuzistan (a partly Arabic-speaking province brought under central control by the Shah's father) and return three small islands in the Strait of Hormuz seized by the Shah in 1971, he was making a bid to be the Arabs' champion.

Saddam was persuaded that the blow he planned to strike against Iran was risk-free and well-timed. But within a very few weeks this was seen to be a misjudgement. His invasion ran out of steam, Iran regrouped its forces, and by late October 1980 the Gulf War had become the static slogging match it was to remain for years, draining away Saddam's ambitions and much else besides. Brzezinski's hopes that the conflict would release the hostages also proved vain. (It was only when the war was stalemated that serious negotiations between the United States and Iran took place through the good offices of Algeria and reached a successful conclusion on 20 January 1981, the day of Ronald Reagan's inauguration.)

As the war ran its course Syria and Israel continued to compete for Iran's favour, thus extending the Arab-Israeli dispute from the Levant to the Gulf. Israel hoped its arms sales to Iran would eventually build a community of interest between them, while Syria, despite pressure from Arab opinion and Sunni establishments, especially in Arabia and the Gulf states, saw no reason to depart from its view that revolutionary Iran must be embraced as an ally.

For neither country was the wooing of Iran a trouble-free policy, and for both gains had to be set against considerable costs. Israel was forced to lie about its arms sales, then face the indignity of public exposure when the Iran-Contra scandal revealed how far it had dragged its American ally into the quagmire of secret dealings with Iran. Asad in turn faced Arab and Sunni criticisms for taking sides with Iran and with the Shi'a and saw his Arab nationalist commitment questioned. Precious financial aid from the Arab Gulf states was much reduced. When in a later phase of the war Iran threatened Kuwait and other Gulf statelets, his claim that his leverage with Tehran protected them from danger looked hollow. But in spite of these costs and embarrassments, he resisted all entreaties to reconsider his fundamental Iranian option.

He was consoled by the fact that his controversial alignment with Iran and Shi'ism brought him two important bonuses: first, the Damascus-Tehran axis which, by freeing him from pressures from Iraq, allowed him to focus all his defences on the Israeli threat; and second the axis of Damascus and the Shi'a of Lebanon, which put at his disposal powerful proxy forces of decisive effect in the coming duel with Begin.

22

Battle with Menachem Begin

Asad and Begin, champions of irreconcilable visions, came to blows, as they were bound some time to do, over Lebanon in what was to be the goriest engagement of the struggle for the Middle East. Lebanon in the 1980s was the hapless arena for the collision between the dominant and expanded Israel which Begin was determined to build and the rival regional order with which Asad tried to stop him. Each man recognized the other as the principal enemy who could put at risk everything he held dear. In shorthand terms, 'Greater Israel' went to war against 'Greater Syria', both controversial concepts of uncertain definition but which certainly ruled each other out. The struggle, in a way the climax of their political lives, very nearly destroyed them both.

They were unevenly matched. At the start of the 1980s Asad was weak, still battling for his life against his Islamic enemies at home, while Begin was at the height of his powers. Moreover, Asad's Levant security doctrine was looking threadbare: he was on extremely bad terms with Jordan, he was struggling without notable success to discipline the Palestinian resistance movement, and in Lebanon he had failed to pacify the country in five years of effort or to limit Israel's involvement with the Christians.

In contrast, Begin could contemplate the results of his first term of office with a good deal of self-congratulation. The peace treaty had taken care of Egypt, while the Gulf War was taking care of Iraq, leaving him with great freedom of action. His hold over the Sinai peninsula provided him with a trump card: he had agreed at Camp David to return Sinai to Egypt, but not fully until April 1982 and, so long as he retained a large slice, no one could be absolutely certain that Egypt would get it back. Wary of upsetting the timetable, the United States and Egypt dared not stand up to him. Their fears were groundless: nothing on earth would have prevented Begin from returning Sinai, since peace with Egypt was the bedrock of his strategy

366

for retaining the West Bank. But this was not widely understood.

Begin's biggest asset was the new American President. From the moment of Ronald Reagan's inauguration in January 1981, even from the moment of his election the previous November, the Israelis sensed a propitious change of climate after the uneasy Carter years. Unlike Carter, Reagan had no interest in Palestinian aspirations and to Begin's satisfaction allowed the autonomy talks to peter out. Begin heartily approved of the Administration's robust anti-Soviet stance, which upgraded Israel's value as a 'strategic asset', and its obsession with 'international terrorism'.

Terrorism preoccupied the Reagan Administration from the start, perhaps not surprisingly since the long incarceration of Americans in the Tehran embassy had done much to destroy Carter and ensure Reagan's election, and the attempted assassinations of the president and of the Pope in 1981 served to increase alarm. Right-wing Republicans in the new team saw a Soviet hand behind every manifestation of anti-Western sentiment. Reagan, Haig, and the CIA chief William Casey gave credence to reports by the American journalist Claire Sterling in *The Terror Network* (1981) of tens of thousands of terrorists, sponsored directly or indirectly by Moscow, being trained in guerrilla camps across the world as 'elite battalions in a worldwide Army of Communist Combat'.[1] The Cubans had a big role in it, but so did the Palestinians – the 'second great magnetic pole for apprentice terrorists'. Intelligence professionals knew that Sterling was talking nonsense, but Begin was happy to encourage the White House and the State Department to see terrorism as the main scourge of the modern world, and Syria, Libya and the PLO as its main practitioners as well, of course, as Soviet proxies.

In the new Administration the Israelis' best hope was the Secretary of State, General Alexander Haig, the excitable soldier-politician who had learned his diplomacy as Kissinger's assistant in the Nixon White House. On his first visit to the Middle East as Secretary in the spring of 1981, Haig offended Asad by deliberately omitting Syria from his itinerary, and denounced the Syrian leader so harshly as a Soviet proxy that his Israeli hosts came to believe Syria was fair game. Haig seemed reassuringly unconcerned about the substance of the Arab-Israeli dispute, pursuing instead the will-o'-the-wisp of a regional 'strategic consensus' against the Soviet Union. Fostering presidential ambitions of his own, Haig was impressed by Israel's muscle in American domestic politics and was much influenced by a pro-Israeli State Department aide, Harvey Sicherman. Indeed so great seemed the concordance of interest between Washington and Jerusalem, so secure the levels of aid, so well-placed Israel's supporters in Congress and the Administration, that Begin came to believe, with some justice, that he could get the United States to tolerate anything he chose to do.

Begin's messianic mission was to unite and make whole the 'Land of Israel' by permanently absorbing into the Jewish state the territories he insisted on calling by the biblical names of Judea and Samaria – in other words the West Bank. To realize this vision meant peopling the West Bank with Jewish settlers and crushing every manifestation of Palestinian nationalism. When he first came to power in 1977 Begin put his bulldozing Minister of Agriculture, General Ariel Sharon, in charge of a crash programme of settlement building. Begin's reading of the bargain struck at Camp David was that, by agreeing to return Sinai to Egypt, he had won a free hand on the West Bank. His success in outwitting both Carter and Sadat appeared to have bred in him a large measure of hubris, leading him to believe that he could safely embark on further expansion.

To make his cherished enterprise safe, however, Begin needed a protected environment. His bold solution was to change the strategic balance of the region, a process which had begun with the removal of Egypt from the battlefield. But this did not resolve the problem altogether. Two enemies remained without whose subjugation Begin could not be certain of lasting success: first there was the PLO, the embodiment of Palestinian nationalism, and then there was Syria, the old opponent to the north, the state marked out by history and geography as the obstacle to the satisfaction of Begin's land hunger and the realization of Israel's regional dominance. Begin did not seek peace with the Palestinians or the Syrians, as he had sought peace with Egypt, because peace involved surrendering captured territory. He wanted to hold the West Bank to complete Eretz Israel, and he needed to retain the Golan in order to protect it. But to hang on to these Arab territories required unchallengeable strength, the key to which lay in containing or, if necessary, defeating Syria. Getting Egypt out had been the aim of Begin's first term as prime minister. Neutralizing Syria became the objective of his second term.

The missile crisis

Such was the context for the first passage of arms between Asad and Begin – the so-called Lebanese missile crisis which opened in April 1981.

The crisis grew out of a struggle for control of the Biqa' valley held by Syria since 1976 and which it considered vital for its defence: the Biqa' was a possible Israeli invasion route and the Damascus-Beirut highway, Syria's lifeline to Lebanon, ran across it. Some months earlier, in December 1980, Christian militiamen allied to Israel had moved into Zahla, the valley's principal town. Such a Christian bridgehead was a threat Asad could not tolerate. His fierce response was to shell Zahla as well as Christian East Beirut and to send commandos to capture strongpoints in the mountains from where he could put further pressure on the Christian heartlands to the north.

Bashir Jumayil, younger son of the Phalanges party founder Shaykh Pierre Jumayil, was the man behind the challenge to Asad. He was said to have been recruited by the CIA when working for a Washington law firm in the early 1970s, and the CIA had in due course introduced him to its Israeli counterpart, Mossad,[2] which was now grooming him for a role as Israel's proconsul in Lebanon. Since the Lebanon civil war he had managed by intimidation and assassination to unite the various Maronite gunmen into a single militia under his command known as the 'Lebanese Forces'. Israel's regional ambitions coincided with Bashir's local ambitions to re-establish Christian dominance in Lebanon.

Israel's contacts with the Christians, seen as its natural allies against Syria and the Palestinians, had greatly expanded since 1976: in the south it openly maintained a Christian border force, while covertly arming, funding and training Bashir's fighters in the northern mountains. An Israeli-Christian alliance was not a new idea, but had attracted both communities since the 1930s in a common fear of the Muslim Arab hinterland. After 1948 the notion that Israel should intervene to redraw Lebanon's borders, seize the south up to the Litani river and encourage the emergence of a friendly Maronite state further north was repeatedly canvassed, notably by David Ben Gurion in 1954 (in his well publicized exchanges with the more cautious Moshe Sharett).[3] But not until the Lebanese civil war of the 1970s did it become practical politics, when Israel started making wider commitments to the Maronites culminating in Begin's promise in 1978, repeated in 1980, to commit the Israeli air force on their side if Syria used its air power against them.[4]

After establishing his strongpoint at Zahla, Bashir in a bid to extend his domain in the early weeks of 1981 brought in bulldozers to build a road connecting the town to Christian Mount Lebanon. Perhaps he gambled on precipitating an Israeli-Syrian clash which he could turn to his advantage. When Asad took up his challenge, shelling Zahla and sending commandos into the mountains, Bashir appealed to Begin for help. Begin urged him to stand firm and then, in honour of his pledge, ordered the IAF north to take on the Syrian air force. On 28 April 1981 two Syrian helicopters ferrying supplies up to their troops were shot down. The following day Asad moved Soviet-built surface-to-air missiles into the Biqa'. The missile crisis had begun.

Begin's instinct was to destroy the SAMs at once, but for a variety of reasons he did not do so. He was busy campaigning for the general elections to be held at the end of June, not a time to go to war. His close associate, Ariel Sharon, did not want war until he himself could take charge of the Defence Ministry, a post Begin had promised him if Likud won the election. The military intelligence chief, Yehoshua Saguy, also recommended caution. But a more substantial reason was probably that, as part of his election campaign, Begin had a spectacular coup up his sleeve and did not want to blunt its impact by opening another front.

On 7 June, in a military and public relations *tour de force*, Israeli aircraft destroyed the French-built Osirak nuclear reactor near Baghdad. For decades Israel had sought to deny the Arabs access to advanced weapons technology – for example, it had carried out acts of terrorism against German scientists working on Egypt's missile programme in the 1960s. But the strike against Iraq, involving a 1,000-km flight by fourteen aircraft over hostile Arab territory, went far beyond this precedent, vastly extending Israel's security frontiers and affirming its intentions to be the sole nuclear power in the region. The prestigious surgical operation helped put Begin back in office three weeks later.

Perhaps the main factor deterring Begin from attacking the SAMs in the Biqa', however, was uncertainty about the American reaction. In spite of his enormous influence over the Reagan Administration, his aggressive behaviour was beginning to meet some resistance. He had embarked on a long tussle with the White House over its plans to sell five AWACS (airborne warning and command systems) to Saudi Arabia, a struggle which was to last much of the year. In October 1981 Reagan at last won consent from the Senate, but the vote was so narrow and the engagement with the Israeli lobby so bruising that the outcome was paradoxically seen as a victory for Begin. The Osirak raid also strained Israel's credit in Washington. While there was considerable sympathy for Begin's motives, there was also annoyance that Israel had used American satellite photography to plan the raid and American-built aircraft and 'smart' bombs to carry it out. The United States condemned the action in the Security Council, but applied no sanctions save to suspend for a few weeks delivery of four more F-16s, the type of aircraft which had carried out the raid. So, when the Syrian missile crisis blew up, Begin prudently decided not to try the Americans further but to accept Washington's suggestion that a presidential envoy, Ambassador Philip Habib, attempt through diplomacy to remove the offending SAMs.

Habib battled throughout the early summer of 1981 to douse the fires in Lebanon. Not only did he need to defuse the dangerous Asad-Begin contest over the SAMs, but he had simultaneously to wrestle with a major flare up in the old conflict between Israel and the Palestinians. For, as if to compensate for the restraint he was showing over Syria's missiles, Begin unleashed his air force and navy in late May and early June against Palestinian positions. When, to his apparent disappointment, this failed to draw PLO fire, he attacked more savagely from 10 July onwards. After five days of Israeli pounding, the Palestinians at last opened up with rocket and artillery fire against Galilee settlements, whereupon, on 17 July, the IAF mounted a twenty-minute raid on the western suburbs of Beirut where the PLO offices were located. About 200 Palestinians and Lebanese were killed and another 700 wounded amid heavy damage to property, to which the PLO responded with more shelling of northern Israel, killing 6 and wounding 59.

This was the unpromising situation from which Habib, with painstaking effort and the assistance of the Saudis, managed to stitch together on 24 July a three-sided 'understanding' between Begin, Asad and 'Arafat.

The essence of the deal was that Syria would keep its missiles in place in the Biqaʿ, but on the understanding that they would not be fired; Israel would continue reconnaissance flights over Lebanon, but would not attack the missiles; and Israel and the Palestinians would stop hitting each other across the Lebanese border, with Asad guaranteeing Palestinian good behaviour. Begin tried to widen the scope of the deal to ban Palestinian attacks on Israeli targets anywhere in the world, but Habib explicitly made clear to him that the understanding was limited to actions originating in Lebanon.[5] In putting this deal together, Habib was not allowed direct contact with 'Arafat – Kissinger's pledge to Israel forbade it – so messages were passed to and fro through the Syrians or the Saudis (often in the person of Crown Prince Fahd's emissary, Shaykh 'Aziz al-Tuwayjari, deputy commander of the National Guard), a roundabout route which did not prevent Begin suspiciously quizzing Habib every time they met on whether he had spoken to the PLO. 'In the end nothing was put in writing but everybody understood what had been agreed', Habib summed up later.

Asad in Damascus felt some momentary satisfaction. The crisis marked his re-entry into the big league of international diplomacy after his exclusion from the peace process four years earlier by Sadat's visit to Jerusalem. He had emerged from the bunker to which the Islamic terrorists had confined him, defied Begin and managed to retain his missiles in Lebanon. He had started a dialogue with the United States. The 'understanding' Habib had negotiated was not an Israeli *diktat* but seemed to him an expression of an American-approved balance of power. To Asad's way of thinking it was a long-overdue step in the right direction.

But Asad had got the wrong signal. Such was Begin's bellicose mood in the summer of 1981 that Asad was lucky not to face an Israeli assault. Perhaps not realizing that the amiable Habib, an American of Lebanese origin, did not reflect the reality of the Administration's indifference to Syria and its commitment to Israel, Asad overestimated Washington's will to restrain Begin. Nor did he wholly appreciate that, to Begin's way of thinking, Habib had forced Israel to make unacceptable compromises: the SAMs in the Biqa' continued to rankle; and in southern Lebanon the hated Palestinians had won a breathing space in which to build up their military strength. More deplorably from Begin's point of view, Habib had given 'Arafat *political* status and, with the ceasefire, Israel had come within an inch of recognizing the 'terrorists'. For the main fear of Israeli hard-liners was not of PLO militancy but of PLO moderation which might force Israel to negotiate – and therefore to make concessions. Yet, for all Begin's objections, Habib's arrangements kept the peace for the next eleven months until Begin would be restrained no longer. His appointment with Asad and 'Arafat was only temporarily deferred.

In October 1981 the shock of Sadat's assassination distracted both American and Israeli attention from Lebanon, but in November Ariel Sharon and US Defense Secretary Weinberger signed a Memorandum of Understanding on strategic co-operation which Sharon at least saw as enhancing his freedom of action against the PLO and Syria. The MOU contributed to persuading the Israeli hawks – not just Begin and Sharon but Chief of Staff Rafael Eitan, Foreign Minister Yitzhak Shamir, and Ambassador Moshe Arens in Washington – that American support for whatever action they envisaged would be forthcoming.

Then, in a high-handed move on 14 December 1981, Begin announced the annexation of the Golan Heights, no doubt in the hope of goading Asad into military action. An embarrassed Washington suspended the MOU, whereupon in a fit of rage Begin annulled it altogether, storming at the US ambassador, Samuel Lewis: 'Are we a banana republic?' Begin's anger could be explained by the fact that American objections to the annexation made an attack on Syria more difficult – if, that is, Asad had allowed himself to be provoked.

Asad could not mistake the signal from the Golan. By claiming it as part of the 'Land of Israel',[6] Begin contemptuously ruled out peace with Syria on the basis of a return of territory. Only capitulation was on offer. Asad read it as a declaration of war – but a war which he was in no condition to fight. He knew that if he made any military move whatsoever, Israel would seize the pretext to hit him, but doing nothing highlighted Syria's humiliating weakness. Asad had to content himself with denouncing the latest Israeli aggression and putting his case to the Security Council and to world leaders – with no tangible result. So he scrupulously observed the ceasefire on the Golan, made no military response to Begin's annexation, and never slackened his efforts to control the Palestinians in Lebanon who he feared would trigger off a conflict at a time not of his choosing.

These were extraordinarily anxious months for Asad as he measured the danger from Israel's hard-line team and the Arabs' chronic feebleness. With the signature of the US-Israel MOU, which he viewed with despondency, he knew how little he could rely on Washington to keep the peace. It was a moment of great frustration.

Sultan Pasha al-Atrash, the Druze chieftain, who with a handful of horsemen had fought the French army in the 1920s, was on his deathbed when Israel extended its law to the Golan, a traditional area of Druze settlement. His son, Mansur, was sitting by him one night when he heard the old man exclaim, 'God curse them!'

'Curse whom?' Mansur asked, thinking Sultan Pasha was referring to someone in the household.

'The Arabs!'

'What have the Arabs done?'

'Nothing! They do nothing! Israel takes their land and they don't move. They have planes, they have guns, they have money, but they do nothing! I spit on these rich Arabs!'[7]

Seeking a *casus belli*

In forming his second cabinet early in August 1981 Begin gave Ariel Sharon the post of Defence Minister which this brutal if brilliant maverick had long coveted. Putting the Israeli Defence Forces in the hands of a notorious Arab-hater and apostle of violence was a clear indication of Begin's intentions. He had three objectives. The first was to annihilate the PLO in Lebanon, destroy it and root it out completely, in order to overcome West Bank resistance to Israeli rule. So the war he planned was essentially a war for the West Bank. But the absorption of the West Bank could not take place in a vacuum. To safeguard Eretz Israel, his second objective was to expel Syrian forces and Syrian influence from Lebanon. And thirdly he intended to instal Bashir Jumayil as president of Lebanon, a Maronite vassal who would sign a peace treaty with Israel. By wrenching Lebanon out of Asad's sphere of influence and into his own, Begin planned to neutralize Syria for good. His overall ambition was to reshape the region so as to allow the building of 'Greater Israel' free from external challenge. Sharon's task was to provide the military means to bring this about.

From his early days as commander of Unit 101, Sharon had built up a reputation as an advocate of bold offensive operations against the Arabs, a reputation consolidated by his Canal crossing in the October War. He maintained that Israel's security interests extended to a vast arc of countries from Turkey, Iraq and Pakistan down through the Persian Gulf and across north and central Africa.[8] He championed the notion that 'Jordan is Palestine', a slogan implying the expulsion of large numbers of Palestinians to Jordan and the overthrow of the monarchy there. No doubt he hoped the Lebanese campaign would provide the opportunity to implement this programme.

Within weeks he had devised a master plan, codenamed Operation Big Pines, far exceeding in scope the existing IDF contingency preparations against the PLO in Lebanon. He understood that the control of Beirut and the defeat of the Syrians were essential to the radical political objectives on which he and Begin were agreed. And the deed had to be done before Lebanon's presidential elections, due in September 1982. Israel had had a long history of covert destabilizing interventions in the Arab world,[9] but the use of the IDF to effect radical political change in an Arab state represented a departure from the vaunted tradition that Israel's wars were defensive or at a stretch pre-emptive. The coming conflict was to be, as Begin later admitted, 'a war by choice'.

However, as Begin and Sharon dared not be candid about their intentions, they had to resort to ruse and deception. Armed forays into Lebanon to protect Israel's northern settlements from cross-border attack, even unprovoked blows against the PLO, were by now tolerated by the Israeli public and international opinion. But an offensive war to destroy the PLO altogether, chase Syria out and remake the Lebanese political system could not be avowed – even to the IDF itself. A pretext for military action was needed.

The trouble was that Habib's ceasefire was holding and the northern frontier was quiet. So, disregarding the objections of their more cautious ministerial colleagues, Begin and Sharon again set about trying to provoke the Palestinians and the Syrians into the armed action which would be seen to justify a large-scale Israeli riposte. Five times between July 1981 and June 1982 Israel massed troops on the frontier, and five times stood them down because the pretext was insufficient and pressures from the cabinet and from Washington too compelling. Begin's warlike moves even managed to alarm Israeli inhabitants of the northern settlements who, far from clamouring for added protection, pleaded for the peace they were enjoying not to be disturbed.[10] It was characteristic of Begin's touchy chauvinism that he gave the Israeli cabinet a first preview of Big Pines on the very day of his angry exchange with Ambassador Sam Lewis over Washington's rebuke for the Golan annexation.

Nevertheless, Begin and Sharon preferred to have US approval for their attack, and made their pitch at their chief ally in the Administration, Secretary of State Haig. In Cairo for Sadat's funeral in October 1981, Begin told Haig that Israel might have to push the PLO back from the border area, but he assured him that care would be taken not to draw Syria into the conflict. Haig responded, 'If you move, you move alone'[11] – a wording curiously close to Lyndon Johnson's elliptical warning before the Six Day War: 'Israel will not be alone unless it decides to go alone', which in the event had not held Israel back.

Washington received a more specific foretaste of what was to come when, on 5 December, an aggressive and impatient Sharon outlined to Philip Habib his solution to the Palestine problem. Habib had returned to the region to explore the chances of expanding his Lebanese ceasefire into a political settlement between Israel and the Palestinians. But when he broached the subject he was given short shrift:[12]

'I'll show you how to deal with the Palestinians', Sharon roared. Spreading out a map of Lebanon in his office at the Defence Ministry in Tel Aviv, he punched at it with his fist here and there, to show how he planned to destroy the PLO and sweep the Palestinians out of Beirut, if not out of Lebanon altogether.

Such an attack was unthinkable, Habib protested. He reported the angry exchange to Haig in Washington, as did Ambassador Lewis.[13]

By his own testimony, Secretary Haig 'over and over again' and 'again and again' cautioned Israel against military action. But the limp formula he used was that the United States would not approve an Israeli attack 'unless there [was] a major, internationally recognized provocation'.[14] Thus Haig sanctioned an attack on Lebanon if the PLO obligingly provided the pretext.

The two allies engaged in a prolonged debate about what would constitute an acceptable provocation, with Israel attempting to rewrite Habib's ceasefire terms, arguing that a Palestinian attack on an Israeli target anywhere in the world could give grounds for an invasion. In February 1982 Israel's military intelligence chief, Yehoshua Saguy, called on Haig in Washington to seek his support for such a redefinition, and Sharon came himself in May to put the case more forcefully. Without spelling out in full detail the scope of Big Pines, he explained how Lebanon could be rescued from Syria and restored to the 'free world', a programme much to Haig's liking. After the meeting Habib warned Haig that Sharon was going away with the wrong impression and he drafted a letter from Haig to Begin urging restraint, a letter Haig later adduced to deny that he had approved the invasion.[15] But in Habib's recollection Haig said and did nothing which could seriously have blunted Sharon's determination to invade. The maps of the planned offensive which he showed Haig were the same ones which had so alarmed Habib in Tel Aviv six months earlier.[16]

Asad was later to hold the United States as responsible as Israel for the carnage and destruction in Lebanon,[17] and not without justification. Although informed of Israeli intentions, at no time did the Administration issue a clear warning that in invading Lebanon Israel would forfeit American backing, and anything short of such an ultimatum could only be taken as a green light.[18] Collusion there was but, to allow for deniability, it was not made explicit. The effect was both to give Israel the clearance it wanted and to rob Washington of effective control over the subsequent course of the war. The US-Israel relationship, precisely because of the intimate interpenetration of the two countries, had spun out of control.

The invasion of Lebanon

When on 3 June 1982 Palestinian gunmen outside London's Dorchester Hotel shot and seriously wounded Israeli ambassador Shlomo Argov, Begin and Sharon grabbed at the opportunity to go to war. That this was not a breach of Habib's ceasefire did not deter them, nor did information from their intelligence that Argov's assailants were men of

Abu Nidal's faction, sworn enemy of the PLO leader, Yasser 'Arafat. 'Abu Nidal, Abu Shmidal', Chief of Staff Eitan scoffed, 'We have to strike at the PLO!'[19] Eitan's loathing for the Palestinians and eagerness to kill them were even greater than Sharon's.

Raring to go, Begin and Sharon had for weeks been trying to provoke the Palestinians into a fight. In April 1982 in response to a mine explosion in southern Lebanon, and in May after two explosive devices were found in Israel, Begin broke the ceasefire to bomb Palestinian targets in the evident hope that the guerrillas would hit back. But in April they held their fire and in May lobbed their shells into empty Galilee fields. On 4 June, however, following the attack on Argov, Begin sent the IAF to bomb West Beirut and southern Lebanon, causing dozens of casualties, and this time the PLO riposted by shelling northern Israel, killing one Israeli and wounding fifteen. This was the signal for an immense barrage of fire to be loosed on Palestinian camps from Israeli aircraft, long-range artillery and naval guns. Begin's Lebanon War had begun.

For public consumption Big Pines was rechristened 'Peace in Galilee' and its objective was said to be to push the PLO back forty kilometres from the Israeli frontier. Both the name and the declared scope of the operation were fictions.

On Sunday 6 June Israeli ground forces surged across the frontier: Israel's Northern Command under Major-General Amir Drori committed to battle a total of 76,000 men, 1,250 tanks, and 1,500 armoured personnel carriers, supported by the air force and navy. Opposite them were regular Syrian and PLA forces under Major-General Sa'id Bayraqdar of about 25,000 men, 300 tanks and 300 APCs, together with some 15,000 PLO fighters fielding a variety of hardware and belonging to at least eight separate guerrilla factions.[20]

Within forty hours, by the morning of 8 June, in a three-pronged strike up the Lebanese coast, into the central mountains, and northeast towards the Biqa', Israel routed the PLO and conquered much of southern Lebanon. The Palestinians had made the mistake of attempting to build conventional forces which could only be outmatched by the IDF. Had they trained and fought as genuine guerrillas, they could have given Israel more trouble. As it was, their best performance was in defending the camps of Rashidiya and 'Ayn al-Hilwa, outside Tyre and Sidon, which held out for days. The Palestinian civilian population was as much an Israeli target as the PLO fighters. From 5 June onwards every major refugee camp in southern Lebanon was subjected to saturation bombardment from land, sea and air, with the apparent intention of flattening the camps to make them permanently

uninhabitable. In annihilating the Palestinians Israel had eager Maronite encouragement. There had been a number of quiet American-
Israeli-Maronite discussions in the months before the invasion about
the future of Lebanon, in which Charles Malik, a former Lebanese
foreign minister and foremost advocate of Lebanon's pro-Western and
Christian Orientation, had played a prominent part.

In the Knesset Begin later defended the massive assault on civilians.
When had the population of southern Lebanon suddenly become
'beautiful people', he asked with heavy sarcasm. Had they not
harboured terrorists? Had not Israel driven one and a half million
Egyptians from the Suez Canal zone during the war of attrition with
Egypt? 'Not for one moment would I have any doubts that the civilian
population deserves punishment.'[21] Palestinian prisoners taken were
often forced to stand bound and blindfolded for days on end, were
exposed to the sun and deprived of food and water, were frequently
beaten and sometimes forced to perform their natural functions where
they stood. Many were taken to Israel for incarceration, crammed into
lorries and buses under the blows and insults of their guards or
bundled together in nets and transported dangling from helicopters.[22]

It was now Asad's turn.

Asad had not expected to fight in Lebanon and did not want to do
so. He was well aware that Israel was planning a strike – by the late
spring so much was common knowledge, reinforced for him by Soviet
warnings – but like the PLO he probably expected a repeat of the
limited 1978 invasion. Ever since 1976 there had been a stand-off
between Syria and Israel in Lebanon, with each tacitly tolerating the
other's presence under the so-called 'red line' agreement. The missile
crisis of 1981 had torn holes in the agreement, but in Asad's mind at
least Habib's 'understanding' had established a new balance, somewhat
more in his favour. Bolstered by his treaty with Moscow and his
alliance with Iran, and by the final defeat of the Muslim Brothers at
Hama in February 1982, he had recovered from the abysmal depths
and was ready to stand up for himself: in April and May he had
attempted to challenge Israel's air supremacy and had lost four MiGs
in the process. But he was not ready for a full-scale fight and his
deployments in Lebanon were modest and defensive.

His Achilles' heel was his relationship with 'Arafat, marked since
their violent clash in 1976 by personal animosity and mutual mistrust
despite a surface display of solidarity. The heart of the matter was, as it
had been since the 1960s, that 'Arafat wanted freedom to make his
own decisions while Asad saw this freedom as a threat to Syria's
security. Asad resented the recognition 'Arafat had won in Europe,

which made him still more difficult to control, and the ties he had established with Saudi Arabia, not least during Habib's negotiations. Before Israel's invasion Syria and the PLO had held some talks but these fell far short of defence co-ordination, and Damascus was not consulted when, on 4 June, the Palestinians opened up against Galilee, falling into Begin's trap. Once again 'Arafat had presented Asad with a *fait accompli*. When therefore Israel's divisions poured across the frontier, the questions uppermost in Asad's mind were: How far are they coming? Will they attack me?

Israel was at pains to reassure him. On 5 June it asked the United States to tell Asad that his units in Lebanon would not be attacked unless they attacked first,[23] and on the 6th Begin wrote a letter to President Reagan promising not to expand the war to the Syrians. On the 7th Begin asked Philip Habib to go to Damascus with the same message. On the 8th Chief of Staff Eitan declared, 'We are making every effort to avoid confrontation with the Syrians. Our business in Lebanon is with the terrorists.' That same day Begin made an emotional personal appeal to Asad from the Knesset:[24]

> We do not want a war with Syria. From this podium, I call on President Asad to instruct the Syrian army not to attack Israeli soldiers, in which case they will not be harmed at all. In fact, we do not want to harm anybody, we only want one thing: that our settlements in the Galilee should not be attacked . . . If we push the line back forty kilometres from our northern border, our job would be completed and all fighting would stop. I make this call on the Syrian president because he knows how to fulfil an agreement.

These assurances and appeals were a ruse intended to lull Asad into a sense of false security, and to silence the criticisms of the United States and of those Israeli cabinet colleagues not privy to the real war aims. Operational plans were ready to deal with the Syrian garrison in Lebanon. On 7 June Syrian radars at Rayak airfield and at Damur were attacked; and even while Begin was speaking formidable task forces were moving to outflank Syrian defences. An armoured and infantry battle group of elite troops was pushing into the Shuf mountains to envelop Syrian positions at Jizzin before heading north, while further east 35,000 men and 800 tanks of the Biqa' Forces Group (BFG) commanded by Major-General Avigdor Ben-Gal (who had checked the Syrian assault on the Golan in 1973) had the mission to seize the Biqa' valley and advance on the Beirut-Damascus road, Syria's umbilical cord to Lebanon. Dealing with the Palestinians alone did not require the deployment of seven mechanized and tank divisions as well as several independent brigades and other specialized units.

Tactically the Israeli General Staff wished to keep Syria out of the battle for the first seventy-two hours while the PLO was smashed, but the routing of the Palestinians was simply the prelude to action against Syria. Whatever they told the cabinet, Begin, Sharon and Eitan were agreed that the aim of the invasion went beyond destroying the PLO to destroying Syria's ability to subvert Israeli intentions regarding both Lebanon and Greater Israel. Whoever willed the ends also willed the means. Hence there was some justification in Sharon's later indignant rebuttals of the charge that he alone was responsible for the Lebanon War.[25] However far-fetched and personal his own strategic visions, the campaign against Syria could not rightly be attributed solely to him but flowed directly from Begin's Greater Israel ambitions.

Sharon's brief was to remove Syria from Lebanon. Could this be accomplished without the military action against Asad which Begin had pledged to avoid and which the United States and much of the Israeli government opposed? Having to conceal his true intentions was undoubtedly inhibiting. Sharon may have thought that a show of force or something short of a major conflict would do the job. At any rate, he fielded enough troops and in threatening enough deployments to impale Asad on the horns of a dilemma: either fight and be defeated or scuttle home and be humiliated. Either way Syria's presence in Lebanon would be ended and Asad's rule put at risk. Throughout the campaign Asad's difficult task was to dodge both options: to avoid either being trapped into a decisive battle or being evicted. This phase of the war was therefore a battle of wits between Asad and Sharon.

For the first two days, 6 and 7 June, it was still possible for Asad to believe that he was not the prime target and, in spite of the provocative movements of Israeli forces, he took great care not to be sucked in. As he later admitted, his first thought was that the Israelis would attack up the coast towards Sidon leaving his central and eastern sectors alone.[26] But by the 8th he could not escape the conclusion, confirmed by Deputy Chief of Staff General 'Ali 'Aslan whom he sent on a reconnaissance, that he was in imminent danger. Israel had overrun 'Fatahland' and was shelling PLO fighters who had fled to Syrian-held territory; Syria's forward defences at Jizzin were being attacked from three directions; and, most ominous of all, an Israeli armoured force racing north had that day reached a village just ten kilometres south of the Beirut-Damascus highway. Syrian troops in Beirut risked being cut off and units in the Biqa' faced encirclement. Swallowing part of Sharon's bait, Asad brought in some reinforcements from the Golan and added three SAM batteries to the sixteen already in the Biqaʿ.

The stage was set for the critical day, 9 June, in the Syrian-Israeli confrontation. Israel's assault on that day was both political and military. Begin asked Philip Habib – whom Reagan had despatched hurriedly to the area 'to cool things down'[27] – to carry a message to Asad which was in effect an ultimatum: Israel would not attack Syrian troops, but Asad must remove his SAMs from Lebanon and pull back all Palestinian units forty kilometres from Israel's border – impossibly humiliating terms. Habib put them to Foreign Minister Khaddam on the morning of the 9th, but in the early afternoon while he was waiting to see Asad, Syria's entire SAM network in the Biqaʿ was attacked and destroyed. Habib's mission had itself been a feint.

The Syrians had some minutes' warning of the attack when their radars observed large Israeli air formations gathering to the west, but almost immediately Israeli electronic countermeasures put the radars out of action. The SAM sites then came under intense attack from air-to-ground and ground-to-ground missiles in co-ordination with long-range artillery. Pilotless drones relayed the damage done, whereupon waves of Phantoms, Skyhawks and Kfirs, escorted by F-15 Eagles and F-16 Falcons, directed by Hawkeye command-and-control aircraft, came in to finish the job with high explosives and fragmentation bombs.[28] Further Israeli air strikes against Syrian SAMs in Lebanon were to follow in July and August. In seven raids the IAF destroyed some twenty-nine SAM batteries and damaged four more.

Asad was utterly outmatched in the air. His Soviet aircraft could not rival the F-15s and F-16s, not to mention their air-to-air missiles, nor did he have the benefit of Soviet early-warning or electronic warfare aircraft to match Israel's Hawkeyes and Boeing 707s. But on 9 June he knew that, whatever the cost, he had to break the Israeli forward momentum if his position in Lebanon was not to collapse like a pack of cards. Syrian interceptors were sent up with the desperate mission of stopping the Israeli raiders. The resulting air battles that afternoon between some 70 Syrian and 100 Israeli supersonic jets were the biggest of contemporary warfare.

Twenty-nine Syrian MiGs were shot down for the loss of not one Israeli plane. An Israeli pilot who fought in the battle reported that the Syrian pilots 'knew they stood no chance against us, yet kept coming in and coming in as if asking to be shot down. They showed such remarkable dedication and courage, and I have nothing but respect and admiration for them.'[29] Commenting on the Biqaʿ valley combat, a senior Israeli air force officer (widely believed to be the IAF commanding general, David Ivri) later remarked: 'Syrian aircraft were fighting from a disadvantage, having to respond to the Israeli threat wherever and whenever it materialized, within a general strategic and tactical situation not in Syria's favour.'[30] In spite of crippling losses on the 9th, the Syrian air force was again massively in battle on the 10th, losing another thirty-five planes. Syria's defence minister later conceded that the 'honourable results' achieved involved heavy sacrifices.[31] Syrian pilots had been defeated by a combination of skill, years of rehearsal and the most sophisticated weapons, electronics and command-and-control systems in the American and Israeli armouries. An Egyptian source added a footnote: in 1981 Egypt secretly delivered to the United States a complete SAM-6 battery, giving American and Israeli technicians the chance to devise ways of jamming its three components, the missiles, the radar, and the command unit.[32]

The Biqa' missile complex was the most prestigious symbol of Syria's presence in Lebanon and of Asad's determination to hold Begin in check. In attacking it, Begin settled a political score, but at the same time, having won total air supremacy and stripped the Syrians naked, he was able to unleash his ground forces in eight columns up the Biqa' valley and its flanking mountain ranges, threatening and enveloping the main Syrian defence line from Lake Qar'un to Rashaya. There was no further Israeli pretence of avoiding combat with the Syrians nor room for doubt in Asad's mind that Israel aimed to destroy him. Now the question for him was: Would Sharon's armies surge forward to the Beirut-Damascus road, cutting off Syrian forces in Beirut and the mountains, or would they turn east and threaten Damascus itself?

Just as he had had to check Israel's air onslaught even at the cost of scores of planes and pilots, so with vital security interests at stake Asad now had to stand and fight. The ground battles of those days were the Syrian army's finest hour. Outnumbered and without air cover, it managed to hold up the Israeli advance and establish new defensive positions. In four days of all-out battle, often using small groups of tanks, anti-tank teams and commando units, it fought its way back in good order, making Israel pay for every metre it won in numerous ambushes and robbing the Israeli high command of the quick, surgical success it had hoped for. On 10 June the second Syrian armoured division, equipped with newly-arrived T-72s, fought a battle with an Israeli armoured brigade in the Rashaya area, pushing the Israelis back several kilometres, destroying thirty-three tanks and capturing some American-built M-60 tanks intact.[33] One was taken to Damascus and promptly flown to Moscow. Among many engagements two were critical. On the central front a single Syrian brigade of tanks and commandos checked the Israelis at the village of 'Ayn Zahalta for more than two days, 8–10 June, preventing them from breaking through to the Beirut-Damascus road, and on the Biqa' front on 10–11 June, at the village of Sultan Ya'qub, Syria's First Tank Division stopped another Israeli thrust from reaching the crucial highway as it snaked its way towards the Syrian border.

Double dealing on the ceasefire

On 11 June 1982 a first ceasefire was negotiated, giving Asad a breathing space. Since the destruction of Syrian missiles on the 9th, international and essentially American pressure had been building up to halt Israel's invasion. At that moment of acute vulnerability, Asad flew secretly to Moscow[34] with an urgent appeal for Soviet protection, prompting Brezhnev to contact Reagan on the hotline. The prospect of superpower involvement rang an alarm bell in Washington. It was on this visit that, because Brezhnev was ailing, Asad had a long meeting with Yuri Andropov, then head of the KGB, who to Asad's relief displayed a detailed understanding of Middle East affairs. The meeting laid the groundwork for the Soviet Union's massive resupply of Syria after the war. Israeli pressure was again to result in an upgrading of Syrian military capability.

Israel's real war aims were now becoming clearer to the world at large and Begin's pledge to go no further than forty kilometres into Lebanon and not to attack the Syrians was seen to be a deception. Secretary Haig still argued that benefits could flow from the campaign, but in the White House fears were growing about where Begin's adventurism might lead. The United States had already voted in the Security Council for Resolution 508 of 5 June which called for an immediate halt to all military activity on either side of the Israeli-Lebanese border, and for Resolution 509 of 6 June which demanded an immediate and unconditional Israeli withdrawal. Time was running out for the Israeli hawks, but reining them in was not to prove easy.

Once again the ceasefire was the work of Philip Habib. After meeting Asad on the evening of the 9 June, he reported to Washington that the Syrian leader was ready to stop fighting provided Israel started to pull back at once and committed itself to withdrawing altogether. Reagan responded with an urgent personal message to both Asad and Begin – delivered at 2 a.m. on the 10th by Habib in Damascus and Ambassador Lewis in Jerusalem – in which he appealed for a ceasefire to begin at 6 o'clock that morning. This suited Asad provided his conditions were met, but Begin's aims were far from being achieved, and Sharon and the generals were clamouring for more time. To delay progress on the ceasefire Begin turned for help to Haig, telephoning him in the early hours to invite him to come immediately to the area on the argument that only high-level US intervention could bring about a settlement. After boasting of the IAF's exploits against the Syrian air force the previous day, Begin laid down Israel's ceasefire terms: all Palestinians would have to leave the forty-kilometre zone, Syrian reinforcements in the Biqa' would have to withdraw, but Israel itself would not budge until security arrangements for its northern border had been agreed. Several hours were lost – or gained from the Israeli point of view – while Haig canvassed for support in Washington for his trip, but in the end Reagan vetoed it. Meanwhile, Israel pressed onward.

In Damascus Habib was in a quandary: Reagan's National Security Adviser, William Clark, signalled him to assure Asad of the president's firm support for an Israeli withdrawal, but Haig simultaneously instructed him to hold his hand and give the Israelis time.[35] Habib, a presidential envoy, chose to obey Clark. Late on 10 June he saw Asad for the second time that day, and passed on Reagan's assurance. He had no means of knowing that a few hours earlier Haig had persuaded Reagan not to send Begin a harsh message drafted by Clark insisting on an unconditional Israeli withdrawal.[36] So Habib had been undercut at home. He had given Asad assurances for which there was little commitment in Washington.

On the strength of Habib's guarantees, Asad agreed to pull back his own troops and to move the PLO fighters northwards. He also approved Habib's proposed timing for a ceasefire. As for the security arrangements in South Lebanon which Begin demanded, Asad made no demur except to say that these could not be part of a ceasefire agreement but would have to be discussed with the Lebanese government.

'Is there anything further you require from us or the Palestinians?' he asked Habib. 'No, nothing at all', Habib answered to Asad's satisfaction.[37]

One way or another, on the night of 10–11 June the Israelis learned of the Asad-Habib understanding. (They may have monitored Habib talking to Washington by satellite. The Damascus embassy communications facility had broken down and he was forced to fall back on voice transmission, not totally secure against eavesdroppers.)[38] On learning what had transpired in Damascus, the Israelis' dilemma was acute: to fall in with the terms Asad had unexpectedly agreed would have meant an immediate ceasefire and the gutting of their grandiose plans. Their way out was to pre-empt Habib – and the American pledges he had given Asad – by declaring a unilateral ceasefire of their own unencumbered by conditions or promises to anyone. The Israeli announcement was broadcast at 8.45 GMT on the morning of 11 June, the ceasefire to come into effect at 10.00 GMT. As Habib had left Damascus for Jerusalem early that morning, Asad, on hearing the news, took it to mean that Israel had agreed to the same terms as he had, underwritten by the United States. Accordingly at 10.10 GMT he broadcast his own acceptance of the ceasefire.

The awakening for Asad – and for Habib – was brutal. As Habib recalled:[39]

> It soon became apparent that Israel's ceasefire didn't mean a thing. Sharon's forces weren't stopping but were moving up fast in the Shuf and were surrounding Beirut. I went to Israel to find out what the hell was going on. When I asked the meaning of this rolling ceasefire, I got bland looks.
>
> Casuistically Begin said, 'Ronald Reagan's message said nothing about a ceasefire in place.'
>
> 'Is this your interpretation?' I stormed at him. 'You cease fire, he ceases fire; you move forward, he shoots, and he has broken the ceasefire! You've invented a new sort of ceasefire. I'll have to get the military attaché to write it up for the record!'

Begin still intended to take control of Beirut to put his man, Bashir Jumayil, in power, so, ignoring the ceasefire, Israeli troops supported by air, sea and artillery bombardments stormed Syrian and Palestinian positions on the outskirts of Beirut and the hills overlooking the capital. The unhappy Habib and a divided Washington were unable to check them. By 13 June Israeli paratroops had linked up with Bashir Jumayil's militiamen in a cordon around West Beirut, bottling up some 14,000 Syrian and PLO troops in an enclave twenty-five kilometres square. A week later, on 22 June, Israel again boldly broke the ceasefire with a full-scale assault on Syrian units defending the Beirut-Damascus highway east of the city. In three days of fierce fighting the Syrians were driven fifteen kilometres back up the road, depriving Asad of any leverage over the battle for the capital. On the evening of the 25th yet another ceasefire was negotiated.

No doubt Asad was saved from a larger-scale defeat in the Biqa‘ and on the approaches to Damascus by the two ceasefires of 11 and 25 June. Sharon was later to complain that he was denied victory by American intervention. But Sharon's own deceptions, differences of focus between him and Begin, and the inhibitions of other members of the government all contributed to his difficulties. There was no consensus in the Israeli cabinet or in the country for a war against Syria to change the regional political map. Had Sharon been able to admit that Syria was his prime target, he could have shaped a more effective strategy, perhaps leapfrogging the PLO at the start to hit Syrian forces first. But Begin was obsessed with the PLO and saw its destruction as the primary objective. So Sharon had to act by stealth, manoeuvring to draw Asad's fire but unable to get in a knockout blow. Sidestepping the trap and keeping the bulk of his forces intact at home, Asad denied Sharon the opportunity to use Israel's full power against him. Sharon did not expel him from Lebanon and so long as he remained there Israel's victory was not sealed. To this extent Asad won the battle of wits.

Yet for several grim weeks Asad was reduced to being little more than a spectator while 'Arafat, besieged in West Beirut, became the focus of world attention. For a man like Asad, who had devoted his entire career to making Syria a central player in the Middle East drama, it was profoundly embarrassing and humiliating to be forced to sit on the sidelines as Israel assaulted an Arab capital a stone's throw away. In accepting the 11 June ceasefire Asad had not consulted the Palestinians and was now accused of abandoning them. In spite of all the sacrifices of the Syrian army and air force, he faced the wounding charge that he had not fought. 'Arafat's accusations on this score were something Asad could never forgive. Driven back from the environs of Beirut, he could do nothing to relieve the agony of its inhabitants or even to rescue his own men cut off in the city. Brigadier-General Muhammad Halal, an October War veteran who commanded the Syrian brigade in Beirut, put up a stout defence. Between bombardments the Israelis dropped leaflets over his positions saying: 'General Halal, we know you are there. Run for your life.' But his orders from Damascus were to fight to the last man.

The siege of Beirut

Curiously, having reached Beirut, Sharon was uncertain what to do next and seemed to flounder in a political and moral vacuum. Begin and Sharon had all along planned to pursue the PLO to the bitter end, to Beirut if need be, but under their deal with Bashir Jumayil it was to be his task not theirs to enter the capital and finish off the 'terrorists'. However, when the Israelis asked him to redeem his promise he backed away hoping the Israelis themselves would do the dirty work. Bashir's hesitations at this critical moment shook the whole basis of the Maronite-Israeli alliance on which Begin's postwar hopes for Lebanon rested.

Sharon had the troops to do the job himself and by now had virtually thrown off any restraint on him from the Israeli cabinet, but the idea of using the IDF to 'clean out' Beirut's shanty-towns alarmed the growing numbers of critics both in Israel and abroad and even some of his field commanders. Fear of further Israeli casualties was an inhibiting factor. Sharon had so far run the war much as he pleased, but even for him the entry of an Arab capital was a daunting threshold to cross. Had he stormed the city at once in hot pursuit of the fleeing PLO, he might have got away with it: his failure to do so meant that the physical annihilation of the PLO, a major Israeli objective of the war, was fudged.

Even hard-liners like Sharon were by now acutely aware of the erosion of their support in Washington. On a visit there on 21 June Begin had faced sharp questioning from President Reagan and Secretary of Defense Weinberger, deriving comfort only from Haig's reluctance to join in. But on 25 June came the news that Haig had been sacked: Israel had lost its foremost champion in the Administration. It was not only or even primarily Israel's war which cost Haig his job and brought George Shultz in to replace him. Haig had clashed repeatedly with White House advisers on other issues such as relations with Europe and economic sanctions against Moscow, earning him a reputation as a poor team player. But the Lebanese War in which he had colluded and his argument (modelled on Kissinger's in 1973) that it opened up opportunities for peace were the last straw. Reagan agreed on the need to evict the PLO from Lebanon but he wanted Lebanon to be freed from both Syria and Israel and restored to being a buffer between them. He did not support Begin's ambition to bring Lebanon under Israel's wing as a Maronite-dominated state.[40]

Having to take account of these new realities, Begin and Sharon reluctantly fell in with Reagan's suggestion to let Philip Habib try his hand at getting the PLO out of Beirut by negotiation. Sharon had no taste for such mealy-mouthed methods believing that 'Arafat would yield only to force, and throughout Habib's summer-long mission he relentlessly pounded the city's teeming southern suburbs where the PLO and Syrian forces had gone to ground. He blockaded them, cutting off water, food and electricity. Time and again, a dozen times in all, Habib had to patch up the ceasefire breached by Sharon, beg like a supplicant for flour and other supplies, and soothe despairing

Lebanese politicians. Sharon, the arrogant victor, could not be restrained. The violence he unleashed on West Beirut in his nine-week siege was intended to bring home to 'Arafat and his fighters as well as to the Lebanese population around them that their options were strictly limited.

The Israeli attacks on the city came roughly in three successive waves: an artillery barrage from 13 to 25 June; air raids from 5 to 12 July; and finally from 22 July to 12 August even more lethal bombardments from air, land and sea. The first two waves seemed designed to bring about an unconditional PLO surrender, and when this failed the third was meant to add Israeli menace to Habib's negotiations for a Palestinian exodus.[41] Israel used concussion bombs to bring down whole buildings as well as phosphorus shells and high explosives and, in at least sixteen locations in West Beirut, American-made cluster bombs.[42] In the brief campaign from 5 June to the end of August some 17,000 to 19,000 Lebanese and Palestinians were killed and another 30,000 to 40,000 wounded.[43]

Sharon's gratuitous cruelty – as in the eleven-hour saturation bombardment of 12 August, *after* the PLO had agreed to go – pointed to his hankering for more radical solutions. What he and Bashir Jumayil had envisaged was not the orderly retreat of PLO combatants, heads held high after a 'heroic stand', but rather the root-and-branch clearing out of the Palestinian presence, the razing of the camps, and the forced deportation of two or three hundred thousand people. Whenever Habib referred to 'PLO combatants', Sharon bellowed his correction: 'PLO terrorists and murderers!' Begin's fear was that the PLO would extract political promises, even recognition, from the United States.

While Habib was struggling to untangle the Beirut mess, Sharon was continuing to press Bashir Jumayyil to join him in a 'cleansing operation'. In Jerusalem on 23 June, Begin had scolded him like an angry schoolmaster for not 'liberating' Beirut. Bashir often came to Habib for advice, developing a dependence on the older, wiser man whom he sometimes addressed as '*Ammo* (uncle). One night late in July he arrived alone at the American ambassador's residence where Habib was staying.

'I'm coming under great pressure. Sharon wants me to clean out the West Beirut camps. He wants me to go in from the east while he comes up from the south. What should I do, '*Ammo*?'

'Well, what do you think you should do?'

'There'd be a lot of killing. It would be tough and I'd lose a lot of men. But how can I resist Sharon?'

'You know, Bashir, that I'm negotiating the withdrawal of the Palestinians. You also know you want to be president one day. If you do what Sharon asks it will damn you. It will make it hard for you to become president of all the Lebanese, Muslims as well as Christians. Don't do it, Bashir. Say no.'[44]

A bully boy and gang leader in his youth, Bashir matured as the presidential election loomed closer into a prudent politician. But while he continued to resist Sharon's pressure, he was still Israel's man. When, aged thirty-four, he was elected president of Lebanon by a simple majority of parliamentary deputies on 23 August 1982 to take office a month later, he owed his position to Israeli guns. However, after the election (which took place in an army barracks near Beirut), and after paying a courtesy call on outgoing President Ilyas Sarkis, he drove up to the American residence to thank Habib, who he knew had softened Muslim opposition to him and saved him from total dependence on Israel.

Habib had by this time also managed to solve the problem of the besieged Palestinians and Syrians. An evacuation plan was ironed out on 19 August in contacts with Israel, 'Arafat, Asad and other Arab leaders. Sharon, the blunt Israeli soldier-patriot, the ultra-nationalist, the centurion of Unit 101, appeared to have won the day, for by 1 September the PLO combatants and the Syrians – over 14,000 people, including some 10,800 Palestinian fighters, 664 Palestinian women and children and 3,600 Syrian troops – had gone. Supervised by a Multinational Force of Americans, French and Italians, the PLO guerrillas embarked by sea while the Syrians and allied PLA units trundled east along the Beirut-Damascus highway. Habib had obtained an assurance from the Israelis that they would let them go without harassment and would keep out of sight while the withdrawal took place. But the Israelis did not stick to the agreement. As he later recalled, 'They could not resist showing they had won. They hoisted Israeli flags along the road and lined it with triumphant Israeli generals.'[45] From a nearby rooftop Bashir Jumayil counted the trucks carrying the Syrians and Palestinians out of his capital.

Refuge for the evacuees

As the drama unfolded, Asad, grimly watching Beirut slip from his grip, struggled to rescue something from the wreckage. He had failed to prevent Bashir Jumayil's election, his unsuccessful efforts to secure a boycott of the vote, to intimidate deputies or put together an anti-

Bashir alliance only serving to highlight the decline of his influence. He knew that Israeli control of Beirut even through a client would pose a threat to him as grave as Sharon's bid to throw him out of the Biqa'. It would be only a matter of time before an Israeli-dominated president brought pressure on him to withdraw, thereby exposing his flank to Israel and undercutting his regional position.

To head off this dread prospect, the permanent bane of his life, Asad had tried to stall Habib's evacuation plan. He had wanted the PLO and indeed his own men to call Sharon's bluff and force him either to come in and get them or to climb down. He had sent passionate appeals to his beleaguered units to keep fighting:[46]

> Beloved ones, I am living with you day and night . . . Beirut's Arabism is a trust in your hands . . . I ask you to remain steadfast: martyrdom or victory!

In the Biqa' he allowed Palestinian raiding parties through the Syrian lines to harass the Israelis, but he had no direct influence over 'Arafat in Beirut. His only lever lay in refusing to co-operate with Habib's increasingly frantic pleas to the Arab states to provide a home for the Palestinians evacuated from the city. Syria would take none, he declared. Throughout the summer Washington put diplomatic pressure on him, while Israel tried to force his hand on 22 July by a surprise bombardment of his entire Biqa' front — allegedly to punish him for guerrilla infiltrations. But when Habib called on him in Damascus the next day, he was adamant in his refusal to co-operate, angry at the spectre of an Israeli proxy ruling in Beirut.

He had a score to settle with the American envoy, as this was Asad's first meeting with Habib since the misunderstandings over the 11 June ceasefire. What had gone wrong, he wanted to know. Why had Habib's assurances of an Israeli withdrawal, given with the authority of an American president, not been honoured?

'It was beyond my powers, Mr President', Habib replied with some embarrassment.

'Is the word of the United States not to be trusted?' Asad asked. 'What then is the meaning of any international agreement?'

According to Asad's aides Habib had little say. 'Mr President, we are living in very bad times', he replied lamely.[47]

By 10 August, it was clear to Asad that, whether he liked it or not, the Palestinians would soon be forced out of Beirut. Intense Israeli military pressure on 'Arafat was compounded by moral pressure from Lebanese leaders to spare the civilian population further hardship.

Asad also suspected that 'Arafat hoped to win future concessions from the United States (an idea Habib may have put into 'Arafat's head through the Lebanese Sunni leader Sa'ib Salam) if he left Lebanon on American terms. Asad thought any such expectations hopelessly gullible but he nevertheless had to consider their likely effect on 'Arafat. So when it seemed that 'Arafat would hold out no longer, he changed his mind and agreed to give refuge in Syria to the bulk of the Beirut evacuees. No doubt he hoped to regain some control over 'Arafat's men who blamed Asad for abandoning them and who now in adversity seemed more independent than ever.

Assassination of Bashir

With Bashir Jumayil elected to the presidency of Lebanon and the Syrians and PLO out of Beirut, Israel began to claim the political rewards of its campaign. Begin, Sharon, Shamir, deputy premier David Levi and others made no bones of their expectation that, freed from Syrian toils, Lebanon would sign a peace treaty with them. Any Syrian obstruction to this programme, Shamir declared, would be 'a brutal, insolent threat to peace'.[48] Bashir himself called for the withdrawal of foreign armies – Syrian, Israeli and Palestinian – committing in Syrian eyes the heinous crime of putting Syria on the same footing as Israel. The late summer of 1982 was a very low point in Asad's fortunes: regionally and domestically his whole position was at risk.

An event then occurred which was greatly to his advantage. On 14 September an immense explosion at the local headquarters of the Phalanges party in East Beirut killed Bashir Jumayil and some thirty of his associates. Shortly afterwards the man who planted the bomb, Habib Tanyus Shartuni, was arrested by the Lebanese Forces. His sister who lived in an apartment just above the Phalanges headquarters inadvertently gave him away by blurting out in a hysterical outburst that he had telephoned a warning to her to leave the building minutes before the explosion. Shartuni was identified as a clandestine member of the Syrian Social Nationalist Party ideologically committed to Damascus and one of Asad's staunchest allies in resisting Israel's ambitions. A branch of Syrian intelligence was rumoured to have assisted Shartuni in placing the bomb, although the link could not be proved. Another man, Nabil 'Alam, also suspected of involvement, took refuge in Syria.[49] Shartuni's act might best be understood in the context of his party's view of Syro-Lebanese relations, as later expounded by the SSNP leader In'am Ra'd:[50]

We had no hope of resisting the Israelis on the basis of Lebanese patriotism divorced from the Syrian axis. I happen to be Lebanese but ideologically I consider myself Syrian. Without Syrian support Lebanon would have been lost.

The killing of Bashir precipitated the notorious revenge massacres of Palestinian civilians in the Sabra and Shatila refugee camps organized with Israeli collusion by Bashir's intelligence chief Elie Hubayka. Within hours of Bashir's death and in breach of Habib's agreement, Sharon on 15 September had ordered the IDF into West Beirut, and by the morning of the 16th it was totally in Israeli hands. No doubt he saw an opportunity to get the Phalanges, anxious to avenge their leader, to do what Bashir had long resisted – that is, clean out the Palestinians from West Beirut. To justify some such action he publicly alleged that 'Arafat had left behind 2,000 PLO fighters lurking under cover in Sabra and Shatila. At 6 p.m. on 16 September Major-General Amir Drori, head of Israel's Northern Command, authorized Hubayka's security force to enter the camps to search for them. The carnage of Palestinian civilians started at once, went on all that night, continued all the next day and night, and did not end until 8 a.m. on 18 September. About a thousand men, women and children were slaughtered. Throughout these forty hours Israeli troops cordoned off the camps, firing flares at night to provide illumination for the Phalangist killers inside. Habib, who by evacuating the Palestinian fighters had left their dependants defenceless, was not the only one to be sickened:[51]

Sharon was a killer, obsessed by hatred of Palestinians. I had given 'Arafat an undertaking that his people would not be harmed, but this was totally disregarded by Sharon whose word was worth nothing.

Lebanon was traumatized by Bashir's death and by its savage aftermath. Although everyone knew he had been Israel's man, it was beginning to be realized that he had sought to distance himself from the Israelis, and it was widely supposed that he might have made a better president than his brutal beginnings suggested. Insiders knew, for instance, that at a meeting with Begin at the border town of Nahariya on 1 September he had resisted peremptory demands for immediate peace talks. It was with something like the relief of a drowning man grasping for a raft that on 21 September the Lebanese welcomed the election as president of Bashir's elder brother, Amin. Amin had no Mossad or CIA links and, if anything, had somewhat disapproved of Bashir's ties, but as a Jumayil and a Phalangist he represented continuity. He was the best the Israelis could hope for in the circumstances.

Begin was cast down by Bashir's death and tarnished by the Sabra and Shatila massacres. In the face of the international outcry, he disclaimed Israeli responsibility with prickly defensiveness: '*Goyim* kill *goyim*, and they immediately come to hang the Jews'. Unconvinced, some 400,000 Israelis took to the streets on 25 September to demand an inquiry in the largest protest demonstration the country had known. The Multinational Force, which had left Lebanon on the heels of the departing PLO, now returned, but without plan or mandate save for a guilty consciousness that, in the anarchy of Lebanon riven by communal hatreds, innocent civilians needed protection. However, the European powers and the United States whose forces constituted the MNF refused to land their troops before the Israeli army had left, and by 29 September Sharon withdrew his men from the city he had fought so hard to seize.

Begin's Lebanon War carried to extravagant lengths an interventionist trend in Israeli politics which from the days of Ben Gurion's premiership aimed at hegemony over the Arabs by military means. But the war and its mishaps demonstrated the inherent limits to the ability of a small country, however wilful and well armed, to force its writ on a whole region. Nevertheless, the more elusive the prize, the more stubborn its pursuit. Asad's duel with Begin was not yet over.

23

The Defeat of George Shultz

The Lebanon was Asad's bitterest war. Rarely had he felt more isolated or unfairly maligned than in the autumn of 1982. Twelve years of risk and effort had led to this: Israeli armies, a mere twenty-eight kilometres from his capital, were imposing a 'new order' on Lebanon which left his security and regional standing in tatters. After the military defeat he had suffered, his call for steadfastness against Israel so often used to upbraid others seemed hollow and his vaunted quest for parity more unrealistic than ever.

He had known adversity in battle before, but not as painfully. In 1967 the disaster was shared by all the Arabs; in 1973, disappointing though the outcome was, he had chosen the place and the time to wage war and was buoyed up by a tide of Arab pride and solidarity. But in 1982 war was forced upon him and he fought alone: Israel was able to put all its energies into a one-front campaign. His losses had been heavy: about 1,200 men dead, 3,000 wounded and 296 taken prisoner; over 300 tanks, 140 armoured personnel carriers, and 80 artillery pieces destroyed. His SAM missile batteries had been smashed and 76 aircraft and six helicopters shot down with, gravest of all, the loss of 60 pilots.[1] In contrast, Israel admitted to losing only one Skyhawk brought down by a Palestinian missile on the first day of the war, and a reconnaissance Phantom downed by a Syrian missile on 11 July. It was little comfort to him that US official estimates put the IAF's losses somewhat higher – 'probably in the region of 11–12 aircraft and three helicopters'.[2] The only thing to cheer him was that by September 1982 the IDF had suffered some 350 men dead and 2,100 wounded, and he knew how sensitive Israel was to casualties.

Much of Asad's unhappiness came from the Arab environment. The Palestinians, his so-called allies, could no more help him than he could help them, while the rest of the Arab world, powerless before the Israeli blitzkrieg, offered him nothing but abuse. 'Gloating and conspiring' as he described them,[3] his Arab enemies sought to exploit his difficulties. Mubarak of Egypt accused him of a secret deal with Begin to divide Lebanon between them, and denied that there had ever been an air battle over the Biqa'; Saddam Husayn of Iraq charged that he was in treacherous collusion with Israel; Husayn of Jordan indicted him for 'liquidating the Palestine cause'. Even his friend Qadhafi of Libya criticized his acceptance of a ceasefire. Only his new Iranian allies extended a friendly hand. Although hard-pressed in their own war against Iraq, they sent 500 volunteers to fight alongside his troops in the Biqa'.

Asad was equally disillusioned with the superpowers. Moscow, with which he had so recently signed a Treaty of Friendship, remained extraordinarily passive throughout the conflict. In spite of his secret wartime visit to Moscow, it was evident that Brezhnev, in his last feeble months of life and distracted by the crises in Afghanistan and Poland, was as anxious as ever to avoid a superpower confrontation. But Asad's deepest grievance was against the United States. Haig's tolerance of the Israeli invasion had blatantly disregarded Syria's security interests, and once Syria had been defeated and the Soviet Union had failed to intervene on its behalf, Washington seemed to write Asad off. It saw no need to make amends to him for Israel's ceasefire violations which undermined Habib's presidential pledges. He was simply ignored. The United States backed the election of Bashir Jumayil whom Asad considered a traitor, and acted as broker in the expulsion of the Palestinian fighters. It was hard for him not to conclude that Washington fully supported Begin's bid to subjugate the Arabs. As for the 'Reagan Plan' of 1 September – the US blueprint for a regional settlement rushed out on the day the last PLO man left Beirut – it failed even to mention Syria or its occupied Golan Heights. By this time, Asad's resentment of the United States was curdling into something like hatred. He was a man to bear grudges, to brood over wrongs done to him, and above all not to be put upon. Even at this dismal time – with his air force crippled, Israel supreme, the Arabs inert and the United States unfriendly, to say the least – he would not admit defeat.

His first priorities were to encourage guerrilla harassment of Israel in Lebanon, while racing to rebuild Syria's own armed strength. He was not ready for an immediate confrontation. In preparing to subvert Israel's designs, he had to lie low and lull his opponents into believing he was finished.

Israel's fear of casualties was a chink in its armour which he could exploit. Hardly had Israeli troops withdrawn from Beirut at the end of

September than they became the targets of snipers, ambushes, booby-trapped cars, hand-grenades lobbed from passing vehicles, in a swelling campaign of irregular warfare. The casualties were not great but the impact of the steady bloodletting on Israeli opinion and IDF morale was considerable. The most spectacular incident was the blowing up of the IDF staff headquarters in Tyre on 11 November 1982 when sixty-seven Israelis died. No firm evidence linked Syria to these operations, but there is little doubt that Asad sent all the help he could to his friends and allies in the Lebanese resistance at this time.

The powerful security agencies which had grown up in Syria between 1977 and 1982 to wage war on the Muslim Brothers were now given new targets. In the struggle for Lebanon, Asad made use of every asset he had, among which were a good many seasoned fighters. The Palestinians evacuated from Beirut to Syria were installed in the Syrian-controlled Biqa' where they joined large numbers of their fellows who had escaped the advancing Israeli columns in the early days of the war. Now they were directed to guerrilla tasks across the Syrian lines. At the same time, inside occupied Lebanon Asad tightened his links with the fighting wings of the Lebanese Ba'th Party, the Lebanese Communist Party, the Syrian Social Nationalist Party, and of course his principal allies, the Shi'a. By devious means, money, weapons and supplies flowed in over the mountains from Damascus. None of these Lebanese resistance groups except the Ba'thists took direct orders from Damascus; each was fighting its own corner. But the common interest in opposing the Israeli occupation served to extend Asad's reach.

When the Israelis first invaded Lebanon many Shi'a in the south welcomed them as deliverers from the high-handed Palestinians, but the brutality of the invasion and the signs that the Israelis were preparing for a long stay exhausted their welcome. Then Israel's attempt to impose Maronite rule drove the Shi'a into outright opposition. They had tilted towards Syria in the early 1970s when Asad befriended their leader, the Imam Musa al-Sadr; now Asad's relations with Iran helped cement the tie. His need for proxies to harass Israel coincided with Iran's eagerness to export its revolutionary message. These overlapping interests served to transform the city of B'albak in the Biqa' into a politico-religious centre of ferment, where some 2,000 Iranians (who had transited Syria with Asad's agreement) were joined by a militant Lebanese faction, Amal al-Islami, several thousand strong under a breakaway Amal commander, Husayn al-Musawi. These Shi'a, whether Iranian or Arab, were imbued with a spirit of martyrdom and consumed with loathing for Israel and the

United States. They made a speciality of suicide attacks. Zealous and fanatical, they were not fully controllable, but they were on Asad's side. In November 1982 they took over the town hall and principal barracks in B'albak. Asad's alliance with Iran which had attracted so much Arab criticism was now paying off where he needed it most – in the life-and-death struggle against Israel.

Such proxies and their terror tactics were useful, but they could be of little avail if Syria itself came under military attack. After the destruction of his missiles and much of his air force between June and August 1982, Asad urgently needed to recover a degree of deterrence. The Soviet Union alone could help, but the war had cast a chill on relations between Damascus and Moscow. For public consumption all was well, but behind the scenes the Syrians were angered by Soviet caution. They also blamed their defeat in the Biqa' air battles on the shortcomings of Soviet equipment, while the Russians charged the Syrians with incompetence. On 13 June, when General Yevgeny Yurasov, first deputy commander-in-chief of the Soviet Air Defence Forces, conducted an on-site inspection of the shattered missile batteries four days after their destruction, there was some acrimony between his team and the Syrian general staff. Relations did not improve in July, August and September, when the IAF with apparently effortless mastery knocked out another dozen newly installed SAMs. On 19 July Marshal Nikolai Ogarkov, Chief of the Soviet General Staff, came in person to assess what by any standards was a major setback for Soviet weapons systems. The Soviet worry was that Israel's know-how in destroying the missiles would be shared with the United States. In these months of frosty argument, Soviet supplies to Syria were restricted to minimal replacements.

The war highlighted an inherent contradiction in the Syrian-Soviet relationship. Asad depended on Moscow for advanced weapons, but at the same time he insisted on full political autonomy: in 1976 he had intervened in Lebanon without consulting the Russians and indeed against their wishes; in 1980 he had massed troops to intimidate Jordan without informing the Russians beforehand; in 1981 he moved missiles into the Biqa', again without consultation, causing Soviet ambassador Vladimir Yukhin to hurry to Moscow and a Soviet deputy foreign minister to hurry to Damascus; and the war of 1982 broke out without co-ordination before the fighting. Whatever the 1980 Treaty of Friendship did for Asad's morale, it was far from being a strategic alliance.[4]

Nevertheless the two countries needed each other, that was a fact of life, and by the autumn of 1982 efforts were being made to patch things up. It was to the advantage of both of them: Asad needed arms, while the Russians needed to restore the reputation of their high-performance weapons as well as their overall political position in the Arab world. To grab the Kremlin's attention, Asad argued that the United States was planning to use Israel and Lebanon as a springboard for further expansion, a thesis which seemed borne out by Reagan's decision in August 1982 to send US marines to Beirut. He knew it would be to his advantage if the Soviet authorities saw the Middle East as a decisive prize in East-West competition. The Kremlin seemed won over but was painfully slow in coming up with the goods. Relations were in this somewhat uneasy state when Leonid Brezhnev's death, announced on 11 November 1982, brought his long stagnant rule to an end. For Asad, who declared seven days' mourning in Syria, it could not have come at a more opportune moment.

Brezhnev's funeral in Moscow on 15 November gave him the chance to renew his acquaintance with Andropov and put his case for more and better weapons. To Asad's relief, Andropov agreed to inaugurate a new era in Syrian-Soviet military co-operation with a deepening of mutual commitment and a vast increase in the quantity and quality of arms deliveries. Defence Minister Tlas, who accompanied Asad to the Soviet Union for the funeral, recalled that it was Andropov himself who insisted that Syria must get the weapons it required, overruling reservations expressed by Soviet Defence Minister Ustinov and Foreign Minister Gromyko. When Ustinov claimed that advanced weapons could not be spared, Andropov said: 'Take them from Red Army stocks. I will not allow any power in the world to threaten Syria.'[5] Andropov was as good as his word: Asad did not have to pay further secret visits to the Soviet Union, as was widely rumoured, but merely sent delegations to negotiate detailed arms contracts. Thus Syria secured the immediate deterrent capability it needed, and this was only the first instalment of a major expansion and upgrading of its armed strength over the next four years. (The armed forces grew from 225,000 in 1982 to 400,000 in 1986, and the complement of armour from 3,200 to 4,400 tanks, of combat aircraft from 440 to 650, of artillery pieces from 2,600 to 4,000, and the air defence sites from 100 to 180, to cite only the main items.)[6]

Over the winter of 1982–3 the first fruits of the new understanding began to appear. A number of advanced weapons systems attracted keen foreign interest because this was the first time Moscow had sold them to a Third World country. The SS-21, a new generation surface-to-surface missile which entered Soviet service in 1982 and was then deployed, to NATO alarm, in Czechoslovakia, was supplied to Syria in

1983. Far more accurate and effective than the Scud already in Syria's armoury, it brought into range Israeli air bases and dockyards. A second innovation was the SSC-1, a long-range anti-ship missile which for the first time gave Syria a coastal defence capability. But the arrivals which in January 1983 caused the most excitement were two batteries of long-range, high-altitude SAM-5 missiles never before deployed outside the Warsaw Pact. They formed the backbone of an integrated air defence system which the Soviet Union now set about constructing, embracing many other types of SAMs, horizon-scanning radar, electronic jammers, and sophisticated command-and-control facilities.[7] Asad thus acquired the means to defend himself against Israeli air attack from the port of Latakia in the north to the Jordan border in the south. (A byproduct of the deal was that Syria had to cancel an intended purchase of three Boeing 757s for its civil airline and buy Tupolev 154s instead. It was a political decision taken reluctantly, but Asad could not afford to say no.)

The advanced weapons changed the Syrian-Soviet relationship in a number of important ways. For one thing, the SAM-5s and the surface-to-surface missiles were operated by Soviet crews. There had been some 2,500 Soviet 'advisers' in Syria in 1982, but by 1984–5 the number had more than doubled to allow for the manning of the new systems as well as the instruction of Syrians in the use of some other new weapons such as the MiG-23 Bis interceptor, the MiG-27 ground attack aircraft, and the T-74 tank, all of which made their first appearance in Syria after the Lebanon War. In addition, Moscow gave Syria a commitment to come to its aid if it were attacked by Israel – an immense boost for Asad and a vital element in his search for strategic balance. 'We have lifted one paw of the Soviet bear and put it down in Syria', Foreign Minister Khaddam boasted.

There was, however, another side to the coin. The Soviet Union wanted greater influence over its protégé, an instinct natural in a patron, so to secure the weapons and protection he needed Asad had to surrender a certain freedom of action. While he retained control over tactical and operational matters, he lost some control over ultimate strategy. His aspiration for parity with Israel had become a Soviet benefaction, to give or withhold. Moreover, with air defences and long-range missiles dependent on Soviet personnel, Syria could no longer consider starting hostilities as it had done in 1973; this too would have to be a Soviet decision. Asad was more constrained than before, but he was also a good deal safer.

These arrangements rested on agreed political foundations. The two allies were at one in seeking to deny Israel the achievement of its war aims, reassert Syria's influence in Lebanon, and prevent the conclusion of an American-brokered Israel-Lebanon peace treaty, which both saw as opening the door to US-Israeli regional hegemony.

Soviet stiffening made Asad bolder. When in the spring of 1983 Israel protested about the SAM-5s, a battle of words blew up which seemed to threaten war. Khaddam complained to the Security Council about Israel's aggressive intentions. And when US Defense Secretary Caspar Weinberger raised the alarm over Syrian missile deployment, Gromyko riposted with a warning that an Israeli attack could endanger world peace. But by this time the IDF's fatal casualties in Lebanon had topped the five hundred mark, and Israel had no stomach for further conflict. 'We have no intention of going to war against Syria over the new missiles or for any other reason', Israel's once bellicose Chief of Staff, General Eitan, protested.[8] But the Syrians were on their mettle. 'We do not fear war. We have enough strength to hit back harder to any blow we receive',[9] declared Dr Najah al-'Attar, Asad's forceful woman Minister of Culture who, with the illness of Information Minister Ahmad Iskandar Ahmad, was emerging as Asad's chief mouthpiece. Such verbal defiance signalled that Syria had begun to chip away at Israel's military advantage.

The Reagan plan

An enemy's mistakes can be as useful as one's own achievements. In climbing up from the abysmal depths of the Lebanon war, Asad was greatly helped by Israel's slowness to exploit its military victory. Had Israel imposed its 'order' on Lebanon in early September 1982 when it was at the height of its power, Asad could have done little about it. But nine long months elapsed before a Lebanese-Israeli agreement was concluded, by which time he was strong enough to contest it. It seemed as if the killing of Bashir Jumayil, the Palestinian massacres, Amin's election, and the forced withdrawal of Israeli troops from West Beirut had weakened Israel's resolve. Its hopes of a pliant Lebanese government ready to do its bidding were fast fading.

Difficulties with the United States were another constraint on Israel. The shock of war had disrupted the close relationship and aroused an impulse in Washington to reassert some control over its runaway ally. President Reagan had been affronted by Israel's cavalier dismissal of his pleas to spare Beirut, and the United States could not be wholly deaf to Arab protests nor be seen to collude in the smashing of an Arab capital. Differences of substance began to emerge between Washington and Jerusalem. Whereas the Administration sympathized with Israel's security concerns, it never fully underwrote nor perhaps even understood Begin's wider objectives of safeguarding Greater Israel by controlling Lebanon and neutralizing Syria. The official American position was still that an independent Lebanon should be restored as a buffer between Syria and Israel, and that the West Bank and Gaza were occupied Arab territories from which at some stage Israel would have to withdraw, in part or in whole.

But independent American thinking on the Middle East had long since been trammelled by fear of the pro-Israeli lobby and by a cupboardful of secret pledges, understandings, and memoranda of agreement extracted by Israel from succeeding Administrations over many years. Whatever the official position, in practice American Middle East policy was characterized by inconsistency and muddle, not wholly surprisingly given the endemic feuds between rival departments of government, the enmeshment of the issues with domestic politics, and the way the Middle East rose and fell on Washington's agenda. A committed pro-Israeli like Kissinger, a liberal lawyer like Vance, an ambitious maverick like Haig inevitably pulled American policy in different directions. This was George Shultz's inheritance when he took over the State Department at the height of the war.

Shultz came to office with mildly pro-Arab views, attributed to his eight years as a senior executive of the giant Bechtel Corporation which did a good deal of construction and engineering business in the Arab world. He had studied economics at Princeton, served in the marines in the Second World War, returned to academia at the Massachusetts Institute of Technology and the University of Chicago, before Nixon brought him into government in 1969 to serve in succession as Secretary of Labor, Director of the Office of Management and Budget and Secretary of the Treasury. After that came the highly paid front man's job at Bechtel. Now this big, bland, largely apolitical Republican without diplomatic experience was pitched into the Middle East quicksands at their most treacherous.

After the trauma of war the whole world, and the Arabs in particular, looked to the United States to give a lead on a broad Middle East settlement including a solution to the Palestine problem. There was also the more specific matter of sorting out relations between Lebanon and its formidable Israeli neighbour whose armies were still camped on its territory. In an effort to get on top of these problems Shultz asked the State Department for a briefing document on the fundamentals of American policy as they had been shaped by his predecessors, and one was compiled under the direction of Nicholas

Veliotes, assistant secretary for Near Eastern and South Asian Affairs.

This paper was the basis for a speech delivered by President Reagan on 1 September 1982 which came to be known as the 'Reagan plan'. For all the interest the speech aroused, the underlying briefing document had not been intended as the foundation of a major US initiative nor was the president's political weight committed to it. Reagan's priorities at this time were essentially domestic, and insofar as he had foreign concerns they were to do with Central America or Asia rather than the Middle East, an area in which he had no background and little interest.[10] The timing of the speech did not reflect an awareness of the urgency of finding solutions to Middle East conflicts. Rather, Washington's instinct was to mollify an Arab world dangerously alienated by the war and to pre-empt condemnation of the United States by Arab leaders who, after anguished paralysis, had at last agreed to hold a summit at the Moroccan city of Fez on 6 September. Such was the rush for Reagan to make his speech that there was no time to fine-tune it, which may have been why Syria and the Golan Heights were not mentioned and why Washington did not consult Israel beforehand – a lapse which breached one of Kissinger's many pledges to Israel, that the United States would never take a Middle East initiative without first clearing it with its ally.

A shocked Begin responded by saying it was 'the saddest day of my life'. He was referring less to the failure to consult than to the content of the speech, for in a few nicely turned phrases Reagan seemed set to rob him of his life's ambition. The American president called for an immediate freeze on Israeli settlements in the West Bank and Gaza, pronounced in favour of Palestinian self-government 'in association with Jordan', and explicitly ruled out Israeli annexation, sovereignty or permanent domination over the occupied territories (as well, of course, as an independent Palestinian state). He affirmed Security Council Resolution 242 as the 'corner-stone' of American peace diplomacy, and interpreted it to mean an Israeli withdrawal on all fronts. Recalling that the Camp David accords had spoken of the legitimate rights of the Palestinian people, Reagan pressed for the Camp David process to be widened to include Jordan and the Palestinians so that a self-governing Palestinian authority could be elected to succeed Israeli rule. His ringing affirmation of America's unshakeable will to protect Israel's security did nothing to soften the blow. From Begin's point of view Israel had fought the 1967 war to 'liberate' the West Bank, had refused to let its grip be shaken in 1973, and had launched war on Lebanon in 1982 to make Greater Israel safe for all time. Now Reagan dared to give voice to Palestinian aspirations and actually proposed handing back the territories to the Arabs! Begin immediately authorized three new settlements on the West Bank. As far as he was concerned, the plan was a total non-starter.

Reagan did not satisfy the Arabs either. The Camp David accords which he held up as a model for a settlement were anathema to them. At their summit at Fez a few days later the Arab leaders set out their principles for a settlement, which in essence restated the plan put forward in 1981 by Crown Prince Fahd of Saudi Arabia. They demanded an Israeli withdrawal to the pre-1967 frontiers; the dismantling of settlements in the occupied territories; the exercise of Palestinian self-determination under PLO leadership, by the creation of a state on the West Bank and Gaza with its capital in East Jerusalem; and the right of Palestinian refugees to return home or to be compensated. The Fez plan implicitly recognized Israel's rights in a clause stating that 'the Security Council will guarantee peace for all the states of the region'.

Asad found himself caught between the Fahd and Reagan plans. He had refused to attend the 1981 Fez summit at which Prince Fahd first outlined his ideas because, with Begin then just back in office and flexing his muscles, it was not in his view the time to signal a readiness to talk. Peace, as he never tired of repeating, was not for the weak. But in 1982 he endorsed Fahd's plan at Fez because, with Israel triumphant, his priority was to deny it the political rewards of the war by closing Arab ranks. Above all, he wanted to prevent Jordan from venturing into negotiations with Israel under the Reagan plan, and supporting the Fahd plan was one way to do it. Asad's concern was to patch up his Levant environment which had been savaged by Israel's invasion of Lebanon. If Jordan were to slip into Israel's sphere of influence through a Camp David-type deal, he would be completely undermined.

Henry Kissinger had advised Shultz that, by weakening the PLO, the Lebanese War had created an opportunity to bring Jordan into the peace process. Taking this advice on board, Shultz encouraged King Husayn to attempt to persuade 'Arafat to give him a mandate for talks. But this was a development Asad felt he had to scotch – and this he did by pressure on the PLO not to yield to the king and on the king not to yield to Israel's embrace.

As a result of these developments, when Shultz came to assess the impact of the Reagan plan he found himself confronting an Israeli rebuff and Arab coolness. As he had expended a good deal of effort in getting Reagan to make the speech on 1 September, he was taken aback by this poor reception and grew wary of State Department

'Arabists' whose briefing document he felt had landed him in trouble. Disappointed on the score of a broad Middle East settlement, Shultz now put his energies into resolving the lesser problem of Israel-Lebanon relations – but here too he was to go seriously astray.

The problem was how best to set about restoring Lebanon's sovereignty, satisfying Israel's security needs and removing foreign armies from the battlefield. On these matters there were widely different points of view in the American camp. The negotiating model preferred by Philib Habib, for example, was the one he had used to good effect in defusing the 1981 missile crisis, that is to say, discreet soundings among the parties to establish what common ground there was leading to an informal 'understanding'. Habib's aim was a bare-bones security agreement between Israel and Lebanon regarding the south of the country which he thought could be put into effect before the end of 1982 while Asad was still weak.[11] But Habib needed a rest from his arduous Lebanese negotiations. He had a heart condition which had not been improved by the slanging matches with Sharon during the Beirut siege. He took off for California for a rest, leaving his assistant, Ambassador Morris Draper, in the field. On his return to Lebanon in December 1982, he discovered to his dismay that the formula he advocated had been dropped in favour of formal direct negotiations between Israel and Lebanon.

The reason was, of course, that Israel, wanting much more out of Lebanon than mere security arrangements in the south, was not satisfied with Habib's informal procedures. It had gone to war for the bigger prize of a peace treaty with a client state. And the more casualties its Lebanese adventure took, the more Israel felt it had to justify it by securing a fully-fledged treaty in face-to-face talks.

Habib made a last effort to head off what he thought a dangerous course. He embarked on a series of probings, first with Amin Jumayil and then with Begin and Sharon, in the hope of moving on to Asad and Fahd. But in Israel he got another nasty shock. He had begun outlining his ideas for a security arrangement when Sharon broke in: 'Wait a minute', he cried, waving a piece of paper, 'We don't need all that stuff you're talking about. I've already gotten an agreement with Amin's signature on it.' To secure his war aims, Sharon had bypassed the American intermediary and conducted secret talks with the Jumayil camp. Habib immediately adjourned the meeting and returned to Beirut.

'What have you done?' he screamed at Amin. 'Why didn't you tell me you were negotiating with the Israelis?'

Amin huffed and puffed. 'There isn't an agreement, only tentative guidelines.' He denied signing anything.[12] But the fact was that his private deal with Sharon had gravely weakened Lebanon's hand and put an end to Habib's attempt to get the rival armies out of Lebanon by informal understandings arrived at quietly.

The debate between advocates of informal soundings and direct talks was then resolved in favour of the latter by Kenneth Dam, deputy Secretary of State, but it is inconceivable that he could have acted without Shultz's support. Accordingly Israel-Lebanon talks opened under US auspices on 28 December 1982, with sessions being held alternately at Kiryat Shemona in Israel and Khalda in Lebanon. They dragged on for four months, in 138 hours of not always amicable bargaining.

A second Camp David?

The course of the negotiations and their eventual outcome owed much to the evolution of Shultz's own position. In the autumn of 1982 the Israelis considered him an enemy, the evil genius behind the Reagan plan, the pro-Arab Bechtel executive; but by the spring of 1983 he was their darling. He had evidently succumbed, like others before him, to the drip-on-stone tactics of the pro-Israel lobby, which had recovered from the embarrassments of the Lebanese War and from the unfavourable television coverage of the Beirut siege and the Sabra and Shatila massacres. American Jews had at first hesitated to endorse Begin's invasion, afraid of being accused of greater loyalty to Israel than to the United States, and the American Israel Public Affairs Committee had even begun by giving the Reagan plan a cautious welcome. It was only when the Arabs at Fez failed to welcome the plan that the lobby recovered its nerve, defended the Lebanon War and focused its campaign on Shultz. This proud but thin-skinned man was not inclined to put up a fight against the great political influence Israel could bring to bear on American decision-making.

The Washington story was that Under-Secretary of State Laurence Eagleburger, an Israeli supporter and Kissinger protégé, played a role in his conversion. 'George', he is alleged to have said to him, 'do you want to be a successful Secretary? Do you want to contribute to arms control, conduct East-West negotiations, save the world economy? Then don't piss with the Israelis. If you do, you won't get anything done.' Moshe Arens, Israel's ambassador in Washington who took over the Defence Ministry in February 1983 when Sharon was forced to resign after the publication of the Kahan Commission's report on the Beirut massacres, also contributed to the Secretary of State's change of heart. An MIT graduate like Shultz and the essence of reasonableness in contrast to Sharon's bluster, Arens was quick to offer the United States access to what Israel had learned about Soviet weapons and strategy during the war, information which Israel had at first withheld in its opposition to the Reagan plan. With such sweeteners Arens may have helped persuade the Secretary to support Israel's demand for a peace treaty. In any event, Shultz came to believe that a second version of the Camp David accords, this time between Israel and Lebanon, was both feasible and desirable.

In lending his weight to the Israel-Lebanon negotiations Shultz may also have been affected by the loss of a trusted adviser at this time. On 18 April 1983, a truck packed with explosives rammed the US embassy in West Beirut, bringing down much of the structure. Among the sixty-three dead were seventeen Americans, and among them the CIA station chief, his deputy, half a dozen CIA officers – and Robert Ames, the agency's chief Middle East analyst, who had flown to Beirut to investigate the new phenomenon of Shi'i terror of which he was almost certainly a victim. Ames had been one of Shultz's key advisers: his death robbed the Secretary of State of sound judgment at a critical moment and hardened his heart against America's critics in the Middle East, chief among whom was Asad's Syria. The CIA was convinced the Iranians were behind the embassy's destruction but suspected the Syrians of complicity.[13]

At the Israel-Lebanon talks the chief Israeli negotiator was David Kimche, Israel's 'Mr Lebanon'. First with Mossad, then as director-general of the Israeli Foreign Ministry, he had been the architect of the Phalanges connection. He was assisted by Major-General Avraham Tamir, Sharon's representative. On the Lebanese side were Antoine Fattal (a man originally of Syrian origin whom Damascus later sought to put on trial), and Brigadier-General 'Abbas Hamdan. In the weeks of nitpicking, Kimche tied up the Lebanese in an elaborate net of legal restrictions and controls. Habib became increasingly exasperated with the daily bickering. 'Let me off the hook', he exploded to Kimche. 'You've got a peace treaty in all but name.'[14]

Yet it required Shultz's personal intervention to bring the negotiations to a conclusion. The problem was that Israel's proposed agreement with Lebanon did not make sense so long as Syrian troops remained strongly entrenched in the country. How to get them out? The dilemma had not been tackled. The question for Shultz when he arrived in the Middle East in April 1983 was whether to engage Asad in negotiations before the Israel-Lebanon accord was finalized or present him with a *fait accompli.* For a week or so Shultz kept his options open.

He summoned American ambassadors in the region to a conference in Cairo to sound out their views. Richard Murphy arrived from Saudi Arabia, Richard Viets from Jordan, Robert Dillon from Lebanon, and from Syria Robert Paganelli who bluntly told Shultz that the blatant disregard of Syria's interests in the proposed accord made Asad's opposition inevitable. Affronted by Paganelli's plain speaking, Shultz dismissed the warning. He had no real grasp of Asad's reasons for dreading an Israeli overlordship in Lebanon, nor did he appreciate the depth of Asad's resentment at what the Syrian saw as Washington's 'betrayal' over the 11 June 1982 ceasefire. He may have remembered that, in Washington in July 1982, Foreign Minister Khaddam had expressed Syria's willingness to withdraw from Lebanon if Israel also did so, and he now believed that Asad would bow to the inevitable. The Saudis and the Lebanese were assuring him that this was so. Perhaps also Shultz could not conceive that a poor Third World country with a population of under ten million could stand up to him. Above all, he failed to realize the extent to which Asad had recovered from the defeat of 1982.

Part of the problem was the lack of American communication with Damascus. Paganelli knew the Syrian mind but Shultz gave him no credence. From the start of the formal Israel-Lebanon talks in December 1982 there had been no attempt to draw the Syrians in. Philip Habib, who had negotiated with Asad over the Biqa' missiles in 1981, over the unfortunate 1982 ceasefire, and again over the PLO evacuation plan, and who knew him better than any other American, was himself out of play at this crucial moment. Asad would not see him. He declared him *persona non grata* claiming that Habib had deceived him over the 11 June ceasefire. The Syrians were disenchanted with the line Habib tended to take in Damascus — that he was on their side, that the Israelis were being tough, that the Syrians should help him to help them. But, such minor irritations apart, Asad refused to let Habib into Syria in May 1983 to express his displeasure with the whole thrust of US policy and particularly with the Israel-Lebanon accord then about to be concluded.

To tie up the loose ends Shultz embarked on a shuttle between Beirut and Jerusalem and by 4 May, after seeing Begin no fewer than six times, he had a draft ready for signature. But the problem of how to get the Syrian army out of Lebanon remained unsolved. To cover themselves the Israelis asked Shultz for a private pledge, incorporated in a side-letter, that they would not be obliged to implement the accord so long as Syrian, and indeed Palestinian, forces had not withdrawn from Lebanon. This was an imprudent move. They had given Asad a veto over the proceedings.

On 7 May, Shultz travelled to Damascus in the hope that he could briskly clear away what he saw as the last obstacle to his peacemaking. He was confident that between the carrot of Saudi aid and the US-Israeli stick Asad would, perhaps after some face-saving rhetoric, end up by endorsing the accord. But he had misjudged his man. Asad would not let himself be bullied by a more powerful adversary and, in characteristic style, he treated the Secretary to a five-hour history lesson. He recited the Arabs' struggle to contain Israel and their resentment at America's indifference to their aspirations and its blind support for their enemy. Now the United States proposed rewarding Israel for its aggression. It was to be allowed to change Lebanon's Arab character, to threaten the security of Arab states such as Syria, and to impose its hegemony on the region. He would not bow to such a US-Israeli *diktat*. He would consider withdrawing his troops from Lebanon only after an unconditional and total Israeli withdrawal. The right way forward, he advised Shultz, lay in the strict implementation of Security Council Resolutions 508 and 509 for which the United States itself had voted.

This interview with Asad was among the least agreeable experiences of Shultz's career. He was not used to such scoldings. Moreover, if Syria stayed put in Lebanon, his accord was in jeopardy, but he realized that to embark on an extended negotiation such as Asad seemed to want would involve reopening the Arab-Israeli dispute in its entirety – the Golan, Palestinian rights, an Israeli withdrawal on all fronts, a comprehensive settlement. So much he learned in Damascus. It was an unthinkable agenda. After a stopover in Riyadh to plead for Saudi pressure on Damascus, Shultz returned to Beirut, angry and affronted but determined to press ahead.

The Secretary of State was not spared a painful encounter with the Lebanese Prime Minister, Shafiq al-Wazzan, with whom he discussed the draft treaty. A sound but simple patriot, the son of a baker, Wazzan saw clearly where Shultz's diplomacy was leading. 'I must tell you, Mr Secretary', he said, 'that I am ashamed and unhappy at the terms of this accord which I will only sign with the utmost reluctance. Is this all that the great United States can secure for us?'[15] Shultz told the Lebanese, to their utter dismay, that it was up to them to talk the Syrians into pulling out. The feeble Lebanese government had looked to the United States to protect it both from Israel's demands and from Syria's pressures. Professor Elie Salem, Lebanon's Foreign Minister at the time, later commented ruefully:[16]

Lebanon was like a child that is taken for a walk by his aunt. We shouldn't have trusted our aunt. I have learned that great powers are often less honest than small ones.

On 17 May the Israel-Lebanon agreement was signed at both Khalda in Lebanon and Qiryat Shemona in Israel. Israel had wanted a lot from its helpless neighbour – diplomatic relations, freedom of movement of goods and persons, a continued Israeli military presence in the south. In the event these stiff terms were trimmed down somewhat as a sop to Lebanon's self-esteem and to its anxiety about Arab reactions, but the final text[17] was nevertheless an astonishing straitjacket on Lebanon's sovereignty.

Instead of official diplomatic relations, Israel secured a 'liaison office' on Lebanese territory, not quite an embassy. Full normalization was to be deferred until after the withdrawal of Israeli troops. But over the whole of the south Israel now exerted considerable control. Its proxy militia under Major Sa'd Haddad, although attached to the Lebanese army, was to remain a separate force patrolling the frontier up to the Zahrani river. (It was privately agreed that Israel would have to approve any successor to Haddad.) In a further zone beyond Haddad's and up to the Awali river, Lebanon could deploy only a single brigade with strict limits on its weapons and equipment. No Lebanese military radars would be allowed to probe into Israel nor would high-altitude SAMs be tolerated. Lebanon would have to give Israel advance notice of flights of any kind over the entire security area. In addition, Israeli military personnel would be present in the south within eight joint Israeli-Lebanese supervisory teams, whose job was to detect and destroy any hostile guerrilla forces.

And this was not the whole of it. The accord formally ended the state of war between Israel and Lebanon, obliged Lebanon to prohibit any manifestation on its territory of hostility to Israel from guerrilla activity to mere propaganda, and banned the passage through Lebanon or its air space of forces, weapons or equipment to or from any state not having diplomatic relations with Israel – in fact the whole Arab world except Egypt. It also enjoined Lebanon to abrogate within a year any treaties, laws or regulations in conflict with its accord with Israel – in fact all the commitments it had assumed at Arab summits and as a member of the Arab League. 'The Israelis are like a thief who gets you to empty your purse, then pauses to tweak the handkerchief from your breast pocket', was Professor Salem's sour comment.[18]

With the publication of the accord a little less than a year after the invasion, it looked as if Israel had won not only the war but also the peace, altering the whole strategic balance of the area. It had been a gory, messy affair, but Lebanon had been brought into its sphere of influence and Syrian power was neutralized. Everyone knew Asad detested the outcome but as so often in the past – over Sinai Two, over Camp David, over the Egypt-Israel peace treaty – he would simply have to put up with it. As Habib commented: 'We know that Syria will not willingly accept the terms and conditions of the accord. It must now accept them unwillingly.'[19] *Pax Hebraica* seemed the new reality.

Battle lines drawn

Israel's new order spelled death to Asad: reduced to insignificance in the region, he risked losing power in Syria itself. The battle of the accord was one he could not evade, and by the summer of 1983, with local allies and Soviet protection, he was in better shape to fight it than his enemies realized. The crisis brought out in sharp relief his characteristic qualities: a conviction of moral and political rectitude, a cool head under fire, colossal stubbornness, and a readiness to fight, even to fight dirty in what he saw as a national cause. Above all, Asad had the patience required for a long haul – a bedouin virtue which could seem more like persistence in revenge. The Arabs tell a story of a tribal chief who bragged to another that he had avenged a slight suffered by his clan forty years earlier. 'You acted hastily', the other chief reproved. Asad's obstinacy had something of this enduring quality.

Into the struggle he threw every resource, every ounce of cunning and nervous energy, setting up at the Presidency something like an operational headquarters from which lines went out to all parts of Lebanon. He had to make his will prevail on every front – in Beirut, East and West, in the northern port of Tripoli, in the Biqa' valley, in the Shuf mountains, and in the devastated south where the Shi'a were beginning to confront the Israeli invaders.

The signature of the accord on 17 May 1983 was the signal for a stream of invective from Damascus against the 'stooges', 'agents' and 'isolationists' who had signed it. The Lebanese government was threatened with a new civil war. The accord was decried as a Phalanges-Israeli agreement designed to give supremacy to the Maronites over every other community in Lebanon and to turn the whole country into an Israeli protectorate. Asad declared the 'contract of submission' stillborn. Four days before the signature Syria's chief Lebanese allies had held a council of war in Zghorta, the north Lebanon fief of Asad's Maronite friend, ex-President Sulayman

Franjiya. There were gathered, apart from Franjiya himself, the Sunni leader from Tripoli Rashid Karami, the Druze Walid Junblatt, George Hawi of the Lebanese Communist Party, In'am Ra'd of the SSNP, and 'Asim Qansuh of the Lebanese Ba'th party. In the coming weeks they coalesced with Asad's encouragement into a National Salvation Front which vowed to fight the accord, overturn Maronite hegemony, confront Israel's occupation and rebuild a 'new Lebanon'.[20] Syria claimed that these men were more representative of the real Lebanon than Jumayil's 'treacherous' government – a point of view it underlined by shelling the main Christian port of Junieh.

Jumayil was not Asad's only target. 'Arafat was another challenger to be put down if Syria was to regain the initiative not just in Lebanon but in the Arab-Israeli conflict as a whole. The long-standing quarrel between Asad and 'Arafat, beginning with 'Arafat's imprisonment in Syria in 1966, and steadily envenomed by Black September in 1970, by the Lebanese crisis of 1976 and by Israel's first invasion of 1978, had been carried to the point of total rupture in the 1982 war. 'Arafat had mortally offended Asad by not giving Syria credit for its military sacrifices and by deciding against going to Damascus when the time came for him to be evacuated from Beirut. Moreover, by toying with the Reagan plan, by negotiating with King Husayn over a formula for peace talks, and more generally by upholding his old claim to an 'independent Palestinian decision', he threatened the very foundations of Asad's regional strategy.

Many Palestinian fighters living under Syrian control in the Biqa' valley, a good number of them members of 'Arafat's own Fatah movement, were critical of the way the Palestinian resistance had quickly collapsed in south Lebanon in the face of Israel's onslaught. They also contested the PLO chairman's decision to leave Beirut and his apparent willingness to consider a political compromise. Led by two Palestinian colonels, Abu Musa and Abu Salih, the dissidents rose against 'Arafat in the Biqa' in May 1983, fought pitched battles with men loyal to him, and with Syrian support gained the upper hand. 'Arafat hurried to the Biqa' and to Damascus to rally his supporters, but Asad, wholly committed to the struggle for Lebanon, would tolerate no such distractions from his main purpose. On 24 June, 'Arafat was expelled from Syria, in a move which dramatized the breach and underlined Asad's own claim to hold the key to the Palestine problem.

By this time Washington was waking up to the failings of its diplomacy: Asad had been allowed to rearm while the Lebanese government which he opposed was woefully precarious. It was time to rethink basic strategy and attempt to engage Asad in a belated dialogue.[21] On 6 July Shultz subjected himself to another gruelling five hours with Asad but without managing to soften his irrevocable rejection of the accord. To maintain contact, Washington found a replacement for Habib in the person of Robert McFarlane, assistant national security adviser, who paid his first visit to Damascus on 6 August, just a month after Shultz. His brief was to discover what exactly were Asad's conditions for withdrawing from Lebanon.

Asad in turn did not want a severance of contact and kept the door open to Washington, agreeing to the formation of a US-Syrian working commission to consult on Lebanon. A couple of weeks later, in an evident gesture of goodwill, he engineered the freeing of David Dodge, the acting president of the American University of Beirut who had been abducted by a pro-Iranian group a year earlier. Syrian agents actually rescued Dodge from Tehran, an index of Asad's interest in a relationship with the United States if it could be on his terms.

Over the years, Asad had developed a negotiating technique which he frequently used with foreign guests, and McFarlane was no exception. He would begin by exchanging a few pleasantries. Then he might ask, 'How is the weather in your country?' A Western guest would usually reply to the effect that at home it was colder than in Syria, giving Asad his opportunity. 'Indeed', he would say, 'it's warm here because the United States is stoking the fire!' There were two sorts of climate in the world, he would explain, one given by God, the other by the United States, and step by step he would make his point that the tensions, crises and wars in the area must all be laid at Washington's door. An American visitor would feel compelled to defend himself, starting the meeting at a disadvantage. Asad's next stratagem was to be extraordinarily digressive and argumentative. If the name of God were mentioned, for example, this might set him off on a long discourse about Islam, Judaism and Christianity before he could be brought back to the matter in hand. Negotiating sessions would last for hours. More than one envoy who suffered this treatment came to the conclusion that Asad raised all sorts of irrelevant subjects simply to tire his visitors the better to control them. At the end of a wearisome session the temptation was to accept what he had to say simply to escape.

Asad's good memory rarely failed to impress. He did not take notes at meetings, never called for pen and paper even in complicated discussions. If a visitor raised six points with him, he might spend an hour answering the first point, then move smoothly through the others in the right order. With Robert McFarlane the unexpected gambit Asad chose was to pose a question about the role of women in American politics, to which McFarlane was at a loss to reply, whereupon Asad launched into a prolonged account of women in Syrian affairs, regretting his failure to advance them further in politics.

When McFarlane got a chance to get down to business he stressed, in line with the new American thinking, that the United States wanted a fair Lebanese settlement which took Syria's interests into account, including a complete Israeli withdrawal. This was not sufficient for Asad. He was open to suggestions but he remained unconvinced that the Americans had grasped the difference between the Syrian and Israeli presence in Lebanon. Syria's influence was legitimate and had to prevail. Syria and Lebanon were one people, one nation, one geography. Israel was an alien presence. On the question of withdrawal McFarlane found him evasive.[22] In a newspaper interview at the time Asad declared:[23]

> It is a mistake for anyone to believe or to think that we will ever leave Lebanon as a morsel which it is easy for the Israelis to swallow because Lebanon is an Arab country to which we are bound by a common history and a common destiny.

This uncompromising tone was predictable because by August Asad and his Lebanese allies were ready to mount a major assault on President Jumayil.

The battle of the accord

On the eve of battle Asad could take heart from clear signs of disarray in the Israeli camp. Some Israelis were beginning to admit that they had been too greedy in negotiating the accord; its implementation was in doubt; and with continuing guerrilla harassment, Israeli leaders were beginning to ponder whether it would not be wise to pull back unilaterally from the Beirut-Damascus road and the Shuf mountains to a more secure line on the Awali river further south.

The clearest signal that Israel's hopes in the war were collapsing was the psychological change which had occurred in Begin himself. As early as July 1982 American envoys noted that, though he remained dogged, his once defiant confidence had leaked away. The 'Chinese torture' of the mounting Israeli casualties seemed to be taking its toll on him. Even hard-line Moshe Arens and leading officials like David Kimche appeared to have lost faith in the overall strategy.[24] For Begin there was also a personal factor. His wife Aliza to whom he was greatly attached died on 14 November 1982, plunging him into deep depression. But the very week which saw Begin brought low, put Asad on the mend. On 15 November the Soviet leader Leonid Brezhnev was buried and, vigorously backed by his successor Andropov, Asad began his climb-back. Ten months later when Asad was ready for battle, Begin had given up the fight. On 29 August 1983 he told his shocked cabinet colleagues of his intention to resign and immediately secluded himself in his modest house on Ben Nun Street in West Jerusalem, not to reappear. The premiership passed to Yitzhak Shamir.

Two crucial engagements were then fought, the first, brief and brutal, in Beirut itself, the second more prolonged in the Shuf mountains overlooking Beirut. From 28 August to 2 September troops of the Amal militia, in the first major Shi'i challenge to President Jumayil, took on the Lebanese army for control of West Beirut. Although they were narrowly defeated, with heavy casualties on both sides, the message of the revolt was that the Shi'a, hitherto on the fence, now openly sided with Syria against Israel and its Lebanese protégés. These were not the B'albak-based Islamic extremists inspired by Iran who were already in Asad's camp, but the Shi'i mainstream of southern Lebanon represented by Nabih Berri's Amal movement.

The battle for the Shuf was the real turning-point in the Syrian-Israeli contest. It began on 3 September as Israel, anxious to minimize its army's exposure, withdrew to the Awali. By this stage Israel had recognized the error of undue reliance on the Maronites and was attempting to reach understandings with the Shi'a and Druzes, but it was too late. In the Shuf the vacuum created by the Israeli withdrawal left the indigenous Druzes of Walid Junblatt face to face with their traditional enemies, the Maronite fighters of the Lebanese Forces whom Israel had brought into the mountains after its invasion.

In the explosion of violence that followed, Druze forces, stiffened by some 2,000 Palestinians and supported by Syrian artillery and tanks (with some tactical advice from Russian officers), routed the Maronite militiamen. The engagement grew into a vast settling of sectarian scores, with mutual massacres of Druzes and Christians, the displacement of tens of thousands on both sides, and the stampeding of about 100,000 Christians towards Beirut and the now besieged Maronite stronghold of Dayr al-Qamar. The Lebanese army joined the fray against the Druzes in mid-September but failed to tip the balance. By the 24th the triumphant Druzes, backed by Syrian heavy guns, had linked up with Amal in the southern suburbs of Beirut, while the presidential palace, foreign embassies, East Beirut, and the Christian heartlands further north were all exposed to artillery bombardment. Syria's proxies had proved more powerful than those of Israel.

The reversal of fortunes aroused intense concern in Israel and the United States, but also in Europe as contingents of French, Italian and British troops were serving in Lebanon in the multinational force. It was now becoming clear that, by forcing Lebanon into an unequal accord with Israel, Shultz had exposed Jumayil's government to ferocious attack, while Israel's withdrawal to a southern defence line had left the United States holding the Lebanese baby. Intervening in support of the beleaguered Jumayil, aircraft from the US Sixth Fleet struck at Druze and Palestinian artillery emplacements in the mountains on 17 and 19 September, and on the 21st naval guns opened up.

On 23 September McFarlane met Asad to insist on a ceasefire and a halt to Palestinian and Syrian reinforcements for the Druzes. Consciously seeking to overcome the 'Vietnam syndrome' – America's doubts about military action in the aftermath of its south-east Asian débâcle – McFarlane shared George Shultz's view that the United States should be ready to use force in support of its diplomacy. So, on taking leave of Asad, he dropped a bombshell of his own: 'By the way', he said casually, 'the USS *New Jersey* will be off Lebanon within twenty-four hours.'[25]

McFarlane came to believe that this veiled threat might have brought about the Shuf ceasefire which was agreed two days later, on 25 September. In fact, Asad had for the moment got everything he wanted and was ready to fall in with ceasefire proposals worked out in several weeks of shuttling between Damascus and Beirut by Prince Bandar ibn Sultan, Saudi Arabia's ambassador to Washington, and the Saudi-Lebanese tycoon, Rafiq al-Hariri. Syria had been projected to centre stage.

Throughout the summer Asad stiffened his terms: he would consider quitting Lebanon only if Israel pulled out unconditionally, if the multinational force withdrew, and if Lebanon were ruled by a government of national unity. The Lebanon-Israel accord had to be torn up: 'America master-minded this agreement. America has to abrogate it.'[26]

In October 1983 Asad's proxies were able to throw Israel and the United States on the defensive. For Israel the turning-point probably came on 16 October when Israeli troops clashed with a crowd of 150,000 Shi'a who had gathered in the southern Lebanese town of Nabatiya for the 'Ashura ceremonies, the annual commemoration of the martyrdom of Husayn, grandson of the Prophet, in 680 AD.[27] The riots which followed, the killings of civilians by Israeli troops and the curfews they tried to impose roused the Shi'i population of the south as never before. The results were seen in a rash of guerrilla assaults which by the end of the year had claimed another forty Israeli lives. A further blow to Israel was the death in January 1984 of its faithful ally in the border region, Major Sa'd Haddad, who was replaced as head of the Israeli-sponsored South Lebanon Army by Colonel Antoine Lahad – promptly labelled a traitor by Syria. The IDF's pull-back continued in 1984 and by 1985 Israel contented itself with a narrow self-proclaimed 'security zone' in Lebanon.

Inevitably Shi'i anger was directed also at Israel's American patron. On 23 October 1983 the marine contingent at Beirut airport, whose ill-defined mission[28] had not protected it from being sucked into the Lebanese turmoil, suffered a calamitous car-bomb attack which at a stroke killed 241 men. On the same morning, in reprisal for an air raid, the French contingent of the MNF was also car-bombed with the loss of 56 men. Pressure mounted for the recall of the Western forces. But the agony was not yet over.

With McFarlane promoted to National Security Adviser early in November (after William Clark had fallen to sniping from Shultz), yet another American envoy was sent out to deal with Asad and rescue what could be salvaged of US policy. Donald Rumsfeld was an able man who had been chief of staff at the White House and ambassador to NATO. But he came to Syria wearing an Israeli shackle: Washington had promised Jerusalem that he would not be permitted to propose amendments of his own to the 17 May accord but would raise with Asad only such ideas as Israel might wish to put forward. This was an odd position for a negotiator to be in. A second constraint on Rumsfeld was the wrangle which raged in the US government about the use of force. Pro-Israeli officials, like the Kissinger protégé Peter Rodman at the National Security Council, thought Rumsfeld should arrive in Damascus after a show of strength. Shultz himself, his policy sabotaged by Asad, was now petulantly anti-Syrian and ready to unleash the Sixth Fleet. But Defense Secretary Weinberger, who had wanted to pull the marines out of Lebanon even before the 23 October carnage, opposed a rogue policy of force. The row paralysed the Administration. Rumsfeld could neither offer Asad inducements because Israel would not let him, nor threaten punishment because Washington was divided.

Asad clung tenaciously to his objectives, and first and foremost the abrogation of the accord. Rumsfeld argued and shuttled, and (in spite of Paganelli's warnings from the Damascus embassy, a lone voice crying in the wilderness), warplanes and naval guns of the Sixth Fleet went into action in December and again in the new year, the *New Jersey* hurling projectiles the size of Volkswagens to crash ineffectually into the Lebanese mountains. With the tide now running strongly his way, Asad remained unmoved.

McFarlane was eventually to concede the American mistake:[29]

> Our people would have been better off if they had taken the advice of that old comic W. C. Fields: Never kick a man unless he is down. Asad was wounded in 1982 but he was not entirely down, and that was the time not to humiliate him but to engage him. I don't pretend that the Syrians would have come to terms right away, but by ignoring them we suffered two casualties. We affronted President Asad, a man with pan-Arab ambitions, and, equally importantly, we allowed him to become stronger. I think it expressed a rather primitive American understanding of the Middle East to assume that a stable outcome in Lebanon could have been forged without Syria's participation. We made it almost certain Asad would be a spoiler.

On one day of particular American humiliation, 4 December 1983, eight more marines were slain at the airport and two US planes were shot down by Syrian gunfire, giving the black Civil rights leader, the Reverend Jesse Jackson, the political bonus at the turn of the year of coming to Damascus to recover a surviving aviator, Robert Goodman. After a good many more alarms the Italian, French, British and American contingents of the MNF were called home in the early months of 1984.

Asad and his allies had won. Asad for one was somewhat incredulous that the United States had given up so easily. He told another Arab ruler: 'The Americans are like children. When we opposed their policy in Lebanon, they launched one or two raids against us. We fired in the air and, lo and behold, two of their planes were shot down. So they pulled out! Well, let them go!' he said in a great gust of laughter. 'Let them go!'

Once his Western protectors had gone, Amin Jumayil was at Asad's mercy and on 29 February 1984 he travelled to Damascus to pay homage and announce his readiness to abrogate the accord. This was formally done five days later.[30] The Biqa' was firmly in Syrian hands, the Shuf controlled by the Druzes, the Shi'a were driving out the Israelis. Much had been gained.

But Asad had also to conduct a whole series of other battles in the second half of 1983 for the control of the northern port of Tripoli, the first of which was against a local Islamic leader, Shaykh Sa'd Sha'ban whose Tawhid movement derived support from Asad's old enemies, Muslim activists who had fled from Hama. Scarcely had Sha'ban been tamed than Yasir 'Arafat appeared in Tripoli in September 1983 and it took weeks of savage fighting by Fatah dissidents backed by Syria to dislodge him.

Part of this swirling current of violence passed Asad by. Strained to breaking point by the fearful struggles of 1982 and 1983, not to speak of five years of deadly combat with the Muslim Brothers before that, and indeed by a lifetime of unremitting labour, he collapsed on 12 November 1983, going into hospital with a heart complaint which threatened to put an end to a tumultuous period of Syrian history. For Asad, however, it was the exhaustion of victory and not, as for Begin, that of defeat.

The balance sheet

Begin's failure in 1982 to impose his terms on the Arabs marked the first involuntary retreat by Israel from the peak of power it had reached in 1967. It meant too that Greater Israel could no longer be built in an unchallenged environment, and it may have been this disappointment which drove Begin from office. Failure to defeat and expel Syria in June 1982 gave Asad the chance to fight back. Failure to obliterate 'Arafat and his movement ensured the PLO's ultimate revival but, this apart, it was an Israeli mistake to imagine that smashing the PLO's Lebanese infrastructure would somehow break the national spirit of the Palestinians in the occupied territories. The uprising in Gaza and the West Bank which began in December 1987 had its roots in Israel's setback in Lebanon in 1983. Other Israeli errors were to try to build a friendly Lebanon, able to deliver a 'second peace treaty', on minority Maronite rule at a time when rival communities like the Shi'a and even the Druzes were on the ascent. Above all, in seeking to compel its weaker neighbour to come to terms, Israel was too brutal in attack, too indifferent to Arab life, too demanding in negotiation and too scornful of Lebanon's sovereignty. Such abuses raised up ferocious enemies on Israel's border. Begin's crude interventionism greatly set back the cause of Arab-Israeli co-existence, causing men like Asad to doubt whether it would ever be possible to live with such a neighbour.

The United States, and George Shultz personally, suffered a mini-Vietnam as America's might was seen to be ineffective and its diplomacy unsuccessful. Having allowed Israel into Lebanon, it was unable to protect the Palestinians from massacre, the Lebanese government from its enemies, the accord from destruction, and even its own marines from maiming and death. The ignominious scuttle from Lebanon in early 1984 marked the lowest point in American fortunes in the Middle East since the Second World War. This nemesis was the result of a steady departure from an independent Middle East policy and the pursuit instead of actions aligned with or manipulated by Israel. The journey down this road began with the Six Day War when the United States condoned Israel's blitz, picked up speed when Henry Kissinger was in the driving seat, and reached collision point in the faltering hands of the Reagan Administration. America's failure was one of omission, of passivity: it allowed its ally to overreach itself – in illegal settlements on Arab land, in raids and annexations from Baghdad to the Golan, in repeated ceasefire violations, and then in the invasion of Lebanon. Washington paid the bills but could exercise no control.

The Lebanese misadventure did not cause Shultz to correct his aim. On the contrary, perhaps because he took the defeat personally, he plunged even deeper into the relationship with Israel, championing a full-blown military alliance and coming to see Arab and Iranian terrorism as a phenomenon quite separate from its causes, a blindness which was to draw the United States into the quagmires of counter-terror, hostage taking, Irangate and other murky enterprises. Just as Carter found himself completing Kissinger's agenda, so Shultz completed Haig's: the ill-fated Israel-Lebanon accord, Israel's reward for its invasion, was in a direct line of descent from Haig's 'green light'.

For Asad, the defeat of Begin and of Shultz was the foreign policy triumph of his presidency. The 1982 war was not only a war for Lebanon or for the West Bank, but also a war to determine whose will was to prevail in the Middle East. Against great odds Asad managed to frustrate Israel's bid for hegemony and hold the line. Almost for the first time in their modern history, the Arabs came to realize that there was no preordained fatality about an Israeli victory or their own defeat.

But Asad's efforts to defend the Arab Levant against Israeli incursions meant riding roughshod over the narrower but no less legitimate interests of those Lebanese, Palestinians and Jordanians who disagreed with his strategy and wished to pursue their own salvation free from the dictates of Damascus. To the extent that these lesser actors continued to defy him, Asad's victory was not total, nor was he able in the coming years to substitute for Israel's proposed new order a stable order of his own.

There was a further consideration. The defeat of Israel and of the United States involved the use of irregular methods: Bashir Jumayil was assassinated, the American embassy blown up, the marines slaughtered, the Israelis harried by hit-and-run guerrillas. Syria was not necessarily directly implicated in these acts of violence but it supported the people who carried them out and above all it benefited from them. Were such methods a resort to terrorism or the legitimate tactics of national resistance? Was Bashir a patriot or a Quisling? Was the multinational force of Americans and Europeans a neutral peacekeeper or did it degenerate into just another militia in the Lebanese civil war, attempting to impose an alien order? Asad was a cautious, responsible leader who for years had painstakingly sought to explain Arab fears and hopes, rights and grievances to a succession of American visitors – Kissinger, Nixon, Carter, Vance, Brzezinski, Shultz, Habib, McFarlane, and the rest. But after all those hours of patient exposition he had not been heard. By condoning Israel's 1982 war the United States had shown a disregard of his interests, convincing him that he was to be driven to the edge of national extinction. With his back to the wall he fought with the means at his disposal. The paradox was that he was a man of order who detested anarchy and was intensely conscious of the risks of using violent and not wholly controllable surrogates. But he felt he had no choice. 'If they really want us to be terrorists, we can be', he told his Druze ally, Walid Junblatt.[31]

In late April 1984 Peter Jennings of ABC asked Asad in a television interview whether he viewed terrorism as a legitimate tool of war. Asad replied:[32]

> We are against terrorism. But what is terrorism? Terrorism is one country invading another, occupying its land and expelling its people. If you mean by terrorism acts committed by gangs of robbers and murderers and the like, we are against it. But the acts of people against the occupiers of their land have not throughout history been known as acts of terrorism. We support the national resistance of all peoples . . .

24

The Brothers' War

On 12 November 1983 after working late in the ground floor office of his residence, Asad felt unwell. He went upstairs to bed, slept poorly and in the morning telephoned his doctor. After examining him, the doctor called in another physician for a second opinion. They recommended immediate treatment for a suspected heart complaint.[1]

Asad was taken to the Shami hospital in Damascus where he was placed in intensive care. Although the specialists detected some irregularity in his heart beat, they could find nothing organically wrong with him. He had long suffered from diabetes, aggravated by a sweet tooth, and as a young man had complained of headaches and eye strain. But these were old complaints which he had come to terms with. The truth was that the once fit pilot officer had undermined his health by years of irregular meals, lack of fresh air and exercise, and unremitting work. The sedentary life had produced varicose veins, for which he had had an operation, and the doctors now feared that phlebitis might set in. But the real cause of his collapse was exhaustion: Asad was simply worn out. The master of Syria for thirteen years was suddenly taken out of play.

His doctors ordered a complete rest and gave him powerful sedatives to enforce it. Asad, who rarely took sleeping pills, found himself dazed and unsteady. This incapacity and the fact that his door was barred by his doctors even to the top men of the regime aroused the wildest uncertainties. Leaderless and panic-stricken, believing him to be on the point of death, his associates sought to gain time by lamely announcing to the public that the president was being treated for appendicitis. The structure Asad had built, wholly dependent on himself, was in danger of breaking down without him.

Asad collapsed at the height of his battle royal for Lebanon. Less than three weeks earlier the American marines had been slaughtered and it seemed that a riposte against Syria, considered an accomplice of

421

the assault, could not be long delayed. US aircraft were overflying Syrian positions in the Lebanese mountains. The armada including the formidable *New Jersey*, symbol of Washington's will to outface him, had already used its guns against his allies. As Asad turned the screw on Amin Jumayil to force him to abrogate the Israel-Lebanon accord, a shooting war with the United States seemed only too probable. And just then Yuri Andropov, the Soviet leader who had given him weapons and guarantees on an unprecedented scale, fell desperately ill. On 11 November Foreign Minister Khaddam returned from an overnight hop to Moscow with the grim news that Andropov was dying and the Kremlin in no shape to take bold or quick decisions. Asad's deterrent posture against Israel was threatened. Worry about Andropov undoubtedly contributed to Asad's own collapse.[2]

The United States was not the only enemy Syria was jousting with that November. Israel was intensifying reprisal raids on the Biqa' and along the Beirut-Damascus highway, following the blowing up in early November of an Israeli intelligence headquarters in Tyre in which twenty-nine people had been killed. President Mitterrand of France had condemned Syrian intervention in Lebanon and vowed that the French contingent car-bombed at the same time as the US marines would be avenged. In Tripoli, the ferocious clash of wills between 'Arafat and Syrian-backed Fatah dissidents was reaching a climax. The Nahr al-Barid camp, an 'Arafat stronghold, had been overrun and the casualties ran into hundreds. To tighten the siege, Syrian artillery had set fire to the refinery and the port, causing damage put at tens of millions of dollars. With 'Arafat holed up in his Tripoli bunker, Damascus had come under intense Arab pressure to end the shameful inter-Arab scrap, but Asad had developed an implacable hatred for the PLO chairman and was determined to throw him into the sea.

In Lebanon as a whole, Israel's order had been defeated but Syria's was by no means imposed. A clutch of leading Lebanese politicians – Maronite, Sunni, Shi'i and Druze – had met in Geneva from 31 October to 8 November, for a 'conference of national reconciliation', in a forlorn attempt to put their shattered country together again. All had come to recognize Syria as the ringmaster, and in deference to it agreed to reaffirm Lebanon's 'Arab identity' and to make Israel's withdrawal a national priority. But as Khaddam reported to Asad on his return from Geneva, David Kimche, Israel's 'Mr Lebanon', had been lurking in the wings and the Lebanese Forces, Israel's proxies, had rejected the conference decisions. Meanwhile, on the ground in Beirut there was anything but harmony: kidnappings, skirmishings, bombardments between East and West, between Maronites and Druzes, between President Jumayil and his enemies continued unabated. Nevertheless Syria was undoubtedly winning, and Jumayil himself was expected in Damascus on 14 November to concede publicly that the accord he had signed with Israel on 17 May was null and void.

It was at this moment, on the eve of his hard-fought victory, that Asad fell ill, leaving everything in the balance. A deeply chagrined Khaddam had to telephone Jumayil and ask him to postpone his trip – in view of the Syrian president's 'appendicitis'. The excuse did not hold water for long, as the foreign press soon unearthed the fact that Asad's appendix had been removed some twenty years earlier.

Asad spent over two weeks in hospital before moving to a private villa in the Ghuta, the Damascus green belt, for a month's convalescence. Although his doctors had been unable to diagnose any definite complaint, he continued to feel very weak. The timing of his collapse, at the peak of the struggle with Israel and the United States, aroused suspicions among those responsible for his safety that he was perhaps the victim of some insidious attack. So for his stay in the country his entire personal staff – cooks, maids, nurses – was changed as were the furnishings and household objects around him. Inevitably his health continued to be the subject of much gossip. He was rumoured to be paralysed down one side, to have been shot in the chest by an assassin, to be incapacitated, to be finished. Syria's habitual secrecy fed the rumours, but in his cunning way Asad may have relished lying low to watch the ripples and confuse his opponents. In due course, to soothe domestic opinion, Syrian television showed him in conference on 27 November and three days later there was a brief somewhat contrived film clip of him opening a new bridge in Damascus.

Fear of a US plot

This picture of business as usual drew a veil not only over Asad's still uncertain health but also over the early rumblings of an internal power struggle.[3] No one had been more thunderstruck by Asad's illness than Rif'at, Lord Protector of the realm, who after three sleepless nights at the hospital looked more ravaged than Asad himself. From his sickbed Asad sent word to form a six-man committee to which he entrusted the day-to-day running of affairs: Khaddam (Foreign Minister), Ahmar (assistant secretary of the party's National Command), Tlas (Defence Minister), Shihabi (Chief of Staff), Kasm (Prime Minister), and Mashariqa (assistant secretary of the Regional Command). But Rif'at, more senior than some, more powerful than any, was not included.

An event then occurred which would have been unimaginable had Asad been on his feet. Fearing that he was dying and alarmed at the changes his death might bring, the country's most powerful generals turned to Rif'at for leadership,[4] perhaps seeing him as the best champion of a system on which they had thrived for a decade and more. As Asad's brother he was a symbol of continuity; as head of the strongest strike force he was a pillar of the regime; he was a victor of the war against the Muslim Brothers, the worst internal danger they had all faced. Above all, Rif'at was the foremost baron in the state and could therefore be counted on to leave undisturbed the baronies and fiefs of others – the security agencies, armoured divisions, state enterprises, missile corps and the like. The last thing the generals wanted was to see the succession pass to the six government and party functionaries on the committee Asad had set up. In their eyes, the members of this committee were no more than talented executives, front men, not the underpinnings of the system which the field commanders and intelligence chiefs saw themselves to be. Appalled at the vacuum which threatened them, the generals now overturned Asad's arrangements.

At their instigation, Shihabi and Khaddam called on Rif'at at his house in Mezze to put it to him that a man of his importance could not be excluded at such a moment of crisis from the ruling councils of the country. Rif'at said that he must bow to the president's wishes, but he was soon persuaded. A full meeting of the Regional Command was then convened – just nineteen members in the absence of Asad himself and of his Information Minister, Ahmad Iskandar Ahmad, then dying of a brain tumour. It voted to substitute itself for Asad's six-man committee. This was a neat way of bringing Rif'at to the centre of affairs.

The success of these manoeuvres depended on Asad's continued incapacity. But he was getting better and when during his convalescence he heard what had happened, he was extremely displeased. Any deviation from unquestioning obedience aroused his suspicions. Summoning the top generals, he berated them for having departed from his express wishes and thus opened the door to unpredictable dangers. They had to be on full alert. Did they not see that the advancement of Rif'at was an American-Saudi plot to unseat him?

How had Asad reached this startling conclusion? In those anxious weeks his greatest worry was the war for Lebanon. While under treatment he had neglected to keep up with domestic affairs, but he had insisted on following the Lebanese crisis by telephone hour by hour. He noted that Yitzhak Shamir had returned from a visit to Washington in late November with a fistful of agreements ushering in (in Shamir's own words) 'a new era in Israeli-US relations'. There were to be joint American exercises with the IDF, US equipment was to be stored in Israel, the embargo on cluster bombs was to be lifted, military aid was to be increased. It appeared that Reagan and Shultz wished to compensate Israel for the aborted accord. At the same time, American accusations against Syria, notably from Caspar Weinberger, for its alleged role in the massacre of the marines became more explicit. When Syrian gunners shot down two US planes on 4 December and an American pilot was captured, Asad was certain that the United States would seek to punish him. His brother Rif'at seemed a possible instrument.

The younger brothers

The relationship between Asad and Rif'at retained something of the pattern of their childhood when across the gap of seven years the elder had compelled respect from the rebellious younger brother. Rif'at bore a noticeable resemblance to his brother, with the same strong heavy body and the same quizzical, sometimes mischievous expression, but their personalities were different: Asad serious and deliberate, Rif'at hedonistic and impulsive, altogether a more physical man but with a quick intelligence nonetheless. He laughed a great deal more than his brother, and in the tradition of Arab chiefs was generous to a fault. While Asad, chained to his desk, became totally absorbed in affairs of state and especially in foreign policy, Rif'at threw himself into building a dedicated following in his Defence Companies and in the country. He exercised arbitrary powers, enriched himself and his cronies, went on confidential missions to friends and enemies alike, and engaged in other murky ventures in the tangled world of Arab politics and business.

Unlike the many yes-men in Asad's entourage, Rif'at could genuinely claim to have shared power with his brother. In the party schism of 1966, the security force he commanded had arrested Amin al-Hafiz and Muhammad 'Umran. In 1969 he had defeated Salah Jadid's security chief, 'Abd al-Karim al-Jundi, paving the way for Asad's seizure of power. He had helped crush the Islamic insurrection in 1980–82, probably saving the regime. These were his credentials. But having triumphed over so many enemies, he began to write his own rules. He had a long arm extending to interests in many parts of the country and across the mountains into Lebanon. His Defence Companies had become a highly mobile private army 55,000-strong, with its own armour, artillery, air defence, and a fleet of troop-carrying helicopters. It was more than a match for any other Syrian unit and the pay and privileges of its men aroused the envy of the rest of the army. Rif'at shared the taste for hunting, womanizing and playing the big shot of his friend and patron Prince 'Abdallah of Saudi Arabia, whose visits to Damascus were the occasion for all-night parties at which in early 1984 Tamara, an American belly dancer, was the star. Perhaps influenced to think dynastically by the Saudi model, Rif'at had married four wives and fathered seventeen children. He inspired loyalty and admiration in his followers, but outside his charmed circle was widely feared and resented. His haste to 'modernize' the country sometimes caused grave offence, as on the occasion in 1983 when his female paratroopers ripped the veils from women in the street, forcing Asad publicly to disown such excess.

Asad had often made use of Rif'at but, with no great confidence in his judgment, it is unlikely that he ever considered him a possible successor. Asad had dedicated his life to the defence of a certain political line on how the struggle with Israel should be conducted. He did not trust his brother with this heritage. He disliked (as did his discreet but influential wife) Rif'at's high living, scorned his weakness for the United States where Rif'at had bought a million-dollar home, and distrusted several of his foreign friendships including those with Yasir 'Arafat and with King Hasan of Morocco, whose covert contacts with Israel were notorious.

To sum up, Asad, believing himself threatened by Western enemies, by Israel and by moderate Arab states, came to see Rif'at as a chink in his armour. The brother who had once been useful, then necessary, then an embarrassment, had become a danger.

In fairness it is unlikely that Rif'at ever seriously aspired to rule in his brother's stead. Psychologically, he longed rather for his brother to recognize his importance – something he felt Asad had denied him from childhood – and of course he wished to live richly and exuberantly without let or hindrance as befitted a member of a ruling family. But essentially he wanted Asad to accept him as a partner, with a free hand on the home front.

However, on Asad's illness in November 1983 when the generals and the party command rallied behind him, Rif'at misinterpreted this gesture as signifying a total commitment to his leadership. Masterful by nature, he now behaved with all the assertiveness of an heir apparent. He started to press for the prime minister's resignation and the formation of a new cabinet. Posters showing him in commanding pose and wearing paratrooper uniform suddenly appeared all over the capital.

He was quickly disabused. No sooner did Asad show signs of recovering than support for Rif'at faded. Taking their cue from Asad, the generals stopped believing that Rif'at could protect their interests and came to see him instead as a threat to the country and to themselves. Suspecting that he truly planned to supplant his brother and assume power, they set about putting obstacles in his way.

The job had to be done discreetly because Rif'at commanded a real army. His four elite brigades – three armoured and one mechanized, all within five miles of Damascus – controlled its approaches with tanks and artillery, whereas the forces of other generals were further out. A head-on challenge was out of the question. There was perhaps another reason for caution. The generals could not be sure how profound and enduring was Asad's animus against Rif'at. Was this a family tiff which would blow over, exposing anyone who rashly took sides? Was the leader putting his generals' loyalty to the test?

An early pointer that Asad meant business came when he disciplined another of his brothers, Jamil, who was known to be close to Rif'at. Mid-way in age between Hafiz and Rif'at, Jamil had become the effective boss of Latakia. An eloquent, ambitious, politically minded man, Jamil had qualified as a lawyer but did not practise. As the president's brother he was elected a member of the People's Assembly by a wide margin over other candidates. An instrument of his power was the *'Ali al-Murtada* association, founded in 1981, a political grouping behind a religious facade. Although it was not a structured movement Jamil may have intended it as a rival to the local Ba'th party, and it certainly provided him with a network of patronage stretching far beyond the town. Scores of buses bringing his supporters into Latakia from as far afield as the Jazira would line up outside his large house and garden where he kept a stable of fine Arab horses, mainly gifts from tribal chiefs. He would slaughter sheep for the visitors and make a grandiloquent speech. In mid-December 1983, as Asad recovered from his illness, the *Murtada* association was closed down on orders from Damascus, an indication that the president was reining in his family.

Containing Rif'at

The task of containing Rif'at fell to the generals. Most were men from 'Alawi peasant families whom Asad had placed – and kept for years –

in positions of great personal influence. Asad liked continuity. His habit was to leave a man in a job if he was satisfied with his performance. On security and intelligence matters, the covert side of the regime, his most trusted associates were 'Ali Duba, head of military intelligence, Muhammad al-Khuly, head of air force intelligence, and Fu'ad 'Absi, the civilian intelligence supremo whose powerful deputy in charge of security was Muhammad Nasif. Despite their titles there were no clear boundaries between these agencies, all three answering directly to Asad himself.

'Ali Duba, a tall, fair man from the village of Qurfays, shared some of Asad's traits: his sardonic humour, his unsocial tastes, his love of literature and his mix of ruthlessness and sentiment. When he was in his twenties his first-born son, to whom he was deeply attached, fell ill after developing an allergy. Rushed down the mountain to a doctor, the child was wrongly diagnosed as suffering from typhoid fever. He was given an injection and died. Crazed with grief Duba summoned his friends to gather threateningly round the doctor's clinic. 'What you do today', his brother cautioned him, 'will determine the sort of man you will be for the rest of your life.' Duba called off his men. Although he later fathered five other children, he was said never to show as much overt affection again.

Muhammad al-Khuly was more pleasure-loving than Duba and more visible in society, while the highly intelligent Muhammad Nasif was the most secretive of the lot, virtually lived in his office and was one of the very few people allowed to telephone Asad at any time. Apart from heading what was in effect the political police, he was one of Asad's key advisers on Shi'i affairs whether in Lebanon or Iran. He had been close to Musa al-Sadr and to Iranian revolutionary leaders such as Qotbzadeh and Tabataba'i, and frequently travelled from Damascus to Bonn and Switzerland, the poles of Iran's Western networks. These covert props of the regime contrasted with the visible trio publicly at the president's side: Foreign Minister Khaddam, Defence Minister Tlas and Information Minister Ahmad Iskandar Ahmad (although the last was soon to die).

Among the generals commanding key units, Rif'at's principal rival was 'Ali Haydar, head of the Special Forces, an elite formation of 10,000–15,000 shock troops who like the Defence Companies had played a prominent role in putting down the Islamic insurrection and who in 1982 had fought Israel in the Lebanon War. Haydar came from the village of Hillat 'Ara – one of the highest in the 'Alawi mountains, two hours' hard walking from the coast when he was a boy. Like Asad he joined the Ba'th before enrolling at the Military Academy. Another of Rif'at's rivals was 'Adnan Makhluf, a cousin of Asad's wife, who commanded the 10,000-strong Presidential Guard. It was responsible for security around the presidential palace, in the Malki residential quarter where the top people lived, and in central Damascus as a whole. Makhluf had originally served in Rif'at's Defence Companies but after a quarrel had been given command of the Presidential Guard on the suggestion of his kinsman, Asad's brother-in-law Muhammad Makhluf. Yet another rival was the president's cousin, 'Adnan al-Asad, who commanded a smaller security force, the Struggle Companies.

In addition, four prominent regular army generals enjoyed Asad's special trust: Shafiq Fayadh and Ibrahim Safi, commanders of the Third and First armoured divisions, 'Ali Salih, head of the missile corps, and 'Ali 'Aslan, chief of operations and deputy chief of staff. Fayadh, a rough bear of a man, came from 'Ayn al-'Arus near Qurdaha, while Safi had made good from humble origins as the son of a landless sharecropper. 'Aslan, widely considered a sober man and one of the ablest members of the officer corps, had a distinguished record in the 1973 war and in the subsequent dramatic expansion of the armed forces. These were the generals who had first rallied round Rif'at, then turned against him, and who in early 1984 began manoeuvring to hold him in check.

Towards the end of December 1983 Asad felt well enough to start seeing foreign visitors again – but without managing to quell speculation that he was suffering from a terminal disease. Two French journalists from the weekly *Le Point*, who interviewed him on 20 December when he was still resting in the Ghuta, reported him as saying, 'I still feel young but my body and my heart don't permit me to stay as young as I would like' – a remark seized upon as evidence that he had suffered a heart attack. In early January 1984, back in Damascus, he handed over the captured US flyer, Lieutenant Goodman, to the Reverend Jesse Jackson, received Britain's Foreign Secretary, Sir Geoffrey Howe, and argued with the American envoy Donald Rumsfeld against the background of gunfire from the Sixth Fleet. In the minds of all these visitors was the question: Was this a dying man?

At this point in the story, Asad's suspicions of foreign intrigue hardened. He became certain that his enemies were seeking to exploit his fragile health and the rift in the regime which foreign embassies were now reporting. His intelligence services were persuaded that Rif'at was being encouraged by King Hasan of Morocco and Prince

'Abdallah of Saudi Arabia – backed discreetly by Washington – to stage a coup timed to coincide with a show of force by the US fleet. Asad instructed 'Ali Duba to put Rif'at and his principal associates under surveillance, while 'Ali Haydar and Shafiq Fayadh were ordered to move troops and tanks into the capital to act as a counterweight to the Defence Companies. Beyond the immediate threat, Asad knew that, if he failed to control Rif'at, he might risk losing control of the other generals also.

On 23 February Prince 'Abdallah flew in to Damascus to a welcome from Rif'at's people which upstaged the formal greetings of Prime Minister Kasm. Had the prince arrived with a chequebook, diplomats speculated, to inaugurate a new regime? To forestall any such mischief, Asad ordered Chief of Staff Shihabi to relieve Rif'at's security aide, Colonel Salim Barakat, of his duties. Asad wanted him out in half an hour. Barakat appealed to Rif'at to protect him and Rif'at telephoned Shihabi to ask for forty-eight hours' grace. But Shihabi could only say that the president's orders were absolutely clear. Refusing to surrender his job, Barakat burst into 'Ali Duba's office brandishing a pistol. He was disarmed, roughed up and taken away. Some hours later Rif'at managed to reach Asad on the telephone.

'What have you done with my man Barakat?'

'I think we've executed him', Asad replied laconically.

'Why should you do that?'

'I gave the order to transfer him but he wouldn't go.'

Some while later Rif'at found Barakat in jail, secured his release and arranged a safer job for him in a university department.

The confrontation

Repeated attempts were made to defuse the crisis through negotiations. Rif'at sent his brother Jamil to intercede with Asad but the president's unforgiving answer was: 'I am your elder brother to whom you owe obedience. Don't forget that I am the one who made you all.' Asad continued to shorten the reins on Rif'at and the latter, now seriously alarmed, sought to protect what freedom he had left.

By 27 February 1984 Syria seemed on the verge of a bloodbath with both sides confronting each other angrily, guns at the ready. At strategic points in the capital, 'Ali Haydar's Special Forces in maroon berets faced Rif'at's Defence Companies in cinnamon berets, while Adnan Makhluf's Presidential Guard put on a show of force in the boulevards around the palace. At night some sporadic shooting was heard but there was no decisive clash of arms.

The irony was that this dangerous turmoil at home coincided with the sealing of victory in Lebanon: on 29 February President Amin Jumayil arrived at last in Damascus to announce his government's decision to abrogate the Israel-Lebanon accord of 17 May 1983. That same night, 29 February-1 March, the Regional Command met in emergency session to find a way out of the internal crisis.

The solution reached was expressed in the appointment, by presidential decree on 11 March, of three Vice-presidents – with Khaddam, Rif'at's enemy and a point of focus for the generals, heading the list. Next came Rif'at himself, named in the decree with no other rank or title save that of 'Doctor' (a reference to a doctorate he had been awarded by Moscow University for a thesis on class struggle in Syria thought to be the work of a Russian-speaking 'Alawi, Ahmad Dawud). The third Vice-president was Zahayr Mashariqa, Asad's assistant on the Regional Command.

Rif'at's promotion to vice-presidential rank was in fact a demotion, seeing that his duties were left unspecified and would now depend on the president's favour. Command of his Defence Companies passed by another presidential decree to Colonel Muhammad Ghanim. Rif'at could not contest his own removal from the job but, summoning his officers, he called on them to elect a new commander – whereupon they chose his son-in-law, Mu'in Nasif. The unfortunate Ghanim, caught between Asad's orders and Rif'at's counter-orders, stepped down.

The Kremlin (where Konstantin Chernenko had emerged as leader on Andropov's death on 10 February 1984) watched developments in Syria with alarm and a good deal of bewilderment. Was their friend Asad in real trouble just when he had seen off the US fleet? Anxious to forestall any violent change which might put at risk hard-won gains in Lebanon, the Russians sent Gaydar Aliyev, Politburo member and first deputy premier, to Damascus to find out at first hand what was going on. Bearing a warm message from Chernenko,[5] he arrived on 10 March and interviewed all the principals, Asad, Rif'at, Khaddam and the others.

But whatever mediatory role Aliyev may have played, the settlement announced on 11 March did not long survive: Asad was still bent on stripping Rif'at of power to rock the boat and Rif'at was equally determined not to be reduced to insignificance. The squeeze on him which had begun in the last weeks of 1983 continued into March 1984 with the transfer and arrest of several of his loyalists and even the death of some.

Rif'at came to feel he was himself in danger when he was told of an anecdote Asad had related at a meeting of his commanders. During the Second World War the Germans had captured Stalin's son, then a young Red Army lieutenant, and proposed exchanging him for a German general held by the Russians. They threatened that if Stalin did not agree to the trade, the lad would be killed. But Stalin would not yield. 'So be it', he answered grimly – and wept. Rif'at's acid comment was: 'My brother's tears are dear to me. I don't want him to shed them on my account.' The Stalin story sounded ominously like a contract on his life.

On 30 March Rif'at could bear the tension no longer. With the noose tightening round his neck and perhaps egged on by sycophants and foreign friends, he ordered his Defence Companies to move in strength on Damascus – and seize power. His tanks drove right into the capital, outgunning the units of his rivals. A squadron of his T-72s took up position outside the General Intelligence headquarters at the Kafar Susa roundabout on the airport road from where they could shell the city. More armour occupied the gardens between the Sheraton Hotel and the new Guest Palace where minefields were also laid. Mechanised infantry surrounded the Meridien Hotel and the compound housing the bureaux of the party's Regional Command. Hastily deployed against this show of force were Shafiq Fayadh's tanks and, in the international fairground along the river, 'Ali Haydar's shock troops. Civilians in the battle zones were bundled out of their houses. It looked like civil war. Foreign military attachés, venturing cautiously on to roof-tops with binoculars, reported that shooting could break out at any moment.

Watching the unfolding drama, diplomats were puzzled by Asad's apparent slowness to react. He seemed almost inactive in the face of his brother's challenge. Had the two sides come to blows in the capital, the destruction would have been very great and the regime's image irreparably tarnished – that is, if it survived at all. All Asad's achievements in thirteen years of effort seemed at risk – and the battle for Lebanon lost after being so nearly won. Yet Asad did not move.

Gambling on his ability to control his brother even *in extremis*, Asad chose not to show his hand. As when he was preparing his counter-attack in Lebanon, he may have wanted to lull his enemies into a sense of false confidence. For this was not a crisis into which he had stumbled unawares, and the outcome was to demonstrate that his ability to master events was unimpaired. In weeks of cat-and-mouse manoeuvring, he had deliberately allowed Rif'at enough rope to hang himself before driving him into open sedition, no doubt to give himself ample justification for removing him altogether. Nor had Asad failed to take family precautions. The day before Rif'at's march on

Damascus, he had arranged for his ailing mother, then in her late eighties, to be flown down from Qurdaha to stay at Rif'at's home. He knew she still exercised a compelling influence over her youngest child. Compared to a player of Asad's astuteness, Rif'at was a political simpleton. The stage was set for the clash of wills.

With Damascus divided between armed camps seemingly on the brink of war, Asad put on full military uniform and, accompanied only by his eldest son Basil, drove without guards or escort through the empty streets to his brother's elaborately defended positions in and around the residential district of Mezze where both Rif'at's residence and the headquarters of his Defence Companies were located. Rif'at had placed tanks in outlying orchards and along the main thoroughfare and artillery on Mount Qasiun overlooking the city. On the way to challenge this concentration of strength, Asad stopped at the Kafar Susa roundabout which was manned by Rif'at's tanks and ordered the officer in charge to return to barracks.

At Rif'at's house in Mezze the brothers came at last face to face. 'You want to overthrow the regime?' Asad asked. 'Here I am. I *am* the regime.' For an hour they stormed at each other but, in his role of elder brother and with his mother in the house, Asad could not fail to win the contest. Rif'at chose to accept Asad's pledge that his interests and assets would be respected, deferring to him as he had so often done in their youth. His friends later reported that he judged the decision to give up the fight to have been the greatest single mistake of his life.

There was a further dimension to the struggle. The Russians intervened on Asad's side, throwing their weight behind him. Rif'at was a brave and daring man, but also a deeply emotional one. He simply could not bring himself to declare open war on a brother whom he admired and respected and whose approval he yearned for, however deeply he resented him.

After the confrontation, Asad toured Rif'at's units deployed in the Mezze area ordering them to stand down, amd in the next day or two, to the vast relief of the populace, the tanks and armed men disappeared from the streets of the capital. Asad's uncontested authority was manifestly restored.

The dénouement

Yet loose ends remained to be tied up. While Rif'at's principal power base was the Defence Companies, he had other centres of influence across the country. He was involved, for example, in numerous businesses and property developments where he had placed protégés as managers, workers and guards. He was also an enthusiastic promoter of young people. One of his controversial schemes was, as has been mentioned, to draft young men and women into parachute training which earned them bonus points in their school-leaving examination, to the resentment of less athletic students. High marks enhanced their chance of a place in the much sought-after medical and engineering faculties. He adopted the romantic word *al-Fursan*, The Knights, as the title of a magazine he published, as the name of a housing estate in Mezze where he lodged some of his followers, and in general as a label for his ideal of energetic youth devoted to both self-improvement and the public good.

Perhaps his most ambitious cultural project was the League of Higher Graduates (*Rabitat al-kharijin al-'ulia*) to which at first only holders of second degrees were admitted but which was later widened to all graduates, although members were accepted only some years after leaving university and if they could point to some success in their careers. The League's fifteen branches round the country, assembling several thousand members, were forums where professional men and women discussed public affairs outside the constraints of the Ba'th party. Rif'at's rationale for drawing educated people into the League was Syria's need in competition with Israel to improve its intellectual life. He was keen on research centres, computers and language-teaching, and a number of such facilities were built under his patronage. But however public-spirited his efforts, his critics saw them as attempts to build a personal power base.

A couple of weeks after Rif'at's bruising encounter with Asad, his aides announced that a League rally would be held on 17 April, Syria's Independence Day, in the amphitheatre of Damascus University. But when Rif'at's public relations men sought permission to televise the occasion, they were denied use of the auditorium. The venue was then switched to the Officers' Club – whereupon the authorities cancelled the rally altogether. The order could have come only from Asad himself. Defiantly Rif'at then gave a lunch at the Sheraton Hotel for some five hundred guests – League members but also ministers and high officials – at which in a two-hour speech he recklessly attacked some of Asad's most fundamental policies.

Rif'at's primary motive was to defend himself against the charge of disloyalty: it was as if, over the heads of the lunch guests, he was speaking to the elder brother in the presidential palace.

My brother doesn't seem to like me any more. When he sees me, he frowns. But I'm not an American agent, I'm not a Saudi agent, I've not plotted against my country. Have you forgotten that ten years ago I was called the 'Red officer'? [a reference to his role as a 'back channel' to the Soviets in the mid-1970s when Asad was negotiating with Kissinger]. When I contacted Prince 'Abdallah and the Saudis agreed to help us, it was because Syria needed money. I was working for Syria, for its economy and government. Why should I now be called a Saudi and American agent?

He could not avoid referring to the near catastrophe two weeks earlier when his tanks and those of 'Ali Haydar and Shafiq Fayadh trained their guns on each other across the squares and gardens of Damascus.

Had I been foolish, I could have destroyed the whole city, but I love this place! My men have been here for eighteen years [a reference to the role his security force played in the intra-party clash of 1966]. The people are used to us, they like us, and now these commandos ['Ali Haydar's men] want to chase us out.

There was more to Rif'at's defence than personal apologetics. Although some saw him as a thug, Rif'at was also the champion of what amounted to a counter-culture. The ideas he promoted conjured up a wholly different vision of Syria and its place in the world from that of Asad. His League was an anti-party group in competition with the Ba'th and his followers were an anti-establishment elite, cleverer and more independent minded than the placemen and party bureaucrats of the regime.

The Sheraton lunch was Rif'at's most spectacular performance, but it was only the last of several. For months, at private and semi-private meetings, he had been developing an indictment of his brother's policies. Why was Syria spending so much in Lebanon when it needed investment at home? Was it wise to risk war with the United States and Europe and earn a reputation for terrorism into the bargain? Why not agree to simultaneous Israeli and Syrian withdrawal from Lebanon? Another favourite theme was Syria's over-dependence on the Soviet Union and on dubious Soviet guarantees. True, the Russians had vastly increased Syrian strength, but the pursuit of parity with Israel had its dangers. It could be achieved only if Syria were fully integrated into Soviet defence plans, but the price of such a full-blown military alliance with Moscow would be to rule out all independence of policy. Khaddam (a man Rif'at had no time for) boasted of having attracted one paw of the Soviet bear to Syrian soil. But what if the other three were to follow? Little Syria would then be tossed helplessly into the air.

On the Palestine question Rif'at made no secret of his opposition to Syria's support for Fatah dissidents such as Abu Nidal and Abu Musa in their war with 'Arafat. What was the sense of the feud with the PLO chairman? Why throw him out of Tripoli? Did he not have the right to be there, seeing that the Israelis were still in Tyre? And why was Syria so ferociously opposed to a Husayn-'Arafat deal which might one day recover much of the West Bank from an Israeli Labour government? Why not allow the Palestinians to proceed down this promising road?

Syria's alliance with Iran was another bone of contention. Rif'at had no love for Iraq's Saddam Husayn, but he rebelled against the close relationship with the Iranian mullahs whom he considered as reactionary and fanatical as the Islamic enemies Syria had fought at home. How could the regime pursue one policy in Hama and another in Tehran? Was the whole struggle against the Muslim Brothers nothing but a sham, without ideological commitment?

Rif'at was no less radical in questioning Syria's domestic orientation. 'We speak of freedom, but we are only free to eat and get married', he would complain. Presenting himself as an advocate of economic and political liberalization, he argued that it was good for Syrians to try to hoist themselves up to the standards of others, to enjoy consumer luxuries as well as the luxury of free speech. Syria, he charged, had deviated from the ideals and principles for which Asad had carried out his Corrective Movement of 1970. With ideas such as this, it was hardly surprising that, in Asad's eyes, Rif'at was guilty not just of heresy but of something close to treachery.

Most Syrians, it should be said, did not regard Rif'at as the liberal and humane pragmatist he made himself out to be. Rather, he was seen as a flagrant example of the abuse of power, of corruption, of loose living, of illicit and extravagant enrichment by such means as control of the Lebanese hashish trade.

On 15 May, in a development seemingly unconnected with the crisis, Asad recalled his ambassador from Morocco, ostensibly because King Hasan had played host at a congress of Moroccan Jews attended by an Israeli delegation which included nine members of the Knesset. Asad was certainly angered by Hasan's gesture of goodwill towards Israel at a time when Israeli troops still occupied large parts of Lebanon, but he must also have wanted to signal his displeasure at what he believed to be a Moroccan hand in Rif'at's rebellion. Rif'at considered Hasan one of the finest Arabs and counted him as a personal friend, while Asad viewed him as a deeply suspect figure whose contribution to Sadat's visit to Jerusalem in 1977 he could not easily forgive.

The dénouement of the brothers' war was a classic example of the ringmaster's art: elegant, unhurried, and demonstrating Asad's control over his fractious underlings. On 28 May, with the help of the Kremlin, he despatched a plane-load of some seventy senior officers to Moscow for a cooling-off period. Among them was Rif'at. They were all banished with no assurance of when they would be allowed back save that it would depend on the will of their master. By expelling them all Asad underlined in the most public way that none of them was indispensable. He later related that some of these generals thought that if they were sent abroad the regime would collapse. 'Fear not for the regime, I told them, fear rather for yourselves.'[6] In the event, all but Rif'at were soon recalled to their duties. Getting rid of him, the richest and most powerful of them all, proved to the whole country that Asad was in control of the others. For face-saving reasons Rif'at's trip to the Soviet Union was described by Damascus Radio as a 'cordial working visit', and Chernenko helpfully granted him an audience on 1 June. But by the 5th Rif'at had set up house in exile in Geneva.

Epilogue

For months thereafter not a word about Rif'at appeared in the Syrian press, although the campaign continued to root out what remained of his influence. His once proud Defence Companies were reduced to a division-sized force about 20,000-strong: large numbers of men were demobilized or switched to other units such as 'Adnan Makhluf's Presidential Guard and 'Ali Haydar's Special Forces. Several of Rif'at's key officers were placed under arrest and a number were said to have been shot. Some civilian loyalists were forcibly evicted from the *Fursan* housing estate. Nothing was more wounding to a liege lord of Rif'at's calibre than to be unable to protect his own. Ba'th party members were instructed to quit the League of Higher Graduates, which withered in the absence of its exuberant patron. Rif'at owned properties all over Damascus which in his heyday, and to the inconvenience of local residents, were sealed off by roadblocks. These were now removed without fanfare, and people were able to enjoy walking up and down streets which had once been forbidden to them.

On 1 August 1984, in another turn of the screw, a handful of prominent party leaders close to Rif'at had their membership of the Regional Command 'frozen'. This was the fate of Muhammad Haydar, a former deputy premier for economic affairs who had acquired vast wealth, built himself a palatial home in Zabadani, a mountain resort near Damascus, and married off one of his daughters to one of Rif'at's sons. Another who fell from grace was the unlucky General Naji Jamil, who ironically had lost his job as air force chief in March 1978 for opposing Rif'at but who now suffered again for having made it up with him. In Latakia some of the properties of the once dominant Jamil al-Asad were confiscated. University places that September were won with *bona fide* marks alone, and some of Rif'at's young parachutists, deprived of their bonuses, had to spend an extra year at school.

Elliptical references to the brothers' war appeared in print and were much talked about. For example, a veteran Ba'thist and former academic, Hafiz al-Jamali wrote a fable in the party newspaper. At a moment of crisis the citizens of an imaginary city are ordered to extinguish all lights. An old woman lights a candle. She is arrested and sentenced to death. Yet at the moment of execution she prays God to grant long life to the ruler. 'If he dies', she explains, 'someone worse may come.' Asad, the fable seemed to say, was preferable to his brother. Another pointer to the *sotto voce* debate was a play by the well-known 'Alawi dramatist Sa'dallah Wannus about a power struggle between a king and his vizier. Entitled 'The Adventure of Slave Jabir's Head' (*Mughamarat ra's al-mamluk Jabir*), it was performed even before the crisis was over.

The ambiguity which surrounded Asad's relations with his brother was officially dispelled on 11 September when the German news magazine *Der Spiegel* published an interview with General Tlas, Asad's Defence Minister, in which he declared Rif'at to be 'permanently *persona non grata*'. The quarrel was at last out in the open.

Rif'at's banishment allowed Syrian society to perform an act of expiation. He left heaped with curses as if he were carrying away not just the sins of his Defence Companies and of his own indulgent lifestyle but also the abuses of the Ba'th revolution. In the public perception, his misdeeds highlighted Asad's virtues. Yet there was something paradoxical about a turbulent Third World country banishing its scapegoat to nice neutral Switzerland.

As befitted a *grand seigneur*, Rif'at was accompanied in Geneva by over a hundred aides and bodyguards, a costly entourage which, it is said, Colonel Qadhafi of Libya helped to finance to keep Rif'at out of Syria. Maintaining a private army in Swiss hotels would strain any purse, even one as deep as Rif'at's. In any event, there were problems with visas which required prolonged negotiation with the Swiss authorities. By September many of Rif'at's men had drifted home and he himself had moved to France with a reduced suite of guards, servants, wives and children. But Damascus was clearly not happy to have this flamboyant and outspoken personage on the loose. When in July Foreign Minister Khaddam narrowly escaped death from a car-bomb, suspicious souls said that this was Rif'at's work. To Asad's great anger Rif'at was also reported to have met Yasir 'Arafat in Geneva. And when it was learned that Rif'at was planning to publish an anti-regime magazine in France and even to start a radio station, Damascus decided it was time to bring him home.

Rif'at still retained the title of vice-president and Asad himself never publicly condemned him, leaving in the public mind a continuing uncertainty about the real nature of their relations. On 10 November 1984 a presidential decree entrusted Rif'at with the supervision of national security – making him in theory the overlord of all his rivals, and on the 26th he returned to Damascus, called at the presidency, and knelt and kissed his brother's hand. But he had not been forgiven. His security job was a sham. He was prevented from renewing contact with his slimmed down Defence Companies and he was hemmed in everywhere he turned. It was painful for a man who had once enjoyed unfettered power to find himself so constrained.

The long-drawn-out struggle between the brothers was brought to its formal conclusion at the Eighth Regional Congress of the Ba'th party, held in Damascus from 5 to 20 January 1985, and attended by 780 delegates from across the country. Rif'at, as a member of the Regional Command, was present, but he was also in a sense in the dock and was exposed to a good deal of criticism. Everyone at the Congress knew how narrowly Syria had escaped fratricidal strife, and to whom they owed renewed serenity.

Party rules stipulated that the Congress elect a Central Committee – hitherto of seventy-five members, now expanded to ninety. These men in turn had the task of electing the new Regional Command, the highest pinnacle of party power. But at the Eighth Congress the rule book was laid aside: Asad, master of the external and the internal scene, victor of the struggle for Lebanon and of the succession crisis, was by acclamation awarded special powers. In recognition of his unchallenged personal pre-eminence the delegates entrusted him with the task of personally naming the ninety Central Committee members. It was a gesture of confidence in the political wizard who had checked the slide into civil war. Benignly, Asad sat through every session of the Congress, enjoying his apotheosis. Three weeks later, on 10 February 1985, he was elected president of Syria for a third seven-year term by 99.97 per cent of the voters.

Asad had triumphed, but in the crisis the institutions of his state had made a poor showing. At the moment of danger he had to go down into the street himself and clear the tanks away. Checks, balances, the People's Assembly, the Popular Organizations, indeed the party itself with its extensive structure in both the country and the army, were all of no avail when ambitious generals threatened to shoot it out. In the end it was his personal authority and that alone which held the country together. He was the only pole holding up the tent. It was not a good augury for the future.

Meanwhile Rif'at took off again for Europe, his hopes of rehabilitation dashed. Asad's severity towards his brother did not abate. Although he was attached to Rif'at and owed him a lot, the defence of the political line to which he was committed overrode sentiment or family attachment. He remained convinced that his brother had, wittingly or not, been involved with foreign powers in an attempted coup against him and against his policies, and this he could not let pass.

In May 1986 Rif'at (who by this time had established himself in Paris in the splendour associated with exiled royalty) paid an unannounced visit to Britain. He was preceded by four armed bodyguards carrying Moroccan passports whom the British authorities quietly detained. Then two private planes landed at Heathrow carrying Rif'at, members of his family, retainers and security men, some forty people in all. Many of these too travelled on Moroccan passports. The British government allowed the party in, but a message was sent to the Syrian government through diplomatic channels requesting clarification of the visitors' status. Asad's response was swift: 'We expect Britain to behave correctly towards holders of valid Syrian passports. What Britain does with holders of other passports is no concern of ours.'

25

Forging a Nation

Like an Arab de Gaulle, imbued with national pride and steeped in diplomacy, Asad seemed not to be over-concerned with internal affairs. Standing up to Israel and other tussles with foreign powers, the main themes of this book, were the causes to which he devoted most of his waking hours. Internal Syrian affairs were if anything a base for external action, for in his mind the two were intimately connected: to be strong abroad he had to be strong at home. But strength on the home front could and did mean different things. On one level Asad felt that he had to be totally unchallenged: any substantial measure of democracy could be a source of weakness, citizens had to be drilled to cheer or to keep silent. On another level he recognized that his foreign policy required an underpinning of real strength, not just military but social and economic, and that this could be achieved only by the efforts of a lively and ambitious society. Throughout his rule he wrestled with the problem of reconciling obedience and dynamism.

In spite of the accent on foreign affairs, Asad and a quarter of a century of Ba'thist rule managed radically to transform Syrian life. The backward, indigent, exploited Syria of his youth was consigned to the past, and in its place emerged a rapidly modernizing, reasonably prosperous and well equipped society performing rather better than most developing countries of the Third World. Grave problems remained but the physical environment changed out of recognition, with roads, railways, dams, bridges and an unprecedented construction boom, and the quality of life was enhanced for the great majority of Syrians, especially the once neglected peasants of the countryside.

The beginnings of the social and political revolution predated Asad and even the Ba'th. In the late 1940s and 1950s the *ancien regime* of the notables came under attack, first from military putschists and homegrown ideological parties, then from Nasser who, as ruler of Syria for over three years from 1958, introduced land reform, central planning – and police control. This was when the notion of a state wielding power over every aspect of its citizens' lives took root. But it was the 1960s which profoundly restructured social and political relations. Following its seizure of power, the Ba'th destroyed the power of the city elites, promoted men from rural backgrounds, made the state the foremost employer, and in spite of the disaster of the Six Day War embarked with Soviet help on major state projects of which the Euphrates dam was the most monumental. These were years in which experienced party cadres and a skilled labour force began to be formed and the country mobilized behind ambitious goals – years on which Asad built.

But the upheavals of the 1950s and 1960s were also deeply divisive. From 1970 it was Asad's task to unify the nation, reconcile the warring classes, and efface Syria's humiliation of 1967 in the October War of 1973. The flood of money reaching Syria after the explosion of oil prices gave him the opportunity to make the 1970s the decade of capital formation, of massive investment in agriculture, industry, infrastructure, health and education. Mistakes were made but much was achieved. In the 1980s, after the hard-fought victories over the Muslim Brothers at home and Israel in Lebanon, Syria won Arab and international weight, a status expressed in greater social cohesion, in spite of inflation and other ills, and in the confidence, even arrogance, of a new ruling elite. Asad's Syria was far from being the equitable socialist society the early Ba'th ideologues had wanted, but it was robust and barring a war or other major upset it looked to be a going concern.

The growth of Damascus

The history of these tormented decades left its mark on Damascus. The paradox was that the capture of the city by the countryside, perhaps the prime achievement of the Ba'th revolution, resulted in an unprecedented burst of urban pride. In striving for reconciliation, Asad lavished funds on the city, gave respect to community and religious leaders and built bridges between the rural newcomers and the commercial bourgeoisie. In gestures to the Sunni Muslim population, he himself made the 'umra or small pilgrimage to Mecca in 1974 and a decade later, in 1983, awarded a prize for reciters of the Qur'an.

In 1945 when Asad was a schoolboy, Damascus was a city of 300,000 inhabitants. When he took power in 1970 it had passed the 800,000 mark,[1] but less than twenty years later, in the late 1980s, the population had exploded fourfold to well over three million, a growth reflecting wars, social revolution, a galloping birth rate of about 3.8 per cent, one of the highest in the world – and the ambitions of Syria's ruler.

Refugees flooded into Damascus when the Golan was lost in 1967; when Lebanon erupted into civil war in 1975, and when it was invaded by Israel in 1982; and of course at every new misfortune in the Palestinian saga – 1948, 1967, 1970, 1982. By the 1980s about 250,000 Palestinians had taken refuge in Syria, most of them in the Damascus area and about a quarter still living in camps, the remainder integrated into Syrian life.[2] As a front-line city constantly under threat of war, Damascus had also to make room for the families of the vast military garrisons on the outskirts. It was a university town, accommodating some 75,000 students in 1972, until the expansion of Aleppo University and the creation of new campuses at Latakia and Homs somewhat relieved the pressure. As the capital of a centralizing state, the seat of party power, the headquarters of many industries and state enterprises, it was a magnet for people from all over the country.

But the single biggest factor in the city's explosive growth was the relentless influx of the rural poor. To house them the city burst the bounds of the plan drawn up in 1968 by the French town planner, Ecochard, ate into the precious orchards of the Ghuta, swallowed up surrounding villages wholesale, strained the resources of 'Ayn al-Fijeh, the spring which has watered Damascus for generations, and snaked out in speculative ribbon development along the access roads until it came hard up against the natural boundaries of Mount Qasiun to the northwest, the Mezze hills to the west, and what remained of the Ghuta oasis to the east. South of the city, along the road to Qunaytra which used to run through scrub and desert, people began to sink wells, lay out vegetable patches and put up small houses. Still the peasants came, and when they could not find lodgings simply squatted in unlicensed shacks at the entrances to the city and on the higher slopes of Mount Qasiun, eight areas which by the mid-1980s had declined into slums housing about a million people. After a vain attempt to check the influx, the authorities acknowledged the squatters as permanent and from 1982 started supplying them with roads, schools, clinics, electricity, and metred water or public taps.

To preserve Damascus from further unplanned growth, satellite towns were built in the 1980s – such as the Mount Qasiun Town for 90,000 people on a 2,600-hectare site or the network of Asad Villages for 60,000 people north of the capital. New road and rail links out of the city introduced Syrians to the commuter habit.

Yet in spite of all this expansion, Damascus still gave the impression of a planned city under control, escaping the rampant, anarchic spread afflicting many a Third World capital. The down-at-heel camps and makeshift slums on the periphery, where the conditions were worst, were far from the squalor of Latin American and African shanty-towns. In most of the city's 67 quarters, life was reasonably well ordered, the streets cleaned and watered, rubbish collected, traffic not impossibly congested, and public services functioning fairly satisfactorily.

In the 1970s and 1980s a modern capital city arose, threaded with underpasses, flyovers and ring-roads linking extensive residential quarters of apartment blocks. Clusters of university buildings, hospitals and research institutes sprang up, as well as international hotels like the Sheraton and the Cham Palace (the creation of Dr 'Usman al-'A'idi, the country's foremost hotelier), two vast parks in east and west Damascus, and show pieces such as the guest palace large enough to house four heads of state and their suites, the massive new presidential palace overlooking the city, the Asad Library, a projected opera and theatre complex, and under construction on the road to the airport a conference centre on a site of many hundreds of acres, a new international fairground, a Cinema City, and a women's military academy – all symbols in their different ways of the swelling ambitions of the country and its president. Asad aspired to make Syria the dominant Arab power of the Levant, the champion in the lists with Israel, a nation on a par with Egypt and Iraq, and he wanted a capital to match.

Rural modernization

Syrian political and economic life was traditionally concentrated along a south-north axis from Damascus through Homs and Hama to Aleppo. Until the 1950s these were the only centres of any importance. The Asad years drew a horizontal line across the old vertical pattern: an east-west axis of road, rail, telephone and air links connected the oil and agricultural wealth of the east and northeast to the consuming and exporting west, bringing on to the economic and demographic map rapidly growing cities on the Euphrates and beyond such as al-Hassaka, Qamishly, Raqqa, Tabqa and Dayr al-Zur, and, on the Mediterranean, Latakia, Tartus, Banyas and Jabla. Development was deliberately decentralized so as to spread the benefits and also perhaps to avoid creating a vertebrate economy which could be paralysed by a single blow.[3]

The Euphrates dam at Tabqa was, with its reservoir Lake Asad, its power station and irrigation network, the most expensive, ambitious and problematic project of the Asad era. Begun in 1968–9 and completed in under ten years, this giant enterprise was seen as the springboard to prosperity. It brought electricity to the most remote hamlets, Lenin's key to rural betterment, but the hopes that 640,000 hectares of land could be made fertile with the waters of the lake were disappointed or at best deferred. The Syrians learned the hard way that building the future involved destroying the past. For one thing Lake Asad engulfed some three hundred villages, displacing 72,000 people with the loss of 25,000 hectares of arable land.

A still greater calamity was the discovery that over 60,000 hectares had been lost to salinity and that the blight was spreading at the rate of ten hectares a day. When Aleppo merchants first opened up the Euphrates basin and the Jazira to cotton growing in the 1940s and 1950s, water was pumped from the river without proper irrigation or drainage. The water level rose and evaporation in the hot dry summers brought salt to the surface. As land was spoiled, the farmers moved on, aggravating the situation by using ever more water in the hope of higher yields. Much time and money went into the search for a solution. Eventually in the 1980s wells were sunk and linked to deep-drainage conduits to lower the water level, while canals were built to bring water to flush the land clean. Another unpleasant discovery was that the soil was rich in gypsum, causing water conduits to collapse. These two problems constituted a major challenge to a developing country in a crucial sector of its economy. Syria might have been better off had it started irrigating the best quality land rather than the worst, seeing that its shortage was not land but water. The sixth five-year plan, 1986–90, absorbed the lesson and diverted Euphrates water westwards to the fertile plains north and south of Aleppo. But while errors were put right, the hope that the dam would double the country's irrigated land area had to be put off for a generation – to Asad's great frustration.

By-products of the project were the twin towns of Tabqa and al-Thawra on the banks of Lake Asad which grew from nothing in 1968 to over 100,000 people by 1985. These frontier settlements were designed by Soviet planners to house the dam workers, but came to serve as dormitory towns for skilled men bused to other projects such as the al-Ba'th dam built 25 kms downstream from Tabqa to produce still more electricity and regulate the flow of the river. The capital of the governorate where all this was taking place was Raqqa, some fifty kms east of the dam and a showpiece of the Ba'th revolution. In ancient times Raqqa had been the summer residence of the Abbasid caliph Harun al-Rashid, but its modern history was undistinguished and by 1960 it was no more than a scruffy township of some 13,000 people. The building of the dam caused it to grow by leaps and bounds to a modern city of 150,000 in the 1980s, more varied in its composition and more free and easy in its temper than anywhere else in Syria.

Presiding over this 'new frontier' governorate from 1980 to 1987 was Governor Muhammad Salman (appointed Syrian Minister of Information in November 1987), who won a reputation as a builder of roads, schools, clinics, power lines and water pipes, not only in the town itself but all across his province the size of Bèlgium. Its population in the mid-1980s was a mere 400,000 – peasants and bedouin, 'submerged' people from the lake area and immigrants in search of work from all parts of the country – but there was room there, according to the governor, for five million. Salman left his mark on Raqqa in numerous remarkable buildings to find in the outback, notably a marble cultural centre and a children's holiday home resembling a luxury hotel with its outdoor theatre and Olympic-sized swimming pool, and in tree planting and public gardens.

It was not an unalloyed success story. A chronicler of the province's upheavals was Dr 'Abd al-Salam al-'Ujayli, country physician, parliamentarian, native son of Raqqa, novelist and thorn in the flesh of officialdom. His novel, *The Submerged* (al-Mughmarun) published in 1977, is about the fate of refugees driven from their homes by the waters of Lake Asad and promised resettlement nearby who found themselves transferred to the far northeast. Wishing to ease rural misery, the government had created another injustice. A second novel, *King River* (al-Nahr Sultan), tells the story of a father who loses his only son to the capricious Euphrates and feels avenged when the tyrant is tamed (the historic moment came on 5 July 1973 when, with Asad in attendance, the flow of the river was diverted to the power station). But in 'Ujayli's story the swarm of officials which descends in the wake of the project brings his hero new trials.[4]

The land reform of the 1960s and the dam-building of the 1970s brought Syria years of confusion before agricultural productivity improved. In the rain-fed plains of Homs and Hama the peasants were undoubtedly better off with the passing of the 'feudal' landowners, at least in years of normal rainfall, but on the irrigated land of the Euphrates basin the picture was more mixed. The new smallholders found they lacked the means of production, notably water pumps, and had to turn for financial help to city merchants or richer peasants – the very people the Ba'th had hoped to eliminate from the production process.[5] Shepherds did not like being turned into farmers, or farmers into state employees. State co-operatives were ineffective, agricultural debt a burden. The acreage allowed each man under the agrarian reform laws was perhaps too small for scientific farming. The whole tangle of relationships between the state, the producer, the market and the various middlemen was by the late 1980s still being painfully sorted out.

Nonetheless, right across the countryside, roads, electricity, piped water, schools and health care transformed village life. Dozens of small dams were built and dozens more planned to trap every drop of rainwater. Grain silos and stores of canned food were sited in each governorate. The ignorant and oppressed sharecropper, so familiar a figure of Asad's youth, very largely disappeared. This was what the Ba'th had come to do. Asad understood that raising the level of the peasant was the essential precondition for building a modern state and a modern army. By the late 1980s all but 2 per cent of the rural population watched television and listened to the radio while refrigerators and washing machines were coming in fast. Before 1963 there was virtually no electricity in the rural areas and only some 2 to 3 per cent of the population owned a refrigerator. In the words of Muhammad Harba, the son of a poor peasant who rose to ministerial rank, 'In a mere twenty-five years Syria experienced a revolution on the land which it took France a century to accomplish'.[6]

Industrialization

Industry was less of a success, largely because big mistakes were made in the rush to industrialize in the boom years after the October War. Israel had inflicted grave damage on the Syrian economy in the war and the urge was to rebuild and do better. Most of the projects which were later to prove headaches were contracted for in the two-year period 1974–6 under the premiership of Mahmud al-Ayyubi. When asked later why he had allowed precious funds to be squandered on unprofitable schemes, Ayyubi replied, 'If we hadn't spent the money on industry, the army would have swallowed it up'. Muhammad Haydar, vice-premier for economic affairs at the time, recounted that he had gone to Saudi Arabia after the 1973 war and King Faysal had asked him what Syria needed. 'Give me a list of your projects with some figures', the king said. Haydar who had come unprepared spent the night working on his pocket calculator to produce some sort of a document. In such haphazard ways was Syria's industrial programme put together.

All too often plants were erected because they offered opportunities for influential middlemen to earn commissions from foreign suppliers, and the middlemen in turn fed a tribe of lesser commission-takers enriching themselves at different stages of public sector projects. Asad had wanted to liberalize the economy but in practice this came to mean the creation of instant millionaires at the nation's expense. Had the plants been viable, such corruption would not have been of crucial importance, but in several cases they proved costly white elephants. Among the most notorious examples was the $110 million paper and pulp plant at Dayr al-Zur, for which the contract was signed with an Austro-Italian consortium in 1976. Its history over the next decade was a series of blunders. It failed to operate on Syrian wheat straw and in any event not enough straw could be delivered to the plant; its large boiler was not designed for Syrian heavy oil; its turbine broke down, causing a five-month stoppage; the foreign personnel walked out; the contractors were taken to the International Court; the raw material was switched to wood and cotton lint involving further expensive adjustments to the machinery. In the end it would have been cheaper to continue importing paper than to build the mill.[7]

Another industrial disaster was the ammonia-urea plant built at Homs by Creusot-Loire of France to be generated by naphtha. After a series of failures, the plant was converted to gas at considerable cost in 1988, requiring the contruction of a $100 million gas pipeline contracted with Bulgaria and Czechoslovakia. Over-ambitious plans were also made for sugar refining in 1975 when it was decided to build four refineries consuming between them 1.7 million tons of beet – which in turn meant turning over some 50,000 hectares of productive land to crop. Encouraged by government incentives, farmers gave up planting cotton and wheat, but in the 1980s with the collapse of the world sugar price much of the new capacity had to be shut down. A giant cement factory, one of the largest in the Middle East, built near Tartus by the German Democratic Republic in the mid-1970s, was not an economic disaster but an environmental one: a valuable stretch of Mediterranean coastline was polluted and thousands of olive trees destroyed. And there were other dismal stories. In time it became evident that several major investments had been made in poorly evaluated projects and that plants had been badly managed. Much of the boom money of the mid-1970s had not been put to good use.

To set against this record there were some distinct successes. Heavy sulphurous oil which had been flowing from fields in the northeast from the early 1970s was supplemented in the mid-1980s by a string of discoveries of good quality light crude along the Euphrates between Dayr al-Zur and Albukamal on the Iraqi border. For the first time Syria had the prospect of a substantial source of independent finance. Gas was found in large quantities in the desert region of Palmyra. Phosphate production rose to over two million tons in 1987, with an annual potential of five million.

A prime instrument in the transformation of the country was the state construction companies, of which there were no fewer than thirteen by the mid-1980s. Of these, by far the most important was the Military Housing Establishment known as Milihouse, an example of free-wheeling enterprise which few state-controlled economies could match. Its creator was a short, stocky, hyper-energetic 'Alawi colonel, Khalil Bahlul, born in 1935 of peasant stock, who first attracted Asad's attention by his efficiency in building aircraft shelters and airfields after the devastation of the 1967 war. He moved on to building housing for the army, recruiting young engineers straight from college, training them at speed on the job, circumventing controls and getting results. In 1975 the basic legislation setting up the state construction companies was passed, launching Bahlul on his spectacular career. Within a decade Milihouse was the largest firm in the country – in fact a conglomerate of sixty-six companies – employing a good half of the 150,000 workers in the Syrian construction industry and responsible for some of the best buildings in the country: the new international airport, the Asad Library, the president's official banqueting hall elaborately decorated in oriental style, the Aleppo Meridien, the sports city in Latakia used for the Mediterranean Games of 1987, numerous schools and university faculties and the 5,000 houses of the Asad Villages, each garden plot planted with two olive trees and a vine, a characteristic Bahlul touch. Examples of his work were to be found all over Syria.

He introduced the management and accounting methods of private business into the public sector, and freed himself from dependence on others by manufacturing or processing almost all his materials – cement, plaster, marble, stone, ceramics, wood and aluminium window-frames, furniture and upholstery. Introducing modern techniques, encouraging engineers, craftsmen and managers to be flexible and innovative, Bahlul contributed as much as any one person could to getting the country moving. In the mid-1980s he branched out further into agriculture, sheep rearing on a large scale and horse breeding. It was said of the Milihouse empire that all it needed was a flag and an anthem, but Bahlul's success and a forceful disrespect for government controls won him enemies. 'What is a sardine?' he mocked. 'It is a whale which has applied all the regulations to the letter.'[8] Eventually his clashes with Prime Minister Kasm brought him down in 1987.

Bahlul played a part in the 1980s in the revival of Aleppo where several of his industrial plants were located. Once a great trading city at the crossroads of caravan routes, larger and richer than Damascus, Aleppo had been in relative decline since the First World War when it was severed from its sea outlet at Alexandretta and from its hinterland in present-day Iraq and Turkey. Feuding between Syria and Iraq over the 1960s and 1970s and the frequent closure of the frontier were also at Aleppo's expense. In any event, the rise of the Ba'thist state in Damascus caused Aleppo to lose its leverage on government and it did not greatly benefit from the post-1973 financial bonanza, nor did its role in the Muslim Brotherhood insurrection endear it to the authorities. It failed in the first dozen years of Asad's rule to acquire an international airport, a top class hotel or a modern business quarter. It suffered from poor sewerage, poor municipal services, and its main street where the historic Baron's Hotel stands became a shabby ghost of the elegant thoroughfare it had once been.

Built by the Mazlumians, a family of Armenian hoteliers, in 1911, Baron's kept a visitors' book which was a sort of footnote to the turbulent century. Mustafa Kamal (Ataturk) made it his headquarters when the Ottoman army was withdrawing from Syria, his rooms passing in due course to General Allenby. King Faysal I stayed at Baron's, as did T. E. Lawrence and Reza Shah of Iran. Under the French Mandate champagne flowed like water to slake the thirst of travellers like Agatha Christie and Amy Johnson arriving on the Taurus Express. Asad too came to Baron's when he visited Aleppo after seizing power.[9] By then the hotel had seen its best days.

In the 1980s Aleppo's prospects improved under its new governor, Muhammad Mawaldi. A local man and the son of a railway worker, he commanded the volunteer People's Army during the Muslim Brothers crisis and afterwards threw himself into rebuilding his city's fortunes. Aleppo's pivotal position on the new road and rail networks, its industries, crafts and lively mercantile tradition, and its hardworking Armenian community all contributed to its revival.

An impressive feature was the growth of Aleppo University from 5,000 students in 1980 to 35,000 five years later, under the direction of the rector, Dr M. A. Hourieh. By then there were fourteen faculties, a teaching staff of 860, some 800 graduates taking higher degrees abroad, and three teaching hospitals. Moreover, precisely because Aleppo escaped both riches and rural invasion on the scale of

Damascus, the city's old quarters were less devastated by property speculators, and the many monuments from the Islamic past – the citadel, the city walls, the covered souks, mosques, baths and khans – made it more visually appealing than its southern rival. About 80 per cent of medieval and Ottoman Aleppo still stood, as compared with only about 20 per cent of old Damascus.

Setbacks to the economy

As the 1980s drew to a close pressures mounted on Asad to re-evaluate the economic record of his presidency. There was a need to recover from the downturn which had afflicted much of the decade following the collapse of world oil prices and the resulting loss of revenue from Syria's own oil exports and from remittances from Syrians working in the Gulf. A severe drought, not really broken until 1986, crippled a country still heavily dependent on rainfall – 30 per cent of Syria's sheep had to be slaughtered in 1983–4 – requiring costly food imports and causing power cuts as the fall in the Euphrates flow reduced electricity generation at the dam. There were political factors as well. Syria's unpopular support of Iran, its quarrels with Jordan and the Palestinians, its tensions with the Gulf countries and its confrontation with the West over terrorism all brought economic penalties. The country was running alarming budget and balance of payments deficits and the population was stunned by inflation which climbed in 1987–8 to over 100 per cent per annum.

It became clear that there could be no immediate salvation from either agriculture or industry. The great investments in both these sectors had not yet provided a viable productive base. Although the mistakes of random industrialization and ill-judged irrigation had been learned and it was widely recognized that Syria's future lay in the exploitation of its own raw materials – oil, gas, phosphates and agro-business – the pay-off was still some years ahead. In the meantime public spending and private consumption were both excessive: government and people had got used to an artificial prosperity based on foreign handouts rather than productivity or savings. The infrastructure and public services such as the free education system, the pride of the Ba'thist state, were arguably more than the country could afford and yet could not easily be trimmed. State employees – over 450,000 of them, one in every five persons employed – made little productive contribution. Badly paid, with poor morale, moonlighting when they could, they had little incentive to work.

The armed services, also numbering over 400,000, made vast claims on resources which could not be reduced because of Syria's front-line position, its role in Lebanon and its regional ambitions. It should be said that the army was itself an instrument of modernization. Military service, officially two and a half years but often extended to four, was not entirely a waste of time. Many conscripts were put to work in state construction companies, others were employed on army farms which produced a significant proportion of the meat, vegetables, fruit and pulses which the troops consumed. Some 20,000 young men were taught to drive each year and thousands of electricians and mechanics were trained. But, although a modest attempt was made to prune the military budget in 1987, the armed services still absorbed over 50 per cent of government expenditure and they were politically untouchable.

Development budgets were also sacrosanct because with the population growing at 3.8 per cent – in the late 1980s an extra 400,000 mouths a year to feed – the government could not slacken in its efforts to provide for their future. In the Asad years Syria benefited from a relatively small population, 5.3 million in 1963 rising to 10.6 million in 1986, but the projection for the end of the century was a staggering 17 million. The dangers of runaway growth dismayed the planners, but policy-makers were reluctant to challenge the Syrian tradition of large families.

Part of Syria's problem seemed to be the lack of a coherent team managing the economy. There was little effective co-ordination between the Ministries of Planning, Finance and Economics, or between these ministries and the party's Bureau of Economic Affairs. Perhaps to reflect his own priorities, Asad chose more vigorous and powerful aides in the fields of foreign affairs and security, men like Khaddam, Shihabi and 'Ali Duba, than in the economic sphere where his appointees tended to lack authority or political weight.

There were also ideological hurdles to clear in the management of the economy, notably the uneasy relationship between the public and private sectors. Men who had overseen the great government-led transformation of the Syrian economy of the 1970s were reluctant to let the private sector expand beyond its existing role in small and medium industry, agriculture and commerce. At the Eighth Regional Congress in February 1985 Asad argued for greater scope for the private sector but clear policy directives did not follow. The government seemed anxious to attract Syrian entrepreneurs and capital back from abroad to invest in tourism, in import replacement of various sorts, and in joint-venture agro-projects. But doubts about the country's political future and the heavy hand of government and party dissuaded many a would-be investor. Denied industrial opportunities, private capital moved into real estate with rocketing property prices as a result.

Syria's economic ills required disagreeable remedies: cutting government spending to reduce budget deficits and stabilize the inflation-stricken currency, the elimination of waste even in taboo areas like the army and the party, the reining in of a parasitical class of over-consumers. Money had to be found to import raw materials to get state factories working again and controls dismantled to release Syria's undoubted mercantile talents. But there was no agreement among policy-makers about the extent or urgency of the crisis. Optimists pointed to the relatively modest level of Syria's external commercial debt, estimated at around $4 billion (excluding sums owed to the Soviet Union for military equipment) and its virtually non-existent internal debt. The Syrian currency, although sharply devalued, had fared no worse than the Israeli shekel or the Turkish pound. Syria's thriving black economy took a lot of the pain out of the official statistics. Moreover, a programme of austerity and liberalization ran counter to the government's declared socialist goals. It risked alienating public sector employees, a key constituency, as well as treading on the toes of the entrenched caste of office holders and others living off the state. Asad encouraged piecemeal reforms but seemed unwilling to sanction a radical change of direction, perhaps anticipating that Syria's long deferred take-off based on oil and a revitalized agriculture would bail him out in the next decade.

'Alawi advancement

The improved fortunes of Syria's 'Alawi community best illustrated the transformations of the Ba'th's quarter century. Although only 12 per cent of the population and formerly the most backward segment of it, the 'Alawis produced not just the president but an important part of the new elite. Coming from far behind and reaching the top, 'Alawis were in the fast lane of Syrian society.

The 'Alawi mountains of the late twentieth century could not present a greater contrast to the picture of poverty and tragic isolation painted by Jacques Weulersse half a century ago.[10] Just as the mountainous hinterland of the Riviera, once one of the poorest parts of France, was brought to life by tourism, so the hinterland of Syria's Mediterranean coast was quickened by the 'Alawi ascent. Hundreds of upland villages were so expanded in an orgy of breeze-block building that scarcely a trace remained of the old rough-stone hamlets of Asad's youth. Traditional dress almost entirely disappeared and the swarms of children wore the track suits, jeans and training shoes of their European contemporaries. The 'Alawis also expanded their domain, spreading down the mountains to the fertile inland farms of the Ghab and westward down to the sea to buy land, build houses, invade and develop the coastal towns of Latakia, Tartus, Banyas and Jabla, and move on to Damascus itself.

In 1970 only 10 per cent of households in the Latakia governorate had piped drinking water; fifteen years later the figure was over 70 per cent and roads had been built to every hamlet. When Asad was at school only a few dozen workers were employed in the sole industrial establishment, the Régie des Tabacs; by the mid-1980s 40,000 workers were employed in public sector companies in food processing and the manufacture of aluminium, cement, textiles, carpets, while a network of dams had irrigated some 50,000 hectares. In the city of Latakia itself, which had grown from 30,000 inhabitants to a quarter of a million in Asad's lifetime, the port was greatly expanded, while a new university, Tishreen ('October' after the 1973 war), created by presidential decree in 1971 and housing 15,000 students by 1985, brought new intellectual standards and patterns of social life.

Immediately after the 1963 revolution 'Alawis started moving eagerly into education. They were clever and worked hard. In increasing numbers they were awarded scholarships and travelled abroad for higher degrees, becoming doctors, engineers, lawyers and university professors, so that twenty-five years later they were strongly represented in the professions and senior cadres of the state, rivalling and sometimes displacing the Sunni and Christian intelligentsia. The 'Alawi thirst to get on was not slaked. In June 1987 an incident in Asad's home village of Qurdaha illustrated how keen it still was. As schoolchildren were sitting their end-year examination some parents, anxious for good results, stormed the hall. The headmaster called the police, a gunfight broke out and a policeman was killed. An angry Asad sent an army unit to surround the building and ensure that the examination proceeded in an orderly fashion. In a study of the peasantry in the flat, newly drained plain of the Ghab, a French social anthropologist, Françoise Métral, discovered that in the western Ghab inhabited by 'Alawis between 34 and 41 per cent of girls attended school, while in the eastern Ghab inhabited by Sunnis the percentage was as low as 0 to 7 per cent.[11]

Although they had no urban tradition of their own, 'Alawi villagers who settled in Damascus were often quicker to adapt to new ideas and modern ways of living than the Sunni *petit peuple*. As befitted mountain people, they tended to be tough and self-reliant but unskilled at commerce or crafts. The humbler among them got jobs as guards, drivers and security personnel at the airport or were recruited by the thousand into the Defence Companies, Special Forces or Presidential Guard, bringing their families to the outlying suburbs of Harasta, Qabun and Mezze.

The advancement of the 'Alawis offended many Syrians who believed they were unduly favoured, but few outside the extremist ranks of the Islamic fundamentalists held their heterodox beliefs against them. Rather, what was resented was the rise of one region over others and of a community hitherto considered inferior. Yet, thanks to their strong position in the army, the security services, the professions, the party, and indeed in every institution across the land, the progress of the 'Alawis seemed irreversible. Having fought and studied their way to the top, they would not easily be dislodged.

Black spots and progress

Black spots in their society and economy preoccupied Syrians in the 1980s, and of these smuggling headed the list. With foreign trade controlled by the government and foreign exchange scarce, there were numerous shortages on the local market – compensated for by thriving contraband from Lebanon. Smuggling across the mountains from free enterprise Lebanon was an old phenomenon, impossible to control because of the long permeable frontier. Whole villages on both sides had lived off it for years. But from 1976 when the Syrian army went into Lebanon, controlling road traffic and even ports like Tripoli and more or less absorbing the Biqa', the traffic became almost institutionalized, with the Syrian army itself heavily involved in it. For the military, from generals to sergeants, a posting to Lebanon was a chance to make a fortune. Alarmed at the erosion of the Syrian *lira*, the loss of customs revenue and the leakage out of the country of price-controlled goods like pharmaceuticals, the authorities tried without much success to clamp down from time to time. The two economies were too interpenetrated, too many people were involved, above all the traffic plugged a gap: smuggled auto parts, for example, helped to keep Syrian cars on the road and for a whole range of consumer products from lavatory paper to washing machines the middle class had nowhere else to turn. The Lebanese town of Shtura in the Biqa', the last staging post before the frontier, became a vast entrepôt for goods destined for the Syrian market. Contraband came in by container truck and for many families a day-trip to Shtura was a commonplace.

If you had money you could buy anything, but if you had only your wages life was austere and limited to basic necessities: comforts, let alone luxuries, were outside your budget. This was the lot of most Syrians. Wages in the large public sector were low right across the scale from street cleaners to university professors, and were scarcely better in the private sector. With inflation rampant, scrambling for a bit extra became the national obsession, and the active and resourceful Syrians resorted to moonlighting and to corruption of all sorts, creating a large black economy which extended deep into government departments and the public sector.

At the summit of the social pyramid arousing envy and resentment was a small conspicuous group of super-rich, a world apart from the struggling masses and even from the reasonably affluent middle class of professional men, private industrialists and merchants. For the most part they were men of peasant or *petit-bourgeois* background who, with Asad, had built the Ba'thist state but who had long since abandoned all pretence of socialist ideals. Drawn from the top echelons of the army, the security services, the party and the government, with legal or illegal access to state revenues, members of this group were distinguished by their ability to buy what they wanted and behave as they wanted without regard to public opinion or state regulation. Over the years the group had milked budgets, taken cuts on government projects, put their sons into private business, struck percentage deals with agents of foreign suppliers, placed protégés in public sector companies, speculated in property, and made money.[12] Some of these transactions were within the law, others were not. So unfettered were their activities and so extensive the networks of patronage and clientelism they built up that some spoke of the emergence of a 'merchant-military complex',[13] even of a new ruling class several thousand strong.

As in many cities, the most desirable place to live in Damascus was to the west. There was said to be a 3°C temperature difference between east and west, with the west being warmer in winter and cooler in summer. Stoves were put away fifteen days earlier in the west. In the late 1940s and 1950s, the 'west end' was the broad tree-lined avenue of Abu Rummaneh, overtaken in the 1960s and 1970s by the Malki quarter which in turn was superseded in the 1980s by the well-guarded glossy apartment blocks of West Malki. This was the home of the country's elite.

There was wealth in Syria beyond this group. The influx of aid funds after the 1973 war created unprecedented liquidity and, within the constraints set by the government, there was still money to be legitimately made in the private sector, in retail trade, building, agriculture, light industry, and in highly paid professions like medicine. Private funds also flowed in from Syrians working or settled abroad. Syria had more rich people under Asad than ever before, as could be seen in the tide of expensive villas swamping fashionable mountain resorts like Bludan. But the private sector had certain grumbles. It felt that for doctrinal and bureaucratic reasons it was being denied the opportunities it deserved. The state still had a prejudice against capitalists, and as a result money which could have been used productively was siphoned off into property speculation. A second complaint was that while honest, thirfty, hardworking merchants and manufacturers were penalized, fortunes were made by profiteers and commission-takers, parasites on government projects in league with the barons of the regime.

A puzzle for many Syrians was why Asad, whose own lifestyle and tastes were so restrained, should tolerate the abuses and gross consumerism of some of his top aides. One explanation offered was that he allowed them to enrich themselves the better to control them, another that their extravagant wealth was a reward for political loyalty. A different view was that these men had become indispensable to Asad, that he could not sack the whole establishment and that, having become in a sense its prisoner, he had no alternative but to put up with its excesses. But a more convincing explanation was that, to govern and modernize Syria, Asad believed he needed a strong monied class of his own men which would supersede the sons of the old Syrian bourgeoisie. Yet Asad seemed to recognize the importance of the traditions and leading families of old Damascus, and it was no accident that when President Carter visited Syria, one of the few places he was taken to was the Shallah farm in the Ghuta, owned by Badr al-Din Shallah, chairman of the Federation of Syrian Chambers of Commerce, a Damascene patriarch in his eighties and the head of a large clan.

In the late 1980s although tensions and jealousies remained, there were signs of reconciliation in the higher reaches of Syrian society. Some children of the new men married into old and once powerful landed or political families, whose names still conferred a unique respectability. On both sides class hatred seemed to give way to a certain grudging interest. In 1984 a son of Vice-President Khaddam married a girl from the distinguished Atasi clan of Homs, a union lavishly celebrated at the Damascus Sheraton, temple of the *nouveaux riches.* The building of luxury hotels such as the Sheraton and the Meridien, which against party opposition Asad had defended as economic necessities, changed social life in the capital.

Yet the emergence of the super-rich, with their privileges, abuses and conspicuous consumption, could not but damage the image of the regime. Egalitarian ideals gave way to unequal treatment. To defend their positions top people grew conservative, their instinct now being to control rather than mobilize popular energies.[14] The achievements of the regime – the dams, roads, railways, industries, schools, institutes and universities, the many opportunities for young people – lost some of their gloss in the light of the excesses of the new elite.

A graver criticism than that of corruption was the regime's human rights record. The arbitrary powers of the security services and cruel conditions of detention, including the resort to torture, were noted by Amnesty International. As a reminder to all, the old prison-fortress of Mezze glowered from its peak above Damascus between the Sheraton Hotel and the new presidential palace. Still incarcerted there in the late 1980s were the men Asad had overthrown in 1970. In Asad's state the notion of individual rights was given little substance in spite of the institutional apparatus. There was no truly independent judiciary, no freedom of information, association or expression, and no autonomous university. In the absence of clear rules governing relations between the individual and the state, the ordinary citizen felt insecure. Even well-to-do Syrians inhabiting the smart quarters of western Damascus feared being denounced by a dissatisfied client or customer and finding themselves under interrogation by one or other of the security agencies. People longed for laws which everyone would respect, and in their absence it seemed as if, at the end of the day, the only protection lay in the Arab tradition of *wasata,* that is, having connections in high places to intervene on one's behalf.

Were there mitigating circumstances for Asad's imperfect state-building? Perhaps his long innings could not have been assured under a liberal regime, nor the Muslim Brothers defeated, nor the assaults of Israel and Arab rivals withstood. Perhaps the explanation lay also in an authoritarian streak in Asad's complex character.

As the regime aged there seemed less room for diversity and more emphasis on conformity in the press, in the state information services, and in the party's Popular Organizations. The Ba'th Vanguard Organization (compulsory for the 6–11 age group), the Union of Revolutionary Youth (schoolchildren in the 12–18 age group, not compulsory but conferring considerable privileges) and the Students' Union endeavoured to shape young minds in the Ba'thist mould. The hugely expanded numbers in schools and universities perhaps explained the regimentation, but also contributed to a decline in intellectual standards. All faculty appointments were vetted by the security services and by the party, which staunchly defended its monopoly control over the universities. Within these constraints there were positive achievements: in 1985 a total of 140,000 students were enrolled in higher education, and in the five years 1984–9 over 7,000 Syrians completed post-graduate studies abroad. To make up for low undergraduate standards, a Science Research Council focusing on military and industrial technology was set up in 1974, followed by a number of other elite and highly secretive institutes.

The emancipation of women, first promoted by the radical Ba'th regime of the late 1960s, was carried forward under Asad. Women were elected to parliament and to office in local government and in trade unions, and became judges and university professors. A woman, Dr Najah al-'Attar (PhD from Edinburgh), was appointed Asad's minister of culture in 1976. Before 1970 there were hardly any kindergartens, and working mothers had to stay at home or leave their children with relatives or friends. By the 1980s kindergartens were numerous, mini-buses collecting children from fixed points in the morning and returning them in the evening. The Ba'th Vanguard Organization put girls into uniform and organized summer camps, mixed since 1983. At about this time co-education started in the main cities and spread gradually into the countryside.

*   *   *   *

'I am always fascinated when people talk about 'the forging of a nation.' Most nations are forgeries...' (Neal Ascherson, *The Observer*, 9 June 1985).

In forging the nation Asad and the Ba'th put to use history, archaeology and the cultural and scientific achievements of the Arabs. A commonly held view was that Syria had been asleep for ten centuries, denatured by alien control, but must now be stirred to life, a prerequisite for which was an understanding of the past. A characteristic occasion was a conference held in April 1985 in the rawly new city of al-Thawra, home of the Euphrates dam, on the History of Science among the Arabs. Attended by several provincial governors, party secretaries, university rectors, poets and assorted intellectuals and presided over by the Minister of Culture, Dr Najah al-'Attar, it celebrated the tenth-century astronomer Abu 'Abdullah ibn Jabir ibn

Sinan al-Battani (855–925 AD) who built an observatory in Raqqa where he lived for half a century. Speaker after speaker, many of whom broke into verse, laid stress on reviving past glories to inspire the citizens of tomorrow.

Archaeological finds at Ebla, south of Aleppo, capital of a trading and military state 2500 years BC, and at Mari on the Euphrates, seat of a Sumerian kingdom of the same millennium, gave a great boost to Syrian national pride. The 15,000 tablets of the Ebla royal archive discovered in 1974–5 were found to be written in a Semitic tongue which Syrian scholars claimed located the origins of the Arabic language and of monotheism itself in their country. Together with the 25,000 tablets of the Mari archive and the 300-room palace of that city, with its heated bathrooms, plumbing and kitchen utensils, the Ebla finds provided Syrians with evidence of their ancient superiority over the Hebrews to the south and of their equality with the great civilizations of Egypt and Mesopotamia. Syrians were often exasperated by Israel's use of the Old Testament to justify its contemporary political actions. But here was comfort. The Ebla archive, in the words of its discoverer, Professor Paolo Matthiae of Rome University, described a world of high civilization 'a thousand years before Abraham'.[15] As Dr 'Afif Bahnassi, Syria's director of antiquities, said in response to the Israeli interpretation:[16]

> As a source of universal history the Bible most often speaks of small cities and minor events compared to the great happenings and personalities recorded in the tablets.

Among the 3,500 archaeological sites identified in Syria, most still underground, Dr Bahnassi was convinced that more Eblas would be found. With Asad's encouragement some thirty museums were built in different parts of the country to house the treasures of its unparalleled heritage.

Syria's promotion of its rich archaeological past was part of Asad's exercise in nation-building. The often heard theme that history had placed Syria at the centre of the world was an indirect way of saying that it lay today at the centre of regional power and decision-making.

26

Dirty Tricks

For all Middle Eastern players dirty tricks were an accepted extension of diplomacy in the 1980s. The fine line between terrorism and the defence of national interests was repeatedly crossed in a region which sank to new depths of violence as a result of the collapse of Lebanon, the Syrian-Israeli contest, the Iranian revolution and the Gulf War. As each state sought to shape anarchic events to its advantage, there was an increasing resort to bombings and massacres, kidnappings and assassinations, suicide missions and punitive raids, detention and torture. A by-product was a vast expansion of the security services in almost every country in the region, to the extent that politics were often reduced to struggles between rival intelligence agencies. No one was blameless, no one could claim to occupy the moral high ground, neither Arabs nor Israelis nor Iranians nor their respective proxies and friends. Asad gave as good or as ill as he got but his entanglement with terror was to prove an albatross which it took him years to shrug off.

The extraordinary turbulence of his life owed much to the fact that no sooner had he mastered one crisis than another blew up to confront him. Even while he was still battling to destroy the Israel-Lebanon accord of 17 May 1983, another front opened up to the south, in the Hashimite Kingdom of Jordan.

Like Lebanon before it, Jordan from late 1983 began contemplating separate negotiations with Israel which, from Asad's point of view, would leave Syria on the sidelines. An Israel-Jordan treaty, inevitably drawing Jordan into Israel's sphere of influence, would radically alter the regional balance of power. He saw it as a replay of the Lebanese campaign – with King Husayn standing in for Amin Jumayil, Shimon Peres taking over where Menachem Begin had left off, and George Shultz seeking revenge for his defeat. Asad was particularly affronted that Jordan should lend itself to a US-Israeli manoeuvre against him just when he had succeeded in inflicting on Israel in Lebanon the first major political setback it had suffered since 1948. The struggle for Jordan was to preoccupy him from 1984 onwards.

For two decades Asad and Husayn had been adversary-partners, who in repeated bouts of vicious jousting had developed a healthy respect for each other. In the 1960s Husayn gave succour to the enemies of the radical Ba'th regime which had seized power in Damascus and bombs and plots became the common currency of the relationship; in 1970 Asad invaded Jordan in support of the Palestinian guerrillas then challenging the king. But the rivals made it up in the mid-1970s when they were drawn together by a common danger posed by Egypt's negotiations with Israel. For a moment they even contemplated union. But they were back to blows again before the end of the decade. Jordan lent covert support to the Muslim Brothers in Syria, while Asad struck back with the threat of another invasion in 1980 and with an attempt on the life of Jordan's prime minister, Mudar Badran. From 1980 too, Asad and Husayn were aligned on opposite sides of the Iraq-Iran War which gave their respective secret services scope for mutual *coups bas*. Husayn depended on the West for the continued existence of his country, especially on Britain, the founder and early patron of his throne. Asad, the militant nationalist with a grudge against the West, cherished ties with Moscow.

There were also local reasons why the two men could not fail to collide: Asad felt he needed to project Syria's influence over the whole Arab Levant, while Husayn was determined to remain an independent player. What primarily divided them was the core problem of the Arab-Israeli dispute, particularly how to recover the occupied territories from Israel and, beyond that, how to dispose of them. Who would inherit them, control them, benefit from them? Ever since losing the West Bank Husayn's ambition had been to restore it to the Hashimite crown, and he had bitterly resented the decision of the 1974 Rabat summit to endorse the PLO's claim to exclusive representation of the Palestinians. With a large Palestinian population within his borders he could not but see the PLO as a rival and a threat and sought to manoeuvre it into dependence on him. Asad too strove to subordinate the PLO but for a different reason – his need to control all the Arab variables in the battle against Israel.

The profoundly different circumstances of Jordan and Syria dictated their different strategies. Militarily dwarfed by Israel, Husayn depended for security on Western protectors, on a balance of power between the Arabs and Israel – and on quiet accommodations with Jerusalem. Beginning in 1967 and over the next two decades, he spent hundreds of hours in secret talks with successive Israeli leaders. As Abba Eban,

Israel's veteran statesman, was to remark: 'No two countries on the face of the globe have more experience of direct, bilateral negotiations than do Israel and Jordan.'[1] These efforts got nowhere because Israel would not contemplate a full return of the territories to the king, wanting him to content himself with part of the West Bank (Labour's preference) or simply with administering the local Palestine Arab population – leaving land, water, security and sovereignty in Israel's hands (the Likud's preference). Nevertheless Husayn clung to the hope that by negotiation he might still recover the occupied territories. He feared that challenging Israel with force would result only in the loss of more land, the expulsion of more Palestinians, and his own downfall.

In contrast, Asad had the will and the means to aspire to stand up to Israel. Believing that there was no sense in negotiating from weakness, he advocated the patient application of physical pressure as the only way to get Israel to disgorge. Differences of personality also contributed to the different strategies. Asad had a stolid talent for waiting, while Husayn restlessly explored one avenue after another, relying on his well-developed political instincts to keep him out of trouble.

For years Husayn had been under sustained American and Israeli pressure to 'solve' the Palestine problem in direct negotiations with Israel. But without an Arab mandate he dared not agree to subdivide the West Bank with Israel, let alone become an Israeli vassal. It was not easy to square the circle between the little that Israel was disposed to yield and what the Arabs would accept. Husayn's preferred formula was for a Jordanian-Palestinian federation, providing in his view an adequate outlet for Palestinian aspirations, protection for his throne and for Israel the security it still professed to need.

In 1982–3, in response to the Reagan plan which seemed to propose just such a solution, he tried to persuade 'Arafat to let him negotiate with Israel on behalf of both Jordan and the Palestinians. 'Arafat was tempted but then backed away under pressure from Asad and hard-line PLO factions. But in 1983–4, when Asad fell ill and Israel beckoned, Husayn thought the time was right to make another attempt – a move which, needless to say, Asad read as an outflanking manoeuvre to neutralize him and give Israel hegemony.

Asad was alerted by a series of danger signals. The first was Husayn's invitation to 'Arafat in December 1983 to visit Amman, just when Syrian-backed forces were throwing him out of Tripoli. Another was 'Arafat's reconciliation with Mubarak of Egypt – for Asad, the hated Egypt of Camp David – two days after sailing from Tripoli. Was 'Arafat about to follow Egypt into 'surrender'? A third worry was the likelihood that Israel's Labour leader, Shimon Peres, prime advocate of the so-called 'Jordan option', would win the Israeli elections of July 1984. If Israel and Jordan managed to strike a deal which satisfied the Palestinians and enjoyed the backing of Arab moderates and the United States, Syria would be isolated and its influence much reduced. All the principal players – Husayn, 'Arafat, Peres, Mubarak and Shultz – seemed united in a desire to clip Asad's wings.

With growing anger and alarm Asad watched Husayn prepare the ground. The king freed Palestinians from his jails, held frequent meetings with 'Arafat throughout 1984, revived joint committees for West Bank affairs, canvassed support in London and Washington, restored diplomatic relations with Egypt in September 1984, and hosted the seventeenth Palestine National Council in Amman that November. The time had come, he told the delegates, for the PLO to abandon its all-or-nothing policy and join with Jordan in an initiative to negotiate a settlement with Israel based on 'land for peace'. The negotiating forum should be a UN-sponsored international conference attended by all five permanent members of the Security Council. On 11 February 1985 after weeks of bargaining Husayn and 'Arafat signed an agreement which seemed to give the king the mandate he needed.

A further ominous sign that Jordan was straying dangerously from what Asad considered nationalist rectitude was the arguments it used in Washington to get US arms and political backing. In overtures to the Jewish lobby, it portrayed Syria as the enemy, Israel as the neighbour with which it was already virtually at peace, and Palestinian radicalism as the danger which Jordan and Israel could together contain. (Unable in all conscience to represent this line of argument Jordan's ambassador to Washington, Ibrahim 'Izzedin, returned to Amman in May 1985 and was replaced by a seventy-year-old Palestinian, Muhammad Kamal, who obediently courted Jewish groups.)[2]

Such was the background to Asad's undeclared war on Husayn in 1983–5.

Jousting with Husayn

In October 1983, the Jordanian ambassadors to India and Italy were wounded in gun attacks; in November a Jordanian official was killed and another seriously wounded in Athens, and three explosive devices defused in Amman; in December a Jordanian consular official was killed and another wounded in Madrid. In March 1984 a bomb exploded outside Amman's Intercontinental hotel and in November the

Jordanian chargé d'affaises in Athens narrowly escaped being shot when his attacker's gun jammed. In December the Jordanian counsellor in Bucharest was shot dead. In April 1985 there was an attack on the Jordanian embassy in Rome and on a Jordanian aircraft at Athens airport. In July the Madrid office of Alia, the Jordanian airline, was machine-gunned and the first secretary of the Jordanian embassy in Ankara was shot dead. In August a Palestinian was arrested in Athens on suspicion of planning a second attempt on the life of the Jordanian chargé. It must be assumed that some at least of these assaults on Jordanians were the work of Syria.

It was widely believed that in his campaign to frighten Husayn Asad used proxies, and in particular the well-known Palestinian hit-man, Sabri al-Banna, better known as Abu Nidal who broke with 'Arafat after the October War of 1973 and set up his own ultra-militant faction, Fatah – the Revolutionary Council. Abu Nidal had waged war against the PLO but had also hired out his guns to various patrons – first to Iraq in 1976–7 which used him against Syria and then to Syria in 1983–5 which used him in its 'coercive diplomacy'[3] against Jordan.

Syria did not escape retaliation, some of it presumably at the hands of Jordan or of its ally Iraq (which had its own reasons for harassing Syria). In December 1984 a Syrian attaché in Athens was attacked but drove off his assailant. In April 1985 the Rome office of Syrian Arab Airlines was bombed and three employees wounded and an attempt was made to kill a Syrian diplomat in Geneva. In May his colleague in Rabat was shot, while in June a bomb was defused outside the Syrian embassy in London. In July large car bombs exploded in Damascus outside the offices of the Syrian Arab News Agency and the Ministry of the Interior, causing dozens of casualties.

Neither Asad nor Husayn admitted that they were waging a terrorist war against each other, but as their differences were well aired, it was public knowledge. The Damascus press thundered that the Jordanian-Palestinian peace plan was as dangerous as the Camp David accords and that the traitors would not go unpunished.[4] In November 1984, when Husayn urged the Palestine National Council to fall in with his negotiating strategy, Damascus launched a 'Jordanian national movement' dedicated to the establishment of a 'democratic and nationalist regime' in Amman – in other words to the overthrow of the king. And following the Husayn-'Arafat accord of February 1985, Abu Nidal and another Syrian-backed Fatah dissident, Abu Musa, publicly set up a joint command to make war on it.

By mid-1985 such pressures were enough to persuade Husayn that it was time to beat a tactical retreat. Asad clearly meant business. Moreover, to Husayn's chagrin Peres had failed to win the Israeli elections and was instead forced to join Shamir in a 'national unity' government in which the Likud frustrated Labour's wish to negotiate a territorial compromise with Jordan. 'Arafat in turn was reined in by his PLO Executive Committee which gutted the February 1985 agreement he had reached with the king. At the same the US Congress prevented the Administration from selling Jordan Stinger air defence missiles despite Husayn's appeasement of the Jewish lobby. In the circumstances, with nothing to gain, it was pointless for Husayn to pursue his murderous quarrel with Asad.

Accordingly a truce was called. The Syrian premier, Dr Kasm, met his Jordanian counterpart Zayd al-Rifa'i in Jidda in mid-September and hostilities were ended. (The Rifa'i family had long had ties with Syria and Husayn was in the habit of appointing Zayd prime minister whenever he needed to defuse a crisis with Damascus.) Moreover, on 10 November in an open letter to his prime minister, the king acknowledged that some Jordanian officials had indeed been involved in the Muslim Brothers' insurrection against Asad – a *mea culpa* which Asad accepted with satisfaction. Rifa'i then came to see Asad and a joint communiqué was issued rejecting direct negotiations with Israel as well as partial or separate solutions. Husayn had conceded defeat. At the end of December 1985 he came himself to Damascus – his first appearance there since 1979; in February 1986 he publicly renounced his accord with 'Arafat; and in May Asad travelled to Amman – his first visit since 1977. He had imposed on Husayn his strategy for dealing with Israel and thereby deflected the threat to his southern flank.

The jousting had been brutal with pawns sacrificed on either side, and after such a contest it was hardly surprising that trust and amity were not fully restored. Husayn had been forced to yield by the realities of power. But the intractable West Bank issue remained unresolved, ensuring that the players would make renewed attempts to secure their preferred solutions. Even while Husayn was bowing to Asad's will, Peres, now Israel's Prime Minister, was hatching new schemes to lure him out of Syria's orbit.

Terrorism rampant

Terror is a sword that can turn in the hand of him who wields it. Asad's doctrine of Levant security demanded that he forcibly dissuade his neighbours from making separate settlements with Israel. In

1982–5 he used terror, among other means, to frighten both Lebanon and Jordan away from such a course. But in waging these battles he unleashed demons which could not be easily controlled. It was all very well using Abu Nidal against Jordan to head off a particular threat if that was the end of it. But Abu Nidal was a killer, with other patrons and an agenda of his own. For example, the killings attributed to him between 1978 and 1983 before Syria took him up – such as the murder of PLO representatives in London, Kuwait, Paris, Brussels and Portugal – were related to his feud with 'Arafat. In fact, so destructive was he of the Palestinian movement that some Arabs came to believe his group had been penetrated by Mossad.

However, some of his other victims were Israeli like the commercial counsellor murdered in Brussels in June 1980, or simply Jewish like the chairman of the Austria-Israel Association murdered in Vienna in May 1981. In August of that year there was an attack on a Vienna synagogue, and in June 1982 the attempted assassination of Ambassador Argov in London which gave Begin the pretext for his Lebanon War.

Asad was to discover that the murderous activities of Abu Nidal's shadowy gunmen could not be turned off at will. They continued to make use of some Syrian facilities – camps, lodgings for their dependants, transit through Damascus airport – in mounting rogue operations which Asad had not authorized, such as the attacks on the El Al counters at Rome and Vienna airports in December 1985 and the hijack of a Pan-Am airliner on the ground at Karachi airport in September 1986 in which more than a score of people were killed. A few days later terrorists machine-gunned a synagogue in Istanbul, again killing more than twenty. In each case there was a link to the mysterious Abu Nidal, but who exactly ordered and funded these missions could not be established.

These attacks served no Syrian interest and fitted into no Syrian strategy. Taken aback by them, Asad expressed great anger when Syria's name was linked to them, and Syrian spokesmen insisted that Abu Nidal's offices in Damascus now dealt only with information and publicity. Western intelligence agencies came to believe that Abu Nidal had turned to Libya for support once Syria had no further need of him. (Fragments of Libyan-supplied Bulgarian hand-grenades found at Rome and Vienna airports and at the Istanbul synagogue appeared to come from the same lot.) Evidently the earlier terror campaign which Asad had waged against Husayn had spilled over into actions gravely detrimental to his reputation.

Equally damaging to him was the overspill of terrorism in Lebanon. To roll back Israeli power Asad had encouraged resistance by militant

Shi'a and other Lebanese radicals. The devastating results were the assassination of Bashir Jumayil, the blowing up of the US embassy, the slaughter of the marines, and the ongoing guerrilla harassment of Israel's invasion force – operations which routed the Americans and drove the Israelis back towards their frontier. But just as Abu Nidal could not be switched off, nor could the Lebanese resistance. It was not a mercenary force taking orders from Damascus but a collection of Lebanese groups, each fighting for its own objectives.

Once Asad had destroyed the Israel-Lebanon accord, continuing violence in Lebanon was not to his advantage. From early 1984 he had no further interest in Shi'i assaults on Western (as opposed to Israeli) targets and tried to impose his own order. But the fully aroused Shi'a of Lebanon had grievances which overlapped only at certain points with his own. Amal, the mainstream Shi'i movement which seized control of West Beirut in February 1984, was at war with the Lebanese state and with the Palestinians whose presence exposed the Shi'a to large-scale Israeli punishment. Moreover, the Shi'i movement in Lebanon was split. Whereas Amal was tactically allied to Syria, the more religiously inspired Hizbullah, concerned with Islamic revolution as much as with Lebanese politics, was umbilically tied to Iran.

A typical Hizbullah hit-man was 'Imad Mughniya, a Shi'i from the B'albak area and nephew of the prominent religious figure, Shaykh Muhammad Jawad Mughniya.[5] In the late 1970s 'Imad had served with 'Arafat's security unit, Force 17, before being recruited by the Iranians when he was believed to have had a hand in the attacks on the US embassy and the marine barracks. He may also have been involved in the kidnapping of William Buckley, the CIA Beirut station chief in March 1984. Buckley, who died presumably under torture in June, was an early victim of the wave of hostage-taking for which Lebanon was to become notorious in 1985–8. In their struggle against Israel and the West, Shi'i militants did not stop at kidnapping, and among their many operations, some drew world attention such as the hijack on 14 June 1985 of a TWA airliner with 244 passengers on board. It was flown back and forth across the Mediterranean, shedding passengers at stops in Algiers before landing at Beirut with a hard-core of thirty-eight American captives on board, one of whom, a navy diver, was then murdered.

None of this served Asad's purpose, but nor did he have the power to stop it. He unequivocally condemned hostage-takers and hijackers as damaging to the Arab cause.[6] He would not allow Hizbullah members in Damascus. He believed their methods blurred the vital distinction between the Arabs' legitimate struggle for national liberation and terrorism. He extolled the guerrilla campaign against

Israel in south Lebanon – praising 'martyrs' like the 16-year-old Lebanese girl, Sana' Yusuf Muhaydli, a member of the pan-Syrian SSNP, who died in a suicide attack on Israel's 'security zone' in April 1985.[7] But random violence against innocent civilians he repudiated.

Yet he was inhibited from tackling the extremists head on for fear of endangering his alliance with Iran and because he wished to make use of every ounce of Shi'i militancy in the continuing struggle against Israel in the south. Whenever he could, he helped secure the release of hostages such as the American correspondent Jerry Levin on 15 February 1985 and others. In the long-drawn-out TWA hijack crisis in June he prevented the hijackers from dispersing their captives, then himself took over the negotiations with them from Amal's leader Nabih Berri and freed the remaining Americans through Damascus on 29 June.

Both Shultz in Washington and the US *chargé d'affaires*, in Damascus, April Glaspie, knew that Asad had gone out of his way to end the TWA hijack, even breaking his own rule by inviting Hizbullah leaders from B'albak to Damascus. The State Department prepared a letter of thanks for Reagan to send him, but Colonel Oliver North of the National Security Council and a pro-Israeli aide, Howard Teicher, replaced the text by another couched in almost insulting terms. Asad was offended: instead of being rewarded, he was rebuffed. When Reagan was prevailed upon to telephone him, he had the North-Teicher letter in front of him and read it out, only compounding the affront. It appeared to Asad that the United States only wanted him to tame the terrorists in Lebanon, while remaining indifferent to his security needs. The State Department persuaded Vice-President George Bush to write a letter in warmer terms to Syrian Vice-President Khaddam, but by then the damage was only partially repaired.

The terrorist slur which Asad earned in his campaign to prevent Lebanon and then Jordan slipping into Israel's orbit continued to dog him and he was all too often held responsible for actions by extremists with which he had no connection. Even his efforts on behalf of Western hostages were often seen as hypocritical gestures cloaking his ongoing use of violence.[8] The terrorist label was to prove a boon to his enemies.

Terrorism and counter-terrorism

Arab terrorism presented Shimon Peres with an opportunity. His long-held ambition to settle the Palestine problem in a separate deal with

Jordan was a consistent strand of his policy as premier from September 1984 to September 1986 and thereafter as foreign minister when he changed places with Shamir in Israel's unity government. But to strike a deal with Jordan it was necessary to release Husayn from Syrian and PLO bonds. So the struggle for Jordan was not unlike the struggle for Lebanon: for Israel to prevail, Syria and the PLO had to be neutralized, even defeated. In Lebanon the defeat of Syria had been fudged. Peres was anxious to demonstrate that he could do better in Jordan – and the terrorist charge against Asad was perhaps a way of achieving this. Peres understood that if he could make the charge stick, Syria and the PLO would be driven beyond the pale and their power to obstruct Israel's aims would be reduced.

Israel's practice had long been to label Palestinian fighters as 'terrorists' so as to justify killing them and deny their cause any legitimacy. The exploitation of the terrorist issue was now to be greatly expanded and to play a vital role in shaping American attitudes. The background was the grave setback which both the United States and Israel had suffered in Lebanon. After this trauma the effort to wrestle with frustrating conflicts in the Middle East was given up for the manly task of fighting 'state-sponsored terrorism'. The US-Israel agreement on strategic co-operation (concluded in 1981, suspended because of the Golan annexation, informally revived by Alexander Haig in 1982 and reactivated by George Shultz in November 1983) gave Israel wide opportunities to steer American policy in this direction. The prescription was to treat the terrorists with their own medicine rather than to trace the roots of the violence to the dispossession of the Palestinians, to the burning Shi'a sense of injustice, to Israel's invasion of Lebanon, or to Syria's need to protect itself against Israeli encroachments. Terrorism became the issue of the day in the United States. Indeed, American policy on the Arab-Israeli dispute dwindled to mere counter-terrorism.

The personal bias of individual officials contributed to the trend. Charlie Hill, the quiet, soft-spoken deputy assistant secretary of the Near East-South Asian Bureau at the State Department, who became Shultz's executive assistant in the summer of 1984, was whole-heartedly committed to Israel. Pro-Israeli staff members such as Howard Teicher, Michael Ledeen and Peter Rodman at the State Department and the National Security Council were also influential, as was the number three man at the State Department in 1982–4, Laurence Eagleburger.

A key factor at the time which influenced President Reagan himself was the proceedings of a conference organized in Washington in June 1984 by Israel's Jonathan Institute, later edited by Israel's UN

ambassador, Benjamin Netanyahu, and published under the title
Terrorism: How the West Can Win.[9] Like Claire Sterling's *The Terror
Network* in the first Reagan years, the conference papers became the
master text of America's obsession with terrorism in Reagan's second
term. Part of an elaborate campaign of psychological warfare directed
against the PLO, Libya and Syria, they helped persuade opinion that
Israel's enemies were also America's, that Arabs in dispute with Israel
were terrorists, and that brute force against them was not only
legitimate but desirable. Netanyahu wrote:[10]

> If a government has harboured, trained and launched terrorists, it
> becomes the legitimate object of a military response. Under no
> circumstances should governments *categorically rule out* a military
> response simply because of the risk of civilian casualties.

George Shultz agreed, arguing in his paper that 'a purely passive
defence' was not a sufficient deterrent. What was required was
'appropriate preventive or pre-emptive actions against terrorist groups
before they strike'.[11] Moshe Arens, then Israel's Defence Minister,
identified Syria as the key terrorist state whose 'world-wide intelligence
apparatus' made use of Palestinians, Armenians, Japanese, and even
Thais![12]

The papers uncoupled terrorism from any political or social context,
treating it 'as a variant of organized crime'.[13] Midge Decter, the pro-
Israeli right-wing publicist, scolded:[14]

> The idea that terrorists embody or represent the interests of groups
> with grievances has freed many in the West from having to assume
> the burden of moral, political, and military action.

Yet only the British writer Paul Johnson was crass enough actually to
congratulate Israel for invading Lebanon in 1982:[15]

> By having had the moral and physical courage to violate a so-called
> sovereign frontier . . . Israel was able for the first time to strike at the
> heart of the cancer.

Acts followed words.

Israeli and US intelligence suspected that Hizbullah's spiritual guide,
Shaykh Muhammad Husayn Fadlallah,[16] was the brain behind the
bombings and kidnappings of Americans in Beirut. A decision was
taken to kill him. On 8 March 1985 a massive car bomb exploded

close to Fadlallah's apartment in a Beirut suburb, killing eighty people and wounding two hundred in a welter of collapsed buildings and shattered vehicles. Fadlallah escaped without injury. Two years later the *Washington Post* reported that the explosion had been set off by a group composed of Lebanese intelligence men and foreigners trained by the CIA under a Reagan-authorized covert action programme.[17] Bob Woodward, in his book on the CIA recounted that Casey had solicited $3 million from the Saudis for the operation, which had been directed on the ground by an English mercenary.[18] The attempt on Fadlallah was a prelude to overt acts of war by Israel and the United States against Arab targets, all justified in the name of the anti-terrorist crusade.

On 1 October 1985 eight Israeli F-16s raided PLO headquarters near Tunis, killing fifty-six Palestinians and fifteen Tunisians and wounding about one hundred others. 'Arafat narrowly escaped death. Reagan condoned the raid as a 'legitimate response' to terrorism, for it was billed as retaliation for the killing of three Israelis (widely believed to be Mossad agents) on a yacht in Larnaca, Cyprus. But the scale of the operation pointed to a more ambitious goal: Israel was seeking not simply to eliminate 'Arafat but to ensure that the PLO, then roped somewhat insecurely to Husayn by the February 1985 agreement, would not be a party to any negotiations. It was later learned that Israel's strike had been made possible by US satellite information on the PLO complex secured by Jonathan Jay Pollard, whose job at the US Naval Security and Investigative Command enabled him to supply Israel with a vast intelligence haul. Pollard was arrested in November 1985 and sentenced to life imprisonment for espionage in March 1987.

In response to the Tunis raid a Palestinian faction led by Abu'l 'Abbas, of the Popular Liberation Front, hijacked an Italian cruise ship, the *Achille Lauro*, on 9 October 1985, and as the operation went wrong murdered Leon Klinghoffer, a crippled American Jew on board. His body was washed up on the Syrian coast and handed over by the Syrians to the US authorities — Asad's way of distancing himself from the outrage.

Making a bogey out of Libya slotted well into Israel's campaign to damn the whole tribe of Arab radicals. An Iranian arms dealer, Manuchehr Ghorbanifar, later identified as an Israeli agent, served to inflame Washington by peddling stories of Qadhafi's terrorist plans, including an alleged plot to kill the US President. When radio intercepts appeared to link Libya with an explosion in a West Berlin discotheque used by American servicemen, Qadhafi's home compound in Tripoli and other targets were bombed on 15 April 1986 by US aircraft flown from British bases. Qadhafi escaped unharmed but dozens of Libyan civilians, including his adopted baby daughter, were killed. Israeli intelligence provided continuous updates on Qadhafi's whereabouts, the last coming at 11.15 p.m. Libyan time, two hours 45 minutes before the attack began.[19] Modelled on Israel's attempt six months earlier to kill 'Arafat in Tunis, the raid on Libya had clearly been intended to kill Qadhafi.

Israel had won wide acceptance for its version of the Arab-Israeli dispute: the violence of its opponents was 'terror', its own was 'legitimate self-defence'. Yet as Richard Rubinstein wrote in his book *Alchemists of Revolution*, 'There is no force more terroristic than a national state at war'.[20]

Attacks on Asad

From Israel's point of view, Asad was a far more important target than either 'Arafat or Qadhafi, and from the late autumn of 1985 he was fed a diet of threats and acts of war. On 19 November 1985 Israel shot down two Syrian MiG-23s over Syrian territory as they made for home after approaching an Israeli surveillance aircraft flying over Lebanon. In what seemed a replay of the 1981 missile crisis, Asad moved SAM batteries up to the frontier and into the Biqa', challenging Israel's control of Lebanese air space. It took much American diplomacy for the Biqa' SAMs to be pulled back.

Pressure on Asad was not only military. In January 1986 a 'tripartite agreement' between Shi'i, Druze and Maronite militia chiefs, which he had stitched together as a basis for Lebanese national reconciliation, was torpedoed by Maronite ultras with Israeli and US encouragement. Syria's order in Lebanon was not to be allowed to prevail. And there were other incidents to needle him. On 4 February 1986 Israeli fighters forced down a Libyan executive jet carrying home to Damascus a Syrian delegation led by the assistant secretary general of the Ba'th party, 'Abdallah al-Ahmar. Syria complained to the Security Council but the United States vetoed the condemnation of Israel. The Syrians vowed revenge.

Syria itself then came under terrorist attack which it variously blamed on Iraq, on Israeli agents from Lebanon, on the Muslim Brothers, and on the CIA. On 13 March 1986 there was a massive car-bomb explosion in central Damascus, the opening shot in a terrorist campaign which seemed designed to destabilize Asad's regime. On 16 April, the day after the US attack on Libya, bombs on trucks and trains in different parts of Syria killed no fewer than 144 people and wounded many more. It may not have been unconnected that in late 1985 the NSC's Colonel Oliver North and Amiram Nir, Peres's counter-terrorism expert, set up a dirty tricks outfit to strike back at the alleged sponsors of Middle East terrorism.[21]

These violent incidents heightened the fears of an Israeli-Syrian war. Contingency plans for an attack on Syria had been prepared by Moshe Arens when he was defence minister under Begin and updated by Rabin who was now in Arens's place. Given US tolerance for Israeli military action, Israeli leaders believed that they could count on quiet applause from Washington if they were able to deliver a 1967-style knockout blow. There was no sympathy in Washington for Asad's ambition to achieve parity with Israel, no understanding of the reasons for his 'spoiling' role in Lebanon and Jordan, nor any liking for his insistence that the Soviet Union be given a role in the peace process. Israel's psychological warfare on the theme of counter-terrorism had prepared Western opinion for the punishment of Asad, as it had for that of 'Arafat and Qadhafi. In the spring of 1986 Syria and Israel seemed on the brink of war.

Yet the Israelis were far from unanimous about the wisdom of attacking Syria. Among the military, Chief of Staff Moshe Levy was a prudent man who recognized that it could be a costly affair. Asad's army of close to half a million men had learned to handle sophisticated weapons and would undoubtedly put up a tremendous fight. Particular Israeli concerns were the air defence wall which the Soviets had built round Syria and the new ground-to-ground missiles, some possibly fitted with chemical warheads, which for the first time raised the spectre of large-scale Israeli civilian casualties.

Urgent US-Soviet exchanges took place in the spring of 1986 against the background of larger than usual Syrian and Israeli ground manoeuvres. Soviet diplomats told the State Department on the personal instructions of General Secretary Gorbachev that the superpowers had a responsibility to draw their respective clients back from the brink.[22] On 28 May Gorbachev publicly reaffirmed the Soviet commitment to defend Syria. Worried by these Soviet signals, Washington urged restraint on Jerusalem. But behind these alarms the political struggle continued.

The assaults on 'Arafat, Qadhafi and Asad in 1985–6 had a prime political purpose; they were designed to create favourable conditions for Peres to press his suit on King Husayn and to allow Israel to solve the Palestine problem on its own terms. Asad had proved himself the greatest single obstacle to Israel's aims in the Levant. Only if he were removed, or at least scared off the scene, could Israel proceed unchallenged. Thus was posed the crucial question which was to underlie Middle East politics as the decade of the 1980s drew to a close: could Israel get its way without first dealing with Asad's Syria?

So, while the fires of war were being stoked on the Syrian front, Shimon Peres embarked from the autumn of 1985 and into 1986 on a highly publicized 'peace initiative' aimed at drawing King Husayn into direct talks. He drummed up support in Europe and the United States, expounding to the UN General Assembly a plan to bring peace 'within thirty days', and showing 'flexibility' by proposing an international forum (a gesture towards the Arabs' demand for an international conference) as a prelude to bilateral negotiations. He called on Husayn to come forward, while making it plain that he considered Syria unready, the PLO unacceptable at any price, and the Soviet Union ineligible unless it restored diplomatic relations with Israel.

Peres found support in the British Prime Minister, Mrs Margaret Thatcher, with whom he struck up a political friendship during his official London visit in January 1986 and on her return visit to Israel in May, the first by a serving British premier. Mrs Thatcher had close relations with King Husayn, and was thus well placed to promote the Jordan-Israel accord that Peres wanted so badly. The fact that some of her close advisers and many of her Finchley constituents were well-wishers of the Israeli Labour party may also have helped. She seemed unable to grasp why Syria objected to such a deal, and to believe that Asad was against peace in general. Mrs Thatcher and the British parliament and press were not well disposed towards Asad who as often as not was depicted as a ruthless, unco-operative ruler for ever threatening Israel. In 1985 anti-Syrian sentiment was further aroused by the long-running and much publicized case of a Syrian diplomat who in defiance of a court order refused to vacate a London flat until his landlord appealed to the Queen.

Such was the pattern of the mid-1980s. Peres in his courtship of Husayn strove to blacken Asad and get him out of the way, while Asad, not eschewing terror, fought to keep Jordan in the Arab camp.

The Hindawi affair

It was during this stalemate that a dramatic terrorist incident brought opprobrium on Asad and seemed to tip the scales in favour of Peres.

At Heathrow on 17 April 1986 shortly after 9 a.m., an Israeli security guard discovered 1.5 kilograms of Semtex, a powerful plastic explosive of Czechoslovak manufacture, in the false bottom of a bag which an Irishwoman, Ann Murphy, was about to carry on to an El Al flight to Tel Aviv. The bomb's detonator was disguised as a pocket calculator. Ann Murphy, a chambermaid at a London hotel, had been given the bag by her Jordanian boyfriend, Nizar Hindawi, by whom she was five months pregnant. He had promised to join her in Israel where they were to be married. The 32-year-old Hindawi had taken his fiancée to the airport in a taxi, priming the bomb on the way by inserting a battery in the calculator. It was timed to go off while the aircraft was in flight.

Leaving his fiancée at Heathrow, Hindawi travelled back to a room in Kensington's Royal Garden Hotel reserved for personnel of Syrian Arab Airlines. Later that morning he boarded the SAA crew bus to return to the airport in order to catch a flight to Damascus leaving at 2 p.m. But before the bus set off news broke that a bomb had been discovered at Heathrow. Hindawi got off hurriedly and went to the Syrian embassy in Belgrave Square where he told the ambassador, Dr Lutfallah Haydar, that he was in trouble and asked for assistance. Haydar passed him on to embassy security men who took him to their lodgings in West Kensington where they attempted to alter his appearance by cutting and dyeing his hair and put him up for the night. But early the next morning, 18 April, Hindawi fled and made for the London Visitors Hotel in Holland Park where he knew the proprietor. The proprietor called in Hindawi's brother (a clerk in the Qatar embassy medical section) who persuaded him to give himself up.

Over the next two days Hindawi was intensively interrogated at Paddington Green police station. He first told the police that he believed the bag he had given Ann Murphy contained narcotics to be smuggled into Israel for a large sum of money. Then, after his sleep was deliberately interrupted several times during the night, he changed his story. He said he was an opponent of King Husayn and had sought Syrian support. In Damascus in January 1986 he had met the head of air force intelligence, General Muhammad al-Khuly, and one of his officers, Colonel Haytham Sa'id. A month later Sa'id gave him a Syrian service passport in the name of 'Issam Share' and instructed him to place a bomb on an El Al aircraft in London. He was sent to Britain on a practice run. On returning to Damascus he had been shown the bag with the secret compartment by Sa'id who had told him how to arm the bomb. On 5 April he had returned once more to London, and at the Royal Garden Hotel was given the bag containing the explosives and the calculator/ detonator by a man whom he believed to be an official of SAA.

This confession was to be the basis of the prosecution's case at Hindawi's trial.

The Heathrow incident occurred two days after the US bombing of Libya and one day after the rash of terrorist explosions in Syria which killed and wounded several hundred people. On hearing of the incident, Asad was certain that he was in danger. The Hindawi affair triggered a world-wide campaign against Syria which he saw as the prelude to a physical attack either by Israel alone or in conjunction with the United States. His enemies wanted to bring him down in order to complete Israel's unfinished business in Lebanon and allow an Israel-Jordan deal to go forward. He believed that Europe, and Britain in particular, had joined the hostile US-Israeli front.[23]

When at the Western summit in Tokyo on 5 May, heads of government of the world's seven leading industrial nations, with Mrs Thatcher in the van, issued a ringing condemnation of 'state-sponsored terrorism', Asad denounced such 'acts of intimidation'. As it happened, the Tokyo summit took place on the day of his visit to Amman which, much to Israel's displeasure, set the seal on his reconciliation with Husayn.

Asad's anxiety grew when both Peres and Rabin made bellicose speeches stressing 'Syria's central role in terrorism',[24] and when Mrs Thatcher arrived in Israel in late May – a visit which he read as expressing British support for Peres's plans for a separate deal with Husayn. To head off what he feared was imminent attack, Asad flew abruptly to Greece on 26 May, and at a dinner given by Prime Minister Papandreou, the one European leader he could count as a friend, made an impassioned speech on the theme of the vital distinction between terrorism and the struggle for national liberation.

Five months later in October 1986 Hindawi went on trial at the Old Bailey and condemnation of Syria reached a climax. However, in court he retracted his account of Syrian involvement and claimed instead to be the victim of a conspiracy which he thought was possibly mounted by Israeli agents. He alleged that Detective Sergeant Will Price who had arrested him and taken part in his interrogation had threatened to turn him over to Mossad and had told him that his father and brother were also under arrest. He complained that the police had made up the statements attributed to him and had forced him to sign them unread.

During the trial, on 20 October Asad gave an interview to *Time* magazine in which he denied Syrian involvement and claimed that Israeli intelligence had planned the Hindawi operation to exploit it for political ends, arranging for it to be uncovered 'at the plane's doorstep'. Unimpressed by Asad's defence and Hindawi's retraction, however, a British jury found Hindawi guilty and he was sentenced on 24 October to forty-five years' imprisonment, the longest sentence in British criminal history. Within hours of the verdict Britain broke off relations with Syria. Although it urged its allies to take stern measures against Asad, none went as far as Mrs Thatcher would have liked: the United States and Canada simply recalled their ambassadors while the European Community, with Greece abstaining, adopted a programme of limited sanctions. Nevertheless, Asad was out in the cold.

The impact on him of the international reproof was blunted by two events. On 10 November, the day the EC sanctions were agreed, the Soviet Foreign Minister warned the West not to use the Hindawi affair as a pretext for reprisals against Syria. And, more unexpectedly but to far greater effect, the French Prime Minister, Jacques Chirac, remarked in an interview with the *Washington Times* that West German Chancellor Kohl and Foreign Minister Genscher both believed, as he tended to do himself, that 'the Hindawi plot was a provocation designed to embarrass Syria and destabilize the Asad regime.' Behind it were 'probably people connected with the Israeli Mossad' in conjunction with Asad's Syrian opponents.[25]

Angry with Chirac for breaking ranks, British officials linked his remarks to French attempts to solicit Syrian aid against terrorists both in France and in Lebanon. In fact, the next day two French hostages were freed in Beirut and handed over to French diplomats in Damascus, earning for Asad Chirac's warm thanks. But Asad was again embarrassed in late November when a West Berlin court sentenced Hindawi's brother, Ahmad Hasi, to fourteen years imprisonment in connection with an explosion eight months earlier in March 1986 at the offices of the German-Arab Friendship Society. Like Hindawi, Hasi first implicated Syria and then retracted the confession in court.

In the wake of the Hindawi verdict, Israel and the United States redoubled their efforts to draw Jordan into separate talks, the high point being the London Agreement of February 1987 reached at a secret meeting between Peres and Husayn at which they approved American-brokered terms for a bilateral negotiation. Peres was later to claim that this agreement was a breakthrough unprecedented since Sadat's visit to Jerusalem in 1977.[26]

> We have a partner . . . Jordan is prepared for direct negotiations after an international opening . . . The international opening will not have the power to impose or intervene in a solution. These are three elements that have never existed before.

Alarmed at these developments Asad strove to break out of the shackles of the damaging terrorist charge which, he claimed in a fighting speech in May 1987, was designed to compel the Arabs to yield their territory and force Syria to renounce its role in the world.[27]

They plotted against us in Lebanon, they plotted against us in an economic siege, and they plotted against us through the Muslim Brotherhood . . . Finally they came up with the idea of terrorism . . . Do we surrender, do these big powers frighten us? They do not.'

Did Asad have reason to feel aggrieved? His resentment that Syria should be singled out was expressed later:[28]

Had British policy really been against terrorism, Mrs Thatcher would have taken harsh measures against the Israelis who tried to kidnap a Nigerian minister in a coffin and who abducted [the dissident Israeli atomic technician] Vanunu.

So what was the extent of Syria's guilt in the Hindawi affair, typical in its murky complexity of the war between hostile services which had come to characterize Middle East politics in the 1980s? It is scarcely in doubt that a Syrian agency, most probably General Khuly's air force intelligence, was involved in the bungled attempt to blow up an El Al airliner. The motive may have been revenge for Israel's forcing down the plane carrying a Syrian delegation two months earlier. Apart from Hindawi's confession which was not in itself conclusive, there was a good deal of independent evidence of a Syrian connection. Hindawi travelled on an official Syrian government passport made out in a false name; the Syrian Ministry of Foreign Affairs had supported his two visa applications to Britain in February and April 1986; Syrian intelligence persuaded a locally recruited clerk at the British embassy in Damascus to submit the second visa application on a day when the consul who had signed the first was away; in London Syrian agents operated under the cover of Syrian Arab Airlines and it was as a member of the crew that Hindawi was to have escaped from Britain.

Furthermore it appeared that British intelligence had intercepted a message from Dr Haydar, the Syrian ambassador, recommending Hindawi to Syrian intelligence some months earlier in 1985. After the bomb was discovered at Heathrow, Hindawi's interview with the ambassador when he asked for help may also have been monitored. Traces of Hindawi's hair and hair dye were found in the London flat of the Syrian security men where he spent the night. And in detention before his trial Hindawi tried to make secret contact with intelligence officials in Damascus, again requesting help. All this amounted to a convincing case.

But it seems equally certain that President Asad, as well as his Prime Minister, Dr Kasm, and the rest of the government knew nothing about the operation until they heard the news on the radio. Quite apart from their own denials, this was the considered judgment of American and European officials, including British officials close to the case, and of well-placed Arab leaders. Rather, the incident suggested that Syrian intelligence (like, on occasion, the secret services of other countries) was not under tight enough political control. Random atrocities were not in Asad's style and, had the destruction of an Israeli civilian aircraft been traced to Syria, his regime and his country would have been put at immense risk. Asad was not in the business of national suicide. Given his consistent anxiety to avoid war with Israel, his sanctioning of the Heathrow bomb made no sense at all.

But was there more to the affair than a bungled rogue operation by an uncontrolled branch of Syrian intelligence? There is some evidence to suggest that Hindawi, and indeed his brother Hasi in West Germany, were double agents who worked for Syria while in fact being controlled by Israel. Hindawi was most probably an *agent provocateur* whose mission was to entrap the Syrian intelligence services so as to smear Syria as a terrorist state. He appeared to be the instrument for an Israeli penetration of Syrian intelligence, a classic exercise of its sort, and through him Israel was able to monitor the Heathrow operation from start to finish, if not to sell it to the Syrians in the first place. Hindawi may have been deliberately planted on the Syrians or indeed spotted as a useful potential double once Syria had recruited him. The British intercept of the Syrian ambassador's coded message recommending him to the intelligence services in Damascus would have been circulated to Israel as to other countries co-operating with Britain on counter-terrorism. If this was true, then the Heathrow bomb was never intended to go off and its discovery was not an accident. A senior Israeli security source interviewed by Ian Black, Jerusalem correspondent of *The Guardian*, went so far as to say that Israeli intelligence had received an advance general warning of an attack on El Al.[29]

In the post-mortem on the Hindawi affair, Syria and Jordan co-operated at the highest level. It was established that the Hindawi family were originally Palestinians who had settled in the East Jordan village of Baqura. They had a history of involvement with Mossad. The father had worked as a cook in the Jordanian embassy in London before being discovered to be an Israeli agent. He was tried in Jordan and sentenced to death *in absentia*,[30] but escaped sentence by staying in Britain. It was in his father's flat in an east London suburb that Hindawi stored the bag and the explosives for ten days in April 1986. According to Syrian and Jordanian sources, Israel used the threat that his father would be sent back to Jordan to win Hindawi's co-operation.[31] Asad was persuaded that British intelligence was protecting the father, although he was a fugitive from Jordanian justice, and must therefore have been aware of what the Israelis were up to. In his opinion, 'It was not an operation which could have been carried out behind the backs of British intelligence'[32].

Much persuasion may not have been necessary to get Hindawi to work for the Israelis, seeing that he had a record as a petty freelance agent, courier and contact man with no ideological commitment. In fact, according to a senior Jordanian official, he had already on a previous occasion done a job for Mossad 'and been paid for it'. He had also worked in various small capacities for Jordan against the Palestinians, for Syria against Jordan, and for the clandestine Jordanian Communist party among other paymasters. It was clear that for some years he had been a pawn in the shadowy middle ground between hostile Middle East services. Because of this background Jordan refused to renew his passport in 1985 and he had then offered his services to Syria.

After Hindawi's arrest, transcripts of his interrogation were quickly passed to Israel, but there was some irritation in British security circles when Israel promptly leaked his 'confession' implicating Syria to the press. A full account appeared in the Israeli newspaper *Ha'aretz* on 9 May 1986.[33]

According to Whitehall source, Britain's decision to break with Syria on the basis of this ambiguous affair was taken by Mrs Thatcher on 21 October, three days before the court's verdict, at a meeting with senior ministers. With the prosecution firmly indicting Syria, she may have believed she would face hostility in parliament and the press if she did not act toughly. No doubt the Prime Minister saw domestic and international advantage in making an example of Syria and, unlike Israel, Syria had few friends in Britain and none in the British cabinet to plead its case. The Foreign Office, according to senior officials, was on the whole against severing diplomatic relations but was overruled by Downing Street. Mrs Thatcher's friendship with Peres and Husayn and her perception that Syria was an obstacle to an accord between them may also have influenced her decision. Certainly Asad came to believe that his intelligence services were entrapped by Israel, with some co-operation from Britain, for political purposes – to put pressure on Syria, to separate it from Europe, and to allow Israel to dominate the situation.[34]

In the months between Hindawi's arrest in April and his trial in October 1986, Asad contented himself with one or two categoric denials of involvement. He did not react to unofficial British promptings that he should recall his ambassador or distance himself from the incident in some public way. Perhaps the messages never got through to him. Perhaps none of his own people dared tell him how gravely Syria was compromised. King Husayn tried to persuade him to give the British Government a private pledge of non-involvement and King Fahd also offered to intercede, but he was too proud to agree. Although Asad was undoubtedly furious with General Khuly for laying himself open to Israeli penetration, he defended him in public, while biding his time to discipline him in his own fashion. Towards the end of 1987 when the dust had settled, he moved Khuly, who had been a trusted aide for more than twenty years, out of intelligence and into an air force sinecure.

In the wake of the damaging affair Asad took a tighter grip on his intelligence services. He also came to regard any lingering connection with Abu Nidal as a liability. After the hijack of the Pan-Am airliner at Karachi in September 1986, President Zia al-Haq of Pakistan sent Syria a dossier showing how the terrorists had made use of Syrian facilities. But it was not until March 1987 when Jimmy Carter, on a private visit to Damascus, raised the Karachi incident with Asad that he called for Zia's dossier and was shocked by what he read there into taking action. On 1 June all Syria-based men belonging to Abu Nidal's outfit, together with their wives and children, were expelled from Syria and their offices closed, a move which opened the way for the return to Damascus in September of the US ambassador, William Eagleton.

In Asad's mind the Hindawi affair was just another battle in his long war to protect the Arab Levant, Lebanon as well as Jordan, from Israel's designs. He could claim a measure of success. Husayn did not cross the forbidden line into a deal with Israel although Peres never gave up trying. Yet Asad would have had to admit that Peres's failure was due as much to Shamir's obstruction as to his own vigorous tugging in the other direction. The weak Reagan Administration professed to want an Israel-Jordan agreement, but it was neither firm enough in reining in Shamir nor steady enough in supporting Husayn to persuade the latter to risk advancing on his own. In the event American vacillation as much as the paralysis of the Israeli government contributed to the explosion of Palestinian frustrations in the occupied territories in the winter of 1987–8.

The Iran-Contra affair

The Levant was not the only front where Asad felt under attack. Israel was also threatening his Gulf flank, or so he interpreted its covert dealings with Iran. He understood that Israel had an interest in fuelling the Iraq-Iran War so as to rule out any possibility that Iraq might turn westwards and combine its military power with that of Syria. So to his way of thinking he faced an Israeli pincer movement aimed both at eroding his vital Levant environment and at denying him a military option on the 'eastern front'.

Fortunately for Asad, there was an in-built contradiction in Israel's two-track policy which involved denouncing Syria *because of* its terrorist record while secretly arming Iran *in spite of* its terrorist record. In fact, Israel's anxiety to maintain the arms flow to Khomayni's Iran at a time when that country was the main inspiration for anti-Western terrorism was to lead to the tortuous intrigues of the Iran-Contra scandal.

As it happened, the first news of covert US arms deals with Iran broke in early November 1986 some ten days after Hindawi was sentenced at the Old Bailey. The 'Irangate' drama which then unfolded crippled the last years of the Reagan Administration but gave Asad some respite. While it undermined America's counter-terrorist pretensions, it helped Asad survive more or less unscathed the bad years of the late 1980s. Because Israel's Gulf policy directly affected Asad, and because, as will be shown, Syria played a crucial part in the Irangate revelations, a summary account of these events must now be given.

It will be recalled that Israel began sending (mainly American) arms secretly to Iran from the start of the Gulf conflict in 1980, even while American hostages were held captive in Tehran and in continuing infringement of the arms embargoes imposed by both the Carter and Reagan Administrations (see Chapter 21). No doubt the framework of US-Israeli strategic co-operation gave Israel leeway for action at variance with declared US policy. Unable to confront Israel on matters directly affecting American security such as the Pollard case, Washington was hardly likely to be stern about arms to Iran for which a long-term benefit could be argued. A view often heard in Washington was that as nothing could be done to stop the trade it was best to keep quiet about it. But when in 1983 it became clear that Iranian-backed groups were behind most of the bombings, kidnappings and hijackings in Lebanon, the State Department launched Operation Staunch to discourage the sale of arms to Iran, and when the US government designated Iran a 'sponsor of international terrorism' in January 1984 additional export controls were imposed.

The dilemma for Israel was acute: it wanted to continue arming Iran for its own regional reasons but its major ally, in increasingly violent confrontation with Iran, was trying to stop the traffic. Something had to be done. How could US policy be redirected to exempt Iran from the anti-terrorist crusade Israel had itself done so much to foster? This was a puzzle Israel and its friends grappled with in 1984.

One friend was Howard Teicher, senior director for political-military affairs on the National Security Council staff, who from late 1984 started criticizing the ban on arms sales to Iran.[35] Even though Khomayni's regime was notoriously anti-Communist, Teicher argued that a new strategy was needed to check Soviet inroads. His views inspired a CIA memorandum in January 1985 by Graham Fuller, vice-chairman of the National Intelligence Council which, by warning of possible Soviet gains in a post-Khomayni Iran, prepared the ground for later Israeli and US arms sales.[36]

A second Fuller memorandum of May 1985 was more specific. Also written with Teicher's help, it argued that the 'twin pillars' of American policy – banning arms sales to Iran and confronting Iranian terrorism – 'may now serve to facilitate Soviet interests more than our own'.[37] Instead, the memo advanced the argument that the way to gain influence in Iran was to allow friendly states – in effect Israel – to sell it arms. These ideas were then embodied by the CIA in a Special National Intelligence Estimate (SNIE) on Iran of 20 May which boldly stated that the degree to which America's allies could 'fill a military gap for Iran will be a critical measure of the West's ability to blunt Soviet influence'.[38]

Basing himself on this SNIE (which he had himself helped compose), Teicher then submitted to Robert McFarlane, the National Security Adviser, on 11 June a draft National Security Decision Directive (NSDD) – a presidential decision document – whose first and main recommendation was that the United States 'encourage Western allies and friends to help Iran meet its import requirements so as to reduce the attractiveness of Soviet assistance . . . This includes provision of selected military equipment as determined on a case-by-case basis'.[39] Teicher's manoeuvres were evidently intended to make Israel's covert arms trade respectable.

When these documents surfaced in the Administration, Shultz and Weinberger reacted with horror and derision. Shultz wrote on 29 June that the proposed policy change was 'perverse' and 'contrary to our interest' while Weinberger scribbled on the margin of the draft, 'This is almost too absurd to comment on'.[40] Both men strongly resisted any easing of restrictions on arms sales to Iran: its complicity in anti-Western terrorism was clear and, in any event, there was no sign that it was moving closer to the Soviet Union. By mid-August 1985 these two senior members of the government had killed Teicher's draft NSDD and it was not submitted to Reagan for his signature.

Even as Teicher's bureaucratic initiative was running into trouble, Michael Ledeen, another of Israel's friends in the Administration, was exploring a different avenue. Ledeen had worked for both Haig and McFarlane at the State Department in the early 1980s before joining the National Security Council in November 1984 as a consultant on Middle East terrorism. On private visits to Israel in the spring and summer of 1985, Ledeen discussed Iran with Prime Minister Peres, who passed him on to a trio of arms dealers active in Israel's covert trade with Iran – Al Schwimmer, the former president of Israel Aircraft Industries who had been appointed a special adviser to Peres in September 1984; Yaacov Nimrodi, formerly Israel's spymaster in Tehran; and an Iranian middleman, Manuchehr Ghorbanifar, a former agent of SAVAK, the Shah's secret police, who had developed ties with Israeli intelligence.[41] All three were eager to explore ways of getting round the tighter American ban – perhaps by involving the United States itself in the trade. As it happened, the three arms dealers had already held meetings in Hamburg in November 1984 with David Kimche, director-general of the Israeli Foreign Ministry, to discuss how to get Washington to open up to Iran, and Ghorbanifar had suggested proposing a weapons-for-hostages trade – a bait which it was hoped the Administration would find more alluring than the alleged Soviet threat which Teicher had canvassed.

But Shultz intervened again. Tipped off by US ambassador Sam Lewis of Ledeen's furtive contacts in Israel which bypassed the State Department, Shultz complained to McFarlane:[42]

> Israel's agenda is not the same as ours, and an intelligence relationship with Israel concerning Iran might not be one upon which we could fully rely . . . I am mystified about the way the situation has been handled and concerned that it contains the seeds of further embarrassment.

McFarlane replied that the initiative was Israel's and that Ledeen was 'acting on his own hook'.[43]

Despite Shultz's qualms, the Israelis moved to exploit the breach Ledeen had opened. On 3 July 1985 Kimche reported to McFarlane that the Iranians believed that they could influence Hizbullah to release hostages in Lebanon – but would want something for their pains, probably weapons.[44] Schwimmer followed Kimche to Washington a week later, lunched with Ledeen and passed on a message through him that seven Americans held in Lebanon could be released for 100 TOW anti-tank missiles from Israel.[45]

Ledeen took his vacation in Israel in July and, in further meetings with Kimche and the three arms dealers, discussed the proposed arms-for-hostages transaction, whereupon Kimche returned to the White House on 2 August to press the argument on McFarlane again. McFarlane responded:[46]

> Look, David, we've known each other a long time. Your interests and ours are not the same. Prolonging the Gulf war which engages Iraq serves your interest, but we want to stop it. We may share an interest in restoring some kind of relationship with Tehran. But our interests are more strategic and yours are more regional.

He told Kimche that easing the arms ban could damage US relations with Arab states and raise problems with Congress. But Kimche had a shrewder sense of how President Reagan would view the chance of getting the hostages out: on 6 August, in the teeth of opposition from Shultz and Weinberger, Reagan gave oral approval for Israel to sell US arms to Iran and agreed to replenish Israeli stocks.[47] To get things moving, McFarlane set up secure communications with Kimche; Ledeen carried a code to him in London.

At the end of August 1985 the first US-approved planeload of TOW missiles took off from Israel for Tehran. By making the United States a party, if a slightly bemused one, to this transaction, Israel obtained political cover for its own ongoing sales. Operation Staunch, which the United States was still pressing on its other allies, was blown wide open and America's counter-terrorist policy was reduced to a hypocritical sham. Not the least of the Administration's contradictions was that it abetted the covert arms shipments to Iran while overtly tilting to Iraq's side in the Gulf War.

The expectation in Washington was that a given number of weapons would free the hostages. These hopes were soon disappointed. In September a single hostage, the Reverend Benjamin Weir, was released, and in spite of increasingly large arms deliveries no one else was freed in the next ten months. The interest of Israel and Iran was not in ending the trade but in continuing it.

In December 1985, at Shultz's insistence, a full-scale meeting was called at the White House at which Shultz protested that the secret arms shipments were 'signalling to Iran that they can kidnap people for profit'.[48] Weinberger objected that the deals laid the United States open to 'blackmail of the very most elementary kind' by both Israel and Iran.[49] A sobered Reagan agreed to call a halt and McFarlane, who had by now been replaced as national security adviser by Admiral John Poindexter, was sent to London to break the bad news to Kimche, Nimrodi and Ghorbanifar.

This was to underestimate Israeli ingenuity, however. Through Teicher Israel had tried to change US policy towards Iran by invoking the Soviet spectre; through Ledeen it had proposed the arms-for-hostages trade. Now it came up with a third idea which could not but tempt an Administration obsessed by Nicaragua. Going to the NSC behind the backs of State and Defense, Peres's adviser on terrorism, Amiram Nir, proposed on 2 January 1986 that the Iranians be overcharged for the weapons and the profits be diverted to the Contras.[50] Nir's brainwave greatly appealed to Poindexter and Oliver North, his specialist in undercover operations, who were anxious to find means of support for the Contras after Congress had cut off funding. Bank accounts were opened in Switzerland, the account numbers communicated to the Israelis, and the money from arms sales began to flow in.

On 17 January 1986 President Reagan signed a Finding which formally relaunched the clandestine arms programme.[51] Much was made in the document of the objectives of promoting a 'moderate' government in Iran and furthering the release of American hostages, but there was no mention of Israel or of the proposed diversion of funds. Congress was kept in the dark. Nir had managed to turn the Iran initiative into an American venture run by North with some CIA back-up through a private network already involved in Contra resupply. Over the next few months four arms deliveries were made to Iran and some $20 million of overpayments found their way to the secret bank accounts – transactions which freed Israel's own sales from all constraint.

No more hostages were released, however, nor were Washington's hopes of a high-level dialogue with Iran realized. When this latest initiative seemed to be running out of steam, it was revived yet again: Nir and Ghorbanifar persuaded North that a visit to Tehran by the still influential former National Security Adviser, Robert McFarlane – with a planeload of Hawk missiles as a sweetener – could yet unlock the impasse and release all the hostages.

McFarlane was brought round to the idea. But on reflection he saw

Israel's own arms sales as something of an obstacle to the plan. If the Iranians could get what arms they wanted from Israel, why do business with the United States? And why release the hostages?[52] The Iranians would have to be convinced that the White House was the only source of arms. Word reached the Administration of a huge Israeli-co-ordinated package worth over $2 billion, dwarfing anything that had gone before, in which a dozen international traders, including the biggest names in the Israeli arms business, planned to provide Iran with warplanes, transport aircraft, helicopters, guided missiles, thousands of anti-tank TOWs, and much more – enough to tip the balance in the Gulf War.

McFarlane realized that if the package was delivered the White House would lose all leverage over Tehran. A high-level decision was taken to abort the deal. Recruiting a spy among the arms merchants, the Iranian Cyrus Hashemi, the Americans were able to monitor the progress of the transaction, and on 22 April 1986 arranged for the principals to be apprehended in Bermuda.[53] Not the least ironic aspect of the affair was that, having been drawn into clandestine trading by Israel, the United States found itself obliged to rein in its ally: thwarting the bumper package allowed McFarlane's more modest Tehran venture to go forward.

With Reagan's approval, McFarlane flew to Iran via Europe and Israel on 23 May.[54] In his party were Oliver North, Howard Teicher, and Amiram Nir posing as an American. They travelled on false Irish passports and carried a Bible signed by Reagan and a key-shaped cake to symbolize the hoped-for opening to Iran. But after hanging around in the former Tehran Hilton for several days and engaging in frustrating arguments with junior Iranian officials, McFarlane and his team returned home having accomplished nothing. A hostage was freed in July, an arms shipment was made in August, another hostage was released in November, but America's Iran initiative declined into low-level contacts and mutual recriminations. Meanwhile, Israel's arms sales continued without further interference from the United States.

When the dirty linen of the Iran-Contra affair came to be washed in public, the main focus of the hearings by the joint House and Senate Committees in the summer of 1987 was on what the president knew and when, on how Congress's ban on military funding for the Contras was flouted, and on the nefarious activities of the secret 'junta'[55] operating at the heart of the US government. Little attention was given to Israel's role or to the reasons which inspired its extraordinary efforts to keep the Gulf War going – essentially enfeebling Syria and denying the Arabs an 'eastern front'.

Senator Daniel Inouye of Hawaii, chairman of the Senate investigating committee and a long-time supporter of Israel, was one of those who protected Israel from exposure. Reporting on the failure to probe Israel's role, the *Wall Street Journal* noted that Inouye had received $48,500 in campaign contributions from pro-Israeli political action committees in 1985–6.[56] And when the independent counsel, Lawrence Walsh, came to investigate the possible criminal aspects of the affair, twelve months of haggling with the Israeli government led to an agreement whereby in exchange for the release of some Israeli documents and bank records Walsh gave up the right to question four key Israeli participants – Kimche, Nimrodi, Schwimmer and Nir.

The Syrian role

By a quirk of fate it was Syria which first blew the affair out of the water. A Syrian intelligence officer in Tehran, 'Iyad al-Mahmud, learned of McFarlane's bizarre mission to Iran. The first instinct of the authorities in Damascus was to keep the story under wraps so as not to embarrass their Iranian allies, but Asad followed the startling development with close attention. It had an obvious bearing on his relations with Iran, on his struggle to check extremist groups in Lebanon, and on his efforts to thwart attempts to ostracize Syria as a 'terrorist state'. It seemed to Asad the height of Western cynicism to put him in the dock over Hindawi, subvert his political position in Lebanon and push Jordan into Israel's arms, while secretly arming Iran and doing deals over hostages in blatant breach of the trumpeted counter-terrorist policy.

On 2 October 1986 Syria's man in Tehran, 'Iyad al-Mahmud, was kidnapped, apparently by a hard-line Iranian faction led by Mehdi Hashemi with close ties to extremist Shi'a in Lebanon. His seizure may have been a protest against Syrian attempts to discipline these factions or it may have been intended to dissuade him from probing further into the US-Iran dealings. The Syrian government made a forceful protest and Mahmud was released within twenty-four hours. But the incident sharpened tensions between Damascus and Tehran over Lebanon where Iran's protégé, Hizbullah, was bucking against Syrian control.

Asad had always been opposed to the taking of hostages amd not unnaturally resented being blamed by the West for terrorism in Lebanon which was mainly the work of pro-Iranian groups. In the immediate aftermath of the Hindawi trial in October 1986, when

international pressure on him was at its peak, he was keen to secure –
and to be seen to secure – the release of at least one hostage in order to
deflect the threat of sanctions against him, if not indeed an armed
attack. When 'Ali Akbar Velayati, the Iranian Foreign Minister, came
to Damascus on 31 October, Asad pressed him to let Syria have a
hostage. It was therefore something of a slap in the face when on 2
November David Jacobsen's pro-Iranian kidnappers released him, not
to Syrian troops, but in front of the US embassy in West Beirut whence
he was immediately whisked to Christian East Beirut – and out to
safety.

An angry Asad was in no doubt that the release was the result of an
arms-for-hostages trade. So, on 3 November, in a snub aimed at both
the United States and Iran, Syria leaked the news of McFarlane's visit
to Tehran and of the covert US-Iran contacts to a friendly newspaper
in Beirut, *Al-Shira'*, little guessing just how momentous an impact the
revelation was to have.

The great stone flung into the Middle East pond left no corner
unaffected. Covered in confusion, the United States retreated into self-
scrutiny in a long-drawn-out examination of how the Reagan
Administration had contrived to get itself into such a mess. Moderate
Arabs were appalled at American perfidy, prompting Washington in a
spectacular about-turn to swing from covert dealings with Iran to
hostile confrontation. A US fleet was despatched to the Gulf and all
semblance of neutrality in the Iraq-Iran conflict was abandoned.

Israel also was thrown on the defensive by the exposure of its arms
traffic and its manipulation of US government policy. It was forced to
focus on damage limitation with both the Administration and the
public. But its image was badly dented and this, on top of the earlier
Pollard scandal, made it vulnerable to sharp international criticism a
year later for its harsh suppression of the Palestinian uprising in the
occupied territories.

All these developments were greatly to Asad's advantage. Israel's
pincer movement against his Levant and Gulf fronts lost its power to
threaten him. For one thing, Irangate distracted the United States and
Israel from the pursuit of an Israel-Jordan settlement, and strains
between the allies prevented them from working effectively together.
The Israeli-inspired Iran initiative had forced Shultz to fight for his
political life – he and the State Department had been isolated and
double-crossed[57] – and he was understandably angry with Peres for
having gone behind his back to plot with the NSC. Peres made profuse
apologies but Shultz was not mollified, and seemed even to tilt towards
Shamir. In any event, he did not throw his weight behind the Peres-

Husayn London Agreement of February 1987 – one reason it came to nothing. Thus to Asad's relief Israel's Gulf intrigues had a negative effect on its Levant ambitions. Mrs Thatcher, who had taken the lead in ostracizing Syria over the Hindawi affair, had reason to feel annoyed when Washington cooled towards the Israel-Jordan settlement it had earlier promoted.

As time passed, Asad was let off the terrorist hook. After the Iran-Contra affair, with its undertones of shabby and even criminal dirty tricks, it was more difficult for Israel to exploit the terrorist issue to its advantage. Not only did Asad see the threat of war recede, but he was gratified to note that the Western political and economic blockade against him was gradually lifted.

By 1988 he had weathered the storm and probably felt more comfortable than he had in years. Nevertheless, his long experience of battle taught him that he could afford neither complacency nor loss of vigilance.

27

Conclusions: the Balance Sheet

More than any Arab statesman of his day, Hafiz al-Asad represents the Arabs' aspiration to be masters of their own destiny in their own region. The aspiration remains largely frustrated, but he has at least ensured that the case for Arab rights and security can no longer be ignored.

This is what his long struggle has been about. Asad is a man of 1967. The defeat made an indelible impression on him and in the agony of it was born his ambition to reach the top and to put things right. For twenty years he has been trying to overturn the verdict of the Six Day War which spelled submission for the Arabs, compelling them to live in the shadow of a small state artificially implanted, as he sees it, in their region by alien settlers funded, armed and supported by an outdated Western imperialism.

Syria is a Ba'thist state and Asad a lifelong party militant. His efforts must be seen in the context of the party's campaign for Arab revival, itself an expression of the much thwarted struggle throughout this century for genuine independence. Having thrown off the Turks, the Arabs fell to the Europeans, and when the Europeans left they found that Israel had taken up the reins. Colonialism went out by the door and came back through the window. In 1956 Israel joined Britain and France in an attempt to destroy Nasser, the Arab champion of his day; then when European nerves failed, it completed the job by itself in 1967. Thereafter, as Asad puts it, Israel strove to perpetuate its supremacy by dividing and subjugating its neighbours. The new imperialism was more dangerous than the old, indeed it was a threat to the Arabs' national existence. This is his version of history.

The need to take up the Israeli challenge has made Asad and modern Syria what they are. Once an exhausted Egypt had left the fray and Iraq had been drawn into battle on another front, Asad saw his country as the sole remaining barrier to Israel's regional hegemony. To

492

hold the line he sought to extend his sway over Jordan, Lebanon and the Palestinians, reaching out by alliances to the Gulf and North Africa, and thus creating a power block in the Arab Levant with Damascus at its centre. The rise of Syria as a regional power rewrote the rules of the Middle East system: Cairo and Baghdad lost importance while the Arab-Israeli dispute, the struggle for the Middle East which is the subject of this book, became essentially a contest between Israel and Syria. Not since Umayyad rule twelve hundred years ago has Syria been so important a political centre of gravity.

Yet Asad's achievements still have a fragile look about them. Too much depends on one man. And insofar as overturning the 1967 verdict is concerned he can claim only partial success. He failed to prevent Israel and the United States from detaching and neutralizing Egypt, the strongest Arab country. He failed to eject Israel from Palestinian or even Syrian territory, so that the Palestinian problem remains entirely unsolved. His vision of a regional settlement in which Israel is held in check behind its pre-Six Day War frontiers by an Arab world of equal strength is still a pipe dream. The notion of parity, central to his ambitions, is rejected by Israel and its superpower backer.

Nevertheless against these unsatisfied aspirations can be set some genuine gains. With real deterrent power, Syria has become a country Israel must hesitate to attack. Moreover, in a whole series of bruising engagements in the 1980s Asad fought off Israeli encroachments into his Levant environment: he foiled attempts to bring Lebanon and Jordon into Israel's orbit – and would resist equally fiercely if in some change of heart Israel were to consider striking a separate political deal with the Palestinians.

For it is a fundamental premise of Asad's policy that piecemeal settlements only confirm Israeli supremacy, and that to defend themselves the Arabs must insist on a comprehensive peace on all fronts or do without peace altogether. This conviction was the basis of his opposition to Camp David, to the Israeli accord with Lebanon, to any species of Jordan option, and to the belated peace efforts of the last months of the Reagan Administration. So, although Asad has not got the regional settlement he wanted, he has proved strong enough to frustrate a solution on Israel's terms. In so doing, he has made Syria the only adversary Israel needs to take seriously.

To many people Syria is an object not just of suspicion but of mystery, and Asad's moves are often seen as both malevolent and impenetrable. In the United States in particular, there is a certain incredulity that a small country with a population of under twelve million should have the effrontery to stand up for itself. Certainly, in defending Arab interests as he sees them, Asad *has* used skill, stealth and brute force to challenge the interests of others – Israel, its Western backers, and even those Arabs who do not endorse his strategy. Yet there is a poignancy about his story in that the task he assumed twenty years ago was larger than the means at his disposal. At the head of a relatively poor and undeveloped country, he has had a basically weak hand, forcing him to play his cards close to his chest, a style which does not make comprehending Syria any simpler.

Asad's sense of limited resources and permanent siege have undoubtedly had an impact on the way he runs his country and conducts his diplomacy. His regime is a very personal one. He insists on controlling everything and in particular foreign affairs and information because, unlike more powerful leaders who walk away from their blunders, he can ill afford to make a mistake. At every stage he risks being knocked out of the game altogether, and that remains the main hope of his enemies.

He was born with or has developed qualities necessary for battle in what is by any standards a tough environment. Although he refuses to be pushed around, he is nevertheless careful not to break irrevocably with an opponent, always leaving open the possibility for an eventual reconciliation. To patience and caution he has added a large dose of courage. It took courage for an 'Alawi to make himself president of a largely Sunni country, courage to attack Israel in 1973, to intervene in Lebanon against Palestinians and the left in 1976, to ally himself with Iran in an apparent break with Arab solidarity, to reject the Israeli-US *diktat* in Lebanon in 1982–3, and throughout the years to buck the trend towards partial settlements with Israel – all dangerous and for the most part unpopular decisions.

Since its birth Israel has sought security in military dominance over the Arabs, a policy which not unnaturally sharpened Arab hostility and stimulated efforts to get even. When from 1977 under Menachem Begin 'Greater Israel' became official policy, the Arabs faced a programme which not only ruled out any Palestinian settlement but by fragmenting and balkanizing the Arab heartlands threatened to put them at a permanent strategic disadvantage. The resulting frustration and destabilization led to wars, massacres, militant fundamentalism, hijackings and kidnappings, terror and counter-terror as described in this book, a wholesale radicalization more dangerous to Israel's long-term future than anything in the past and which surely adds up to an indictment of US-Israeli policies in the Middle East. *Pax hebraica*, funded and armed by Washington, has only produced mayhem on a large scale.

Asad's Syria represents the rejection of an Israeli-dominated Middle East order, offering instead one based on the supremacy of neither Arabs nor Israelis but on a balance of power between an Arab Levant centred on Damascus and an Israel within its 1948–9 boundaries. It is a mistake to suppose that the Arabs would find Israeli hegemony more acceptable once Asad himself passes from the scene. No doubt the solution he offers presupposes some radical rethinking in the opposite camp: Israel would have to substitute a will to co-exist for its ambition to dominate. It would have to accept an Arab negotiating partner strong enough to help the Lebanese and the Palestinians rebuild their shattered societies and strong enough too to keep the peace.

In the meantime, when asked how he would wish this chronicle to be concluded, Asad replied: 'Say simply that the struggle continues'.[1]

Notes

Chapter 1 Coming Down the Mountain

1 Interview with Jabir al-Asad, President Asad's cousin, Qurdaha, 15 April 1985.
2 Hala (b 1909); Ahmad (b 1910, d 1975); Ibrahim (b 1911, d 1968); Husayba (b 1912); Isma'il (b 1913); Bahija (b 1918); Muhammad (b 1920, d 1976); Bahjat (b 1923, d 1942); Hafiz (b 1930); Jamil (b 1933); Rif'at (b 1937).
3 Interviews with Qurdaha village elders, April 1985.
4 The information in the following paragraph is derived from the Qurdaha municipal records.
5 Tabitha Petran, *Syria* (London, 1972) p. 69.
6 J. Weulersse, *Le Pays des Alaouites* (Tours, 1940) p. 328; H. A. R. Gibb and J. H. Kramers, *Shorter Encyclopaedia of Islam* (Leiden 1953) pp. 453–456.
7 Interview with the head of the Qurdaha municipality, 15 April 1985.
8 Reverend Samuel Lyde, *The Ansyreeh and Ismaeleeh* (London, 1853); *The Asian Mystery* (London, 1860); René Dussaud, *Histoire et Religion des Nosairis* (Paris, 1900); Sulayman Efendi al-Adhana, *Kitab al-bakura al-sulaymaniya fi kashf asrar al-diyana al-nusayriya* (Beirut, 1863) (Partial English translation by Edward E. Salisbury, 'The Book of Sulaiman's First Ripe Fruit: Disclosing the Mysteries of the Nusairian Religion', in *Journal of the American Oriental Society*, vol. viii, 1864); Henri Lammens, *Etudes religieuses* (Paris, 1899); *Syrie* (Paris, 1921); *L'Islam, croyances et institutions* (Beirut, 2nd ed. 1941); Gibb and Kramers, *Shorter Encyclopaedia of Islam*; Heinz Halm, *Die islamische Gnosis: die extreme Schia und die 'Alawiten* (Zurich and Munich, 1982); Martin Kramer, 'Syria's Alawis and Shi'ism', in Martin Kramer (ed.) *Shi'ism, Resistance and Revolution* (Boulder, Colorado, 1987).
9 Philip K. Hitti, *History of Syria* (London 1951) p. 586.
10 Interview with President Asad, Damascus, 13 September 1984.
11 Ibid.
12 Ibid.
13 Ibid.
14 Appendix to a letter from Ibrahim el-Kinj, Chairman of the Representative Council of the Latakia Government, to the French Prime Minister, 11 June 1936. French Foreign Ministry Archives, Levant 1918–1930, Syrie-Liban, doc. E-492, fol. 195.

15 Captain E. E. Evans-Pritchard, 'A Note on the Nosairis of Syria', Beirut 1942, unpublished. The tribal lists in the Note were authoritative as they were prepared for Evans-Pritchard by the well-known 'Alawi poet and politician Badawi al-Jabal, son of Shaykh Sulayman al-Ahmad.

Chapter 2 The French Legacy

1 R. Montagne, 'La crise politique de l'arabisme', *La France méditerranéenne et africaine* (Paris, 1938); Stephen H. Longrigg, *Syria and Lebanon under French Mandate* (London, 1958); André Raymond, 'La Syrie, du royaume arabe à l'indépendance', in André Raymond (ed.), *La Syrie d'aujourd'hui* (Paris, 1980); Philip S. Khoury, *Syria and the French Mandate: The Politics of Arab Nationalism, 1920–1945* (London, 1987) p. 12.
2 Interview with the historian Gabriel Saadé, Latakia, April 1985, who was largely responsible for turning the building into a museum.
3 Evans-Pritchard, 'Note on the Nosairis'.
4 Weulersse, *Le Pays des Alaouites*, pp. 334–6; Khoury, *Syria and the French Mandate*, pp. 523–5.
5 Michel Seurat, 'Les populations, l'état et la société', in Raymond, *La Syrie d'Aujourd'hui*, p. 92. The killing that year of a leading 'Alawi officer, Colonel Muhammad Nasir, also attributed to men in Shishakli's entourage, may have served to stimulate 'Alawi political consciousness. Whatever the sectarian consequences of his murder, the motives for it were probably political: Nasir was associated with Shukri al-Quwatli's National Party, seen as a political rival by Shishakli. Nasir's daughter, Siba Nasir, was in 1988 appointed the first woman ambassador in the Syrian foreign service.
6 Richard Pearse, *Three Years in the Levant* (London, 1949) pp. 149–150, quoted in Petran, *Syria*, p. 71.

Chapter 3 Party School and Army College

1 Interview with President Asad, Damascus, October 1984.
2 Interview with Ahmad Rustum (one of the lucky ones), Surghaya, 29 August 1984. In 1946 there were only 8,000 places in Syrian secondary schools; by 1953 this had risen to 50,000.
3 Interview with Ghazi Abu 'Aql, a school friend of Asad, later an army general and head of the Defence Factories Establishment, Damascus, 1 May 1985.
4 Interview with 'Adnan 'Umran (a former Syrian ambassador in London and later assistant secretary-general of the Arab League), May 1982.
5 Interview with President Asad, Damascus, October 1984.
6 Ibid.
7 Interview with Dr Wahib al-Ghanim, Latakia, 15 April 1985.
8 Raymond, *La Syrie d'Aujoud'hui*, p. 75; Elizabeth Picard, 'Retour au Sandjak', *Maghreb Machrek*, 99 (January March, 1983) pp. 47–64.
9 Interview with Dr Shakir Fahham, Damascus, 14 May 1985. See also Sami al-Jundi, *Al Ba'th* (Beirut, 1969) p. 29.
10 Interview with Dr Wahib al-Ghanim, 15 April 1985.

11 *al-'Abqariya al-'arabiya fi lisaniha* (Damascus, 1943).
12 Interview with Dr Wahib al-Ghanim, 15 April 1985.
13 Ibid.
14 Of the considerable literature on the Ba'th, see the Bibliography for works by Tanios Abou-Rejeily, K. S. Abu Jaber, Michel 'Aflaq, M. S. Agwani, Zaki al-Arsuzi, Shibli al-'Aysami, Hanna Batatu, Salah al-Din Bitar, Bashir Da'uq (ed.), John F. Devlin, Sylvia G. Haim, Simon Jargy, Sami al-Jundi, Nabil M. Kaylani, Moshe Ma'oz, Tabitha Petran, Itamar Rabinovich, André Raymond (ed.), Munif al-Razzaz, Eric Rouleau, Muta' Safadi, Ibrahim Salama, Jalal al-Sayyid, Gordon H. Torrey, Nikolaos van Dam, Jean Pierre Viennot.
15 Interview with Dr Shakir Fahham, university rector and former Minister of Education, Damascus, 14 May 1985.
16 Interview with Ahmad Rustum, Surghaya, 29 August 1984.
17 Ibid.
18 Ibid.
19 President Asad to the Ninth General Congress of the National Union of Syrian Students, Damascus, 4 May 1985.
20 Interview with President Asad, Damascus, May 1985.
21 Interview with Dr Wahib al-Ghanim, Latakia, 15 April 1985.
22 Ibid.
23 Interview with Dr 'Abd al-Ra'uf al-Kasm, Damascus, 13 March 1988.
24 Interview with President Asad, Damascus, May 1985.
25 See the testimony of 'Abd al-Karim al-Jundi, a later colleague of Asad, in *Le Monde*, 13–19 October 1966.
26 Interview with Air Force General (Retired) Fu'ad Kallas, Damascus, 13 September 1984.
27 Interview with President Asad, Damascus, 13 September 1984.
28 Ibid.
29 Ibid.

Chapter 4 The Peasants' Revolt

1 Interview with Dr 'Abd al-Salam al-'Ujayli, Raqqa, 22 April 1983.
2 Interview with Muhammad Ibrahim al-'Ali, a writer and the commander of the People's Army, Damascus, 19 March 1988.
3 Interview with Dr 'Aziz al-Saqr, Latakia, 15 April 1985.
4 J. Weulersse, *Paysans de Syrie et du Proche Orient* (Paris, 1946) p. 314.
5 Mohammed Harba, 'Organisations agraires, population rurale et développement en Syrie', vol. I, unpubl. doctoral thesis, Montpellier, 1978, pp. 132 ff. (In April 1985 Harba was appointed Minister of Local Administration, then, in November 1987, Minister of the Interior.)
6 *The Economic Development of Syria* (a World Bank report) (Baltimore, 1955); Doreen Warriner, *Land Reform and Development in the Middle East* (London, 1957); Abdul-Qader al-Nayal, 'Industrialisation and Dependency, Syria 1920–1957', Unpubl. thesis, Institute of Social Studies, The Hague, 1974.
7 For a detailed account see Patrick Seale, *The Struggle for Syria* (Oxford, 1965) pp. 24–99; new edn (London, 1986).

Chapter 5 The Cairo Conspiracy

1 Interview with President Asad, Damascus, 13 September 1984.

2 For a detailed account see 'The Baghdad Pact and Its Enemies, II', in Seale, *The Struggle for Syria*, pp. 213–37.

3 Interview with President Asad, Damascus, 13 September 1984.

4 Ibid.

5 Ibid.

6 Interview with Air Force General (Retired) Fu'ad Kallas, Damascus, 13 September 1984.

7 Interview with President Asad, Damascus, 13 September 1984.

8 Ibid.

9 Hanna Batatu, *The Old Social Classes and the Revolutionary Movements of Iraq* (Princeton, 1978) pp. 866–89.

10 Interview with President Asad, Damascus, May 1985.

11 Ibid.

12 Ibid.

13 Some informants say the leader of the group at the start was a Druze, Lt-Col. Mazyad Hunaydi. However, shortly afterwards he was transferred to the diplomatic service and posted out of harm's way to the UAR embassy in Jakarta. He died unsung in Suwayda on 29 August 1983.

14 Interview with President Asad, Damascus, May 1985.

15 Ibid.

16 The network included two Druzes, Salim Hatum and Hamad 'Ubayd; an 'Alawi, Sulayman Haddad; and a number of Sunnis including 'Uthman Kan'an from Alexandretta, a group from the Hawran in southern Syria – Musa al-Zu'bi, Mustafa al-Hajj 'Ali and Ahmad al-Suwaydani – Muhammad Rabah al-Tawil from Latakia, and Mustafa Tlas from Rastan near Homs. (See Nikolaos Van Dam, *The Struggle for Power in Syria* (London, 1979), p. 49, n. 51; Elisabeth Picard, 'Clans militaires et Pouvoir Ba'thiste en Syrie', *Orient* (Hamburg) (3rd quarter, 1979) pp. 54–5.) These men only joined the Military Committee once the seizure of power in 1963 ended the first phase of clandestinity.

17 See John F. Devlin, *The Ba'th Party: A History of its Origins to 1966* (Stanford, 1976) pp. 105–14, for the expansion of the party outside Syria.

18 One of the casualties along the way was Jalal al-Sayyid, a member of the party's first four-man executive committee and founder of the party branch in his home town of Dayr al-Zur. Sayyid left the party in 1955 because he did not like Hawrani's class warfare or the pressure for union with Egypt. Landowning and tribal influences were strong in Dayr al-Zur and, situated on the Euphrates with close ties to Iraq, it viewed with anxiety Syria's move into Egypt's orbit.

19 Interview with Dr Munif al-Razzaz, Kuwait, 15 February 1971.

20 See Gideon Rafael, *Destination Peace* (London, 1981) pp. 36 ff. for an account of Nasser's early readiness to negotiate.

21 Interview with 'Abd al-Ghani Qannut, Damascus, 27 February 1977.

22 'Abd al-Karim Zahr al-Din, *Mudhakkarati 'an fatrat al-infisal fi Suriya* (My Memoirs of the Secessionist Period in Syria) (Beirut, 1968); Van Dam,

The Struggle for Power, pp. 40–41; Itamar Rabinovich, *Syria under the Ba'th, 1963–66* (Tel Aviv, 1972) pp. 18–20; Petran, *Syria*, pp. 149–50.

23 Interview with President Asad, Damascus, October 1984.

24 Interview with Jabir al-Subh al-Hamadani, himself one of the Aleppo mutineers, London, 8 March 1986.

25 In addition to their daughter Bushra, born in Cairo in 1960, and to Basil, Asad and Aniseh went on to have three more boys, Bashar (b 11 September 1965), Majd (b 18 December 1966) and Maher (b 8 December 1967).

26 Interview with President Asad, Damascus, May 1985.

Chapter 6 Capturing the State

1 Interview with President Asad, Damascus, May 1985.

2 Interview with Ahmad Rustum, Damascus, 3 September 1984.

3 *Nidal al Ba'th*, vi, 'Internal Circular on the Fifth National Congress', pp. 81 and 86, quoted in Devlin, *The Ba'th Party*, p. 200.

4 Dr Munif al-Razzaz, *al-Tajruba al-murra* (The Bitter Experience) (Beirut, 1967) p. 90.

5 Interview with President Asad, Damascus, May 1985.

6 Ibid.

7 Interview with Mansur al-Atrash, Quraya, 28 April 1985.

8 Salim Hatum, Ahmad al-Suwaydani, Muhammad Rabah al-Tawil, Hamad 'Ubayd and Musa al-Zu'bi. There was a further small expansion of the Committee in the summer of 1963, but according to Asad, 'The highest number we ever arrived at was thirteen'.

9 Interview with Dr Saber Falhut, Damascus, 11 May 1985.

10 Interview with Amin al-Hafiz, London, 10 May 1986.

11 Interview with President Asad, Damascus, May 1985.

12 The Cairo talks were held in three series: 14–16 March, 19–21 March, and 6–17 April. Nasser, flanked by Marshal 'Amer and others, was present throughout and did most of the talking. Iraq was represented by 'Ali Salih al-Sa'di, Talib Shabib, Salah Mahdi 'Ammash and Ahmad Hasan al-Bakr. The Syrian delegation changed each time. In the first series it consisted of four NCRC officers, Hariri, Qutayni, Fahd al-Sha'ir and Fawwaz Muharib, and three cabinet ministers, Deputy Prime Minister Nihad al-Qasim, Agriculture Minister 'Abd al-Halim Suwaydan, and Economy Minister 'Abd al-Karim Zuhur. At the second series 'Aflaq and Bitar joined Lu'ayy al-Atasi and Sha'ir. At the third series no fewer than seventeen Syrians attended representing the NCRC, the cabinet, the Nasserist factions and, in the case of Muhammad 'Umran, the Military Committee. See Devlin, *Ba'th Party*, pp. 240–1; Malcolm Kerr, *The Arab Cold War*, 3rd edn (New York, 1971) pp. 44–76.

13 Interview with Talib Shabib, London, 25 July 1984.

14 Led by Hani al-Hindi and Jihad Dahi. The other two Nasserist groupings were the Socialist Unionist Movement led by Sami Sufan, a loosely structured group of ex-Ba'thist intellectuals who split with the party on the first breach with

Nasser in 1959, and the United Arab Front led by Nihad al-Qasim and ʿAbd al-Wahab Hawmad, out-and-out Nasserists.

15 Interview with President Asad, Damascus, May 1985.
16 Ibid.

Chapter 7 Capturing the Party

1 Batatu, *The Old Social Classes*, pp. 1013–14.
2 Interview with Tawfiq ʿUbayd (Baʿth party leader in Suwayda during the Shishakli dictatorship), Suwayda, 29 April 1985.
3 The eight-man Command comprised Shufi and three other 'Marxists', a trade unionist Khalid al-Hakim, a radical Aleppo lawyer, Ahmad Abu Salih, and an engineer, Muhammad Nawfal; three members of the expanded Military Committee, Asad, Muhammad Rabah al-Tawil, and Hamad ʿUbayd; and Dr Nur al-Din Atasi, the socialist son of a Homs landowning family.
4 Interview with Khalid al-Fahum, Damascus, 7 September 1984.
5 A. Ben-Tsur, 'The Neo-Baʿth Party of Syria', *Journal of Contemporary History* (III, 1968); Itamar Rabinovich, *Syria Under the Baʿth 1963–66* (Jerusalem, 1972).
6 'Baʿd al-muntalaqat al-nazariya', *Nidal al-Baʿth*, vi, pp. 232–91. An abridged English translation is in Rabinovich, *Syria under the Baʿth*, pp. 243–64.
7 See Ronald R. Macintyre, 'The Arab Baʿth Socialist Party: Ideology, Politics, Sociology and Organisation', Unpubl. doct. thesis, Australia National University, 1969, pp. 310–407, for an account of Baʿth party structure.
8 Zaki al-Arsuzi, *Muʾallafat kamila* (Complete Works), vols v and vi (Damascus, 1975–76).
9 Interview with President Asad, Damascus, May 1985.
10 Interview with Ahmad al-Asʿad (a Cairo contemporary of Hadid, later Hama party secretary), Hama, 25 April 1985.
11 Interview with Ahmad Rustum, Surghaya, 29 August 1984.
12 Interview with President Asad, Damascus, May 1985.
13 Ibid.
14 Interview with Mansur al-Atrash, Quraya, 28 April 1985.
15 Interview with President Asad, Damascus, 8 May 1985.
16 *Le Monde*, 8 July 1966.
17 Asad's report to the Extraordinary Session of the Fourth Regional Conference, 20–31 March 1969, reported in *al-Anwar*, Beirut, 15 November 1970.

Chapter 8 Blindly to the Brink

1 Foreign Ministry officials who survived the purge included: Muwaffaq ʿAllaf, Adib al-Daoudi, Dia Fattal, Sabah Kabbani, Farid Lahham and Zuhayr Murabit. From 1974 onwards these Damascene and Sunni diplomats were promoted by Asad and appointed to prominent posts abroad.
2 *Le Monde*, 13 July 1966.

3 Information about Hatum's background and the course of his conspiracy was derived in part from interviews in Suwayda on 29 April 1985 with Najib al-Bahri, former secretary of Sultan Pasha al-Atrash, and with Tawfiq 'Ubayd, a childhood friend of Hatum.
4 Razzaz died in Iraq in 1984 while under house arrest.
5 Interview with Ahmad Rustum, Surghaya, 29 August 1984.
6 Van Dam, *The Struggle for Power*, p. 77.
7 Amos Perlmutter, 'Some Spies Can Fool Them Too,' *International Herald Tribune*, 8 July 1985.
8 Interview with As'ad Kamil Elyas, Damascus, 14 August 1984, then secretary to the Syrian delegation.

Chapter 9 The Six Day Walkover

1 Carl Von Horn, *Soldiering for Peace* (London, 1966) Chapter 21.
2 Ze'ev Schiff, 'The dispute on the Syrian-Israeli border', *New Outlook* (February 1967); Avner Yaniv, 'Syria and Israel: The Politics of Escalation', in Moshe Ma'oz and Avner Yaniv (eds), *Syria Under Assad* (London, 1986) pp. 160–64; Yitzhak Rabin, *The Rabin Memoirs* (London, 1979) p. 40.
3 Sa'd Jum'a, *The Conspiracy and the Battle of Destiny* (Beirut, 1968) pp. 119–20 (in Arabic); Wasfi Tal, *Writings on Arab Affairs* (Amman, 1980) p. 326 (in Arabic).
4 Fuad Jabber, 'The Resistance Movement before the Six Day War', in William B. Quant et al., *The Politics of Palestinian Nationalism* (Berkeley, 1973) p. 174.
5 Interview with President Asad, Damascus, 12 May 1985.
6 Interview with Shafiq al-Hut, the PLO representative in Beirut, London, 15 February 1987.
7 Abu Iyad, *Palestinien sans patrie* (Paris, 1978) p. 76.
8 Interview with Shafiq al-Hut, London, 15 February 1987.
9 Yaariv's statement was made on 12 May 1967. Quoted in John K. Cooley, *Green March, Black September* (London, 1973) p. 160.
10 Ibid.
11 Yoram Peri, *Between Battles and Ballots, Israel's Military in Politics* (Cambridge, 1983) pp. 237, 246.
12 *Arab Report and Record* (1967, issue 11) p. 178.
13 As early as September 1966 Rabin had proposed dealing with guerrilla raids by striking at the 'Syrian regime itself'. Interview in *Bamahane* (Israel's army magazine), 11 September 1966.
14 Ritchie Ovendale, *The Origins of the Arab-Israeli Wars* (London, 1984) p. 178.
15 Nasser's resignation speech, 9 June 1967, quoted in Robert Stephens, *Nasser* (London, 1971, Pelican edn 1973) p. 506.
16 Interview with Mohamed Heikal, London, 11 March 1986.
17 Ibid.
18 Speech to Arab trade unionists, 26 May 1967, quoted in Stephens, *Nasser*, p. 479.

19 Press conference, 28 May 1967, quoted in ibid. p. 479.
20 For example, Richard Crossman, *The Diaries of a Cabinet Minister*, Vol. 2 (London, 1976) pp. 355–9; Barbara Castle, *The Castle Diaries 1964–70* (London, 1984) pp. 257–62.
21 Rabin, *Memoirs*, p. 69.
22 Abba Eban, *An Autobiography* (London, 1977) p. 349.
23 William B. Quandt, *Decade of Decisions* (Berkeley, 1977) pp. 49–50; Eban, *Autobiography*, pp. 352, 359.
24 Quandt, *Decade*, p. 61.
25 One such back-channel was Abe Fortas, a presidential adviser. (See Louis Gomolak, unpub. doctoral thesis on Lyndon Johnson's presidency, Univ. of Texas at Austin.) Johnson is also believed to have conveyed his approval of Israel's coming campaign through the number two man at the Israeli Embassy in Washington, Ephraim ('Eppi') Evron, with whom he was on closer terms than with Ambassador Avraham Harman.
26 It has been asserted that the United States provided Israel with covert aerial reconnassiance assistance during the Six Day War. Stephen Green, *Taking Sides: America's Secret Relations with a Militant Israel* (New York, 1984) pp. 204–11.
27 This was the view of Under Secretary of State Eugene Rostow (Quandt, *Decade*, p. 38); and of some quarters in the Israeli Foreign Ministry (Rafael, *Destination Peace*, pp. 130–31).
28 Peri, *Between Battles and Ballots*, p. 245, quoting Ezer Weizman, *On Eagles' Wings* (London, 1976) p. 219.
29 Ibid. pp. 259–60.
30 Interview with an Israeli former intelligence officer who wishes to remain anonymous.
31 For example, General Ezer Weizman, *Haaretz*, 29 March 1972.
32 Rabin, *Memoirs*, p. 90.
33 Ibid. p. 88.
34 Anthony H. Cordesman, *The Arab-Israeli Military Balance and the Art of Operations* (Washington, 1986) p. 15.
35 Lawrence L. Whetten, *The Canal War* (Cambridge, Mass., 1974) p. 44.
36 Galya Golan of the Hebrew University, interviewed in *New Outlook*, Tel Aviv, September 1987, p. 22.
37 Petran, *Syria*, pp. 199–200; see *Maghreb Machrek*, vol. 95 (January-March, 1982) pp. 99–106, for Golan history and bibliography.

Chapter 10 The Fight to the Top

1 Interview with 'Abd al-Majid Farid (then the director of Nasser's office), London, 14 January 1986.
2 Interview with Amin al-Hafiz, London, 10 May 1986.
3 Interview with Mansur al-Atrash, Damascus, 28 April 1985.
4 This and subsequent quotations in this chapter from President Asad are from an interview with the President, Damascus, 12 May 1985.
5 Eberhard Kienle, 'The Conflict between the Baath Regimes of Syria and Iraq

prior to their Consolidation', *Ethnizität und Gesellschaft* (Occasional Paper No. 5, Free University of Berlin, 1985) p. 17.

6 Interview with President Asad, Damascus, 12 May 1985.

7 Van Dam, *The Struggle for Power*, pp. 78–82.

8 General Mustafa Tlas, quoted in Lucien Bitterlin, *Hafez el-Assad: Le Parcours d'un Combattant* (Paris, 1986) p. 80.

9 Interview with Air Force General Fu'ad Kallas, Damascus, 13 September 1984.

10 Interview with Dr Munif al-Razzaz, Kuwait, 15 February 1984.

11 Interview with As'ad Kamil Elyas, Damascus, 14 August 1984.

Chapter 11 The Black September Fiasco

1 Interview with President Asad, Damascus, 12 May 1985.

2 Riad el-Rayyes and Dunia Nahhas, *Guerrillas for Palestine* (London, 1976) p. 144.

3 Interview with Khalid al-Fahum, chairman of the Palestine National Council, Damascus, 7 September 1984.

4 Interview with President Asad, Damascus, 12 May 1985.

5 Ibid.

6 Interviews with 'Abd al-Ghani Qannut, Damascus, 27 February 1977, and with Khalid al-Fahum, Damascus, 7 September 1984.

7 Interview with President Asad, Damascus, 12 May 1985.

8 Henry Kissinger, *White House Years* (Boston, 1979) p. 618.

9 Quandt, *Decade*, pp. 115–18; Rabin, *Memoirs*, pp. 146–8.

10 Rabin, *Memoirs*, p. 148.

11 Uri Avnery, *My Friend, The Enemy* (London, 1986) pp. 29, 85.

12 Quandt, *Decade*, p. 126.

13 Interview with Lakhdar Brahimi, London, October 1985.

14 *Le Monde*, 18 November 1970.

15 When Asad took over the party and government newspapers in February 1969, the Jadidists founded a paper in Beirut, *al-Rayya*, as a platform for their views. On 15 November 1970 it denounced the 'handful of military deviationists' who had rebelled against the party's authority and its declared aim of liberating Palestine. Several months later, in June and July 1971, *al-Rayya* published the Jadidist version of what happened at the November 1970 emergency congress.

16 Interview with As'ad Kamil Elyas, Damascus, 14 August 1984.

17 Interview with President Asad, Damascus, May 1985.

18 Interview with Talib Shabib, London, 25 July 1984.

Chapter 12 Asad's State

1 Interviews with Mansur al-Atrash (son of Sultan Pasha) and Najib al-Bahri (aide to Sultan Pasha from 1954 to 1982), Quraya and Suwayda, 28–29 April 1985.

2 Interview with Colette Khury, Damascus, September 1984.

3 Interview with Hani Rumani (who acted in the play), Damascus, 8 May 1985.

4 Interview with Ahmad Iskandar Ahmad (Minister of Information from 1 September 1974 to his death on 29 December 1983), Damascus, 3 March 1977.

5 R. Santucci, 'La Syrie avant l'affrontement', *Maghreb Machrek*, no. 60 (October-December, 1983) pp. 73–4.

6 Interview with President Asad, Damascus, 18 March 1988.

7 The diversity of opinion was illustrated by the fact that the Ba'th was given 87 seats, the Nasserist Arab Socialist Union 11, the Communists 8, 'progressive' independents 7, independent Ba'thists 5, Socialist Unionists 4, Akram al-Hawrani's Arab Socialists 4, former Ba'thists 3, independent Nasserists 2, Muslim religious leaders 3, businessmen 3 and representatives of the General Union of Peasants 36. *Arab Report and Record* (1971) p. 117.

8 The General Confederation of Trade Unions (founded in 1938 but brought under Ba'th control in 1966), the General Union of Peasants, the General Union of Students, the Revolutionary Youth Organization and the General Women's Federation (founded 1967). See Raymond A. Hinnebusch, 'Local Politics in Syria: Organization and Mobilization in Four Village Cases', *Middle East Journal*, 30, no. 1 (winter 1976).

9 Michel Seurat, 'Les populations, l'Etat et la société', in Raymond, *La Syrie d'Aujourd'hui*, p. 124.

10 Interview with Basil al-Asad, Damascus, 19 March 1988.

11 Interview with Fu'ad Ballat, a former director-general of Syrian television, Bludan, August 1984.

Chapter 13 Sadat, the Unsound Ally

1 Interview with President Asad, Damascus, May 1985.

2 Ghali Shoukri, *Egypt: Portrait of a President* (London, 1981) p. 36.

3 Lt-Gen. Sa'd El Shazly, *The Crossing of the Suez* (San Francisco, 1980) pp. 164–6.

4 Mohamed Heikal, *The Road to Ramadan* (London, 1976) pp. 172–3; Shazly, *Crossing of the Suez*, pp. 175–6; Anwar al-Sadat, *In Search of Identity* (London, 1978) p. 230.

5 Interview with 'Adnan 'Umran, London, 17 March 1976.

6 *al-Nahar*, Beirut, 10 August 1972.

7 Ibid.

8 Interview with President Asad, Damascus, May 1985.

9 Colonel Trevor N. Dupuy, *Elusive Victory: The Arab-Israeli Wars, 1947–1974* (London, 1978) p. 441.

10 Shazly, *Crossing of the Suez*, p. 29.

11 Henry Kissinger, *Years of Upheaval* (London, 1982) pp. 297–9.

12 Shazly, *Crossing of the Suez*, p. 202.

13 Interview with President Asad, Damascus, May 1985.

14 Heikal, *Road to Ramadan*, p. 119; Ismail Fahmy, *Negotiating for Peace in the Middle East* (London, 1983) p. 8.
15 For a detailed account of Egyptian–US relations in 1971–3 see Quandt, *Decade*, pp. 128–64.
16 Kissinger, *Years of Upheaval*, pp. 196, 203, 296; Quandt, *Decade*, pp. 147, 153, 161–2.
17 Kissinger, *Years of Upheaval*, p. 220.
18 Ibid., p. 461.
19 Heikal, *Road to Ramadan*, p. 180.
22 Interview with President Asad, Damascus, May 1985.
21 Shazly, *Crossing of the Suez*, p. 31.
22 Heikal, *Road to Ramadan*, p. 22.
23 Interview with President Asad, Damascus, May 1985.
24 Shazly, *Crossing of the Suez*, p. 37.
25 The senior Western source for this information does not wish to be identified.
26 Kissinger, *Years of Upheaval*, pp. 494, 500.
27 Ibid., p. 506.

Chapter 14 The October Illusion

1 Dupuy, *Elusive Victory*, p. 417.
2 Interview with As'ad Kamil Elyas, Damascus, 14 August 1984.
3 Dupuy, *Elusive Victory*, p. 433.
4 Rafael, *Destination Peace*, p. 290.
5 Lt-Gen. Mordechai Gur in Louis Williams (ed.), *Military Aspects of the Arab-Israeli Conflict* (Tel Aviv, 1975) p. 202.
6 Moshe Dayan, *Story of My Life* (London, 1976) p. 467.
7 Heikal, *Road to Ramadan*, pp. 217, 214.
8 Shazly, *Crossing of the Suez*, pp. 245–6.
9 Interview with President Asad, Damascus, May 1985.
10 Kissinger, *Years of Upheaval*, pp. 481–3.
11 Dayan, *Story of My Life*, pp. 486–7.
12 Ibid., p. 474.1
13 Dupuy, *Elusive Victory*, p. 450.
14 Maj-Gen. Binyamin Peled, in Williams, *Military Aspects*, p. 242.
15 Louis Duclos, 'L'équilibre militaire israélo-arabe', *Maghreb Machrek*, 67 (1975) p. 42.
16 Abu Iyad, *Palestinien sans patrie*, p. 197.
17 Dayan, *Story of My Life*, p. 528.
18 Shazly, *Crossing of the Suez*, p. 248; Dupuy, *Elusive Victory*, p. 491; Chaim Herzog, *The Arab-Israeli Wars* (London, 1982) p. 261.
19 Shazly, *Crossing of the Suez*, p. 248; Dupuy and Herzog suggest Egypt and Israel sent into battle up to 1,000 tanks each.
20 Shazly, *Crossing of the Suez*, p. 266.
21 Interview with President Asad, Damascus, May 1985.
22 Ibid.

23 Heikal, *Road to Ramadan*, p. 216.
24 Rabin, *Memoirs*, p. 114.
25 Kissinger, *Years of Upheaval*, p. 203. For his Middle East views, see ibid. pp. 195–205; for the evolution of his pro-Israeli policy, see Quandt, *Decade*, pp. 143–48, 159–64.
26 David Kochav, Economic Adviser, Israeli Ministry of Defence, in Williams *Military Aspects*, p. 183.
27 Quandt, *Decade*, pp. 102, 146–7.
28 Kissinger, *Years of Upheaval*, p. 625.
29 Ibid., p. 196.
30 Heikal, *Road to Ramadan*, pp. 207–8; Dupuy, *Elusive Victory*, p. 473; Kissinger, *Years of Upheaval*, p. 497; Abu Iyad, *Palestinien sans patrie*, pp. 196–7; Ismail Fahmy, *Negotiating for Peace in the Middle East* (London, 1983) pp. 25–6.
31 Kissinger, *Years of Upheaval*, p. 502.
32 Ibid., pp. 473, 493.
33 Ibid., p. 519.
34 Heikal, *Road to Ramadan*, p. 230.
35 Ibid., pp. 237–8.
36 Interview with As'ad Kamil Elyas, Damascus, 14 August 1984.
37 Heikal, *Road to Ramadan*, p. 238.
38 Kissinger, *Years of Upheaval*, p. 544.
39 Interview with President Asad, Damascus, May 1985.
40 Ibid.
41 Ibid.
42 Kissinger, *Years of Upheaval*, p. 583.

Chapter 15 Duel with Henry Kissinger

1 Interview with President Asad, Damascus, May 1985.
2 Ibid.
3 Quandt, *Decade*, p. 220; Kissinger, *Years of Upheaval*, p. 752; Matti Golan, *The Secret Conversations of Henry Kissinger* (New York, 1976) pp. 120–1.
4 Interview with President Asad, Damascus, May 1985.
5 Kissinger, *Years of Upheaval*, pp. 769–73.
6 Interview with Harold H. Saunders, London, June 1985.
7 Interview with 'Adnan 'Umran, Tunis, 27 December 1987.
8 Interview with As'ad Kamil Elyas, Damascus, 11 August 1984.
9 Kissinger, *Years of Upheaval*, p. 783.
10 Interview with President Asad, Damascus, May 1985.
11 Ibid.
12 Kissinger, *Years of Upheaval*, pp. 1249–50.
13 *al-Ahram*, 16 November 1973.
14 Mohamed Heikal, *Autumn of Fury* (London, 1983, paperback edition, 1984) pp. 79–80.
15 Shazly, *Road to Ramadan*, p. 290.

16 Interview with President Asad, Damascus, May 1985.
17 Ibid.
18 Kissinger, *Years of Upheaval*, p. 849.
19 Interview with President Asad, Damascus, May 1985.
20 Interview with Dr Sabah Kabbani, London, 15 February 1987.
21 Quandt, *Decade*, p. 237.
22 Kissinger, *Years of Upheaval*, p. 850.
23 See an admission by Menachem Begin, Israel Home Service, 29 September 1980, BBC *Summary of World Broadcasts*, ME/6537, 1 October 1980.
24 *The Village Voice*, New York, 23 February 1976; The Bertrand Russell Peace Foundation (Nottingham, 1977). See also Gerard Chaliand (ed.) *People without a Country: the Kurds and Kurdistan* (London, 1980) pp. 183–7.
25 Kissinger, *Years of Upheaval*, p. 941.
26 Interview with Harold Saunders, London, June 1985.
27 Interview with President Asad, Damascus, May 1985.
28 Kissinger, *Years of Upheaval*, pp. 1090–1, 1098.
29 See Asad's interview with Arnaud de Borchgrave in *Newsweek*, 2 June 1974; Kissinger, *Years of Upheaval*, p. 1133.
30 Ibid., p. 578.
31 Marvin and Bernard Kalb, *Kissinger* (Boston, 1974) pp. 526–7.
32 Edward R. F. Sheehan, 'Step-by-step in the Middle East', *Foreign Policy*, No. 22 (Spring, 1976).
33 Ibid.
34 Ze'ev Schiff, 'Dealing with Syria', *Foreign Policy*, No. 55 (Summer, 1984).
35 Stanley Hoffman, 'A New Policy for Israel', *Foreign Affairs*, Vol. 53, No. 3 (April, 1975).
36 Interviews with Dr Adib Daoudi (a former Syrian presidential adviser), Geneva, 2 November 1984, and As'ad Kamil Elyas, Damascus 11 August 1984; Kissinger, *Years of Upheaval*, pp. 1133–5.

Chapter 16 The Year Things Fell Apart

1 *Newsweek*, 2 June 1974.
2 Interview with Harold Saunders, London, June 1985.
3 Seymour M. Hersh, *Kissinger: The Price of Power* (London, 1983) Chapter 22, 'Chile: Get Rid of Allende'; William Shawcross, *Sideshow: Kissinger, Nixon and the Destruction of Cambodia* (London, 1979).
4 Kissinger, *Years of Upheaval*, p. 628.
5 Ibid, pp. 624–9, pp. 1036–8.
6 BBC *Summary of World Broadcasts*, ME/4811, 23 January 1975.
7 *Newsweek*, 24 February 1975.
8 President Asad's speech to the National Union of Syrian Students, Damascus, 26 February 1975, BBC *Summary of World Broadcasts*, ME/4842/A, 28 February 1975.
9 Interview with Harold Saunders, Washington, 26 September 1986.

10 *Washington Post*, 6 March 1975.
11 BBC *Summary of World Broadcasts*, ME/4861, 22 March 1975.
12 Quoted in Quandt, *Decade*, p. 267.
13 Texts in *Arab Report and Record* (1975) pp. 517–19.
14 *International Herald Tribune*, 11 September 1975; *Washington Post*, 16 September 1975; *New York Times*, 17 and 18 September 1975; Sheehan, 'Step by Step in the Middle East'; Quandt, *Decade*, pp. 273–6; Quandt, *Camp David* (Washington, 1986) pp. 59n, 201; Gerald R. Ford, *A Time to Heal* (London, 1979) p. 308.
15 *Arab Report and Record* (1975) p. 540.
16 Yitzhak Rabin in Williams, *Military Aspects*, pp. 212, 216.

Chapter 17 The Lebanese Trap

1 BBC *Summary of World Broadcasts* ME/4927, 12 June 1975.
2 President Asad's interview with Salim al-Lawzi of *al-Hawadith*, 22 June 1975, BBC *Summary of World Broadcasts*, ME/4941, 28 June 1975.
3 Kissinger, *Years of Upheaval*, p. 788.
4 Frederic C. Hof, *Galilee Divided: The Israel-Lebanon Frontier, 1916–1984* (Boulder and London, 1985) p. 75.
5 Kissinger, *Years of Upheavel*, p. 1082.
6 Hof, *Galilee Divided*, p. 74, quoting Michael Hudson, 'The Palestine Factor in the Lebanese Civil War', *Middle East Journal*, Vol. 32, No. 3 (Summer, 1978).
7 Speech by President Asad to members of newly elected Syrian Provincial Councils, Damascus, 20 July 1976, BBC *Summary of World Broadcasts*, ME/5266, 22 July 1976.
8 BBC *Summary of World Broadcasts*, ME/5140, 21 February 1976.
9 Ibid., ME/5157, 12 March 1976.
10 Ibid., ME/5171, 29 March 1976.
11 Winslow Peck writing in *Anti*, an Athens magazine, 17 April 1976, quoted in *Arab Report and Record* (1976) p. 256.
12 BBC *Summary of World Broadcasts*, ME/5266, 22 July 1976.
13 President Asad's speech in Damascus on 20 July 1976, BBC *Summary of World Broadcasts*, ME/5266, 22 July 1976.
14 Ze'ev Schiff, 'Dealing with Syria', *Foreign Policy*, No. 55 (Summer, 1984).
15 Itamar Rabinovich, 'The Lebanese Crisis', in Colin Legum, Haim Shaked and Daniel Dishon (eds), *Middle East Contemporary Survey V, 1980–81* (London, 1982) p. 172.
16 Interview with Khalid al-Fahum, Damascus, 7 September 1984.
17 Jonathan Randal, *The Tragedy of Lebanon* (London, 1983) p. 178.
18 *Arab Report and Record* (1976) p. 185; *Al-Nida'*, Beirut, 21 March 1976, quoted in Walid Khalidi, *Conflict and Violence in Lebanon* (Harvard, 1979) p. 55.
19 Interview with Walid Junblatt, London, 30 December 1986.
20 Interview with Khalid al-Fahum, Damascus, 7 September 1984.
21 BBC *Summary of World Broadcasts*, ME/5266, 22 July 1976.

22 Interviews with Sa'id Hamami, the late PLO representative in London, 5 July 1976; Khalid al-Fahum, chairman of the Palestine National Council, Damascus, 1 March 1977 and 7 September 1984; Shafiq al-Hut, the PLO representative in Beirut, London, 15 February 1987.

23 BBC *Summary of World Broadcasts*, ME/5185, 14 April 1976.

24 Interview with Shafiq al-Hut, London, 15 February 1987.

25 BBC *Summary of World Broadcasts*, ME/5225, 4 June 1976.

26 *Arab Report and Record* (1976) p. 344.

27 Ibid., p. 411.

28 Interview with Walid Junblatt, London, 30 December 1986.

29 *Le Monde*, 21 September 1976, quoted in Elizabeth Picard, 'L'engagement syrien au Liban', *Maghreb Maehrek*, No. 74, October-December, 1976, p. 5.

30 Interview with Salim al-Lawzi, London, 1 July 1976.

31 BBC *Summary of World Broadcasts*, ME/5185, 14 April 1976.

32 Interview with As'ad Kamil Elyas, Damascus, 14 August 1984.

33 *Arab Report and Record* (1976) p. 362.

34 Interview with Qasim Ja'far, contributing editor of *al-Taqrir*, London, 11 April 1987.

35 BBC *Summary of World Broadcasts*, ME/8144, 31 December 1985.

36 Interview with President Asad, Damascus, 4 March 1977.

37 Interview with Walid Junblatt, London, 30 December 1986.

38 Hof, *Galilee Divided*, pp. 80–81.

Chapter 18

1 Quandt, *Camp David*, p. 31.

2 BBC *Summary of World Broadcasts*, ME:/5357, 6 November 1976.

3 Cyrus Vance, *Hard Choices* (New York, 1983) p. 23. Interview with Cyrus Vance, New York, 31 July 1987.

4 Zbigniew Brzezinski, *Power and Principle* (London, 1983) p. 85.

5 Brookings Institution, *Towards Peace in the Middle East* (Washington, 1975).

6 Quandt, *Decade*, p. 161.

7 Vance, *Hard Choices*, p. 186.

8 Jimmy Carter, *Keeping Faith* (London, 1982) p. 280.

9 Rabin, *Memoirs*, p. 234.

10 Interview with presidential adviser Dr Adib Daoudi, Geneva, 2 November 1984.

11 Carter was accompanied by Vance, Brzezinski, William B. Quandt (Middle East expert on the National Security Council staff), Richard Murphy (US ambassador to Syria), and 'Isa Sabbagh (interpreter); Asad's team was Khaddam, 'Abdallah al-Khani (assistant foreign minister), Adib Daoudi (presidential adviser), Sabah Kabbani (Syrian ambassador in Washington), and As'ad Kamil Elyas (interpreter).This account of the meeting is based on the official record of the talks in the Syrian Presidential Archive; on interviews with Dr Adib Daoudi, Geneva, 2 November 1984; Dr Sabah Kabbani, London, 15 February 1987; As'ad Kamil Elyas, Damascus, 11 August 1984; William Quandt, Washington, 26 September 1986. See also Carter, *Keeping Faith*, pp.

285–6; *The Blood of Abraham* (Boston, 1985) pp. 67–73; Vance, *Hard Choices*, pp. 176–7; Brzezinski, *Power and Principle*, pp. 94–5; Quandt, *Camp David*, pp. 56–8.

12 Vance, *Hard Choices*, pp. 188–9.

13 Interview with Talcott Seelye, US ambassador to Syria 1978–81, Washington, 30 July 1987.

14 Vance, *Hard Choices*, p. 163.

15 Interview with Talcott Seelye, Washington, 30 July 1987.

16 Interview with William Quandt, Washington, 26 September 1986.

17 Quandt, *Camp David*, p. 83, n. 22.

18 Brzezinski, *Power and Principle*, pp. 108–10; Quandt, *Camp David*, pp. 125–31.

19 Quandt, *Camp David*, pp. 129, 134.

20 Interview with Cyrus Vance, New York, 31 July 1987.

21 Interview with Talcott Seelye, Washington, 30 July 1987.

22 Gabriel Ben-Dor, 'The Middle East in 1981: A Year of Political Disorder', in Legum et al., *Middle East Contemporary Survey* V, p. 13.

23 Eitan Haber, Ze'ev Schiff and Ehud Ya'ari, *The Year of the Dove* (New York, 1979) pp. 3–4; Quandt, *Camp David*, p. 109.

24 Shmuel Segev, *Sadat – ha-Derekh la-Shalom* (Sadat – The Road to Peace) (Tel Aviv, 1979) p. 55.

25 Moshe Dayan, *Breakthrough: A Personal Account of the Egypt-Israel Peace Negotiations* (New York, 1981) pp. 38–54.

26 *Time*, 6 August 1978.

27 *October* (Cairo), 11 December 1977.

28 Interview with As'ad Kamil Elyas, Damascus, 11 August 1984.

29 Karim Pakradouni, *La Paix Manquée* (Lebanon, 1984) pp. 126–9.

30 Interview with Dr Adib Daoudi, Geneva, 2 November 1984.

31 *Arab Report and Record* (1977) pp. 923, 938.

32 Interview with William Quandt, Washington, 29 September 1986.

33 Interview with Nasser's son-in-law, Dr Ashraf Marwan, London, 2 June 1986.

34 Interview with Harold Saunders, London, June 1985.

35 Quandt, *Camp David*, pp. 247–53.

36 Interview with Herman Eilts, Washington, 26 September 1986.

37 *Arab Report and Record*, 1978, p. 620.

38 Interview with Cyrus Vance, New York, 31 July 1987.

39 Revealed by Iraqi President Ahmad Hasan al-Bakr in a message to Arab leaders on 29 November 1977, made public on 1 February 1978. BBC *Summary of World Broadcasts*, 3 February 1978.

40 *Arab Report and Record*, 1978, p. 141.

41 Interview with Mansur al-Atrash, Damascus, 7 May 1985.

42 Interview with Dr Saber Falhut, Damascus, 11 May 1985.

43 George W. Ball, *The Past has Another Pattern* (New York, 1982) p. 466.

44 Interview with Dr Ashraf Marwan, London, 2 June 1986.

Chapter 19 The Enemy Within

1 Radio Damascus, 22 June 1979, quoted in BBC *Summary of World Broadcasts*, 25 June 1979; *al-Ba'th*, 24 June 1979.
2 Olivier Carré and Gérard Michaud, *Les Frères Musulmans (1928–1982)* (Paris, 1983) p. 135.
3 David W. Carr, 'Capital Flows and Development in Syria', *The Middle East Journal*, Vol. 34, No. 4 (Autumn, 1980).
4 Michel Chatelus, 'La croissance économique: mutations des structures et dynamismes du déséquilibre', in Raymond, *La Syrie d'Aujourd'hui*, p. 267.
5 Seurat, 'Les populations, l'etat et la société', p. 132.
6 In Damascus, *Al-Shubban al-muslimun* (Muslim Youth); in Homs, *Jam'iyat al-hidaya al-islamiya* (Society for the Propagation of Islam); in Aleppo *Dar al-arqam*, named after a meeting place of the Prophet and his Companions.
7 Interview with Dr Shakir Fahham, Damascus, 14 May 1985.
8 Interview with Nadim 'Akkash, Governor of Dayr al-Zur, 23 April 1985. 'Akkash was a former head of security in Hama and later in Aleppo.
9 Interview with Ahmad al-As'ad, Hama party secretary, Hama, 25 April 1985.
10 Ibid.
11 Interview with 'Ali Badawi, Aleppo, 16 April 1985.
12 Interviews with Muhammad Muwaldi, Governor of Aleppo, 18 April 1985; Nadim 'Akkash, Governor of Dayr al-Zur, 23 April 1985; Anwar Ahmadov, Soviet consul in Aleppo, 20 April 1985.
13 *al-Nadhir*, No. 10, 1 February 1980, quoted in Carré and Michaud, *les Frères Musulmans*, pp. 151–3.
14 Interview with Badr al-Din al-Shallah at his family farm in the Ghuta, 12 April 1985.
15 Oral sources; also *al-Nadhir*, No. 12, 26 February 1980 (which claimed to have secured a copy of Rif'at's speech), quoted in Carré and Michaud, *Les Frères Musulmans*, pp. 139–40.
16 *Tishrin*, 1 July 1980.
17 Interview with Anwar Ahmadov, Aleppo, 20 April 1985.
18 Carré and Michaud, *les Frères Musulmans*, pp. 144–5.
19 *Tishrin*, 8 March 1980.
20 Based on an account by one of the soldiers, 'Isa Ibrahim Fayyad, on Jordanian television in February 1981, quoted in Carré and Michaud, *Les Frères Musulmans*, pp. 147–8. As well as participating in the Palmyra massacre, Fayyad was a member of a Syrian hit-team sent by Rif'at al-Asad to kill the Jordanian Prime Minister and former intelligence chief, Mudar Badran, who, as Syria knew, was providing the Islamic terrorists with arms and training camps. The Syrians were apprehended at the frontier, suggesting that Jordanian intelligence had penetrated Rif'at's organization.
21 *Report from Amnesty International to the Government of the Syrian Arab Republic* (London, 1983) pp. 35–6.
22 See the Kuwait weekly, *al-Mujtama'*, 21 July 1981, for an interview with Shaykh Bayanuni.

23 Interview with Basil al-Asad, Damascus, 19 March 1988.

24 This account of the battle for Hama is based in part on interviews with Muhammad Harba, then Governor of the city (Damascus, 2 May 1985), and with Ahmad al-As'ad, Hama party secretary, and 'Ali Sharaf, his secretary-bodyguard (Hama, 25 April 1985), as well as on the testimony of other citizens and on published sources, specifically *al-Nadhir*, No. 44, 27 February 1982 and No. 46, 8 May 1982, for the guerrillas' side of the story.

25 Interview with President Asad, Damascus, 12 May 1985.

26 Report from Hama by Robert Fisk, *The Times*, 19 February 1982.

27 Interview with President Asad, Damascus, 12 May 1985.

28 The phrase originated with Dr 'Abd al-Ra'uf al-Kasm, Prime Minister from January 1980 to November 1987. Interview with Dr Kasm, Damascus, 13 March 1988.

29 *The Times*, 17 March 1980; *Le Monde*, 18 March 1980.

30 Interview with Anwar Ahmadov, Soviet consul in Aleppo, 20 April 1985.

31 Daniel Dishon and Bruce Maddy-Weitzman, 'Inter-Arab Relations', in Legum et al., *Middle East Contemporary Survey V*, p. 231.

32 See King Husayn's public admission in his letter to Prime Minister Zaid al-Rifa'i, *The Times*, 12 November 1985.

33 Asad's speech at the revolution anniversary rally, 7 March 1982, BBC *Summary of World Broadcasts*, 9 March 1982.

34 Interview with President Asad, Damascus, 12 May 1985.

35 Ibid.

36 Asad's speech at the revolution anniversary rally, 7 March 1982, BBC *Summary of World Broadcasts*, 9 March 1982.

Chapter 20 Standing Alone

1 Interview with As'ad Kamil Elyas, Damascus, 14 September 1984.

2 Interview with Dr 'Abd al-Ra'uf al-Kasm, Damascus, 13 March 1988.

3 Interview with President Asad, Damascus, 18 March 1988.

4 Interview with Basil al-Asad, Damascus, 19 March 1988.

5 Pakradouni, *La Paix Manquée*, p. 74.

6 For Syrian arguments on the need for parity, see for example an article in the Damascus daily, *Tishrin*, 28 November 1981; Asad's interview with the Kuwait daily, *al-Ra'y al-'Amm*, 13 December 1981; and Foreign Minister Khaddam's speech to the People's Assembly following Israel's annexation of the Golan Heights, 16 December 1981, BBC *Summary of World Broadcasts*, 18 December 1981.

7 Interview with As'ad Kamil Elyas, Damascus, 14 August 1984.

8 Interview with SSNP leaders 'Isam al-Mahaiyri and In'am Ra'd, Damascus, 15 August 1984.

9 Asad's speech to the Syrian Peasants' Congress, 26 April 1981, BBC *Summary of World Broadcasts*, 28 April 1981.

10 Report of a speech by Asad to a Lebanese Forces delegation, Voice of Lebanon, 29 December 1985, BBC *Summary of World Broadcasts*, 31 December 1985.

Chapter 21 Ally of the Ayatollah

1 For a detailed account of Sadr's career see Fouad Ajami, *The Vanished Imam: Musa al-Sadr and the Shia of Lebanon* (Ithaca and London, 1986).
2 Interview with Zuhayr Jannan (Syrian Ministry of Information), who accompanied Ahmad Iskandar Ahmad to Tehran, Damascus, 10 April 1985.
3 Interview in *Keyhan*, 19 August 1979, BBC *Summary of World Broadcasts*, 21 August 1979.
4 President Asad's note of his visit to Tehran, 28–31 December 1975, Presidential Archive, Damascus.
5 Laurent Chabry, 'La mise en service de l'oléoduc Irak-Turquie et la mésentente syro-irakienne', *Maghreb Machrek*, No. 77 (July-September 1977).
6 Joint statement by Iraq's RCC and party Regional Command on 28 July 1979, BBC *Summary of World Broadcasts*, 30 July 1979.
7 President Bakr himself, 'Adnan Husayn, head of Saddam's private office, Muhyi 'Abd al-Husayn al-Mashhadi, secretary-seneral of the RCC, an RCC member Muhammad 'Ayish, and others who were to perish in the bloodbath.
8 The source for this sentence and the next wishes to remain anonymous.
9 Chibli Mallat, 'Le féminisme islamique de Bint al-Houda', *Maghreb Machrek*, No. 116 (1987).
10 Ofra Bengio, 'Iraq', in Legum et al. *Middle East Contemporary Survey IV 1979–80*, pp. 518–21.
11 Damascus Radio, 24 September 1980, BBC *Summary of World Broadcasts*, 26 September 1980.
12 *Pravda*, 11 October 1980, quoted in Dilip Hiro, *Iran Under the Ayatollahs* (London, 1985) p. 287.
13 Mikha'el Gurdus, Israel's famous radio monitor, Israeli television, 9 October 1980, BBC *Summary of World Broadcasts*, 11 October 1980.
14 Aaron S. Klieman, *Israel's Global Reach: Arms Sales As Diplomacy* (New York and Oxford, 1985) p. 158; Benjamin Beit-Hallahmi, *The Israeli Connection* (London, 1988) pp. 9–12.
15 Klieman, *Israel's Global Reach*, p. 159.
16 Interview with Cyrus Vance, New York, 31 July 1987; Brzezinski, *Power and Principle*, p. 504.
17 *Washington Post*, 29 November 1986, quoted in The National Security Archive, *The Chronology* (New York, 1987) p. 3.
18 Bob Woodward, *Veil: The Secret Wars of the CIA 1981–1987* (London, 1987) p. 501.
19 *The Chronology*, p. 6.
20 Interview with Dr Ahmad al-Khatib, the Kuwaiti opposition leader, London, 12 September 1986.
21 Gary Sick, *All Fall Down: America's Fateful Encounter with Iran* (London, 1985) p. 90.
22 Joint House and Senate Hearings into the Iran-Contra scandal, 6 May 1987 (Secord).
23 Sick, *All Fall Down*, p. 353, n. 7.

24 Reprinted in *The Guardian*, 9 October 1980.

25 Sick, *All Fall Down*, pp. 170, 303, 305.

26 Interview with Muhammad Ali Hashemi, 12 April 1987.

27 King Husayn on Amman television, 4 October 1980, BBC *Summary of World Broadcasts*, 6 October 1980.

Chapter 22 Battle with Menachem Begin

1 Claire Sterling, *The Terror Network* (New York and London, 1981) pp. 1–24.

2 Woodward, *Veil*, pp. 204, 217.

3 Moshe Sharett, *Yoman Ishi* (Personal Diary) (Tel Aviv, 1980) pp. 377, 398–400.

4 Rabinovich, 'The Lebanese Crisis', p. 171; Ze'ev Schiff and Ehud Ya'ari, *Israel's Lebanon War* (London, 1985) pp. 29–30.

5 Interview with Philip Habib, Washington, 27 September 1986.

6 Begin's speech to the Knesset on the annexation of the Golan Heights, 14 December 1981, BBC *Summary of World Broadcasts*, ME/6907, 16 December 1981.

7 Interview with Mansur al-Atrash, Suwayda, 28 April 1985.

8 Lecture by Ariel Sharon at the Center of Strategic Studies, Tel Aviv University, December 1981.

9 Avi Shlaim, 'Israeli Interference in Internal Arab Politics: the Case of Lebanon', in Giacomo Luciani and Ghassan Salamé (eds), *The Politics of Arab Integration* (London, 1988) pp. 232–5.

10 Uzi Benziman, *Sharon, an Israeli Caesar* (London, 1987) p. 234.

11 Alexander M. Haig, Jr, *Caveat: Realism, Reagan, and Foreign Policy* (London, 1984) pp. 326–7.

12 Interview with Philip Habib, Washington, 27 September 1986.

13 *International Herald Tribune*, 25–26 May 1985.

14 Haig, *Caveat*, pp. 188, 326–7.

15 Ibid., p. 330.

16 Interview with Philip Habib, Washington, 27 September 1986.

17 Statement issued by the Central Command of Syria's National Progressive Front, chaired by President Asad, 19 June 1982, BBC *Summary of World Broadcasts*, 22 June 1982.

18 Ze'ev Schiff, 'Green Light, Lebanon', *Foreign Policy*, No. 50 (Spring, 1983).

19 Schiff and Ya'ari, *Israel's Lebanon War*, p. 98.

20 Trevor N. Dupuy and Paul Martell, *Flawed Victory: The Arab-Israeli Conflict and the 1982 War in Lebanon* (Fairfax, Virginia, 1986) pp. 86–90.

22 Israel Home Service, 12 August 1982, BBC *Summary of World Broadcasts*, 14 August 1982.

22 Sean MacBride (chairman), *Israel in Lebanon*: The report of the International Commission to enquire into reported violations of International Law by Israel during its invasion of the Lebanon (London, 1983) pp. xiv–xv, 123–8.

23 Haig, *Caveat*, p. 337.

24 Israel Home Service, 8 June 1982, BBC *Summary of World Broadcasts*, 10 June 1982.
25 In a four-hour lecture at Tel Aviv University on 11 August 1987, *International Herald Tribune*, 13 August 1987; *The Guardian*, 13 August 1987.
26 Interview with President Asad, Damascus, 18 March 1988.
27 Interview with Philip Habib, Washington, 27 September 1986.
28 General Mustapha Tlass et al., *L'Invasion israélienne du Liban* (Paris, 1986) pp. 131–3.
29 *Flight International*, 21 August 1982, p. 404.
30 Ibid., 16 October 1982, pp. 1108–11.
31 Tlass, *L'Invasion*, p. 134.
32 Interview with Dr Ashraf Marwan, London, 2 June 1986.
33 *The Times*, 26 July 1982; *The Middle East Military Balance 1983*, Jaffee Center for Strategic Studies (Tel Aviv, 1983) p. 260.
34 Interview with President Asad, Damascus, 18 March 1988.
35 Interview with Philip Habib, London, 25 September 1987.
36 Haig, *Caveat*, p. 341.
37 Interview with As'ad Kamil Elyas, Damascus, August 1984; see also Asad's interview with Lally Weymouth, *Los Angeles Times*, 14 August 1983.
38 Interview with the late Sir David Roberts, at that time British ambassador in Damascus, London, July 1984.
39 Interview with Philip Habib, Washington, 25 July 1987.
40 Interview with Robert McFarlane, former national security adviser, Washington, 30 July 1987.
41 MacBride, *Israel in Lebanon*, p. 145.
42 Ibid., p. 226.
43 *Washington Post*, 3 September 1982, quoting a Lebanese survey based on police and hospital records; *L'Orient le Jour*, Beirut, 30 November 1982, quoting official Lebanese estimates; also estimates by the Washington-based Near East Refugee Organization quoted in Roger Owen, 'The Lebanese Crisis: Fragmentation or Reconciliation?', *Third World Quarterly*, Vol. 6, No. 4 (October 1984) pp. 934–49; from 4 June to 15 August 1982, UNICEF counted 29,500 dead and wounded in Beirut alone, 40% of whom were children, quoted in Michael Johnson, *Class and Client in Beirut* (London, 1986) p. 204 n.
44 Interview with Philip Habib, Washington, 27 September 1986.
45 Ibid.
46 Text of President Asad's message to Syrian armed force in Beirut, 2 August 1982, BBC *Summary of World Broadcasts*, 4 August 1982.
47 Interview with As'ad Kamil Elyas, Damascus, August 1984; Lally Weymouth's interview with President Asad, *Los Angeles Times*, 14 August 1983.
48 Israel Home Service, 26 August 1982, BBC *Summary of World Broadcasts*, 27 August 1982.
49 *Le Monde*, 11 September 1985.
50 Interview with In'am Ra'd, Damascus, August 1984.
51 Interview with Philip Habib, Washington, 27 September 1986.

Chapter 23 The Defeat of George Shultz

1 Richard A. Gabriel, *Operation Peace for Galilee* (New York, 1984) p. 121; *Flight International*, 17 April 1983.
2 Clarence L. Robinson, 'Surveillance Integration Pivotal in Israeli Successes', *Aviation Week and Space Technology*, 5 July 1982, p. 17.
3 National Progressive Front Central Command statement, 19 June 1982, BBC *Summary of World Broadcasts*, 22 June 1982.
4 Qasim Ja'far, 'The Soviet Union in the Middle East: a case study of Syria', in Robert Cassen (ed.), *Soviet Interests in the Third World* (London, 1985) pp. 271–3.
5 Interview with General Mustafa Tlas, Damascus, 14 May 1984.
6 Interview with Qasim Ja'far, London, 11 April 1987.
7 Cynthia A. Roberts, 'Soviet Arms-transfer Policy and the Decision to Upgrade Syrian Air Defences', *Survival*, Vol. xxv, No. 4 (July-August 1983) p. 154.
8 Israeli television service, 18 March 1983, BBC *Summary of World Broadcasts*, 21 March 1983.
9 Editorial in *Tishrin*, quoted in *International Herald Tribune*, 22 March 1983.
10 Interview with Robert McFarlane, Washington, 30 July 1987.
11 Interview with Philip Habib, Washington, 25 July 1987.
12 Ibid.
13 Woodward, *Veil*, p. 247.
14 Interview with Philip Habib, Washington, 25 July 1987.
15 Interview with Professor Elie Salem, London, 22 January 1984.
16 Ibid.
17 Text in Legum et al., *The Middle East Contemporary Survey, VII, 1982–83*, pp. 690–7.
18 Interview with Professor Elie Salem, London, 22 January 1984.
19 Interview with Philip Habib, London, 4 June 1983.
20 The National Salvation Front's charter was broadcast on Damascus Home Service, 23 July 1983, BBC *Summary of World Broadcasts*, 26 July 1983.
21 For a contribution to the Washington debate at the time, see Talcott W. Seelye (US ambassador to Syria, 1978–81), 'A more careful look at Assad's Syria', *International Herald Tribune*, 21 July 1983.
22 Interview with Robert McFarlane, Washington, 30 July 1987.
23 Asad interview with Lally Weymouth, *Los Angeles Times*, 14 August 1983.
24 Interview with Robert McFarlane, Washington, 30 July 1987.
25 Ibid.
26 Asad interview with Lally Weymouth, *Los Angeles Times*, 14 August 1983.
27 See Yves Gonzalez-Quijano, 'Les interprétations d'un rite: célébrations de la 'Achoura au Liban', *Maghreb Machrek*, 115, (January-March, 1987) pp. 5–28.
28 See Brian Hocking and Michael Smith, 'Reagan, Congress and foreign policy: a troubled partnership', *The World Today*, (May 1984) pp. 190–4.
29 Interview with Robert McFarlane, Washington, 30 July 1987.
30 Lebanese government statement on abrogation, 5 March 1984, BBC *Summary of World Broadcasts*, 6 March 1984.

31 Interview with Walid Junblatt, London, 30 December 1986.
32 Damascus television service, 25 April 1984.

Chapter 24 The Brothers' War

1 Interview with President Asad, Damascus, 18 March 1988.
2 Interview with General Mustafa Tlas, Damascus, 14 May 1984.
3 The following account, except where otherwise indicated, is based on the
    testimony of leading participants in the crisis as well as on the recollection of
    diplomatic observers who wish to remain anonymous.
4 Interview with former deputy premier for economic affairs, Muhammad
    Haydar, Damascus, 16 April 1984.
5 Interview with President Asad, Damascus, May 1984.
6 Interview with President Asad, Damascus, 18 March 1988.

Chapter 25 Forging a Nation

1 Anne-Marie Bianquis, 'Damas et la Ghouta', in Raymond, *La Syrie
    d'Aujourd'hui*, pp. 359–406.
2 Laurie Brand, 'The Palestinians in Syria: the Politics and Economics of
    Integration'. Unpubl. paper, 1988.
3 Alisdair Drysdale, paper presented at a conference on Syria, School of Oriental
    and African Studies, London, 20 May 1987.
4 Interview with Dr 'Abd al-Salam al-'Ujayli, Raqqa, April 1985.
5 Jean Hannoyer, 'Campagnes et Pouvoir en Syrie: Essai d'histoire socio-
    économique sur la région de Deir ez-Zor'. Unpubl. thesis, Ecole des Hautes
    Etudes en Sciences Sociales, Paris, 1982.
6 Interview with Dr Muhammad Harba, Damascus, 2 May 1985. Harba was
    appointed minister of the interior in November 1987.
7 Interview with Dr Muwaffaq Habbal, production manager of the General
    Company for the Paper Industry, Dayr al-Zur, 23 April 1985.
8 Interview with Khalil Bahlul, Damascus, 1 May 1985.
9 Interview with Coco Mazlumian, Aleppo, April 1985.
10 Weulersse, *Le Pays des Alaouites*.
11 Françoise Métral, paper delivered at a conference on Syria, School of Oriental
     and African Studies, London, 20 May 1987.
12 Elizabeth Longuenesse, 'Syrie: secteur public industriel, les enjeux d'une crise',
     Maghreb Machrek, No. 109 (1985) pp. 5–24.
13 Interview with Professor Sadiq al-'Azm, author and political scientist,
     Damascus, 27 April 1985.
14 Raymond A. Hinnebusch, 'Class and State in Ba'thist Syria', paper delivered at
     a symposium on Syria at State University of New York at Binghamton, 22–23
     April 1988.
15 Quoted in Michael Jenner, *Syria in View* (London, 1986) p. 12.
16 Interview with Dr 'Afif Bahnassi, Damascus, 12 May 1985.

Chapter 26 Dirty Tricks

1 Abba Eban, 'It's not like it was with Sadat', *Yediot Ahronot*, 3 December 1987, quoted in *Israel Press Briefs*, No. 56 (December 1987-January 1988) p. 5. The *New York Times Magazine* of 23 April 1984 reported that Husayn had held eleven secret meetings with Israeli leaders between 1967 and 1977.

2 See Claudia Wright in the *New Statesman*, 7 June 1985, on the 'Izzedin affair.

3 The expression is Gérard Chaliand's. See his 'Terrorisme "publicitaire", terrorisme "diplomatique"', *Le Monde*, 25–26 May 1986.

4 *al-Thawra*, 31 July 1985; *Tishrin*, 5 August 1985.

5 For an account of Shaykh Jawad Mughniya's life and political ideas see Chibli Mallat, *Shi'i Thought from the South of Lebanon* (Centre for Lebanese Studies, Oxford, 1988).

6 Interview with President Asad, Damascus, May 1985.

7 President Asad addressing a national conference of Syrian students, Damascus, 4 May 1985.

8 For examples of such accusations see the cover stories, 'The Terror Broker: Syria's Assad', *The Washington Times Insight* magazine, 23 September 1985, and 'Syria's President Assad: Master of Terror', *U.S. News and World Report*, 10 November 1986.

9 Benjamin Netanyahu, *Terrorism: How the West Can Win* (New York, 1986). The Institute was named after Netanyahu's brother who was killed leading the 1976 Entebbe rescue mission.

10 Ibid. pp. ix, 221.

11 Ibid. p. 23.

12 Ibid. p. 95.

13 Ibid. p. 204.

14 Ibid. p. 192.

15 Ibid. p. 36.

16 For Shaykh Muhammad Fadlallah's ideas see Mallat, *Shi'i Thought*; Martin Kramer, 'La morale de Hizbollah et sa logique', *Maghreb Machrek* 119, (January-March 1988) pp. 39–59.

17 *Washington Post*, 22 February 1987.

18 Woodward, *Veil*, pp. 395–7.

19 *Washington Post*, 17 April 1986.

20 Quoted in Shau! Bakhash, 'The Riddle of Terrorism', *New York Review of Books*, 27 September 1987.

21 *International Herald Tribune*, 27–28 February 1988.

22 Private communication from a US diplomatic source.

23 Interview with President Asad, Damascus, 18 March 1988.

24 BBC *Summary of World Broadcasts*, 16 and 28 May 1986.

25 *Washington Times*, 10 November 1986.

26 Israeli television, 30 December 1987, BBC *Summary of World Broadcasts*, 1 January 1988. Peres argued that, had Likud not killed his peace bid, the December 1987 uprising in the occupied territories would not have occurred.

27 Damascus Home Service, 26 May 1987, BBC *Summary of World Broadcasts*, 28 May 1987.

28 Interview with President Asad, Damascus, 18 March 1988.
29 Ian Black, *The Guardian*, 15 November 1986.
30 Interview with a very senior Jordanian source, Amman, 4 March 1988.
31 Interview with Dr 'Abd al-Ra'uf al-Kasm, Damascus, 13 March 1988.
32 Interview with President Asad, Damascus, 18 March 1988.
33 Charles Glass, 'Who Was Hindawi Working For?', *Spectator*, 1 November 1986.
34 Interview with President Asad, Damascus, 18 March 1988.
35 *Report of the President's Special Review Board*, 26 February 1987 (The Tower Report), quoted in *Chronology*, p. 68.
36 *New York Times*, 17 December 1986, *Washington Post*, 21 December 1986.
37 Graham Fuller to Director of Central Intelligence, 'Toward a Policy on Iran', 17 May 1985, quoted in *Chronology*, p. 103.
38 The Tower Report, pp. B-7, B-8.
39 Ibid., p. B-9.
40 Ibid., p. B-9; Senate Select Committee on Intelligence: 'Report on Preliminary
.   Inquiry', 29 January 1987, quoted in *Chronology*, p. 118.
41 *New York Times*, 25 December 1986; *Washington Post*, 27 December 1986 and 12 January 1987; Tower Report, quoted in *Chronology*, pp. 93, 99–100.
42 Tower Report, quoted in *Chronology*, p. 110.
43 Ibid., p. 111.
44 Ibid., pp. 122–3.
45 Ibid., pp. 129–30.
46 Interview with Robert McFarlane, Washington, 30 July 1987.
47 *Washington Post*, 9 December 1986.
48 Tower Report, quoted in *Chronology*, p. 208.
49 Ibid., p. 211.
50 *Washington Post*, 16 and 27 December 1986, 10 and 12 January 1987; Senate Select Committee on Intelligence, quoted in *Chronology*, pp. 235–7.
51 Tower Report, quoted in *Chronology*, pp. 261–2.
52 Interview with Robert McFarlane, Washington, 30 July 1987.
53 Patrick Seale, 'The Banker and the $2.5 billion arms sting', *The Observer*, 27 April 1986. The case was dropped in the wake of the Irangate revelations.
54 *Chronology*, pp. 379–80.
55 The phrase is Theodore Draper's. See his article 'Reagan's Junta', *New York Review of Books*, 29 January 1987, and subsequent articles on 8 and 22 October 1987 and 17 December 1987.
56 *Wall Street Journal*, 3 August 1987.
57 *Washington Post*, 24 July 1987.

Chapter 27 Conclusions: the Balance Sheet

1 Interview with President Asad, Damascus, 18 March 1988.

Select Bibliography

I. Works in Arabic

'Abd Allah, King. *Mudhakkarat* (Memoirs), Amman, 1947.

'Abd al-Da'im, 'Abd Allah. *al-Qawmiya wa'l-'insaniya* (Nationalism and Humanity), Beirut, 1957.

—— *al-Ishtirakiya wa'l-dimuqratiya* (Socialism and Democracy), Beirut, 1961.

—— *al-Jil al-'arabi al-jadid* (The New Arab Age), Beirut, 1961.

'Abd al-Karim, Ahmad. *Adwa' 'ala tajrubat al-wahda* (Elucidation of the Experience of Unity), Damascus, 1962.

'Abd al-Nasir, Jamal. *Falsafat al-thawra*, Cairo, n.d. (Eng. trans. Abdel-Nasser, G. *The Philosophy of the Revolution*. Cairo, n.d.).

Abu Mansur, Fadl Allah. *A'asir dimashq* (Damascus Storms), Beirut, 1959.

al-Adhana, Sulayman Efendi. *Kitab al-bakura al-sulaymaniya fi kashf asrar al-diyana al-nusayriya*, Beirut, 1863. (Partial Eng. trans by E.E. Salisbury, 'The Book of Sulaiman's First Ripe Fruit: Disclosing the Mysteries of the Nusairian Religion', *Journal of the American Oriental Society*, vol. viii, Paris, 1924.)

'Aflaq, Michel. *Ma'rakat al-masir al-wahid* (Battle for the One Destiny), Beirut, 1958.

—— *Fi sabil al-ba'th* (In the Cause of the Ba'th), Beirut, 1959. Revised and expanded edition, Beirut, 1963.

al-'Ajlani, Munir. *Difa' al-doctor Munir al-'Ajlani amam al-mahkama al-'askariya fi dimashq* (The Defence of Dr Munir al-'Ajlani Before the Military Court in Damascus), Damascus, 1957.

al-'Alami, Musa. *'Ibrat filastin*. Beirut, 1949. (Eng. trans. 'The Lesson of Palestine', *Middle East Journal*, no. 3 (1949) pp. 373–405).

'Allush, Naji. *al-Thawra wa'l-jamahir* (The Revolution and the Masses), Beirut, 1962.

al-Amin, F. *Hafiz al-Asad wa dawruhu al-qawmi fi lubnan* (Hafiz al-Asad and his National Role in Lebanon), Beirut, 1983.

Arab League. *Jam'iyat al-duwal al-'arabiya: mithaquha wa nubdha tarikhiya 'anha* (The League of Arab States; its Charter together with a Short Historical Account), Cairo, 1947.

al-Arsuzi, Zaki. *al-'Abqariya al-'arabiya fi lisaniha* (Arab Genius in Language), Damascus, 1942.

—— al-Umma al-'arabiya (The Arab Nation), Damascus, 1958.

—— Mashakiluna al-qawmiya (Our Nationalist Problems), Damascus, 1958.

—— al-Mu'allafat al-kamila (The Collected Works), Damascus, 1972–1974.

al-Atasi, Jamal (ed.) Fi'l-fikr al-siyasi (On Political Thought), 2 vols, Damascus, 1963.

al-Atrash, Fu'ad. al-Duruz, mu'amara wa tarikh wa haqa'iq (The Druze, Conspiracy, History and Facts), Beirut, 1975.

al-'Aysami, Shibli. Fi'l-thawra al-'arabiya (On the Arab Revolution), 2nd edn, Beirut, 1969.

—— al-Wahda al-'arabiya min khilal al-tajruba (Arab Unity through Experience), Beirut, 1971.

—— Hawl al-wahda al-'arabiya (Concerning Arab Unity), 2nd edn, Beirut, 1974.

—— Hizb al-ba'th al-'arabi al-ishtiraki, 1, marhalat al-arba'inat al-ta'sisiya 1940–1949 (The Arab Socialist Ba'th Party, 1, The Foundation Stage of the 1940s, 1940-1949), 2nd edn, Beirut, 1975. (French. trans. Baghdad, 1977.)

Ayyub, S. al-Hizb al-shuyu'i fi suriya wa lubnan, 1922–58 (The Communist Party in Syria and Lebanon, 1922–58), Beirut, 1959.

al-'Azm, 'Abd al-Qadir. al-'Usra al-'Azmiya (The 'Azm family), Damascus, 1951.

al-'Azm, Khalid. Mudhakkarat Khalid al-'Azm, (The Memoirs of Khalid al-'Azm), 3 vols, Beirut, 1973

al-'Azm, Sadiq. Al-Naqd al-dhati ba'd al-hazima (Self-Criticism after the Defeat), Beirut, 1968.

B'albaki, Layla. Ana 'ahya (I Live), Beirut, 1958. (French.trans. Je vis, Paris, 1961).

Bakdash, Khalid. al-Hizb al-shuyu'i fi'l-nidal li 'ajl al-'istiqlal wa'l-siyada al-wataniya (The Communist Party in its Struggle for Independence and National Sovereignty), Beirut, 1944. Report delivered by Bakdash to the National Congress of the CP of Syria and Lebanon, Dec.-Jan. 1944.

—— al-Shuyu'iya wa'l-qawmiya (Communism and Nationalism), Beirut, 1944.

—— Suriya ba'd al-jala' (Syria after the Evacuation), Damascus, 1946.

—— al-Shuyu'iya fi suriya (Communism in Syria), Damascus, 1946.

—— Dawr suriya al-tarikhi fi'l-'alam al-'arabi (Syria's Historic Role in the Arab World), Damascus, 1955.

al-Barudi, Fakhri. Mudhakkarat al-Barudi (Memoirs of al-Barudi), Beirut, 1951.

Bitar, Salah al-Din. al-Siyasa al-'arabiya bayn al-mabda' wa'l-tatbiq (Arab Politics between Principle and Practice), Beirut, 1960.

—— and Michel 'Aflaq. al-Qawmiya al-'arabiya wa mawqifuha min al-shuyu'iya (Arab Nationalism and its Attitude towards Communism), Damascus, 1944.

—— al-Ba'th wa'l-hizb al-shuyu'i (The Ba'th and the Communist Party), Damascus, 1944.

al-Bizri, 'Afif. al-Nasiriya fi jumlat al-isti'mar al-hadith (Nasserism: Part of the New Imperialism), Damascus, 1962.

Dalil al-jumhuriya al-suriya, 1939–1940 (Handbook of the Syrian Republic, 1939–1940), Damascus, n.d.

Darwaza, al-Hakam. al-Shuyu'iya al-mahalliya fi ma'rakat al-'arab al-qawmiya (Local Communism in the National Struggle of the Arabs), Beirut, 1961.

al-Da'uq, Bashir (ed). Nidal al-ba'th fi sabil al-wahda al-huriya wa'l-ishtirakiya (The Struggle of the Ba'th for Unity, Freedom and Socialism), 11 vols, Beirut, 1963–1974.

Faris, George (ed.) *Man huwa fi suriya 1949* (Who's Who in Syria, 1949), Damascus, 1949. See also companion vols for 1951 and 1957.

Fawzi, Gen. Muhammad and Mahmud Hafiz. *Dirasat fi'l-qawmiya al-'arabiya* (Studies in Arab Nationalism), Cairo, n.d. (c. 1959).

Hadhihi hiya suriya al-kubra (This is Greater Syria), Damascus, n.d. A collection of documents.

al-Haffar, Lutfi. *Dhikrayyat* (Reminiscences), 2 vols. Damascus, 1954.

al-Haffar, Wajih. *al-Dustur wa'l-hukm* (The Constitution and Governance), Damascus, 1948.

al-Hafiz, Yasin (ed.) *Fi'l-fikr al-siyasi* (On Political Thought), Damascus, 1963.

al-Hakim, Hasan. *Mudhakkarati. Safahat min tarikh suriya al-haditha 1920–1958* (My Memoirs. Pages from Modern Syrian History, 1920–1958), 2 vols, Beirut, 1965–1966.

al-Hasani, 'Abd al-Razzaq. *Tarikh al-wizarat al-'iraqiya* (History of the Iraqi Cabinets), vol. viii, Sidon, 1955.

al-Hawrani, Akram. *Ra'y al-ustadh Akram al-Hawrani fi'l-wahda al-'arabiya* (The Views of Mr Akram al-Hawrani on Arab Unity), Damascus, 1962.

Haykal, Muhammad Hasanayn. *Ma alladhi jara fi suriya?* (What Happened in Syria?), Cairo, 1962.

al-Hindi, Hani. *Jaysh al-inqadh* (The Army of Rescue), Beirut, 1974.

al-Hizb al-Suri al-Qawmi al-Ijtima'i (The Syrian Social Nationalist Party, sometimes known as the Parti Populaire Syrien). *Ila al-nayu-raj'iyin al-'urubiyin* (To the Arabizing Neo-reactionaries), Beirut, 1949.

al-Husri, Sati'. *Yawm maysalun* (The Day of Maysalun), Beirut, 1947.

—— *Ara' wa ahadith fi'l-qawmiya al-'arabiya* (Views and Addresses on Arab Nationalism), Cairo 1951.

—— *Ara' wa ahadith fi'l-wataniya wa'l-qawmiya* (Views and Addresses on Patriotism and Nationalism), Cairo, 1954.

—— *Difa' 'an al-'uruba* (Defence of Arabism), Beirut,1956.

—— *Al-Iqlimiya judhuruha wa budhuruha* (Particularism, its Roots and Seeds), Beirut, 1963.

Ibrahim, Sa'd al-Din. *Itijahat al-rai' al-'am al-'arabi nahwa mas'alat al-wahda* (Attitudes of Arab Public Opinion on the Question of Unity), Beirut, 1980.

'Indani, Tawfiq. *al-Ba'th fi durub al-nidal* (The Ba'th on the Paths of Struggle), Damascus, 1965.

Iraq Government. *Majra al-hawadith al-muta'atiya min al-inqilab fi dimashq bima yata'allaq bi'l-hukuma al-'iraqiya* (The Course of Events Resulting from the Damascus Coup d'Etat which Relate to the Iraq Government), Baghdad, 1949.

Iraq Ministry of Defence. *Mahkamat al-sha'b* (The People's Court), Baghdad, 1958.

'Isa al-Fil, Ahmad. *Suriya al-jadida fi'l-inqilabayn al-awwal wa'l-thani* (The New Syria in the First and Second Coups d'Etat), Damascus, 1949.

Junblatt, Kamal. *Hadhihi wasiyati* (This Is My Testimony), Beirut, 1978.

al-Jundi, Sami. *'Arab wa yahud* (Arabs and Jews), Beirut, 1968.

—— *Sadiqi Ilyas* (My Friend Ilyas), Beirut, 1969.

—— *al-Ba'th* (The Ba'th), Beirut, 1969.

—— *Atahadda wa attahim* (I Challenge and I Accuse), Beirut, 1970.

Kahaleh, Habib. *Dhikrayat na'ib* (Memoirs of a Deputy), Damascus, n.d.

al-Kawtharani, Wajih. *Bilad al-sham* (The Lands of Damascus), Beirut, 1980.

al-Kayyali, 'Abd al-Rahman. *Marahil fi'l-intidab al-faransi wa nidalina al-watani* (Stages in the French Mandate and in our National Struggle), vols I-IV, Aleppo, 1958–1960.

al-Khuri, Sami. *Radd 'ala Sati' al-Husri* (Reply to Sati' al-Husri), Beirut, n.d.

Kishk, Muhammad Jalal. *al-Naksa wa'l ghazw al-fikri* (The Setback and Cultural Invasion), Beirut, 1969.

—— *al-Qawmiya wa'l ghazw al-fikri* (Nationalism and Cultural Invasion), Beirut, 1970.

Kurd 'Ali, Muhammad. *al-Mudhakkarat* (Memoirs), 4 vols, Damascus 1948–1951

Maqsud, Clovis. *Nahwa ishtirakiya 'arabiya* (Towards Arab Socialism), Beirut, 1957.

—— *Azamat al-yasar al-'arabi* (The Crises of the Arab Left), Beirut, 1960.

Murqus, Ilyas. *Tarikh al-ahzab al-shuyu'iya fi'l-watan al-'arabi* (History of the Communist Parties in the Arab Homeland), Beirut, 1964.

al-Nafuri, Amin. *'Abd al-Nasir bada'a fi dimashq wa-intaha fi shtura* ('Abd al-Nasir Began in Damascus and Ended in Shtura), Damascus, 1962.

Nasrallah, Muhammad 'Izzat. *al-Radd 'ala Sadiq al-'Azm* (An Answer to Sadiq al-'Azm), Beirut, 1970.

Nassur, Dr Adib. *Qabla fawat al-'awan* (Before It Is Too Late), Beirut, n.d.

al-Qal'aji, Qadri. *Tajrubat 'arabi fi'l-hizb al-shuyu'i* (The Experience of an Arab in the Communist Party), Beirut, n.d.

al-Qasimiya, Khayriya (ed.) *Mudhakkarat Fawzi al-Qawaqji 1914-1932* (The Memoirs of Fawzi al-Qawaqji), vol. I, Beirut 1975.

—— *Filastin fi mudhakkarat Fawzi al-Qawaqji 1936–1948*˙ (Palestine in the Memoirs of Fawzi al-Qawaqji), vol. II, Beirut, 1975.

al-Quwatli, Shukri. *Majmu'at khutab* (Collected Speeches), Damascus, 1957.

al-Razzaz, Munif. *Ma'alim al-hayat al-'arabiya al-jadida* (Characteristics of the New Arab Life), 5th edn, Beirut, 1966.

—— *al-Tajruba al-mura* (The Bitter Experience), Beirut, 1967.

al-Rikabi, Fu'ad. *'Ala tariq al-thawra* (On the Road to Revolution), Cairo, 1962.

—— *al-Hall al-awhad* (The Only Solution), Cairo, 1963.

al-Rimawi, 'Abd Allah. *al-Mantiq al-thawri li'l-haraka al-qawmiya al-'arabiya al-haditha* (The Revolutionary Logic of the Modern Arab Nationalist Movement), Cairo, 1961.

—— *al-Haraka al-'arabiya al-wahida* (The Sole Arab Movement), Beirut, 1964.

al-Rumi, Shamil. *al-Fatayir* (Pancakes), Damascus, 1960.

Sa'ada, Antun. *Nushu' al-umam* (The Rise of Nations), vol. I, Beirut, 1938.

—— *al-Ta'alim al-suriya al-qawmiya al-ijtima'iya* (Syrian National Social Teaching), 4th edn, Beirut, 1947.

al-Sadat, Anwar. *Qissat al-wahda al-'arabiya* (The Story of Arab Unity), Cairo, 1957.

al-Safadi, Muta'. *Jil al-qadar* (The Generation of Fate), Damascus, 1960.

—— *Hizb al-Ba'th ma'sat al-mawlid ma'sat al-nihaya* (The Ba'th Party, its Tragic Birth, its Tragic Death), Beirut, 1964.

al-Sa'id, Rif'at. *Hasan al-Banna*, Cairo, 1977.

Salama, Ibrahim. *al-Ba'th min al-madaris ila'l-thakanat* (The Ba'th from the Schools to the Barracks), Beirut, 1969.

Sayigh, Anis. *al-Fikra al-'arabiya fi misr* (The Arab Idea in Egypt), Beirut, 1959.

al-Sayyid, Jalal. *Hizb al-ba'th al-'arabi* (The Arab Ba'th Party), Beirut, 1973.

al-Shahbandar, Dr 'Abd al-Rahman. *al-Thawra al-suriya al-wataniya* (The Syrian National Revolution), Damascus, 1933.

—— *al-Qadaya al-ijtima'iya al-kubra fi'l-'alam al-'arabi* (The Great Social Issues in the Arab World), Cairo, 1936.

Shmays, 'Abd al-Na'im. *al-Qawmiyun al-suriyun* (The Syrian Nationalists), Cairo, 1958.

—— *Shuruh fi'l-'aqidah* (Explanations on Ideology), Beirut, 1958.

al-Siba'i, Badr al-Din. *Adwa' 'ala al-r'asmal al-ajnabi fi suriya 1850–1958* (Elucidation on Foreign Capital in Syria, 1850–1958), Damascus, 1958.

Zahr al-Din, 'Abd al-Karim. *Mudhakkarati 'an fatrat al-infisal fi suriya* (My Memoirs of the Separatist Period in Syria), Beirut, 1968.

Zurayk, Dr Qustantin. *Ma'na al-nakba* (The Meaning of the Disaster), Beirut, 1948.

II. Works in other languages

Abdel-Malek, A. *Egypte: société militaire*, Paris, 1962. (US edn *Egypt: Military Society*, New York, 1968).

Abdullah ibn Hussein. *The Memoirs of King Abdullah of Transjordan*, ed. P. P. Graves, London, 1950.

Abou Iyad. *Palestinien Sans Patrie*, Paris, 1978.

Abouchdid, E. E. *Thirty years of Lebanon and Syria, 1917–1947*, Beirut, 1948.

Abu Jaber, K. S. *The Arab Ba'th Socialist Party, History, Ideology and Organisation*, Syracuse, N.Y., 1966.

Abul-Fath, A. *L'Affaire Nasser*, Paris, 1962.

Ahmed, J. M. *The Intellectual Origins of Egyptian Nationalism*, Oxford, 1960.

Ajami, F. *The Arab Predicament: Arab Political Thought and Practice since 1967*, Cambridge, 1981.

—— *The Vanished Imam: Musa al Sadr and the Shia of Lebanon*, Ithaca N.Y, London, 1986.

al-Akhrass, S. *Revolutionary Change and Modernisation in the Arab World: a Case from Syria*, Damascus, 1972.

Amin, S. *The Arab Nation*, London, 1978.

Amine, M. 'Le Développement des partis politiques en Syrie entre 1936 et 1947', Unpubl. thesis, University of Paris, 1950.

Amnesty International Publications, *Report from Amnesty International to the Government of the Syrian Arab Republic*, London, 1983.

—— *Syria: Torture by the Security Forces*, London, 1987.

Antonius, G. *The Arab Awakening*, London, 1938.

Asfour, E. W. *Syria: Development and Monetary Policy*, Cambridge, Mass., 1959.

Ashour, I. Y. 'The Remnants of the Feudal System in Palestine, Syria and the Lebanon', Unpubl. thesis, American University of Beirut, 1946.

Avnery, U. *My Friend, The Enemy*, London, 1986.

Baer, G. *Population and Society in the Arab World*, New York, 1964.

Bagh, S. *L'Industrie à Damas entre 1928 et 1959, Etude de géographie économique*, Damascus, 1961.

Bakhash, S. *The Reign of the Ayatollahs: Iran and the Islamic Revolution*, New York and London, 1985.

Ball, G. W. *The Past Has Another Pattern*, New York, 1982.

—— *Error and Betrayal in Lebanon: an Analysis of Israel's Invasion of Lebanon and the implications for US-Israeli Relations*, Washington D.C., 1984.

Batatu, H. *The Old Social Classes and the Revolutionary Movements of Iraq*, Princeton N.J., 1978.

Be'eri, E. *Army Officers in Arab Politics and Society*, New York, 1970.

Begin, M. *The Revolt: Story of the Irgun*, Jerusalem, 1977.

Beit-Hallahmi, B. *The Israeli Connection: Whom Israel Arms and Why*, London, 1988.

Bekdash, K. *La Charte national du parti communiste en Syrie et au Liban*, Beirut, 1944.

Benziman, U. *Sharon: An Israeli Caesar*, London, 1985.

Berger, M. *The Arab World Today*, New York, 1962.

Berque, J. *Les Arabes d'hier à demain*, Paris, 1960.

Betts, R. B. *Christians in the Arab East*, Athens, 1975.

Birdwood, Lord. *Nuri as-Said: a Study in Arab Leadership*, London, 1959.

Bitterlin, L. *Hafez el-Assad: Le Parcours d'un Combattant*, Paris, 1986.

Brenner, L. *The Iron Wall: Zionist Revisionism from Jabotinsky to Shamir*, London, 1984.

Breuilly, J. *Nationalism and the State*, Manchester, 1982.

Brookings Institution, The. *Toward Peace in the Middle East*, Washington D.C., 1975.

—— *Toward Arab-Israeli Peace*, Washington D.C., 1988.

Brown, L. C. *International Politics and the Middle East: Old Rules, Dangerous Game*, Princeton N.J. and London, 1984.

Brzezinski, Z. *Power and Principle*, New York and London, 1983.

Campbell, J. C. *Defense of the Middle East*, rev. edn. New York, 1960.

Carré, O. and G. Michaud. *Les Frères Musulmans (1928–1982)*, Paris, 1983.

Carrère d'Encausse, H. *La politique soviétique au Moyen-Orient 1955–1975*, Paris, 1975.

Carter, J. *Keeping Faith*, New York and London, 1982.

—— *The Blood of Abraham*, Boston, Mass., 1985.

Castle, B. *The Castle Diaries 1964–70*, London, 1984.

Chaliand, G. (ed.) *People Without a Country: the Kurds and Kurdistan*, London, 1980.

Chatty, D. *From Camel to Truck: the Bedouin in the Modern World*, New York, 1986.

Childers, E. B. *The Road to Suez*, London, 1962.

Chomsky, N. *Peace in the Middle East?*, New York, 1974, London, 1975.

—— *The Fateful Triangle: The United States, Israel and the Palestinians*, Boston, Mass. and London, 1983.

Cleveland, W. L. *The Making of an Arab Nationalist: Ottomanism and Arabism in the Life and Thought of Sati' al-Husri*, Princeton N.J., 1971.

—— *Islam against the West: Shakib Arslan and the Campaign for Islamic Nationalism*, Austin Texas, 1985.

Cobban, H. *The Palestinian Liberation Organisation: People, Power and Politics*, Cambridge, 1984.

—— *The Making of Modern Lebanon*, London, 1985.

Colombe, M. *L'Evolution de l'Egypte, 1924–1950*, Paris, 1951.

—— *Orient arabe et non-engagement*, 2 vols, Paris, 1973.

Cooley, J. K. *Green March, Black September: The Story of the Palestinian Arabs*, London, 1973.

Copeland, M. *The Game of Nations*, London, 1969.

Cordesman, A. H. *The Arab-Israeli Military Balance and the Art of Operations*, Washington D.C., 1986.

Crossman, R. *The Dairies of a Cabinet Minister*, London, 1976.

Crow, R. 'A Study of Political Forces in Syria based on a survey of the 1954 elections', Unpubl. Beirut, 1955.

Daker, N. *Sédentarisation des bedouins nomades en Syrie*, Paris, 1973.

Davis, H. M. *Constitutions, Electoral Laws, Treaties of States in the Near and Middle East*, 2nd edn Durham, 1953.

Dawisha, A. I. *Egypt in the Arab World: the Elements of Foreign Policy*, London, 1976.

—— *Syria and the Lebanese Crisis*, London, 1980.

—— and I. W. Zartman (eds) *Beyond Coercion: the Durability of the Arab State*, London, 1988.

Dawn, C. E. *From Ottomanism to Arabism: Essays on the Origins of Arab Nationalism*, Urbana, Ill. 1973.

Day, A. R. *East Bank/West Bank: Jordan and the Prospects for Peace*, New York, 1986.

Dayan, Maj.-Gen. M. *Diary of the Sinai Campaign, 1956*, London, 1967.

Dayan, M. *Story of My Life*, London, 1976.

—— *Breakthrough: A Personal Account of the Egypt-Israel Peace Negotiations*, New York, 1981.

Devlin, J. F. *The Ba'th Party: a History from its Origins to 1966*, Stanford, Cal., 1966.

—— *Syria: Modern State in an Ancient Land*, Boulder, Col. and London, 1983.

Dubertret, L. and J. Weulersse. *Manuel de géographie, Syrie, Liban et Proche-Orient*, Beirut, 1940.

Dupuy, T. N. *Elusive Victory: The Arab-Israeli Wars, 1947–1974*, New York, 1978.

—— and P. Martell. *Flawed Victory*, Washington D.C., 1985.

Dussaud, R. *Histoire et Réligion des Nosairis*, Paris, 1900.

Eban, A. *An Autobiography*, New York, 1977, London, 1978.

Ecochard, M. and G. Banshoya, *Plan Directeur de Damas*, Damascus, 1968.

Eden, Sir A. *The Memoirs of the Rt Hon. Sir Anthony Eden KG, PC, MC, iii: Full Circle*, London, 1960.

Egypt Min. of Foreign Affairs. *Records of conversations, notes and papers exchanged between the Royal Egyptian Government and the United Kingdom Government, March 1958-November 1951*, Cairo, 1951.

Eshel, D. *The Lebanon War*, Tel Aviv, 1982.

Evans-Pritchard, Capt. E. E. 'A Note on the Nosairis of Syria', unpubl. Beirut, 1942.

Eveland, W. C. *Ropes of Sand: America's Failure in the Middle East*, New York, 1980.

Evron, Y. *War and Intervention in Lebanon: The Israeli-Syrian Deterrence Dialogue*, London, 1987.

Fahmy, I. *Negotiating for Peace in the Middle East*, London, 1983.

Faris, N. A. and M. T. Husayn. *The Crescent in Crisis: an interpretative study of the modern Arab world*, Kansas, 1955.

Fedden, R. *Syria: an Historical Appreciation*, London, 1946. Revised edn London, 1955.

Fisher, S. N. (ed.) *Social Forces in the Middle East*, Ithaca N.Y., 1955.

Fisher, W. B. *The Middle East, a Physical, Social and Regional Geography*, London, 4th edn, 1961.

Flapan, S. *Zionism and the Palestinians*, New York and London, 1979.

Ford, G. R. *A Time to Heal*, New York and London, 1979.

Frye, R. N. (ed.) *The Near East and the Great Powers*, Cambridge, Mass., 1951.

Gabby, R. E. *A Political Study of the Arab-Jewish Conflict*, Geneva, 1959.

Gabriel, R. A. *Operation Peace for Galilee*, New York, 1984.

Ghalioun, B. 'Etat et luttes de classes en Syrie, 1945–1970', Unpubl. thesis, Paris, 1974.

Gibb, Sir A. & Partners. *The Economic Development of Syria*, London, 1947.

Gibb H. A. R. and J. H. Kramers, *Shorter Encyclopaedia of Islam*, Leiden, 1953.

Gilmour, D. *Dispossessed: The Ordeal of the Palestinians 1917–1980*, London, 1980.

—— *Lebanon: the Fractured Country*, Oxford, 1983.

Glubb, J. B. *A Soldier with the Arabs*, London, 1957.

—— *Britain and the Arabs: a Study of Fifty Years, 1908–1958*, London, 1959.

Golan, G. *Syria, Lebanon, Jordan*, London, 1967.

—— *Yom Kippur and After: The Soviet Union and the Middle East Crisis*, London, 1977.

Golan, M. *The Secret Conversations of Henry Kissinger*, New York, 1976.

Gordon, D. C. *The Republic of Lebanon: Nation in Jeopardy*, Boulder, Col. and London, 1983.

Green, S. *Taking Sides: America's Secret Relations with a Militant Israel*, New York, 1984.

Haber, E., Ze'ev Schiff and Ehud Ya'ari, *The Year of the Dove*, New York, 1979.

Haddad, G. *Fifty Years of Modern Syria and Lebanon*, Beirut, 1950.

—— *Revolutions and Military Rule in the Middle East*, New York, 1965.

al-Hafez, M. A. *La Structure et la Politique économique en Syrie et au Liban*, Beirut, 1953.

Haig, A. M. Jr. *Caveat: Realism, Reagan and Foreign Policy*, London, 1984.

Haim, S. G. *Arab Nationalism: An Anthology*, Los Angeles and London, 1962. Paperback edition 1976.

Halm, H. *Die islamische Gnosis: die extreme Schia und die 'Alawiten*, Zurich and Munich, 1982.

Halpern, M. *The Politics of Social Change in the Middle East and North Africa*, Princeton, N.J., 1963.

Hamide, A. R. *La Région d'Alep: étude de géographie rurale*, Paris, 1959.

—— *La ville d'Alep: étude de géographie urbaine*, Paris, 1959.

Hannoyer, J. 'Campagnes et pouvoir en Syrie: Essai d'histoire socio-économique sur la région de Deir ez-Zor', Unpubl. thesis, Paris, 1982.

Hansen, B. *Economic Development of Syria*, Santa Monica, Cal. 1969.

Harba, M. 'Organisations agraires, population rurale et développement en Syrie', Unpubl. thesis, Montpellier, 1978.

Heikel, M. *The Cairo Documents*, New York, 1973.

—— *The Road to Ramadan*, New York and London, 1975.

—— *The Sphinx and the Commissar*, New York and London, 1978.

—— *Autumn of Fury*, New York and London, 1983.

Helbaoui, Y. *La Syrie: Mise en valeur d'un pays sous-développé*, Paris, 1956.

Hersh, S. M. *Kissinger: The Price of Power*, New York and London, 1983.

Herzog, C. *The Arab-Israeli Wars*, London, 1982.

Heyworth-Dunne, J. *Religious and Political Trends in Modern Egypt*, Washington D.C., 1950.

Hilan, R. *Culture et développement en Syrie et dans les pays retardés*, Paris, 1969.

Hiro, D. *Iran Under the Ayatollahs*, London, 1985.

Hirst, D. *The Gun and the Olive Branch: the Roots of Violence in the Middle East*, New York and London, 1977.

Hirst, D. and I. Beeson. *Sadat*, London, 1981.

Hirszowicz, L. *The Third Reich and the Arab East*, London, 1966.

Hitti, P. K. *History of Syria, including Lebanon and Palestine*, New York and London, 1951.

Hof, F. C. *Galilee Divided: The Israel-Lebanon Frontier, 1916–1984*, Boulder, Col. and London, 1985.

Holt, P. M. *Egypt and the Fertile Crescent, 1516–1922*, London, 1966.

Hourani, A. H. *Syria and Lebanon*, London, 1946.

—— *Minorities in the Arab World*, Oxford, 1957.

—— *A Vision of History*, Beirut, 1961.

—— *Arabic Thought in the Liberal Age, 1798–1939*, London, 1962.

—— *Europe and the Middle East*, London, 1980.

—— *The Emergence of the Modern Middle East*, London, 1981.

Hudson, M. C. *Arab Politics: the Search for Legitimacy*, New Haven, Conn., 1977.

Humbaraci, A. *Middle East Indictment*, London, 1958.

Hurewitz, J. C. *Middle East Dilemmas: the Background of United States Policy*, New York, 1953.

—— *Diplomacy in the Near and Middle East; a Documentary Record, ii: 1914–1956*, Princeton, N.J., 1956.

Husaini, I. M. *The Moslem Brethren*, Beirut, 1956.

International Bank for Reconstruction and Development. *The Economic Development of Syria*, Baltimore, 1955.

Ionides, M. *Divide and Lose: the Arab Revolt 1955–8*, London, 1960.

Issawi, C. (ed.) *The Economic History of the Middle East 1800–1914*, Chicago, 1966.

Jamowitz, M. *The Military and the Political Development of New Nations*, Chicago, 1964.

Jansen, M. *The Battle of Beirut: Why Israel Invaded Lebanon*, London, 1982.

Jargy, S. *Syrie*, Paris, 1962.

Jenner, M. *Syria in View*, London, 1986.

Johnson, M. *Class and Client in Beirut: The Sunni Muslim Community and the Lebanese State 1840–1985*, London, 1986.

Junblatt, K. *Pour le Liban*, Paris, 1978.

Kalb, M. and B. *Kissinger*, Boston, Mass., 1974.

Kaminsky, C. and S. Kruk. *La Syrie: Politiques et Stratégies de 1966 à nos jours*, Paris, 1987.

Karanjia, R. K. *Arab Dawn*, Bombay, 1958.

Karpat, K. H. (ed.) *Political and Social Thought in the Contemporary Middle East*, London, 1968.

Kamel, M. I. *The Camp David Accords*, London, 1986.

Kedourie, E. *England and the Middle East: the Destruction of the Ottoman Empire 1914–1921*, London, 1956.

—— *The Chatham House Version and other Middle Eastern Studies*, London, 1970.

—— *Arabic Political Memoirs and Other Studies*, London, 1974.

—— *In the Anglo-Arab Labyrinth: the McMahon-Husayn Correspondence and its Interpretations, 1914–39*, Cambridge, 1976.

—— *Islam in the Modern World*, London, 1980.

Kepel, G. *The Prophet and Pharaoh: Muslim Extremism in Egypt*, London, 1985.

Kerr, M. *The Arab Cold War, 1958–64: a Study of Ideology in Politics*, Oxford, 1965. 3rd edn subtitled *Gamal 'Abd al-Nasir and his Rivals, 1958–70*, Oxford, 1971.

Khadduri, M. *Independent Iraq 1932–1958*, 2nd edn Oxford, 1960.

—— *Republican Iraq*, Oxford, 1969.

—— *Arab Contemporaries: the Role of Personalities in Politics*, Baltimore, 1973.

Khalidi, W. 'Political Trends in the Fertile Crescent', in W. Z. Laqueur (ed.) *The Middle East in Transition*, London, 1958.

—— *Conflict and Violence in Lebanon*, Cambridge, Mass., 1984.

Khalidi, R. *Under Siege*, New York, 1986.

Khoury, P. S. *Urban Notables and Arab Nationalism: the Politics of Damascus 1860–1920*, Cambridge, 1983.

—— *Syria and the French Mandate: The Politics of Nationalism 1920–1936*, Cambridge, Mass. and London, 1987.

Kirk, G. E. *A Short History of the Middle East*, London, 1948.

—— *The Middle East in the War, 1939–1946*, London, 1952.

—— *The Middle East, 1945–1950*, London, 1954.

—— *Contemporary Arab Politics*, New York, 1961.

Kirkbride, Sir A. *A Crackle of Thorns*, London, 1956.

Kissinger, H. *White House Years*, New York and London, 1979.

—— *Years of Upheaval*, New York and London, 1982.

Klieman, A. S. *Israel's Global Reach: Arms Sales as Diplomacy*, New York and Oxford, 1985.

Kramers, M. (ed.) *Shi'ism, Resistance and Revolution*, Boulder, Col., 1987.

Lacouture, J. and S. *L'Egypte en mouvement*, Paris, 1956.

Lacouture, J. *Nasser*, Paris, 1971.

Laissy, M. *Du Panarabisme à la Ligue Arabe*, Paris, 1948.

Lammens, H. *Etudes réligieuses*, Paris, 1899.

—— *La Syrie et sa mission historique* Cairo, 1915.

—— *La Syrie: précis historique*, Beirut, 1921, 2 vols.

—— *L'Islam, croyances et institutions*, Beirut, 2nd edn 1941.

Laqueur, W. Z. *Communism and Nationalism in the Middle East*, London, 1956.

—— (ed.) *The Middle East in Transition*, London, 1958.

—— *The Soviet Union and the Middle East*, New York, 1959.

Legum, C. et al. (eds). *Middle East Contemporary Survey*, London, vol. i, 1976–77;
vol. ii, 1977–78; vol. iii, 1978–79; vol. iv, 1979–80; vol. v, 1980–81; vol. vi, 1981–82; vol vii, 1982–83.

Lerner, D. *The Passing of Traditional Society*, New York, 1964.

Lewis, B. *The Arabs in History*, London, 1958.

—— *The Middle East and the West*, New York, 1964.

—— *The Assassins: a Radical Sect in Islam*, London, 1967. Paperback edn London, 1985.

Little, T. *Egypt*, London, 1958.

Longrigg, S. H. *Iraq, 1900 to 1950: a political, social and economic history*, London, 1953.

—— *Syria and Lebanon under French Mandate*, London, 1958.

—— *The Middle East, a Social Geography*, London, 1963.

Love, K. *Suez the Twice-Fought War*, New York, 1969.

Luttwak, E. and D. Horowitz. *The Israeli Army*, New York, 1975.

Lyde, the Rev. S. *The Ansyreeh and Ismaeleeh*, London, 1853.

—— *The Asian Mystery*, London, 1860.

Maalouf, A. *The Crusades Through Arab Eyes*, London, 1984.

MacBride, S. et al. *Israel in Lebanon: The Report of the International Commission*, London, 1983.

Macintyre, R. R. 'The Arab Ba'th Socialist Party: Ideology, Politics, Sociology and Organisation', Unpubl. thesis, Australian National University, 1969.

Majdalani, G. 'The Arab Socialist Movement', in W. Z. Laqueur (ed.) *The Middle East in Transition*, London, 1958.

Mansfield, P. *The Arabs*, London, 1976.

Ma'oz, M. *Ottoman Reform in Syria and Palestine, 1840–1861: the Impact of the Tanzimat on Politics and Society*, Oxford, 1968.

Ma'oz, M. and A. Yaniv (eds). *Syria under Assad: Domestic Constraints and Regional Risks*, London, 1986.

Marlowe, J. *Arab Nationalism and British Imperialism*, London, 1961.

Melia, J. *Chez des Chrétiens d'Orient*, Paris, 1929.

Meir, G. *My Life*, New York, 1976.

Milson, M. (ed.) *Society and Political Structure in the Arab World*, New York, 1973.

Mitchell, R. P. *The Society of the Muslim Brothers*, London, 1969.

Monroe, E. *Britain's Moment in the Middle East, 1914–56*, London, 1963.

Mutawi, S. A. *Jordan in the 1967 War*, Cambridge, 1987.

Nashabi, H. A. 'The Political Parties in Syria 1918–1933', Unpubl. thesis, American University of Beirut, 1952.

National Security Archive, The. *The Chronology: The Documented Day-by-Day Account of the Secret Military Assistance to Iran and the Contras*, New York, 1987.

al-Nayal, M. A. K. 'Industrialisation and Dependency, Syria 1920–1957', Unpubl. thesis, The Hague, 1974.

Neguib, M. *Egypt's Destiny*, London, 1955.

Netanyahu, B. (ed.) *Terrorism: How the West Can Win*, New York, 1986.

Nir, A. *The Soviet-Syrian Friendship and Cooperation Treaty: Unfulfilled Expectations*, Tel Aviv, 1983.

Nuseibeh, H. Z. *The Ideas of Arab Nationalism*, Ithaca, N.Y., 1956.

Nutting, A. *Nasser*, London, 1972.

Orgels, B. *Contribution à l'étude des problemes agricoles de la Syrie*, Brussels, 1962.

Ovendale, F. *The Origins of the Arab-Israeli Wars*, London, 1984.

Owen, R. (ed.) *Essays on the Crisis in Lebanon*, London, 1976.

Patai, R. (ed.) *The Republic of Syria*, New Haven, Conn., 2 vols, 1956.

Pakradouni, K. *La Paix Manquée: Le Mandat d'Elias Sarkis (1976–1982)*, Beirut, 1984.

Pearse, R. *Three Years in the Levant*, London, 1949.

Peri, Y. *Between Battles and Ballots: Israeli Military in Politics*, Cambridge, 1983.

Petran, T. *Syria*, London, 1972.

—— *The Struggle Over Lebanon*, New York, 1987.

Polk, W. R. 'America in the Middle East 1947–1958', in *St Antony's Papers* no. 11, London, 1961.

—— *The United States and the Arab World*, Cambridge, Mass., 1965.

Porath, Y. *In Search of Arab Unity 1930–1945*, London, 1986.

Quandt, W. B., F. Jabber and A. M. Lesch, *The Politics of Palestinian Nationalism*, Berkeley and London, 1973.

Quandt, W. B., *Decade of Decisions: American Policy Toward the Arab-Israeli Conflict 1967–1976*, Berkeley and London, 1977.

—— *Camp David: Peacemaking and Politics*, Washington D.C., 1986.

Rabbath, E. *Les Etats-Unis de Syrie*, Aleppo, 1925.

—— *Unité syrienne et devenir arabe*, Paris, 1937.

Rabin, Y. *The Rabin Memoirs*, London, 1979.

Rabinovich, I. *Syria under the Ba'th 1963–66; the Army-Party Symbiosis*, Jerusalem, 1972.

—— *The War for Lebanon, 1970–1985*, Ithaca N.Y. and London, revised edn 1985.

Rafael, G. *Destination Peace*, London, 1981.

Randal, J. *The Tragedy of Lebanon: Christian Warlords, Israeli Adventurers and American Bunglers*, London, 1983.

el-Rayyes, R. and D. Nahas. *Guerrillas for Palestine*, London, 1976.

Raymond, A. (ed.) *La Syrie d'Aujourd'hui*, Paris, 1980.

Razzaz, M. *The Evolution of the Meaning of Nationalism*, New York, 1963.

Riad, M. *The Struggle for Peace in the Middle East*, London, 1981.

Rodinson, M. *Israel et le refus arabe, 75 ans d'histoire*, Paris, 1969.

Rondot, P. *La Syrie*, Paris, 1978.

Rondot, P. *Le destin du Proche-Orient*, Paris, 1959. (Eng. trs. *The Changing Patterns of the Middle East 1919–1958*, London, 1961).

Royal Institute of International Affairs (RIIA). *Survey of International Affairs, 1951, 1952, 1953, 1954, 1955–6 and 1957–8*, London.

—— *The Middle East: a political and economic survey* 3rd edn London, 1958.

—— *British Interests in the Middle East; a report by a Chatham House study group*, London, 1958.

Saab, E. *La Syrie ou la révolution dans la rancoeur*, Paris, 1968.

Sadat, A. *In Search of Identity*, London, 1978.

Safran, N. *Egypt in Search of Political Community*, Cambridge, Mass., 1961.

Said, E. W. *The Question of Palestine*, New York, 1979.

as-Said, Nuri Pasha. *Arab Independence and Unity*, Baghdad, 1943.

Salibi, K. S. *The Modern History of Lebanon*, London, 1965.

—— *Crossroads to Civil War: Lebanon 1958–1976*, London, 1976.

Saunders, H. H. *The Other Walls: The Politics of the Arab-Israeli Peace Process*, Washington D.C., 1985.

Sauvaget, J. *Esquisse d'une histoire de la ville de Damas*, Paris, 1934.

—— *Alep: essai sur le développement d'une grande ville syrienne des origines au milieu du XIXe siecle*, 2 vols, Paris, 1941.

Sayegh, F. A. *Arab Unity: Hope and Fulfilment*, New York, 1956.

Schatkowski Schilcher, L. *Families in Politics: Damascene Factions and Estates of the 18th and 19th Centuries*, Stuttgart, 1985.

Schiff, Z. and E. Ya'ari. *Israel's War in Lebanon*, New York and London, 1984.

Seale, P. *The Struggle for Syria: A Study of Post-War Arab Politics, 1945–1958*, London, 1965; new edn London, 1986.

Segev, S. *Sadat – ha-Derekh la-Shalom* (Sadat – the Road to Peace), Tel Aviv, 1979.

Shadid, M. K. *The United States and the Palestinians*, London, 1981.

Sharett, M. *Yoman Ishi* (Personal Diary), Tel Aviv, 1980.

Shawcross, W. *Sideshow: Kissinger, Nixon and the Destruction of Cambodia*, London and New York, 1979.

El Shazly, Lt-Gen. S. *The Crossing of the Suez*, San Francisco, 1980.

—— *The Arab Military Option*, San Francisco, 1986.

Shoukri, G. *Egypt: Portrait of a President, 1971–1981*, London, 1981.

Sick, G. *All Fall Down: America's Fateful Encounter with Iran*, New York and London, 1985.

Sid-Ahmed, M. *After the Guns Fall Silent: Peace or Armageddon in the Middle East*, London, 1976.

Sluglett, M. F. and P. *Iraq Since 1958: from Revolution to Dictatorship*, London and New York, 1987.

Smolansky, O. M. *The Soviet Union and the Arab East under Khrushchev*, Lewisburg, 1974.

Spears, E. *Fulfilment of a Mission*, London, 1977.

Stephens, R. *Nasser*, London, 1971. Paperback edn. London, 1973.

Sterling C. *The Terror Network*, New York and London, 1981.

Stirling, Col. W. F. *Safety Last*, London, 1953.

Syrian Social Nationalist Party Information Bureau. *Antoun Sa'adeh: Leadership and Testimony*, n.d.

Tarazi, S. al-D. *Les Services publics libano-syriens*, Beirut, 1946.

Thoumin, R. *Histoire de Syrie*, Paris, 1929.

Tibawi, A. L. *A Modern History of Syria including Lebanon and Palestine*, London, 1969.

Tibi, B. *Arab Nationalism. A Critical Inquiry*, New York, 1981.

Timermann, J. *The Longest War*, New York 1982.

Tivnan, E. *The Lobby: Jewish Political Power and American Foreign Policy*, New York, 1987.

Tlass, General M. et un groupe de chercheurs syriens. *L'Invasion israélienne du Liban*, Paris, 1986.

Tomeh, R. G. 'Landowners and Political Power in Damascus 1858–1958', Unpubl. thesis, American University of Beirut, 1977.

Torrey, G. H. *Syrian Politics and the Military 1945–1958*, Columbus, Ohio, 1964.

U.S. Army Area Handbook for Syria, Washington D.C., 1965.

U.S. Dept. of State. *United States Policy in the Middle East: September 1956-June 1957: Documents*, Washington D.C., 1957.

Van Dam, Nikolaos. *The Struggle for Power in Syria: Sectarianism, Regionalism and Tribalism in Politics, 1961–1978*, London, 1979.

Van Dusen, M. H. 'Intra- and Inter-Generational Conflict in the Syrian Army', Unpubl. thesis, Johns Hopkins University, 1971.

Vance, C. *Hard Choices*, New York, 1983.

Vatikiotis, P. J. *The Egyptian Army in Politics*, Indiana, 1961.

—— (ed.) *Revolution in the Middle East and other Case Studies*, London, 1972.

Vaucher, G. *Gamal Abdel-Nasser et son équipe*, 2 vols, Paris, 1959–60.

Vernier, B. *Armée et Politique au Moyen-Orient*, Paris, 1966.

Von Horn, C. *Soldiering for Peace*, London, 1966.

Warriner, D. *Land Reform and Development in the Middle East*, London, 1957.

Waters, R. T. 'A Social-Political Analysis of Syria 1943–1958', Unpubl. thesis, American University of Beirut, 1962.

Weinberger, N. J. *Syrian Intervention in Lebanon*, Oxford, 1986.

Weizman, E. *On Eagles' Wings*, New York, 1976.

Weulersse, J. *Le Pays des Alaouites*, 2 vols, Tours, 1940.

—— *Paysans de Syrie et du Proche-Orient*, Paris, 1946.

Wheelock, K. *Nasser's New Egypt*, New York and London, 1957.

Whetten, L. L. *The Canal War: Four Power Conflict in the Middle East*, Cambridge, Mass., 1974.

Williams L. (ed.) *Military Aspects of the Arab-Israeli Conflict*, Tel Aviv, 1975.

Wint, G. and P. Calvocoressi. *Middle East Crisis*, London, 1957.

Wirth, E. *Syrien, Eine Geographische Landeskunde*, Darmstadt, 1971.

Woodward, B. *Veil: The Secret Wars of the CIA 1981–1987*, New York and London, 1987.

Wynn, W. *Nasser of Egypt; the Search for Dignity*, Cambridge, Mass., 1959.
Yermiya, D. *My War Diary: Israel in Lebanon*, London and New York, 1984.
Yodfat, A. *Arab Politics in the Soviet Mirror*, Jerusalem, 1973.
Zeine, Z. N. *Arab-Turkish Relations and the Emergence of Arab Nationalism*, Beirut, 1958.
—— *The Struggle for Arab Independence*, Beirut, 1960.
Ziadeh, N. A. *Syria and Lebanon*, London, 1957.
Zuwiyya-Yamak, L. *The Syrian Social Nationalist Party: an Ideological Analysis*, Cambridge, Mass., 1966.

III. Articles

Abou el-Haj, R. 'Identité et histoire: leur utilisation sociale dans l'historiographie arabe de la période ottomane', *Maghreb Machrek* no. 97, 1982.
Abou-Rejeily, A. 'La pédagogie du Ba'th selon Michel Aflaq', *Travaux et Jours*, 51, 1974.
Abu-Lughod, I. and E. Ahmad (eds). 'The Invasion of Lebanon', *Race and Class*, vol. xxiv, no. 4, spring 1983.
Agwani, M. S. 'The Ba'th: A Study in Contemporary Arab Politics', *International Studies*, III, 1961.
Baldissera, E. 'La composizione dei Governi Siriani dal 1918 al 1965', *Oriente Moderno*, 1972.
Batatu, H. 'Some Observations on the Social Roots of Syria's Ruling Military Group and the Causes of its Dominance', *Middle East Journal*, vol. 35, no. 3, summer 1981.
Ben-Dor, G. 'The Middle East in 1981: A Year of Political Disorder', in Colin Legum et al. (eds), *Middle East Contemporary Survey*, vol. v, 1980–1981, New York and London, 1982.
Bengio, O. 'Iraq', in Colin Legum et al. (eds) *Middle East Contemporary Survey*, vol. iv, 1979–1980, New York and London, 1981.
Ben Tsur, A. 'Composition and Membership of the Ba'th Party in the Qunaytra Region', (in Hebrew, English summary), *Hamizrah Hahedash*, Jerusalem xviii, 1968.
—— 'The Neo-Ba'th Party of Syria', *Journal of Contemporary History*, III, 1968.
Berque, J. 'L'Univers politique des arabes', *Encyclopédie française* xi, Paris, 1957.
Binder, L. 'Radical Reform Nationalism in Syria and Egypt', *Muslim World*, xlix/2–3, 1959.
Carleton, A. 'The Syrian Coups d'Etat of 1949', *Middle East Journal*, vol. 4, no. 1 1950.
Carr. D. W . 'Capital Flows and Development in Syria', *Middle East Journal*, vol. 34, no. 4, autumn 1980.
Chabry, L. 'Le Ba'th et l'armée en Irak et en Syrie', *Maghreb Machrek*, no. 71, 1976.
—— 'La mise en service de l'oléoduc Iraq-Turquie et la mésentente syro-iraquienne', *Maghreb Machrek*, no. 77, 1977.

Chatelus, M. 'La Croissance économique: mutations des structures et dynamismes du déséquilibre', in André Raymond (ed.), *La Syrie d'aujourd'hui*, Paris, 1980.

Chevalier, F. 'Forces en presence dans la Syrie d'aujourd'hui', *Orient*, no. 4, 1957.

Colombe, M. 'L'Egypte et les origines du nationalisme arabe', *L'Afrique et l'Asie*, no. 14, 1951.

—— 'La nouvelle politique arabe de la République Arabe Unie', *Orient*, no. 11, 1959.

—— 'La mission à Damas du Maréchal égyptien Abd al-Hakim Amer', *Orient*, no. 3, 1959.

—— 'Particularismes et nationalisme arabes à la suite du coup d'état syrien', *Orient*, no. 5, 1961.

Couland, J. 'Le parti communiste libanais cinquante ans après', *Maghreb Machrek*, no. 68, 1975.

David, J-C. 'L'urbanisation en Syrie', *Maghreb Machrek*, no. 81, 1978.

Dawisha, A. 'Syria under Asad, 1970–78: the Centres of Power', *Government and Opposition*, vol. 13, no. 3, summer 1978.

Dawn, C. E. 'The Rise of Arabism in Syria', *Middle East Journal*, vol. 16, no. 2, 1962.

Devlin, J. 'The Political Structure in Syria', *Middle East Review*, vol. 17, no. 1, fall 1984.

—— 'Syria: Consistency at Home and Abroad', *Current History*, February 1986.

Dishon, D. and B. Maddy-Weitzman. 'Inter-Arab Relations', in Colin Legum et al. (eds), *Middle East Contemporary Survey*, vol. v, 1980–1981. New York and London, 1982.

Drysdale, A. 'The Regional Equalization of Health Care and Education in Syria since the Ba'thi Revolution', *International Journal of Middle East Studies*, vol. 13, 1981.

—— 'The Syrian Political Elite, 1966–1976: A Spatial and Social Analysis', *Middle Eastern Studies*, vol. 17, no. 1, 1981.

—— 'The Succession Question in Syria', *Middle East Journal*, vol. 39, no. 2, spring 1985.

Duclos, L. 'L'équilibre militaire israélo-arabe', *Maghreb Machrek*, no. 67, 1975.

Elisseef, N. 'Dimashq' and 'Ghuta' in *The Encyclopaedia of Islam*, new edn.

Garfinkle, A.M., 'The Forces behind Syrian Politics', *Middle East Review*, vol. 17, no. 1, fall 1984.

Glass, C. 'Who was Hindawi working for?' *Spectator*, 1 November 1986.

Golan, G. 'Syria and the Soviet Union since the Yom Kippur War', *Orbis*, vol. 21, 1978.

Golan, G. and I. Rabinovich. 'The Soviet Union and Syria: the Limits of Co-operation', in Y. Ro'i (ed.) *The Limits to Power: Soviet Policy in the Middle East*, London, 1979.

Gonzalez-Quijano, Y. 'Les interprétations d'un rite: célébrations de la 'Achoura au Liban', *Maghreb Machrek*, no. 115, 1987.

Grassmuck, G. 'The Electoral Process in Iraq, 1952–1958', *Middle East Journal*, vol. 14, 1960.

Hannoyer, J. 'Grands projets hydrauliques en Syrie', *Maghreb Machrek*, no. 109, 1985.

Hinnebusch, R. A. 'Local Politics in Syria: Organization and Mobilization in Four Village Cases', *Middle East Journal*, vol. 30, no. 1, 1976.

—— 'Party and Peasant in Syria', *Cairo Papers in Social Science*, vol. 3, no. 1, 1979.

—— 'Rural Politics in Ba'thist Syria', *The Review of Politics*, vol. 44, no. 1, 1982.

—— 'Syria under the Ba'th: State Formation in a Fragmented Society', *Arab Studies Quarterly*, vol. 4, no. 3, 1982.

—— 'Syria under the Ba'th: Social Ideology, Policy and Practice', in L. Michalak and J. Salacuse (eds) *Social Legislation in the Contemporary Middle East*, Berkeley, 1986.

—— 'Syria', in S. Hunter (ed.) *The Politics of Islamic Revivalism*, Bloomington, Indiana, 1988.

Hocking B. and M. Smith. 'Reagan, Congress and foreign policy: a troubled partnership', *The World Today*, May 1984.

Hoffman, S. 'A New Policy for Israel', *Foreign Affairs*, vol. 53, no. 3, April 1975.

Hottinger, A. 'How the Arab Bourgeoisie Lost Power', *Journal of Contemporary History*, III, 1968.

Hourani, A. 'The Decline of the West in the Middle East', *International Affairs* Jan.–Apr. 1953.

Hourani, C. 'The Arab League in Perspective', *Middle East Journal*, vol. 1, no. 2 1947.

Hudson, M. 'The Palestine Factor in the Lebanese Civil War', *Middle East Journal*, vol. 23, no. 3, summer 1978.

Jabber, F. 'The Resistance Movement before the Six Day War', in W. B. Quandt et al, *The Politics of Palestinian Nationalism*, Berkeley, 1973.

Ja'far, K. 'The Soviet Union in the Middle East: a case study of Syria', in Robert Cassen (ed.) *Soviet Interests in the Third World*, London, 1985.

Jargy, S. 'La Syrie province de la RAU', *Orient*, no. 8, 1958.

—— 'Declin d'un parti', *Orient*, no. 2, 1959.

Kaylani, N. M. 'The Rise of the Syrian Ba'th 1940–1958: Political Success, Party Failure', *International Journal of Middle Eastern Studies*, vol. 3, no. 1, 1972.

Kelidar, A. R. 'Religion and State in Syria', *Asian Affairs*, vol. 61, no. 1, 1974.

—— and M. Burrell, 'Lebanon: the Collapse of a State', *Conflict Studies*, no. 74, August 1976.

Kerblay, B. 'La Pénetration économique des pays du bloc sovietique au Moyen-Orient', *Orient*, no. 13, 1960.

Kerr, M. H. 'Hafiz Asad and the Changing Patterns of Syrian Politics', *International Journal*, vol. 28, 1973.

Khadduri, M. 'Constitutional Developments in Syria', *Middle East Journal*, 1951.

Khader, B. 'Structures et reforme agraires en Syrie', *Maghreb Machrek*, no. 65, 1974.

Khalidi, W. 'A Sovereign Palestinian State', *Foreign Affairs*, 56, summer 1978.

—— 'Toward Peace in the Holy Land', *Foreign Affairs*, 66, spring 1988.

Khoury, P. S. 'Factionalism among Syrian Nationalists during the French Mandate', *International Journal of Middle Eastern Studies*, 13, 1981.

—— 'The Tribal Shaykh, French Tribal Policy and the Nationalist Movement in Syria between Two World Wars', *Middle Eastern Studies*, 18, 1982.

Kienle, E. 'The Conflict Between the Baath Regimes of Syria and Iraq prior to their Consolidation', *Occasional Papers*, 7, Ethnizität und Gesellschaft, Free University of Berlin, 1985.

Kirk, G. E. 'Cross Currents within the Arab League: the Greater Syria Plan', *The World Today*, January 1948.

Klat, P. J. 'The Origins of Landownership in Syria', *Middle East Economic Papers*, 1958.

Kramer, M. 'La morale de Hizbollah et sa logique', *Maghreb Machrek*, no. 119, 1988.

Laurent, F. 'L'URSS et le Moyen-Orient', *Orient*, no. 2, 1957.

Lewis, N. 'The Frontier of Settlement in Syria, 1800–1950', *International Affairs*, January 1955.

Longuenesse, E. 'La Classe Ouvrière au Proche Orient: La Syrie', *Pensées*, no. 197, February 1978.

—— 'Bourgeoisie, Petite-bourgeoisie et Couches moyennes en Syrie', *Peuples méditerranéens*, no. 4, July-September 1978.

—— 'The Class Nature of the State in Syria', *MERIP Reports*, vol. 9, no. 4, 1979.

—— 'Syrie, secteur public industriel: les enjeux d'une crise', *Maghreb Machrek*, no. 109, 1985.

Macintyre, R. R. 'Syrian Political Age Differentials 1958-1966', *Middle East Journal*, vol. 29, no. 2, 1975.

Mallat, C. 'Le féminisme islamique de Bint al-Houda', *Maghreb Machrek*, no. 116, 1987.

—— 'Shi'i Thought from the South of Lebanon', *Papers on Lebanon*, 7, Centre for Lebanese Studies, Oxford, 1988.

Ma'oz, M. 'Attempts at Creating a Political Community in Modern Syria', *Middle East Journal*, vol. 26, no. 4, 1972.

—— 'Syria under Hafiz al-Asad: New Domestic and Foreign Policies', *Jerusalem Papers on Peace Problems*, 1975.

—— 'Hafiz al-Asad: A Political Profile', *Jerusalem Quarterly*, 8, 1978.

Mégarbané, C. 'L'enseignement en Syrie', *Travaux et Jours*, 51, 1974.

Métral, F. 'Etat et paysans dans le Ghab en Syrie', *Maghreb Machrek*, no. 109, 1985.

Montagne, R. 'La Crise politique de l'arabisme', *La France Méditerranéenne et africaine*, Paris, 1938.

Oron, Y. 'History and Ideas of the Arab Socialist Renaissance Party', *New East*, ix, 1959.

Owen, R. 'The Lebanese Crisis: Fragmentation or Reconciliation?' *Third World Quarterly*, vol. 6, no. 4, October 1984.

Palmer, M. 'The United Arab Republic - An Assessment of its Failure', *Middle East Journal*, vol. 20, no. 1, 1966.

Perlmutter, A. 'Begin's Rhetoric and Sharon's Tactics', *Foreign Affairs*, fall 1982.

—— 'Some Spies Can Fool Themselves Too', *International Herald Tribune*, 8 July 1985.

Picard, E. 'L'engagement syrien au Liban', *Maghreb Machrek*, no. 74, 1976.

—— 'Syria returns to democracy', in G. Hermet, R. Rose, and A. Rouquie (eds) *Elections Without Choice*, London, 1978.

—— 'Clans militaires et Pouvoir Ba'thiste en Syrie', *Orient*, (Hamburg), 3e trim. 1979.

—— 'Ouverture économique et renforcement militaire en Syrie', *Oriente Moderne*, 59, nos 7–12, 1979.

—— 'Clivages et consensus au sein du Commandement Militaire Ba'thiste syrien (1970–1979)', in Alain Rouquie (ed.) *La Politique de Mars*, Paris.

—— 'Retour au Sandjak', *Maghreb Machrek*, no. 99, 1983.

—— 'La politique de la Syrie au Liban', *Maghreb Machrek*, no. 116, 1987.

Rabinovich, I. 'The Lebanese Crisis', in Colin Legum et al. (eds) *Middle East Contemporary Survey*, vol v, 1980–81.

Rastier, J. 'A la Recherche du socialisme syrien', *Orient*, no. 4, 1957.

Raymond, A. 'La Syrie, du Royaume arabe à l'indépendance (1914–1946)', in A. Raymond (ed.) *La Syrie d'Aujourd'hui*, Paris, 1980.

Roberts, C. A. 'Soviet Arms-transfer Policy and the Decision to Upgrade Syrian Air Defences', *Survival*, vol. xxv, no. 4, 1983.

Robinson, C. L. 'Surveillance Integration Pivotal in Israeli Success', *Aviation Week and Space Technology*, 5 July 1982.

Rondot, Pierre. 'L'experience du Mandat Français en Syrie et au Liban, 1918–1945', *Revue Generale de Droit International Public*, 1948.

—— 'Les Etats-Unis devant l'Orient d'aujourd'hui', *Orient*, no. 2, 1957.

—— 'Tendances particularistes et tendances unitaires en Syrie', *Orient*, no. 5, 1958.

—— 'Quelques remarques sur le Ba'th', *Orient*, no. 31, 1964.

—— 'Trente années d'histoire', *Le Monde*, 14–15 March 1976.

Rouleau, E. 'La Syrie ba'thiste ou la fuite à gauche', *Le Monde*, 13–19 October 1966.

—— 'The Syrian Enigma: What is the Ba'th?', *New Left Review*, no. 45, 1967.

Sadowski, Y. 'Cadres, Guns and Money: the Eighth Regional Congress of the Syrian Ba'th', *MERIP Reports*, vol. 15, no. 6, 1985.

Santucci, R. 'La Syrie avant l'affrontement', *Maghreb Machrek*, no. 60, 1973.

Schiff, Z. 'The dispute on the Syrian-Israeli border', *New Outlook*, February 1967.

—— 'The Green Light', *Foreign Policy*, spring 1983.

—— 'Dealing with Syria', *Foreign Policy*, summer 1984.

Seurat, M. 'Les populations, l'état et la société', in A. Raymond (ed.) *La Syrie d'aujourd'hui*, Paris, 1980.

Seymour, M. 'The Dynamics of Power in Syria since the break with Egypt', *Middle Eastern Studies*, vol. 6, no. 1, 1970.

Sharabi, H. 'The Transformation of Ideology in the Arab World', *Middle East Journal*, vol. 19, no. 4, 1965.

al-Shawi, H. 'Le Ba'th, sa technique d'action politique', *Maghreb Machrek*, no. 59, 1973.

—— 'Le Contenu de la contestation communiste en Irak et en Syrie', *Maghreb Machrek*, no. 63, 1974.

—— 'Le Ba'th et l'armée en Irak et en Syrie', *Maghreb Machrek*, no. 71, 1976.

Sheehan, E. R. F., 'Step by Step in the Middle East', *Foreign Policy*, no. 22, spring 1976.

Shlaim, A. 'Israeli Interference in Internal Arab Politics: the Case of Lebanon', in

G. Luciani and G. Salamé (eds) *The Politics of Arab Integration*, New York and London, 1988.

Torrey, G. H. 'The Ba'th - Ideology and Practice', *Middle East Journal*, vol. 23, 1969.

Van Dam, N. 'Sectarian and Regional Factionalism in the Syrian Political Elite', *Middle East Journal*, vol. 32, no. 1, 1978.

Van Dusen, M. H. 'Political Integration and Regionalism in Syria', *Middle East Journal* vol. 26, no. 2, 1972.

—— 'Downfall of a Traditional Elite', in F. Tachau (ed.) *Political Elites and Political Development in the Middle East*, Cambridge, Mass., 1975.

Vernier, B. 'Le Role politique de l'armée en Syrie', *Politique Etrangère* vol. 24, no. 5, 1964.

Viennot, J-P. 'Le Ba'th entre la théorie et la pratique', *Orient*, no. 30, 1964.

—— 'Le role du Ba'th dans la genèse du nationalisme arabe', *Orient*, no. 35, 1965.

Wakebridge, C. 'The Syrian side of the Hill', *Military Review*, vol. 56, no. 2, February 1976.

Weulersse, J. 'Régime agraire et vie agricole en Syrie', *Bulletin de l'Association de Géographes français*, no. 113, 1938.

Winder, B. 'Syrian Deputies and Cabinet Ministers, 1919–1959', *Middle East Journal*, vol. 16, no. 4, 1962; vol. 17, 1963.

Yaniv, A. 'Syria and Israel: The Politics of Escalation', in Ma'oz, M. and A. Yaniv (eds) *Syria Under Assad*, London, 1986.

Yared, M. 'Le Baas ou la quête de l'unité arabe et du socialisme', *Le Monde*, 14–15 March 1976.

Index